THE INTERNATIONAL LAW OF ENERGY

The world's energy structure underpins the global environmental crisis and changing it will require regulatory change at a massive level. Energy is highly regulated in international law, but the field has never been comprehensively mapped. The legal sources on which the governance of energy is based are plentiful but they are scattered across a vast legal expanse. This book is the first single-authored study of the international law of energy as a whole. Written by a world-leading expert, it provides a comprehensive account of the international law of energy and analyses the implications of the ongoing energy transformation for international law. The study combines conceptual and doctrinal analysis of all the main rules, processes and institutions to consider the past, present and likely future of global energy governance. Providing a solid foundation for teaching, research and practice, this book addresses both the theory and real-world policy dimension of the international law of energy.

Jorge E. Viñuales is the Harold Samuel Chair of Law at Cambridge, the Founding Director of the Cambridge Centre for Environment, Energy and Natural Resources Governance, and a Member (Associé) of the Institut de Droit International. He has published extensively on international law and has wide experience as counsel, expert and adjudicator.

CAMBRIDGE STUDIES IN INTERNATIONAL AND COMPARATIVE LAW: 164

Established in 1946, this series produces high quality, reflective and innovative scholarship in the field of public international law. It publishes works on international law that are of a theoretical, historical, cross-disciplinary or doctrinal nature. The series also welcomes books providing insights from private international law, comparative law and transnational studies which inform international legal thought and practice more generally.

The series seeks to publish views from diverse legal traditions and perspectives, and of any geographical origin. In this respect it invites studies offering regional perspectives on core *problématiques* of international law, and in the same vein, it appreciates contrasts and debates between diverging approaches. Accordingly, books offering new or less orthodox perspectives are very much welcome. Works of a generalist character are greatly valued and the series is also open to studies on specific areas, institutions or problems. Translations of the most outstanding works published in other languages are also considered.

After seventy years, Cambridge Studies in International and Comparative Law sets the standard for international legal scholarship and will continue to define the discipline as it evolves in the years to come.

A list of books in the series can be found at the end of this volume.

THE INTERNATIONAL LAW OF ENERGY

JORGE E. VIÑUALES
University of Cambridge

CAMBRIDGE
UNIVERSITY PRESS

CAMBRIDGE
UNIVERSITY PRESS

University Printing House, Cambridge CB2 8BS, United Kingdom

One Liberty Plaza, 20th Floor, New York, NY 10006, USA

477 Williamstown Road, Port Melbourne, VIC 3207, Australia

314–321, 3rd Floor, Plot 3, Splendor Forum, Jasola District Centre, New Delhi – 110025, India

103 Penang Road, #05–06/07, Visioncrest Commercial, Singapore 238467

Cambridge University Press is part of the University of Cambridge.

It furthers the University's mission by disseminating knowledge in the pursuit of education, learning, and research at the highest international levels of excellence.

www.cambridge.org
Information on this title: www.cambridge.org/9781108415835
DOI: 10.1017/9781108235273

First published 2022

A catalogue record for this publication is available from the British Library.

ISBN 978-1-108-41583-5 Hardback

To my friends and colleagues of the Cambridge Centre for Environment, Energy and Natural Resource Governance (C-EENRG) – I could not have hoped for a better intellectual home in which to develop the ideas leading to this book.

CONTENTS

An Online Bibliography can be accessed at http://cambridge.org/9781108415835.

FIGURES

TABLES

PREFACE

There are many drivers of the epoch-defining environmental crisis that the biosphere – and humankind as part of it – faces today, as we embark on the critical 2020–2030 decade. The main one, by many accounts, is the reliance by one species, humans, on a certain form of energy, derived from fossil fuels, as the backbone of its modern conception of 'civilisation'. Burning fossil fuels is not only at the roots of the environmental crisis but also at the foundation of how humans produce shelter, heat, food, transportation and most of their cultural products, including technology.

From the narrow lenses of the social practice we call international law, energy may appear as a sub-topic, alongside so many others. In reality, international law is but one aspect of a wider order shaped, since the dawn of the so-called Industrial Revolution in the late eighteenth century, by fossil fuel energy. This fossil fuel-based socio-technical regime is, however, not like its predecessors. Contrary to the latter, the fossil fuel-based order has come to encompass, by its Earth-shaping effects, the entire biosphere, including humanity. And we now understand that it challenges a much more profound layer of 'regulation', a resilient but threatened biospheric balance that was, for too long, taken for granted.[1]

Energy, not *international law*, is the pivotal term around which an account of the international law of energy must be organised. It is, more specifically, the socio-technical regime, built upon certain forms of energy, fossil fuels and its ongoing transformation into a new socio-technical regime, which provides the backbone of the entire account. This account is intended to show that the international law of energy is the entirety of international law as it concerns 'energy' and that clarifying how it does so is important to understand the ongoing energy

[1] I have outlined this other layer in some previous work: J. E. Viñuales, 'Two Layers of Self-Regulation' (2020) 11 *Transnational Legal Theory* 16; J. E. Viñuales, *The Organisation of the Anthropocene: In Our Hands?* (The Hague: Brill Research Perspectives, 2018).

transformation, which may contribute to reversing – or not – the dire consequences of the fossil fuel–based energy order.

This explains why this account is presented as a monographic study, an analysis of energy and the energy transformation from the disciplinary lenses of international law. This disciplinary perspective deserves attention because international law has been instrumental in expanding the socio-technical energy order that has pushed the biospheric balance to the brink of 'change', which, for humans and so many other species, may mean collapse. By understanding how energy is governed in international law as a whole, I hope to shed light on how international law built and sustained the fossil fuel energy regime and failed to sufficiently restrain its adverse consequences; but my goal is also to show how international law may be playing a role in the emergence of a new energy regime which is less unsettling for the resilience mechanisms of the biosphere.

The discussion in the book is overall technical, with sufficient references to the relevant rules, case law and commentary, in the doctrinal tradition, blended with theoretical material, including an analytical framework introduced for this purpose. As a result, the book could be used as a textbook in a variety of academic and professional training contexts. Yet, the main reason to pay sufficient attention to the technical material is that, without sufficient command of the law, the understanding that I aim to provide in this book could never be empowering or contribute to the ongoing transformation.

ABBREVIATIONS

AB	Appellate Body of the WTO Dispute Settlement Body
AFDI	Annuaire français de droit international
African Commission	African Commission of Human and Peoples' Rights
African Court	African Court of Human and Peoples' Rights
AJIL	*American Journal of International Law*
ASILProc	American Society of International Law Proceedings
BIT	Bilateral Investment Treaty
BYIL	*British Yearbook of International Law*
CESCR	UN Committee on Economic, Social and Cultural Rights
CFR	US Code of Federal Regulations
COP (COPs)	Conference(s) of the Parties
ECT	Energy Charter Treaty
ECtHR	European Court of Human Rights
EJIL	*European Journal of International Law*
EPA	US Environmental Protection Agency
FTA	free trade agreement
GA (or UNGA)	United Nations General Assembly
GAOR	*United Nations General Assembly Official Records*
GATS	General Agreement on Trade in Services
GATT	General Agreement on Tariffs and Trade
GYIL	*German Yearbook of International Law*
HRC	United Nations Human Rights Committee
IAEA	International Atomic Energy Agency
ICJ	International Court of Justice
ICLQ	*International and Comparative Law Quarterly*
ICommHR	Inter-American Commission on Human Rights
ICSID	International Centre for Settlement of Investment Disputes
ICtHR	Inter-American Court of Human Rights
IDI	Institut de droit international
IEA	International Energy Agency
IEF	International Energy Forum

IIA(s)	international investment agreement(s)
IJMCL	*International Journal of Marine and Coastal Law*
ILM	international legal materials
IMO	International Maritime Organisation
IPR(s)	intellectual property right(s)
IRENA	International Renewable Energy Agency
ITLOS	International Tribunal for the Law of the Sea
JDI	*Journal du droit international*
JIDS	*Journal of International Dispute Settlement*
JIEL	*Journal of International Economic Law*
JWELB	*Journal of World Energy Law and Business*
MEA(s)	multilateral environmental agreement(s)
MPEPIL	*Max Planck Encyclopedia of Public International Law*
OAS	Organisation of American States
OECD	Organisation for Economic Co-operation and Development
OJ	*Official Journal of the European Union*
OLADE	Latin American Organization for Energy Cooperation
OPEC	Organization of the Petroleum Exporting Countries
PCA	Permanent Court of Arbitration
RCADI	Recueil des cours de l'Académie de droit international de La Haye
RGDIP	*Revue générale de droit international public*
RIAA	Reports of International Arbitral Awards
SC (or UNSC)	United Nations Security Council
SFDI	Société française pour le droit international
TFDD	Transboundary Freshwater Dispute Database, www.transboundarywaters.orst.edu
UN	United Nations
UNCITRAL	United Nations Commission on International Trade Law
UNCTAD	United Nations Commission on Trade and Development
UNECE	United Nations Economic Commission for Europe
UNEP	United Nations Environment Programme
UNTS	United Nations Treaty Series
WMO	World Meteorological Organization
WTO	World Trade Organization
YbILC	*Yearbook of the International Law Commission*

INSTRUMENTS

Date	Full reference	Abbreviation	Pages
4 October 1913	Convention entre la France et la Suisse pour l'aménagement de la puissance hydraulique du Rhône entre l'usine projetée de la Plaine et un point à déterminer en amont du pont de Pougny-Chancy	Rhône Agreement	251
20 April 1921	Convention and Statute on Freedom of Transit, 7 LNTS 11		95
9 December 1923	Convention relating to the Development of Hydraulic Power affecting more than one State, 35 LNTS 75		246
27 August 1926	Convention pour le règlement des rapports entre la Suisse et la France au sujet de certaines clauses du regime juridique de la future derivation du Rhin à Kembs	Rhine/Kembs Agreement	249
19 November 1930	Convention entre la France et la Suisse concernant la concession de la chute du Chatelot sur le Doubs, signed at Paris		251

(*cont.*)

Date	Full reference	Abbreviation	Pages
25 February 1938	Agreement between the Governments of Brazil and Bolivia on the exportation and use of Bolivian petroleum, 51 UNTS 256	Brazil/Bolivia Agreement	271
12 October 1940	Convention on Nature Protection and Wild Life Preservation in the Western Hemisphere, 56 Stat. 1354, TS 981	Western Hemisphere Convention	168
6 February 1941	Convention on Construction of Oil Pipelines signed by Argentina, Bolivia, Brazil, Paraguay, and Uruguay	Oil Pipeline Convention	271
14 November 1944	Treaty between the United States of America and Mexico relating to the utilization of the waters of the Colorado and Tijuana Rivers, and of the Rio Grande (Rio Bravo) from Fort Quitman, Texas, to the Gulf of Mexico, and supplementary protocol, 3 UNTS 313	1944 US–Mexico Agreement	250
30 and 31 May 1949	Exchange of notes constituting an agreement between the Government of the United Kingdom of Great Britain and Northern Ireland and the Government of Egypt regarding the construction of the Owen Falls Dam		249

(cont.)

Date	Full reference	Abbreviation	Pages
18 June 1949	Accord entre la Suisse et l'Italie au sujet de la concession de forces hydrauliques du Reno di Lei, avec protocole additional	Reno di Lei Agreement	251
25 April 1950	State treaty between the Grand Duchy of Luxembourg and the Land Rhineland-Palatinate in the Federal Republic of Germany concerning the construction of a hydroelectric powerplant on the Sauer (Sure) at Rosport/ Ralingen		252
16 October 1950	Agreement between the Federal Government of the Republic of Austria and the Free State of Bavaria concerning the Österreichisch-Bayerische Kraftwerke AG (Austrian Bavarian Hydroelectric Company)	Österreichisch-Bayerische Kraftwerke Agreement	251
4 November 1950	Convention for the Protection of Human Rights and Fundamental Freedoms, 4 November 1950, 213 UNTS 221	ECHR	149, 172
18 April 1951	Treaty establishing the European Coal and Steel Community, 261 UNTS 140	ECSC Treaty	376

(*cont.*)

Date	Full reference	Abbreviation	Pages
12 January 1952	'Integrated economic development and commercial agreements', UN Doc. A/RES/523(VI)	Resolution 523 (VI)	24, 45, 351
13 February 1952	Agreement between the Government of Republic of Austria and the Government of the Federal Republic of Germany and of the Free State of Bavaria concerning the Donaukraftwerk-Jochenstein-Aktiengellschaft (Danube Power-Plant and Jochenstein Joint-Stock Company)		251
25 April 1954	Agreement between the Government of India and the Government of Nepal on the Kosi project		249
12 May 1954	International Convention for the Prevention of Pollution of the Sea by Oil, 327 UNTS 3	OILPOL	
23 October 1956	Statute of the International Atomic Energy Agency, 276 UNTS 3	IAEA Statute	294–295, 303, 304, 309, 321–322, 324
27 October 1956	Convention entre la République fédérale d'Allemagne et la République française sur l'aménagement du cours supérieur du		249

(*cont.*)

Date	Full reference	Abbreviation	Pages
	Rhin entre Bàie et Strasbourg et protocole annexé à la convention		
25 March 1957	Treaty Establishing the European Atomic Energy Community, 298 UNTS 167	EURATOM Treaty	302
25 March 1957	Treaty establishing the European Economic Community, 298 UNTS 3	EEC Treaty	377
27 May 1957	Convention entre la Confédération suisse et la République italienne au sujet de l'utilisation de la force hydraulique du Spöl et protocole additionnel	Spöl Agreement	251
20 December 1957	Convention on the Establishment of a Security Control in the Field of Nuclear Energy, OECD/LEGAL/0020		304
22 February 1958	Bahrain-Saudi Arabia Frontier Agreement, 1733 UNTS 3	Bahrain–Saudi Arabia Frontier Agreement	201
29 April 1958	Convention on the Continental Shelf, 499 UNTS 311	CCS	201
29 April 1959	Agreement between the Government of the Union of Soviet Socialist Republics, the Government of Norway and the	Kaitakoski Agreement	249

(*cont.*)

Date	Full reference	Abbreviation	Pages
	Government of Finland concerning the regulation of Lake Inari by means of the Kaitakoski hydroelectric power station and dam, 346 UNTS 192/167		
29 April 1959	Additional Protocol between the Union of Soviet Socialist Republics and Finland concerning compensation for loss and damage and for the works to be carried out by Finland in connection with the implementation of the Agreement of 29 April 1959 between the Government of the Union of Soviet Socialist Republics, the Government of Finland and the Government of Norway concerning the regulation of Lake Inari by means of the Kaitakoski hydroelectric power station and dam, 346 UNTS 212	Kaitakoski Protocol	249
1 July 1959	Agreement on the Privileges and Immunities of the IAEA, INFCIRC/9/Rev.2	IAEA Immunities	294

(cont.)

Date	Full reference	Abbreviation	Pages
1 December 1959	The Antarctic Treaty, 402 UNTS 71	Antarctic Treaty	168, 331
4 December 1959	Agreement between Nepal and India on the Gandak Project		253
23 January 1960	Agreement concerning the principles of geological co-operation between the Czechoslovak Republic and the Republic of Austria, 495 UNTS 99		207
29 July 1960	Convention on Third Party Liability in the Field of Nuclear Energy, 956 UNTS 251	Paris Convention	305
10–14 September 1960	Statute of the Organization of the Petroleum Exporting Countries (OPEC), adopted at the second conference, held in Caracas in January 1961, Resolution II.6	OPEC Statute	294, 352
19 September 1960	The Indus Waters Treaty concluded between India and Pakistan	Indus Water Treaty	252
14 December 1960	UN General Assembly Resolution 1514 (XV), 'Declaration on the Granting of Independence to Colonial Countries and Peoples', A/RES/1514 (XV)		48
17 January 1961	Treaty between Canada and the United States of America relating to cooperative	Columbia River Treaty	250

(*cont.*)

Date	Full reference	Abbreviation	Pages
	development of the water resources of the Columbia River basin, 592 UNTS 272		
14 December 1962	'Permanent sovereignty over natural resources', UN Doc. A/RES/1803 (XVII)	Resolution 1803 (XVII)	24, 45, 212, 352
31 January 1963	Convention Supplementary to the Paris Convention of 29 July 1960 on Third Party Liability in the Field of Nuclear Energy, 1041 UNTS 358 Supplementary Convention	Brussels	335
21 May 1963	Convention on Civil Liability for Nuclear Damage, 1063 UNTS 265	Vienna Convention	305
29 July 1963	Convention entre le Gouvernement de la République française et le Gouvernement espagnol relative a l'aménagement du cours supérieur de la Garonne, JORF of 29 May 1964, p. 4571	Garonne Agreement	249
23 August 1963	Convention entre la République française et la Confédération suisse au sujet de l'aménagement hydroélectrique d'Emosson (avec modification)	Emosson Agreement	251

(cont.)

Date	Full reference	Abbreviation	Pages
30 November 1963	Convention between the Government of the Socialist Federal	Iron Gates Agreement	250
	Republic of Yugoslavia and the Government of the Romanian People's Republic concerning the execution of works for the Iron Gates water power and navigation system on the river Danube, 559 UNTS 364		250
30 November 1963	Exchange of letters constituting an agreement between the Romanian People's Republic and the Socialist Federal Republic of Yugoslavia concerning the adjustment of the frontier on the Danube		252
10 February 1965	Convention on Transit Trade of Land-locked States, 597 UNTS 3		95
20 August 1966	Helsinki Rules on the Uses of the Waters of International Rivers, art IV; adopted by the International Law Association at its fifty-second conference, Helsinki		245
16 December 1966	International Covenant on Civil and Political Rights, 999 UNTS 171	ICCPR	48, 172
16 December 1966	International Covenant on Economic, Social and Cultural Rights, 993 UNTS 3	ICESCR	48, 172

(*cont.*)

Date	Full reference	Abbreviation	Pages
19 December 1966	Amended Agreement between His Majesty's Government of Nepal and the Government of India concerning the Kosi project	Kosi Project Agreement	249
14 February 1967	Treaty for the Prohibition of Nuclear Weapons in Latin America, 634 UNTS 281	Treaty of Tlatelcoco	318
1 July 1968	Treaty on the Non-Proliferation of Nuclear Weapons, 729 UNTS 161	NPT	295, 304–305, 308, 309, 310, 317, 319
15 September 1968 (revised 11 July 2003)	African Convention on the Conservation of Nature and Natural Resources, 1001 UNTS 3	African Conservation Convention	168
20 March 1969	Agreement between Qatar and Abu Dhabi on the settlement of maritime boundaries and ownership of islands (with declarations and map)	Qatar/Abu Dhabi Agreement	209
23 May 1969	Vienna Convention on the Law of Treaties, 1155 UNTS 331	VCLT	8
4 July 1969	Convention entre la République française et la République fédérale d'Allemagne au sujet de l'aménagement du Rhin entre Strasbourg/ Kehl et Lauterbourg/ Neuburgweier	Rhine/ Strasbourg/ Lauterbourg Agreement	251

(*cont.*)

Date	Full reference	Abbreviation	Pages
22 November 1969	American Convention on Human Rights, 1144 UNTS 123	ACHR	172
29 November 1969	Convention on Civil Liability for Oil Pollution Damage, 973 UNTS 3	CLC 69	189
29 November 1969	International Convention Relating to Intervention on the High Seas in Cases of Oil Pollution Casualties, 970 UNTS 211	Intervention Convention	181
24 October 1970	UN General Assembly Resolution 2625 (XXV), 'Declaration on Principles of International Law concerning Friendly Relations and Cooperation among States in accordance with the Charter of the United Nations', Annex	Friendly Relations Declaration	48
2 February 1971	Convention on Wetlands of International Importance especially as Waterfowl Habitat, 996 UNTS 245	Ramsar Convention	138
16 December 1971	Agreement between the Government of the Socialist Republic of Romania and the Government of the Union of Soviet Socialist Republics on the joint construction of the Stinca-Costesti hydraulic engineering	Stinca-Costesti Agreement	250

(cont.)

Date	Full reference	Abbreviation	Pages
	scheme on the River Prut and the establishment of the conditions of its operation (with protocol), 890 UNTS 3		
17 December 1971	Convention Relating to Third Party Liability in the Field of Maritime Carriage of Nuclear Material, 944 UNTS 255		336
18 December 1971	International Convention on the Establishment of an International Fund for Compensation for Oil Pollution Damage, 1110 UNTS 57	FUND/71	189
16 June 1972	'Declaration of the United Nations Conference on the Human Environment', Stockholm, UN Doc. A/CONF 48/14/Rev.1, pp. 2ff.	Stockholm Declaration	62
23 June 1972	Convention entre la Suisse et l'Italie relative à l'aménagement hydraulique du torrent Breggia à la frontière italo—suisse		250
16 November 1972	Convention for the Protection of the World Cultural and Natural Heritage, 1037 UNTS 151	World Heritage Convention or WHC	170
29 December 1972	Convention for the prevention of marine	London Convention	155, 297

(*cont.*)

Date	Full reference	Abbreviation	Pages
	pollution by dumping of wastes and other matter		
17 February 1973 (modified 17 February 1978)	International Convention for the Prevention of Pollution from Ships, as modified by the Protocol of 1978 relating thereto, UNTS 1340 I-22484	MARPOL 73/78 or MARPOL	153, 161, 168, 181, 220
26 April 1973	Treaty between the Federative Republic of Brazil and the Republic of Paraguay concerning the hydroelectric utilization of the water of the Paraná River owned in condominium by the two countries, from and including the Salto Grande de Sete Quedas or Salto del Guaira, to the mouth of the Iguazú River, 923 UNTS 57	Itaipú Agreement	250
22 May 1973	Agreement between the Government of the United Kingdom of Great Britain and Northern Ireland and the Government of the Kingdom of Norway relating to the Transmission of	Ekofisk Agreement	271
	Petroleum by Pipeline from the Ekofisk Field and Neighbouring		271

(*cont.*)

Date	Full reference	Abbreviation	Pages
	Areas to the United Kingdom		
27 August 1973	Crude Oil Pipeline Agreement between the Government of the Turkish Republic and the Government of the Iraqi Republic	Kirkuk-Ceyhan Agreement	271
14 September 1973	Agreement Between Belgium, Denmark, the Federal Republic of Germany, Ireland, Italy, Luxembourg, the Netherlands, the European Atomic Energy Community and the Agency in Connection with the Treaty on the Non-Proliferation of Nuclear Weapons, INFCIRC/193		318
2 November 1973	Protocol relating to Intervention on the High Seas in Cases of Marine Pollution by Substances other than Oil, 1313 UNTS		181
2 November 1973	Convenio Constitutivo de la Organización Latinoamericana de Energía [Agreement Establishing the Latin American Energy Organization], 1000 UNTS 129	Lima Agreement	388
3 December 1973	Treaty of Yacyretá between the Republic	Treaty of Yacyretá	250, 293

(cont.)

Date	Full reference	Abbreviation	Pages
	of Paraguay and the Argentine Republic, 13 UNTS 80		
29 January 1974	Convention between France and Spain on the delimitation of the territorial sea and the contiguous zone in the Bay of Biscay (Golfe de Gascogne/Golfo de Vizcaya) (with map)	Bay of Biscay Convention	209
30 January 1974	Agreement Between Japan and the Republic of Korea concerning joint development of the southern part of the continental shelf adjacent to the two countries (with map, appendix, agreed minutes and exchange of notes)	Japan/Korea Agreement	210
1 May 1974	'Declaration on the Establishment of a New International Economic Order', Res. 3201 (S-VI)		45
16 May 1974	Agreement between Sudan and Saudi Arabia relating to the joint exploitation of the natural resources of the sea-bed and sub-soil of the Red Sea in the Common Zone		210
17 September 1974	Council Resolution of 17 September 1974 concerning the new energy policy strategy for the Community		377

(cont.)

Date	Full reference	Abbreviation	Pages
1 November 1974	International Convention for the Safety of Life at Sea, 1185 UNTS 2	SOLAS Convention	306
18 November 1974	OECD Council Decision Establishing an International Energy Agency, OECD Document C(74)203 (Final)		358
18 November 1974	Agreement on an International Energy Program, 1040 UNTS 272	IEA Statute	294, 358
12 December 1974	'Charter of Economic Rights and Duties of States', UN Doc. A/ RES/3281/XXIX		45
13 February 1975	Council Directive 75/ 404/ EEC of 13 February 1975 on the restriction of the use of natural gas in power stations		377
14 April 1975	Directive 75/405/EEC of 14 April 1975 concerning the restriction of the use of petroleum products in power stations		377
20 May 1975	Council Directive 75/ 339/ EEC of 20 May 1975 obliging the Member States to maintain minimum stocks of fossil fuel at thermal power stations		377
15 October 1975	Memorandum of Understanding on the ASEAN Council on Petroleum, Jakarta, Indonesia		391

(*cont.*)

Date	Full reference	Abbreviation	Pages
15 October 1975	Declaration of the ASEAN Council on Petroleum, Jakarta, Indonesia		391
10 May 1976	Agreement between the Government of the United Kingdom of Great Britain and Northern Ireland and the Government of the Kingdom of Norway relating to the exploitation of the Frigg Field Reservoir and the transmission of gas therefrom to the UK, 1977 Great Britain TS 113	Norway/UK Frigg Agreement	219
16 May 1976	Crude Oil Pipeline Protocol between the Government of the Turkish Republic and the Government of the Iraqi Republic	Kirkuk-Ceyhan Protocol	271
12 June 1976	Convention on the Conservation of Nature in the South Pacific, available at: www.ecolex .org (TRE-000540)	Apia Convention	168
28 January 1977	Agreement between the Government of Canada and the Government of the United States of America concerning transit pipelines, 28 UST 7449	Transit Pipelines Agreement	274
20 September 1977	Agreement between the United States of America and Canada	Northern Pipeline Agreement	271

(*cont.*)

Date	Full reference	Abbreviation	Pages
	on Principles Applicable to a Northern Natural Gas Pipeline, 29 UST 3581		
24 April 1978	Protocol concerning regional cooperation in combating pollution by oil and other harmful substances in cases of emergency		183
23 August 1978	Vienna Convention on the Succession of States in Respect of Treaties, 1946 UNTS 3	VCST	226, 253
21 February 1979	Memorandum of Understanding Between Malaysia and the Kingdom of Thailand on the Establishment of the Joint Authority for the Exploitation of the Resources of the Sea Bed in a Defined Area of the Continental Shelf of the two Countries in the Gulf of Thailand	Malaysia/ Thailand MOU	210, 294
19 September 1979	Convention on the Conservation of European Wildlife and Natural Habitats, E.T. S. No. 104	Bern Convention	168
19 October 1979	Agreement on Parana River projects (Argentina-Brazil-Paraguay), 19 ILM 615 (1980)		255

(*cont.*)

Date	Full reference	Abbreviation	Pages
13 November 1979	Convention on Long-Range Transboundary Air Pollution, 1302 UNTS 217	LRTAP Convention	162
18 December 1979	Convention on the Elimination of All Forms of Discrimination Against Women, 1249 UNTS 13	CEDAW	54–55
3 March 1980	Convention on the Physical Protection of Nuclear Material, 1458 UNTS 125	Physical Protection Convention	305
17 May 1980	Treaty between the Government of the Federative Republic of Brazil and the Government of the Argentine Republic for developing the shared water resources of the frontier sections of the Uruguay River and its tributary, the Pepiri-Guaçu (Pepirí-Guazú) River, 1333 UNTS 62	Uruguay River Agreement	250
27 June 1981	African Charter on Human and Peoples' Rights, 21 ILM 58 (1982)	African Charter	51, 172
22 October 1981	Agreement on the Continental Shelf between Iceland and Jan Mayen (Iceland/Norway), 21 ILM (1982) 1222	Iceland/Norway Agreement	219

(*cont.*)

Date	Full reference	Abbreviation	Pages
10 December 1982	United Nations Convention on the Law of the Sea, 1833 UNTS 397	UNCLOS	46–48, 58, 95, 98, 101, 138–142, 145, 152–158, 164, 181, 187, 197, 207–208, 215, 220–228, 230–239, 260, 263, 266–269, 277, 278, 290
14 June 1983	International Convention on the Harmonized Commodity Description and Coding System, 1503 UNTS 167	HS Convention	19
13 September 1983	Agreement for Cooperation in Dealing with Pollution of the North Sea by Oil and Other Harmful Substances		182
28 September 1984	Protocol to the 1979 Convention on Long-Range Transboundary Air Pollution on the longterm Financing of the Cooperative Programme for Monitoring and Evaluation of the Long-Range Transport of Air Pollutants in Europe (EMEP), 1491 UNTS 167	EMEP Protocol	162
29 June 1985	Completing the Internal Market. White Paper from the Commission to the European Council, Milan, 28-29 June 1985, COM (85) 310 final		377

(*cont.*)

Date	Full reference	Abbreviation	Pages
8 July 1985	Protocol on the Reduction of Sulphur Emissions or their Transboundary Fluxes, 27 ILM 707	Sulphur Protocol I	163
9 July 1985	ASEAN Agreement on the Conservation of Nature and Natural Resources, 15 EPL 64	Kuala Lumpur Agreement	168
30 July 1985	Addendum to the Crude Oil Pipeline Agreement of 27 August 1973 between the Government of the Iraqi Republic and the Government of the Turkish Republic	Kirkuk-Ceyhan Addendum	271
6 August 1985	South Pacific Nuclear Free Zone Treaty, 1445 UNTS 177	Treaty of Rarotonga	318
17 February 1986	*Single European Act*, 17 February 1986, 1987 O.J. (L 169) 1		378
24 June 1986	Agreement on ASEAN Energy Cooperation Manila		392
24 June 1986	ASEAN Petroleum Security Agreement Manila		392
26 September 1986	Convention on Early Notification of a Nuclear Accident, 1439 *UNTS* 275	Convention on Early Notification	306, 333
26 September 1986	Convention on Assistance in Case of a Nuclear Accident or Radiological Emergency, 1457 UNTS 133	Convention on Assistance	306, 333
24 October 1986	Treaty on the Lesotho Highlands Water Project between the	Lesotho Highlands Agreement	250

(*cont.*)

Date	Full reference	Abbreviation	Pages
	Government of the Kingdom of Lesotho and the Government of the Republic of South Africa, available at : www.ecolex.org (TRE- 152232)		
23 July 1987	Council Regulation (EEC) No 2658/87 of 23 July 1987 on the tariff and statistical nomenclature and on the Common Customs Tariff		19
28 July 1987	Agreement relating to the Central African Power Corporation, 25 November 1963 and Agreement between the Republic of Zimbabwe and the Republic of Zambia concerning the utilization of the Zambezi River	Zambezi River Agreement	250
16 September 1987	Montreal Protocol on Substances that Deplete the Ozone Layer, 1522 UNTS 29	Montreal Protocol	164
13 November 1987	GATT, *Note by the Secretariat, Summary of Statements and proposals made concerning negotiations on natural resource-based products*, MTN.GNG/NG3/8	Negotiations on natural resource-based products	75
2 May 1988	The Internal Energy Market (Commission		377

(*cont.*)

Date	Full reference	Abbreviation	Pages
	Working Document), Brussels, 2 May 1988, COM (88) 238 final		
2 June 1988	Convention on the Regulation of Antarctic Mineral Resource Activities	Wellington Convention or CRAMRA	168
8 September 1988	Agreement on the Establishment of the ASEAN – EC Energy Management Training and Research Centre Brussels, Belgium		393
27 September 1988	Joint Protocol Relating to the Application of the Vienna Convention and the Paris Convention, 1672 UNTS 293	Joint Protocol	336
31 October 1988	Protocol concerning the Control of Emissions of Nitrogen Oxides or their Transboundary Fluxes, 28 ILM 214	NOx Protocol	163
16 November 1988	Additional Protocol to the American Convention on Human Rights in the Area of Economic, Social and Cultural Rights, O.A.S. Treaty Series No. 69	Protocol of San Salvador	55
22 March 1989	Basel Convention on the Control of Transboundary Movements of Hazardous Wastes and their Disposal, 1673 UNTS 57	Basel Convention	331

(*cont.*)

Date	Full reference	Abbreviation	Pages
27 June 1989	Convention (No. 169) concerning Indigenous and Tribal Peoples in Independent Countries, 28 ILM 1382 (1989)	ILO Convention 169	151, 255, 432
19 October 1989	IMO Resolution A.672 (16), 'Guidelines and Standards for the Removal of Offshore Installations and Structures on the Continental Shelf and in the Exclusive Economic Zone'		157
9 December 1989	Treaty between Australia and the Republic of Indonesia on the zone of cooperation in an area between the Indonesian province of East Timor and Northern Australia, 9 December 1989, 29 ILM (1990) 469	Timor Gap Treaty	225
30 May 1990	Agreement Between the Government of Malaysia and the Government of the Kingdom of Thailand on the Constitution and Other Matters Relating to the Establishment of the Malaysia-Thailand Joint Authority	Malaysia/ Thailand Agreement	210
29 June 1990	Council Directive 90/ 377/ EEC of 29 June 1990 concerning a Community procedure		378

(*cont.*)

Date	Full reference	Abbreviation	Pages
	to improve the transparency of gas and electricity prices charged to industrial end-users		
29 October 1990	Council Directive 90/ 547/ EEC of 29 October 1990 on the transit of electricity through transmission grids		378
30 November 1990	International Convention on Oil Pollution Preparedness, Response and Cooperation, available at www.ecolex.org (TRE-001109)	OPRC Convention	182
30 January 1991	Bamako Convention on the ban on the Import into Africa and the Control of Transboundary Movement and Management of Hazardous Wastes within Africa, 30 ILM 773	Bamako Convention	331
25 February 1991	Convention on Environmental Impact Assessment in a Transboundary Context, 1989 UNTS 310	Espoo Convention	142, 297
31 May 1991	Council Directive 91/ 296/ EEC of 31 May 1991 on the transit of natural gas through grids		378

(*cont.*)

Date	Full reference	Abbreviation	Pages
4 October 1991	Protocol on Environmental Protection to the Antarctic Treaty, 30 ILM 1455 (1991)	Madrid Protocol	168
18 November 1991	Protocol concerning the Control of Emissions of Volatile Organic Compounds or their Transboundary Fluxes, 31 ILM 573	VOC Protocol	163
13 December 1991	Committee on Economic, Social and Cultural Rights, General Comment No. 4: The Right to Adequate Housing, E/1992/23		54
13 December 1991	Agreement between the Republic of Argentina, the Federative Republic of Brazil, the Brazilian- Argentine Agency for Accounting and Control of Nuclear Materials and the International Atomic Energy Agency for the Application of Safeguards, INFCIRC/435		315, 318
17 December 1991	Concluding Document of the Hague Conference on the European Energy Charter		69
7 February 1992	Treaty of Maastricht on European Union, 7 February 1992, *OJ C 191, 29.7.1992, p. 1–112.* Now Treaty on	TEU	385

(cont.)

Date	Full reference	Abbreviation	Pages
	European Union, consolidated, 13 December 2007, 2008/C 115/01 [TEU]		
13 March 1992	Treaty on the development and utilization of the water resources of the Komati River Basin between the Government of the Kingdom of Swaziland and the Government of the Republic of South Africa	Komati Agreement	251
18 March 1992	Convention on the Protection and Use of Transboundary Watercourses and International Lakes, 1936 UNTS 269	UNECE Water Convention or Helsinki Convention	246
9 April 1992	Convention on the Protection of the Marine Environment of the Baltic Sea Area, available on www.ecolex.org (TRE-001153)		159
9 May 1992	United Nations Framework Convention on Climate Change, 31 ILM 849	UNFCCC	120, 163, 164, 415
5 June 1992	Convention on Biological Diversity, 1760 UNTS 79	CBD	
13 June 1992	'Rio Declaration on Environment and Development', UN Doc. A/CONF.151/26. Rev.1	Rio Declaration	62, 237, 343

(*cont.*)

Date	Full reference	Abbreviation	Pages
13 June 1992	Report of the United Nations Conference on Environment and Development, A/ CONF.151/26/Rev.l (Vol. l), Resolution 1, Annex 2: Agenda 21	Agenda 21	342
17 June 1992	Pipeline Consortium Agreement between the Government of the Republic of Kazakhstan and the Government of the Sultanate of Oman, joined by Russia in July 1992	CPC Agreement	272
22 September 1992	Convention for the Protection of the Marine Environment of the North-East Atlantic, 2354 UNTS 67	OSPAR Convention	159
27 November 1992	Protocol amending the International Convention on Civil Liability for Oil Pollution Damage, available at: www. ecolex.org (TRE-001 177)	CLC/92	189–193
27 November 1992	Protocol to Amend the International Convention on the Establishment of an International Fund for Compensation for Oil Pollution Damage, available at: www . ecolex.org (TRE-001 176)	FUND/92	189, 192

(*cont.*)

Date	Full reference	Abbreviation	Pages
17 December 1992	North American Free Trade Agreement, 32 ILM 296	NAFTA	92, 419
30 April 1993	Agreement between the Government of the United Kingdom of Great Britain and Northern Ireland and the Government of the Republic of Ireland relating to the Transmission of Natural Gas by Pipeline between the United Kingdom of Great Britain and Northern Ireland and the Republic of Ireland	UK/Ireland Agreement	273
14 September 1993	North American Agreement on Environmental Cooperation, 32 ILM 1480 (1993)	NAAEC	124
14 September 1993	North-American Agreement on Labor Cooperation, 32 ILM 1499 (1993)	NAALC	124
12 November 1993	Maritime treaty between Jamaica and the Republic of Colombia (with chart)	Colombia/ Jamaica Agreement	209
14 October 1993	Management and Cooperation Agreement between the Government of the Republic of Senegal and the Government of the Republic of Guinea-Bissau	Guinea-Bissau/ Senegal Agreement	44, 210–211, 293

(*cont.*)

Date	Full reference	Abbreviation	Pages
15 April 1994	Agreement establishing the World Trade Organisation, 1867 UNTS 154	Marrakesh Agreement	293
15 April 1994	General Agreement on Tariffs and Trade 1994, Marrakesh Agreement Establishing the World Trade Organization, Annex 1A, 1867 UNTS 187	GATT	35, 70, 74–75, 78, 79, 81, 83–88, 92–93, 95–98, 102, 104, 109–110, 113, 114, 116, 117–124, 199, 200, 286, 289, 357
15 April 1994	General Agreement on Trade in Services, Marrakesh Agreement Establishing the World Trade Organization, Annex 1B, 1869 UNTS 183	GATS	78, 123
15 April 1994	Agreement on Technical Barriers to Trade, 1868 UNTS 120	TBT Agreement	121
15 April 1994	Agreement on Subsidies and Countervailing Measures, 1867 UNTS 14	SCM Agreement	408
15 April 1994	Agreement on Trade-Related Investment Measures, Marrakesh Agreement Establishing the World Trade Organization, Annex 1A, 1868 UNTS 186	TRIMs or TRIMs Agreement	88, 408
15 April 1994	Agreement on Trade-Related Aspects of Intellectual Property Trade, 1869 UNTS 299	TRIPs or TRIPs Agreement	15
14 June 1994	Protocol to the LRTAP Convention on	Sulphur Protocol II	163

(*cont.*)

Date	Full reference	Abbreviation	Pages
	Further Reduction of Sulphur Emissions, 33 ILM 1540		
17 June 1994	Convention on Nuclear Safety, 1963 UNTS 293	CNS or Convention on Nuclear Safety	306
27 July 1994	Exchange of Notes between the Government of the United Kingdom of Great Britain and Northern Ireland and the Government of the Kingdom of Norway amending the Agreement relating to the Transmission of Petroleum by Pipeline from the Ekofisk Field and Neighbouring Areas to the United Kingdom	Ekofisk Amendment	271
28 July 1994	Agreement relating to the implementation of Part XI of the United Nations Convention on the Law of the Sea of 10 December 1982, 1836 UNTS 3 Implementation Agreement	1994	141
15 September 1994	Agreement between the Government of the Federative Republic of Brazil and the Government of the Russian Federation for the Cooperation on the Peaceful Uses of Nuclear Energy	Russia-Brazil NCA	315

(*cont.*)

Date	Full reference	Abbreviation	Pages
14 October 1994	Protocol for the Protection of the Mediterranean Sea against Pollution Resulting from Exploration and Exploitation of the Continental Shelf and the Seabed and its Subsoil, available on www.ecolex.org (TRE-001206)		159
7–8 December 1994	Southern African Power Pool (SAPP) Inter-Utility Memorandum Memorandum	SAPP Inter-Utility	287
17 December 1994	Final Act of the European Energy Charter Conference, Lisbon	Final Act	18
17 December 1994	Energy Charter Treaty, 2080 UNTS 100	ECT	15, 18–19, 25, 32, 68, 69–73, 77, 81, 88, 89, 98–102, 104, 107–108, 111–112, 116, 124–127, 199–200, 286, 289, 294, 347, 411
17 December 1994	Protocol on Energy Efficiency and Related Environmental Aspects, 2081 UNTS 3	PEEREA	106
11 January 1995	European Commission, *Green Paper – For a European Energy Policy*, 11 January 1995, COM(95) 659 Final		378
27 March 1995	Accord entre le Gouvernement de la	Norway/France Agreement	273

(*cont.*)

Date	Full reference	Abbreviation	Pages
	République française et le Gouvernement du Royaume de Norvège portant sur le transport par gazoduc de gaz du plateau continental norvégien et d'autres secteurs vers la France		
10 June 1995	Convention for the Protection of the Mediterranean Sea against Pollution, 16 February 1976, as amended and later becoming the Convention for the Protection of the Marine Environment and the Mediterranean Coastal Environment, available on www.ecolex.org (TRE- 001284)	Barcelona Convention	159
12 June 1995	Protocol of Agreement relating to the organization and operation of the Agency for Management and Cooperation	Guinea-Bissau/ Senegal Protocol	44, 211, 293
13 December 1995	European Commission, *White Paper - An Energy Policy for the European Union*, Brussels, 13 December 1995, COM(95) 682 Final		385
15 December 1995	Protocol Amending the Agreement on ASEAN Energy Cooperation Bangkok		393

(cont.)

Date	Full reference	Abbreviation	Pages
15 December 1995	Treaty on the Southeast Asia Nuclear Weapon-Free Zone, INFCIRC/548	Treaty of Bangkok	318
8 February 1996	Agreement between the Government of the Republic of Chad and the Government of the Republic of Cameroon Relating to the Construction and Operation of a Transportation System of Hydrocarbons by Pipeline	Chad/Cameroon Agreement	273
12 February 1996	Treaty concerning the integrated development of the Mahakali River (India-Nepal), 36 1LM 531 (1996)	Mahakali River Agreement	253
11 April 1996	African Nuclear Weapon-Free Zone Treaty, 35 ILM 698 (1996)	Treaty of Pelindaba	318
3 May 1996	European Social Charter (Revised), ETS No. 163	ESC	55
3 May 1996	International Convention on Liability and Compensation for Damage in Connection with the Carriage of Hazardous and Noxious Substances, amended by the Protocol of 30 April 2010, available at: www.ecolex.org (TRE-001 245)	HNS Convention 2010	297

(*cont.*)

Date	Full reference	Abbreviation	Pages
8 March 1996	Agreement between the Azerbaijan Republic and Georgia relating to the Development and Refurbishment of certain existing Petroleum Transportation Facilities, the Development of New Petroleum Transportation Facilities, and the Transportation of Petroleum via such Facilities beyond the Territory of Georgia		272
24 August 1996	Protocol on Energy in the Southern African Development Community (SADC) Region	SADC Energy Protocol	68
17 September 1996	Harare Declaration on Solar Energy and Sustainable Development, A/53/395		26
7 November 1996	Protocol of 7 November 1996 to the Convention of 1972 on the Prevention of Marine Pollution by Dumping of Wastes and Other Matter, 1046 UNTS 120	London Protocol	155, 297
6 December 1996	Agreement on the Establishment of Closed Joint Stock Company 'Caspian	CPC Hybrid Agreement	272

(*cont.*)

Date	Full reference	Abbreviation	Pages
	Pipeline Consortium-R' and Closed Joint Stock Company 'Caspian Pipeline Consortium-K' and Caspian Pipeline Consortium Restructuring and Shareholders' Agreement among the Government of the Russian Federation, the Government of the Republic of Kazakhstan, the Government of the Sultanate of Oman, Oman Oil Coompany Ltd. and Chevron Overseas Petroleum Inc., Open Joint Stock Oil Company Lukoil, Mobil Corporation, Open Joint Stock Oil Company Rosneft, Agip SPA, British Gas Exploration and Production Ltd., State Holding Company Munaigaz, Oryx Energy Company and Caspian Pipeline Consortium Ltd		
19 December 1996	*Directive 96/92/EC* of 19 December 1996 concerning common rules for the internal market in electricity		382
20 May 1997	Committee on Economic, Social and Cultural Rights (CESCR),		54

(*cont.*)

Date	Full reference	Abbreviation	Pages
	General Comment No. 7: The right to adequate housing (Art.11.1): forced evictions, E/1998/22		
21 May 1997	United Nations Convention on the Law of the Non-Navigational Uses of International Watercourses, 36 ILM 700	UN Watercourses Convention	63, 204, 246
5 September 1997	Joint Convention on the Safety of Spent Fuel Management and on the Safety of Radioactive Waste Management, available at: www.ecolex.org (TRE-001273)	Joint Convention	329
12 September 1997	Protocol to amend the Vienna Convention on Civil Liability for Nuclear Damage, 2241 UNTS 302	1997 Protocol	12 September 1997
12 September 1997	Convention on Supplementary Compensation for Nuclear Damage, IAEA INFCIRC/567	Complementary Vienna Convention	12 September 1997
26 September 1997	Protocol of 1997 to amend the International Convention for the Prevention of Pollution from Ships of 2 November 1973, as modified by the Protocol of 17 February 1978		161

(*cont.*)

Date	Full reference	Abbreviation	Pages
12 November 1997	'World Solar Programme 0^1996-2005', UNESCO, Records of the General Conference, Twenty-ninth Session, Paris, 21 October–12 November 1997, vol. 1: Resolutions		26
10 December 1997	Agreement between the Government of the Kingdom of Belgium and the Government of the United Kingdom of Great Britain and Northern Ireland relating to the Transmission of Natural Gas through a Pipeline between the Kingdom of Belgium and the United Kingdom of Great Britain and Northern Ireland	UK/Belgium Agreement	273
11 December 1997	Kyoto Protocol to the United Nations Framework Convention on Climate Change, Kyoto, 2303 UNTS 148	Kyoto Protocol	129–131, 163–165, 410
22 May 1998	Agreement on the Establishment of the ASEAN Centre for Energy		393
22 June 1998	*Directive 98/30/EC* of 22 June 1998 concerning common rules for the internal market in natural gas		382

(*cont.*)

Date	Full reference	Abbreviation	Pages
24 June 1998	Protocol on Persistent Organic Pollutants to the LRTAP Convention, 37 I.L.M .513	POP Protocol	163
24 June 1998	Protocol on Heavy Metals to the LRTAP Convention, available at : www.unece.org/env/lrtap/hm_h1.html	Metals Protocol or HM Protocol	163
25 June 1998	Convention on Access to Information, Public Participation in Decision-making and Access to Justice in Environmental Matters, 2161 UNTS 447	Aarhus Convention	147, 297, 431
22–23 July 1998	OSPAR Decision 98/3 on the Disposal of Disused Offshore Installation, Sintra, Portugal	Decision 98/3	160
25 September 1998	Regional Cooperation Agreement for the Promotion of Nuclear Science and Technology in Latin America and the Caribbean, INFCIRC/ 582	ARCAL Agreement	316
17 June 1999	Protocol on Water and Health to the 1992 Convention on the Protection and Use of Transboundary Watercourses and International Lakes, 2331 UNTS 202	Protocol on Water and Health	246
25 October 1999	UN Security Council Resolution 1272 (1999), UN Doc. S/RES/1272 (1999)		43

(*cont.*)

Date	Full reference	Abbreviation	Pages
18 November 1999	Agreement among the Azerbaijan Republic, Georgia and the Republic of Turkey Relating to the Transportation of Petroleum Via the Territories of the Azerbaijan Republic, Georgia and the Republic of Turkey Through the Baku-Tbilisi-Ceyhan Main Export Pipeline	BTC IGA	272
30 November 1999	Protocol to the 1979 Convention on Long-Range Transboundary Air Pollution on the Reduction of Acidification, Eutrophication and Ground-Level Ozone, Document of the Economic and Social Council EB.AIR/1999/1	Gothenburg Protocol	163
10 February 2000	Exchange of Notes Constituting an Agreement between the Government of Australia and the United Nations Transitional Administration in East Timor (UNTAET) concerning the Continued Operation of the Treaty between Australia and the Republic of Indonesia on the Zone of Cooperation in an		44

(*cont.*)

Date	Full reference	Abbreviation	Pages
	Area between the Indonesian Province of East Timor and Northern Australia of 11 December 1989		
2 July 2000	Agreement between the Kingdom of Saudi Arabia and the State of Kuwait concerning the submerged area adjacent to the divided zone		210
11 August 2000	General Comment No. 14: The Right to the Highest Attainable Standard of Health (Art. 12), Document E/ C.12/2000/4		54
13 September 2000	'Millennium Declaration', UN Doc. A/RES/55/2	Millennium Declaration	28
20 December 2000	'World Solar Programme 1996-2005', UN Doc. A/RES/55/205	Resolution 55/ 205	26
18 January 2001	Acordo entre o Governo da República Federativa do Brasil e o Governo da República da Coréia para Cooperção nos Usos Pacíficos da Energia Nuclear	Korea-Brazil NCA	315
21 February 2001	Treaty between the Federal Republic of Nigeria and the Democratic Republic of Sao Tome e Principe on the Joint Development of Petroleum and other Resources, in respect of Areas of the	Nigeria/Sao Tome e Principe Agreement	220

(*cont.*)

Date	Full reference	Abbreviation	Pages
	Exclusive Economic Zone of the two States		
23 March 2001	International Convention on Civil Liability for Oil Pollution Damage, available at: www.ecolex.org (TRE-001 377)	BUNKERS	189, 190
12 December 2001	Draft articles on the prevention of transboundary harm from hazardous activities, G.A. Res. 56/82, U.N. Doc A/RES/56/82	ILC Prevention Articles	134
12 December 2001	Responsibility of States for Internationally Wrongful Acts, G.A. Res. 56/83, U.N. DOC A/RES/56/83	ILC State Responsibility Articles	8, 185
25 January 2002	Protocol Concerning Cooperation in Preventing Pollution from Ships and, in Cases of Emergency, Combating Pollution of the Mediterranean Sea, available on www.ecolex.org (TRE- 001402)		183
20 May 2002	Timor Sea Treaty Between the Government of East Timor and the Government of Australia, 2258 UNTS 3 (2005)	Timor Sea Treaty	220
5 July 2002	ASEAN Memorandum of Understanding (MoU) on the Trans-ASEAN Gas Pipeline, Bali		393

(*cont.*)

Date	Full reference	Abbreviation	Pages
4 September 2002	'Political declaration', Report of World Summit on Sustainable Development in Johannesburg (South Africa), 26 August to 4 September 2002. UN Doc. A/CONF.199/20, p. 1, 2002	Political declaration	
4 September 2002	'Plan of Implementation', Report of the World Summit on Sustainable Development at Johannesburg (South Africa), 26 August-4 September 2002. UN Doc. A/CONF.199/20 Implementation	Plan of	27, 369
26 November 2002	Committee on Economic, Social and Cultural Rights, General Comment No. 15 (2002), The Right to Water (Articles 11 and 12 of the International Covenant on Economic, Social and Cultural Rights), UN ESCOR DOC. E/C.12/ 2002/11	GC 15	
31 January 2003	ECOWAS Energy Protocol A/P4/1/03	ECOWAS Energy Protocol	68, 101
31 January 2003	Treaty on the West African Gas Pipeline Project between the Republic of Benin and the Republic of Ghana and the Federal	West African Pipeline Agreement	273

(*cont.*)

Date	Full reference	Abbreviation	Pages
	Republic of Nigeria and the Republic of Togo		
16 May 2003	Protocol to the International Convention on the Establishment of an International Fund for Compensation for Oil Pollution by oil, available at: www.ecolex.org (TRE-001 401)	FUND/2003	189, 192
21 May 2003	Protocol on Civil Liability and Compensation for Damage Caused by the Transboundary Effects of Industrial Accidents on Transboundary Waters, Doc. ECE/MP.WAT/11-ECE/CP.TEIA/9	Kyiv Protocol	142
26 June 2003	Directive 2003/54/EC of 26 June 2003 concerning common rules for the internal market in electricity and repealing Directive 96/ 92/EC		382
26 June 2003	Directive 2003/55/EC of 26 June 2003 concerning common rules for the internal market in natural gas and repealing Directive 98/ 30/EC		382
26 June 2003	Regulation (EC) No 1228/ 2003 of 26 June 2003 on conditions for access to the network		382

(*cont.*)

Date	Full reference	Abbreviation	Pages
	for cross-border exchanges in electricity		
13 October 2003	Directive 2003/87/EC of the European Parliament and of the Council of 13 October 2003 establishing a scheme for greenhouse gas emission allowance trading within the Community and amending Council Directive 96/61/E, OJ 2003 L 0087, 25 June 2009 (consolidated version)	ETS Directive	130
2 December 2003	Exclusive Economic Zone Co-operation Treaty Between the State of Barbados and the Republic of Guyana Concerning the Exercise of Jurisdiction in Their Exclusive Economic Zones in the Area of Bilateral Overlap Within Each of their Outer Limits and Beyond the Outer Limits of the Exclusive Economic Zones of Other States, 2277 UNTS 202	Barbados/ Guyana Agreement	220
26 May 2004	Human Rights Committee, General Comment No. 31: The Nature of the General Legal Obligation Imposed on States		173

(*cont.*)

Date	Full reference	Abbreviation	Pages
	Parties to the Covenant, CCPR/C/ 21/Rev.1/Add. 13		
21 August 2004	Berlin Rules on Water Resources, adopted at the 71nd conference of the ILA (2004)	Berlin Rules	246
24 September 2004	Agreement Relating to the Transmission of Natural Gas through a Second Pipeline between the United Kingdom of Great Britain and Northern Ireland and Ireland and through a Connection to the Isle of Man	UK/Ireland Second Pipeline Agreement	273
26 September 2004	Agreement between the Government of the State of Qatar and the Government of the United Arab Emirates relating to the Transmission of Gas by Pipeline between the State of Qatar and the United Arab Emirates	Dolphin Gas Pipeline Agreement	273
13 April 2005	International Convention for the Suppression of Acts of Nuclear Terrorism, 2445 UNTS 89	Nuclear Terrorism Convention	305
19 January 2006	US-Oman Free Trade Agreement	US-Oman FTA	114
13 March 2006	'Promotion of new and renewable sources of energy, including the		27

(*cont.*)

Date	Full reference	Abbreviation	Pages
	implementation of the World Solar Programme', A/RES/60/199		
8 September 2006	Treaty on a Nuclear-Weapon-Free Zone in Central Asia, 2212 UNTS 257	Semipalatinsk Treaty	318
4 December 2006	Draft principles on the allocation of loss in the case of transboundary harm arising out of hazardous activities, G.A. Res. 61/36, UN Doc A/RES/61/36	ILC Principles on Loss	
23 August 2007	Memorandum of Understanding on the ASEAN Power Grid		393
13 September 2007	UN General Assembly Resolution 61/295, 'Declaration on the Rights of Indigenous Peoples'	UNDRIP	50, 151, 255
26 November 2007	Accord d'application de l'accord de coopération du 15 mai 1997 entre le Gouvernement de la République française et le Gouvernement de la République Populaire de Chine pour le développement des utilisations pacifiques de l'énergie nucléaire	France-China NCA	314
13 December 2007	Treaty of Lisbon amending the Treaty	Treaty of Lisbon	379

(*cont.*)

Date	Full reference	Abbreviation	Pages
	on European Union and the Treaty establishing the European Community, OJ C 306, 17.12.2007, pp. 1–271		
13 December 2007	Treaty on the Functioning of the European Union, OJ C 83 - 30.3.2010	TFEU	55–56, 378–381, 385
24 March 2008	Accord de coopération entre le Gouvernement de la République algérienne démocratique et populaire et le Gouvernement de la République populaire de Chine pour le développement des utilisations pacifiques de l'énergie nucléaire	China-Algeria NCA	314
10 October 2008	Agreement for Cooperation between the Government of the United States of America and the Government of India concerning Peaceful Uses of Nuclear Energy		313
11 December 2008	'Draft Articles on the Law of Transboundary Aquifers', G.A. Res. 63/ 124, UN Doc A/ RES/ 63/124	ILC Aquifers Draft	246
26 January 2009	Statute of the International Renewable Energy	IRENA Statute	294, 371

(*cont.*)

Date	Full reference	Abbreviation	Pages
	Agency (IRENA), IRENA/FC/Statute		
1 March 2009	ASEAN Petroleum Security Agreement, Cha-am, 1 March 2009		392
21 May 2009	Agreement for Cooperation between the Government of the United States of America and the Government of the United Arab Emirates concerning Peaceful Uses of Nuclear Energy	US-UAE NCA	312
3 July 2009	Accord intergouvernemental entre la République algérienne démocratique et populaire, la République fédérale du Nigéria et la République du Niger, relatif au projet trans-saharien-gaz-pipeline	Trans-Saharan Pipeline Agreement	273
13 July 2009	Directive 2009/72/EC of 13 July 2009 concerning common rules for the internal market in electricity and repealing Directive 2003/54/EC		382
13 July 2009	Directive 2009/73/EC of 13 July 2009 concerning common rules for the internal		382–383

(*cont.*)

Date	Full reference	Abbreviation	Pages
	market in natural gas and repealing Directive 2003/55/EC		
13 July 2009	Regulation (EC) No 713/2009 of 13 July 2009 establishing an Agency for the Cooperation of Energy Regulators (ACER)		383, 385
13 July 2009	Regulation (EC) No 714/2009 of 13 July 2009 on conditions for access to the network for crossborder exchanges in electricity and repealing Regulation (EC) No 1228/2003		101, 383, 386
13 July 2009	Regulation (EC) No 715/2009 of 13 July 2009 on conditions for access to the natural gas transmission networks and repealing Regulation (EC) No 1775/2005		101, 383, 386
13 July 2009	Agreement among the Republic of Austria, the Republic of Bulgaria, the Republic of Hungary, Romania and the Republic of Turkey regarding the Nabucco Project, 385 der Beilagen XXIV. GP - Staatsvertrag - Abkommenstext	Nabucco IGA	198

(*cont.*)

Date	Full reference	Abbreviation	Pages
	in englischer Sprache (Normativer Teil)		
29 September 2009	Agreement between Georgia and the Azerbaijan Republic relating to the Transit, Transportation and Sale of Natural Gas in and Beyond the Territories of Georgia and the Azerbaijan Republic through the South Caucasus Pipeline System	SCP Agreement	272
25 November 2009	Agreement on the functioning of the Gas Exporting Countries Forum, 23 December 2008, Qatar Official Gazette, vol. 11, p. 45ff; the GECF Statute is attached to the GECF Agreement	GECF Agreement and GECF Statute	365
7 December 2009	North Seas Countries' Offshore Grid Initiative, available at: www.benelux.int	NSCOGI Declaration	263
30 April 2010	Consolidated text of the International Convention on Liability and Compensation for Damage in Connection with the Carriage of Hazardous	HNS Convention	297

(*cont.*)

Date	Full reference	Abbreviation	Pages
	and Noxious Substances by Sea, 1996,and the Protocol of 2010 to the Convention		
10 December 2010	The North Seas Countries' Offshore Grid Initiative, 'Memorandum of Understanding'	NSCOGI MoU	263
11 December 2010	Gas Pipeline Framework Agreement between the Government of the Islamic Republic of Afghanistan, the Government of the Republic of India, the Government of the Islamic Republic of Pakistan and the Government of Turkmenistan	TAPI Framework Agreement	273
16 February 2011	'International Year of Sustainable Energy for All', A/RES/65/151	Resolution 65/151	27
22 February 2011	International Energy Forum Charter, 51 ILM 201 (2012).	IEF Charter	363
25 May 2011	OECD, Guidelines for Multinational Enterprises, Annex I to the Declaration on International Investment and Multinational Enterprises	OECD Guidelines	171
16 June 2011	Guiding Principles on Business and Human	UN Guiding Principles	171

(*cont.*)

Date	Full reference	Abbreviation	Pages
	Rights: Implementing the United Nations 'Protect, Respect and Remedy' Framework, HRC Resolution 17/4		
7 September 2011	European Commission, Communication – The EU Energy Policy: Engaging with Partners beyond our Borders, 7 September 2011, COM(2011) 539 final		381
22 September 2011	Memorandum of Understanding on Energy Cooperation between the Association of Southeast Asian Nations and the International Energy Agency		393
18 October 2011	Commonwealth of Independent States, Agreement on the Creation of a Free Trade Area		101
1 January 2012	International Finance Corporation, Performance Standards on Environmental and Social Sustainability	IFC Performance Standards	146
30 May 2012	Memorandum of Understanding between the Ministry of Industry, Energy		285

(*cont.*)

Date	Full reference	Abbreviation	Pages
	and Tourism in Iceland and the Department for Energy and Climate Change in the United Kingdom on Cooperation in the Energy Sector		
26 June 2012	Intergovernmental Agreement between the Government of the Republic of Turkey and the Government of the Republic of Azerbajian concerning the Trans Anatolian Natural Gas Pipeline System		272
13 February 2013	Agreement among the Republic of Albania, the Hellenic Republic and the Italian Republic relating to the Trans-Adriatic Pipeline Project	Trans-Adriatic Pipeline Agreement	272
17 April 2013	Regulation (EU) No 347/2013 of 17 April 2013 on guidelines for trans-European energy infrastructure (TEN-E Regulation)		101
24 April 2013	Framework Agreement between the Republic of Iraq and the Hashemite Kingdom of Jordan to implement a project to transport Iraqi crude oil through the	Iraq/Jordan Agreement	273

(*cont.*)

Date	Full reference	Abbreviation	Pages
	territory of the Kingdom of Jordan to the export terminal port (Aqaba) on the Red Sea coast for export with a parallel gas pipeline		
29 May 2014	Treaty on the Eurasian Economic Union		101
21 October 2014	Agreement between the Government of Nepal and the Government of the Republic of India on Electric Power Trade Cross-Border Transmission Interconnection and Grid Connectivity	India-Nepal IGA	285
21 May 2015	Concluding Document of the Ministerial ('The Hague II') Conference on the International Energy Charter		73
21 October 2015	Resolution 70/1, 'Transforming our World: The 2030 Agenda for Sustainable Development', UN Doc. A/RES/70/1	2030 Agenda	4, 28, 369
12 December 2015	Adoption of the Paris Agreement, Decision 1/CP.21, FCCC/CP/2015/L.9, Annex	Paris Agreement	131, 163–166, 401, 432
18 March 2016	Regional Cooperative Agreement for Research, Development and Training Related to Nuclear Science and	RCA Agreement	316

(*cont.*)

Date	Full reference	Abbreviation	Pages
	Technology for Asia and the Pacific, INFCIRC/919		
6 October 2016	Carbon Offsetting and Reduction Scheme for International Aviation (CORSIA), ICAO Assembly, Resolution 22/2 'Consolidated statement of continuing ICAO policies and practices relating to environmental protection - Global Market-Based Measure (GMBM) scheme', Doc. ICAO/A/39-WP/ 530	CORSIA	410
30 October 2016	Comprehensive Economic and Trade Agreement (CETA) between Canada and the European Union and its Member States, OJ L 11, 14.1.2017, pp. 23–1079	CETA	113
30 November 2016	European Commission, *Communication – Clean Energy for All Europeans*, 30 November 2016, COM (2016) 860 Final		381, 385
10 December 2016	Declaration of Cooperation OPEC and non-OPEC, adopted at the first	DoC	355, 356

(*cont.*)

Date	Full reference	Abbreviation	Pages
	OPEC and non-OPEC Ministerial Meeting		
13 January 2017	Nordic Saami Convention		52
19 September 2017	Cooperative Agreement for Arab States in Asia for Research, Development and Training related to Nuclear Science and Technology, INFCIRC/ 929	ARASIA Agreement	316
4 March 2018	Regional Agreement on Access to Information, Public Participation and Justice in Environmental Matters in Latin America and the Caribbean	Escazú Agreement	147, 431
6 March 2018	Maritime Boundary Treaty, Annex 28 to the Conciliation Commission Report: Conciliation Between the Democratic Republic of Timor-Leste and the Commonwealth of Australia, Report and Recommendations of the Compulsory Conciliation Commission Between Timor-Leste and Australia on the Timor Sea (9 May 2018)	Australia/ Timor-Leste Boundary Treaty	210

(*cont.*)

Date	Full reference	Abbreviation	Pages
30 May 2018	Directive (EU) 2018/844 of 30 May 2018 amending Directive 2010/31/EU on the energy performance of buildings and Directive 2012/27/EU on energy efficiency		383
30 October 2018	Memorandum of Understanding between the Association of Southeast Asian Nations and the International Renewable Energy Agency		393
11 December 2018	Directive (EU) 2018/2002 of 11 December 2018 amending Directive 2012/27/EU on energy efficiency		383
11 December 2018	Directive (EU) 2018/2001 of 11 December 2018 on the promotion of the use of energy from renewable sources		383
11 December 2018	Regulation (EU) 2018/1999 of 11 December 2018 on the Governance of the Energy Union and Climate Action		384
5 June 2019	Directive (EU) 2019/944 of 5 June 2019 on common rules for the		383–384

(*cont.*)

Date	Full reference	Abbreviation	Pages
	internal market for electricity and amending Directive 2012/27/EU		
5 June 2019	Regulation (EU) 2019/943 of 5 June 2019 on the internal market for electricity		384
5 June 2019	Regulation (EU) 2019/941 of 5 June 2019 on risk-preparedness in the electricity sector and repealing Directive 2005/89/EC		384
5 June 2019	Regulation (EU) 2019/942 of 5 June 2019 establishing a European Union Agency for the Cooperation of Energy Regulators		384
2 July 2019	Charter of Cooperation, adopted at the 6th OPEC and non-OPEC Ministerial Meeting	CoC	355
20 September 2019	African Regional Cooperative Agreement for Research, Development and Training related to Nuclear Science and Technology, INFCIRC/ 935	AFRA Agreement	316
21 September 2020	Commission Implementing Regulation (EU) 2020/1577 of 21 September		19

(*cont.*)

Date	Full reference	Abbreviation	Pages
	2020 amending Annex I to Council Regulation (EEC) No 2658/87 on the tariff and statistical nomenclature and on the Common Customs Tariff		
19 November 2020	Energy Transition Towards Sustainable Development, Joint Ministerial Statement of the thirty-eighth ASEAN Ministers on Energy Meeting	2020 AMEM Statement	33

CASES

Permanent Court of International Justice and International Court of Justice

Maritime Delimitation in the Black Sea (Romania v Ukraine), Judgment, ICJ Reports 2009, p. 61, 58, 59

Maritime Delimitation and Territorial Questions between Qatar and Bahrain, Jurisdiction and Admissibility, Judgment, ICJ Reports 1994, 223

Military and Paramilitary Activities in and against Nicaragua (Nicaragua v. *United States of America), Merits, Judgment*, I.C.J. Reports 1986, p. 14, 45

North Sea Continental Shelf (Federal Republic of Germany/Denmark; Federal Republic of Germany/Netherlands), Judgment, ICJ Reports 1969, p. 47, 232, 233

Nuclear Tests (New Zealand v. France), Request for the Indication of Interim Measures of Protection, Order (22 June 1973), ICJ Reports 1973, p. 135, 241

Nuclear Tests (Australia v. France) (New Zealand v. France), Judgments, ICJ Reports 1974, p. 268, 232

Obligation to Negotiate Access to the Pacific Ocean (Bolivia v. Chile), Judgment, ICJ Reports 2018, p. 507, 233

Oil Platforms case (Islamic Republic of Iran v. United States of America), ICJ Reports 2003, p. 161, 36, 185

Pulp Mills on the River Uruguay (Argentina v. Uruguay), Judgment, ICJ Reports 2010, p. 14, 133, 134, 232, 251

Railway Traffic between Lithuania and Poland, 1931 PCIJ Series A/B No. 42, 232

Sovereignty over Pulau Ligitan and Pulau Sipadan (Indonesia/Malaysia), Judgment, ICJ Reports 2002, p. 625, 225

Temple of Preah Vihear (Cambodia v. Thailand), Judgment, ICJ Reports 1962, p. 6, 225

International Tribunal for the Law of the Sea and Other UNCLOS-Related Mechanisms

Conciliation between The Democratic Republic of Timor-Leste and The Commonwealth of Australia, PCA Case No. 2016-10, Press Release No. 9, 1 September 2017, 50

Dispute Concerning Coastal State Rights in the Black Sea, Sea of Azov, and Kerch Strait (Ukraine v. Russian Federation), PCA Case No. 2017-06, Award concerning the preliminary objections of the Russian Federation (21 February 2020), 134, 240

Dispute concerning delimitation of the maritime boundary between Bangladesh and Myanmar in the Bay of Bengal (Bangladesh/Myanmar), ITLOS Case No. 16, Judgment (14 March 2012), 59

Dispute Concerning Delimitation of the Maritime Boundary Between Ghana and Cote D'Ivoire in the Atlantic Ocean (Ghana/Cote D'Ivoire), ITLOS Case No. 23 (Provisional measures), Order (25 April 2015), 61, 134, 230

Dispute Concerning Delimitation of the Maritime Boundary Between Ghana and Cote D'Ivoire in the Atlantic Ocean (Ghana/Cote D'Ivoire), ITLOS Case No. 23, Judgment (23 September 2017), 59, 229

Dispute concerning delimitation of the maritime boundary between Mauritius and Maldives in the Indian Ocean (Mauritius/Maldives), ITLOS Case No. 28, Preliminary Objections, Judgment (28 January 2021), 188

WTO Dispute Settlement Body

Other Interstate Arbitrations (or Assimilated)

Eritrea Ethiopia Claims Commission

United Nations Compensation Commission

Investment Disputes

European Court of Human Rights

European Committee of Social Rights

Inter-American Court of Human Rights

African Commission and African Court on Human and Peoples' Rights

Human Rights Committee

Decisions of Compliance Committees

Inspection and Advisory Panels (by Date)

European Union Courts

Domestic Case Law (by Country and Date)

Introduction

Energy is highly but not clearly regulated in international law. The legal sources on which the governance of energy is based are plentiful but scattered around a vast legal expanse, which has so far been addressed – with very rare exceptions[1] – through separate specialised accounts devoted to specific topics or branches. The purpose of this book is twofold: to provide an overall account of the international law of energy understood as the entirety of international law seen from the prism of energy; and to rely on this account to analyse the implications of the ongoing energy transformation for international law.

Traditionally, only a limited part of the international legal aspects of energy attracted the attention of commentators. Most notable among these aspects were agreements for the joint development of hydrocarbons,[2] certain international proceedings relating to the expropriation of

[1] See, in particular, C. Redgwell, 'International Regulation of Energy Activities', in M. M. Roggenkamp et al. (eds.), *Energy Law in Europe: National, EU and International Regulation* (Oxford: Oxford University Press, 3rd ed. 2016), pp. 13–136; K. Talus (ed.), *Research Handbook on International Energy Law* (Cheltenham: Edward Elgar, 2014); R. Leal-Arcas, A. Filis, E. S. Abu Gosh, *International Energy Governance: Selected Legal Issues* (Cheltenham: Edward Elgar, 2015); J. E. Viñuales, 'Vers un droit international de l'energie: Essai de cartographie', in M. G. Kohen, D. Bentolila (eds), *Mélanges en l'honneur du professeur Jean-Michel Jacquet: le droit des rapports internationaux économiques et privés* (Paris: LexisNexis, 2013), pp. 321–344; A. A. Fatouros, 'An International Legal Framework for Energy' (2007) 332 *RCADI* 355.

[2] See e.g. V. Becker-Weinberg, *Joint Development of Hydrocarbon Deposits in the Law of the Sea* (Berlin: Springer, 2014); N. Bankes, 'Recent Framework Agreements for the Recognition and Development of Transboundary Hydrocarbon Resources' (2014) 29 *International Journal of Marine and Coastal Law* 666; C. Scholfield, 'Blurring the Lines: Maritime Joint Development and the Cooperative Management of Ocean Resources' (2008) 7 *Issues Legal Scholarship* 1; A. E. Bastida et al, 'Cross-Border Unitization and Joint Development Agreements: An International Law Perspective' (2007) 29 *Houston International Law Journal* 355; D. M. Ong, 'Joint Development of Common Offshore Oil and Gas Deposits: "Mere" State Practice or Customary International Law?' (1999) 93 *American Journal of International Law* 771; H. Fox, *Joint Development of Offshore Oil and Gas* (London: BIICL, 1990); W. T. Onorato, 'Apportionment of an International Common

oil investments structured under 'State contracts',[3] disputes relating to the delimitation of maritime areas,[4] the prevention and compensation of oil spills[5] or some nuclear energy-related transactions.[6] More recently, there have been attempts to clarify the international law of energy

Petroleum Deposit' (1977) 26 *International and Comparative Law Quarterly* 324; W. T. Onorato, 'Apportionment of an International Common Petroleum Deposit' (1968) 17 *International and Comparative Law Quarterly* 85.

[3] See e.g. Ch. Leben, 'La théorie du contrat d'Etat et l'évolution du droit international des investissements' (2004) 302 *RCADI* 197; S. Toope, *Mixed International Arbitration: Studies in Arbitration between States and Private Persons* (Cambridge: Grotius, 1990); C. Greenwood, 'State Contracts in International Law – The Libyan Oil Arbitrations' (1983) 53 *British Yearbook of International Law* 27; R. von Mehren, N. Kourides, 'International Arbitrations between States and Foreign Private Parties: The Libyan Nationalization Cases' (1981) 75 *American Journal of International Law* 476.

[4] For a recent comprehensive statement of the law of maritime delimitation see Y. Tanaka, *Predictability and Flexibility in the Law of Maritime Delimitation* (Oxford: Hart, 2nd ed. 2019). For discussions focussed on energy see: K. Noussia, 'On International Arbitrations for the Settlement of Boundary Maritime Delimitation Disputes and Disputes from Joint Development Agreements for the Exploitation of Offshore Natural Resources' (2010) 25 *International Journal of Marine and Coastal Law* 63; M. Miyoshi, C. Schofield, *The Joint Development of Offshore Oil and Gas in relation to Maritime Boundary Delimitation* (Durham: International Boundaries Research Unit, 1999); G. H. Blake et al. (eds.), *The Peaceful Management of Transboundary Resources* (Berlin: Springer, 1995); R. Lagoni, 'Oil and Gas Across National Frontiers' (1979) 73 *American Journal of International Law* 215.

[5] See e.g. C. M. De la Rue, C. B. Anderson, *Shipping and the Environment: Law and Practice* (London: Routledge (Informa Law), 2nd ed. 2009); K. Le Couvreur, *La responsabilité civile à l'épreuve des pollutions majeures resultant du transport maritime* (Aix-en-Provence: PUAM, 2007); M. Jacobsson, 'The International Oil Pollution Compensation Funds and the International Regime of Compensation for Oil Pollution Damage', in J. Basedow, U. Magnus (eds.), *Pollution of the Sea: Prevention and Compensation* (Berlin: Springer, 2007), pp. 137–150; A. K.-J. Tan, *Vessel-Source Marine Pollution* (Cambridge: Cambridge University Press, 2005); E. Franckx (ed.), *Vessel-Source Pollution and Coastal State Jurisdiction The Work of the ILA Committee on Coastal State Jurisdiction Relating to Marine Pollution (1991–2000)* (The Hague: Kluwer, 2001); C. Wu, *Pollution from the Carriage of Oil by Sea: Liability and Compensation* (The Hague: Kluwer, 1996); D. Brubaker, *Marine Pollution and International Law: Principles and Practice* (London: Belhaven Press, 1993); J. W. Kindt, *Marine Pollution and the Law of the Sea* (Getzville NY: Hein & Co, 1986); A. Boyle, 'Marine Pollution under the Law of the Sea Convention' (1985) 79 *American Journal of International Law* 342; D. Abecassis, *The Law and Practice Relating to Oil Pollution from Ships* (London: Butterworths, 1978).

[6] See e.g. S. Tromans, *Nuclear Law: The Law Applying to Nuclear Installations and Radioactive Substances in Its Historic Context* (Oxford: Hart, 2nd ed. 2010); OECD, *International Nuclear Law. History, Evolution and Outlook* (Paris: OECD, 2010); F. Nocera (ed.), *The Legal Regime of Nuclear Energy: A Comprehensive Guide to International and European Union Law* (Cambridge: Intersentia, 2005).

through the prisms of trade,[7] foreign investment,[8] environmental protection,[9] human rights[10] or the law of the sea.[11] These accounts are based on the familiar framing of 'branches' of international law, following which energy issues are analysed branch-by-branch. Despite their contribution, the traditional and the more recent framings have an important shortcoming: they keep the conceptual siloes standing. Yet, it is not possible to understand the legal implications of the major energy transformation[12] the world is undergoing with partial or segmented analytical tools. This is for three main reasons.

First, different bodies of international law pursue multiple, different and potentially conflicting goals. The prevailing branch-based view of

[7] See e.g. A. Marhold, *Energy in International Trade Law* (Cambridge: Cambridge University Press, 2021); I. Espa, T. Cottier (eds.), *International Trade in Sustainable Electricity: Regulatory Challenges in International Economic Law* (Cambridge: Cambridge University Press, 2017); V. Pogoretskyy, *Freedom of Transit and Access to Gas Pipeline Networks under WTO Law* (Cambridge: Cambridge University Press, 2017); D. Azaria, *Treaties on Transit of Energy via Pipelines and Countermeasures* (Oxford: Oxford University Press, 2015); Y. Selivanova (ed.), *Regulation of energy in International Trade Law: WTO, NAFTA and Energy Charter* (Alphen aan den Rijn: Wolters Kluwer, 2011).

[8] See e.g. P. D. Cameron, *International Energy Investment Law: The Pursuit of Stability* (Oxford: Oxford University Press, 2nd ed. 2018); M. Scherer, C. Amirfar (eds.), *International Arbitration in the Energy Sector* (Oxford: Oxford University Press, 2018); H. G. Burnett, L.-A. Brett, *Arbitration of International Mining Disputes* (Oxford: Oxford University Press, 2017); M. Erkan, *International Energy Investment Law: Stability through Contractual Clauses* (Alphen aan den Rijn: Wolters Kluwer, 2011).

[9] See e.g. D. Bodansky, J. Brunnée, L. Rajamani, *International Climate Change Law* (Oxford: Oxford University Press, 2017); P. D. Park, *International Law for Energy and the Environment* (London: Routledge, 2nd ed. 2013); A. J. Bradbrook et al. (eds.), *The Law of Energy for Sustainable Development* (Cambridge: Cambridge University Press, 2005); Gao Zhiguo (ed.), *Environmental Regulation of Oil and Gas* (London: Kluwer, 1998).

[10] See e.g. J. Ezirigwe, 'Human Rights and Property Rights in Natural Resources Development' (2017) 35 *Journal of Energy & Natural Resources* 201; D. N. Zillman et al. (eds.), *Human Rights in Natural Resource Development: Public Participation in the Sustainable Development of Mining and Energy Resources* (Oxford: Oxford University Press, 2002).

[11] N. Bankes, S. Trevisanut (eds.), *Energy from the Sea: An International Law Perspective on Ocean Energy* (Leiden: Martinus Nijhoff, 2015); H. Esmaeili, *The legal regime of offshore oil rigs in international law* (Aldershot: Ashgate, 2001). See further n. 1 and 2.

[12] Global Commission on the Geopolitics of the Energy Transformation, *A New World: The Geopolitics of the Energy Transformation* (IRENA, 2019) [*Geopolitics of the Energy Transformation*] (speaking of an 'irreversible momentum for a global energy transformation' and reviewing the evidence and the main drivers of the transformation, such as technological change relating to efficiency, transportation and renewable energy, environmental constraints and increasing public support).

international law does not capture the complex interactions arising from what economists call the 'energy trilemma',[13] i.e. the trade-offs presented by the pursuit of energy security, equity (access and affordability), and sustainability (mainly decarbonisation). By way of illustration, in *India – Solar Cells*,[14] the Appellate Body of the World Trade Organization (WTO) confirmed the panel's findings that the local content requirements (LCRs) introduced by India as a condition for renewable energy generators to benefit from an advantageous support scheme was in violation of trade disciplines. This is a correct – yet not uncontroversial – application of international trade law, which typically restricts LCRs because of the inefficiencies and distortions they create.[15] However, unless India – as the second most populous country in the world and the third largest emitter of greenhouse gases – moves massively and rapidly into renewable energy, the mitigation goals pursued by the climate change regime will not be reachable. In an ideal world, India would do so without reverting to industrial policy to promote its own industry. But it may be politically unrealistic to expect such massive transfers of public money to producers of foreign equipment, even if the latter is cheaper and better. If one adds to this two-branch picture access to energy from a human rights perspective, as contemplated in Sustainable Development Goal 7 (SDG 7),[16] or the collective entitlement to the development of energy resources arising from the principle of self-determination,[17] then the trade-off is even more complex. The analysis of

[13] See World Energy Council, *World Energy Trilemma Index 2020* (London: WEC, 2020). This index has been prepared annually by the WEC since 2010, together with two consultancies.

[14] *India – Certain Measures Relating to Solar Cells and Solar Modules* (Complainant: United States), AB Report, 16 September 2016, WT/DS456/AB/R, WT/DS456/AB/R/Add.1.

[15] G. C. Hufbauer, J. J. Schott, C. Cimino-Isaacs, M. Vieiro and and E. Wadam, *Local Content Requirements: A Global Problem* (New York: Columbia University Press, 2013).

[16] Resolution 70/1, 'Transforming our World: The 2030 Agenda for Sustainable Development', 21 October 2015, UN Doc. A/RES/70/1, including a statement of 17 sustainable development goals (SDGs). On SDG 7 see S. Bruce, J. E. Viñuales, 'SDG 7: Access to Affordable, Reliable, Sustainable and Modern Energy for All', in J. Ebbesson, E. Hey (eds.), *The Cambridge Handbook on the United Nations Sustainable Development Goals and International Law* (Cambridge: Cambridge University Press, 2021), chapter 7.

[17] The dispute regarding the hydrocarbon deposits in the Timor Sea provides a good illustration of this complexity, as illustrated by Portugal's unsuccessful claim before the ICJ in connection with the 1989 Timor Gap Treaty between Australia and Indonesia: *East Timor (Portugal v. Australia), Judgment, I.C.J. Reports 1995*, p. 90. The status of the resources in the area remained highly disputed after Timor Leste's independence, and it was only settled recently by means of conciliation process: *Conciliation between The*

how energy is relevant for a certain 'branch' of international law, such as trade law, or that of certain recurring tensions between branches, such as trade and environment, are important steps; but partial ones.

Secondly, the need for an integrative approach is even more acute at a time when the world seems already engaged in a necessary yet daunting energy transition of civilisational proportions from a fossil fuel-based energy matrix to a low-carbon one. Law is a strategic battlefront in this transition. As we learn from the literature on socio-technical transitions,[18] the early movers that thrive in a given socio-technical regime (e.g. the generation of electricity predominantly from the combustion of fossil fuels) normally struggle to move into a new regime (e.g. one based on renewable energies), whereas latecomers can more easily leapfrog. This is sometimes summarised with the expression 'first in, last out; last in, first out'.[19] In such a context, law is a key instrument used by those industries and States attached to the present energy matrix to hinder the transition to a new one where they are less competitive. For example, the energy transition in Germany (*Energiewende*) has led to investment claims from foreign companies holding substantial investments in coal-fired and nuclear power plants.[20] Conversely, law is also used by the newcomers to accelerate the transition and thereby challenge the position of market leaders. Dozens of investment claims brought against countries such as Canada,[21] the Czech

Democratic Republic of Timor-Leste and The Commonwealth of Australia, PCA Case No. 2016–10, Press Release No. 9, 1 September 2017. For an overview of this process see G. Le Moli, J. E. Viñuales, 'A Foundational Experiment: The Timor Leste-Australia Conciliation', in C. Tomuschat, M. Kohen (eds.), *Flexibility in International Dispute Settlement* (Leiden: Nijhoff, 2020), pp. 156–177.

[18] See A. Grubler, 'Energy transitions research: Insights and cautionary tales' (2012) 50 *Energy Policy* 8; F. W. Geels, 'Socio-Technical Transitions to Sustainability: A Review of Criticisms and Elaborations of the Multi-Level Perspective' (2019) 39 *Current Opinion in Environmental Sustainability* 187.

[19] Grubler, *Energy transitions research*, at 12.

[20] See *Vattenfall AB, Vattenfall Europe AG, Vattenfall Europe Generation AG v. Federal Republic of Germany*, ICSID Case No. ARB/09/6, Award (11 March 2011) (embodying the parties' settlement agreement of the same date); *Vattenfall AB and others v. Federal Republic of Germany*, ICSID Case No. ARB/12/12, pending. See also the related domestic proceedings: Judgment of the Federal Constitutional Court (6 December 2016), BVerfGE 143, 246; Order of the Federal Constitutional Court (29 September 2020), 1 BvR 1550/19. These and other cases are discussed in Chapter 8.

[21] See *Mesa Power Group, LLC v. Government of Canada*, UNCITRAL, PCA Case No. 2012–17, Award (24 March 2016); *Windstream Energy LLC v. Government of Canada*, PCA Case No. 2013–22, Award (27 September 2016).

Republic,[22] Italy[23] or Spain[24] for amounts that reach billions of Euros illustrate the complexities entailed by this dimension of the energy

[22] See *Natland Investment Group N.V. and others v. Czech Republic*, PCA Case No. 2013–35, Partial Award (20 December 2017); *Antaris Solar GmbH and others v. Czech Repulic*, UNCITRAL Rules, Award (2 May 2018); *Voltaic Network GmbH v. Czech Republic*, UNCITRAL Rules, Award (15 May 2019); *I.C.W. Europe Investments Limited v. Czech Republic*, UNCITRAL Rules, Award (15 May 2019); *Photovoltaik Knopf Betriebs-GmbH v. Czech Republic*, UNCITRAL Rules, Award (15 May 2019); *WA Investments-Europa Nova Limited v. Czech Republic*, UNCITRAL Rules, Award (15 May 2019); *Mr Jürgen Wirtgen, Mr Stefan Wirtgen, and JSW Solar (zwei) GmbH & Co.KG v. Czech Republic*, UNCITRAL Rules, Final Award (11 October 2017).

[23] See *Blusun S.A., Jean-Pierre Lecorcier and Michael Stein v. Italy*, ICSID Case No. ARB/14/3, Final Award (27 December 2016), Decision on Annulment (13 April 2020); *Eskosol S.p.A. in liquidazione v. Italy*, ICSID Case No. ARB/15/50, Award (4 September 2020); *CEF Energia BV v. Italy*, SCC Case No. 158/2015, Award (16 January 2019); *Belenergia S.A. v. Italy*, ICSID Case No. ARB/15/40, Award (6 August 2019); *Greentech Energy Systems A/S & Ors. v. Italy*, SCC Arbitration V (2015/095), Award (23 December 2018); *ESPF Beteiligungs GmbH, ESPF Nr. 2 Austria Beteiligungs GmbH, and InfraClass Energie 5 GmbH & Co. KG v. Italy*, ICSID Case No. ARB/16/5, Award (14 September 2020).

[24] See *Charanne and Construction Investments v. Spain*, SCC Rules, Award (21 January 2016); *Isolux Netherlands, BV v. Spain*, SCC Case V2013/153, Final Award (17 July 2016); *Eiser Infrastructure Limited and Energia Solar Luxembourg S.a.r.l. v. Spain*, ICSID Case No. ARB/13/36, Award (4 May 2017); *Masdar Solar & Wind Cooperatief U.A. v. Spain*, ICSID Case No. ARB/14/1, Award (16 May 2018); *Antin Infrastructure Services Luxembourg S.à.r.l. and Antin Energia Termosolar B.V. v. Spain*, ICSID Case No. ARB/13/31, Award (15 June 2018), Decision on the rectification of the award (29 January 2019); *NextEra Energy Global Holdings B.V. and NextEra Energy Spain Holdings B.V. v. Spain*, ICSID Case No. ARB/14/11, Decision on Jurisdiction, Liability and Quantum Principles (12 March 2019), Final Award (31 May 2019); *9REN Holding S.a.r.l v. Spain*, ICSID Case No. ARB/15/15, Award (31 May 2019); *Cube Infrastructure Fund SICAV and others v. Spain*, ICSID Case No. ARB/15/20, Decision on Jurisdiction, Liability and Partial Decision on Quantum (19 February 2019), Final Award (26 June 2019); *SolEs Badajoz GmbH v. Spain*, ICSID Case No. ARB/15/38, Award (31 July 2019); *InfraRed Environmental Infrastructure GP Limited and others v. Spain*, ICSID Case No. ARB/14/12, Award (2 August 2019); *OperaFund Eco-Invest SICAV PLC and Schwab Holding AG v. Spain*, ICSID Case No. ARB/15/36, Award (6 September 2019); *BayWa r.e. Renewable Energy GmbH and BayWa r.e. Asset Holding GmbH v. Spain*, ICSID Case No. ARB/15/16, Decision on Jurisdiction, Liability and Directions on Quantum (2 December 2019); *Stadtwerke München GmbH, RWE Innogy GmbH et al. v. Spain*, ICSID Case No. ABR/15/1, Award (2 December 2019); *RREEF Infrastructure (G.P.) Limited and RREEF Pan-European Infrastructure Two Lux S.à r.l. v. Spain*, ICSID Case No. ARB/13/30, Award (11 December 2019); *RWE Innogy GmbH and RWE Innogy Aersa S.A.U. v. Spain*, ICSID Case No. ABR/14/34, Decision on jurisdiction, liability and certain issues of quantum (30 December 2019); *Watkins Holdings S.à r.l. and others v. Spain*, ICSID Case No. ARB/15/44, Award (21 January 2020); *The PV Investors v. Spain*, PCA Case No. 2012–14, Final Award (28 February 2020); *Hydro Energy 1 S.à r.l. and Hydroxana Sweden AB v. Spain*, ICSID Case No. ARB/15/42, Decision on Jurisdiction, Liability and Directions on Quantum (9 March 2020); *Cavalum SGPS, S.A. v. Spain*, ICSID Case No. ARB/15/34,

transition. Last but not least, law must accommodate the legitimate concerns of those who may be left behind by the transition. The political up-rise of the so-called *gilets jaunes* (yellow vests) against an attempted increase in fuel taxes by the French government is a stark reminder of the social dimension of the transition.[25] From the standpoint of international law and policy, this 'inclusiveness' dimension has gained prominence in the last two decades, whether through the rise of participatory rights or through explicit calls to ensure a just transition of the workforce.[26] These different pieces of the international legal puzzle can all be mobilised at the same time, with unclear interactional effects, in the struggles emerging from the energy transition, and focussing on only some of them may result in a skewed picture of how international law affects or is affected by this transition.

Thirdly, an overall view of the international law of energy would be useful in practice for the design and evaluation of energy policies from a legal standpoint. Depending on their legal form, energy policies may be consistent or inconsistent with different international norms and hence challenged before international courts and tribunals.[27] At present, such consistency is mainly assessed from a sectoral point of view (e.g. consistency with trade disciplines, investment disciplines, human rights or environmental law). In the absence of a transversal analytical framework, practicing lawyers are ill-equipped to provide more general assessments, despite the fact that the possibility of legal inconsistencies arising from different international obligations is far from theoretical. Some illustrations include the inconsistencies between the EU rules banning State aid and certain obligations arising from investment treaties[28] or the

Decision on Jurisdiction, Liability and Directions on Quantum (31 August 2020); *STEAG GmbH v. Spain*, ICSID Case No. ARB/15/4, Decision on Jurisdiction, Liability and Principles on Quantum (8 October 2020).

25 See A. Chrisafis, 'Who Are the Gilets Jaunes and What Do They Want?', *The Guardian* (7 December 2018).

26 See e.g. the 'Silesia Solidarity and Just Transition Declaration', adopted on the side of the twenty-fourth Conference of the Parties of the UN Framework Convention on Climate Change, held at Katowice, Poland, in December 2018, available at: https://cop24.gov.pl/presidency/initiatives/just-transition-declaration/. On the political context of the just transition see K. E. H. Jenkins, B. K. Sovacool, A. Blachowicz, A. Lauer, 'Politicising the Just Transition: Linking global climate policy, Nationally Determined Contributions and targeted research agendas' (2020) 115 *Geoforum* 138.

27 See A. Boute, 'Energy Trade and Investment Law. International Limits to EU Energy Law and Policy', in M. M. Roggenkamp et al. (eds.), *Energy Law in Europe: National, EU and International Regulation* (Oxford: Oxford University Press, 3rd ed. 2016), pp. 137–185.

28 This is at stake in many arbitration proceedings brought against EU Member States. See n. 22, 23 and 24. The intricate questions arising from these relations are epitomised by the

mismatch between non-discrimination obligations in trade and investment treaties[29] or, still, tensions between obligations arising from human rights or environmental law and obligations arising from trade or investment law.[30] Broad and facilitated consistency assessments would be useful because international claims often result from measures adopted by sub-national entities, with less resources for – and interest in – such assessments, for which the national State as such is responsible in international law.[31]

Against this background, this book reframes, in two main ways, how energy is analysed in international law. It moves the focus (1) away from certain specific techniques (such as joint development agreements) or branches of international law (trade, investment, environment etc.) and onto a transversal perspective: the international law of energy as the entirety of international law read through the prism of energy; and (2) away from a predominant emphasis on fossil fuels, particularly oil, and onto the ongoing energy transformation towards a more efficient and low-carbon energy matrix. It does so as a means to make a more general theoretical point, namely that the energy transformation is increasingly finding expression in the laws shaping international energy transactions (entitlements over resources and the ability to conduct the activities to put them to use) and not only in those which regulate to 'negative

decision of the Court of Justice of the European Union in *Slovakia v. Achmea*, JEU, 'C-284/16' (2018). For an analysis of the wider implications see J. R. Basedow, 'The *Achmea* Judgment and the Applicability of the Energy Charter Treaty in Intra-EU Investment Arbitration' (2020) 23 *Journal of International Economic Law* 271.

29 See N. DiMascio, J. Pauwelyn, 'Nondiscrimination in Trade and Investment Treaties: Worlds Apart or Two Sides of the Same Coin?' (2008) 102 *American Journal of International Law* 48.

30 See E. Vranes, *Trade and the Environment: Fundamental Issues in International Law, WTO Law, and Legal Theory* (Oxford: Oxford University Press, 2009); T. Cottier, J. Pauwelyn, E. Burgi (eds.), *Human Rights and International Trade* (Oxford: Oxford University Press, 2005); P.-M. Dupuy, E.-U. Petersmann, F. Francioni (eds.), *Human Rights in International Investment Law and Arbitration* (Oxford: Oxford University Press, 2009); Viñuales, *Foreign Investment and the Environment* (Cambridge: Cambridge University Press, 2012).

31 See Vienna Convention on the Law of Treaties, 23 May 1969, 1155 UNTS 331 [VCLT], Article 27 ('A party may not invoke the provisions of its internal law as justification for its failure to perform a treaty'; International Law Commission, Responsibility of States for Internationally Wrongful Acts, UN General Assembly Resolution 56/83, 12 December 2001, Annex, Article 4(1) ('The conduct of any State organ shall be considered an act of that State under international law ... whatever its character as an organ of the central Government or of a territorial unit of the State').

externalities' (the adverse effects on those not participating in the transactions and the environment).

Making this point and fleshing out its implications requires a long analytical detour, which can be summarised as follows. Chapter 1 of the book introduces the conceptual foundations of the international law of energy, namely the characterisation of energy as a legal object (a resource, a product, a technology, and an activity), the purposes of global energy governance (availability, security of supply, diversification, efficiency, safety, access and sustainability), the structure of international energy transactions (entitlements over energy, the enabling and protection of the transactions, and the regulation of its negative externalities), and the main approaches or patterns followed in their regulation (the foundational, ad hoc and centralised approaches). Chapters 2 to 7 rely on this conceptual architecture to study the entirety of international law from the prism of energy as a legal object. Each approach is presented in two chapters. Chapters 2 and 3 introduce the foundational approach, highlighting the rules that confer and allocate entitlements over energy, those that enable and protect investment, trade and transit in energy, and those that seek to regulate the negative externalities of such transactions. Chapters 4 and 5 analyse the ad hoc approach focussing on agreements for the joint development of hydrocarbons, hydroelectric projects in shared watercourses, pipelines, offshore windfarms and cross-border electricity transmission lines. Chapters 6 and 7 examine the centralised approach focussing first on the international legal regime for nuclear energy and then on certain regimes which are organised along the lines of producer/consumer (e.g. the Organization of Petroleum Exporting Countries and the International Energy Agency), promotion (e.g. the International Renewable Energy Agency) and regional organisations (e.g. the EU energy union, the Latin American Energy Organization and the ASEAN). In each chapter, the analysis fleshes out the implications of the ongoing energy transformation. But all these different strands are brought together and expanded in Chapter 8, which is specifically devoted to international law and the energy transformation. The conclusion summarises all these strands and highlights the current legal 'front lines' in the struggle between a well-established but dangerous sociotechnical regime based on fossil fuels and an emerging one based on renewable energies, which is full of promise but also of uncertainty.

1

Energy in International Law

I The Internationalisation of Energy Transactions

The history of energy can be written from myriad perspectives, depending on the object emphasised in each account. A household, a river, an activity, an event, a specific resource, a given technology, a country, a region, a global process or combinations thereof are some of the objects around which an energy narrative has been built.[1] As a result, the periodisation used, and the inflexion points selected as milestones are naturally not the same, and nor is their relevance for other disciplines. From the standpoint the social practice and discipline we call international law, three broad inflexion points are particularly noteworthy.

The first is the slow and multifaceted process known as the Industrial Revolution, which unfolded from the late eighteenth century onwards in

[1] Selected examples of this varying focus include: P. Warde, 'The Hornmoldt Metabolism: Energy, Capital, and Time in an Early Modern German Household' (2019) 24 *Environmental History* 472; R. White, *The Organic Machine: The Remaking of the Columbia River* (New York: Hill and Wang, 1995); C. F. Jones, *Routes of Power: Energy and Modern America* (Cambridge: Harvard University Press, 2014); M. I. Santiago, *The Ecology of Oil: Environment, Labor, and the Mexican Revolution, 1900–1938* (Cambridge: Cambridge University Press, 2006); D. Yergin, *The Prize: The Epic Quest for Oil, Money, and Power* (New York: Free Press, 2009); G. Hecht, *The Radiance of France: Nuclear Power and National Identity after World War II* (Cambridge: MIT Press, 1998) or D. Nye, *Electrifying America: Social Meanings of a New Technology, 1880–1940* (Cambridge: MIT Press, 1990); E. A. Wrigley, *The Path to Sustained Growth: England's Transition from an Organic Economy to an Industrial Revolution* (Cambridge: Cambridge University Press, 2016) or S. H. Schurr, B.C. Netschert, *Energy in the American Economy 1850–1975* (Baltimore: Johns Hopkins University Press, 1960); A. Kander, P. Malanima, P. Warde, *Power to the People: Energy in Europe over the Last Five Centuries* (Princeton: Princeton University Press, 2013); J. R. McNeill, P. Engelke, *The Great Acceleration: An Environmental History of the Anthropocene since 1945* (Cambridge, MA: Belknap Press, 2016) or V. Smil, *Energy Transitions: History, Requirements, Prospects* (Santa Barbara: Praeger, 2010).

England.[2] The Industrial Revolution is of critical importance for the study of the international law of energy first and foremost because it marked the transition from a mainly 'organic' (human-, animal-, wood- or charcoal-based) to a mainly 'mineral fuel' coal-based economy.[3] Whereas the search for 'stocks' of mineral energy resources in foreign lands for use in the metropolis remained limited, the Industrial Revolution added a measure of internationalisation in energy transactions both directly and indirectly. Directly, the turn to coal and the increasing use of oil mainly after the First World War meant that energy resources had to be extracted where their deposits were found. As long as that location fell within a territory controlled by a State, including colonial possessions, that measure of legal internationalisation remained limited. However, energy transactions were also internationalised in an indirect manner, through the possibilities coal offered for long-distance transportation (for market access, resource extraction and military expeditions) and the heavy reliance on slaves as part of the human energy supporting the 'triangular trade' mechanism that enabled and sustained the Industrial Revolution in England. In an influential book,[4] economic historian K. Pomeranz asks why the Industrial Revolution happened in England rather than the Yangzi Delta, despite propitious conditions in both regions. His answer rests on two main factors, namely the fortuitous availability of large coal reserves in England[5] and, no less importantly, the triangular trade between England (exporting manufactures to its American colonies and former colonies), West Africa (from which slaves were sent to the Americas) and the Americas (which relied on cheap

[2] On this major – and highly debated – subject of historiographical research see: Wrigley, *The Path to Sustained Growth;* R. C. Allen, *The British Industrial Revolution in a Global Perspective* (Oxford: Oxford University Press, 2014); E. A. Wrigley, *Energy and the English Industrial Revolution* (Cambridge: Cambridge University Press, 2010); D. S. Landes, *The Unbound Prometheus. Technological Change and Industrial Development in Western Europe from 1750 to the Present* (Cambridge: Cambridge University Press, 2nd ed. 2003); R. P. Sieferle, *The Subterranean Forest: Energy Systems and the Industrial Revolution* (Cambridge: White Horse Press, 2001). For three partial surveys of a vast literature see: E. Griffin, *A Short History of the British Industrial Revolution* (London: Palgrave, 2010); S. A. Beaudoin, 'Current Debates in the Study of the Industrial Revolution' (2000) 15 *OAH Magazine of History* 7; D. Cannadine, 'The Past and the Present in the English Industrial Revolution, 1880–1980' (1984) 103 *Past and Present* 114.

[3] Wrigley, *The Path to Sustained Growth*, at 2–3.

[4] K. Pomeranz, *The Great Divergence: China, Europe, and the Making of the Modern World Economy* (Princeton: Princeton University Press, 2000).

[5] This is a classic line of argument epitomised by the work of W. S. Jevons, *The Coal Question* (London: Macmillan, 1865).

slave labour to produce the raw materials acquired by Britain in exchange for manufactures). These two factors, the abundance of coal in England and the 'natural bounty' imported from abroad enabled a capital and manufacture intensive path, with a growing population fed by natural resources from overseas grown/extracted by slaves. Thus, slavery as a form of traded human energy served as a catalyst for the transition to the fossil fuel energy matrix.

The second inflexion point relevant for an international law perspective also unfolded over several decades, but mainly in the aftermath of the Second World War. The post-war reconstruction effort required growing amounts of energy resources, mainly coal and oil, which could not be satisfied only by domestic inland deposits. The assertion of sovereign powers over the resources of the continental shelf, triggered by US President Truman's proclamation of 1945,[6] and the internal allocation of powers over oil in submerged lands between the federal government and the States of the Union,[7] both illustrate an increasingly acute understanding of this imperative. More generally, the exploitation of fossil fuel resources in foreign lands was an extremely profitable activity, and it was essentially under the control of international oil companies from either colonial powers or the US.[8] In a post-1945 decolonisation context

[6] Proclamation 2667 of 28 September 1945: 'Policy of the United States with Respect to the Natural Resources of the Subsoil and Sea Bed of the Continental Shelf', 10 Fed. Reg. 12305 (1945). The initiative for this proclamation, which came both from the State Department and the Department of the Interior as early as 1943, was directly related to the possibility of drilling for oil offshore. Even before Truman came to power, in a letter of 1943, President Roosevelt noted '[f]or many years I have felt that the old three-mile limit . . . should be superseded by a rule of common sense. For instance the Gulf of Mexico is bounded on the South by Mexico and on the North by the United States. In parts of the Gulf, shallow water extends very many miles offshore. It seems to me that the Mexican Government should be entitled to drill for oil in the Southern half of the Gulf and we in the Northern half of the Gulf. That would be far more sensible than allowing some European nation, for example, to come in there and drill', reproduced in D. C. Watt, 'First steps in the enclosure of the oceans: The origins of Truman's proclamation on the resources of the continental shelf, 28 September 1945' (1979) 3 *Marine Policy* 211, at 213.

[7] In 1947, in *United States v. California*, the US Supreme Court concluded that the federal government had 'paramount rights in full dominion over the resources of the soil under the water area, including oil', 322 US 19 (1947), at 38–39. This principle was confirmed in *United States v. Texas*, 339 US 707 (1950) and *United States v. Louisiana*, 339 US 699 (1950). It was eventually reversed by statute, with the adoption in 1953 of the Submerged Lands Act, 43 USC §§ 1301–15 (1953). R. B. Krueger, 'The Background of the Doctrine of the Continental Shelf and the Outer Continental Shelf Lands Act' (1970) 10 *Natural Resources Journal* 442, at 452–453.

[8] A vivid account of the struggle for oil is provided in Yergin's classic book *The Prize.*

characterised by the emergence of numerous newly independent States eager to use their own resources for their national development,[9] this configuration led to a further degree of internationalisation of energy transactions. Two main questions arose, which underpin the legal foundations of international energy transactions. One was the question of *entitlements over energy* and, more generally, the determination of the rules conferring such entitlements and allocating powers in case of competing claims. The other was the *organisation of the energy transaction* based on such entitlements. The *geographical mismatch between the countries where energy deposits were mainly located and those where the resources were consumed* required indeed substantial amounts of foreign investment by the latter in the former in order to exploit the relevant deposits. It also rested on the assumption that the movement of capitals, equipment and the energy resources (or the refined product) thus produced would be enabled and protected.

At present, a third inflexion point is unfolding before our very eyes as a result of much more profound and long neglected implication of the 'mineral fuel' economy, namely its environmental implications, of which climate change is the most salient manifestation.[10] This multifaceted process of transition from carbon-intensive to low-carbon forms of energy and processes, often called the low-carbon transition or the energy 'transformation', has very important implications for the international law of energy. One 2019 report provides one of several characterisations of this transformation.[11] Its main markers are the substantial improvements in energy efficiency, the rapidly growing reliance on modern renewable energies for electricity production, and the growing electrification of sectors (e.g. transportation) traditionally based on fossil fuels. The drivers, according to this report, must be sought in the

[9] See the discussion of the emergence of the Organization of Petroleum Exporting Countries in Chapter 7.

[10] As noted by the prominent environmental historian J. R. McNeill: 'Cheap and abundant energy has probably done more to shape the human–environment relationship than anything else in the last 150 years. Cheap and abundant energy has proven a potent historical force in almost every sphere, from the conduct of housework to international struggles for power', J. R. McNeill, 'Cheap Energy and Ecological Teleconnections of the Industrial Revolution, 1780–1920' (2019) 24 *Environmental History* 492.

[11] Global Commission on the Geopolitics of the Energy Transformation, *A New World: The Geopolitics of the Energy Transformation* (IRENA, 2019), at 15–23. See further International Renewable Energy Agency (IRENA), *Global Energy Transformation: A Roadmap to 2050 (2019 Edition)* (IRENA, 2019).

declining costs of renewable energies, climate change and other forms of pollution, proactive renewable energy policies (such as targets and support schemes), technological innovation, corporate and investor action and, last but not least, a shift in public opinion.

The implications of this third inflexion point will be discussed throughout this book both in the context of each the three 'approaches' to energy governance and, more specifically, in Chapter 8. Their international legal dimensions can only be assessed if we first shed light on the overall phenomenon studied in this book, the international law of energy. That, in turn, requires a clear understanding of what is 'energy' as a legal object (II), the purposes pursued over time by the international law of energy (III), the overall structure of international energy transactions (IV), and the main patterns that can be extracted from a detailed and comprehensive analysis of the relevant rules, instruments and institutions (V).

II Energy as a Legal Object

2.1 Overview

From the perspective of international law, 'energy' is understood not as a physical quantity or an enabler of other human activities but as a legal object. International law is a language and, as such, it projects a certain ontology on the world. Defining energy as a legal object is therefore an inductive exercise. It amounts to scanning international law to track the different forms in which energy is governed, explicitly or implicitly. This scan has been conducted as part of the groundwork for this study and the main conclusion and submission is that energy, as an object of international law, has four facets: energy as a resource; as a product or service; as a technology or the components and equipment on which the technology relies; and as an activity.

Defining energy as a legal object is necessary in order to both (1) identify the rules most relevant for energy and (2) bring them together under an integrated analytical framework. The identification of the relevant materials implies no circularity in the analysis. It is true that the initial characterisation of energy relies on a scan of the relevant sources. Yet, this initial characterisation – which reflects the legal materials relied upon – has been tested and adjusted through subsequent applications. This trial-and-error process is not reproduced here, as it is part of the groundwork for the study. But one example can help to understand what it consisted of. Initially, my definition of energy as a legal object had only three facets (resource, product, activity). However, a range of legal materials (e.g. the technologies and equipment expressly contemplated under the Energy Charter Treaty (ECT), the provisions on scientific cooperation, information exchange and technology transfer appearing in a wide body of bilateral energy agreements,[12] and the international law relating to the protection of intellectual property rights (IPRs)[13]) strongly suggested that the technology facet of energy could not be adequately subsumed under the other facets. Although one cannot be certain that further testing of the definition may not require additional adjustments, the fact that, by now, this characterisation has been tested for a decade suggests that, as a conceptual tool, this definition is sufficiently mature.

The circularity caveat aside, the purpose of this definition is to federate very diverse bodies of international law, whether they specifically refer to energy or not, whether they were developed to cover energy or not, under a single analytical framework capable of clarifying which international rules and processes are relevant for energy governance and why.

2.2 *Energy as a Resource*

Energy as a 'resource' is perhaps the most intuitive facet of all. The term resource applies to stocks, such as those of fossil fuels (coal, oil and gas) or of minerals from which fissile materials can be derived (mainly uranium), as well as to flows, such as the flow of a watercourse, solar radiation or wind power used for renewable energy. It also applies to related stocks of resources, such as those on which renewable energy systems (e.g. cobalt, copper, lithium, manganese, nickel and zinc) and batteries (e.g. lithium, cobalt, graphite and nickel) rely. The resources underlying the generation of so-called bioenergy (solid biomass as well as liquid and gaseous biofuels) vary significantly. They include forests, a range of crops (such as corn, wheat, soy or sugarcane) and other materials (from algae to carcasses to waste). As a general matter, bioenergy resources are mainly stocks.

[12] See Chapters 4 and 5.
[13] Most notably the provisions of the Agreement on Trade-Related Aspects of Intellectual Property Rights, 15 April 1994, Marrakesh Agreement Establishing the World Trade Organization, Annex 1C, 1869 UNTS 299 [TRIPS Agreement].

The distinction between 'stocks' and 'flows' is meaningful from a geopolitical perspective, as noted by the aforementioned 2019 report from the Global Commission on the Geopolitics of the Energy Transformation,[14] as well as from a legal one. International law confers and allocates entitlements over energy resources in a static or 'spatial' form. By way of illustration, whereas coal, oil, gas and uranium stocks or 'deposits' can be appropriated through legal concepts such as 'territorial sovereignty' or the exclusive 'sovereign rights' over the continental shelf (for offshore oil and gas), flows such as solar radiation, wind power or stream power (for tidal energy) present both spatial (location) and non-spatial (flow) dimensions. Solar radiation cannot be fully appropriated, although solar energy installations are certainly territorial.

To clarify this facet, three additional observations are in order. First, the same energy resource may be governed both as a stock and as a flow. For example, oil and gas are stocks for purposes of power allocation but they may also be treated as flows in the regulation of transportation and transit. Electricity is left out for now, because this is discussed under the product/service facet. Secondly, the tension between stock/flow governance is well illustrated by the rules applicable to the non-navigational uses of international watercourses, such as the generation of hydroelectricity,[15] as well as by the need for unitisation of shared oil and gas deposits, which present some 'flow' characteristics before they are extracted from a well.[16] Thirdly, in addition to the stock/flow distinction, it is useful to categorise energy as a resource using a tripartite intuitive distinction between: 'fossil' (coal, oil and gas), nuclear (mainly uranium) and renewable resources (mostly hydro, solar, wind and bioenergy).

The use of these terms will facilitate the presentation later on, for example when discussing the 'centralised approach' used to describe the international legal regime of nuclear energy or the 'ad hoc approach' used for oil and gas, hydroelectricity or offshore wind.

[14] According to this report, growing reliance on modern renewable energies will transform the geopolitics of energy because 'renewable energy resources are available in one form or another in most countries, unlike fossil fuels which are concentrated in specific geographic locations' and 'most renewables take the form of flows, whilst fossil fuels are stocks. Energy stocks can be stored, which is useful; but they can be used only once. In contrast, energy flows do not exhaust themselves and are harder to disrupt', *The Geopolitics of the Energy Transformation*, at 23.

[15] See Chapter 5.

[16] See Chapter 4.

2.3 Energy as a Product

The second facet of energy as a legal object is that of an 'end product or service'. Energy resources undergo a process of transformation into usable products or services. The latter can be categorised essentially as 'electricity' (or electrical power), thermal services (heating or cooling, for many different purposes), and a range of 'fuels' (including gasoline, diesel, jet fuel and several types of biofuels, including ethanol, biodiesel and biogas). In this categorisation, hydrogen must also be seen as an energy 'product', despite its versatility for a variety of uses (e.g. fertilisers). This is because most hydrogen is produced from fossil fuels (mainly natural gas) in dedicated facilities of which hydrogen is the primary product.[17] Even when produced by electrolysis, the resource itself is water and the primary product is hydrogen.

These end products and services are not the only ones that can be derived from energy resources. For example, the petrochemical industry uses energy resources to produce a range of products such as plastics. But the focus in this study is on energy end products and services. Another clarification concerns how 'end' products and services are characterised. Some accounts of energy refer to 'transportation' as the end service of most fuels. However, in international law, transportation is governed as an 'activity' by a range of instruments specifically addressing tankers,[18] pipelines[19] and electrical transmission lines.[20]

The distinction between energy resources and end products/services is legally significant in certain contexts because it reflects the scope of application of certain instruments (e.g. agreements relating to electricity as such) as well as the different legal regime governing trade in goods and trade in services.[21]

2.4 Energy as a Technology

Thus characterised, neither energy resources nor energy end products and services clearly cover a significant object of international law, namely the 'technologies' used to generate end products (or to enable certain activities) on the basis of resources.

[17] See IEA, *The Future of Hydrogen. Seizing Today's Opportunities* (June 2019), at 31.
[18] See Chapter 3.
[19] See Chapter 4.
[20] See Chapter 5.
[21] See Chapter 2.

By technologies one must understand the knowledge of the processes, whether protected by IPRs or not, as well as the physical components (materials, equipment, machinery) enabling such processes. Article 1 (4bis) of the ECT and its related annexes offer a long list of relevant illustrations under the heading 'Energy-Related Equipment'. Although heavily focussed on fossil fuels and nuclear energy, this list provides many examples such as tubes, pipes and hollow profiles used for pipelines or sea lines protection, reservoirs, tanks and containers, steam, vapour and hydraulic turbines, centrifuges, nuclear reactors, cranes, self-propelled bulldozers and excavators, drilling equipment, taps, processors, and many others. Article 1(12) of the ECT further refers to IPRs, which are broadly defined as encompassing 'copyright and related rights, trademarks, geographical indications, industrial designs, patents, layout designs of integrated circuits and the protection of undisclosed information'. In an understanding relating to Article 1(12), the Parties 'recognize[d] the necessity for adequate and effective protection of Intellectual Property rights according to the highest internationally-accepted standards'.[22] The ECT is mentioned only as an example.

The Agreement on the Trade-Related Aspects of Intellectual Property Rights (TRIPS), concluded under the aegis of the WTO,[23] also contains general disciplines requiring States to adopt a national system of IPRs protection consistent with international standards.[24] Certain bilateral and regional trade agreements also include provisions relating to IPRs which are relevant for energy as a technology.[25]

2.5 *Energy as an Activity*

The fourth facet concerns energy as an 'activity'. In international law, the clearest general characterisation of energy activities so far is provided in Article 1(5) of the ECT: '"Economic Activity in the Energy Sector" means an economic activity concerning the exploration, extraction, refining,

[22] Final Act of the European Energy Charter Conference, Lisbon, 17 December 1994 [Final Act], Understanding 5.

[23] See n. 13.

[24] TRIPS Agreement, Article 1(1) and (3), which refer to the standards set in Part II of the Agreement for IPRs such as industrial designs, patents, and layout-designs of integrated circuits, among others.

[25] See M. Handler, B. Mercurio, 'Intellectual Property', in S. Lester, B. Mercurio, L. Bartels (eds.), *Bilateral and Regional Trade Agreements. Commentary and Analysis* (Cambridge: Cambridge University Press, 2nd ed. 2016), pp. 324–363.

production, storage, land transport, transmission, distribution, trade, marketing, or sale of Energy Materials and Products'. Energy Materials and Products are in turn defined by a global legal 'ontology' developed through the Harmonized System of the World Customs Organization[26] as well as a regional one, the Combined Nomenclature of the then European Communities.[27] In an 'Understanding' appearing in the Final Act of the European Energy Charter Conference, two important clarifications are added. First, 'Economic Activities in the Energy Sector' include not only those activities relating to fossil fuels, nuclear energy and electricity, but also renewable energies.[28] Secondly, some other activities, such as the removal and disposal of waste, the decommissioning of facilities, and a range of consulting services are also included.[29] Such understanding is confirmed by Article 19(3)(a) of the ECT when it defines the 'Energy Cycle'.[30]

These analytical distinctions enshrined in the ECT are of broader relevance for international law. Energy activities can be generally characterised as encompassing 'exploration, extraction, refining, production, storage, land transport, transmission, distribution, trade, marketing, or sale', as well as waste removal and disposal, decommissioning of facilities, and a range of energy-related services. These activities are sometimes further summarised (based on the example of the petroleum industry) into three categories of activities: upstream (exploration and production),

[26] This is based on the International Convention on the Harmonized Commodity Description and Coding System, 14 June 1983, 1503 UNTS 167 [HS Convention], Article 3(1)(a) and the Annexed Nomenclature, which is regularly updated. The current version dates from the 2017 Amendments, and a new version (HS 2022) has been agreed and will enter into force on 1 January 2022. A discussion of how energy falls within the Harmonised System is provided in Chapter 2.

[27] This nomenclature was established by Council Regulation (EEC) No. 2658/87 of 23 July 1987 on the tariff and statistical nomenclature and on the Common Customs Tariff, in pursuance of the HS Convention, of which the EU is a party. It is updated every year and published as a European Commission implementing regulation. The latest edition is Commission Implementing Regulation (EU) 2020/1577 of 21 September 2020 amending Annex I to Council Regulation (EEC) No. 2658/87 on the tariff and statistical nomenclature and on the Common Customs Tariff.

[28] Final Act, Understanding with respect to Article 1(5), at para. (b)(ii).

[29] Final Act, Understanding with respect to Article 1(5), at paraa. (b)(iv), (v) and (vii).

[30] Article 19(3)(a) of the ECT provides the following definition: '"Energy Cycle" means the entire energy chain, including activities related to prospecting for, exploration, production, conversion, storage, transport, distribution and consumption of the various forms of energy, and the treatment and disposal of wastes, as well as the decommissioning, cessation or closure of these activities, minimising harmful Environmental Impacts'.

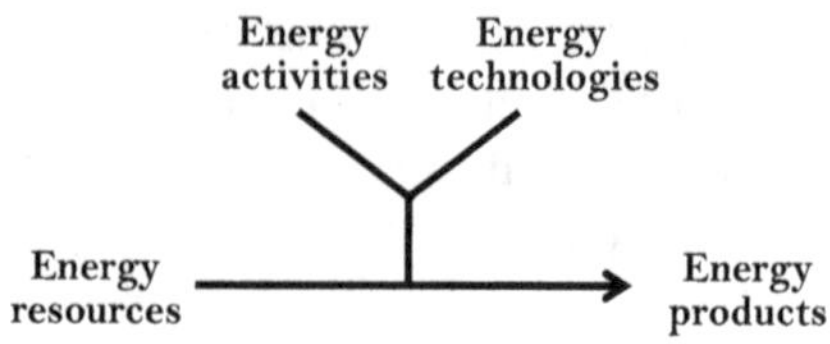

Figure 1.1 Energy as a legal object.

midstream (processing, storing, and transporting), and downstream (refining and conversion, distribution, retail).

Some of the activities are specifically regulated by either global or *ad hoc* legal regimes. Examples include the transportation of energy resources, which is governed *inter alia* by global treaties on the prevention and compensation of oil pollution damage,[31] or the treatment of energy-related 'services' under market access rules in trade and investment agreements,[32] or still the differences between 'exploration' and 'exploitation' of resources in undelimited areas.[33]

Energy activities may also be addressed *en bloc* in the same footing as many other activities relating to an 'investment' by a foreign investor falling under one or more investment agreements.[34] The latter point is yet another example of how international law may govern energy as a legal object with specifically addressing it. As discussed later in this chapter (see Section V), what shall be called the 'foundational approach' to energy governance is, with few exceptions, unspecific.

2.6 *Energy as a Legal Object: Summary*

The four dimensions of energy as a legal object are summarised graphically in Figure 1.1. In essence, *international law frames energy as resources converted into products through a range of activities relying on certain technologies*:

This simple framing shows that 'energy' as a legal object is distinct from energy as a physical force and focuses on the legal organisation of

[31] See Chapter 3.
[32] See Chapter 2.
[33] On the different regime of 'exploration' and 'exploitation' in undelimited and/or disputed maritime areas see Chapters 2 and 4.
[34] See Chapter 2.

the processes that generate and harness that force for certain purposes pursued by States and many other actors on the international plane. These purposes are discussed next.

III The Purposes of Energy Governance

3.1 Overview

Given energy's role as an enabler, the overall purpose of energy governance is the availability of sufficient energy to achieve a range of goals, which can be broadly encompassed by the term prosperity. Yet, this statement is overly simplistic. There are many steps involved in making energy available, from access to the resources and technology necessary for the extraction and conversion of energy to the adequate distribution of energy end products. There are also side effects in such processes, including the wider impact of all the activities performed to make energy available. Moreover, different actors at different levels pursue different goals depending on their needs, interests and ability to influence the policy process. In order to move from this level of abstraction to a more meaningful discussion of the purposes of energy governance, the analysis follows four steps.

I begin by stating, with reference to some representative instruments, what the main purposes of energy governance are at the international level (2.2). I then place this basic statement in historical perspective (2.3), flesh out the ways in which the energy transition has found expression in pursuance of different purposes (2.4), and connect these different goals and their deeper roots and implications to the development of international law since the second half of the twentieth century, emphasising the interactions between the purposes of energy governance (2.5). The competing nature of the different purposes of energy governance will become apparent at each stage of the discussion.

3.2 Main Purposes of Energy Governance

The overarching and most rudimentary purpose of energy governance is the 'availability' of sufficient energy to fuel prosperity. One associated – and intermediate – purpose concerns the uninterrupted supply of energy (energy security), which has itself been pursued, from a supply side, through the diversification of source countries and energy resources (energy diversification) and, from a demand side, through policies to

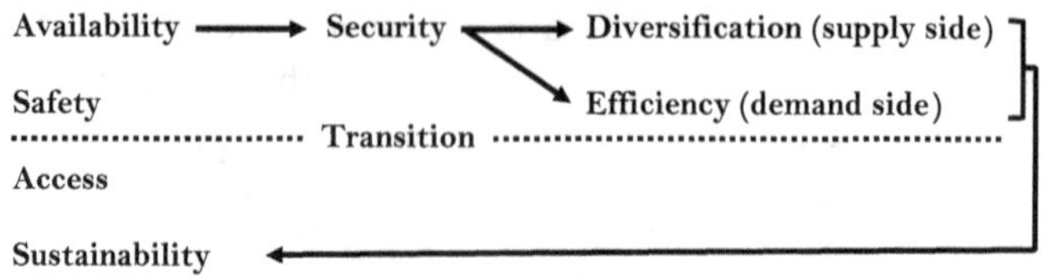

Figure 1.2 The purposes of energy governance.

make energy use more efficient, i.e. to perform the same tasks using less energy (energy efficiency).

Importantly, neither 'availability' nor its intermediate purposes require a specific allocation of energy among groups and/or individuals. Matters of distributive justice and, more specifically, of individual and collective entitlements are captured by another purpose, namely 'energy access'. Moreover, the quest for prosperity is not unconstrained. Energy activities may have deleterious effects both on human beings (calling for 'energy safety') and the environment, through oil spills, acidification, air pollution, and emissions of greenhouse gases (placing 'sustainability' constraints). The latter purpose has, in fact, led to a reorientation of two intermediate goals (diversification and efficiency) to serve not only energy security but also environmental and climate change policy. This reorientation is conveyed by the change of terminology from 'alternative' sources of energy to 'renewable', 'sustainable' or 'low-carbon' energy sources. The purposes of energy governance are summarised graphically in Figure 1.2.

These are not the only purposes that energy policies can pursue. For example, the military implications of the resources and technologies used to generate nuclear energy (which can be used to enrich uranium to weapon-grade level) present specific characteristics that do not fit entirely under the above-mentioned goals.[35] Moreover, the purposes of energy policy may be stated in other terms, as in the case of the EU energy policy, which has sought through several 'energy packages' to increase the integration of and competition within the internal energy market.[36]

The quest for *'availability', 'security', 'diversification', 'efficiency', 'safety', 'access' and 'sustainability'* through a range of policies formulated

[35] See Chapter 6. In the nuclear energy context, energy security is not understood as only a matter of security of supply but as international security (physical protection, non-diversion of nuclear materials and ultimately non-proliferation).

[36] See the discussion of EU energy law in Chapter 7.

in legal terms, including through international law, presents synergies and conflicts. 'Availability' and 'sustainability' may be at odds with each other, although the energy transition is changing that tension. 'Efficiency', which at first sight appears as consistent with all the other goals, may require the adoption of equipment and appliances by end users that are too expensive for some sectors of the population, thus thwarting energy access. Enjoying energy 'security' may also come at a price, requiring inefficient but strategically important investments. Similarly, energy 'safety' typically requires contingency systems and a range of other regulatory requirements that may also add costs to energy production. Synergies are also possible. Reliance on renewable energies in the 1970s was seen as a potential means to ensure energy security in the wake of unreliable supplies of energy resources from the Middle East. The interrelations between these different purposes can be better understood by reference to some historical developments.

3.3 *The Primacy of Availability and Security*

In the early 1950s, the assertion of a right to exploit natural resources in the national interest was not as obvious as it may appear today. Schrijver[37] provides an illuminating example by reference to the drafting history of what became UN General Assembly Resolution 523 (VI).[38] The draft proposed by Poland stated that 'under-developed countries' have the full right to determine freely the use of their natural resources. The United States opposed this formulation and proposed an amendment adding a reference to 'the interests of an expanding world economy'. Underlying this proposal was an attempt, by several industrialised countries, to secure some level of access to the energy resources located mostly in the Middle East. The final compromise text, brokered by Egypt, India and Indonesia, referred to both the national interest and that of the world economy.[39] As noted by Schrijver, this resolution is remarkable in

[37] See N. Schrijver, *Sovereignty over Natural Resources. Balancing Rights and Duties* (Cambridge: Cambridge University Press, 1997), at 37ff.

[38] 'Integrated economic development and commercial agreements', 12 January 1952, UN Doc. A/RES/523(VI) [Resolution 523 (VI)].

[39] Resolution 523 (VI), first preambular paragraph ('under-developed countries have the right to determine freely the use of their natural resources and that they must utilize such resources in order to be in a better position to further the realization of their plans of economic development in accordance with their national interests, and to further the expansion of the world economy').

that it stated for the first time the 'right' of under-developed countries to determine freely the use of their natural resources and for the first *and last* time the expectation that such resources be used not only in their national interest but also to further the expansion of the world economy.

Resource sovereignty gained increasing recognition in subsequent years, finding expression in a stream of UN General Assembly resolutions, most notably Resolution 1803 (XVII).[40] But the latent tension between the pursuit of national prosperity by resource-rich countries and energy security concerns by oil importing countries remained a major issue. It has characterised the geopolitics of oil ever since, as suggested by the vivid debate ignited by the ongoing works for the Nord Stream 2 pipeline project, which many see as a political lever allowing Russia to circumvent Ukraine in its gas exports to the EU and increase the reliance of the latter on Russian exports, thus also thwarting US exports of shale gas to Europe.[41]

The first major expression of the use of energy exports as a political instrument was the oil embargo imposed by the Organization of Arab Petroleum Exporting Countries (OAPEC)[42] in October 1973 against the United States and other industrialised countries, as a result of their support of Israel in the Yom Kippur War. Oil supply was wielded as a weapon, with powerful effects over the economies of the affected importing countries. By March 1974, when the embargo was lifted, the nominal price of the oil barrel had increased by almost 300 per cent.[43]

The 1973 oil crisis acted as a catalyst for importing countries to realise the need to give energy security both an institutional and a technological solution. Two noteworthy and related consequences[44] were the creation

[40] 'Permanent sovereignty over natural resources', 14 December 1962, UN Doc. A/RES/1803(XVII) [Resolution 1803 (XVII)]. See further Chapters **4** and **7**.

[41] See A. Goldthau, 'Assessing Nord Stream 2: Regulations, Geopolitics & Energy Security in the EU, Central Eastern Europe & the UK', *Strategic Paper 10 – European Centre for Energy and Resource Security* (2016); R. L. Morningstar, D. Fried, O. Khakova, 'Reinforcing transatlantic ties amidst Nord Stream 2 sanctions: a way forward', *Atlantic Council* (18 December 2020).

[42] On this organisation and its links to the Organization of Petroleum Exporting Countries (OPEC) see Chapter 7.

[43] See R. A. Johnson, 'The Impact of Rising Oil Prices on the Major Foreign Industrial Countries' (1980) 66 *Federal Research Bulletin* 817. The 'nominal price' is the average quarterly OPEC price in USD, adjusted for spot market transactions.

[44] For a survey of the responses in West Germany, Japan, France and the United States see G. J. Ikenberry, 'The irony of state strength: comparative responses to the oil shocks in the 1970s' (1986) 40 *International Organization* 105.

of the International Energy Agency (IEA) in 1974, involving a 'Sharing System' or buffer against oil shocks,[45] and a trend towards energy diversification, both from Middle East sources and from oil as such.[46] The goal pursued by these initiatives was energy security, but at the same time it created momentum for the development of renewable energies, at the time called – from an energy security perspective – 'alternative' energies.

Energy security and, specifically, access to fossil fuel resources (oil and gas) has remained an important driver of international legal developments in the field of energy. With the first signs of disaggregation of the Soviet bloc, the then European Communities launched a negotiation process that culminated with the adoption of the ECT in 1994.[47] Although the ECT pursues several purposes, the overall aim of the European initiative was to secure a continued flow of energy resources and products from the former Soviet republics in exchange for access to European markets and foreign investment.

Since the early 1990s, however, a stream of policy developments has introduced a new dimension of global energy governance, which is no longer seen only as an energy availability framework but also as an approach to transitioning from a carbon-intensive to an inclusive (access) and low-carbon (sustainability) energy matrix. This new transitional dimension is represented in Figure 1.2 with the dotted line between the classic and the more recent purposes of energy governance.

3.4 *The Rise of Access and Sustainability*

The transition to a low-carbon inclusive energy matrix has found expression in global governance mostly in the form normative statements adopted by UN bodies as well as some selected major conferences. Four main and sometimes overlapping phases can be identified in the process of mainstreaming of renewable energies in global governance, corresponding to the introduction, consolidation, institutionalisation, and expansion of the issue.

[45] See Chapter 7.

[46] Ikenberry, *The Irony of State Strength*, at 107.

[47] The idea of a European Community for Energy was championed by the former Prime Minister of the Netherlands, Ruud Lubbers, at the Dublin European Council held on 25–26 June 1990 and subsequently taken up by the Commission, which conducted the negotiation process leading to the adoption of the ECT in 1994. On the negotiating history of the ECT see generally K. Hober, *The Energy Charter Treaty. A Commentary* (Oxford: Oxford University Press, 2020), pp. 13–24.

The introduction phase unfolded over two decades, from 1981 to 2002. A first attempt was made in the 1980s with the convening[48] of a UN Conference on New and Renewable Sources of Energy, held in Nairobi in 1981, but at the time the 'energy transition' was understood mostly from the lenses of diversification for energy security purposes.[49] The sustainability dimension gained ground over the ensuing decade and was recognised in Chapter 9 of the action plan adopted at the 1992 Rio 'Earth Summit', i.e. Agenda 21, which referred to '[t]he need to control atmospheric emissions of greenhouse and other gases and substances' as part of the explanation for a 'growing reliance on environmentally sound systems, particularly new and renewable sources of energy'.[50] On this basis, the UN Educational, Scientific and Cultural Organization (UNESCO) launched, at a 'World Solar Summit' held in Harare, in September 1996, a 'World Solar Programme 1996–2005'[51] aimed to catalyse and promote cooperation among governments and the private sector for the development of renewable energies. At the nineteenth special session of the UN General Assembly in 1997, dubbed 'Earth Summit + 5', the Commission on Sustainable Development (CSD), established to oversee the implementation of Agenda 21, was asked to address 'energy issues' in its ninth session.[52] Then, in December 2000, the UN General Assembly adopted Resolution 55/205 endorsing the UNESCO initiative.[53]

[48] 'United Nations Conference on New and Renewable Sources of Energy', 16 December 1980, UN Doc. A/RES/35/204 [Resolution 35/204].

[49] See the article by the Conference's Secretary-General, E. V. Iglesias, 'Objectives of the United Nations Conference on New and Renewable Sources of Energy' (1981) 5 *OPEC Review* 12.

[50] Report of the United Nations Conference on Environment and Development, A/CONF.151/26/Rev.1 (Vol. 1), Resolution 1, Annex 2: Agenda 21 [Agenda 21], Basis for Action 9.9.

[51] Harare Declaration on Solar Energy and Sustainable Development, 17 September 1996, A/53/395, annex, section II. The Declaration led to the adoption by the UNESCO of its 'World Solar Programme 1996–2005', UNESCO, Records of the General Conference, Twenty-ninth Session, Paris, 21 October–12 November 1997, vol. 1: Resolutions.

[52] Resolutions and Decisions adopted by the General Assembly during its nineteenth special session, 23 to 28 June 1997, Supplement No. 2 (A/S-19/33), para. 46(a). The CSD undertook this task and proposed a draft decision to ECOSOC. See Commission on Sustainable Development, Report on the ninth session (5 May 2000 and 16–27 April 2001), ECOSOC Official Records 2001, Supplement No. 9, E/2001/29E/CN.17/2001/19, Draft Decision 9/1: Energy for Sustainable Development.

[53] 'World Solar Programme 1996–2005', 20 December 2000, UN Doc. A/RES/55/205 [Resolution 55/205].

The endorsement of the UN General Assembly, the work of CSD and reliance on it during the 2002 Johannesburg Summit on Sustainable Development,[54] marks the transition to the consolidation phase, which can be broadly situated between 2002 and 2005. This period is of note for two main reasons. First, although the main resolutions continued to refer to cleaner and more advanced fossil fuel technologies, UN General Assembly Resolution 60/199 made the 'promotion of new and renewable sources of energy' a specific sub-item of the agenda of the UN General Assembly.[55] Secondly, certain global meetings held during this period laid the ground for the institutional expression of renewable energy at the global level.

This institutionalisation phase unfolded approximately between 2004 and 2011. Indeed, the impetus given by the Johannesburg Summit as well as by two other conferences held in Bonn (2004), Beijing (2005) and then again in Bonn (2009) led to the establishment in 2004 of a 'global policy network' on renewable energy, REN21, and that of an International Renewable Energy Agency (IRENA), in 2009.[56] In addition to decarbonisation, the 'access' dimension was emphasised by UN General Assembly Resolution 65/151, which declared 2012 the 'International Year of Sustainable Energy for All'.[57] Under this umbrella, in September 2011, UN Secretary-General Ban Ki-moon announced the launch of a 'Sustainable Energy for All' initiative (SE4ALL or SEforALL),[58] which later became an independent body.[59]

The expansion phase is marked by the inclusion of a specific Sustainable Development Goal (SDG 7) in the 2030 Agenda for Sustainable Development aimed to 'ensure access to affordable, reliable,

[54] Report of the World Summit on Sustainable Development at Johannesburg (South Africa), 26 August–4 September 2002, UN Doc. A/CONF.199/20, Plan of Implementation, para. 20.

[55] 'Promotion of New and Renewable Sources of Energy, Including the Implementation of the World Solar Programme', 13 March 2006, A/RES/60/199, para. 13.

[56] See the discussion of promotion organisations in Chapter 7.

[57] 'International Year of Sustainable Energy for All', 16 February 2011, A/RES/65/151 [Resolution 65/151].

[58] A Vision Statement of Ban Ki-moon, Secretary General of the United Nations, Sustainable Energy for All (November 2011), available at: www.seforall.org/sites/default/files/gather-content/SG_Sustainable_Energy_for_All_vision.pdf.

[59] It was established under Austrian law in the form of a Quasi-International Organization (*Quasi-Internationale Organisation*). Federal Law on the Granting of Privileges to Non-Governmental International Organisations, Federal Law Gazette No. 174/1992, as later amended, section 7(2).

sustainable and modern energy for all'.[60] Unlike the Millennium Development Goals (MDGs),[61] which contained no stand-alone goal on energy, the SDG thus turned access to energy into a global priority which concerns not only developing countries (as did the MDGs) but all countries (as the SDGs do).

3.5 Competition among Purposes

The many goals now pursued by global energy governance have introduced significant complexity in the international legal norms and instruments that give expression to them.

Different bodies of international law pursue different and potentially conflicting goals. For example, the requirement to provide wide and affordable access to energy, as part of certain human rights,[62] may collide with efforts at decarbonising the economy, as required by climate change law,[63] or with the disciplines arising from investment law (e.g. if low-cost access is pursued by imposing a tariff cap on an electricity utility owned by foreign investors). Similarly, the requirement to decarbonise the energy sector under climate change law may, in some circumstances, collide with the disciplines arising from trade law (e.g. if the low-carbon policy relies on discriminatory local content requirements).[64] More generally, the special joint development and related agreements or watercourse-specific agreements between two States may prioritise the availability and security of energy over considerations of human rights or environmental protection, whether in their letter or in practice.[65]

[60] Resolution 70/1, 'Transforming Our World: The 2030 Agenda for Sustainable Development', 21 October 2015, UN Doc. A/RES/70/1, including a statement of 17 sustainable development goals (SDGs). On SDG 7 see S. Bruce, J. E. Viñuales, 'SDG 7: Access to Affordable, Reliable, Sustainable and Modern Energy for All', in J. Ebbesson, E. Hey (eds.), *The Cambridge Handbook on the United Nations Sustainable Development Goals and International Law* (Cambridge: Cambridge University Press, 2021), chapter 7.

[61] 'Millennium Declaration', 13 September 2000, UN Doc. A/RES/55/2.

[62] See the discussion of the entitlements of individuals in Chapter 2.

[63] See the discussion of climate change law in Chapter 3.

[64] See *Canada – Certain Measures Affecting the Renewable Energy Generation Sector*, Panel Report (19 December 2012), WT/DS412/R and *Canada – Measures Relating to the Feed in Tariff Program*, WT/DS426/R, AB Report (6 May 2013), WT/DS412/AB/R and WT/DS426/AB/R; *India – Certain Measures Relating to Solar Cells and Solar Modules*, AB Report (16 September 2016), WT-DS456/AB/R. For a discussion of trade law as it relates to energy see Chapter 2.

[65] See *In the matter of the Indus Waters Kishenganga Arbitration before the Court of Arbitration constituted in accordance with the Indus Waters Treaty 1960 between the*

The analysis has to proceed on a case-by-case basis because two or more norms that appear incompatible on their face may be reconciled through interpretation and, conversely, two apparently compatible norms may, in practice, be applied in an inconsistent manner. What is important is the ability to recognise that different energy goals may be supported by different norms of international law. Analytically, an account of the international law of energy must encompass all these normative sources and, insofar as possible, spell out their interrelations.

IV The Structure of International Energy Transactions

4.1 *Overview*

The theory of externalities can be used to understand the structure of international energy transactions because it provides a simple distinction between the core purpose of different international norms and instruments. It may be useful to recall, in intuitive terms, why this is so, before elaborating on the different aspects of this proposition. Simply stated, there are rules of international law that are mainly concerned with conferring and allocating entitlements over energy and with the legal organisation of the energy transactions, whereas some other rules operate as a sort of additional layer mainly addressing the negative externalities generated by such transactions rather than the transactions themselves. This apparently simple statement requires significant elaboration to be properly understood. One must clarify what is meant by 'transaction' generating 'externalities' on 'third parties' as well as identify the international legal rules mainly concerned with the 'transaction' and the 'externalities'.

4.2 *'Transactions' and 'Externalities'*

The first step is to clarify what is meant by the 'externalities' of a 'transaction'. For present purposes, rather than the classical contributions

Government of India and the Government of Pakistan signed on 19 September 1960 (Islamic Republic of Pakistan v. Republic of India), PCA, Final Award (20 December 2014), para. 111 (where the tribunal, while admitting the relevance of environmental protection, gave priority to the express language of a 1960 treaty apportioning the water flow between India and Pakistan). The relevant principles are briefly discussed in Chapters 2 and 3 and then in more detail in Chapter 5.

of Pigou[66] or Coase[67] on this topic, we can rely on the broad characterisation of externalities provided by J. E. Meade in a 1973 study:

> [a]n external economy (diseconomy) is an event which confers an appreciable benefit (inflicts an appreciable damage) on some person or persons who were not fully consenting parties in reaching the decision or decisions which led directly or indirectly to the event in question.[68]

A negative externality (a 'diseconomy') is thus the harm caused by a transaction (a 'decision or decisions which led directly or indirectly to' such harm) on third parties (a 'person or persons who were not fully consenting parties' in the transaction).

This characterisation has the merit of emphasising the composite nature, indeed the complexity, of the concept of 'transaction'. A transaction could mean something as narrow and specific as a contract between two companies for the sale of given product or something as broad, composite and complex as the set of policies and private transactions encompassed by an economic development model, with many other examples in between. The dividing line between the 'transaction' and the 'externality' has profound implications for the validity of economic theory. As noted by a commentator who positively but objectively reviewed Meade's work '[i]f a theory relegates some of the most important contemporary issues to the category of externalities that, by definition, lie outside the theory's boundaries, then what is its value?'[69] For present purposes, however, it is not the theory of externalities but the conceptual distinction between 'transactions' and 'externalities' as it has permeated the framing and design of international law that warrants attention.[70]

66 See A. C. Pigou, *The Economics of Welfare* (London: Mcmillan, 1920).

67 See R. Coase, 'The Problem of Social Cost' (1960) 3 *Journal of Law and Economics* 1.

68 See J. E. Meade, *The Theory of Economic Externalities: The Control of Environmental Pollution and Similar Social Costs* (Geneva: IUHEI, 1973). This is the written version of a set of lectures delivered at the Institut universitaire de hautes études internationales in Geneva.

69 R. Morgenstern, 'Book Review' (1976) 14 *Journal of Economic Literature* 66, at 68.

70 For a critique see J. E. Viñuales, *In Our Hands? The Organisation of the Anthropocene* (The Hague: Brill Research Perspectives, 2018) (arguing that environmental law is overwhelmingly structured as the law of negative externalities); J. E. Viñuales, J.-F. Mercure, 'Pathway to Reframing Environmental Law' (2020) 50(6) *Environmental Policy and Law* 63 (with J.-F. Mercure) (Special issue for the fiftieth anniversary, guest-edited by B. Desai).

Meade, as others who have theorised externalities, saw third parties through an anthropocentric prism. Those 'persons who were not fully consenting parties' included humans who suffer from the environmental degradation of certain transactions, but not the environment as such, as it lacks agency to 'fully consent'. Conceptually, however, third parties could also include certain non-human entities, such animals, trees, the 'environment', legal persons, States etc., as well as non-present human persons, individual or collective, such as future generations. Being a 'third party' to a transaction may be clear-cut for narrow and specific transactions (e.g. a one-off sale of goods) but as the term transaction is used to refer to more composite and complex phenomena (e.g. a foreign investment transaction in the extractive industries sector or the trade flows of a range of goods between two countries) that requires a more complex understanding of third parties. In a town where most of the population works in a coal-fired power plant generating electricity for the entire town, they may all be considered as part of the polluting transaction (the production of electricity from coal) while, at the same time, they are third parties suffering from polluted air and water. Similarly, in a global economy still based on the burning of fossil fuels, States (at least most of them) are both parties to the production and consumption transactions organised globally and third parties suffering from global environmental degradation. The distinction between 'participants' and 'third parties' in broad and composite transactions is thus not one of 'agency' (full consent) but one of 'role'. The same agent, e.g. a State, may perform both the role of participant and of third party at the very same point in time. If we allow for agent heterogeneity, the situation becomes more complex but the distinction between agents and roles stands.

Analytically, one may try to disentangle who exactly participates in a specific transaction and to what extent. For example, in the aforementioned example of the town, a major producer of furniture which does not work in the coal-fired power plant and which relies on solar panels to generate the electricity it consumes would clearly be a third party suffering from air and water pollution. But what if it sells all its furniture to the local power plant or if it relies entirely for its business on the electricity provided by the plant and is one of the main clients? Even more complex, what if the local government is both the main client of the plant and derives most of its tax revenue from it? Analytically, one may still define the relevant transactions separately and target one of them (e.g. the generation of electricity) as the transaction resulting in the negative externality, but this analytical cut would not accurately represent reality.

In global energy governance, most States are in a position analogous to those of the furniture producer and the local government. The transactions they are involved in are complex and interdependent networks of relations organised by a range of legal instruments. The negative externalities of some of these transactions are also addressed by legal instruments. The agents, whether States, international organisations, companies, groups, peoples and/or individuals, are all interrelated in such transactions, performing at times the role of participants and at times that of third parties.

4.3 The Rules Governing International Energy 'Transactions' and their 'Externalities'

The international legal rules mainly concerned with the 'transaction' and the 'externalities' can only be identified if the search is conducted within the context of 'energy' transactions. It is useful at this stage to recall the 'legal' definition of energy provided earlier in this chapter (see Section II). One component of that definition looks at energy as a set of 'activities'. Article 1(5) of the ECT characterises an 'Economic Activity in the Energy Sector' as 'an economic activity concerning the exploration, extraction, refining, production, storage, land transport, transmission, distribution, trade, marketing, or sale of Energy Materials and Products'. As noted earlier, this specific characterisation provides an indication of the type of activities that constitute the heart of international energy transactions.

The bulk of the law organising these activities is domestic and transnational (e.g. corporate structures, international contracts, joint ventures, employment contracts), but some important dimensions remain the province of international law. Specifically, the conferral of legal *entitlements* over resources (on which the ability to explore and produce relies) is based on a range of customary and treaty norms allocating sovereignty over land and water as well as sovereign rights over certain maritime areas (the exclusive economic zone and the continental shelf).[71] Such powers are the foundations over which energy transactions are organised. As noted earlier in this chapter (see Section I), international law plays an important role in this organisation because energy transactions have become internationalised. This means, specifically, that there is a

[71] See Chapter 2.

substantial mismatch between the States where energy is produced and the States where energy is consumed. As a result, energy as a legal object (resources, products, technology, activities) must cross borders. That, in turn, requires *enabling and protecting* such movements. A wide range of rules and treaties relating to foreign investment (to develop the resources located abroad), trade (to enable access to markets and level the playing field of exports/imports) and transit (to minimise hindrances to the movement of the relevant energy resources and products) organise these movements. IPRs relating to these flows are also protected, although international law only requires the granting of a minimum level of protection, relying on domestic law to do so. Thus, the international law mainly concerned with international energy transactions can be seen as those rules *(1) confer and allocate entitlements over energy and (2) that organise the cross-border movements entailed by such transactions by 'enabling' and 'protecting' foreign investment, trade and transit.*

In addition to this first layer of international law, another layer places limitations on how these transactions are conducted in order to prevent, most notably, adverse effects (negative externalities) on humans and the environment as 'third parties'. Two important observations are in order here. First, the limitations are not intended to ban or impede the transactions. Quite to the contrary, they are specifically designed not to excessively interfere with them.[72] For this reason, the rules introducing such limitations can be said to operate as an 'additional layer'. Secondly, the fact that these norms are 'additional' from the perspective of energy transactions does not mean that they are not constitutive in other contexts. A good example is provided by international human rights law. The fact that, in the energy context, human rights may operate mostly to prevent or mitigate the negative effects of energy activities on the integrity, private life and/or cultural expression of individuals,[73] does not mean that international human rights law is 'additional' as a general matter. In fact, the prism of 'branches' is only partly adequate as 'international human rights law' does not only impose 'additional' limitations on the conduct of energy activities; it also generates entitlements over energy resources (e.g. the collective right over natural resources or the extension of a people's right to self-determination through permanent sovereignty over natural resources).[74]

[72] See the discussion in the studies in n. 70.

[73] See Chapter 3.

[74] See Chapter 2.

These two observations introduce important caveats and must be kept in sight when stating that, from an energy perspective, *the international law regulating the negative externalities of international energy transactions is mainly – but certainly not only – provided by international human rights and environmental law.*

V Three Approaches to the Regulation of International Energy Transactions

5.1 Overview

Three main approaches to the regulation of international energy transactions can be extracted from an examination of international legal practice. I shall refer to them as the *foundational*, *ad hoc*, and *centralised* approaches. Before presenting each of them and their interactions, two clarifications are in order.

First, the term 'approach' is used as a synonym of a conceptual or analytical 'prism' through which a set of rules, whether expressly interrelated or not, are considered together from the perspective of their relevance for energy as a legal object. For example, the right of peoples to self-determination, the rules relating to State powers over the continental shelf, the rights and duties of an occupying power over the resources in the occupied territory, the principle of prevention of environmental harm, and bilateral investment treaties have little in common as regards their emergence, content and application. Yet, as discussed in Chapters 2 and 3 of this book, through the prism of the foundational model, they are sources from which to derive the rules shaping three main issues: the conferral and allocation of entitlements over energy, the enabling and protection of international energy transactions, and the regulation of the negative externalities of such transactions on humans and/or the environment. Thus, through this prism, an unconnected set of rules is analysed together from the perspective of its relevance to energy as a legal object. The three approaches must be understood as artificial analytical lenses, the only purpose of which is to bring into view the relevance of a certain set of rules for energy as a legal object.

Secondly, the distinctive features of each approach can be derived from three main criteria, namely (1) the level of specificity of the relevant rules, which ranges from broad and unspecific sets of rules which were not designed to apply to energy but nevertheless do so (e.g. non-discrimination standards in international trade law or general human rights) to very specific sets of rules expressly designed to govern one or more aspects of energy as a legal object (e.g. a joint development agreement or a pipeline agreement); (2) the 'transversality' or 'verticality' of the relevant rules, with 'transversality' understood as rules that govern certain aspects of energy as a legal object (e.g. 'trade' in energy goods or services; protection of energy 'investments'; conditions for the maritime transportation of oil to prevent 'operational' or 'accidental discharges'; human rights to life, health, private and family life, culture, property etc. of populations affected by energy-related activities) and 'verticality' understood as narrower but deeper regulation (e.g. general legal framework applicable to a specific hydrocarbons deposit or to a hydroelectric project, under which maritime disputes are suspended, joint ventures are formed, licences are issued, contracts are entered into, proceeds are distributed); and (3) the spatial scope of application of the relevant set of rules, which ranges from universal application (e.g. some customary norms), to multilateral application (with a wider – e.g. the GATT, the ICCPR or the ECT – or narrower – e.g. some pipeline agreements – scope depending on the treaty), to bilateral application (e.g. joint development agreements).

These criteria are intended to describe the 'sets of rules' brought into sight by each one of the three approaches, rather than the approaches as such. Thus, the *foundational approach* encompasses rules that are typically – but not exclusively – unspecific, transversal and from universal to bilateral, the *ad hoc approach* covers rules that are specific, vertical and narrowly multilateral or bilateral, and the *centralised approach* encompasses rules that are specific, transversal and multilateral. It also relies on bilateral agreements concluded under the aegis of or to support the multilateral regime. Figure 1.3 summarises this basic characterisation.

The way in which the features of this comparative characterisation find expression in each approach requires further elaboration to be properly

Approaches	Specificity		Angle of incidence		Spatial scope			
	Unspecific	Specific	Transversal	Vertical	Universal	Multilateral		Bilateral
						Wide	Narrow	
Foundational								
Ad hoc								
Centralised								

Figure 1.3 Comparative characterisation of approaches.

understood. This is discussed next and in each of the two chapters examining in detail each approach.

5.2 *Foundational Approach*

The foundational approach covers a range of otherwise unconnected sets of rules which are typically – but not exclusively – unspecific, transversal and range from universal to bilateral. These rules govern (1) the conferral and allocation of entitlements over energy, (2) the enabling and protection of international energy transactions (issues such as investment, trade and transit), and/or (3) the regulation of the negative externalities of such transactions on humans and/or the environment.

Given the nature and importance of the questions governed by this broad set of rules, the lack of specificity is a particularly salient feature. It explains why a very significant part of the international law of energy remained, until recently, beyond the radar of legal scholars working on energy or was analysed in an issue- or branch-specific manner. In the last decade, a significant body of scholarship has clarified the relevance for energy of subjects such as trade law, foreign investment law, environmental law, human rights or the law of the sea.[75] It also explains why the rules covered by this approach are fragmented, i.e. derived from a wide range of sources mostly with a universal or multilateral scope, and fragmentary, i.e. addressing only certain transversal areas rather than fully governing a given energy project.

A complex question arising from the lack of specificity is where to draw the line between relevant and irrelevant rules. The answer is twofold. From a practical perspective, the answer will depend on the factual circumstances that call for the application of international law. For example, the rules circumscribing the right to self-defence in general international law were relevant to decide the dispute arising from the destruction, by US forces, of two Iranian oil platforms in the late 1980s. To the extent that the incidents disrupted oil supply, the determination of their legality was relevant from an energy governance perspective.[76] Yet, such practical relevance is case-specific and, therefore, insufficient to identify the rules that are generally relevant for global energy governance.

[75] See the extensive body of scholarship referred to in the introduction with respect to these subjects. More specific topical studies are mentioned in Chapters 2 and 3.

[76] See *Oil Platforms (Islamic Republic of Iran v. United States of America)*, Judgment, ICJ Reports 2003, p. 161.

From a theoretical perspective, a clearer line is therefore needed to delimitate the rules of international law that, although unspecific, are generally relevant for energy. The criteria for the recognition of such rules stem from the regulated objects. As noted earlier in this chapter: (1) some rules *confer* and *allocate* entitlements over energy as a legal object, (2) other rules *enable* and *protect* international energy transactions, and (3) yet other rules *place limitations on the adverse effects* that such transactions may have on humans and the environment.

The interconnections between these three categories of rules are fleshed out in Chapters 2 and 3, but, for present purposes, it can be summarised as follows: norms conferring entitlements are constitutive of powers over energy, but they also entail prerogatives over the conduct of energy transactions. Yet, such prerogatives are subject to two types of limitations, depending on their overall goal. Some limitations constrain the exercise of prerogatives in order to enable and protect international energy transactions. Some other limitations constrain the previous type of (enabling/protecting) limitations in order to pursue other goals, i.e. the protection of humans and the environment from adverse side effects. From the perspective of the distinction between transactions and externalities, the rules conferring and allocating entitlements over energy and those enabling and protecting international energy transactions organise the 'transaction' as a whole, whereas those placing limitations on the transaction address its negative externalities.

Importantly, considered together, the rules relevant for all three categories lay the foundations for other much more specific rules to operate, including the rules that will be examined in the context of the *ad hoc* and *centralised* approaches. Hence the 'foundational' character of these broader rules.

5.3 *Ad Hoc Approach*

Compared to the foundational approach, the rules encompassed by the *ad hoc* approach are specific, vertical and either bilateral or narrowly multilateral. They have, for this reason, received sustained attention in the literature.[77] But this initial characterisation must be further elaborated upon in order to understand how these rules govern energy.

[77] See the extensive body of scholarship referred to in the introduction with respect, most notably, to joint development agreements. More specific topical studies are mentioned in Chapters 4 and 5.

As regards their specificity, the focus is not merely on 'energy' but on a specific energy deposit (e.g. an oil or gas field stranding the land or maritime areas of two or more States or located in a disputed area) or even a project (e.g. a specific binational or plurinational hydroelectricity project, a specific pipeline project or, more recently, a jointly undertaken project to develop an offshore windfarm and/or electricity transmission lines). The organisation of the exploitation of a specific deposit or the development of a specific project often requires a deeper – vertical – body of rules under the umbrella of the relevant agreement. This takes the form of a layered set of arrangements bringing together not only States as such but a range of other entities, such as public and/or private companies, financiers, contractors and consultants, and affected stakeholders, which may all be given a role in the relevant arrangements. Also as a result of the deposit- or project-specific focus, the agreements on which such regulation is based tend to be bilateral or narrowly multilateral in scope, encompassing only those States which participate in the project. In some cases, the limited scope of such agreements is, as such a problem, if it leaves out States that may be affected by the project. Such States can only rely on the broader rules encompassed by the foundational approach, which remain generally applicable to an extent which is sometimes undefined.

The latter point raises a common difficulty arising from *ad hoc* approaches to energy governance, namely that specificity of the arrangements may deliberately or inadvertently result in some degree of 'insulation' of the project from the generally applicable international and domestic law. That, in turn, requires some clarification of the interactions between different norms – general and specific – particularly those aimed at limiting the negative externalities of the energy transaction envisioned in the *ad hoc* instruments. Figure 1.4 represents graphically the relations

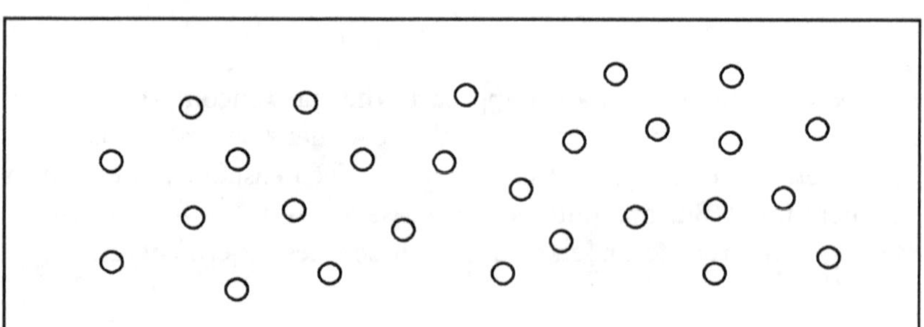

Figure 1.4 Relations between approaches.

between the rules covered by the foundational (overall rectangle) and *ad hoc* approaches (small circles).

As noted in the previous section, one definitional feature of the rules encompassed by the foundational approach is precisely their foundational character: they are the building blocks upon which more specific rules can be developed for a given deposit and/or project. The specific articulation of these rules is not legally organised at the level of the approach. Approaches are mere analytical lenses to bring into sight a certain set of rules to be considered together. As further discussed in Chapters 4 and 5, normative interactions must be analysed in most cases at the level of each norm to determine whether one displaces the other or both apply together in a certain manner.

5.4 *Centralised Approach*

Compared to the foundational and *ad hoc* approaches, the centralised approach encompasses rules that are specific, transversal and multilateral. However, as noted earlier, it also relies on bilateral agreements concluded by States participating in the centralised or proto-centralised regime in order to support this regime or complement it in aspects not covered by it (e.g. nuclear cooperation agreements or safeguard agreements).[78] Thus, the spatial dimension of the rules encompassed by this approach are necessarily multilateral to some extent and possibly bilateral, but – unlike the *ad hoc* approach – they cannot be limited to the latter. Another related difference with the *ad hoc* approach is that, due to their overall supportive character, these bilateral agreements do not seek to insulate the transaction from the broader centralised or proto-centralised regime.

As regards differences between the centralised and the foundational approaches, although both rely on multilateral agreements, the rules covered by the centralised approach focus specifically on the governance of energy. Such specificity is not organised around a deposit or a project either, but focuses on particular energy resource (nuclear energy, oil, gas, renewable energies etc.). Importantly, such focus defines the mandate and functional scope of the institutional component of the regime. Centralised and proto-centralised approaches are indeed characterised by the establishment of an international organisation (e.g. the

[78] See Chapter 6.

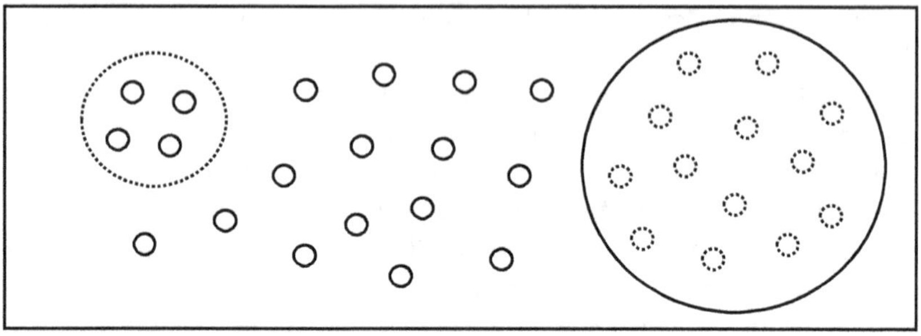

Figure 1.5 Relations between approaches (suite).

International Atomic Energy Agency (IAEA)) designed to serve as the epicentre of the efforts to govern a certain energy resource at the international level. Such efforts are fleshed out legally in form of a transversal governance framework which is sufficiently comprehensive, encompassing the 'life-cycle' of the relevant form of energy, rather than a specific aspect or activity. In order to perform its steering role, the organisation enjoys some measure of formal or informal normative power.

In centralised regimes, such as the governance of nuclear energy, these distinctive features are more clearly fleshed out than in proto-centralised regimes, such as those concerning oil (based on a combination of the OPEC, the IEA and the International Energy Forum (IEF)) or renewable energy (based on the IRENA but also on the IEA, with the two organisations in a relation of partial cooperation and partial competition).[79] The different levels of centralisation are depicted in Figure 1.5 by the use of a full line in the large circle (centralisation, e.g. the IAEA) and a dotted line in the smaller circle (proto-centralisation, e.g. the OPEC/IEA/IEF or the IRENA). The small circles represent the deposit- or project-specific ad hoc arrangements. Some of them are drawn with a dotted line to represent the different role of bilateral agreements which are supportive of a broader centralised regime (e.g. a safeguards agreement is clearly different in nature from a joint development agreement in its scope and function). The emphasis is placed here on the large circle (drawn with a full line) which provides the centre of gravity of the regulation. Conversely, for proto-centralised regimes relating, for example, to oil, gas or renewable energies, the centre of gravity is clearly on the *ad hoc* regime (hence the full line in the small circles) rather than in the broader

[79] On these and other organisations see Chapter 7.

cooperative framework (drawn with a dotted line). The overall rectangle represents, as before, the rules covered by the foundational approach.

Whereas Figure 1.5 offers only a very broad representation of the overall structure of the international law of energy, it has the advantage of being simple and encompassing. A more granular representation would admittedly require shades that Figure 1.5 cannot possibly capture. Moreover, the question of normative interactions mentioned in the previous section becomes even more complex when the additional layers of the centralised approach are considered. Ultimately, legal analysis is – and must be – case-specific, and no overarching representation can be fully accurate. But the goal of the analytical framework introduced in this chapter and summarised in Figure 1.5 is only (and specifically) intended to frame the field or, in other words, to frame how international law as a whole regulates international energy transactions.

2

Foundational Approach

International Energy Transactions

I Overview

In Chapter 1, I discussed the basic driver of the internationalisation of energy transactions, namely the geographical mismatch, in a 'mineral fuel' energy matrix, between the countries where energy resources are mainly located and those where energy products are mainly consumed.

That mismatch intervenes in an international system structured around sovereign States but also including other legally recognised entities, such as international organisations, peoples, other groups and individuals. In this context, one important aspect of international energy transactions concerns the entitlements of these different entities over energy, understood as resources converted into products through a range of activities relying on certain technologies. International law contains rules which confer such entitlements and organise allocation among competing uses. Such rules are the legal infrastructure upon which international energy transactions are organised. Other rules organise the cross-border movements necessary to access resources where they are located and process them – through certain activities and technologies – for consumption in the form of products in other countries. Enabling access and protecting the processes of conversion and transfer are key aspects of a range of rules governing foreign investment, trade and transit relating to energy.

These two sets of rules, taken together, organise international energy transactions. They are the focus of this chapter. There is an additional layer of rules which aim to keep the adverse effects of such transactions on humans and the environment within certain bounds. These other rules are examined in Chapter 3.

When the rules organising international energy transactions and those regulating their 'negative externalities' are considered together, they can be seen as laying the foundations, the *droit commun* or background law, of international energy transactions. Hence their analytical characterisation, in the account provided in this book, as the 'foundational' approach. Their identification requires an examination of the entirety of international law from the prism of energy as a legal object. Chapters 2 and 3 provide such an examination, relying on the conceptual categories introduced in Chapter 1. Of course, these two chapters cannot be expected to cover such a vast corpus of rules in detail. Their focus is on the identification and function of the most relevant rules, including references to more detailed legal commentary and analysis.

II Legal Entitlements over Energy as a Legal Object

2.1 Rules Conferring Entitlements

2.1.1 Introductory Observations

Some rules define and allocate entitlements over energy, mostly as a resource, although such rules also entail powers and prerogatives that are relevant from a wider regulatory perspective encompassing both the legal organisation of international energy transactions (foreign investment, trade and transit) and the regulation of their negative externalities.

The rules defining powers can be briefly introduced by reference to the entitlement-holders. Entitlement-holders are of two types, originary (those who are conferred entitlements directly from a rule of international law) and derivative (those who receive their entitlements from a delegation by an originary entitlement-holder). *Originary entitlement-holders* include States, peoples, other collective subjects (e.g. indigenous and tribal peoples), and individuals, whereas *derivative entitlement-holders* include international organisations (e.g. the European Union) or their organs (e.g. a tribunal entitled by a delegation in a treaty to delimitate an area). The rules concerning these entitlement-holders are examined in the next sections.

There are some entities which, due to their peculiarities, are difficult to categorise, such as the UN Transitional Administration in East Timor (UNTAET),[1] which operated as a quasi-government, the International

[1] Established by UN Security Council Resolution 1272 (1999), 25 October 1999, UN Doc. S/RES/1272 (1999). The resolution was expressly adopted '[a]cting under Chapter VII of the Charter of the United Nations', which entitles the UN Security Council to adopt binding decisions. UNTAET was granted a broad mandate. One aspect of the transitional administration was the negotiation with Australia of the ongoing fossil fuel activities conducted under the controversial 1989 Timor Gap Treaty between Australia and Indonesia.

Seabed Authority (ISA),[2] which manages the 'Area' (the seabed and subsoil beyond national jurisdiction) as common heritage of mankind, and some binational entities.[3] Technically, these entities are derivative entitlement-holders, because their powers are exercised as a delegation from States, but their entitlements present the peculiar feature that the delegation encompasses some degree of entitlement over energy resources as such and not only over powers and prerogatives to regulate energy.

UNTAET and Australia entered into an arrangement whereby UNTAET stood in place of Indonesia in the Timor Gap Treaty 'without prejudice to the position of the future government of an independent East Timor'. See Exchange of Notes Constituting an Agreement between the Government of Australia and the United Nations Transitional Administration in East Timor (UNTAET) concerning the Continued Operation of the Treaty between Australia and the Republic of Indonesia on the Zone of Cooperation in an Area between the Indonesian Province of East Timor and Northern Australia of 11 December 1989, 10 February 2000. On the context of this arrangement see G. Triggs, 'Proposed Timor Sea Arrangements between Australia and the East Timor Transitional Administration' (2002) 20 *Journal of Energy & Natural Resource Law* 41.

[2] The International Seabed Authority (ISA) was established by Section 4 of Part XI of the United Nations Convention on the Law of the Sea, 10 December 1982, 1833 UNTS 397 [UNCLOS]. Article 157(1) of UNCLOS provides that 'The Authority is the organization through which States Parties shall, in accordance with this Part, organize and control activities in the Area, particularly with a view to administering the resources of the Area'. The delegation of powers therefore explicitly concerns the administration of resources. Article 153(1) of UNCLOS states that the '[a]ctivities in the Area shall be organized, carried out and controlled by the Authority on behalf of mankind as a whole'. Two systems are envisioned. One where the Authority acts through its own 'Enterprise' and the other where public or private companies from States parties and sponsored by them act in association with the Authority. In practice, the latter regime prevailed raising difficult questions regarding the responsibility of States sponsoring such activities. See *Responsibilities and Obligations of States sponsoring Persons and Entities with respect to Activities in the Area*, Case No. 17, ITLOS (Seabed Dispute Chamber), Advisory Opinion (1 February 2011) [*Responsibilities in the Area*].

[3] See for example the international Agency created by the Management and Co-operation Agreement between the Government of the Republic of Senegal and the Government of the Republic of Guinea-Bissau, 14 October 1993, to 'exploit the Area' (Article 4) and which 'succeeds' the parties 'in the rights and obligations deriving from the Agreements concluded by each State and relating to the exploitation of the resources in the Area' (Article 5). This Agreement was followed by a Protocol of Agreement relating to the organization and operation of the Agency for Management and Co-operation, 12 June 1995, according to which the Agency is 'an international organization responsible for managing the resources of the Area, directly through the Enterprise or its subsidiaries or through other companies' (Article 4). Article 6 confers upon the Agency 'exclusive rights to mining and petroleum titles [...] in the Area'.

2.1.2 States

By virtue of their *sovereignty*, within their territory States hold two main entitlements over energy, namely (1) permanent sovereignty over their natural resources (against irrevocable appropriation from colonial powers, foreign occupying powers and private entities),[4] (2) the sovereign prerogative to exploit their natural resources for their own national development[5] and set energy policies as they see fit (against economic coercion).[6]

[4] The most prominent recognition of this principle is found in UN General Assembly Resolution 1803 (XVII) on 'Permanent Sovereignty over Natural Resources', 14 December 1962, UN Doc. A/RES/1803/XVII, subsequently considered to reflect customary international law. Such recognition first came in *Texaco Overseas Petroleum Company and California Asiatic Oil Company v. The Government of the Libyan Arab Republic*, Arbitral Award (19 January 1977), 17 ILM 1978, para. 87, and it was subsequently confirmed, most notably in *Armed Activities on the Territory of the Congo (Democratic Republic of the Congo v. Uganda)*, Judgment (19 December 2005), ICJ Reports 2005, p. 168, paras. 244–245. In the latter case, the Court recognised the customary character of the norm but not its relevance on the facts of the case (foreign occupation of the territory of a sovereign State). Thus, in case of foreign occupation outside of the decolonisation context, it is the broader principle of respect for sovereignty that should be invoked. See *Military and Paramilitary Activities in and against Nicaragua (Nicaragua v. United States of America), Merits, Judgment*, I.C.J. Reports 1986, p. 14 [*Nicaragua*], paras. 202, 212–213, 251–252.

[5] 'Permanent sovereignty' and the 'right to exploit resources for national development' are clearly linked. As noted by in *China – Raw Materials*: 'An important element of the principle of state sovereignty is the principle of sovereignty over natural resources, recognized as a principle of international law, and allowing states to 'freely use and exploit their natural wealth and resources wherever deemed desirable by them for their own progress and economic development', *China – Measures Related to the Exportation of Various Raw Materials*, Panel Report, 5 July 2011, WT/DS394/R WT/DS395/R WT/DS398/R [*China – Raw Materials – Panel Report*], para. 7.380. However, the right to exploit natural resources for the exclusive benefit of the State was not always obvious. Historically, there were attempts by the United States to use such resources not only for the national interest of the country where they were located but also for 'the interests of an expanding world economy', epitomised by the debates leading to the adoption of UN General Assembly Resolution 523 (VI) on the 'Integrated economic development and commercial agreements', 12 January 1952, UN Doc. A/RES/523(VI).

[6] The persistent question of what constitutes economic 'coercion' rather than mere economic 'cooperation' was discussed throughout the 1960s, including in the specific context of natural resources, in several UN General Assembly resolutions. See Resolution 3016 (XXVII) on 'Permanent Sovereignty over Natural Resources of Developing Countries' of 18 December, UN Doc. A/RES/3016(XVII), paras. 2 and 3; 'Declaration on the Establishment of a New International Economic Order', 1 May 1974, UN Doc. A/RES/S-6/3201, operative part, paras. 4(d) and 4(e) in fine; 'Charter of Economic Rights and Duties of States', 12 December 1974, UN Doc. A/RES/3281/XXIX, Charter, chapter II, Article 1, 2(1). More recently, this sovereign prerogative to set energy policy has been

They also hold '*sovereign rights*' over certain maritime spaces adjacent to their territory, i.e. the exclusive economic zone (EEZ)[7] and the continental shelf.[8] The recognition of the latter was largely triggered by attempts to assert powers over offshore energy resources, starting with the 1945 Truman Proclamation.[9] The UNCLOS affirmed the exclusive 'sovereign rights [of coastal States] for the purpose of exploring and exploiting its natural resources'[10] of the continental shelf. As for the exclusive economic zone, although its main purpose concerned the assertion of powers over fisheries, Article 56(1)(a) of the UNCLOS expressly grants exclusive sovereign rights over 'non-living' natural resources 'of the seabed and its subsoil' (a clause overlapping with the powers under the continental shelf regime) and, importantly for the energy transition, also 'the production of energy from the water, currents and winds'.

The *difference* between 'sovereignty', which encompasses the spatial basis of the State up to the limits of the territorial sea, and the 'sovereign rights' accorded over the EEZ and the continental shelf is significant in several respects relevant to energy. Although in some matters, e.g. *drilling* of the seabed 'for all purposes' (Article 81), the two regimes are largely equated, in some others there are significant differences. Two must be mentioned here due to their particular relevance for energy transactions.

The first concerns the status of *'artificial islands', 'installations' and 'structures'*, which include most of the infrastructures and equipment used for energy exploration and exploitation. Article 60 of the UNCLOS regulates the matter for the EEZ, but it is also applicable to the continental shelf.[11] A distinction is made between, on the one hand, 'artificial islands' and, on the other hand, 'installations' and 'structures'. The construction and operation of the former, irrespective of their purpose, are subject to the coastal State's authorisation and jurisdiction (hence a

recognised in the context of trade and investment disputes. See e.g. *China – Raw Materials – Panel Report*, para. 7.380; *Crystallex International Corporation v. Bolivarian Republic of Venezuela*, ICSID Case No. ARB(AF)/11/2, Award (4 April 2016), para. 581.

[7] UNCLOS, Part V.

[8] UNCLOS, Part VI.

[9] 'Policy of the United States with Respect to the Natural Resources of the Subsoil and Sea Bed of the Continental Shelf', Presidential Proclamation No. 2667, 28 September 1945, 327 Dept of State Bulletin 485.

[10] UNCLOS, Article 77(1)–(2).

[11] UNCLOS, Article 80.

regime akin to sovereignty), whereas that of the latter are only subject to such powers if they pursue an economic purpose (which expressly include – through the reference to Article 56 – energy-related installations and structures) or interfere with the coastal State's enjoyment of its sovereign rights over the resources of the EEZ. This wording leaves out installations and structures for other purposes and raises doubts as to the legal regime applicable to the construction and operation of such installations and structures. In signing, ratifying or acceding to the UNCLOS, several States made declarations addressing this issue, either stating that the consent of the coastal State is required[12] or, conversely, emphasising that the jurisdiction of the coastal State does not extend to them.[13]

The second difference concerns the powers of coastal States over the authorisation and regulation of *offshore pipelines and cables* (for electricity transmission). There is no right of immersion (the right of laying submarine pipelines and cables) of third States in the territorial sea.[14] Here, the authorisation of the coastal State is required. The laying of the Nord Stream pipeline required the authorisation of the three States (Russia, Denmark and Germany) whose territorial seas are crossed by the pipeline.[15] By contrast, there is a right of immersion beyond the territorial sea, in the EEZ,[16] the continental shelf[17] and beyond.[18] This right is not unconstrained. Article 79 of the UNCLOS, to which Articles 58(1) and 87(1)(c) refer, strikes a balance between the prerogatives of the coastal State (based not on sovereignty but on sovereign rights) and the right of immersion. In essence, (1) the laying of the pipelines and cables is not subject to the consent of the coastal State, (2) but the delineation of the course of a pipeline (not of a cable) requires such consent. Moreover, the coastal State (3) has 'the right to take reasonable measures' for the

[12] See e.g. the declarations of Brazil (paragraph V; declaration upon ratification, para. III); Cabo Verde (paragraphs VI); Ecuador (paragraph IV, 3); Germany (Statement, paragraphs not numbered); Uruguay (paragraph E). All available at: https://treaties.un.org/.

[13] See the declarations of Italy (declaration upon signature, paragraphs not numbered); The Netherlands (Objections, II, 3); United Kingdom (section (a)). All available at: https://treaties.un.org/.

[14] UNCLOS, Articles 2 and 79(4).

[15] See C. Redgwell, 'International Regulation of Energy Activities', in M. M. Roggenkamp et al. (eds.), *Energy Law in Europe: National, EU and International Regulation* (Oxford: Oxford University Press, 3rd ed. 2016), pp. 13–136, at 66.

[16] UNCLOS, Article 58(1).

[17] UNCLOS, Article 79(1).

[18] UNCLOS, Article 87(1)(c).

enjoyment of its sovereign rights over natural resources – without impeding the laying and maintenance of the pipelines and cables – and for the prevention and control of marine pollution from pipeline (Article 79(2) of the UNCLOS). Furthermore, and importantly, (4) when the cables and pipelines concern the exploitation of the coastal State's sovereign rights (by contrast with cables and pipelines for mere transit of resources and products from elsewhere), its jurisdiction is not confined to the bounds set by Article 79(2) of the UNCLOS.

2.1.3 Peoples

Peoples, as an international legal subject, enjoy the right to self-determination recognised as such (i.e. not as a mere principle) since the adoption of UN General Assembly Resolution 1514 (XV) in 1960,[19] subsequently confirmed by common Article 1 of the two 1966 International Covenants[20] and by the 1970 Friendly Relations Declaration.[21] In its 2019 Advisory Opinion on the *Chagos Archipelago*, the ICJ confirmed that Resolution 1514 (XV) codified, already in 1960, a right of peoples under general international law.[22] This is not the place to discuss which group qualifies as a 'people' entitled to the right to self-determination. International law recognises the existence of different entities, sometimes using the word 'people' to describe a group that may not necessarily constitute a people for the purpose of the right to self-determination.[23]

UN General Assembly Resolution 1803 (XVII)[24] concerns the latter, and it expressly affirms the permanent sovereignty of peoples over their natural resources, as an economic extension of the political right to self-determination. In this context, the principle and the right to permanent sovereignty over natural resources were designed as an instrument of

[19] UN General Assembly Resolution 1514 (XV), 'Declaration on the Granting of Independence to Colonial Countries and Peoples', 14 December 1960, A/RES/1514(XV).

[20] See ICESCR, Article 1; ICCPR, Article 1.

[21] UN General Assembly Resolution 2625 (XXV), 'Declaration on Principles of International Law concerning Friendly Relations and Co-operation among States in accordance with the Charter of the United Nations', 24 October 1970, Annex.

[22] *Legal Consequences of the Separation of the Chagos Archipelago from Mauritius in 1965*, Advisory Opinion, ICJ Reports 2019, p. 95, para. 152–154.

[23] Such is the case of certain collective subjects such as indigenous and tribal peoples or minorities, which are discussed later in this article. See M. G. Kohen, 'Self-determination', in J. E. Viñuales (ed.), *The UN Friendly Relations Declaration at 50. An Assessment of the Fundamental Principles of International Law* (Cambridge: Cambridge University Press, 2020), pp. 133–165, at 158–163.

[24] See n. 4.

economic emancipation against the existing (but not against the subsequently agreed) asymmetries in the ownership and control of natural resources by colonial and post-colonial interests, both colonial States and the private investors, hence the need to stress the 'permanence'. In normal situations, it overlaps with the right of States to exploit their natural resources in the national interest, but in some exceptional cases – when there is a tension between the government and the people – this overlap hides a tension between legal entitlements.[25]

Although some commentators have expressed scepticism regarding the legal traction of this principle with respect to the exploitation of natural resources, the fact remains that, as noted by Dolzer, the 'Permanent Sovereignty' movement was extremely successful politically and economically in capturing oil and gas resources, displacing foreign interests from concession-holders, to contractors in production-sharing agreements and eventually to mere service providers.[26] Even at the legal level, permanent sovereignty has served to protect the entitlements of certain peoples over energy. The principle played a significant role in the long process of preservation, then of recognition and finally of implementation of the entitlement of the East Timorese people over their energy resources in the Timor Sea. In the *East Timor* case, although the ICJ did not enter into the merits of Portugal's claim, Judge Weeramantry discussed in some detail the implications of the principle of permanent sovereignty over natural resources in his dissenting opinion. The following observation is particularly apposite:

> In the present case, it is impossible to venture a prediction as to how long it will be before the East Timorese people achieve self-determination. [. . .] Should a period of years elapse until such time, and the Treaty [the 1989 Timor Gap Treaty] is in full operation in the meantime, a substantial segment of this invaluable resource may well be lost to East Timor for all time. This would be a loss of a significant segment of the sovereignty of the people. [. . .] At such time as the East Timorese people exercise their right to self-determination, they would become entitled as a component of their sovereign right, to determine how their wealth and natural resources should be disposed of. *Any action prior to that date which may in effect*

[25] The most common hypothesis is the so-called resource curse. See e.g. J. E. Viñuales, 'The Resource Curse: A Legal Perspective' (2011) 17 *Global Governance* 197. But there are also more complex configurations. See G. Le Moli, 'President of the Republic et al. v. Ali Ayyoub et al'. (2019) 113 *American Journal of International Law* 798.

[26] R. Dolzer, 'International Co-operation in Energy Affairs' (2015) 372 *RCADI* 395, at 419–420.

> *deprive them of this right must thus fall clearly within the category of acts which infringe on their right to self-determination, and their future sovereignty, if indeed full and independent sovereignty be their choice.*[27]

The dispute was eventually resolved more than twenty years later through a conciliation procedure under the UNCLOS leading to a treaty, which addressed also the interests from the companies involved in the activities in the relevant area of the Timor Sea.[28]

2.1.4 Other Collective Subjects

The peoples discussed in the previous paragraphs are not the only collective subjects which hold legal entitlements over natural resources, including energy resources. 'Indigenous' and 'tribal' peoples have been recognised such entitlements in a number of instruments and cases, within certain limits.[29] The ILO Convention 169 on the Rights of Indigenous and Tribal Peoples recognises indigenous land and resource rights, with a combination of possessive use and management rights.[30] Article 14(1) of the Convention affirms that 'the rights of ownership and possession of [indigenous peoples] over the lands which they traditionally occupy shall be recognized'. In the same vein, the UN Declaration on the Rights of Indigenous Peoples states that '[i]ndigenous peoples have the right to the lands, territories and resources which they have traditionally owned, occupied or otherwise used or acquired' and States have the obligation to 'provide effective mechanisms for prevention of, and redress for [. . .] [a]ny action which has the aim or effect of dispossessing [indigenous peoples] of their lands, territories or resources'.[31]

[27] See *East Timor (Portugal v. Australia)*, Judgment, ICJ Reports 1995, p. 90 [*East Timor*], Dissenting Opinion of Judge Weeramantry, at 198 (emphasis added).

[28] See *Conciliation between The Democratic Republic of Timor-Leste and The Commonwealth of Australia*, PCA Case No. 2016–10, Press Release No. 9, 1 September 2017.

[29] UNDRIP, Article 46(1) of the Declaration expressly states that '[n]othing in this Declaration may be interpreted as implying for any State, people, group or person any right to engage in any activity or to perform any act contrary to the Charter of the United Nations or *construed as authorizing or encouraging any action which would dismember or impair, totally or in part, the territorial integrity or political unity of sovereign and independent States*' (emphasis added).

[30] Indigenous and Tribal Peoples Convention, ILO, 27 June 1989 [ILO Convention 169]; previosuly, Indigenous and Tribal Populations Convention, ILO, 26 June 1957 (no longer in force).

[31] UNDRIP, Articles 26(1) and 8(2)(b).

In the context of the African Charter on Human and Peoples' Rights,[32] the African Court has made a distinction between the entitlement of such peoples to self-determination, as understood in the previous section, which is not recognised, and their entitlement to other collective rights, which is recognised. According to the Court:

> It is generally accepted that, in the struggle against foreign domination in all its forms, the Charter primarily targets the peoples comprising the populations of the countries struggling to attain independence and national sovereignty. [...] In the circumstances, the question is whether the notion of 'people' used by the Charter covers not only the population as the constituent elements of the State, but also the ethnic groups or communities identified as forming part of the said population within a constituted State. In other words, the question that arises is *whether the enjoyment of the rights unquestionably recognised for the constituent peoples of the population of a given State can be extended to include sub-state ethnic groups and communities that are part of that population.* [...] In the view of the Court, *the answer to this question is in the affirmative, provided such groups or communities do not call into question the sovereignty and territorial integrity of the State without the latter's consent.* It would in fact be difficult to understand that the States which are the authors of the Charter intended, for example, to automatically recognise for the ethnic groups and communities that constitute their population, the right to self-determination and independence guaranteed under Article 20(1) of the Charter, which in this case would amount to a veritable right to secession. On the other hand, *nothing prevents other peoples' rights* [...] *from being recognised, where necessary, specifically for the ethnic groups and communities that constitute the population of a State.* [...] In the instant case, *one of the rights at issue is the right of peoples to freely dispose of their wealth and natural resources guaranteed under Article 21 of the Charter.*[33]

In an earlier case, the African Commission had expressly recognised the collective right of the Ogoni people to their energy resources under Article 21 of the African Charter, which *in casu* had been violated by the Nigerian government:

> [c]ontrary to its Charter obligations [...] the Nigerian Government ha[d] given the green light to private actors, and the oil Companies in particular, to devastatingly affect the well-being of the Ogonis [... and that ...]

[32] African Charter on Human and Peoples' Rights, 27 June 1981, 21 ILM 58 (1982) [African Charter].

[33] *African Commission on Human and Peoples' Rights v. Republic of Kenya* ('Ogiek case'), ACtHPR App. 006/2012, Judgment of 26 May 2017, paras. 197–200 (emphasis added).

> [b]y any measure of standards, its practice falls short of the minimum conduct expected from governments, and therefore, is in violation of Article 21 of the African Charter.[34]

Similar reasoning can be found in the case law of the Inter-American Court of Human Rights in connection with the broad interpretation of the right to property of indigenous communities under Article 21 of the American Convention. In *Kichwa of Sarayaku v. Ecuador*, the Court recognised the collective entitlement of the Kichwa over their land and the natural resources therein.[35] In this case, the Ecuadorian government had granted oil exploration and exploitation concessions to an Argentine company, which began its seismic exploration without the consent and even without consulting the indigenous community. The Court concluded that by allowing such action the government had violated the collective right of the Kichwa indigenous people protected by Article 21 of the American Convention.[36]

In the European context, although the case law of the European Court of Human Rights on the property rights of indigenous peoples is limited and confined essentially to the admissibility stage,[37] some recognition has been granted by the adoption of the Nordic Saami Convention by Finland, Norway and Sweden on 13 January 2017.[38] The 'Saami people' are expressly recognised as 'the indigenous people of Finland, Norway and Sweden' (Article 2) and so is their right to self-determination 'in accordance with the rules and provisions of international law and of this Convention', which includes '[i]n so far as it follows from these rules and provisions [...] the right to determine [...] to dispose, to their own benefit, over its own natural resources' (Article 3). The Convention also contains specific provisions relating to the rights of the Saami over land and water, including a provision on the 'Utilization of natural resources'

[34] *Social and Economic Rights Action Center (SERAC) and others v. Nigeria*, African Commission Application No. 155/96 (2001–2002), para. 58.

[35] *Case of the Kichwa Indigenous People of Sarayaku v. Ecuador*, ICtHR Series C No. 245, Judgment (merits and compensation) (27 June 2012) [*Kichwa de Sarayaku v. Ecuador*], paras. 145–147. The leading case the paved the way for this line of jurisprudence is *Mayagna (Sumo) Awas Tingni Community v. Nicaragua*, ICtHR Series C No. 79, Judgment (31 August 2001).

[36] *Kichwa de Sarayaku v. Ecuador*, para. 231.

[37] On the European practice see P. Kovács, 'Indigenous Issues under the European Convention of Human Rights, reflected in an Inter-American Mirror' (2016) 48 *George Washington International Law Review* 781.

[38] Nordic Saami Convention, 13 January 2017, available at: www.sametinget.se/105173.

(Article 36). This provision introduces a consultation requirement before permits for prospecting or extraction of minerals or other sub-surface resources are granted by one of the States Parties. When the interference with Saami cultural activities reaches a certain level, such permits cannot be granted 'unless so consented by the Saami parliament and the affected Saami'. At the time of writing, this instrument had not yet entered into force. It requires the approval of the Saami parliaments and the Saami Council's position has called for the renegotiation of the text with them.[39] Yet, the degree of domestic recognition of the rights of the Saami has seen significant developments, as suggested by the decision of Sweden's Supreme Court recognising that a Saami village has exclusive rights to grant hunting and fishing rights in their traditional land.[40]

2.1.5 Individuals

Individuals also hold certain entitlements over energy under international law. A distinction must be introduced regarding the concessions and other rights granted by a State (in which case the entitlement is recognised to the State) to a foreign investor or another economic operator. Such rights are granted under domestic law and they may be protected under certain investment protection disciplines. But they are not entitlements originally conferred on them by international law. There has been some controversy regarding the nature of investment disciplines. Despite some variations in the conceptions endorsed by different tribunals,[41] it is unquestionable that they are not conferred on the basis

[39] See Report of the Saami Council to the Committee on Economic, Social and Cultural rights – supplementing and commenting on Finland's seventh periodic report of States parties due in 2020 (E/C.12/FIN/7), para. 5.

[40] See Swedish Supreme Court, Case No. T 853–18, Decision (23 January 2020).

[41] See *Archer Daniels Midland Company and Tate & Lyle Ingredients Americas, Inc. v. The United Mexican States*, ICSID Case No. ARB (AF)/04/5, Award (21 November 2007), para. 171 ('the fundamental difference between Chapter Eleven of the NAFTA and human rights treaties in this regard is, besides a procedural right of action under Section B, that Chapter Eleven does not provide individual substantive rights for investors, but rather complements the promotion and protection standards of the rules regarding the protection of aliens under customary international law'.); *Cargill Incorporated v. United Mexican States*, ICSID Case No. ARB(AF)/05/2, Award (18 September 2009), paras. 424–426 ('With due respect to the majority in ADM and Respondent in this case, the Tribunal does not agree that investors under Chapter 11 are granted mere procedural rights of access. [. . .] The Tribunal acknowledges that the rights of investors under Chapter 11 derive from the agreement of the State Parties and that they may to some extent, at least as far as the reach of Chapter 11, be dependent on the continuation of that agreement. But this situation is no different from rights of

of human dignity (but merely of reciprocal concessions based on nationality[42]) and they are not constitutive (i.e. they only exist to protect an entitlement otherwise granted).

A different question is whether there is a human right to energy. Such entitlement has been conceptualised as a stand-alone 'right to access to energy',[43] i.e. a right to 'a sufficient, regular, reliable, efficient, safe, and affordable supply of (ideally clean and sustainable) energy',[44] or the 'right to electricity' itself.[45] At the very least, such right embodies 'a shared objective in poverty eradication and human development',[46] and it is widely acknowledged as a component part of the rights to an adequate standard of living and adequate housing[47] as well as the right to health.[48] It is also recognised by the Convention on the Elimination of All Forms

individuals within many municipal legal systems. That the origin of individual rights may be found in the act of a sovereign, or in the joint act of sovereigns, does not negate the existence of the rights conferred. It is the view of this Tribunal that Chapter 11 creates a framework within which it is the investor that acts upon and benefits from the obligations which are set forth in Chapter 11').

42 See *Barcelona Traction, Light and Power Company, Limited*, Judgment, ICJ Reports 1970, p. 3, at 33; *Sawhoyamaxa Indigenous Community v. Paraguay*, ICtHR Series C No. 146 (29 March 2006), para. 140 ('the Court considers that the enforcement of bilateral commercial treaties negates vindication of non-compliance with state obligations under the American Convention; on the contrary, their enforcement should always be compatible with the American Convention, which is a multilateral treaty on human rights that stands in a class of its own and that generates rights for individual human beings and does not depend entirely on reciprocity among States').

43 See A. J. Bradbrook, J. G. Gardam, 'Placing Access to Energy Services within a Human Rights Framework' (2006) 28 *Human Rights Quarterly* 389.

44 Bradbrook/Gardam, *Access to Energy*, at 409.

45 See S. Tully, 'Access to Electricity as a Human Right' (2006) 24 *Netherlands Quarterly of Human Rights* 557.

46 Redgwell, *International Regulation*, at 1077.

47 ICESCR, Article 11 (1); Report of the Special Rapporteur on adequate housing as a component of the right to an adequate standard of living, 1 March 2002, UN Doc. E/CN.4/2002/59, paras. 35, 46(b); Committee on Economic, Social and Cultural Rights (CESCR), General Comment No. 7: The right to adequate housing (Art.11.1): forced evictions, 20 May 1997, E/1998/22, paras. 1, 17; CESCR, Conclusions and Recommendations of the CESCR, Dominican Republic, 19 December 1994, UN Doc. E/C.12/1994/15, para. 11; CESCR, General Comment No. 4: The Right to Adequate Housing, 13 December 1991, E/1992/23, para. 8(b).

48 ICESCR, Article 12; CESCR, General Comment No. 14: The Right to the Highest Attainable Standard of Health (Art. 12), 11 August 2000, Document E/C.12/2000/4, paras. 3, 4, 11, 15, 36, 43(c) (repeatedly referring to housing as an underlying determinant of health).

of Discrimination against Women (CEDAW).[49] At the regional level, some authority can be found in the San Salvador Protocol to the ACHR,[50] the African Charter,[51] and the European Social Charter.[52] At the domestic level, the decision of the Constitutional Court of South Africa in the *Grootboom case* provides an apposite illustration.[53] The case concerned the scope of social and economic rights (particularly the rights to housing and children's right to shelter) under the South African Constitution. The complainant, Mrs Grootboom, was one of over 800 adults and children living in very poor conditions in an informal settlement, who had illegally occupied nearby land and been evicted. The Court concluded that the State was obliged to provide inter alia access to food, water and housing, which may include access to services 'such as water, sewage, electricity and roads'.[54]

2.1.6 International Organisations

Unlike the four entitlement-holders reviewed so far, derivative entitlement-holders receive their entitlements from a delegation from an originary entitlement-holder, normally made by treaty.

The most representative illustration is provided by Articles 4(2)(i) and 194 of the Treaty on the Functioning of the European Union (TFEU),[55] according to which 'energy' is a 'shared competence' between the Union and Member States. This means that EU Member States exercise their

[49] Convention on the Elimination of all Forms of Discrimination against Women, 18 December 1979, 1249 UNTS 1, Article 14(2)(h). See Committee on the Elimination of Discrimination Against Women (CEDAW), CEDAW General Recommendation No. 34: Article 12 of the Convention (Women and Health), 2016, CEDAW/C/GC/34, paras. 21–28 (listing 'water, sanitation and energy' as three essential needs to fulfill the right to adequate living conditions).

[50] Additional Protocol to the American Convention on Human Rights in the Area of Economic, Social and Cultural Rights, 17 November 1988, 28 ILM 156, Article 11.

[51] African Charter, Article 16; *Free Legal Assistance Group et al. v. Zaire*, African Commission, Communications No. 25/89, 47/90, 56/91 & 100/93 (1995), paras. 1–4, 47.

[52] ESC, Article 31(1); *European Roma Rights Centre v. France* (51/2008), European Committee of Social Rights, Complaint No. 51/2008, Decision on the merits (19 October 2009), para. 46.

[53] *Government of the Republic of South Africa and Others v. Grootboom and Others* (CCT11/00) [2000] ZACC 19; 2001 (1) SA 46; 2000 (11) BCLR 1169 (4 October 2000) [*Grootboom case*].

[54] *Grootboom*, para. 37.

[55] Previously the EC Treaty and, before it, the EEC Treaty. Its current name dates to the adoption of the Treaty of Lisbon, 13 December 2007). On the EU Energy Union see Chapter 7.

competence when the Union has not exercised – or has decided not to exercise – its own competence. It must be noted, however, that even in this context, Article 194(2) TFEU *in fine* reserves a Member State's 'right to determine the conditions for exploiting its energy resources, its choice between different energy sources and the general structure of its energy supply'. The choices relating to energy supply can be limited by the Union acting by a unanimous decision of the Council (Article 192(2)(c) TFEU) and, in practice, it is also limited by EU policy on renewable energy. The distinction between the entitlement over energy resources and energy policy is a reminder that, out of the two entitlements of States flowing from sovereignty (see Section 2.1.2), only sovereign prerogative is constrained by the delegation or, in other words, the powers delegated to the Union concern mostly energy as a product, technology or activity, rather than as a resource.

Other examples of international organisations with some measure of energy entitlements include the aforementioned special cases of the UNTAET,[56] the ISA[57] and certain agencies established in joint development and watercourse agreements.[58]

2.2 *Rules Allocating Entitlements*

2.2.1 Introductory Observations

In addition to *conferring* entitlements, international law contains *allocative rules* of direct relevance in case of competing entitlements. The two main challenges posed by these rules concern their scope of application (e.g. whether rules developed in one context, e.g. of international watercourses or groundwater resources, can be extrapolated to shared oil and gas resources) and the frequent use of rules formulated in the form of 'reasonableness', 'diligence', 'cooperation' or other similar terms which, effectively, amount to an open-textured standard delegating the final decision to the adjudicator or to the agreement of the relevant parties. In the specific area of shared oil and gas resources, efforts within the context of the ILC to distil principles from State practice have so far been unsuccessful, indeed resisted by most States.[59]

[56] See n. 1.
[57] See n. 2.
[58] See n. 3 and Chapters 4 and 5.
[59] See Chapter 4.

The main consequence from both a theoretical and a practical perspective, is that the allocation of powers over energy, when there are competing claims over certain energy resources (whether onshore or offshore) are governed by unspecific rules, unless the relevant States reach an agreement on the delimitation of the relevant areas or, at least, the 'joint development' of the relevant resources. In the following paragraphs, four main sets of rules are briefly noted, namely the rules concerning the relations between title and *effectivités*, the broad principles on maritime delimitation, the principles applicable to the use of energy resources as well as to other natural resources, and the rules relating to what can be broadly called asymmetric claims (e.g. between a colonial or occupying power and a people, or between a government and a collective subject holding powers over energy). Some of these sets are analysed in detail in Chapters 4 and 5.

2.2.2 Energy between Title and *Effectivités*

Energy activities, whether onshore or offshore, may have some relevance for the determination of entitlements over energy. This is because the granting of rights over the energy resources in an area may, depending on the circumstances, be relevant to determine title or to delimitate an area. Such relevance depends on the legal context – as well as the circumstances – in which it intervenes.

In the context of onshore resources, the main question concerns the relations between title to territory and so-called *effectivités*, i.e. acts that display the intention of a government to behave like the sovereign of a given area, including the management of natural resources. The relations between title and *effectivités* were clarified by a chamber of the ICJ in 1986, in the *Frontier Dispute* between Burkina Faso and Mali.[60] There are four main hypotheses. First, when the holder of formal title also exercises the relevant acts, then such acts or *effectivités* confirm and possibly specify the specific expanse of the title. Secondly, when the *effectivités* are exercised by a State other than the holder of the title, the latter prevails despite the *effectivités*. That means that the display of energy activities is not enough, as such, to override a formal title by another State. The third and fourth hypotheses are particularly relevant for energy. When there is no formal title, then the *effectivités* could potentially amount to title and assertion of powers over energy resources and/

[60] *Frontier Dispute (Burkina Faso/Mali)*, Judgment, ICJ Reports 1986, p. 554 [*Burkina Faso/Mali*], para. 63.

or activities would count as acts *à titre de souverain*, i.e. assertion of governmental authority. Also, when there is title but its specific territorial expanse is not clearly circumscribed, *effectivités* 'play an essential role in showing how the title is interpreted in practice'.[61] In the latter case, then, actual practice on the ground will be key to determine the specific scope of the title.

2.2.3 Energy and Maritime Delimitation

For offshore resources, the rules of maritime delimitation are particularly relevant. Some aspects of these rules are analysed in detail in Chapter 4 of this book. For present purposes, the allocation of entitlements can be examined at three main levels.

The first and most basic level concerns maritime boundaries that have been agreed, and which are straddled by a transboundary energy deposit. These rules are discussed in more detail in Chapter 4 but, generally speaking, they often take the form of joint development agreements (agreement to jointly exploit a known deposit) allocating matters such as financial contributions and rents.

The second level concerns the principles on the basis of which maritime delimitation is to be conducted and the role played by energy deposits and activities within them. The principles of maritime delimitation have been mostly developed in the case law of international courts and tribunals, given the open-textured nature of the applicable provisions found in the UNCLOS (Articles 15 (territorial sea), 74(1) (exclusive economic zone), and 83(1) (continental shelf)).[62] The standard approach, fleshed out by the International Court of Justice in the case concerning the *Maritime Delimitation in the Black Sea*, between Romania and Ukraine, consists of three steps: (1) drawing an equidistance line between the spaces to be delimited (adjacent or opposite territorial seas, exclusive economic zones and/or continental shelves) from the appropriate basepoints, (2) then adjusting the line to take into account 'special' or 'relevant' circumstances and (3) then, if necessary, correcting the result to avoid 'any marked disproportion between the ratio of the respective coastal lengths and the ratio between the relevant maritime area of each

[61] *Burkina Faso/Mali*, para. 63.

[62] For detailed studies see Y. Tanaka, *Predictability and Flexibility in the Law of Maritime Delimitation* (Oxford: Hart, 2nd ed. 2019); M. Lando, *Maritime Delimitation as a Judicial Process* (Cambridge: Cambridge University Press, 2019).

State'.[63] Within this approach, government action relating to oil and gas resources and activities (e.g. issuing licences) has been invoked as a 'special' or 'relevant' circumstance, but the ICJ has rejected this view and confined consideration of such practice within narrow bounds:

> although the existence of an express or tacit agreement between the parties on the siting of their respective oil concessions may indicate a consensus on the maritime areas to which they are entitled, oil concessions and oil wells are not in themselves to be considered as relevant circumstances justifying the adjustment or shifting of the provisional delimitation line. Only if they are based on express or tacit agreement between the parties may they be taken into account.[64]

Moreover, such practice in and of itself has been deemed insufficient to establish the existence of a tacit agreement on the maritime boundary.[65] Thus, the role of such oil and gas practice is akin to that of *effectivités* in the context of the third and fourth hypotheses reviewed earlier (*effectivités* as the sole basis for title, in the absence of a formal title; and *effectivités* to clarify the scope of a recognised title).

The third level at which the allocation of powers over offshore resources can be assessed concerns the rights and obligations in the period before an agreement on delimitation and/or on the development of the resource has been reached. As noted before, efforts within the ILC to codify principles for shared oil and gas resources, which would encompass this situation, have been resisted by States. Articles 74(3) (exclusive economic zone) and 83(3) (continental shelf) of UNCLOS require States, pending final delimitation, to make 'every effort to enter into provisional arrangements of a practical nature' and to make 'every effort [. . .] not to jeopardize or hamper the reaching of the final agreement'. The specific content and implications of these obligations are analysed in detail in Chapter 4. But the next paragraphs offer a

[63] *Maritime Delimitation in the Black Sea (Romania v. Ukraine)*, Judgment, ICJ Reports 2009, p. 61, paras. 115–122. The International Tribunal for the Law of the Sea (ITLOS) has followed this approach in its first maritime delimitation case, the *Dispute Concerning Delimitation of the Maritime Boundary between Bangladesh and Myanmar in the Bay of Bengal (Bangladesh/Myanmar)*, ITLOS Case No. 16, Judgment (14 March 2012), paras. 233–240.

[64] *Land and Maritime Boundary between Cameroon and Nigeria (Cameroon v. Nigeria: Equatorial Guinea intervening)*, Judgment, ICJ Reports 2002, p. 303, para. 304. See further *Dispute Concerning Delimitation of the Maritime Boundary Between Ghana and Cote D'Ivoire in the Atlantic Ocean (Ghana/Cote D'Ivoire)*, ITLOS Case No. 23, Judgment (23 September 2017) [*Ghana/Cote D'Ivoire – Judgment*], paras. 452–455.

[65] *Ghana/Cote D'Ivoire – Judgment*, para. 215.

concise statement and a comparison with other allocative rules applicable to the analogous case of shared waterbodies.

2.2.4 Principles Governing Competing Uses of Energy

The principles governing the exploitation of natural resources are a composite set of rules that stem from different sources. This raises difficult questions regarding their scope of application.

Articles 74(3) and 83(3) of the UNCLOS have been interpreted in the *Guyana/Suriname* arbitration in such a manner as to permit two types of activities in a disputed area, namely 'activities undertaken by the parties pursuant to provisional arrangements of a practical nature' and 'acts which, although unilateral, would not have the effect of jeopardizing or hampering the reaching of a final agreement on the delimitation of the maritime boundary'.[66] Importantly, the latter category encompassed, according to the arbitral tribunal 'unilateral acts which do not cause a physical change to the marine environment'.[67] Such acts, e.g. seismic exploration, are permitted under Articles 74(3) and 83(3) of the UNCLOS, whereas acts such as the physical exploitation of oil and gas reserves, which lead to a permanent physical change, are not. The reason why they are not is their effect, typically the change in the conditions for extraction that are imposed on the other State once a State has drilled (and hence changed the pressure conditions of) a reservoir. Conversely, if such effects can be prevented (due to a new type of technology or to the solid nature of the resource, e.g. solid minerals, rather than oil and gas), then there would be no prohibition as a matter of principle unless the rights of the other State are otherwise hampered or the environment is significantly harmed.

A broadly similar distinction was drawn by the ICJ in 1976 in the *Aegean Sea Continental Shelf* case between Greece and Turkey, at the stage of interim relief.[68] The Court declined to order the provisional measures requested by Greece because (1) the seismic exploration conducted by Turkey did not involve 'any risk of physical damage to the seabed or subsoil or to [the] natural resources', (2) the activities were of a 'transitory character' and did not involve the 'establishment of installations' and (3) Turkey had not embarked on any activity amounting to

[66] *In the matter of an arbitration between Guyana and Suriname*, PCA Case 2004/04, Award (17 September 2007) [*Guyana/Suriname*], para. 466.

[67] *Guyana/Suriname*, para. 467.

[68] *Aegean Sea Continental Shelf, Interim Protection*, Order, ICJ Reports 1976, p. 3 [*Aegean Continental Shelf*].

the 'actual appropriation or other use of the natural resources of the areas' in dispute.[69] Although similar, this test is more demanding than the one set by the arbitral tribunal in *Guyana/Suriname*, because the absence of physical damage is not, as such sufficient, to make the activity permissible. It is not seismic exploration but the manner in which it is conducted that matters, as the ICJ noted by the reference to its potential findings on the merits.[70] Risk of damage is also covered and, even in the absence of damage/risk, permanent installations, appropriation or use would make the activity cross the line of permissibility.

The fact that the more demanding test was formulated outside the context of Articles 74(3) and 83(3) of the UNCLOS could suggest that the latter are less demanding than general international law. The order on provisional measures rendered by the Special Chamber of the ITLOS in *Ghana/Côte d'Ivoire* has not removed this impression of discrepancy. The Chamber noted that the exploration activities leading to the acquisition and use of information about the resources in the disputed area may, as such, suffice to 'create a risk of irreversible prejudice to the rights of Côte d'Ivoire'.[71] The Chamber thus went beyond the ICJ in the *Aegean Continental Shelf* case, although both decisions concern the preservation of the rights of parties in litigation and not the hampering of the possibility to reach agreement, which is a different question. The Special Chamber allowed existing exploitation operations conducted by Ghana to continue, on the condition that no new drilling would be authorised, and Ghana would take measures to ensure that information derived from such operations would not be used in a way that hampered *Côte d'Ivoire*'s interests.[72] Thus, the Chamber admitted the possibility that mere unilateral exploration may be unlawful and that unilateral exploitation in a disputed area may be lawful. Of particular note, the latter point was confirmed in the decision on the merits, in which the Chamber rejected the claim that Ghana's exploitation activities in the disputed area engaged its international responsibility.[73]

[69] *Aegean Continental Shelf*, para. 30.

[70] *Aegean Continental Shelf*, para. 31.

[71] *Dispute Concerning Delimitation of the Maritime Boundary Between Ghana and Cote D'Ivoire in the Atlantic Ocean (Ghana/Cote D'Ivoire)*, ITLOS Case No. 23 (Provisional measures), Order (25 April 2015) [*Ghana/Côte d'Ivoire – Provisional measures*], paras. 95–96.

[72] *Ghana/Côte d'Ivoire – Provisional measures*, paras. 99, 108(1)(a).

[73] *Ghana/Côte d'Ivoire – Judgment*, paras. 589–592, 633. For a detailed discussion see Chapter 4.

The logic underpinning these principles is broadly similar to two other sets of rules governing the use of natural resources. The first set applies to all resources and all areas, and concerns the limits arising from the need to protect the environment. I will revert to this set in Chapter 3, as its focus is on limiting the negative externalities of energy activities on the environment. But the starting point of these rules is the assertion of 'the sovereign right [of States] to exploit their own resources',[74] which is thereafter limited by the principle of prevention of significant environmental harm. This principle encompasses inter alia the procedural obligations to conduct an environmental impact assessment of the activity and to notify and consult with potentially affected States.[75] Such principles have been deemed to be applicable irrespective of the geographical location of harm,[76] including in disputed areas.[77]

The other set of principles applies to international watercourses. As further discussed in Chapter 5, the initial focus was the use of such watercourses for navigational purposes and subsequently the so-called non-navigational uses, including hydroelectricity but also other energy uses. The allocation of entitlements over a shared watercourse was first conceived of as a 'community of interest' placing each riparian State on an equal footing as regards navigational uses.[78] This approach was transposed by the ICJ to non-navigational uses, specifically hydroelectricity, in the case concerning the *Gabčíkovo-Nagymaros Project*.[79] In this case, the Court equated the 'community of interest' with the principle of

[74] See 'Declaration of the United Nations Conference on the Human Environment', Stockholm, 16 June 1972, UN Doc. A/CONF 48/14/Rev.1, pp. 2ff., Principle 21; 'Rio Declaration on Environment and Development', 13 June 1992, UN Doc. A/CONF.151/26. Rev.1, Principle 2.

[75] *Certain Activities Carried Out by Nicaragua in the Border Area (Costa Rica v. Nicaragua) and Construction of a Road in Costa Rica along the San Juan River (Nicaragua v. Costa Rica)*, Judgment, ICJ Reports 2015, p. 665 [*Costa Rica/Nicaragua*], para. 104.

[76] *Request for an Advisory Opinion Submitted by the Sub-Regional Fisheries Commission (SRFC)*, Advisory Opinion of 2 April 2015, ITLOS Case No. 21 [*IUU Advisory Opinion*], paras. 111, 120.

[77] *Ghana/Côte d'Ivoire – Provisional measures*, paras. 68–73; *In the matter of the South China Sea Arbitration before and Arbitral Tribunal constituted under Annex VII of the United Nations Convention on the Law of the Sea*, PCA Case No. 2013–19, Award (12 July 2016) [*South China Sea Arbitration*], para. 927.

[78] *Case relating to the territorial jurisdiction of the International Commission on the River Oder*, PCIJ Series A No. 23, Judgment (10 September 1929), p. 27.

[79] *Gabčíkovo-Nagymaros Project (Hungary v. Slovakia)*, Judgment, ICJ Reports 1997, p. 7 [*Gabčíkovo-Nagymaros Project*], para. 85.

reasonable and equitable utilisation of the watercourse[80] enshrined in the 1997 New York Convention on the Non-Navigational Uses of International Watercourses.[81] States – typically those situated upstream – have a right to unilateral utilisation of a watercourse[82] as long as they do not deprive the downstream State of 'equitable and reasonable share' of the natural resource.[83] This is assessed at three levels: (1) by reference to certain factors (e.g. geological features, economic and broader social factors, current and potential uses, vital human needs),[84] (2) within the overall bounds of the duty of no harm, i.e. the due diligence duty not to cause 'significant' harm to the interests of the other State[85] and (3) even if significant harm occurs without fault, the due diligence duty requires the upstream State to proactively bring the situation back to the level of permissible (reasonable and equitable) bounds as well as to discuss the possibility of compensation.[86] There are several examples of the application of these principles – on a stand-alone basis or together with watercourse-specific treaties – arising from hydroelectric projects in shared watercourses.[87] However, disputes over the construction and operation of hydroelectric dams raise complex political and economic issues which call for a range of political means, as suggested by the ongoing dispute between Brazil and Paraguay over the Itaipú Dam[88]

[80] *Gabčíkovo-Nagymaros Project*, para. 85.

[81] United Nations Convention on the Law of the Non-Navigational Uses of International Watercourses, 21 May 1997, 36 ILM 700 [UN Watercourses Convention], Article 5.

[82] See *Lake Lanoux Arbitration (Spain* v. *France)*, Award of 16 November 1957, RIAA, vol. XII, pp. 281ff. [*Lake Lanoux Arbitration*].

[83] *Gabčíkovo-Nagymaros Project*, para. 85.

[84] UN Watercourses Convention, Articles 6(1) and 10.

[85] UN Watercourses Convention, Article 7(1).

[86] UN Watercourses Convention, Article 7(2).

[87] See e.g. *Lake Lanoux Arbitration* and *Gabčíkovo-Nagymaros Project*. In addition to these inter-State cases, hydroelectric projects have given rise to several commercial and investment arbitration disputes, but they are governed by different rules. See e.g. *Transglobal Green Energy, LLC and Transglobal Green Panama, S.A. v. Republic of Panama*, ICSID Case No. ARB/13/28, Award (2 June 2016); *Alpiq AG v. Romania*, ICSID Case No. ARB/14/28, Award (9 November 2018) (unpublished); *Hydro S.r.l. & Ors. v. Republic of Albania*, ICSID Case No. ARB/15/28, Award (24 April 2019) (unpublished); *ENERGO-PRO a.s. v. Republic of Bulgaria*, ICSID Case No. ARB/15/19, pending.

[88] See 'A Dam Mess. A Secret Hydropower Deal with Brazil Causes a Political Crisis in Paraguay', *The Economist*, 22 August 2019. See generally C. Folch, *Hydropolitics. The Itaipu Dam, Sovereignty and the Engineering of Modern South America* (Princeton: Princeton University Press, 2019).

and that between Ethiopia, Egypt and Sudan over the Grand Ethiopian Renaissance Dam.[89]

2.2.5 Asymmetric Conditions

Disputes regarding the allocation of entitlements over natural resources may also arise under asymmetric conditions, understood as situations of colonialism, foreign occupation and/or oppression of certain collective subjects. Although such situations are not infrequent, they have only been expressly addressed in the case law of international tribunals in a handful cases. Four illustrations can help to clarify the applicable rules and their operation.

The first two illustrations concern inter-State relations. Following the 1990–1991 Gulf War, the UN Security Council adopted Resolution 687 (1991), which 'reaffirmed that Iraq [. . .] is liable under international law for any direct loss, damage, including environmental damage and the depletion of natural resources [. . .] as a result of Iraq's unlawful invasion and occupation of Kuwait'.[90] The UN Compensation Commission established by this resolution to manage these claims focussed on the ascertainment of claims but not the principle of Iraq's liability.[91] Thus, although there were several instalments of claims brought by corporations, private legal entities and public sector enterprises specifically in the oil sector (called 'E1' claims), including by Kuwaiti petroleum companies, as well as by governments, including by Kuwait itself (called 'F3' claims), they are only informative as to the process that may be followed in such circumstances rather than the underlying substantive principles.

[89] See 'Egypt-Ethiopia Row over Nile Dam', BBC News, 7 November 2019. See generally Z. Yihdego, A. Rieu-Clarke, A. E. Cascao (eds.), *The Grand Ethiopian Renaissance Dam and the Nile Bassin: Implications for Transboundary Water Cooperation* (London: Routledge, 2017).

[90] UN Security Council Resolution 687 (1991), 3 April 1991, UN Doc. S/RES/687(1991), para. 16.

[91] In the *Well Blowout Control Claim*, an E1 claim, the panel recalled that 'The Security Council having determined, under Chapter VII of the Charter, that compensation in accordance with international law should be provided to foreign Governments, nationals and corporations for any direct loss, damage or injury sustained by them as a result of Iraq's unlawful invasion and occupation of Kuwait, in order to restore international peace and security, *the issue of Iraq's liability has been resolved by the Security Council and constitutes part of the law applicable before the Commission*', *Report and Recommendation made by the Panel of Commissioners Appointed to Review the Well Blowout Control Claim*, S/AC.26/1996/5/Annex, 18 December 1996, para. 68 (emphasis added).

Conversely, the second example does not concern energy, but it clarifies the applicable substantive principles. In 1999, the Democratic Republic of the Congo (DRC) brought an action before the ICJ against Uganda in connection with the latter's occupation of the DRC's North-Eastern territory and claiming inter alia that Ugandan troops and other entities collaborating with them were engaged in the looting of natural resources, including diamonds, gold and coffee. In *DRC v. Uganda*, the Court concluded that Uganda had violated its 'duty of vigilance' by failing to prevent its military forces from engaging in the 'looting, plundering and exploitation of the DRC's natural resources',[92] which were prohibited under certain rules of international humanitarian law (Article 47 of the 1907 Hague Regulations and Article 33 of the Fourth Geneva Convention, prohibiting pillage) and human rights (Article 21(2) of the African Charter, which protects against the spoliation of property).[93] In addition, as the occupying power in the Ituri district, Uganda's failure to its duty of vigilance extended also to 'all acts of looting, plundering and exploitation of natural resources in the occupied territory' (Article 43 of the 1907 Hague Regulations), including those committed by entities other than Ugandan forces.[94] Of note, the encroachment on peoples was only viewed through the prism of human rights law and the Court expressly rejected the relevance of the principle of permanent sovereignty over natural resources, implying that it was confined to the decolonisation context.[95]

The third and fourth illustrations confirm the relevance of human rights and the right to self-determination for natural resources. In the aforementioned *Ogoni*[96] and *Kichwa of Sarayaku*[97] cases, the entitlement of indigenous peoples over their natural resources were deemed to be protected by human rights (Articles 21 of the African Charter and 21 of the American Convention), and the granting by the government of energy concessions over such resources may therefore be unlawful under international law. As for the right to self-determination, the attempts since the mid 1970s by Indonesia and Australia to assert powers over the petroleum resources of East Timor were eventually defeated by the

[92] *Armed Activities on the Territory of the Congo (Democratic Republic of the Congo v. Uganda)*, Judgment, ICJ Reports 2005, p.168 [*DRC v. Uganda*], para. 246.
[93] *DRC v. Uganda*, para. 245.
[94] *DRC v. Uganda*, paras. 248–250.
[95] *DRC v. Uganda*, para. 244.
[96] See n. 34.
[97] See n. 35.

recognition, exercise and fleshing out (through a lengthy and convoluted process leading to delimitation of maritime boundaries between East Timor and Australia[98]) of the East Timorese people's right to self-determination. A key legal step in this long process was the statement by the ICJ in the 1995 *East Timor* case that the 'assertion that the right of peoples to self-determination, as it evolved from the Charter and from United Nations practice, has an *erga omnes* character, is irreproachable'.[99] In context, that meant that, although Portugal's claim in that case was inadmissible, both Australia and Indonesia were bound to respect this right despite their attempts at appropriating East Timor's oil and gas resources.

III Rules Enabling and Protecting International Energy Transactions

3.1 Analytical Distinctions

Some rules organise certain aspects (foreign investment, trade and transit) of international flows in energy (as a resource, product, technology and/or activity). These rules place certain limitations or disciplines on the 'prerogatives' enjoyed by entitlement-holders, above all States (but also organisations such as the EU[100]), over the conduct of energy transactions. But they do not confer or allocate 'entitlements' over energy.[101] As discussed in more detail next, the rules relating to foreign investment, trade and transit do not confer any entitlements over energy resources as such. They assume such entitlements and the ensuing prerogatives, and they aim to enable certain energy transactions whose regulation would

98 See n. 28.

99 *East Timor*, para. 29.

100 See e.g. *Nord Stream 2 AG v. European Union*, PCA Case No. 2020–07, Notice of Arbitration (26 September 2019), pending. In this case, Nord Stream 2 claims that, by adopting Directive (EU) 2019/692 of 17 April 2019 amending Directive 2009/73/EC concerning common rules for the internal market in natural gas, the EU has violated the non-discrimination provisions of the ECT. The Amending Directive extends the application of the Gas Directive, including its unbundling, third-party access and tariff regulation obligations, to third-country (non EU) offshore import pipelines, such as Nord Stream 2, which spans the territorial seas and exclusive economic zones of Russia, Finland, Sweden and Germany.

101 This difference is expressly recalled in Article 18(1) ECT according to which: 'The Contracting Parties recognise state sovereignty and sovereign rights over energy resources [i.e. entitlements]. They reaffirm that these must be exercised in accordance with and subject to the rules of international law [i.e. limitations on prerogatives]'.

otherwise be at the entire discretion of the State, e.g. granting market access, ensuring transit, protecting established activities.

As noted in Chapter 1, from the perspective of the distinction between transactions and externalities, these rules, together with the rules that define and allocate powers over energy, complete the organisation of international energy transactions. Their adoption was prompted by the internationalisation of energy markets,[102] i.e. the need to access energy resources located in countries which are not the main consumers of the products stemming from such resources. By way of illustration, whereas in 2018 China consumed a total of 3164 millions of tonnes of oil equivalent (Mtoe), it only produced 2534 Mtoe.[103] Similarly, whereas India consumed 929 Mtoe, it only produced 588 Mtoe. As for the United States, its production (2175 Mtoe) and consumption (2258 Mtoe) are more closely aligned, although that does not mean that domestic consumption is based on domestic production. Indeed, even if one compares production and consumption, the 'net' results will often hide a significant amount cross-border transactions. Mismatches between consumption and production have historically driven foreign investment in resource-rich countries and associated transboundary movements of technologies to conduct energy activities therein and send back their results (in the form of resources or products). Such movements rely on international law to be enabled (e.g. access and transit) and protected (e.g. treatment of activities). By contrast, other rules, which will be discussed in Chapter 3, place limitations on the organisation of energy transactions to address their negative externalities.

Although the rules enabling and protecting international energy transactions largely overlap with the fields covered by investment, trade and transit law as 'branches', assimilating the two levels would be misleading. There are rules which are normally studied under such branches and that, as noted earlier, are not intended to enable or protect international energy transactions but to preserve the State's ability to regulate for other purposes (e.g. addressing their negative externalities on humans and the environment or protecting national security). Even when the focus is only on enabling and protective rules, some key rules are derived from

[102] See I. Overland, 'Energy: The Missing Link in Globalization' (2016) 14 *Energy Research & Social Science* 122 (building a quantitative index to measure the globalisation of energy with consistent data relating to three indicators during the period 1992–2011).

[103] See Global Energy Statistical Yearbook 2019, available at: https://yearbook.enerdata.net/total-energy/world-consumption-statistics.html.

other 'branches', e.g. the rules on transit arising from the law of the sea. In order to understand the overall articulation of the rules enabling and protecting international energy transactions, it is useful to begin with the examination of a particular instrument, the ECT, which lays down a range of 'transversal' norms relating to investment, trade and transit at a multilateral (but regional) level with a specific focus on energy.

An analogous transversal configuration of rules can also be found in other regional agreements, such as the Protocol on Energy in the Southern African Development Community Region (SADC)[104] and, much more clearly, the Energy Protocol of the Economic Community of West African States (ECOWAS),[105] which was deliberately modelled on the ECT.[106] In addition, a vast network of free trade agreements (FTAs) also combine aspects of trade, investment and transit regulation at the bilateral or multilateral level, sometimes with specific provisions governing energy.[107]

My discussion in this chapter is limited to the rationale and configuration of the rules enshrined in the ECT as a fully fledged illustration of how international energy transactions are enabled and protected in international law. I then look for an analogous configuration at the global level based on the wider network of rules and instruments governing foreign investment, trade and transit.

[104] Protocol on Energy in the Southern African Development Community (SADC) Region, 24 August 1996, available at: www.sadc.int/files/3913/5292/8363/Protocol_on_Energy1996.pdf. This instrument is essentially a framework agreement setting up an institutional structure to facilitate the development of an energy market in the SADC.

[105] ECOWAS Energy Protocol A/P4/1/03, 31 January 2003, available at: http://erera.arrec.org/wp-content/uploads/2016/08/ECOWAS-Energy-Protocol.pdf. Like the ECT, this instrument contains a specific chapter devoted to commerce (chapter II), including a provision on transit (Article 7), another chapter focussing of investment protection (chapter III), a chapter on miscellaneous provisions (chapter III) asserting, inter alia, sovereignty over natural resources (Article 18) and providing for environmental protection (Article 19), and a full chapter of dispute settlement (chapter V).

[106] E. Denters, T. Gazzini, 'The Role of African Regional Organizations in the Promotion and Protection of Foreign Investment' (2017) 18 *Journal of World Investment and Trade* 449, at 461.

[107] See E. Cima, 'Promoting Renewable Energy through FTAs? The Legal Implications of a New Generation of Trade Agreements' (2018) 52 *Journal of World Trade* 663; M. W. Gehring et al., 'Climate Change and Sustainable Energy Measures in Regional Trade Agreements (RTAs). An Overview', *ICTSD Issue Paper No. 3* (August 2013); A. Marhold, *Energy in International Trade Law* (Cambridge: Cambridge University Press, 2021), pp. 141-155.

3.2 *A Partial Synthesis: The Energy Charter Treaty*

The ECT stems from a European initiative to secure its imports of energy resources, particularly oil and gas, from the former Soviet bloc. The impulsion came from the then Dutch Prime Minister, Ruud Lubbers, at the European Council held in Dublin, on 25 June 1990. Amidst growing concerns for the instability of European energy supplies generated by the events in Eastern Europe, Lubbers launched the idea of reformulating the energy relationship with the Soviet bloc to develop what he called, in a Memorandum shared with other leaders, a 'European Energy Community'.[108] Western European countries had become major importers of 'red' oil and gas, particularly in the 1970s,[109] and the political turbulence underwent by the Soviet bloc created both great uncertainty and great opportunities. The initiative was entrusted to the European Commission and it led, first, to the adoption of a non-binding instrument, the European Energy Charter, on 17 December 1991,[110] and later to the negotiation and adoption of the ECT, on 17 December 1994.

It is important to recall this context to understand the grand bargain underpinning the ECT system, which is entirely designed to tackle the aforementioned mismatch between energy consumption (in European countries) and energy resources (located in countries of the former Soviet bloc, particularly Russia, Kazakhstan and Azerbaijan). The latter needed investment to develop their resources and access to European markets ('security of demand'), whereas the former pursued 'security of supply' and investment opportunities. As one commentator has put it, the ECT can be pinned down to the formula 'access to markets for access to resources'.[111] That, in turn, required an instrument transversally organising trade, investment and transit, in addition to some other aspects.

[108] On the origins and negotiation of the European Energy Charter and the ECT see T. W. Wälde (ed.), *The Energy Charter Treaty: An East-West Gateway for Investment and Trade* (The Hague: Kluwer, 1996), particularly the foreword by Ruud Lubbers recounting the origins of the idea and chapter 5, by J. Doré, 'Negotiating the Energy Charter Treaty'. See also K. Hobér, *The Energy Charter Treaty. A Commentary* (Oxford: Oxford University Press, 2020), pp. 13–24.

[109] See J. Perović and D. Krempin, 'The Key Is in Our Hands: Soviet Energy Strategy during Détente and the Global Oil Crises of the 1970s' (2014) 39(4) *Historical Social Research* 113–144 (discussing the reasons driving the USSR increasing role in supplying energy to Europe from the 1970s).

[110] Concluding Document of the Hague Conference on the European Energy Charter, 17 December 1991.

[111] A. A. Fatouros, 'An International Legal Framework for Energy' (2007) 332 *RCADI* 355, at 412.

And because European countries were interested in extending such concessions for energy security purposes only, the ECT was designed as an energy-specific instrument, as emphasised in the Final Act of the Conference in which it was adopted.[112]

For present purposes, it is this articulation of trade, investment and transit in the ECT, as enablers of international energy transactions, which must be fleshed out.[113] Trade aspects are addressed in Parts II and VI of the ECT. In essence, Member States grant access into their markets to 'Energy Materials and Products'[114] and 'Energy-Related Equipment',[115] which, in the analytical framework provided in this study, means that former Soviet republics are able to export energy resources and products and, in turn, import energy technologies and activities (foreign investment). Two noteworthy aspects of the ECT trade rules are the extension of many GATT[116] trade disciplines 'by reference' to States which were not members of the GATT[117] and the express application of such GATT trade rules to energy materials and products and Energy-Related Equipment.[118]

The condition for satisfying energy-imports by European countries was the provision of sufficient investment, technology and credit to producer countries. Foreign investment is encouraged by Part III of the

[112] Final Act of the Conference, Understanding IV, 1 (a): 'The representatives underline that the provisions of the Treaty have been agreed upon bearing in mind the specific nature of the Treaty aiming at a legal framework to promote long-term cooperation in a particular sector and as a result cannot be construed to constitute a precedent in the context of other international negotiations'.

[113] For a detailed analysis of the ECT see R. Leal-Arcas (ed.), *Commentary to the Energy Charter Treaty* (Cheltenham: Edward Elgar, 2018); Hobér, *The Energy Charter Treaty*; Marhold, *Energy in International Trade Law*, pp. 110-141.

[114] ECT, Article 1(4) and Annexes EM I and II. The ECT also applies to 'Economic Activity in the Energy Sector' (Article 1(5), characterised by reference to 'Energy Materials and Products' but excluding some, e.g. aromatic oils, listed in Annex NI).

[115] ECT, Article 1(4bis) and Annexes EQ I and II.

[116] GATT, Annex 1A.

[117] ECT, Article 29(2). Several key States arising from the former USSR (including Russia and Kazakhstan, but not Azerbaijan or Turkmenistan) have become, in the meantime, Members of the WTO. Trade among States which are Members of the WTO (even if also ECT parties) is governed by the WTO rules (Article 29(1)–(2) ECT). The main difference is that, under the ECT system, certain WTO rules are not applicable (see ECT, Annex W).

[118] ECT, Articles 1(4) and 1(4bis) expressly refer to the Harmonized System of the Customs Cooperation Council and the Combined Nomenclature of the European Communities to characterize the categories under which different materials, products and equipment fall. This is spelt out in Annexes EM I and II and EQ I and II.

ECT, which addresses both the pre-investment (admission) and post-investment (treatment) stages, although with different levels of specificity. Negotiations on the first aspect, which has been traditionally a bastion of sovereign prerogative,[119] were a major stumbling block, particularly because Russia did not want to undertake commitments in an area where it had no settled practice or experience.[120] Eventually, at the initiative of the European Union, some soft language was negotiated for inclusion in the text, with the understanding that it would be further specified in a subsequent 'supplementary treaty',[121] which has not been adopted.[122] Article 10(2) only requires a party 'to endeavour to accord' investors of other parties non-discriminatory treatment (i.e. national treatment and MFN treatment) as regards the 'Making of Investments in its Area'.[123] This 'best efforts' obligation is circumscribed, however, in several ways, which gives it more traction than a mere exhortation.[124]

[119] One important aspect of this prerogative is reaffirmed in ECT Article 18(2): 'Without affecting the objectives of promoting access to energy resources, and exploration and development thereof on a commercial basis, the Treaty shall in no way prejudice the rules in Contracting Parties governing the system of property ownership of energy resources'.

[120] The position of Russia within the ECT is peculiar. It signed but did not ratify the treaty. However, until 18 October 2009, the ECT was provisionally applicable to it in accordance with Article 45 ECT. Russia's termination of its provisional application, in accordance with Article 45(3)(a) ECT, was prompted by a series of arbitrations arising from the take-over of Yukos. See T. Voon, A. Mitchell, 'Ending International Investment Agreements: Russia's Withdrawal from Participation in the Energy Charter Treaty' (2017) 111 *American Journal of International Law* 461.

[121] ECT, Article 10(4).

[122] Pre-investment protection is one of the issues included by the ECT Conference's list of issues to be discussed as part of the ongoing ECT modernisation process. See Decision of the Energy Charter Conference, 27 November 2018, CCDEC201821, Annex, para. 6. On 6 November 2019, a 'Modernisation Group' was established to conduct negotiations on this and other issues (CCDEC2019 10). Pre-investment was discussed during the Third Negotiation Round (3–6 November 2020), on the basis of a discussion paper and the positions expressed by certain Parties. The focus was on non-discrimination in granting access.

[123] The terms 'Making of Investments' are defined in Article 1(8) of the ECT as 'establishing new Investments, acquiring all or part of existing Investments or moving into different fields of Investment activity'.

[124] The ECT text adds three main qualifications: a best efforts obligation to limit to the minimum exceptions to non-discrimination regarding access and to progressively remove existing ones (Article 10(5)(a)–(b) ECT); requirement to notify to the Secretariat any measures restricting admission (Article 10(9)(a) ECT); and the possibility to commit firmly, by a simple declaration, not to introduce new exceptions and/or to accord non-discriminatory treatment at the admission stage (Article 10(6)(a)–(b) ECT), see Fatouros, *International Legal Framework*, at 421–422.

Regarding post-investment treatment, the ECT provides, as most bilateral investment treaties (BITs), for both absolute (e.g. fair and equitable treatment, constant protection and security, observance of commitments (Article 10(1) ECT)[125] or protection against expropriation (Article 13 ECT)) and relative (national treatment and MFN (Article 10(7), (8) and (9)(b) ECT)) standards of protection. Importantly, Part V of the ECT provides for investor-State arbitration (Article 26) as a means to enforce the obligations under Part III.

The system of market access through trade rules and capacity development through foreign investment protection is completed by a key provision on transit, Article 7 ECT.[126] Securing transit was important for two reasons. First, unlike the integrated top-down regime imposed by the USSR, the carriage of energy materials and products from distant places (e.g. Siberia) and now involving several independent countries (e.g. Azerbaijan, Kazakhstan or Turkmenistan) to Europe required strong disciplines on transit. Secondly, carriage of energy is peculiar due to the substantial amounts of investment it entails (e.g. building pipelines), which also calls for stability and predictability. In this context, Article 7 subjects 'Transit'[127] of 'Energy Materials and Products', including through fixed installations (e.g. pipelines or transmission lines[128]), to the principles of freedom of transit, non-discrimination, and facilitation.[129] Significantly, it also prohibits interruption or reduction of transit in the event of dispute.[130] Specific agreements are expressly reserved.[131] Of note, Article 7(2) reflects the fact that transit infrastructures are often in the hands of separate public or private entities, and it requires States to encourage such entities to modernise their infrastructures to facilitate

[125] Of note, the wording of Article 10(1) ECT refers to 'conditions' for foreign investors to 'make Investments'. Although the verb 'make' is not capitalized (hence, it does not seem to refer to Article 1(8) ECT), the wording is broad enough to sustain the argument that such absolute standards may apply to the pre-investment phase.

[126] See Fatouros, *International Legal Framework*, at 430–437.

[127] This term is defined in Article 7(10)(a)(i) ECT as 'the carriage through the Area of a Contracting Party, or to or from port facilities in its Area for loading or unloading, of Energy Materials and Products originating in the Area of another state and destined for the Area of a third state, so long as either the other state or the third state is a Contracting Party'. Moreover, Article 7(10)(a)(ii) contemplates an additional, rather rare, situation where the State of origin is also the State of destination.

[128] ECT, Article 7(10)(b).

[129] ECT, Article 7(1) and (3).

[130] ECT, Article 7(6).

[131] ECT, Article 7(3) and (6).

transit. Moreover, Article 7(4) strikes a balance between the need to ensure the existence of adequate transit infrastructure operating in commercial terms and sovereign prerogative. States are required not to place obstacles on the establishment of new capacity (i.e. competition), except in accordance with their laws and only to the extent that such laws are consistent with the principles of Article 7(1) (freedom of transit, non-discrimination, facilitation).

Overall, the ECT provides the most developed example of a specific transversal framework enabling and protecting international energy transactions. Whereas its scope remains regional, the ECT is open for accession by States and regional economic integration organisations which have signed the European Energy Charter or which meet certain terms approved by the Energy Charter Conference.[132] In practice, significant efforts have been made to globalise the ECT, including the adoption of a political instrument, the International Energy Charter, in 2015,[133] and outreach efforts by the Secretariat. The ECT is now binding on more than fifty countries and organisations (the EU and EURATOM) from Europe to Central Asia and, more recently, the Middle East, with the accessions of Yemen and Jordan, and soon elsewhere, with the ongoing accession processes of countries such as China, Morocco and Niger.[134] However, certain key countries, such as Russia, have expressly communicated their intention neither to ratify nor apply the ECT provisionally and others, such as the United States, have not even signed it. It is therefore important to assess whether, beyond the ECT, international law generally provides an analogous configuration of investment, trade and transit rules governing aspects of international energy transactions.

3.3 *An Inchoate Global Framework for Energy Trade, Investment and Transit*

3.3.1 Introductory Observations

Although the three aspects combined under the ECT's system are covered by a dense network of international instruments, the global framework for energy investment, trade and transit remains inchoate.

[132] ECT, Article 41.
[133] Concluding Document of the Ministerial ('The Hague II') Conference on the International Energy Charter, 21 May 2015.
[134] See International Energy Charter, Annual Report 2018, at 10–11.

This is for three main reasons. First, trade rules, although applicable to energy as a legal object, are not energy-specific. That raises questions with respect to the application of the WTO agreements to energy. Secondly, the bodies of rules governing trade and investment at the global level are disconnected: on the one hand, the global governance of trade flows relies mostly on a global system organised under the aegis of the WTO, as well as on a significant number of more specific free trade agreements (FTAs); on the other hand, the promotion and protection of foreign investment relies mostly on a bilateral model, embodied in BITs and investment chapters in FTAs. Thirdly, the parties to all these pieces of the normative mosaic are not the same, which introduces great complexity in the analysis. This is particularly clear in the area of transit rules. In the following paragraphs, trade, investment and transit are examined in turn.

3.3.2 Energy Trade under the WTO Agreements

3.3.2.1 From 'Whether' to 'How' Express references to energy are conspicuously absent from the text of WTO Agreements, as they were from the GATT.[135] For decades, trade in energy was *de facto* removed from the GATT's remit, although there were no clear legal grounds for doing so aside from the fact that some major petroleum-exporting countries (e.g. Iraq, Iran, Saudi Arabia, the USSR and Venezuela) were not parties to the GATT. Although several reasons have been given to

[135] See generally Marhold, *Energy in International Trade Law*; I. Espa, T. Cottier (eds.), *International Trade in Sustainable Electricity: Regulatory Challenges in International Economic Law* (Cambridge: Cambridge University Press, 2017); Y. Selivanova, 'The WTO Agreements and Energy', in K. Talus (ed.), *Research Handbook on International Energy Law* (Cheltenham: Edward Elgar, 2017), pp. 275–307; A. Boute, 'Energy Trade and Investment Law. International Limits to EU Energy Law and Policy', in M. M. Roggenkamp et al. (eds.), *Energy Law in Europe: National, EU and International Regulation* (Oxford: Oxford University Press, 3rd ed. 2016), pp. 137–185; A. Marhold, 'Fragmentation and the Nexus between the WTO and the ECT in Global Energy Governance: A Legal Institutional Analysis Twenty Years Later' (2015) 16 *Journal of World Investment and Trade* 389; Y. Selivanova (ed.), *Regulation of energy in International Trade Law: WTO, NAFTA and Energy Charter* (Alphen aan den Rijn: Wolters Kluwer, 2011); G. Marceau, 'The WTO in the Emerging Energy Governance Debate' (2010) 5 *Global Trade and Customs Journal* 83; H. Abdallah, 'Oil exports under GATT and the WTO' (2005) 29 *OPEC Review* 267; M. Desta, 'The Organization of Petroleum Exporting Countries, the World Trade Organization, and Regional Trade Agreements' (2003) 37 *Journal of World Trade* 523; UNCTAD, *Trade Agreements, Petroleum and Energy Policies*, UNCTAD/ITCD/TSB/9 (New York: United Nations Publications: 2000).

explain this situation, the more fundamental one is that the GATT was designed to limit the ability of States to place foreign goods at a disadvantage in domestic markets or give an advantage to domestic goods in foreign markets. Both practices had been pursued in the 1930s through increases in tariffs, discrimination and competitive devaluations, and they were widely believed to have contributed to the outbreak of hostilities. The possibility for a State to make its own goods more expensive in foreign markets, through export measures, was a marginal problem. This, together with the fact that the few petroleum producing countries which were parties to the GATT (Indonesia, Kuwait and Nigeria) had an interest in exporting their resources, made the issue of marginal concern.

After the oil embargo of 1973, the perception changed, and the issue of export restrictions was indeed raised during the Tokyo round (1973–1979) of trade negotiations, although with no concrete results.[136] During the Uruguay Round (1986–1994), energy exporting policies were discussed again. Several energy-related issues were identified as concerns, including 'dual-pricing practices and resulting subsidies', 'government ownership and management of natural resource products trade', 'natural resource development policies and practices' and 'export restrictions and export taxes'.[137] Moreover, with respect to 'product coverage', some delegations proposed the addition of a 'product group' under the Negotiating Group on Natural Resource-Based Products focussing on 'energy and energy-based products, including natural gas, petroleum, coal, uranium, petrochemicals, oil and gas processing'.[138] Yet, these and other attempts to introduce restrictions on the conduct of energy policy were resisted and eventually unsuccessful.[139] On the issue of dual pricing, i.e. the practice whereby a State sells its energy resources and products at a higher price in foreign markets than in its own domestic market, a standoff between the United States, which sought to restrict the practice in the Negotiating Groups on Natural Resource-Based Products and on Subsidies and Countervailing Duties, and Mexico, who argued for the

136 Understanding Regarding Export Restrictions and Charges, GATT Multilateral Trade Negotiations, Group 'Framework', MTN/FR/W/23.

137 See GATT, *Note by the Secretariat, Summary of Statements and Proposals Made Concerning Negotiations on Natural Resource-Based Products*, MTN.GNG/NG3/8, 13 November 1987, para. 5.

138 GATT, *Negotiations on Natural Resource-Based Products*, para. 14.

139 See UNCTAD, *Trade Agreements, Petroleum and Energy Policies*, at 15–19.

protection of the comparative advantages of resource-endowed countries, was settled in favour of the latter position.[140]

Despite some regain of interest in the context of services negotiations under the Doha Round[141] and, above all, in the negotiation of accession protocols with certain key energy exporting and transit countries,[142] the WTO is lagging far behind in this area. In a speech opening a joint ECT-WTO workshop on the role of intergovernmental agreements in energy policy, held in Geneva in April 2013, the former WTO Director-General, Pascal Lamy, noted indeed that given the importance of energy for trade and of trade for energy 'it [was] paradoxical that the multilateral trading system has not done more for energy'.[143] He then identified several types of trade-restrictive practices of particular relevance to energy, such as trade-distorting subsidies, certain practices (i.e. dual pricing) by State trading enterprises, protectionism in government procurement, transit restrictions and restrictions of energy exports, investment and services, before candidly observing that:

> WTO disciplines address many of these issues, although not always by design, and certainly not as part of an overarching approach that takes into account multilaterally agreed energy policy objectives. Thus, when thinking about how the WTO can most effectively contribute to the energy goals of the international community, the relevant question is not whether the existing WTO framework is relevant and applicable to trade in energy goods and services, for it clearly is. Instead, we need to ask ourselves how the WTO's contribution can be further improved given rapid changes in the energy policy landscape and the international community's goals regarding energy. The question is therefore one of coherence.[144]

These observations depict an accurate picture of the situation. With some specific caveats, it is unquestionable that the WTO framework, specifically its market access and non-discrimination disciplines, apply to energy

[140] UNCTAD, *Trade Agreements, Petroleum and Energy Policies*, at 18–19.

[141] See Council for Trade in Services, Special Session, Report by the Chairman to the Trade Negotiations Committee, 28 November 2005, TN/S/23, summarizing previous iterations and including a Heading 11 (Energy Services).

[142] For an analysis of energy issues in the accession protocols of six countries (Ecuador, Oman, China, Saudi Arabia, Ukraine, Russia and Kazakhstan) see A. Marhold, F. Weiss, 'Energy and Fossil Fuels as a Topic of WTO Accession Protocols' (2018) 9 *European Yearbook of International Economic Law* 61.

[143] Lamy calls for dialogue on trade and energy in the WTO, 29 April 2013 [Lamy, speech], available at: www.wto.org/english/news_e/sppl_e/sppl279_e.htm.

[144] Lamy, speech.

as a legal object, i.e. a resource, a product, a technology and an activity. A recent dispute concerning trade in gas and in gas-related services between Russia and the EU,[145] has largely settled the 'whether' question and turned it entirely into one of 'how' the WTO framework applies.

The conceptual categories certainly differ. In the trade context, the object energy must be fitted within the categories of 'goods', 'services' or 'IPRs'. To take the example of energy 'resources' and 'products', these are clearly 'goods' under the Harmonized System (HS), which is equal for all WTO Members up to the level of 'sub-headings'.[146] Indeed, the HS contains a category or 'chapter' 27 on 'Mineral fuels, mineral oils and products of their distillation; bituminous substances; mineral waxes', with headings on 'coal; briquettes, ovoids and similar solid fuels manufactured from coal' (heading 2701), 'petroleum oils and oils obtained from bituminous minerals, crude' (heading 2709), 'petroleum gases and other gaseous hydrocarbons' (heading 2711) and 'electrical energy' (heading 2716). Also, under chapter 26 on 'Ores, slagh and ash', heading 2612 covers 'uranium and thorium ores and concentrates', and under chapter 28 on 'Inorganic chemicals; organic or inorganic compounds of precious metals, of rare-earth metals, of radioactive elements or isotopes', heading 2844 covers 'radioactive chemical elements and radioactive isotopes (including the fissile or fertile chemical elements and isotopes) and their compounds; mixtures and residues containing these products'. These and other chapters, headings and sub-headings are, in fact, relied upon in Annex EM I of the ECT to define 'Energy Materials and Products'.

Unsurprisingly, major energy importers have set low tariffs on the imports of these 'goods'. For example, the 2017 tariffs set by the main energy importer, China, on coal imports (heading 2701) were on average (of its four sub-headings) 4.4 per cent ad valorem (i.e. 0.044 of the value of the good). Those on natural gas (heading 2711) were on average (of its seven sub-headings) also of 4.4 per cent ad valorem. As for oil (heading 2709) and uranium ore (heading 2612), the tariff was zero. Even when tariffs are unbound (i.e. there is no agreed maximum cap on the tariff for

[145] *European Union and Its Member States – Certain Measures Relating to the Energy Sector* (Complainant: Russia), Panel Report (10 August 2018), WT/DS476/R [*EU – Energy Package*].

[146] World Customs Organization's internationally agreed 'Harmonized System' codes (which up to six digits is equal for all members); chapter (two digits), heading (four digits), sub-heading (six digits), tariff-line (eight or more digits).

a certain heading), non-discrimination standards would continue to apply to whatever level of tariff is set by the importing country and so would the national treatment obligation to internal measures.

In *EU – Energy Package*, the supply of 'gas' was 'unquestionably' considered as involving trade in goods,[147] subject to the GATT, and certain related 'services', such as transmission of natural gas via pipeline or liquefied natural gas (LNG) services were deemed to be a matter for the GATS,[148] subject to each country's schedule of concessions.[149] Thus, as noted before, the application of the WTO framework to energy is no longer a matter of 'whether'. It is now well settled that the system does apply to energy. The mains questions concern the extent of the coverage (3.3.2.2) and the modalities of the framework's application (3.3.2.3).

3.3.2.2 Extent of the Coverage Matters relating to the extent of the coverage concern two main issues, namely the existence of *significant lacunae* in the main agreements and *membership of key countries* for energy trade. Both are related because some lacunae have been filled in the protocols of accession to the WTO of certain countries. On the issue of possible lacunae, three main examples of lacunae stand out: export measures, trade in energy services, and network-bound transit.

3.3.2.2.1 Export Measures Regarding export measures, the adoption of both restrictions and duties on exports is frequent in practice, accounting for an average of 15 per cent of all trade-restrictive measures reported between 2012 and 2018.[150] Article XI of the GATT expressly prohibits the adoption by States of 'prohibitions or restrictions [. . .] on the exportation or sale for export of any product destined for the territory of any other contracting party'. This prohibition also applies to export restrictions adopted by State trading enterprises (STEs).[151]

[147] *EU – Energy Package*, para. 7.269.

[148] GATS, Annex 1B.

[149] *EU – Energy Package*, para. 7.338.

[150] Author's calculation based on Trade Policy Review Body, Overview of developments in the international trading environment – annual report by the Director-General – Mid-October 2018 to mid-October 2019, WT/TPR/OV/22, at 30.

[151] See GATT, Art XVII(1)(a), and Ad to Articles XI, XII, XIII, XIV and XVIII: 'Throughout Articles XI, XII, XIII, XIV and XVIII, the terms 'import restrictions' or 'export restrictions' include restrictions made effective through state trading enterprises'. State trading enterprises are characterized as those 'which have been granted exclusive or special rights or privileges [. . .] in the exercise of which they influence through their purchases

However, export 'duties, taxes or other charges' are not prohibited. That allows countries not having undertaken specific commitments in this regard to apply sometimes high export duties to key energy exports. For example, Russia applies a 30 per cent duty to exports of natural gas.[152] In addition, it is unclear which enterprises qualify as STEs. One would intuitively expect Gazprom (Russia) and Saudi Aramco (Saudi Arabia) to be treated as STEs and, yet, despite assurances given during its accession process,[153] Russia has not made the requisite notification on STEs, and Saudi Arabia has notified that it does not have any such enterprises.[154]

Moreover, the system of production quotas allocated among members of the Organization of Petroleum Exporting Countries (OPEC),[155] which is the organisation's approach to reduce overall production, hence supply, and thereby increase the price of petroleum, is not as such an export restriction. It would be too much of a constraint on both energy entitlements and sovereign prerogative to consider that a State has an obligation, under the GATT, to maintain a certain level of production simply because its resources and products are demanded abroad.[156]

Furthermore, even if OPEC quotas were to be characterised as export restrictions, they may still fall under the carve-out in Article XI(2)(a) of 'restrictions temporarily applied to prevent or relieve critical shortages of [...] other products essential to the exporting contracting party' or, still, under the more tightly circumscribed exceptions of Articles XX(g) ('conservation of exhaustible natural resources')[157] or XXI(b) ('essential

or sales the level or direction of imports or Exports', Understanding on the Interpretation of Article XVII of the GATT 1994.

152 See Trade Policy Review Body, *Trade policy review – Report by the Secretariat – Russian Federation*, 6 December 2016, WT/TPR/S/345/Rev.1, at 67. Russia has undertaken in its Accession Protocol to bind and reduce the export duties applied to 703 tariff lines (at the 10 digit level).

153 Marhold/Weiss, *Energy and Fossil Fuels*, at 74.

154 Working Party on State Trading Enterprises – State trading – New and full notification pursuant to article XVII:4(a) of the GATT 1994 and para. 1 of the [...] XVII – Kingdom of Saudi Arabia, 11 April 2018, G/STR/N/16/SAU.

155 On the OPEC see Chapter 7.

156 See Selivanova, *The WTO Agreements and Energy*, at 287–288 (referring on this point to S. A. Broome, 'Conflicting Obligations for Oil Exporting Nations? Satisfying Membership Requirements of both OPEC and the WTO' (2006) 38 *George Washington International Law Review* 409. See also ECT, Article 18.

157 These exceptions have never been invoked in an OPEC-related case, as no such case has been brought before WTO dispute settlement organs. But an apposite illustration of the

security interests').[158] These exceptions are discussed in Chapter 3 of this book, as they reserve policy space for measures aimed to limit the negative externalities of trade transactions on humans and the environment.

3.3.2.2.2 Energy Services Another partial lacuna concerns the coverage of energy services,[159] which is not only dependent upon the willingness of each WTO Member to undertake specific commitments under the GATS but, more generally, it also lacks a specific energy services section in the WTO service sectoral classification list.[160] Both issues are linked because the absence of a specific classification has been used as an argument not to make concessions in this sector. The sector is very important in practice because, with the rise and consolidation of the resource sovereignty movement, international contractors, including the major international oil companies, often intervene as service providers. Moreover, some major energy exporters, such as Russia, operate through vertically integrated companies that provide both goods (the resource or product) and services (transmission through pipelines). Services are also a key area for renewable energies, which are labour and services-intensive.[161]

In the context of the Doha Round, attempts to specify the classification were steered by an informal group of 'Friends of Energy Services' but with no concrete results. There are, however, some sub-sectors in the classification list that touch directly upon energy, such as 'services incidental to mining' (1.F.h/CPC 883, 5115), 'services incidental to energy distribution' (1.F.j/CPC 887) and 'pipeline transport' (11.G/CPC 713), or on general services sectors, such as transport (11), distribution (4), construction and related engineering services (3) or rental (1.E). Yet, commitments undertaken in the area of energy services are limited and

operation of Articles XI(2)(a) and XX, letters (b) and (g) is provided by *China – Raw Materials – Panel Report*, paras. 7.238–7.617.

[158] The only application of this provision so far was in *Russia – Measures concerning Traffic in Transit* (Complainant: Ukraine), Panel Report (5 April 2019), WT/DS512/R [*Russia – Traffic in Transit*], paras. 7.59–7.149.

[159] For an overview of the issues see WTO Secretariat, *Energy Services, Background Note by the Secretariat*, 9 September 1998, S/C/W/52.

[160] Services Sectoral Classification List, Note by the Secretariat, 10 July 1991, MTN.GNS/W/120.

[161] See IRENA, *Renewable Energy and Jobs. Annual Review 2019* (IRENA 2019) (showing a steady increase in employment in renewable energy sectors, particularly photovoltaic and bioenergy, between 2012 and 2018).

sparse. In resource-rich countries, commitments are confined essentially to sub-sectors 1.F.h, 1.F.j and, to a lesser extent, 11.G.a. Sparse coverage makes the specific classification of the service a very important issue.

In *EU – Energy Package*, Russia argued for an integrated consideration of gas supply, LNG services and pipeline transmission as one category of services. The Panel rejected the argument and observed that gas supply amounted to trade in goods, hence not subject to the GATS, and that LNG services (e.g. the liquefaction of natural gas for its transportation or its regasification) was distinct from transmission of natural gas via pipeline.[162]

3.3.2.2.3 Network-Bound Transit Another partial lacuna that has attracted significant attention concerns the scope of Article V of the GATT on transit. Article V(1) of the GATT provides that 'goods [. . .] and also vessels and other means of transport, shall be deemed to be in transit [. . .]'. This definition thus applies both to goods (but not to services)[163] and to means of transport that are mobile, but not to fixed transport infrastructure such as pipelines or transmission lines. As noted earlier, the ambiguity in the application to fixed infrastructures was expressly addressed in the context of Article 7(10)(b) of the ECT, but not in the context of Article V(1) of the GATT.

Of the two disputes over the application of Article V of the GATT decided so far,[164] none has addressed specifically transit through fixed infrastructures. The reasoning of the panel in *EU – Energy Package* did not address Article V. Yet, it clarified that other provisions, such as Articles I, III and XI apply to aspects of trade in goods (natural gas) through pipelines.[165] It may be possible to rely on this reasoning to argue that Article V also applies to fixed infrastructures, particularly in the light of the panel's recognition of 'the fixed nature of pipeline infrastructure and the necessity for natural gas transported by pipeline to flow along predetermined paths and to be imported through a limited number of fixed entry points'.[166] The complexities raised by transit regulation are discussed in Section 3.3.4.

162 *EU – Energy Package*, para. 7.338.

163 On whether electricity is a good or a service, see the discussion in Section 3.3.2.3.1.

164 *Colombia – Indicative Prices and Restrictions on Ports of Entry*, Panel Report, 27 April 2009, WT/DS366/R; *Russia – Measures Concerning Traffic in Transit*, Panel Report, 5 April 2019, WT/DS512/R.

165 *EU – Energy Package*, paras. 7.827, 7.994–7.996, 7.1300–7.1301, 7.1312–7.1313.

166 *EU – Energy Package*, paras. 7.994–7.996.

3.3.2.2.4 Membership and Commitments of Key Countries Aside from these lacunae in the subject-matter coverage of the agreements, there are also lacunae concerning the membership of key countries.

Since the establishment of the WTO in 1994, a number of energy-relevant countries have joined as Members. These include Ecuador (1996), Oman (2000), Georgia (2000, important for transit of Caspian fossil fuels), China (2001, which is major importer of fossil and nuclear resources and products, and a major exporters of renewable energy equipment), Saudi Arabia (2005), Ukraine (2008, a key transit country for exports of Russian gas to the EU), Russia (2012), Tajikistan (2013) and Kazakhstan (2015). Although some important countries, such as Algeria, Azerbaijan, Iran, Iraq and Turkmenistan, remain for now outside, the country coverage has changed dramatically as compared to the pre-WTO situation. As noted earlier in this chapter, negotiation of WTO accession offers a platform to add or clarify commitments in areas (e.g. export duties, energy services, transit through fixed infrastructures) which are not (or not clearly) covered by the WTO Agreements.

A study of the energy-related commitments in the accession protocols of seven key countries shows that, over time, energy matters have featured much more prominently in such protocols.[167] Another study identifies five key energy-related areas addressed in these instruments, namely freedom of transit (e.g. Ukraine, Russia, Tajikistan), export duties (China), STE (most countries, although with varying degrees of specificity), energy pricing policies (e.g. Russia, Saudi Arabia, Tajikistan) and energy services (commitments under the GATS are more frequent in acceding members than in original members).[168] Of note, such commitments overwhelmingly concern fossil fuels, likely as a result of their less clear coverage under the WTO Agreements than the goods (certain resources and technologies) on which renewable energies and efficiency measures rely, and the historical and strategic reluctance to subject energy to trade disciplines.

The potentially far-reaching implications of such commitments were uncovered in a much-debated case against China's export measures:

[167] Marhold/Weiss, *Energy and Fossil Fuels.*

[168] See J. Lee, A. Okenwa, G. Tebagana, P. Baral, 'Energy-Related Rules in Accession Protocols: Where Are They?', in C. Osakwe and U. Dadush (eds), *WTO Accessions and Trade Multilateralism: Case Studies and Lessons from the WTO at 20* (Cambridge: Cambridge University Press, 2015), pp. 701–728.

China – Raw Materials[169] where Article 11.3 of China's Protocol of Accession was interpreted to bar 'export duties' on mineral resources and, more controversially, to exclude reliance on the general exceptions contemplated in Article XX of the GATT.[170]

3.3.2.3 Modalities of Application The latter controversy provides a fitting transition to the other main challenge posed by energy to the WTO Agreements, which concerns not the extent of their coverage but the modalities of their application. Difficulties have emerged on several issues, among which the following stand out: the treatment of certain energy resources and products (e.g. electricity, natural gas and LNG), the business practices of STEs, the peculiarities of energy transportation in the context of certain GATT disciplines, and a range of questions concerning differentiation of products on the basis of their environmental footprints.

3.3.2.3.1 Characterisation of Electricity With respect to matters of characterisation, one illustration concerns the characterisation of electricity as a good or a service. This characterisation has profound regulatory implications because goods are more comprehensively regulated under the GATT (including for Article V on transit, which applies to 'goods') than services under the GATS. In practice, electricity is treated as a good, whereas transmission and distribution are treated as services.

There are several grounds for this solution. The HS contains an express, albeit optional, heading for electricity as a good (heading 2716 on 'electrical energy') and it is widely used in the cross-border trade of electricity.[171] Moreover, the treatment of electricity as a 'good' has been confirmed by the case law.[172] A similar issue arose in *EU – Energy*

[169] *China – Raw Materials – Panel Report*, paras. 7.52–7.160; *China – Raw Materials*, AB Report (30 January 2012), WT/DS394/AB/R, WT/DS395/AB/R, WT/DS398/AB/R, paras. 278–307.

[170] For a discussion of the reasons underpinning these challenges see I. Espa, 'Chinese Natural Resources Disputes: A Never-Ending Story ?' (2018) 9 *European Yearbook of International Economic Law* 39.

[171] M. Sanchez Miranda, 'Liberalization at the Speed of Light: International Trade in Electricity and Interconnected Networks' (2018) 21 *Journal of International Economic Law* 67, at 94.

[172] See *Municipality of Almelo v. NV Energiebedrijf Ijsselmij*, ECJ Case C-393/92, Judgment of 27 April 1994, para. 28 (referring further to *Costa v. ENEL*) and *Commission v. Italy*, Case C-158/94, Judgment of 23 October 1998, para. 17 (confirming Almelo). See generally P. Pierros, 'Exploring Certain Trade Related Aspects of Energy under

Package regarding the characterisation of gas supply, which Russia sought to integrate with LNG services and pipeline transportation of natural gas. However, the panel clearly distinguished the supply of gas, which it characterised as trade in goods, from the other two services.[173]

3.3.2.3.2 Business Practices of State Trading Enterprises With respect to the business practices of STEs, as noted earlier, Article XVII(1)(a) of the GATT and the Ad to Articles XI, XII, XIII, XIV and XVIII extend the application of a number of trade disciplines, including non-discrimination and the prohibition of quantitative restrictions, to measures adopted by STEs.

The identification and formal notification of State instrumentalities as STEs has been a key area in the WTO accession negotiations of a number of petroleum-exporting countries. Even when Article XVII(1) is formally applicable, the requirements on STEs involved in energy trading are to make 'purchases or sales solely in accordance with commercial considerations' (XVII(1)(b) of the GATT).[174] The issue received significant attention during the negotiations concerning the accession of Russia. The EU and the United States sought confirmation that Gazprom, 51 per cent of the shares of which are owned by Russia, 'would act on the basis of commercial considerations' in setting gas prices in foreign markets.[175] Russia resisted the imposition of tight commitments as contrary to its sovereignty over natural resources and merely agreed that prices charged to industrial users would be set on a commercial basis.[176] Yet, Gazprom's business practices (e.g. export ban clauses, destination clauses and restrictions on re-exports) in some Central and Eastern European countries (Bulgaria, the Czech Republic, Estonia, Hungary, Latvia, Lithuania, Poland and Slovakia) have led the European Commission to open an anti-trust inquiry for abuse of dominant position.[177] The influence of Gazprom has also been addressed in the Third EU Energy Package

GATT/WTO: Demarcation Questions regarding Electricity' (1999) 5 *International Trade Law & Regulation* 26.

173 *EU – Energy Package*, para. 7.338.

174 On the general understanding of 'commercial considerations' see *Canada – Wheat Exports and Grain Imports*, AB Report (30 August 2004), WT/DS276/AB/R, paras. 144–145, 149.

175 Report of the Working Party on the Accession of the Russian Federation, 17 November 2011, WT/ACC/RUS/70, WT/MIN(11)/2 [*Report Working Party – Russia*], para. 122.

176 *Report Working Party – Russia*, para. 132.

177 See Marhold/Weiss, *Energy and Fossil Fuels*, at 75–76. See further European Commission, *Factsheet, Antitrust: Commission send Statement of Objections to Gazprom*, Brussels, MEMO/15/4829, 22 April 2015.

through a range of measures requiring unbundling (of production and transmission), capacity limits (in the use of a key pipeline), and diversification (from Russian gas). It is also an aspect of the claim brought by Nord Stream 2 against the EU in relation with the extension of the Gas Directive to third-country offshore import pipelines.[178]

Shortly after its accession to the WTO, Russia brought a claim against the EU in connection with these measures. In *EU – Energy Package*, the panel rejected most but not all the contentions. In particular, the panel sided with Russia in connection with the discriminatory nature of certain requirements imposed on the operator of the OPAL pipeline as a condition to benefit from an infrastructure exemption (which effectively limited Gazprom's ability to use the pipeline to sell its gas to 50 per cent of the pipeline's capacity)[179] and of the criteria to benefit from the 'project of common interest' (PCI) status (which effectively conditioned the granting of such advantageous status on the need to move away from Russian gas).[180] As some observers have noted, this could potentially amount to using WTO law to protect Gazprom's dominant position from measures designed to steer competition.[181]

3.3.2.3.3. Operation of Substantive Standards A third issue where the operation of the WTO framework is in need of clarification concerns the application of some key substantive standards. Two examples drawn from *EU – Energy Package* are noteworthy.

The first relates to the operation of the prohibition of quantitative restrictions in Article XI of the GATT. The GATT introduces a dividing line between quantitative restrictions, which must be applied at the border to be covered by Article XI(1), and internal measures, which are governed by Article III(4) (national treatment). The reason for this dividing line is that many internal measures may operate as quantitative restrictions and subjecting them to Article XI would go too far in limiting the ability of States to regulate.[182] In the context of the dispute, the

[178] See n. 100.

[179] *EU – Energy Package*, paras. 7.994–7.997.

[180] *EU – Energy Package*, paras. 7.1300–7.1301, 7.1312–7.1313, 7.1348–7.1350.

[181] See V. Pogoretskyy, K. Talus, 'The WTO Panel Report in EU–Energy Package and Its Implications for the EU's Gas Market and Energy Security' (2020) 19 *World Trade Review* 531.

[182] *Canada – Administration of the Foreign Investment Review Act*, Panel Report, L/5504 (7 February 1984), BISD 30S/140, par. 5.14, referred to in Pogoretskyy/Talus, *The WTO Panel Report in EU-Energy Package*, at 543.

question was whether a measure restricting the supply of a good through a given path, i.e. the pipeline at stake, can constitute a quantitative restriction to the import of that good. The specificities of the transportation of gas, which *in casu* was bound by the need for pipeline capacity, led the panel to conclude that the measure, a cap of 50 per cent on how much gas from a dominant company (i.e. Gazprom) could exit the pipeline in the Czech market, was a quantitative restriction in breach of Article XI(1) of the GATT. The key reasons given by the panel were the fixed nature of pipelines and the need for natural gas to be transported through them and therefore to follow a specific route.[183] This finding raises the broader question of how to set the dividing line between the scopes of application, respectively, of Articles III(4) and XI(1), in case of network-bound imports of gas or electricity.[184]

The second illustration concerns the interpretation of 'like products' in the context of Article I(1) of the GATT (MFN). In *EU – Energy Package*, Russia argued that the unbundling measure imposed on operators of natural gas transmission pipelines – but not on liquefied natural gas (LNG) operators – by the Third EU Energy Package was in breach of Article I(1) of the GATT (MFN) because it treated natural gas less favourably than LNG. The panel applied the standard test of likeness, derived from *EC – Asbestos*,[185] to compare natural gas and LNG, and it observed that three out of the four prongs of this test led to the conclusion that natural gas and LNG were not 'like products'. On this basis, it rejected the claim.[186] The analysis of the panel on this issue is debatable because, as noted in the literature, it neglects that both products have the same chemical structure and that the end-use of LNG as vessel fuel – which the panel saw as evidence of different end uses – remains niche.[187] This debate notwithstanding, the case illustrates the complexities presented by energy as an object for the operation of core trade standards.

3.3.2.3.4 Differentiation The fourth and, possibly, most representative issue concerns the limited scope for differentiation under WTO disciplines between goods with a different environmental and/or social

[183] *EU – Energy Package*, paras. 7.994–7.997.

[184] Pogoretskyy/Talus, *The WTO Panel Report in EU-Energy Package*, at 544.

[185] *European Communities – Measures Affecting Asbestos and Products Containing Asbestos*, AB Report (12 March 2001), WT/DS135/AB/R, para. 101.

[186] *EU – Energy Package*, para. 7.855.

[187] Pogoretskyy/Talus, *The WTO Panel Report in EU-Energy Package*, at 542.

footprint. This issue opens a range of sub-questions which have received substantial attention in practitioner and academic circles, such as the definition of likeness under Articles I and III, particularly to treat differently goods on the basis of their processes and production methods (PPMs),[188] or the operation in these and other cases (e.g. trade-related measures imposed or induced by a multilateral environmental agreement[189]) of the general exceptions clause (Article XX of the GATT),[190] or the possibility to ingrain differentiation in schedules of tariff concessions by setting low bounds for 'environmental goods'[191] or the possibility to set sustainability criteria in government procurement[192] or, still, the possibility to subsidise electricity generation from renewable energy facilities.[193]

The debate on each of these sub-questions has a dual nature: it concerns both the enabling and protection of energy transactions and the limitation of their negative externalities on humans, the environment and other values, such as national security. In all cases, the main problem is determining whether the application of the relevant trade disciplines should be bent to favour products and industries with lower environmentally and/or socially negative externalities. In some cases, e.g. negotiated reductions on tariffs imposed on certain goods or sustainability criteria in government procurement, such differentiation presents no inconsistency with trade disciplines. In other cases, however, the relevant

188 See D. Sifonios, *Environmental Processes and Production Methods (PPMs) in WTO Law* (Berlin: Springer, 2018).

189 See WTO, *Matrix on trade-related measures pursuant to selected multilateral environmental agreements*. Note by the Secretariat (19 March 2021) WT/CTE/W/160/Rev.9, TN/TE/S/5/Rev.7.

190 See S. Zleptnig, *Non-Economic Objectives in WTO Law* (The Hague: Brill, 2009); T. Cottier, 'Renewable energy and WTO law: more policy space or enhanced disciplines?' (2014) 1 *Renewable Energy Law and Policy Review* 40; A. Rutherford, *Energy Security and Green Energy* (Cham: Springer, 2020) pp. 103–139.

191 See P. C. Mavroidis, D. J. Neven, 'Greening the WTO Environmental Goods Agreement, Tariff Concessions, and Policy Likeness' (2019) 22 *Journal of International Economic Law* 373.

192 See L. Tosoni, 'The Impact of the Revised WTO Government Procurement Agreement on the EU Procurement Rules from a Sustainability Perspective' (2013) 8 *European Procurement & Public Private Partnership Law Review* 41.

193 See, among many other contributions on this topic, I. Espa, G. Marin Duran, 'Renewable Energy Subsidies and WTO Law: Time to Rethink the Case for Reform Beyond Canada – Renewable Energy/Fit Program' (2018) 21 *Journal of International Economic Law* 621; H. B. Asmelash, 'Energy Subsidies and WTO Dispute Settlement: Why Only Renewable Energy Subsidies Are Challenged' (2015) 18 *Journal of International Economic Law* 261.

measures have been considered inconsistent with non-discrimination standards.[194] But given that such measures, even when they pursue protectionist and trade-restrictive purposes, place limitations on the negative externalities of energy transactions, rather than enabling or protecting them, they will be analysed in Chapter 3. Subsidies to renewable energy are also analysed in Chapter 8, in the specific context of the energy transition.

3.3.3 Investment Protection, Bilateralism and Misalignment

3.3.3.1 Foreign Investment and Trade Disciplines Unlike the ECT, the WTO Agreements do not govern foreign direct investment directly. They do so indirectly and only to a limited extent through four main channels.

The first and most basic channel concerns investment operations whose business model relies on trade, either because they export their products or because they rely heavily on imported inputs. In this case, basic trade disciplines, such as market access commitments and non-discrimination standards, provide some measure of protection of their business model. In a global trade system characterised by global supply chains,[195] trade regulation remains an essential component of investment regulation.

The second channel concerns trade-related investment measures or TRIMs. The TRIMs Agreement,[196] which is part of the WTO multilateral agreements, introduces some specifications regarding the interpretation of two standards of the GATT, national treatment (Article III) and the prohibition of quantitative restrictions (Article XI), with the aim to exclude certain trade-distortive practices such as local content requirements. It is, in earnest, a modulation of the first channel, as it does not introduce new disciplines and, in addition, it only applies in the context of the GATT (hence to trade in goods, not in services).

194 See e.g. *Canada – Certain Measures Affecting the Renewable Energy Generation Sector* (Complainant – Japan), AB Report (6 May 2013), WT/DS412/AB/R, WT/DS426/AB/R; *India – Certain Measures Relating to Solar Cells and Solar Modules* (Complainant: United States), AB Report (16 September 2016), WT/DS456/AB/R, WT/DS456/AB/R/Add.1.

195 See R. Baldwin, 'Global Supply Chains: Why They Emerged, Why They Matter, and Where They Are Going?' (2012) *Centre for European Policy Research (CERP) Discussion Paper 9103*.

196 Agreement on Trade-Related Investment Measures, 15 April 1994, Marrakesh Agreement Establishing the World Trade Organization, Annex 1A, 1868 UNTS 186.

The third channel is provided by the commitments entered into by certain members under the GATS. Certain energy activities conducted by foreign investors (e.g. exploration, storing, liquefaction and/or gasification, transportation, processing, consulting) may take the form, legally, of a service and, in such case, their regulation may fall under the sector or sub-sector commitments, if any, made by the relevant State. Even considering these three vectors together, the protection offered to foreign investment under the multilateral trading system is far less extensive than under the ECT.

It is only when the fourth channel is taken into account, namely FTAs, that a comprehensive regulation of foreign investment is brought together with trade rules. Investment chapters in FTAs are, together with bilateral investment treaties (BITs), the main pillars of foreign investment enabling and protection at the international level. They are, however, bilateral or narrowly multilateral in their application and, as a result, they do not compensate for the inchoate nature of the global trade, investment and transit regime.

3.3.3.2 Foreign Investment and Investment Disciplines As noted in the previous section, the function performed by the ECT's rules on investment promotion and protection is performed at the global level by a dense network of BITs and investment chapters in bilateral or narrowly multilateral FTAs. This is very important given the capital-intensive nature of the investments required in the energy sector, which call for a significant degree of stability and predictability, as well as by the need to make such investments where the relevant resources are found, even under volatile political and legal conditions.[197]

The development of the international law of foreign investment was closely connected to the needs of the energy industry, first through the development of specific contractual forms (the so-called State contracts[198]) and later in BITs and FTAs. There is a significant body of literature on the early petroleum arbitrations arising from nationalisation

[197] See generally P. D. Cameron, *International Energy Investment Law: The Pursuit of Stability* (Oxford: Oxford University Press, 2nd ed. 2018); M. Scherer, C. Amirfar (eds.), *International Arbitration in the Energy Sector* (Oxford: Oxford University Press, 2018); H. G. Burnett, L.-A. Brett, *Arbitration of International Mining Disputes* (Oxford: Oxford University Press, 2017).

[198] See M. Erkan, *International Energy Investment Law: Stability through Contractual Clauses* (Alphen aan den Rijn: Wolters Kluwer, 2011); Ch. Leben, 'La théorie du contrat d'Etat et l'évolution du droit international des investissements' (2004) 302 *RCADI* 197;

processes in the Middle East and North Africa.[199] More recently, the literature has focussed on the degree of stability and predictability provided by BITs and investment chapters in FTAs to energy activities through an internationalised system of investment protection.[200]

This system is typically sector-neutral and, hence, not specifically tailored to the needs of the energy industry. It is based on three main components:[201] (1) a definitional component circumscribing the scope of application of the treaty, notably through the definition of the term 'investment' and of the requisite holder, a 'foreign' investor; (2) certain standards of protection of an absolute (fair and equitable treatment, full protection and security, protection against unlawful expropriation etc.) and relative (MFN and national treatment) nature; (3) a dispute settlement component typically allowing investors to directly bring a claim against a host State before an international arbitration tribunal. These components are broadly similar across treaties, including the ECT, although there are certainly differences of wording at the level of specific clauses.

Some commentators have argued that convergence in the content of BITs and investment chapters of FTAs, together with the operation of certain connecting clauses (MFN) and a substantial body of case law interpreting these treaties turns this network of bilateral instruments into a multilateral investment governance framework.[202] There is some evidence for this view, even if deep cleavages persist in the case law

P. Weil, 'Problèmes relatifs aux contrats passés entre un Etat et un particulier' (1969) 128 *RCADI* 94.

199 For an overview of the main cases see Leben, *La théorie du contrat d'Etat*, at 215–234. See also C. Greenwood, 'State Contracts in International Law – The Libyan Oil Arbitrations' (1983) 53 *British Yearbook of International Law* 27.

200 See n. 197.

201 See J. E. Viñuales, 'Foreign Direct Investment: International Investment Law and Natural Resource Governance', in E. Morgera and K. Kulovesi (eds.), *Research Handbook on International Law and Natural Resources* (Cheltenham: Edward Elgar, 2016), pp. 26–45. On investment law in general see C. McLachlan, L. Shore, M. Weiniger, *International Investment Arbitration: Substantive Principles* (Oxford: Oxford University Press, 2nd ed. 2017); Z. Douglas, J. Pauwelyn, J. E. Viñuales (eds.), *Foundations of International Investment Law* (Oxford: Oxford University Press, 2014); R. Dolzer, C. Schreuer, *Principles of International Investment Law* (Oxford: Oxford University Press, 2nd ed. 2012). On the process see Z. Douglas, *The International Law of Investment Claims* (Cambridge: Cambridge University Press, 2009).

202 See S. Schill, *The Multilateralization of International Investment Law* (Cambridge: Cambridge University Press, 2009); J. W. Salacuse. 'The Treatification of International Investment Law' (2007) 13 *Law and Business Review of the Americas* 155.

regarding basic tenets of the system, such as the definition of investment[203] and even the very interpretation given to the multilateralising device, MFN clauses.[204] For present purposes, however, the most important features to be noted are that, although this body of treaties does perform the function of providing stability and predictability, it is separate, in its parties, procedures, operation and overall dynamics, from the multilateral trade system. Thus, unlike the rules on the promotion and protection of foreign investment in the ECT, the international law of foreign investment is not part of a broader synthesis of trade, investment and transit rules providing clear foundations for the organisation of energy transactions. This is a significant challenge, because it introduces mismatches or misalignments between trade and investment regulation, including in the understanding of the very idea of non-discrimination.[205]

3.3.3.3 Misalignments A relevant illustration of misalignments between trade and investment regulation in the specific area of energy is provided by the feed-in-tariff scheme (FIT) introduced by the province of Ontario, for which Canada came under cross-fire from both WTO trading partners[206] and foreign investors.[207]

In *Canada – Renewables*, the WTO Appellate Body held that by attaching local content requirements regarding domestic equipment to the FIT, Canada had breached the national treatment standard (Article

[203] See M. Waibel, 'Subject Matter Jurisdiction: The Notion of Investment', in J. E. Viñuales, M. Waibel (eds.), *ICSID Reports: The Meaning of Investment*, vol. 19 (Cambridge: Cambridge University Press, 2021), pp. 25-82.

[204] See McLachlan/Shore/Weiniger, *International Investment Arbitration*, paras. 7.298–7.317. The contrasting positions are illustrated, on the one hand, by *RosInvest Co UK Ltd v. Russian Federation*, SCC Case No. V079/2005, Award on Jurisdiction (5 October 2007), paras. 73–75, 124–139 (where the scope of an arbitration clause is extended by means of the MFN clause) and, on the other hand, *Austrian Airlines v. Slovakia*, UNCITRAL, Award (9 October 2009), paras. 117–141 (concluding that the MFN clause cannot be used to import an arbitration clause from another treaty).

[205] See N. DiMascio, J. Pauwelyn, 'Nondiscrimination in Trade and Investment Treaties: Worlds Apart of Two Sides of the Same Coin?' (2008) 102 *American Journal of International Law* 48.

[206] See *Canada – Certain Measures Affecting the Renewable Energy Generation Sector* (Complainant – Japan), Request for consultation (Japan), 13 September 2010, AB Report, 6 May 2013, WT/DS412/AB/R, WT/DS426/AB/R [*Canada – Renewables – AB*] (proceedings also addressed a separate complaint from the EU filed 2011).

[207] See *Mesa Power Group, LLC v. Government of Canada*, UNCITRAL, PCA Case No. 2012–17, Award (24 March 2016) [*Mesa v. Canada*]; *Windstream Energy LLC v. Government of Canada*, PCA Case No. 2013–22, Award (27 September 2016) [*Windstream v. Canada*].

III(4)) of the GATT and Article 2(1) of the TRIMs Agreement. Of note, the Appellate Body reversed the panel's finding on the application of the public procurement carve-out (Article III(8)(a) of the GATT) concluding that the local content requirements on equipment were not 'laws, regulations or requirements governing the procurement by governmental agencies' of electricity within the meaning of the carve-out.[208]

In *Mesa v. Canada*, a similar question was put to an arbitral tribunal constituted under chapter 11 of the NAFTA[209] to hear a dispute arising from the Ontario FIT. The investor claimed that the FIT had been unfairly designed and implemented as a result of which it had not been awarded a contract to sell electricity to Ontario. Canada invoked the public procurement carve-out of Article 1108(7)(a) of the NAFTA. The wording of this provision is broadly similar to that of Article III(8)(a) of the GATT but with some significant differences. WTO law and jurisprudence, as well as the provisions of the trade, procurement and competition chapters of the NAFTA featured prominently in the arguments of the parties.[210] The tribunal did consider the conclusions of the panel and the Appellate Body in *Canada – Renewables*, mainly to confirm that the term procurement had to be interpreted broadly.[211] Yet, it observed that the term had a specific meaning under chapter 11 of the NAFTA, different from the meaning given elsewhere in trade law and in the trade, procurement, and competition chapters of the NAFTA, particularly Article 1001(5) (chapter 10 on 'Government Procurement'). According to the tribunal, 'the term [procurement] must be interpreted differently depending on the chapter and the specific context in which it is used'.[212] It then carefully distinguished what it saw as a qualified definition of procurement in Article III(8)(a) of the GATT, Article 1(2) of the WTO Government Procurement Agreement (GPA) and Canada's notes annexed to the latter (i.e. requiring the purchase to be for governmental use) from the unqualified terms used in Article 1108(7)(a) (no requirement of governmental use, hence not excluding procurement for commercial resale).[213] Moreover, it noted that, unlike Article III(8)(a) of the GATT, Article 1108(7)(a) applied to both 'goods' and 'services'.[214]

[208] *Canada – Renewables – AB*, para. 5.79.
[209] North American Free Trade Agreement, 17 December 1992, 32 ILM 289 and 605 (1993).
[210] See *Mesa v. Canada*, paras. 378–391.
[211] *Mesa v. Canada*, paras. 412–414.
[212] *Mesa v. Canada*, para. 417.
[213] *Mesa v. Canada*, para. 431–439.
[214] *Mesa v. Canada*, para. 455.

Furthermore, the tribunal dismissed the relevance, in the investment context, of an aspect which had been decisive in *Canada – Renewables*, namely the lack of a nexus between the goods procured (electricity) and the measures challenged (local content requirements regarding equipment). It is true that the formulation of the investment claim was not limited to the local content requirements, but the conclusion of the tribunal is nevertheless noteworthy:

> because Article 1108(7)(a) of the NAFTA is broader than Article III:8(a) of the GATT. Once it is established that there has been 'procurement' by a Party or state enterprise, Article 1108(7)(a) excludes all claims of NT, MFN and domestic content in connection with such procurement.[215]

The tribunal eventually concluded that the public procurement carve-out of Article 1108(7)(a) was available and rejected the investor's claim.[216]

Irrespective of whether one agrees or not with what is an overall well-reasoned award, the main conclusion to be drawn from this illustration is the existence of some degree of misalignment, on several points, between trade law (including not only the GATT and the GPA but also the trade disciplines in the NAFTA) and investment law. Such misalignment stems from the different terms and design of the relevant treaties and also, possibly, from the existence of two different dispute settlement approaches leading to a divergent jurisprudence. It is this misalignment, and its roots in the separate laws and processes of trade and investment law, that explains the lack of continuity between the global regulation of trade and investment. These barriers may be undergoing a process of erosion as a result of the economic forces driving the liberalisation of trade and investment.[217] In this process, the energy sector is likely to be a driving force. Yet, at the global level, the process has yet to reach the level of consolidation displayed by the ECT.

3.3.4 The Transit Mosaic

3.3.4.1 Overarching Principles The regulation of transit provides a clear illustration of the complexity of legal arrangements existing at the global level to govern an issue which is fundamental to energy. As discussed in Chapter 1, the geographical mismatch between resource

215 *Mesa v. Canada*, para. 459.
216 *Mesa v. Canada*, para. 465.
217 See J. Kurtz, *The WTO and International Investment Law. Converging Systems* (Cambridge: Cambridge University Press, 2016).

extraction/production and consumption is the foundation of the internationalisation of energy markets, with the associated need for foreign direct investment (to develop the resources where they are located) and trade (to enable the necessary exports/imports). Transit sits at the heart of this system due to the specificities of energy, which generally requires specific forms of carriage, e.g. through long-distance (sometimes offshore) pipelines for oil and gas, special tankers and terminals (e.g. for LNG), or transmission networks for electricity. In addition, transit introduces three additional problems: the need for special infrastructure in transit countries; the structure of ownership/control of such infrastructure (often deemed a 'natural monopoly' and regulated as such); and the possible hurdles that transit countries may introduce between transactions organised by exporting and importing countries.

Overall, the rules on transit, like those on trade and investment, have to balance the sovereign prerogative of transit States with the needs of international energy transactions (i.e. the interests of exporting and importing countries and the relevant companies). The system that has been developed to address transit issues is relatively simple at a conceptual level but highly scattered and ad hoc, hence complex, at a legal and practical level. The global level is discussed here, whereas the regimes applicable to specific pipeline projects are discussed in Chapter 5. Conceptually, the general system rests on one main principle, (1) the freedom of transit, and a handful of supporting principles: (2) non-discrimination on the basis of origin, ownership or destination of the goods in transit, (3) prohibition of imposing customs duties on the goods in transit, (4) reasonableness and proportionality of transit charges, (5) due diligence in avoiding delays and other obstacles to transit and (6) cooperation in developing adequate infrastructures for transit and/or granting access to them.[218]

Legally, these principles are applied, with some variations, at the multilateral, regional and bilateral levels, and they are largely organised depending on their relevance to specific forms of carriage: road, railways, maritime and air transport.[219] Some of these methods remain important for the transportation of energy resources (e.g. coal transported by trucks,

[218] See V. Pogoretskyy, *Freedom of Transit and Access to Gas Pipeline Networks under WTO* (Cambridge: Cambridge University Press, 2017), at 79.

[219] For a concise overview of the main instruments see E. M. Giemulla, 'Traffic and Transport, International Regulation', in *Max Planck Encyclopedia of Public International Law* (April 2013).

railway and cargoes), products (fuels transported through these means) and technologies (e.g. equipment transported through these means). In addition, energy transportation presents the special issue of fixed infrastructures, such as pipelines and transmission networks, with their own regulatory specificities. To illustrate this complexity, it is useful to make an inroad into the transit 'mosaic' moving from the multilateral (UNCLOS and the GATT) to the regional (the ECT) and then the bilateral level (pipeline agreements), with a focus on fixed infrastructures or 'network-bound' energy transit.

3.3.4.2 Global Level At the global level, several instruments are relevant for network-bound energy transit. The conceptual approach described in the previous paragraph operates as a constraint on transit States' prerogatives arising from both sovereignty and 'sovereign rights'. The latter are more limited than sovereignty and a 'right of immersion' is expressly contemplated in the UNCLOS (see Section 2.1.2 of this chapter). Some of the instruments that place constraints on these entitlements are unspecific to energy and therefore present additional complexities. The three main unspecific instruments are the 1921 Barcelona Convention on Freedom of Transit,[220] the GATT and the UNCLOS, the latter as regards the rights of land-locked States, which place constraints on the entitlements of transit States.[221]

The Barcelona Convention resulted from the codification efforts of the League of Nations in view of the implementation of Article 23(e) of the League's Covenant (freedom of transit).[222] Article 2 of the Statute annexed to the Convention states the principles of freedom of transit ('shall facilitate free transit') and non-discrimination. This provision has a broad scope (it is sector-neutral) but it is limited in the extent of the principles it asserts.

In the context of the GATT, the formulation of Article V on transit was inspired by Article 2 of the Barcelona Statute.[223] Article V of the

[220] Convention and Statute on Freedom of Transit, 20 April 1921, 7 LNTS 11 (still in force).

[221] A prior treaty on this specific point was adopted in 1965 but binds a narrower group of 43 States. See Convention on Transit Trade of Land-locked States, 10 February 1965, 597 UNTS 3.

[222] See Pogoretskyy, *Freedom of Transit*, at 75.

[223] United Nations – Economic and Social Council – Preparatory Committee of the International Conference on Trade and Employment – Committee II – Technical Sub-Committee – Report of the Technical Sub-Committee, E/PC/T/C.II/54/Rev.1 (28 November 1946), at 7.

GATT begins by defining 'traffic in transit' and then states the principles of (1) freedom of transit ('there shall be freedom of transit'), (2) non-discrimination, (3) prohibition of imposing customs duties on the goods in transit, (4) reasonableness and proportionality of transit charges and (5) due diligence in avoiding delays and other obstacles to transit. However, two elements of the conceptual matrix remain unaddressed, namely whether the fixed infrastructures (pipelines and transmission networks) used for energy fall under the definition of 'traffic in transit' and the issue, very important in practice, of cooperation in developing adequate infrastructures for transit and/or granting access to them. With respect to the definition of 'traffic in transit', Article V(1) expressly covers goods (e.g. energy resources, products and technologies (equipment)) and their means of transport 'in transit', hence mobile. Although several provisions of the GATT apply to network-bound transportation of energy resources and products,[224] it remains unclear whether Article V is one of them, given its specific wording. This highlights the importance of more specific agreements regulating transit. The other issue arising from the lack of specificity of Article V concerns the availability of and access to adequate fixed infrastructures for energy transit. States are not generally 'required' to develop transit infrastructure to respond to the needs of other States or to provide a right of access to third parties (operators from other States) when such infrastructures exist. The GATT is silent on this issue. The 2013 Trade Facilitation Agreement (TFA), a plurilateral treaty applicable only to WTO Members who have accepted it,[225] adds some mild clarity. As a general matter, this agreement specifies, in its Articles 10 and 11, the broad principles set out in Article V of the GATT. Article 11(5) of the TFA encourages Members 'to make available, where practicable, physically separate infrastructure (such as lanes, berths and similar) for traffic in transit'. The emphasis is on the 'separate' character of the infrastructure rather than on its existence. Also, pursuant to Article 11(16) of the TFA, Members 'shall endeavour to cooperate and coordinate with one another with a view to enhancing freedom of transit', but this is a soft-worded provision.

Of the two disputes decided so far addressing Article V of the GATT, none has addressed network-bound transit. The findings in *Colombia –*

[224] See the discussion in Section 3.3.2 of this chapter.

[225] Among the transit-relevant Members who are parties, one finds the EU, Georgia, Russia, Turkey, and Ukraine. See www.wto.org/english/tratop_e/tradfa_e/tradfa_agreeacc_e.htm

Ports of Entry, which concerned textiles, apparel and footwear, cannot be simply transposed as such to network-bound energy transit, as they would misleadingly suggest the recognition of third-party access to them.[226] In the more recent *Russia – Traffic in Transit*, the panel only addressed the scope and operation of Article V in a limited manner (with regard to V(2)), on the grounds that such a discussion was overridden by Russia's invocation of the national security exception of Article XXI of the GATT.[227] Network-bound energy transportation was addressed in *EU – Energy Package* but not from the angle of Article V of the GATT. The relevance of this important decision for transit remains latent, although it does shed light on the legality of restrictions to access to pipelines under Article XI(1) of the GATT.[228]

Part X of the UNCLOS regulates in some detail the freedom of transit by land-locked States. Like the GATT, the provisions of Part X do not address specifically the situation of network-bound transit. Yet, the lack of specificity in this case is not an oversight but a deliberate choice. Article 124(2) of the UNCLOS specifically states that '[l]and-locked States and transit States may, by agreement between them, include as means of transport pipelines and gas lines and means of transport other than those included in paragraph 1 [i.e. mobile ones]'. Thus, in the absence of such an agreement, references to 'means of transport' in Part X do not include fixed transit infrastructures. But this does not mean that land-locked States do not enjoy freedom of transit. This principle, indeed this right, is recognised in Article 125(1) of the UNCLOS. Paragraph (2) of this provision states that the 'terms and modalities' for the exercise of such right must be set by agreement, which provides the opportunity to address the issue of fixed transit infrastructures. Such agreements are not a condition for 'the right of access to and from the sea' to exist. In addition to (1) the principle of freedom of transit, Part X also recognises other principles of the transit conceptual matrix, namely (2) non-discrimination (although only 'positive' discrimination is expressly reserved),[229](3) prohibition of imposing customs duties on the goods in transit,[230] (4) reasonableness and proportionality

[226] See D. Azaria, 'Energy Transit under the Energy Charter Treaty and the General Agreement on Tariffs and Trade' (2009) 27 *Journal of Energy and Natural Resources Law* 559.

[227] *Russia – Traffic in Transit*, para. 7.108.

[228] See the discussion in Sections 3.3.2.3.2 and 3.3.2.3.3 of this chapter.

[229] UNCLOS, Articles 126 and 131.

[230] UNCLOS, Article 127.

of transit charges (although only implicitly[231]) and (5) due diligence in avoiding delays and other obstacles to transit.[232] Of particular note, unlike the GATT, Part X of the UNCLOS explicitly addresses the availability of adequate infrastructures. Article 129 provides that:

> Where there are no means of transport in transit States to give effect to the freedom of transit or where the existing means, including the port installations and equipment, are inadequate in any respect, the transit States and land-locked States concerned may cooperate in constructing or improving them.

Access to fixed transit infrastructures is expressly excluded by the combined operation of Articles 125(1) and 124(1)–(2) of the UNCLOS. Article 125(1) provides that 'land-locked States shall enjoy freedom of transit through the territory of transit States by all means of transport'. Article 124(2) clarifies that, absent a specific agreement, the term 'means of transport' does not include 'pipelines and gas lines and means of transport other than those included in paragraph 1'. Paragraph (1)(d) of Article 124 defines 'means of transport' as 'railway rolling stock, sea, lake and river craft and road vehicles' and 'where local conditions so require, porters and pack animals'. Thus, like in other general instruments, the issue of access to fixed transit infrastructure is left open.

3.3.4.3 Regional Level: The ECT Moving from the global and unspecific rules to the regional and specific ones, Article 7 of the ECT is a key provision of this instrument. First of all, unlike the instruments discussed earlier, it expressly covers network-bound infrastructure in the definition of transit. Article 7(10)(b) defines 'Energy Transport Facilities' as:

> high-pressure gas transmission pipelines, high-voltage electricity transmission grids and lines, crude oil transmission pipelines, coal slurry pipelines, oil product pipelines, and other fixed facilities specifically for handling Energy Materials and Products.

This definition is used in formulating the principles by which 'Transit of Energy Materials and Products' is governed, namely (1) freedom of transit,[233] including an overarching obligation 'to secure established flows of Energy Materials and Products',[234] (2) non-discrimination on

[231] UNCLOS, Article 127.
[232] UNCLOS, Article 130.
[233] ECT, Article 7(1).
[234] ECT, Article 7(5) *in fine*.

the basis of origin, ownership or destination of the goods in transit, but the more favourable treatment granted through special agreements is reserved,[235] (3) prohibition of imposing customs duties on the goods in transit, (4) reasonableness and proportionality of transit charges,[236] (5) due diligence in avoiding delays and other obstacles to transit,[237] including a key commitment not to interrupt or reduce transit in the event of dispute,[238] and (6) cooperation in developing adequate infrastructures for transit and/or granting access to them.[239] The focus of the ECT on energy explains why principle (6) on infrastructure and access is specifically regulated through a regime that strikes a careful balance between, on the one hand, the interests of the exporting/importing countries and, on the other hand, the sovereign prerogative of the transit country.

To understand this regime, it is useful to recall the basic idea underpinning the ECT, namely that foreign investment would be used to generate capacity, i.e. production but also transit capacity, and then trade and transit rules would allow the exports/imports of energy resources and products. The importance of these issues made them the focus of lengthy negotiations on a Transit Protocol, but these were discontinued in 2011. Thus, the ECT regulation of capacity and access rests on Article 7. Regarding capacity, mindful that transit infrastructure may not exist or be inadequate in a transit country, and that it may be in the hands of entities separate from the State, the drafters formulated two obligations and two safeguard clauses in Article 7(2), (4), (5) and (9). The first obligation is for Members 'to encourage the relevant entities to cooperate' in the modernisation and development of adequate infrastructures.[240] The second obligation concerns situations where the transit through 'Energy Transport Facilities' cannot be achieved in commercial terms (e.g. an entity holds a monopoly over the use of the pipeline or the transmission line). In such case, Members 'shall not place obstacles in the way of new capacity being established, except as may be otherwise provided in applicable legislation which is consistent with paragraph (1)'.[241] An understanding added to this provision notes that 'the applicable legislation would include provisions on environmental protection,

[235] ECT 7(1) and (3).
[236] ECT 7(1).
[237] ECT 7(1).
[238] ECT 7(6).
[239] ECT 7(2), (4), (5) and (9).
[240] ECT 7(2).
[241] ECT 7(4).

land use, safety, or technical standards'. Thus, there is no obligation to develop new capacity; the obligation is to refrain from placing obstacles to such development except for recognised reasons. One such reason is the application of certain pieces of legislation. Another is provided in Article 7(5), which is a safeguard clause reserving the power of the transit State not to allow new capacity or an increase in the flows if it can show that it 'would endanger the security or efficiency of its energy systems, including the security of supply'. Article 7(9) is a more general safeguard clause stating that, except for the obligation in Article 7(4), nothing in Article 7 obliges a party 'to take any measure' with respect to the development or availability of Energy Transport Facilities.

The regulation of third-party access to fixed transit infrastructures also arises from these provisions. Article 7(3) provides for non-discrimination in the use of Energy Transport Facilities, except when there is an international agreement providing more favourable terms. Such non-discrimination does not entail a 'right of access', which would be impracticable given that fixed transit infrastructures have limited capacity. Article 7(5)(b) emphasises this point stating that a Member 'shall not be obliged to [. . .] permit new or additional Transit through existing Energy Transport Facilities' if that 'would endanger the security or efficiency of its energy systems'. Only 'established flows of Energy Materials and Products' must be 'secure[d]'. The main questions that remain open concern the development of additional capacity, which is subject to the regime discussed earlier, and access by 'new or additional' flows which can be accommodated within existing capacity without danger, which is subject to the freedom, non-discrimination and facilitation obligations (but not to an explicit right of access).

3.3.4.4 Project/Route-Specific Level Despite its specific focus on energy, the ECT remains an umbrella agreement. It is not the only one, as one finds analogous umbrella regulation of transit activities in some regional treaties,[242] most notably the EU,[243] the CIS Free Trade

[242] See generally Pogoretskyy, *Freedom of Transit*, at 90–95 (the following examples are given by Pogoretskyy).

[243] See TFEU, Part III, title II, on the prohibition of quantitative restrictions on imports (Article 34) and exports (35) between Member States. See *Administration des douanes et droits indirects*, Case C-115/02, Judgment of the Court (23 October 2003), para. 18 ('It is therefore necessary, as a consequence of the Customs Union and in the mutual interest of the Member States, to acknowledge the existence of a general principle of freedom of transit of goods within the Community'). In addition, the EU has enacted specific

Agreement,[244] Eurasian Economic Union,[245] and the ECOWAS Energy Protocol.[246] Yet, the ECT remains unique in its spatial scope, energy-specificity and transversal focus.

As an umbrella, it expressly contemplates the possibility for States to enter into specific agreements relating to fixed transit infrastructures. Such agreements are common. A comparative survey of the agreements applicable to ten oil and gas pipelines, prepared by the ECT Secretariat, provides an overview of their main terms.[247] These agreements are part of what this study calls the *ad hoc* approach, namely governance frameworks developed for specific projects, and they will be discussed in Chapter 5. For present purposes, we should note that such agreements have a vertical dimension, i.e. they consist of a set of arrangements that go deeper in laying out the rights and obligations of participating companies and entities, and they also address in more specific terms matters of capacity and access.

3.3.4.5 Interactions between Levels One important aspect of the transit normative mosaic that remains to be discussed is the interactions amongst all these normative layers. Such interactions are typically addressed in broad terms, which go some way in determining the priority of application of different instruments but do not fully clarify the situation.

By way of illustration, Article 132 of the UNCLOS gives express priority over the entire UNCLOS to existing or subsequent agreements granting greater transit facilities. One would therefore expect that the transit provisions of the ECT would take priority over those of the UNCLOS. Yet, priority of application would depend on the ascertainment of the terms 'greater transit facilities', and it would also have to

instruments for energy infrastructure. See Regulation (EC) No. 714/2009 of 13 July 2009 on conditions for access to the network for cross-border exchanges in electricity and repealing Regulation (EC) No. 1228/2003; Regulation (EC) No. 715/2009 of 13 July 2009 on conditions for access to the natural gas transmission networks and repealing Regulation (EC) No. 1775/2005; Regulation (EU) No. 347/2013 of 17 April 2013 on guidelines for trans-European energy infrastructure (TEN-E Regulation).

244 Commonwealth of Independent States, Agreement on the Creation of a Free Trade Area, 18 October 2011, Article 7(1).

245 Treaty on the Eurasian Economic Union, 29 May 2014, Article 79 and Annex 22.

246 ECOWAS Energy Protocol, Article 7.

247 R. Leal-Arcas, *Energy Transit Activities: Collection of Intergovernmental Agreements on Oil and Gas Transit Pipelines and Commentary* (ECT Secretariat, 2015).

take into account the express reservation in Article 7(8) of the ECT regarding Members' 'rights and obligations under international law including customary international law, existing bilateral or multilateral agreements, including rules concerning submarine cables and pipelines', which reflects the declaration of the EU and certain European States that Article 7 is subject to and does not affect the international rules on jurisdiction over submarine cables and pipelines.[248] Regarding the interactions with Article V of the GATT, Article 4 of the ECT expressly reserves the application of the WTO Agreement (which incorporates the GATT) between ECT Members which are also WTO Members ('[n]othing in this Treaty [ECT] shall derogate [...]'). The priority of application of the GATT is specifically recalled for transit by Article 7(8) of the ECT. However, such priority does not necessarily mean that Article V of the GATT entirely excludes the application of Article 7 of the ECT, particularly for matters addressed by the latter which are not covered in the former, such as infrastructure capacity and access and, possibly, the full issue of fixed transit infrastructures. The priority only comes into play when the ECT provides for WTO-minus treatment (e.g. Annex W of the ECT). Thus, Article V of the GATT remains the 'floor', but it is not meant as the 'ceiling'. A proper understanding of the articulation of Articles V of the GATT and 7 of the ECT is important because Article 29(1) and (2)(a) extends the regime on 'trade' (i.e. Part II of the ECT, which includes Article 7 on transit) applicable between WTO Members also to ECT Members which are not WTO Members, subject to some exclusions that have either elapsed or do not concern transit (Annex W of the ECT). If the reservation was improperly understood as exclusion, then the ECT provision on transit would be deprived of *effet utile*.

These specific interactions have not been clarified in the case law, unfortunately, but the practice concerning the relations between the ECT provisions on investment and EU law suggests that they could raise significant complications.[249] For this reason, the adoption of specific

[248] Final Act of the European Energy Charter Conference, Declaration 3 (with respect to Article 7).

[249] See J. R. Basedow, 'The Achmea Judgment and the Applicability of the Energy Charter Treaty in Intra-EU Investment Arbitration' (2019) 23 *Journal of International Economic Law* 271.

agreements can add much clarity. However, an *ad hoc* approach has also some significant disadvantages because it amounts to piece-meal regulation of a general question and its relations with the rules underpinning the foundational approach of energy governance are unsettled, not only as regards the rules organising the transaction but also those addressing its negative externalities.

3

Foundational Approach

Regulating Negative Externalities

I Overview

A large number of instruments and rules of international law address what was referred to in Chapter 1 as the negative externalities of international energy transactions on certain protected objects, mainly human beings (human physical, social and cultural integrity), the environment (whether from an 'anthropocentric' perspective or a more general 'ecocentric' one), as well as on some human values, such as national security, public order and peace.

It may be tempting, for the sake of analytical habit, to equate these rules to 'branches', such as human rights law and international environmental law, but it would be a mistake to do so, and one with significant practical consequences. This is for three main reasons. First, there are rules (e.g. clauses reserving regulatory powers in investment agreements; Articles XX and XXI of the GATT; Articles 7(4)–(5) and 19 of the Energy Charter Treaty) within other 'branches', e.g. investment, trade and transit law, which specifically aim to protect certain values from the negative externalities of the energy transactions enabled or protected by the core standards of such branches. Secondly, human rights law may go a long way in protecting the environment, much like international environmental law can promote the protection of human rights.[1] Thirdly, not every rule of international human rights law as a 'branch' places limits on the negative externalities of energy transactions. Some of them confer entitlements over energy resources, products or the conduct of certain activities (see Chapter 2). Some others, such as the right to property, should be understood as part of the rules 'enabling' and 'protecting' international energy transactions discussed in Chapter 2, because they operate in a form analogous (although not fully similar) to investment

[1] See P.-M. Dupuy, J. E. Viñuales, *International Environmental Law* (Cambridge: Cambridge University Press, 2nd ed. 2018), chapter 10.

protection disciplines. This is a deceptively simple point because the operation of a human right, indeed of an international rule, depends on how it is used. For example, the right to property can operate to assert an entitlement over natural resources,[2] or to protect an energy transaction[3] or, still, to limit the negative externalities of extractive industries on human rights.[4] Thus, one could find the right to property across the full span of the foundational approach (conferring entitlements, enabling/protecting the transaction, limiting negative externalities). But the distinction is significant because not every rule presents the same versatility.

With these caveats in mind, this chapter examines the rules that place limits on the negative externalities of international energy transactions. I begin with a discussion of certain rules which appear in the very instruments enabling and protecting the transaction (investment, trade and transit). The advantages and disadvantages of including these 'special' externality-relevant rules in such instruments are analysed in the light of some illustrations. Subsequently, I examine the 'general' externality-relevant rules, namely those laid down in instruments whose main effect, in the energy context, is not the organisation of international energy transactions but the regulation of their negative externalities.

II The Operation of Special Rules

2.1 *Legal Proximity*

Special externality-relevant rules are understood here by reference to two main features. First, they are part, technically, of an instrument whose main purpose is to organise one or more aspects of international energy transactions or have an express legal connection to it (e.g. a protocol or a side-agreement). Second, they reserve the sovereign prerogative of the State within an instrument which – on the contrary – aims to constrain it. Such prerogative is reserved to shield specific measures, situations and/or purposes other than the enabling/protection of international energy transactions. They are 'special' in that they have a closer connection (technically defined as a wider and express set of legal grounds requiring

[2] See e.g. *Mayagna (Sumo) Awas Tingni Community v. Nicaragua*, ICtHR Series C No. 79, Judgment (31 August 2001).

[3] See e.g. *Case of OAO Neftyanaya Kompaniya Yukos v. Russia*, ECtHR Application no. 14902/04, Judgment (20 September 2011).

[4] See e.g. *Case of Kursun v. Turkey*, ECtHR Application no. 22677/10, Judgment (30 October 2018).

their consideration, typically a treaty provision,[5] shared treaty 'context'[6] and shared institutions,[7] which are additional to the broader technique of systemic integration[8] or applicable law considerations in a dispute[9]) with the rules organising the transaction. Yet, this connection varies according to the nature and operation of different special rules.

One can distinguish several degrees of proximity, from the closest to the more distant special (and indeed general) rules.[10] The closest category of special externality-relevant rules is provided by rules defining the scope of application of a treaty or a clause and excluding certain measures, situations and/or purposes from it. The next category of special rules does not concern the question of whether a certain energy facilitation discipline applies or not but the question of how it applies. Specifically, it concerns the interpretation of the primary rules whose main function is to enable or protect energy transactions in a way that circumscribes their understanding to protect certain values. The third category consists of clauses that identify exceptional grounds on the basis

[5] See e.g. Protocol on Energy Efficiency and Related Environmental Aspects, 17 December 1994, 2081 UNTS 3 [PEEREA], Preamble and Articles 10, 11, 13 and 16.

[6] See VCLT, Article 31(1)–(2). For an application see *Adel A Hamadi Al Tamimi v. Sultanate of Oman,* ICSID Case No. ARB/11/33, Award (3 November 2015), para. 389 (referring to another chapter of the same treaty).

[7] The main example is provided by the dispute settlement organs of the WTO. For a well-known application, which had significant influence on subsequent decisions, see *United States – Import Prohibition of Certain Shrimp and Shrimp Products,* Report of the Appellate Body (12 October 1998), WT/DS58/AB/R [*Shrimp – Turtle*], paras. 129–132 (referring to the preamble of the Marrakesh Agreement). In the absence of a link, one argument often levelled is that the externality-relevant rule belongs to an external legal context. See e.g. *Philip Morris Brand Sàrl (Switzerland), Philip Morris Products S.A. (Switzerland) and Abal Hermanos S.A. (Uruguay) v. Oriental Republic of Uruguay*, ICSID Case No. ARB/10/7, Award (8 July 2016), Concurring and dissenting opinion, para. 181 ('First, as noted above, I do not agree with the Tribunal's conclusion that 'the "margin of appreciation" is not limited to the context of the [ECHR] but "applies equally to claims arising under BITs"'. In my view, *this conclusion is impossible to sustain with regard to the BIT at issue in this arbitration and also impossible to justify more generally, with regard to other investment instruments*'.) (emphasis added).

[8] VCLT, Article 31(3)(c).

[9] See J. E. Viñuales, 'Customary Law in Investment Regulation' (2013/2014) 23 *Italian Yearbook of International Law* 23 (specifically on the matter of 'supplementing' rules).

[10] I rely here on my previous work on defences J. E. Viñuales, 'Defence Arguments in Investment Arbitration', in J. E. Viñuales, M. Waibel (eds.), *ICSID Reports*, vol. 18 (Cambridge: Cambridge University Press, 2020), pp. 9–108, itself an application to investment disputes of a wider account: J. E. Viñuales, 'Seven Ways of Escaping a Rule: Of Exceptions and their Avatars in International Law', in L. Bartels, F. Paddeu (eds.), *Exceptions in International Law* (Oxford: Oxford University Press, 2020), pp. 65–87.

of which a measure inconsistent with the aforementioned primary rules can be excused. These clauses come into play once the latter have been deemed to be breached, and their role is to excuse the breach. The last and more distant category of special rules are those laid down in a separate instrument, e.g. a protocol or a side-agreement, which is directly and expressly linked to the instrument organising energy transactions. The proximity of such separate instruments is normally assessed from the perspective of the primary instrument.

The following paragraphs analyse the extent to which the 'special' character of these rules allows them to place limitations on the negative externalities of energy transactions. The overall conclusion is nuanced. The initial advantages of proximity to the instrument organising the transaction are counterbalanced by the emphasis of the instrument – and of specialised dispute settlement organs – on enabling and protecting the transaction. That, in turn, restricts the scope and operation of these special rules to perform their ultimate purpose of limiting negative externalities. Specifically, these special rules perform their function only to the extent that they do not interfere with the instrument's overall purpose to organise energy transactions. Often, there are no general legal grounds for such *de facto* hierarchy, and the balance tends to shift at the pace of the credibility and legitimacy gained by the values protected by special externality-relevant rules.

2.2 Carve-outs

The first group of provisions are frequent in practice, although their diversity (ranging from provisions defining the spatial, temporal, personal and subject-matter application of a treaty to specific carve-outs within one single clause) and their characterisation as such is not always given full effect in the case law. The following examples are intended to illustrate this point. Some of the cases concern energy-related disputes whereas some others concern a different sector but are nevertheless relevant for the operation of such clauses in an energy context.

2.2.1 Taxation Carve-outs (Article 21 ECT)

One illustrative clause is Article 21 of the ECT which carves-out 'Taxation Measures' from the ambit of the treaty. This carve-out shields one important aspect of the State's sovereign prerogative, taxation, from the ECT disciplines facilitating energy transactions. Taxation is one of the main instruments to internalise the cost of negative externalities. Yet, the case law on Article 21 of the ECT has sometimes excluded its application to taxes that are not specifically aimed to raise revenue.

In *Antaris v. Czech Republic*, an arbitral tribunal hearing a dispute for breach of the investment provisions of the ECT concluded that a levy imposed on renewable energy generators (amounting to a reduction of the benefits the latter derived from a feed-in-tariff scheme) was not a Taxation Measure under Article 21 of the ECT. The reason was that this provision 'was not intended to encompass measures which had principal objectives other than the raising of revenue'.[11]

There are factual specificities that may explain this otherwise debatable conclusion, but the fact remains that the focus on the 'principal objectives' of the tax provided a basis to exclude externality corrective taxes from the carve-out and thereby subjected them to the investment disciplines of the ECT.

2.2.2 Non-Precluded Measures (Article XI Argentina–US BIT)

A similarly restrictive stance was taken by certain tribunals addressing the level of gas tariffs charged by foreign investors in Argentina following the economic crisis of 2002.

In three cases, *CMS v. Argentina*,[12] *Enron v Argentina*[13] and *Sempra v Argentina*,[14] the arbitral tribunals constituted under the BIT between Argentina and the United States addressed, among others, arguments about the operation of Article XI of the Argentina–US BIT, according to which:

> This Treaty shall not preclude the application by either Party of measures necessary for the maintenance of public order, the fulfilment of its obligations with respect to the maintenance or restoration of international peace or security, or the Protection of its own essential security interests.

Argentina argued that certain measures which limited the increase of gas tariffs were necessary to provide gas to its population and were outside

[11] *Antaris Solar GmbH and Dr. Michael Göde v. Czech Republic*, PCA Case No. 2014-01, Award (2 May 2018), para. 248.

[12] *Sempra Energy International v. The Argentine Republic*, ICSID Case No. ARB/02/16, Award (28 September 2007), paras. 325–397.

[13] *CMS Gas Transmission Company v. The Republic of Argentina*, ICSID Case No. ARB/01/8, Award (12 May 2005) [*CMS v. Argentina - Award*], paras. 353–378.

[14] *Enron Corporation and Ponderosa Assets, L.P. v. Argentine Republic*, ICSID Case No. ARB/01/3, Award (22 May 2007) [*Enron v. Argentina - Award*], paras. 322–342.

the scope of the BIT. The three tribunals rejected the argument and analysed Article XI as an exception, rather than a carve-out, subject to exacting conditions akin to those governing the customary defence of necessity.

The characterisation of Article XI by these tribunals was severely criticised by Ad Hoc Committees established under the ICSID Convention to review these awards, two of which were annulled on this specific point.[15] In *CMS v. Argentina*, the award was not annulled on this point, but the Ad Hoc Committee introduced an important conceptual distinction between the operation of Article XI and that of the necessity defence in customary international law (which is an excuse for an acknowledged breach), namely that if Article XI applied, there could be no breach capable of being excused by the necessity defence.[16] A similar understanding of Article XI as a threshold provision has been retained in other cases, some relating to energy[17] and some others to other sectors.[18] In none of them, however, the carve-out has operated to exclude the jurisdiction of the tribunal,[19] as it has in the context of Article 21 of the ECT.[20]

2.2.3 Public Procurement Carve-out (Article III(8)(a) GATT)

The specific effect (exclusion of jurisdiction or defence on the merits) has also emerged in the case law of the WTO dispute settlement organs. In some cases, the carve-out only excludes the application of a specific provision.

An example is the public procurement carve-out or 'derogation' in Article III(8)(a) of the GATT. If the conditions of this carve-out are met

[15] *Sempra Energy International v. The Argentine Republic*, ICSID Case No. ARB/02/16, Decision on the Argentine Republic's Application for the Annulment of the Award (29 June 2010) [*Sempra v. Argentina – Annulment*], para. 159; *Enron Corporation and Ponderosa Assets, L.P. v. Argentine Republic*, ICSID Case No. ARB/01/3, Decision on the Application for Annulment of the Argentine Republic (30 July 2010) [*Enron v. Argentina – Annulment*], para. 405.

[16] *CMS Gas Transmission Company v. Argentine Republic*, ICSID Case No. ARB/01/08, Decision on Annulment (25 September 2007) [*CMS v. Argentina – Annulment*], para. 129.

[17] *LG&E Energy Corp, LG&E Capital Corp, LG&E International Inc. v. Argentine Republic*, ICSID case No. ARB/02/1, Decision on Liability (3 October 2006), paras. 226–244.

[18] *Continental Casualty Company v. The Argentine Republic*, ICSID Case No. ARB/03/9, Award (5 September 2008), paras. 160–236.

[19] See *Continental Casualty v. Argentina*, paras. 164 and 167.

[20] See *Antaris v. Czech Republic*, para. 217.

(e.g. the government favours domestic producers of greener products over producers of foreign 'like products'), then the national treatment clause is simply not applicable, and the government is free to treat domestic goods more favourably than foreign ones. Article III(8)(a) was unsuccessfully invoked in *Canada – Renewable Energy*[21] and *India – Solar Cells*[22] to shield the local content requirements introduced by the respondent States in their feed-in-tariff schemes.

2.2.4 National Security (Article XXI GATT)

In some other cases, however, the availability of the carve-out would exclude the application of the entire treaty, hence raising the question of whether this is a jurisdictional objection or a defence on the merits.

The matter arose in *Russia – Traffic in transit*, which, although not an energy-related dispute, is relevant for global energy governance.[23] In this case, Ukraine challenged certain transit restrictions introduced by Russia as incompatible with Articles V and X of the GATT and Russia's commitments in its Accession Protocol. Russia argued that the panel had no jurisdiction to review the measures because they had been adopted to protect national security, under Article XXI(b)(iii). The panel concluded that it had jurisdiction to hear the claim, as the availability of Article XXI(b)(iii) was a matter that could be reviewed by the panel. Yet, after asserting jurisdiction, the panel considered that the operation of Article XXI(b)(iii) was such that it had to be analysed before determining the existence of a breach. It did note that, had the measures been taken outside a context of international crisis, Ukraine would have established a *prima facie* case for violation of Article V(2).[24] But it reasoned that the nature of Article XXI(b)(iii) required its consideration before the assessment of breach and, if available, there was no need for such an assessment.[25]

[21] *Canada – Certain Measures Affecting the Renewable Energy Generation Sector* (Complainant – Japan), AB Report, 6 May 2013, WT/DS412/AB/RWT/DS426/AB/R, [*Canada – Renewables*], paras. 5.54–5.85.

[22] *India – Certain Measures Relating to Solar Cells and Solar Modules* (Complainant: United States), AB Report, 16 September 2016, WT/DS456/AB/R, WT/DS456/AB/R/Add.1 [*India – Solar Cells*], paras. 5.17–5.44.

[23] *Russia – Measures Concerning Traffic in Transit*, Panel Report, 5 April 2019, WT/DS512/R [*Russia – Traffic in Transit*].

[24] *Russia – Traffic in Transit*, para. 7.183.

[25] *Russia – Traffic in Transit*, paras. 7.108–7.109.

In doing so, it expressly distinguished the operation of Article XXI(b)(iii) from that of Article XX (general exceptions), which will be discussed later. The wider space provided to the operation of this national security carve-out was explained by the formulation of the clause, which exempts measures adopted under certain circumstances ('taken in time of war or other emergency in international relations') but does not require the assessment of the degree of deviation as compared to normal circumstances. A no less important explanation, of a political nature, may be that national security considerations are more easily accepted as a consideration overriding the organisation of energy transactions than environmental or human protection considerations.

2.3 *Modulations of Primary Norms*

Special externality-relevant rules may take the form of modulations of certain core terms of trade, investment and transit disciplines. Such modulations may be express, with actual wording in the provision (or elsewhere in the instrument) referring to the need to take into account such negative externalities, or implicit, i.e. based on a reinterpretation of a core term.

2.3.1 Environmental Aspects (Article 19 ECT)

It is useful to begin the examination with the ECT due to its focus on energy. Part IV on 'Miscellaneous provisions' contains a long provision, Article 19, entitled 'Environmental Aspects'.

This provision is drafted in hortatory language and, in many ways, it epitomises the shortcomings of special externality-relevant rules. Its overall purpose is to 'minimise' the harmful 'Environmental Impacts', understood broadly as encompassing environmental protection, human health and also cultural expressions.[26] The drafting of the provision makes clear, however, that such considerations must not 'interfere' with energy transactions. The overall obligation, stated in the chapeau of Article 19(1) is formulated as follows:

> [E]ach Contracting Party shall strive to *minimise* in an *economically efficient* manner harmful Environmental Impacts occurring either within or outside its Area from all operations within the Energy Cycle in its Area,

[26] ECT, Article19(3)(b).

> taking proper account of safety. In doing so each Contracting Party shall act in a *Cost-Effective manner* (emphasis added).

The provision then recalls the precautionary and polluter-pays principles and adds, echoing Principle 16 of the Rio Declaration on Environment and Development, that action to internalise the cost of negative externalities must not 'distor[t] Investment in the Energy Cycle or international trade'.

In addition to the hortatory language used in the formulation of environmental standards ('strive to', 'take into account', 'promote', 'have regard', 'encourage'), the priority of the organisation of the transaction over measures to tackle negative externalities is further confirmed in several provisions. The definition of the 'Energy Cycle' in Article 19(3)(a) refers, again, to 'minimising harmful Environmental Impacts' of an otherwise undisturbed 'energy chain'. The characterisation of 'Improving Energy Efficiency' in Article 19(3)(c) emphasises the need to maintain 'the same unit of output (or a good or service) without reducing the quality or performance of the output'. In an understanding regarding Article 19(1)(i), which concerns the assessment of environmental impacts, it is expressly stated that '[i]t is for each Contracting Party to decide the extent to which the assessment and monitoring of Environmental Impacts should be subject to legal requirements'.

This order of priority is unsurprising. Despite references to environmental protection, the ECT's underlying bargain was about access to resources in exchange for access to markets. The regulation of negative externalities was not allowed to interference with this overall transaction. No dispute has arisen so far regarding the implementation of Article 19 of the ECT. The environmental and efficiency aspects of the ECT have been further developed through a protocol and they could also be covered, albeit to a limited extent, by the general exception clause of Article 24 of the ECT. Both will be discussed in later sections. For now, the brief examination of Article 19 of the ECT serves to illustrate the possible shortcomings of this type of special externality-relevant rules, which are formulated in such a way as to avoid interfering with the main goal of the instrument, namely enabling and protecting international energy transactions.

2.3.2 Revised Government Procurement Agreement

Another example of an express modulation is provided by the 2012 revised Government Procurement Agreement, which is a plurilateral agreement within the WTO which restricts, for Members having accepted it, the scope of the public procurement carve-out of Article III(8)(a) of the GATT. In 2012, the GPA was revised to apply to a larger group of government entities as well as to smaller contract values, thus expanding its coverage.

But the revision was not only aimed at facilitating market access to foreign providers but also to reserve the possibility of differentiation depending on the environmental and social impact of providers.[27] Thus, Article X on 'Technical Specifications and Tender Documentation' specifically emphasises, at paragraph (6), that '[f]or greater certainty, a Party [...] may, in accordance with this Article, prepare, adopt or apply technical specifications to promote the conservation of natural resources or protect the environment'. Similarly, Article X(9) provides that the 'evaluation criteria' on the basis of which bids are selected 'may include, among others [...] environmental characteristics'.

Given the economic importance of public procurement and of allowing for efficiency and other forms of minimisation of negative externalities in energy goods, products, technologies and activities, the modulations appearing the revised GPA are significant. At the same time, however, they intervene in an instrument which, above all, places constraints on what is otherwise a carve-out (or derogation) from the national treatment discipline in Article III of the GATT.

Beyond the GATT, another illustration is provided by the Comprehensive Economic Trade Agreement (CETA) between the EU and Canada.[28] Chapter 19 of the CETA concerns government procurement. Articles 19(9)(6) and 19(9)(9) contain wording similar to that of Article X(6) and (9) of the revised GPA.

2.3.3 Interpretive Annexes (Annex 10-B(4)(b) US–Oman FTA)

Similar considerations also apply in the investment context. By way of illustration, Annex 10-B(4)(b) of the US–Oman FTA provides that: '[e]-xcept in rare circumstances, non-discriminatory regulatory actions by a Party that are designed and applied to protect legitimate public welfare objectives, such as public health, safety, and the environment, do not

[27] See M.-A. Corvaglia, 'Public Procurement and Private Standards: Ensuring Sustainability under the WTO Agreeement on Government Procurement' (2016) 19 *Journal of International Economic Law* 607.

[28] CETA, pp. 23–1079.

constitute indirect expropriations'.[29] The operation of this interpretive annex has been addressed in a case concerning the extractive industries, although not in the energy sector.

In *Al-Tamimi v. Oman*, an arbitral tribunal constituted under the US–Oman FTA had to decide a dispute concerning State measures affecting the operation of a limestone quarry in violation of domestic environmental law. The claimant claimed that its investment had been expropriated in violation of the expropriation clause of the FTA (Article 10.6.1) to which the aforementioned annex was attached. The tribunal rejected the claim observing, among other things, that the claim would have 'to confront the express stipulation' in the annex non-discriminatory regulatory actions to protect the environment 'do not constitute indirect expropriations'.[30]

2.3.4 Implicit Modulations

Aside from express modulations of the wording of trade, investment and transit disciplines, a number of cases have also addressed the possibility of introducing implicit modulations of such disciplines through the interpretation of basic terms, such as the reference to 'like products' or 'like circumstances' in non-discrimination standards, the interpretation of the domestic laws that condition the protection of a foreign investment transaction or that of the fair and equitable treatment standard or of the international minimum standard of treatment.

In these modulations, the scope for human rights or environmental protection recognised in the case law is limited. Regarding the understanding of 'like products' under Articles I (MFN) and III (national treatment) of the GATT, although it varies in different provisions and circumstances,[31] the case law has retained four main criteria to determine whether two products are alike: (1) physical properties, (2) functionality, (3) consumer perception and (4) tariff classification.[32] A particularly complex question concerns the possibility to take into account the so-called different processes and production methods (PPMs) of a good,

[29] US–Oman Free Trade Agreement, 19 January 2006, available at: https://ustr.gov/trade-agreements/free-trade-agreements/oman-fta.

[30] *Adel A Hamadi Al Tamimi v. Sultanate of Oman*, ICSID Case No. ARB/11/33, Award (3 November 2015), para. 368.

[31] *Japan – Taxes on Alcoholic* Beverages, AB Report (4 October 1996), WT/DS8/AB/R,WT/DS10/AB/R, WT/DS11/AB/R [*Japan Alcoholic Beverages*], p. 21.

[32] *European Communities – Measures Affecting Asbestos and Products Containing Asbestos*, AB Report (12 March 2001), WT/DS135/AB/R [*EC – Asbestos*], para. 101.

including their different social and environmental footprints, to consider that the two products are not 'alike' (on their exceptional justification see Section 2.4.6 of this chapter). This is different from the possibility of taking into account the products own physical characteristics, which has been accepted as a sufficient basis for them not to be considered alike.[33]

The key question is whether the same good (e.g. electricity) procured from two sources (e.g. a domestic company and a foreign company, or two foreign companies from different countries) which produce it relying on processes with different social and environmental footprints (e.g. from photovoltaics instead of burning fossil fuels) can be considered not to be alike. The issue has not been addressed in the context of energy. But in two disputes relating to animal welfare, *EC – Seal products* and *US – Tuna II*, the products were considered to be alike and the measures to be in breach of Articles I and III of the GATT[34] and Article 2.1 (national treatment) of the TBT Agreement.[35] The analysis in both cases suggests that there is reluctance to address the issue of PPMs at the level of 'likeness', i.e. of the primary norm, and the preference is to confine it to the level of general exceptions.

In the investment context, the variability of the case law makes it difficult to identify settled solutions. There is, however, one case in which the different impact of two investment projects (car parks) on a site protected under the World Heritage Convention, i.e. their different negative externalities, led an arbitral tribunal to conclude that the two projects were not in like circumstances for purposes of the MFN clause in

[33] *EC – Asbestos*, paras. 109–132.

[34] *European Communities – Measures Prohibiting the Importation and Marketing of Seal Products*, AB Report (22 May 2014), WT/DS400/AB/R, WT/DS401/AB/R [*EC – Seals*], paras. 5.96 and 5.130.

[35] In *United States – Measures Concerning the Importation, Marketing and Sale of Tuna and Tuna Products*, AB Report (16 May 2012), WT/DS381/AB/R [*US – Tuna II*]. In this case, the measure was essentially discussed under the TBT Agreement, which does not contain a general exception clause. Subsequently, the United States modified the measure to bring it into compliance. At this stage, there was agreement between the Parties that the measure was in breach of Articles I(1) and III(4) of the GATT and the disagreement concerned the availability of the general exceptions clause in Article XX, particularly the chapeau. The AB upheld the panel's conclusion that Article XX excused the measure. See *United States – Measures Concerning the Importation, Marketing and Sale of Tuna and Tuna Products – Recourse to article 21.5 of the DSU by the United States – Second recourse to article 21.5 of the DSU by Mexico*, AB Report (14 December 2018), WT/DS381/AB/RW/USA, WT/DS381/AB/RW2 [*US – Tuna II – 14 December 2018*], paras. 6.288–6.290.

the applicable BIT.[36] More frequently, the issue of negative externalities has been integrated into the analysis through the interpretation of core investment standards such as the fair and equitable treatment clause (or the international minimum standard of treatment in the NAFTA)[37] or the requirement for investments to be made in accordance with domestic law.[38] In addition, there are also cases, including in the energy sector, in which a State has brought a counterclaim against the investor for violation of human rights[39] or environmental law.[40] But the laws relied on by the State as the basis for the counterclaim in such cases are not part of the BIT as such and, therefore, they cannot shed light on the operation of special externality-relevant rules.

2.4 Exceptions

2.4.1 Overview

The third type of special externality-relevant rules intervene once a violation of a primary norm (enabling/protecting international energy transactions) has been ascertained. They operate as 'excuses' for what is otherwise conduct inconsistent with the energy facilitative disciplines laid out in the instrument. Such understanding regarding their operation reflects the order of priority between the organisation of energy transactions and the limitation of their negative externalities.

Some representative illustrations of these exception clauses include Article XX of the GATT, Articles 7(5) and 24 of the ECT and a number of similar clauses in FTAs and BITs. Virtually all the cases that have

[36] *Parkerings-Compagniet AS v. Republic of Lithuania,* ICSID Case No. ARB/05/8, Award (11 September 2007), para. 392.

[37] *Plama Consortium Ltd v. Republic of Bulgaria,* ICSID Case No. ARB/03/24, Award (27 August 2008), paras. 219–221; *Chemtura Corporation (formerly Crompton Corporation) v. Government of Canada,* UNCITRAL, Award (2 August 2010), paras. 133–143.

[38] *Mamidoil Jetoil Greek Petroleum Products Societe Anonyme SA v. Republic of Albania,* ICSID Case No. ARB/11/24, paras. 359–495; *Cortec Mining Kenya Limited, Cortec (Pty) Ltd and Stirling Capital Ltd v. Republic of Kenya,* ICSID Case No. ARB/15/29, Award (22 October 2018), paras. 310–387.

[39] *Urbaser S.A. and Consorcio de Aguas Bilbao Biskaia, Bilbao Biskaia Ur Partzuergoa v. Argentine Republic,* Award (8 December 2016), paras. 1143–1155, 1182–1210.

[40] *Perenco Ecuador Ltd. v. The Republic of Ecuador and Empresa Estatal Petróleos del Ecuador (Petroecuador),* ICSID Case No. ARB/08/6, Interim Decision on the Environmental Counterclaim (11 August 2015); *Burlington Resources Inc. v. Republic of Ecuador,* ICSID Case ARB/08/5, Decision on Counterclaims (7 February 2017).

discussed the operation of exception clauses, including in the context of energy-related disputes, concern Article XX of the GATT.

2.4.2 Article XX of the GATT

Article XX has two components: a preamble or chapeau and ten letters defining specific types of 'measures' characterised in various ways by reference to the protection of public morals, public order, human, animal or plant life or health, or exhaustible natural resources. Both the letters and the chapeau state certain requirements that a measure challenged as inconsistent with a GATT discipline has to meet to be excused.

The overall operation of Article XX was clarified by the WTO Appellate Body in *US – Reformulated Gasoline*,[41] a leading case concerning the environmental and health externalities of gasoline. At stake was a challenge brought by Venezuela against certain administrative measures adopted by the United States in the implementation of the Clean Air Act to limit the levels of air pollution from vehicles. The effect of the measures was that domestically refined gasoline would benefit from a tailored regime whereas imported gasoline was subject to a general standard (a baseline). In practice, that gave an advantage to the sale in the United States of domestic gasoline. The United States invoked Article XX, notably letter (g) (conservation of exhaustible natural resources) to justify its measure.

The Appellate Body made a number of statements regarding the operation of this general exception clause which are important to understand the scope and limitations of this special externality-relevant rule in an energy context. First, the AB noted that Article XX comes into play to justify (the term 'excuse' would be more accurate) an inconsistency with a substantive rule of the GATT.[42] Secondly, the nature of Article XX thus carried significant implications for the burden of proof, which is allocated to the State invoking the exception.[43] Thirdly, the exceptions of Article XX are available for breaches of any substantive provision of the GATT.[44] Fourthly, the analysis of Article XX has to follow two steps, starting with the determination of whether the measure falls under one of

[41] *United States – Standards for Reformulated and Conventional Gasoline*, AB Report (29 April 1996), WT/DS2/AB/R [*US – Reformulated Gasoline*],

[42] See e.g. *US – Reformulated Gasoline*, at 23; *EC – Asbestos*, para. 115; *Thailand – Customs and Fiscal Measures on Cigarettes from the Philippines*, WT/DS371/AB/R (17 June 2011), para. 173.

[43] *US – Reformulated Gasoline*, at 22–23.

[44] *US – Reformulated Gasoline*, at 24.

the letters and then moving to whether the requirements of the chapeau are met.[45]

In practice, the requirements of the chapeau have been a formidable obstacle to the justification of domestic environmental protection measures. In *US – Gasoline*, the US invocation of Article XX(g) failed at the level of the chapeau.[46] Mindful of the restrictive implications of this analysis of the clause, the AB concluded its assessment with a significant observation on what its finding did *not* mean:

> that the ability of any WTO Member to take measures to control air pollution or, more generally, to protect the environment, is at issue [...] WTO Members have a large measure of autonomy to determine their own policies on the environment. [...] So far as concerns the WTO, that autonomy is circumscribed only by the need to respect the requirements of the General Agreement and the other covered agreements.[47]

In practice, the operation of Article XX has left limited room for the limitation of the underlying transaction for the sake of environmental or human health protection.

To understand such limits, it may be useful to briefly discuss the interplay between Article XX and certain issues of particular relevance for energy governance, such as export measures on raw materials, support schemes for renewable energy, technical barriers to trade (particularly as regards efficiency), PPMs, and energy security as a ground for justifying restrictions to trade in goods and services.

2.4.3 Export Measures and Article XX

Article XI of the GATT prohibits export restrictions but not export duties. Two issues have arisen in this context, namely whether export restrictions can be justified under Article XX and whether limitations agreed in accession protocols on (otherwise lawful) export duties can also be justified under Article XX.

The answer to the first question is that Article XX is indeed available to justify export restrictions in violation of Article XI of the GATT. Of course, whether the measure is justified or not depends on the specific circumstances of the case, but Article XX can be invoked. In *China – Raw Materials*, certain restrictions adopted by China on the exports of several

[45] *US – Reformulated Gasoline*, at 22.
[46] *US – Reformulated Gasoline*, at 24.
[47] *US – Reformulated Gasoline*, at 29–30.

raw materials (bauxite, coke, fluorspar, magnesium, manganese) were – considered collectively – in breach of Article X(1) of the GATT. China argued that they were necessary to protect the environment due to the negative externalities caused by their extraction. The panel considered that the exceptions of Article XX(b) and (g) could be invoked to justify some of them, but that the requirements of these exceptions were not met.[48]

Regarding the second question, the Appellate Body confirmed the panel's finding that Article XX could not be invoked to justify violations of Article 11.3 of China's Accession Protocol, under which China had undertaken commitments with respect to export duties.[49] This is a systemically important issue because it would mean that commitments in accession protocols, as a result of their *lex specialis* character, leave less room to accommodate measures to limit negative externalities, which is inconsistent with the overall rationale of the aforementioned statement of the Appellate Body in *US – Gasoline.*

2.4.4 Renewable Energy Support Schemes and Article XX

Article XX has also been invoked, albeit unsuccessfully, to justify renewable energy support schemes involving local content requirements.

In *India – Solar Cells*,[50] the United States claimed that India's Jawaharlal Nehru National Solar Mission (NSM), which conditioned participation in the scheme by renewable energy producers to certain local content requirements, was in breach of the national treatment clauses in Article III(4) of the GATT and 2.1 of the TRIMS.[51] India sought to justify its measure by reference to Article XX letters (d) (measures necessary to secure compliance with laws and regulations) and (j) (products in general or local short supply). Both defences were rejected at the level of the letter, without reaching the level of the chapeau. But the reasoning of the Appellate Body in connection with Article XX(d) is of particular relevance to prepare the discussion of

[48] *China – Measures Related to the Exportation of Various Raw Materials*, Panel Report (5 July 2011), WT/DS394/R, WT/DS395/R, WT/DS398/R [*China – Raw Materials – Panel*], paras. 7.613 and 7.615.

[49] *China – Measures Related to the Exportation of Various Raw Materials*, AB Report (30 January 2012), WT/DS394/AB/R, WT/DS395/AB/R, WT/DS398/AB/R 30 [*China – Raw Materials – AB*], para. 307.

[50] *India – Certain Measures Relating to Solar Cells and Solar Modules*, AB Report (16 September 2016), WT-DS456/AB/R [*India – Solar Cells*].

[51] TRIMS, Annex 1A.

'external' externality-relevant rules. India argued that the local content requirements in the measure were necessary to secure compliance, among other things, with the UN Framework Convention on Climate Change (UNFCCC).

The Appellate Body identified a series of criteria to assess the degree of normativity of the 'laws and regulations' contemplated in Article XX(d)[52] and then concluded that the UNFCCC (and the other legal bases invoked by India) did not have sufficient normative force to require compliance. As a result, the requirements of letter (d) were not met. Although this outcome may be due to the specific circumstances of the case (nothing in the UNFCCC requires, indeed, the adoption of a local content requirement), the test crafted by the Appellate Body would leave out a large part of environmental and human rights norms and treaties and even domestic constitutional and statutory provisions. Environmental norms, due to the constantly evolving conditions they face – scientifically, politically and environmentally – are necessarily formulated in broad terms. The same can be said of at least certain human rights provisions, such as those concerning economic, social and cultural rights.

The reasoning of the Appellate Body in *India – Solar Cells* means not only that Article XX(d) is unsuitable to ensure the respect of 'external' externality-relevant rules but, more generally, it emphasises the obstacles posed by the GATT to the energy transition. Local content requirements are frequently used in feed-in-tariff schemes for renewable energy for political economy reasons.[53] Politically, the massive transfers of taxpayer money that such schemes involve cannot be expected to be made without some measure of 'green' industrial policy favouring the transition of local industries to a low-carbon economy. Upholding trade liberalisation over the energy transition, even at the level of a single case,

[52] *India – Solar Cells*, para. 5.113 (this test includes '(i) the degree of normativity of the instrument and the extent to which the instrument operates to set out a rule of conduct or course of action that is to be observed within the domestic legal system of a Member; (ii) the degree of specificity of the relevant rule; (iii) whether the rule is legally enforceable, including, e.g. before a court of law; (iv) whether the rule has been adopted or recognized by a competent authority possessing the necessary powers under the domestic legal system of a Member; (v) the form and title given to any instrument or instruments containing the rule under the domestic legal system of a Member; and (vi) the penalties or sanctions that may accompany the relevant rule').

[53] See J.-C. Kuntze, T. Morenhout, *Local Content Requirements and the Renewable Energy Industry – A Good Match?* (Geneva: ICTSD, 2013).

unveils a deeper tension between the rules organising energy transactions and those limiting their negative externalities.

2.4.5 Technical Barriers to Trade and Article XX

The question of technical barriers to trade under the TBT Agreement[54] has been mentioned with respect to the modulation of substantive disciplines. A range of technical regulations, standards and conformity assessment processes may influence the access and commercialisation of energy products (different types of fuels) and equipment (e.g. setting efficiency requirements).

At the level of Article XX, the main difficulty is the absence in the TBT Agreement of a general exception clause which could be invoked to justify non-compliant measures. The preamble of the TBT Agreement contains language resembling that of the chapeau of Article XX. Yet, this has not been deemed sufficient to make Article XX available for the justification of a breach of Article 2.1 of the TBT Agreement (national treatment and MFN), although such language does provide a basis for relying on the case law relating to Article XX for the interpretation of Article 2.1.[55]

Article 2.1 of the TBT is not an exception but a substantive provision, a primary norm. Its scope is in many ways narrower than the substantive provisions of the GATT, because it only applies to certain types of measures. Yet, in the light of the definition of a 'technical regulation' in Annex I.1 of the TBT Agreement, such measures could potentially introduce regulatory distinctions between two products on the basis of their PPMs, i.e. on the different level of negative externalities caused by production of the goods targeted by the regulation. This is the main ambiguity between the two chessboards, i.e. the GATT and the TBT Agreement. Under the latter, PPMs would be analysed at the level of the primary norm. The main inquiry is whether the regulatory distinction made by the measure is legitimate.[56] By contrast, as discussed next, under the GATT, non-product-related PPMs (those which leave no trace on the product) can only be analysed at the level of the general exceptions clause, not that of substantive standards (e.g. Articles I, III and XI of the GATT).

[54] Agreement on Technical Barriers to Trade, 15 April 1994, 1868 UNTS 120 [TBT Agreement].

[55] *EC – Seals*, paras. 5.310–5.313; *US – Tuna II – 14 December 2018*, paras. 7.345 and 7.347.

[56] *US – Tuna II – 14 December 2018*, paras. 284 and 286.

2.4.6 Processes and Production Methods under Article XX

The question of PPMs has been discussed in a number of prominent disputes, although not related to energy. For present purposes, the key question concerns the extent to which the different environmental or human footprint of two 'like products' (e.g. their respective level of emissions of GHGs involved in their products, or their respective pollution of land and waterbodies, or still their different labour standards) can provide a basis to justify, under Article XX, their different treatment.

The matter was addressed before the establishment of the WTO in the well-known *tuna-dolphin* cases in connection with the incidental killing of dolphins by tuna harvesters who sold their catch in the United States. The measure adopted by the United States in this regard was found to be in violation of Article XI of the GATT and the two exceptions invoked to justify it, under Article XX(b) (protection of animal life), (g) (conservation of exhaustible natural resources) and (d) (compliance with laws and regulations), were rejected.[57] The matter arose again in three other disputes, all focussing on differential treatment of certain products on the grounds of the different environmental footprint (the higher impact on certain species or animal welfare) of their PPMs.

In the famous *US – Shrimp* case,[58] the United States sought to justify a measure (a PPM certification requirement for the importation of shrimp into the US market) found in violation of Article XI of the GATT by reference to Article XX(g). The Appellate Body found that the measure met the requirements of letter (g), i.e. it was related to the conservation of exhaustible natural resources (endangered turtles caught in shrimp nets), but not those of the chapeau of Article XX.[59] Subsequently, the United States modified the measure to bring it into compliance.

A similar outcome was reached in *US – Tuna II* in a dispute akin to the previous tuna-dolphin cases, this time in relation to 'dolphin-safe' labelling standards. Yet, the dispute was mainly decided under the TBT Agreement, which does not contain a general exception clause (see Section 2.4.5).

[57] See *United States – Restrictions on Imports of Tuna*, Panel Report, DS21/R-39S/155 (3 September 1991), paras. 5.17–5.34, 5.34–5.40, 7.1, and *United States – Measures Concerning the Importation, Marketing and Sale of Tuna and Tuna Products*, Panel report (16 June 1994), DS29/R, paras. 5.6–5.41, 6.1.

[58] *United States – Import Prohibition of Certain Shrimp and Shrimp Products*, AB Report (12 October 1998), WT/DS58/AB/R [*US – Shrimp*].

[59] *US – Shrimp*, paras. 125–145 (letter (g)), 146–186 (inconsistency with the chapeau).

The third dispute, *EC – Seals* concerned European Regulations that prohibited the importation and commercialisation of seal products except from hunts by Inuit or indigenous communities (IC exception) or hunts conducted for marine resource management purposes (MRM exception). This time, the dispute was argued at the level of both the TBT Agreement and the GATT. On the latter, the measures were found to be in violation of Article I(1) (MFN) and III(4) (national treatment).[60] The EU invoked the exception in Article XX(a) (measures necessary to protect public morals). The panel and the Appellate Body accepted the defence at the level of letter (a) but, once again, the requirements of the chapeau were not deemed to be met.[61] All in all, the case law reviewed highlights the limited scope, under Article XX, for environmental differentiation on the basis of PPMs.

2.4.7 Energy Security and Article XX

The last issue to be mentioned concerns the protection of energy security or 'security of supply' under general exception clauses. There is a difference between the protection of 'national security' under Article XXI of the GATT and the protection of energy security under Articles XX of the GATT and XIV of the GATS.[62] As noted earlier by reference to *Russia – Traffic in transit*, the operation of Article XXI is more accurately described as a carve-out or a threshold measure. By contrast, Articles XX of the GATT and XIV of the GATS are exceptions and they operate as such, i.e. they presuppose a violation of a substantive discipline.

In *EU – Energy Package*, both provisions were tested in the specific context of energy security. In order to justify certain measures (diversification and certification requirements seeking to limit Gazprom's dominance) found in breach of the GATT and the GATS, the EU invoked Articles XX(j) of the GATT ('measures essential to the acquisition or distribution of products in general or local short supply') and XIV(a) of the GATS (measures 'necessary to protect public morals or to maintain public order'). On the first, the EU argued that gas could suddenly become in short supply in case of disruption because, due to the infrastructures necessary for its transport, it cannot be secured on short notice. The panel rejected this argument noting that Article XX(j)

[60] *EC – Seals*, paras. 5.78–5.130.

[61] *EC – Seals*, paras. 5.289–5.290 (on letter (a)), 5.291–5.339 (inconsistency with the chapeau).

[62] GATS, Annex 1B.

requires the product to be 'presently in short supply', not in the future.[63] On the second issue, the panel granted significant discretion to the EU in adopting measures to maintain energy security, as part of the maintenance of public order, but the exception was rejected at the level of the chapeau of Article XIV of the GATS, which is similar to that of Article XX of the GATT.[64] This case confirms the limited space left by these general exception provisions to encroach on the organisation of international energy transactions.

2.5 *Separate but Formally Linked Instruments*

2.5.1 Overview

The fourth type of special externality-relevant rules are characterised by two main features: (1) they are laid down in an instrument which is separate from that embodying the rules organising energy transactions, but (2) they are expressly linked to the latter instrument, typically by a specific clause and/or by the existence of shared institutions and/or by the use of the same definitional terms.

Most examples are provided by instruments which are not energy-specific, such as the North American Agreement on Environmental Cooperation (NAAEC), the North American Agreement on Labor Cooperation (NAALC), the two seminal side agreements to the NAFTA. However, the ECT has a Protocol, the PEEREA mentioned earlier in this chapter,[65] which is aimed to elaborate on ECT Article 19 (particularly paragraph (1)(d)) and promote energy efficiency, thereby also some measure of environmental protection.

2.5.2 The PEEREA

For present purposes, the two main aspects of the PEEREA concern its link with the ECT and its subordination to the organisation of energy transactions, both conceptual and legal.

The first aspect is manifest in several provisions of the PEEREA, which conditioned its entry into force to the entry into force of the ECT,[66] was

[63] *European Union and its Member States – Certain Measures Relating to the Energy Sector* (Complainant: Russia), Panel Report (10 August 2018), WT/DS476/R [*EU – Energy Package*], paras. 7.1348–7.1350.

[64] *EU – Energy Package*, paras. 7.1241–7.1254.

[65] See n. 5.

[66] PEEREA, Article 18(1). Both instruments entered into force together.

open for signature and is open to accession only by States which are parties to the ECT,[67] relies on the ECT's Conference and Secretariat as the PEEREA's institutions[68] and uses the same definitions as the ECT of terms such as 'Energy Cycle', 'Environmental Impacts', 'Improving Energy Efficiency' and 'Cost-Effective[ness]'.[69] Moreover, the PEEREA contains a specific provision clarifying its relations with the ECT. Pursuant to Article 13(1) of the PEEREA: 'In the event of inconsistency between the provisions of this Protocol and the provisions of the Energy Charter Treaty, the provisions of the Energy Charter Treaty shall, to the extent of the inconsistency, prevail'.

The latter provision embodies the second aspect to be discussed, namely the subordination of the PEEREA to the ECT or, in other words, the subordination of the efficiency and related environmental measures adopted under the PEEREA to the organisation of the energy transactions. More generally, the PEEREA is drafted so as to avoid possible interference with energy transactions. The priority sequence underpinning the PEEREA can be defined as follows: (1) organisation of energy transactions, (2) improvement of their efficiency, and (3) environmental benefits arising from such improvements. This is clear from the formulation of its preamble, which refers to the 'economic and environmental gains' resulting from 'cost-effective efficiency measures', and from the very definition of the PEEREA's scope and objective in Article 1(1): 'This Protocol defines policy principles for the promotion of energy efficiency as a considerable source of energy and for *consequently* reducing adverse Environmental Impacts of energy systems'.[70]

The closer the PEEREA comes to giving environmental norms a role which is not mediated by efficiency measures, themselves based on the assumption of the continued operation of energy transactions, is Article 3 (7), according to which '[c]o-operative or coordinated action shall take into account relevant principles adopted in international agreements, aimed at protection and improvement of the environment, to which Contracting Parties are parties'. Yet, the PEEREA has so far remained at the margin of the ECT system,[71] thereby epitomising the limited

[67] PEEREA, Articles 14 and 15.
[68] PEEREA, Article 10(1) and 11(1) of PEEREA.
[69] See ECT, Article 19(3)(a)–(d) and PEEREA, Article 2(4)–(7).
[70] Emphasis added.
[71] The actual operation of the Protocol has attracted almost no attention from commentators. See e.g. P. Vajda, V. Aleksic, T. Hunter, 'Article 19: Environmental Aspects', in R. Leal-Arcas (ed.), *Commentary on the Energy Charter Treaty* (Cheltenham: Edward

incidence of the rules regulating negative externalities in a legal context designed first and foremost to enable and protect international energy transactions.

III 'General' Rules Limiting Negative Externalities

3.1 Stages of Intervention

The negative externalities of energy transactions are more generally addressed by a substantial number of 'general' rules of international law, whether treaty-based or customary, energy-specific or unspecific, concerned with environmental and/or human protection. Their 'general' character is understood as the absence of an explicit legal connection (e.g. a treaty provision, a shared 'context' or shared institutions) and therefore the need to rely on unspecific connectors such as the rule of systemic integration (Article 31(3)(c) of the VCLT), general rules of conflict (*lex specialis, lex posterior, lex superior*) or considerations of applicable law in a given dispute. As a result of their diversity, some of these rules are often excluded from accounts of energy governance. The main difficulty in dealing with such diversity is to strike a balance between what is genuinely relevant and what is not and, with respect to the former, how to organise the analysis in a way that the relevance to energy governance is readily understood.

To tackle this problem, the following discussion is structured around a spectrum defined by two criteria: whether the negative externality (a single event or a continuous flow) is 'tolerated', i.e. allowed to occur, or not, i.e. considered to be in violation of a rule; and whether the non-tolerated harm caused by the externality has materialised or not. On this basis, four broad stages of intervention can be identified in the rules and instruments discussed in this section: cost internalisation (addressing tolerated negative externalities); prevention (preventing the occurrence of a non-tolerated negative externality); response (containment of the negative externalities of an event which has occurred); reparation (allocating *ex post facto* the costs of the harmful event). The examination of the main rules relating to the protection of both human beings (with their many associated values) and the environment is organised around this spectrum.

Elgar, 2018), para. 19.08; K. Hober, *Energy Charter Treaty. A Commentary* (Oxford: Oxford University Press, 2020), pp. 350–352.

3.2 *Cost Internalisation*

The rules operating at this stage of intervention are a direct expression of the distinction between transactions and (negative) externalities. Their purpose is to tackle the negative externalities without impeding the transaction. The economic rationale is to correct what the relevant theory sees as a sub-optimal operation of market forces, which places a cost on third parties to a transaction rather than on the transaction participants (producers and consumers) themselves. The intervention seeks to reflect in the price of the good or service exchanged in the transaction the full cost of such transaction for the wider society (third parties), including the environment as such. Such correction can be introduced by means of a market mechanism, such as a tax or a trading scheme. In both cases, the assumption is that the negative externality, i.e. the side effect, is tolerable and does not warrant the outright suspension, modification or termination of the transaction.

3.2.1 The Polluter-Pays Principle

The idea of cost internalisation found legal expression in the early 1970s in the form of the 'polluter-pays principle'.[72] This principle has been formulated in an authoritative manner in Principle 16 of the Rio Declaration:

> National authorities should endeavour to promote the internalization of environmental costs and the use of economic instruments, taking into account the approach that the polluter should, in principle, bear the cost of pollution, with due regard to the public interest and without distorting international trade and investment.

This principle features in some energy-specific treaty instruments discussed earlier, such as the ECT[73] and – indirectly – in its PEEREA,[74] as well as in many other instruments relating to environmental protection in general.[75] Importantly, the operation of the polluter-pays principle

[72] See P. Schwartz, 'Principle 16', in J. E. Viñuales (ed.), *The Rio Declaration on Environment and Development. A Commentary* (Oxford: Oxford University Press, 2015), pp. 429–450.

[73] ECT, Article 19(1) (chapeau).

[74] PEEREA, Articles 1(2)(b) (indirectly by reference to a full reflection of costs in pricing), 3(2)(a) (indirectly by reference to a full reflection of costs in pricing), 3(7) (indirectly by reference to principles).

[75] See A. Boyle, 'Polluter Pays', *Max Planck Encyclopedia of Public International Law* (March 2009).

differs from that of other principles discussed later in that it seeks to guide the domestic action of States rather than inter-State relations. This is clearly stated in the first sentence of Principle 16, which emphasises '*national authorities* should endeavour [...]' (emphasis added). It is therefore unsurprising that most cost internalisation schemes are found at the domestic level.

Historically, a pioneering application of this approach was the acid rain tradable permits system introduced by the 1990s amendments of the Clean Air Act in the United States.[76] This scheme focussed on emissions of sulphur dioxide arising from coal-fired electricity plants. It required the Environmental Protection Agency to subject significant electricity plants to a system of SO_2 tradable allowances initially allocated on the basis of prior fuel use. Each regulated entity was required to submit allowances for its emissions, if necessary, purchasing them from other entities. Over time, the overall cap would decline, and a certain percentage of the allowances would be auctioned (rather than allocated free of charge). The ultimate goal was to achieve a SO_2 emissions reduction of 50 per cent as compared to 1980 levels.

Significant levels of emission reduction (approximately 36 per cent between 1990 and 2004) were achieved despite an increase by 25 per cent of electricity generation from regulated utilities over the same period. The cost of such reduction was comparatively lower, according to Schmalensee and Stavins, than what achieving such reduction through command-and-control regulation would have costed. Hence the economic efficiency argument underpinning cost internationalisation through market mechanisms.

3.2.2 Pricing Mechanisms

Pricing mechanisms, including not only trading schemes (which create a market and therefore a price) but also taxes (which reflect the social cost of a transaction), have significantly developed in the context of climate change policies. The World Bank's annual *State and Trends of Carbon Pricing* offers an overview of the regional, domestic and sub-national mechanisms of carbon pricing. In its 2019 edition,[77] it reports fifty-seven

[76] See R. Schmalensee and R. N. Stavins, 'Policy Evolution under the Clean Air Act' (2019) 33 *Journal of Economic Perspectives* 27, at 37–38, which I follow in the discussion of this scheme.

[77] World Bank, *State and Trends of Carbon Pricing 2019* (Washington, DC: World Bank, 2019).

carbon pricing mechanisms around the world, either established or planned (twenty-eight trading systems and twenty-nine carbon taxes). However, such mechanisms cover only 20 per cent of global annual emissions and, importantly, only 5 per cent of them set a sufficiently high price of carbon (USD 40–80 per tonne of CO_2 by 2020 and USD 50–100 per tonne of CO_2 by 2030). Although the carbon price may change, the latter point emphasises one of the key considerations that must be taken into account when assessing cost internalisation as an approach to reduce negative externalities, namely that the relevant mechanisms may be too deferent to the pursuit of the underlying transaction. In other words, the correction entirely depends on whether the set price is genuinely capable of changing behaviour and curbing emissions.

At the international level, the main market mechanisms envisioned by international rules and relevant for energy concern the trading of certain rights to emit greenhouse gases. Article 17 of the Kyoto Protocol[78] established a system according to which States Parties subject to emission-reduction commitments can buy and sell their allowances (assigned amount units) as well as some other units resulting from certain activities (removal units or RMUs from land-use, land-use change and forestry activities, emission reduction units or ERUs from joint implementation activities under Article 6, and certified emission reduction units or CERs from the clean development mechanism established by Article 12) by means of a system of registries overseen by an international transactions log (ITL).[79] The purpose of international emissions trading under Kyoto was to improve flexibility and efficiency in achieving the commitments undertaken by countries listed in Annex B. Such commitments were formulated in the form of quantified emission-reduction targets of a basket of greenhouse gases listed in Annex A. The Kyoto Protocol and the relevant decisions of its institutions provide the basis for the trading system. Of note, the Protocol does not require, specifically, the adoption of a trading system by its States Parties at the regional, domestic or sub-national levels, although States are free to do so.

[78] Decision 11/CMP.1, Modalities, rules and guidelines for emissions trading under Article 17 of the Kyoto Protocol, FCCC/KP/CMP/2005/8/Add.2; Decision 13/CMP.1, Modalities for the accounting of assigned amounts under Article 7, paragraph 4, of the Kyoto Protocol, FCCC/KP/CMP/2005/8/Add.2.

[79] The checks performed by the administrator of the ITL before a transaction is allowed to proceed are described in the DES (*Data Exchange Standards for Registry Systems under the Kyoto Protocol*, 24 November 2013), section 4.6.

That was confirmed by the Court of Justice of the European Union in *Air Transport Association of America v. Secretary of State.*[80] In this case, an association of air carriers challenged before UK courts the extension of the Emissions Trading Directive,[81] which establishes the European trading system, to cover aviation and, more specifically, to require the offsetting of emissions generated by flights taking off or landing in EU territory. The High Court of England and Wales requested a preliminary ruling to the European Court. The latter examined several arguments regarding the legality of the extension under both EU and international law. With respect to the Kyoto Protocol, it noted that:

> even though the Kyoto Protocol imposes quantified greenhouse gas reduction commitments with regard to the commitment period corresponding to the years 2008 to 2012, the parties to the protocol may comply with their obligations in the manner and at the speed upon which they agree.[82]

It further noted that Article 2(2) of the Kyoto Protocol, which provides that States Parties are to pursue the limitation of emissions from aviation through the International Civil Aviation Organization (ICAO), was not specific enough for the applicants to rely on as a ground to challenge the extension of the ETS.[83] More generally, the ECJ concluded that the extension was lawful.

The matter was subsequently settled politically and through the development, within the context of ICAO, of an offsetting system known as CORSIA (Carbon Offsetting and Reduction Scheme for International Aviation). Like Kyoto's emissions trading system, CORSIA is an international mechanism based on a set of decisions of ICAO's Assembly.[84]

[80] *Air Transport Association of America and Others v. Secretary of State for Energy and Climate Change*, CJEU Case C-366/10 (21 December 2011).

[81] Directive 2003/87/EC of the European Parliament and of the Council of 13 October 2003 establishing a scheme for greenhouse gas emission allowance trading within the Community and amending Council Directive 96/61/E, OJ 2003 L 0087, 25 June 2009 (consolidated version) [ETS Directive].

[82] *Air Transport Association*, para. 76.

[83] *Air Transport Association*, para. 77.

[84] CORSIA is based on three resolutions of the ICAO Assembly, namely Resolution A40–19: *Consolidated statement of continuing ICAO policies and practices related to environmental protection – Carbon Offsetting and Reduction Scheme for International Aviation (CORSIA)*; Resolution A40–17: *Consolidated statement of continuing ICAO policies and practices related to environmental protection – General provisions, noise and local air quality*, and Resolution A40–18: *Consolidated statement of continuing ICAO policies and practices related to environmental protection – Climate change*. On

Its implementation is spread in three phases: pilot (2021–2023), first phase (2024–2026), and second phase (2027–2035). Up to 2026, participation is voluntary, and the massive impact of the coronavirus outbreak on aviation will likely discourage widespread participation.

Unlike the Kyoto Protocol or CORSIA, the Paris Agreement does not provide for a global emissions trading system or for other specific cost internalisation measures. But it expressly acknowledges the possibility of their adoption at the regional, domestic or sub-national level, most notably in Article 6(2), which refers to internationally transferred mitigation outcomes or, in other words, to the possibility of using carbon units issued under a given trading system to meet the obligations under another. The modalities and legal bases for such recognition vary from one case to another. As a general matter, they may rest either on international agreements (e.g. the Article 6(2) agreements concluded by Switzerland with countries such as Georgia, Ghana, Peru or Senegal[85]) or on contractual practices, records of understanding or other arrangements which are not directly governed by international law. That makes them part of the wider phenomenon of carbon pricing systems regularly charted by the World Bank's *State and Trends of Carbon Pricing* series.

3.3 Prevention of Harm

3.3.1 Overview

The centre of gravity of the general rules addressing the negative externalities of energy transactions is clearly on the prevention of harm to the protected objects. A wide body of rules, both of customary international law and treaty law, protect humans and the environment from excessive (non-tolerated) harm but, in most cases, they are unspecific (to energy), and their general character sometimes limits their practical operation in the context of energy transactions.

Given the fact that international energy transactions sometimes take place in disputed areas, it is useful to make a distinction in the analysis between principles of customary international law, which are applicable to all States, and treaty-based regulation. This distinction is further

the operation of CORSIA see ICAO *Environmental Report* (2019), chapter 6: 'Climate Change Mitigation: CORSIA'.

[85] Available at <https://www.bafu.admin.ch/bafu/en/home/topics/climate/info-specialists/climate-international-affairs/staatsvertraege-umsetzung-klimauebereinkommen-von-paris-artikel6.html>

warranted because the operation of these 'general' rules can only rely on general connectors, such as the systemic integration rule (Article 31(3)(c) of the VCLT) or broader considerations of applicable law, which are both sensitive to the scope of application of the relevant rules (universal for general international law and party-specific for treaties). The following paragraphs discuss, first, the operation of customary international environmental law in the context of energy disputes (3.3.2) and then briefly surveys a number of treaty-systems which set both procedural (3.3.3) and substantive limitations (3.3.4) on energy transactions.

3.3.2 Principles of Customary International Environmental Law

The identification of the content and nature of the main principles of international environmental law has been fraught with disagreement and contradiction. Part of the problem came from the relative novelty of the norms, which despite their anchor in traditional concepts of international law such as due diligence,[86] no harm[87] and the prohibition of *abus de droit*,[88] were often seen as either aspirational considerations or, conversely, blunt instruments of little practical use in a high-stakes energy context.

That has now changed. In the last several years, a body of case law arising from a range of international courts and tribunals, and most notably from the ICJ, has shed light on the main principles of international environmental law which have customary grounding.[89] The core principles are stated in paragraph 104 of the ICJ's 2015 judgement in the case *Costa Rica/Nicaragua*, where the Court noted that:

> to fulfil its obligation to *exercise due diligence in preventing significant transboundary environmental harm*, a State must, before embarking on an

[86] See J. E. Viñuales, 'Due diligence in international environmental law: A fine-grained cartography', in H. Krieger, A. Peters, L. Kreuzer (eds.), *Due Diligence in the International Legal Order* (Oxford: Oxford University Press, 2020), pp. 111–128; S. Besson, 'La Due Diligence en droit international' (2020) 409 *RCADI* 153.

[87] See L.-A. Duvic-Paoli, *The Prevention Principle in International Environmental Law* (Cambridge: Cambridge University Press, 2018); Xue Hanqin, *Transboundary Damage in International Law* (Cambridge: Cambridge University Press, 2003).

[88] See J. Paulsson, *The Unruly Notion of Abuse of Rights* (Cambridge: Cambridge University Press, 2020); A. Kiss, *L'abus de droit en droit international* (Paris: LGDJ, 1952).

[89] *Certain Activities Carried Out by Nicaragua in the Border Area (Costa Rica v. Nicaragua) and Construction of a Road in Costa Rica along the San Juan River (Nicaragua v. Costa Rica)*, Judgment, ICJ Reports 2015, p. 665 [*Costa Rica/Nicaragua – Judgment*].

> activity having the potential adversely to affect the environment of another State, *ascertain if there is a risk of significant transboundary harm, which would trigger the requirement to carry out an environmental impact assessment.* [...] If the environmental impact assessment confirms that there is a risk of significant transboundary harm, the State planning to undertake the activity is required, in conformity with its due diligence obligation, *to notify and consult in good faith* with the potentially affected State, where that is necessary to determine the appropriate measures to prevent or mitigate that risk.[90]

This concise statement has many merits and some problems. As a general matter, it states three main principles, namely the principle of prevention of environmental harm (an application of the duty of due diligence), the requirement to conduct an environmental impact assessment (EIA) prior to the launching of activities of a certain scope, and the duty to cooperate in good faith through notification of and consultation with the affected States. These three principles are of great importance for the regulation of the negative externalities of energy transactions. I will, first, briefly characterise them, and then discuss some specific illustrations of their relevance derived from the case law.

The principle of prevention of environmental harm is solidly rooted in customary international law.[91] Its main formulation is found in Principle 2 of the Rio Declaration on Environment and Development, which reproduces, with a minor (but not insignificant) modification, the text of Principle 21 of the Stockholm Declaration on the Human

[90] *Costa Rica/Nicaragua – Judgment*, para. 104 (emphasis added).

[91] *Legality of the Threat or Use of Nuclear Weapons,* ICJ Reports 1996, p. 226, para. 29; *Gabčíkovo-Nagymaros Project (Hungary v. Slovakia),* Judgment, ICJ Reports 1997, p. 7, para. 140; *Pulp Mills on the River Uruguay (Argentina* v. *Uruguay),* Judgment, ICJ Reports 2010, p. 14, para. 101; *Costa Rica/Nicaragua – Judgment,* para. 104, 118; *Iron Rhine Arbitration (Ijzeren Rijn) (Belgium/Netherlands),* Award (24 May 2005), RIAA XXVII, pp. 35–125 [*Iron Rhine arbitration*], paras. 59, 222; *In the matter of the Indus Waters Kishenganga Arbitration before the Court of Arbitration constituted in accordance with the Indus Waters Treaty 1960 between the Government of India and the Government of Pakistan signed on 19 September 1960 (Islamic Republic of Pakistan v. Republic of India),* PCA, Partial Award (18 February 2013) [*Indus Water Kishenganga – Partial Award*], paras. 448–451; *Ghana/Côte d'Ivoire – Provisional measures,* para. 71; *In the matter of the South China Sea Arbitration before an Arbitral Tribunal constituted under Annex VII of the United Nations Convention on the Law of the Sea (Republic of the Philippines v. People's Republic of China),* PCA Case No. 2013–19, Award (12 July 2016) [*South China Sea Arbitration*], para. 941. See generally L.-A. Duvic Paoli and J. E. Viñuales, 'Principle 2: Prevention', in J. E. Viñuales (ed.), *The Rio Declaration on Environment and Development. A Commentary* (Oxford: Oxford University Press, 2015), pp. 107–138.

Environment: 'States have … the sovereign right to exploit their own resources … and the responsibility to ensure that activities within their jurisdiction or control do not cause damage to the environment of other States or of areas beyond the limits of national jurisdiction'. This formulation contains three main components, namely the right to exploit natural resources, the no harm principle (reformulated in an environmental light) and the duty to prevent harm to the global commons. The latter component highlights that prevention is no longer about good neighbourliness or, in other words, about the interest of the potentially affected State but about the protection of the environment *per se*. This point is confirmed by several decisions which have considered that the duty applies irrespective of the territorial situation of the relevant areas, even when they are disputed.[92] Thus, the exploration and exploitation of energy resources must respect the prevention principle, even if the area is considered to be within the territory of the State conducting or permitting the activity (see further Chapter 4). Two additional specifications regarding the scope of the principle concern the characterisation of the requisite 'harm' and the relevance of 'risk', even in the absence of actual harm. The Draft Articles on Prevention adopted in 2001 by the UN International Law Commission[93] clarify these two aspects stating that harm must be 'significant'[94] and that the creation of 'risk' of such harm may be sufficient to breach the principle.[95]

From a procedural standpoint, the prevention principle is extended by the EIA requirement and the duty to cooperate. These two extensions do not exhaust the content of prevention, which remains operative together

[92] *Dispute Concerning Delimitation of the Maritime Boundary between Ghana and Côte d'Ivoire in the Atlantic Ocean (Ghana/Côte d'Ivoire)*, ITLOS Case No. 23, Order (25 April 2015) [*Ghana/Côte d'Ivoire – Provisional measures*], paras. 68–73; *Request for an Advisory Opinion Submitted by the Sub-Regional Fisheries Commission (SRFC)*, Advisory Opinion (2 April 2015), ITLOS Case No. 21 [*IUU Advisory Opinion*], paras. 111, 120; *South China Sea Arbitration*, paras. 927 and 940; *Dispute Concerning Coastal State Rights in the Black Sea, Sea of Azov, and Kerch Strait (Ukraine v. Russian Federation)*, PCA Case No. 2017–06, Award concerning the preliminary objections of the Russian Federation (21 February 2020), para. 295. All these cases refer to Article 192 of the UNCLOS together with the prevention principle.

[93] Draft Articles on the Prevention of Transboundary Harm from Hazardous Activities, 12 December 2001, GA Res. 56/82, UN Doc. A/RES/56/82 [ILC Prevention Articles], Articles 2(a) and 3.

[94] *Trail Smelter Arbitration*, RIAA, vol. III, pp. 1905–1982 (*Trail Smelter*), p. 1965, at 1980; ILC Prevention Articles, Art 2(a); *Pulp Mills on the River Uruguay (Argentina v. Uruguay)*, Judgment, ICJ Reports 2010, p. 14, para. 101.

[95] ILC Prevention Articles, Article 3.

with, as well as beyond these two procedural duties. The most authoritative formulation of the EIA requirement in international law is provided in Principle 17 of the Rio Declaration: 'Environmental impact assessment, as a national instrument, shall be undertaken for proposed activities that are likely to have a significant adverse impact on the environment and are subject to a decision of a competent national authority'. In this formulation, the requirement has been deemed to result from customary international law.[96] Some additional comment is necessary to clarify the requirement's content, spatial scope of application and relations with prevention and cooperation. Regarding the *content*, the ICJ identified some basic parameters, such as the application to 'activities' (by contrast to policies or plans)[97] and the need for the EIA to be conducted 'prior' to the approval of the relevant activity and for the impact to remain monitored.[98] Yet, beyond this basic content, the ICJ considered that the specific content of the assessment is for each State to define in its domestic laws and regulations.[99] Moreover, the actual 'trigger' of the requirement is not entirely clear. In their English version, both Principle 17 and the ILC Prevention Articles speak of 'significant adverse impact', thereby equating the trigger with the 'significant' environmental harm that must be prevented under the prevention principle. However, the French and Spanish versions use a higher threshold, a distinction of wording which was preserved in the case law.[100] Given these differences of wording, it appears that more than mere risk of significant harm is needed to trigger the EIA requirement. With respect to the *spatial scope* of the norm, although the ICJ initially recognised it as applying in a transboundary context,[101] other tribunals have also

[96] *Pulp Mills*, para. 204; *Responsibilities and Obligations of States sponsoring Persons and Entities with respect to Activities in the Area*, Case No. 17, ITLOS (Seabed Dispute Chamber), Advisory Opinion (1 February 2011) [*Responsibilities in the Area*], paras. 145, 148; *Costa Rica/Nicaragua*, para. 104.

[97] N. Craik, 'Principle 17: Environmental Impact Assessment', in J. E. Viñuales (ed.), *The Rio Declaration on Environment and Development. A Commentary* (Oxford: Oxford University Press, 2015), pp. 451–70, at 456.

[98] *Pulp Mills*, para. 205.

[99] *Pulp Mills*, para. 205.

[100] The French version of Principle 17 refers to 'effets nocifs importants' (rather than to dommage 'significatif') and the ICJ has spoken of 'impact préjudiciable important' (*Pulp Mills*, para. 204) or 'risque de dommage transfrontière important' (*Costa Rica/Nicaragua*, para. 104). The Spanish version of Principle 17 uses the word 'considerable' (rather than 'sensible') to qualify the risk of harm.

[101] *Pulp Mills*, paras. 204–205; *Costa Rica/Nicaragua*, para. 104.

recognised it as applying to activities in the global commons[102] and, importantly, in disputed areas.[103] Finally, concerning the relations with prevention and cooperation, in *Costa Rica/Nicaragua*, the ICJ suggested the existence of a sequence whereby the duty to notify and consult cannot emerge until an EIA has ascertained the requisite risk. In turn, the EIA would not be required unless a preliminary assessment signals its need. Such a sequence would, in practice, mean that the State of origin of the activity is entitled to unilaterally conduct a preliminary assessment (the content of which is also defined by its laws), then as the case may be to unilaterally conduct an EIA (the content of which is, again, defined by its laws), and only then a duty to notify and consult would emerge. A more consistent solution would place the entire conduct of the State of origin under the due diligence requirements arising from the prevention principle, which depending on the circumstances, may call for notification and consultation earlier in the process and indeed require the content of both the preliminary assessment and the EIA to meet international standards.

As for the duty to cooperate, a distinction must be made between cooperation in a transboundary context (Rio Declaration, Principles 19 and 18) and cooperation 'in a spirit of global partnership' (Rio Declaration, Principles 7 and 27). Only the former has been recognised as having customary grounding.[104] Principle 19 of the Rio Declaration formulates this duty as follows: 'States shall provide prior and timely notification and relevant information to potentially affected States on activities that may have a significant adverse transboundary environmental effect and shall consult with those States at an early stage and in good faith'.[105] Principle 18, which emerged from the Chernobyl disaster, further states, in its first sentence, that: 'States shall immediately notify other States of any natural disasters or other emergencies that are likely to produce sudden harmful effects on the environment of those States'. Although the trigger of the duty, as noted earlier, is subject to

[102] *Responsibilities in the Area*, paras. 145, 148.

[103] *South China Sea Arbitration*, paras. 947–948.

[104] *Pulp Mills*, paras. 77, 102, 144–146; *Costa Rica/Nicaragua*, paras. 104, 106; *IUU Advisory Opinion*, para. 139–140; *Ghana/Côte d'Ivoire – Provisional measures*, para. 73; *South China Sea Arbitration*, paras. 946, 984–985.

[105] See L. Boisson de Chazournes and K. Sangbana, 'Principle 19: Notification and consultation on activities with transboundary impact', in J. E. Viñuales (ed.), *The Rio Declaration on Environment and Development. A Commentary* (Oxford: Oxford University Press, 2015), pp. 492–507.

some ambiguities, the key consideration remains the existence of the requisite risk. The commentary to Article 4 of the ILC Prevention Articles, notes that '[t]he requirement of cooperation of States extends to all phases of planning and of implementation' because the potentially affected State 'may know better than anybody else ... which features of the activity in question may be more damaging to it, or which zones of its territory close to the border may be more affected by the transboundary effects of the activity, such as a specially vulnerable ecosystem'.[106] With respect to the content of the duty, it encompasses the procedural requirements to notify and consult as well as other procedural steps, including requests of assistance,[107] information exchange regarding the state of a shared resource,[108] consultations even in the absence of notification[109] etc. Thus, there is no necessary sequence between these procedural steps. The ultimate goal, as noted before, is the display of due diligence in preventing significant environmental harm.

The operation of these principles in the specific context of energy-related disputes can be illustrated by reference to some cases. They are selected to show the operation of these broad 'general' norms in three main contexts, namely hydrocarbon extraction, hydroelectricity projects in shared watercourses, and seabed mining of critical minerals. In the context of hydrocarbon exploration and extraction, the matter arose in a dispute between *Ghana* and *Côte d'Ivoire* submitted to a Special Chamber of the International Tribunal for the Law of the Sea (ITLOS).[110] The dispute concerned what Ghana argued to be a mere demarcation (by virtue of an alleged 'tacit agreement') and Côte d'Ivoire an actual single line delimitation of both countries' territorial seas, exclusive economic zones and continental shelfs in the Atlantic Ocean. Oil activities, including the granting of oil concessions, seismic surveys and drilling operations, had been ongoing for several years in the disputed area. At the beginning of the proceedings, Côte d'Ivoire requested the Special Chamber to order the suspension of Ghana's oil activities in the disputed area. The request aimed to preserve the rights of Côte d'Ivoire over the resources in that area, and it specifically referred to

[106] *ILC Prevention Articles*, commentary ad Article t 4, para. 1.
[107] *ILC Prevention Articles*, commentary ad Article 4, paras. 5 and 6.
[108] *ILC Prevention Articles*, Article 12.
[109] *ILC Prevention Articles*, Article 11.
[110] *Ghana/Côte d'Ivoire – Provisional measures* and Judgment (23 September 2017) [*Ghana/Côte d'Ivoire – Judgment*].

the need to prevent serious harm to the environment pending the proceedings on the merits.[111] According to Côte d'Ivoire, Ghana's environmental legislation did not meet international standards and the activities threatened wetlands and a national park protected under the Ramsar Convention[112] and the World Heritage Convention. The Special Chamber recalled Articles 192 (duty to protect and preserve the marine environment) and 193 (right of States to exploit natural resources 'in accordance with their duty to protect and preserve the marine environment') and, of particular note, it also recalled the customary international law principles of prevention and cooperation.[113] The effect of these principles was, however, nuanced. The Special Chamber ordered the suspension of new drilling activities only and allowed the continuation of existing activities inter alia because:

> the suspension of ongoing activities conducted by Ghana in respect of which drilling has already taken place would entail the risk of considerable financial loss to Ghana and its concessionaires and could also pose a serious danger to the marine environment resulting, in particular, from the deterioration of equipment [. . .] such an order could also cause harm to the marine environment.[114]

In the subsequent proceedings, Côte d'Ivoire argued that Ghana's continued activities were in breach of the environmental protection requirements set in the order. But the Special Chamber rejected the argument noting that Ghana had not conducted any 'new' drilling.[115] The interest of this case for present purposes lies in the Special Chamber's reliance, however limited, on customary international environmental law and, more specifically, in the understanding that the relevant principles apply to a disputed area. This point is significant, and it has been restated by an arbitral tribunal constituted under Annex VII of the UN Convention on the Law of the Sea in a pending dispute between *Ukraine and Russia* concerning, in part, fossil fuel extraction in a disputed (occupied) area.[116] Ukraine argues that Russia is unlawfully exploring and extracting

[111] Request for the prescription of provisional measures submitted by the Republic of Côte d'Ivoire under Article 290, paragraph 1, of the United Nations Convention on the Law of the Sea [*Request of Côte d'Ivoire*], paras. 3 and 46–52.

[112] Convention on Wetlands of International Importance especially as Waterfowl Habitat, 2 February 1971, 996 UNTS 245 [Ramsar Convention].

[113] *Ghana/Côte d'Ivoire – Provisional measures*, paras. 69–73.

[114] *Ghana/Côte d'Ivoire – Provisional measures*, paras. 99 and 101.

[115] *Ghana/Côte d'Ivoire – Judgment*, paras. 650–652.

[116] See *Ukraine v. Russia*.

hydrocarbons in the occupied area, whereas Russia contends that the UNCLOS is not relevant because the disputed area falls in internal waters. In its decision on preliminary objections, the tribunal left the determination of this argument to the merits, but it noted that 'the obligation to protect and preserve the marine environment under Article 192 applies to "all maritime areas". Such areas, in the Arbitral Tribunal's view, undoubtedly include internal waters'.[117]

The operation of customary international environmental law has been fleshed out in some more detail in the context of the *Indus Water Kishenganga* arbitration.[118] This case concerned a dispute between India and Pakistan regarding India's Kishenganga Hydro-Electric Project (KHEP). Both India and Pakistan planned to exploit the hydro-electric potential of a river (named Kishenganga in India's administered portion of Kashmir and Neelum in Pakistan's administered portion), but India moved first. The Kishenganga/Neelum is a tributary of the Jhelum river and thereby a part of the Indus system of rivers. Pakistan argued that the KHEP was in breach of the 1960 Indus Water Treaty between the two countries and, more specifically, of the obligations under Articles III (2) (to let flow the waters of the Western rivers and not permit any interference with those waters) and IV(6) (maintenance of natural channels) (first dispute) and that India could not bring the level of the reservoir below a certain threshold (Dead Storage Level) except in an unforeseen emergency (second dispute). The environmental dimension of the dispute is noteworthy because the Indus Water Treaty makes no reference to environmental protection. Paragraph 29 of Annexure G of the Treaty directs, however, the arbitral court seized of a dispute to apply 'whenever necessary for [the Treaty's] interpretation or application, but only to the extent necessary for that purpose [...] customary international law'. The court relied on this provision as well as on some

[117] *Ukraine v. Russia*, para. 295, relying on *Request for Advisory Opinion Submitted by the Sub-Regional Fisheries Commission*, Advisory Opinion of 2 April 2015, ITLOS Reports 2015, p. 4, para. 120 (referring to Article 192 of the UNCLOS). The same paragraph was relied upon for the same purpose by another Annex VII tribunal in *South China Sea Arbitration*, para. 940. This tribunal further noted, by reference to the prevention principle, that customary international law informs the content of Article 192 of the UNCLOS, *South China Sea Arbitration*, para. 941.

[118] *In the matter of the Indus Waters Kishenganga Arbitration before the Court of Arbitration constituted in accordance with the Indus Waters Treaty 1960 between the Government of India and the Government of Pakistan signed on 19 September 1960 (Islamic Republic of Pakistan v. Republic of India)*, PCA, Partial Award (18 February 2013) [*Indus Water Kishenganga – Partial Award*].

previous decisions, most notably those rendered in the *Iron Rhine* arbitration[119] and the case concerning the *Gabčíkovo-Nagymaros Project*,[120] to interpret the Treaty in the light of customary international environmental law[121] so as to ensure the maintenance of a minimum environmental flow downstream of the KHEP. Because such flow could not be quantified with the information provided in the proceedings leading to the first partial award, the court requested further information and determined the minimal flow in the final award. Three main conclusions must be derived from this case. First, the arbitral court confirmed that it had to interpret the 1960 'in light of the customary international principles for the protection of the environment in force today'.[122] Secondly, the court provided two bases for such an interpretation, i.e. paragraph 29 of the Annexure G but also the established principle that 'international environmental law must be taken into account even when (unlike the present case) interpreting treaties concluded before the development of that body of law'.[123] Thirdly, the effects of this interpretation were specifically quantified in the final award requiring a certain number of extra cubic metres per second (cumecs) of water to maintain the minimum downstream environmental flow. The court made clear that environmental considerations remained subject to the agreement of the parties, which *in casu* meant that the flow set on the basis of environmental considerations alone (twelve cumecs) had to be adjusted down (to nine cumecs) to reflect the bargain in the Treaty.[124]

The third illustration concerns the risks posed by the growing interest in the exploration and extraction of certain minerals used for batteries, wind and photovoltaic equipment (see further Chapter 8) from the seabed and subsoil beyond national jurisdiction, i.e. the Area. In a 2011 *Advisory Opinion on the Responsibility of States sponsoring activities in the Area*,[125] the ITLOS Seabed Chamber clarified the implications of

[119] *Iron Rhine Arbitration.*
[120] *Gabčíkovo-Nagymaros Project.*
[121] *Indus Water Kishenganga – Partial Award*, paras. 445–454.
[122] *Indus Water Kishenganga – Partial Award*, para. 452.
[123] *Indus Water Kishenganga – Partial Award*, para. 452.
[124] *In the matter of the Indus Waters Kishenganga Arbitration before the Court of Arbitration constituted in accordance with the Indus Waters Treaty 1960 between the Government of India and the Government of Pakistan signed on 19 September 1960 (Islamic Republic of Pakistan v. Republic of India)*, PCA, Final Award (20 December 2014), para. 112–116.
[125] *Responsibilities in the Area.*

several principles of customary international environmental law for such activities. The opinion was requested by the Council of the International Seabed Authority (ISA), itself prompted by a letter of Nauru. The broader context of the request[126] is provided by the system of Part XI of the UNCLOS (the Area), as effectively amended by the 1994 Implementation Agreement.[127] In order to obtain an exploration or exploitation licence, an entity must be sponsored by a State Party to the UNCLOS,[128] and it must submit two areas for consideration. The ISA decides which area is granted to the applicant and the other area is reserved for activities 'in association with developing States'.[129] Nauru and Tonga made proposals for activities in reserved areas, but they soon grew concerned about their potential legal exposure in case of harm. For this reason, Nauru wrote to the ISA for it to request an advisory opinion to the ITLOS Seabed Chamber to clarify such exposure. The request identified three main questions, which can be summarised as follows: (1) What are the obligations of sponsoring States? (2) What is the extent of liability of a sponsoring State in case a sponsored entity fails to comply with the applicable standards? (3) What are the 'necessary and appropriate' measures a sponsoring State must adopt to comply with its obligations? The Seabed Chamber replied, in essence, that sponsoring States are not strictly liable (although they could be made so in the future[130]) for the harm caused by sponsored entities but that they are subject to a high level of due diligence determined by the UNCLOS (Articles 139(1), 153 (4), 206 and Annex 3, Article 4(4)), the ISA's regulations (Nodules Regulations, Sulphides Regulations), the 1994 Implementation Agreement (annex, section 1(7)) and, of particular note, also by customary international environmental law, including the prevention

[126] See D. Freestone, 'Responsibilities and Obligations of States Sponsoring Persons and Entities with Respect to Activities in the Area' (2011) 105 *American Journal of International Law* 755.

[127] Agreement relating to the implementation of Part XI of the United Nations Convention on the Law of the Sea of 10 December 1982, 28 July 1994, 1836 UNTS 3 [1994 Implementation Agreement].

[128] UNCLOS, Article 153(2)(b).

[129] UNCLOS, Annex III, Article 8. The other option, i.e. development by the Enterprise envisioned in Part XI, was effectively shelved following the 1994 Implementation Agreement.

[130] *Responsibilities in the Area*, paras. 209, 211.

principle,[131] the requirement to conduct an EIA,[132] and the precautionary approach (deemed a custom in *statu nascendi*).[133] On whether developing countries were subject to a lower bar, the Seabed Chamber's answer was a clear no, most likely to avoid the risk of sponsoring States of 'convenience'.[134]

3.3.3 Procedural Requirements

3.3.3.1 Impact Assessments In addition to the customary norm requiring the conduct of an EIA, several treaties require States to assess the environmental impact of a proposed activity (EIA) and, in some cases, of plans and policies. The latter assessments are called 'Strategic Environmental Assessments' (SEAs). The practice emerged in the late 1960s, with the adoption in the United States of the National Environmental Policy Act, and it was widely adopted around the world.[135]

On the international plane, the main instrument was adopted within the context of the UN Economic Commission for Europe, namely the 1991 Espoo Convention on Environmental Impact Assessment in a Transboundary Context (Espoo Convention)[136] and its 2003 Kyiv Protocol on Strategic Environmental Assessment (Kyiv Protocol).[137] Article 2(1) of the Espoo Convention places the entire system under the broad duty of prevention, albeit narrowly formulated in a transboundary context: '[t]he Parties shall, either individually or jointly, take all appropriate and effective measures to prevent, reduce and control significant adverse transboundary environmental impact from proposed

131 *Responsibilities in the Area*, paras. 110–120 (the Seabed Chamber refers here to the ICJ's judgment in *Pulp Mills* as well as to the *ILC Prevention Articles*).

132 *Responsibilities in the Area*, paras. 148–149.

133 *Responsibilities in the Area*, paras. 131–132, 135.

134 *Responsibilities in the Area*, para. 159.

135 See N. Craik, *The International Law of Environmental Impact Assessment* (Cambridge: Cambridge University Press, 2008); N. A. Robinson, 'EIA Abroad: The Comparative and Transnational Experience', in S. G. Hildebrand and J. B. Cannon (eds.), *Environmental Analysis: The NEPA Experience* (Boca Raton: Lewis, 1993), pp. 679–702.

136 Convention on Environmental Impact Assessment in a Transboundary Context, 25 February 1991, 1989 UNTS 310 [Espoo Convention]. At the time of writing, the Espoo Conventnion was binding on the EU and 44 States of the Pan-European region. The United States and Russia are signatories but they have not ratified it. Article 17(3) contemplates the possibility of accession by any UN Member State with approval of the Meeting of the Parties to the Convention.

137 Kyiv Protocol on Strategic Environmental Assessment, 21 May 2003, 2685 UNTS 140 [Kyiv Protocol].

activities'. Within this broad duty, Article 2(2) requires each Party to implement the Convention 'including, with respect to proposed activities listed in Appendix I that are likely to cause significant adverse transboundary impact, the establishment of an environmental impact assessment procedure' with a certain minimal content. The focus is on 'proposed activities', defined as 'any activity or any major change to an activity subject to a decision of a competent authority in accordance with an applicable national procedure' (Article 1(v)). But the key requirement arising from the Convention is to subject to an EIA procedure certain types of proposed activities (listed in Appendix I), which include a range of energy activities.[138] The EIA procedure must be conducted within certain parameters, including the requirement to conduct the EIA prior to authorising or undertaking the activity (Article 2(3)), public participation without discrimination on the basis of location (Article 2(2) and (6)) and some minimal content (Appendix II). The Convention establishes a system of notification (Articles 2(4) and 3) and consultation (Article 5) for proposed activities listed in Appendix I, and it also provides a legal basis for consultations regarding whether a proposed activity not listed in Appendix I should be treated as listed and hence subject to the EIA procedure (Article 2(5)). Article 6 makes clear that the EIA obligation is procedural in nature, i.e. that as long as the outcome of the EIA is duly taken into account, it is for the State of origin to take a decision on the proposed activity. Thus, the outcome of the EIA does not predetermine whether the proposed activity will be approved or undertaken. Article 7 contemplates the possibility of subsequent monitoring the impact of the project.

In 2003, the Kyiv Protocol, in force since 2010, extended the obligation (Article 4(1)) to conduct an assessment of environmental impact, including health, to certain 'plans and programmes' identified in Article 4(2), (3) and (4), which include 'plans and programmes which are prepared for [. . .] energy' and which set the framework for the development of the proposed activities in Appendix I of the Espoo Convention as well as some others.[139] The assessment must provide for public participation

[138] Such as crude oil refineries, gasification and liquefaction installations, thermal power stations, installations for the production, enrichment or reprocessing of nuclear fuels, large diameter oil and gas pipelines, large dams and reservoirs, major extraction of coal, offshore hydrocarbon production, major storage of petroleum.

[139] Annex II of the Kyiv Protocol lists, e.g. nuclear power stations and nuclear reactors, including their decommissioning, construction of overhead electrical power lines, industrial installations for the production of electricity or the carrying of gas, surface storage

(Article 8) and for some minimal content (Article 7), and – like the EIA – it does not predetermine the final decision (Article 11).

The operation of the Espoo Convention has been tested in several occasions, including in the context of an Undersea Methane Pipeline between Italy and Croatia,[140] a Hydropower Station on the border between France and Switzerland,[141] nuclear power plants and expanded spent fuel repositories in Finland[142] or the high-profile Nord Stream pipeline project.[143] The planned construction of a nuclear power plant in England, the Hinkley Point C project (HPC), offers an illustration of how the Espoo Convention operates in a context where different countries disagree as to the potential transboundary impact of a proposed activity. Between November 2009 and December 2012, the United Kingdom made public consultations on six draft energy infrastructure National Policy Statements, including one on nuclear energy, and examined impact assessments submitted by the proponent of the activity, EDF. On this basis, the United Kingdom's Planning Inspectorate considered that the HPC was not likely to have significant effects on the environment of other States of the European Economic Area (EEA) and therefore refrained from entering into transboundary consultations. This prompted reactions from several States as well as from civil society, which highlighted that the public outside the United Kingdom had not been consulted. In March 2013, despite the expressions of concern, the UK Secretary of State for Energy and Climate Change approved the project. The approval was unsuccessfully challenged before UK courts. Subsequently, a member of the German parliament, certain civil society organisations as well as several States Parties to the Espoo Convention submitted information to the Implementation Committee of the Espoo Convention noting that the United Kingdom had failed to appropriately notify potentially affected countries or consult the public therein. On the

of fossil fuels and natural gas, installations for hydroelectric energy production, wind farms, deep geothermal drilling.

140 Undersea Methane Pipeline between Italy and Croatia, Case study factsheet no. 2 (March 2004), available at: www.unece.org/.

141 Chancy-Pougny Hydropower Station, on the border between France and Switzerland, Case study factsheet no. 4 (August 2008), available at: www.unece.org/.

142 Nuclear Power Plants in Finland, Case study factsheet no. 5 (March 2009), and Expansion of a planned spent nuclear fuel repository in Finland, Case study factsheet no. 6 (March 2009), both available at: www.unece.org/.

143 T. Koivoruva and I. Polonen, 'Transboundary Environmental Assessment in the Case of the Baltic Sea Gas Pipeline' (2010) 25 *IJMCL* 151.

basis of the information received and noting that 'there was a profound suspicion of non-compliance', the Committee launched a non-compliance procedure.[144] In its findings, it recalled that, given the aim of the Convention, as stated in Article 2(1), 'even a low likelihood of [transboundary impact] should trigger the obligation to notify affected Parties in accordance with article 3'.[145] It further recalled 'the need to enhance international cooperation in assessing environmental impact as well as the principle of prevention, as referred to in [. . .] the Convention Preamble'.[146] It then observed that the construction of a nuclear power plant was included in Appendix I to the Convention and that the United Kingdom should have notified, in accordance with Articles 2(4) and 3(1) of the Convention, potentially affected countries.[147] This conclusion suggests that the triggering of the processes laid down in the Convention are not a purely unilateral matter.

In addition to the Espoo Convention, other international instruments provide for the requirement to conduct an EIA. As noted earlier, the ITLOS Seabed Chamber recalled the obligation to conduct an EIA under Article 206 of the UNCLOS, section 1(7) of the annex to the 1994 Implementation Agreement and the Nodules (Regulation 31(6)) and Sulphides (Regulation 33(6)) Regulations.[148] Of particular note, the assessment of the environmental (and sometimes also social) impact of an activity may also be required by the operational guidelines of multilateral funding agencies, which often take part in financing operations of energy projects. For example, Performance Standard 1 of the International Finance Corporation (IFC)'s Performance Standards on Environmental and Social Sustainability, require the 'Client' (the receiver of funding) to: 'conduct a process of environmental and social assessment, and establish and maintain an [Environmental and Social Management System] appropriate to the nature and scale of the project and commensurate with the level of its environmental and social risks

[144] *Findings and recommendations further to a Committee initiative concerning the United Kingdom of Great Britain and Northern Ireland* (EIA/IC/CI/5) [*UK – HPC – Espoo*], para. 7. The Implementation Committee has examined other complains under the Espoo Convention relating to proposed nuclear power plants, e.g. in Metsamor, Armenia (EIA/IC/S/3) and Ostrovets, Belarus (EIA/IC/S4).

[145] *UK – HPC – Espoo*, paras. 51 and 57.

[146] *UK – HPC – Espoo*, para. 59.

[147] *UK – HPC – Espoo*, para. 66.

[148] *Responsibilities in the Area*, paras. 141–145.

and impacts'.[149] Failure to comply with this and other requirements may be brought to the attention of the IFC's Compliance Advisor Ombudsman (CAO). Energy-related projects, including hydroelectricity,[150] oil and gas exploration and extraction,[151] pipelines[152] and others have featured prominently in the case law of the CAO. Similar guidelines and procedures exist for regional development banks[153] as well as for other lending institutions. As discussed next, one important aspect in these procedures, which overlaps with other procedural requirements arising from human rights law, concerns public participation.

[149] International Finance Corporation, Performance Standards on Environmental and Social Sustainability (1 January 2012) [IFC Performance Standards], para. 5.

[150] See e.g. *Assessment Report, Assessment by the Office of the Compliance Advisor/Ombudsman in relation to a complaint filed against IFC's investment in ENDESA Pangue S.A., Chile* (May 2003); *Assessment Report, Complaint regarding Allain Duhangan Hydropower Project Himachal Pradesh, India* (23 March 2004); *Stakeholder Assessment and Framework, Ambuklao-Binga Hydroelectric Power-01/Binga, Philippines* (30 July 2008); *Assessment Report: Complaint Regarding the Albania Hydros Project (IFC Project #583387), Tirana, Albania* (April 2013); *Assessment Report, Regarding Community concerns in relation to IFC's Kurum Project (#33378) in Albania* (September 2015); *Assessment Report: Regarding concerns in relation to the Bujagali Energy Ltd. Project (IFC # 24408 & # 33022& MIGA #6732) in Jinja, Uganda* (March 2018).

[151] See e.g. *Assessment Report, Complaint Regarding the Lukoil Overseas Project (Kazakhstan – Karachaganak/03), Western Kazakhstan Oblast, Kazakhstan* (27 April 2009); Appraisal Report: Case of IFC's Involvement Linked to the Jubilee Oil Field, Ghana (June 2011); *Assessment Report: Complaint Regarding the Bankers Petroleum Project (IFC #27306), Patos, Albania* (August 2013).

[152] See e.g. the 33 complaints filed against various organisations related to the Baku-Tbilisi-Ceyhan (BTC) oil and gas pipeline, most recently *Assessment and Conclusion Report, Complaint Regarding the Baku Tbilisi-Ceyhan (BTC) Pipeline (Project #11251), Vale, Georgia* (December 2011); *Assessment Report: Regarding Community and Civil Society concerns in relation to the Chad-Cameroon Petroleum Development and Pipeline Project (#11125) in Chad* (October 2012); *Assessment Report, Regarding concerns in relation to MIGA's Investment in Trans-Anatolian Natural Gas Pipeline (TANAP)Project#13661, in Azerbaijan* (August 2019).

[153] See e.g. European Bank for Reconstruction and Development (EBRD), *Environmental and Social Performance Requirements* (Environmental and Social Policy, 2019), EBRD Performance Requirement 1; Inter-American Development Bank (IADB), *Environment and Safeguards Compliance Policy* (19 January 2006), B.3 Screening and Classification (paragraph 4.17 distinguishing Categories A, B and C, on the basis of the environmental impact of operations); Asian Development Bank, *Safeguard Policy Statement* (June 2009), Appendix 1: Safeguard Requirements 1: Environment (section D, requirement 1: Environmental Assessment); African Development Bank Group's Integrated Safeguards System, *Policy Statement and Operational Safeguards* (December 2013), Operational safeguard 1 – Environmental and social assessment.

3.3.3.2 Procedural Human Rights The procedural dimension of human rights has found expression in three main ways of particular interest to energy,[154] namely the emergence of procedural environmental rights, the reinterpretation of general human rights as encompassing a procedural dimension, and certain specific rights of indigenous and tribal peoples.

3.3.3.2.1 Procedural Environmental Rights The impulsion for the recognition of procedural environmental rights came from Principle 10 of the Rio Declaration, according to which:

> Environmental issues are best handled with the participation of all concerned citizens, at the relevant level. At the national level, each individual shall have appropriate access to information concerning the environment that is held by public authorities, including information on hazardous materials and activities in their communities, and the opportunity to participate in decision-making processes. States shall facilitate and encourage public awareness and participation by making information widely available. Effective access to judicial and administrative proceedings, including redress and remedy, shall be provided.

Although the principle avoids references to ‘rights’, its implementation through the 1998 Aarhus Convention on Access to Information, Public Participation in Decision-Making and Access to Justice in Environmental Matters,[155] the 2018 Escazú Regional Agreement on Access to Information, Public Participation and Justice in Environmental Matters in Latin America and the Caribbean,[156] and, more generally, the case law of regional human rights bodies has removed any ambiguity as to the existence of such environmental procedural rights.

These systems recognise three main clusters of rights: access to environmental information; participation in environmental decision-making

[154] See generally G. Pring and S. Y. Noé, ‘The Emerging International Law of Public Participation Affecting Global Mining, Energy, and Resources Development’, in D. N. Zillman, A. R. Lucas, G. Pring (eds), *Human Rights in Natural Resource Development* (Oxford: Oxford University Press, 2002), pp. 11–76.

[155] Aarhus Convention on Access to Information, Public Participation in Decision-making and Access to Justice in Environmental Matters, 25 June 1998, 2161 UNTS 447 [Aarhus Convention].

[156] Regional Agreement on Access to Information, Public Participation and Justice in Environmental Matters in Latin America and the Caribbean, 4 March 2018 [Escazú Agreement].

processes; and access to justice in environmental matters. The Escazú Agreement further provides express protection to environmental defenders,[157] in light of the particular risk they undergo in the region. The most mature system, at present, is that of Aarhus Convention, which has been widely discussed in the case law of the Aarhus Compliance Committee.[158]

The first cluster of rights provided in this instrument concerns the right of access to environmental information (Articles 4 and 5), a term which is broadly understood (Article 2(3)) as including inter alia '[f]actors, such as substances, energy, noise and radiation, and activities or measures'[159] (letter (b)). The second cluster relates to public participation in decision-making processes regarding activities (Article 6), plans, programmes and policies (Article 7) and executive regulations or legally binding instruments of general application (Article 8). Different processes are subject to different participation requirements.[160] Specifically, Annex I of the Convention lists activities (including several activities from the 'energy sector') which are subject to the requirements of Article 6 (Article 6(1)(a)). Activities which are not listed (Article 6(1)(b)) may still be subject to these requirements if they are significant enough.[161] The third cluster concerns access to justice on environmental matters (Article 9). Of particular note, Article 9(3) empowers members of the public 'to challenge acts and omissions by private persons and public authorities which contravene provisions of its national law relating to the environment'.[162] The reference to laws 'relating to the environment' is

[157] Escazú Agreement, Article 9.

[158] See A. Andrusevich and S. Kern (eds.), *Case Law of the Aarhus Convention Compliance Committee (2004–2014)* (Lviv: RACSE, 3rd ed. 2016) (references made in this section to the case law of the Committee are derived from Andrusevich/Kern).

[159] See *Moldova* ACCC/C/2008/30, ECE/MP.PP/C.1/2009/6/Add.3 (8 February 2011), para. 29; *European Community* ACCC/C/2007/21, ECE/MP.PP/C.1/2009/2/Add.1 (11 December 2009), para. 30.

[160] See *United Kingdom* ACCC/C/2010/53, ECE/MP.PP/C.1/2013/3 (11 January 2013), para. 82.

[161] See *Czech Republic* ACCC/C/2010/50, ECE/MP.PP/C.1/2012/11 (2 October 2012), para. 82; *United Kingdom* ACCC/C/2010/45 and ACCC/C/2011/60, ECE/MP.PP/C.1/2013/12 (23 October 2013), para. 75; *Czech Republic* ACCC/C/2012/70, ECE/MP.PP/C.1/2014/9 (4 June 2014), para. 53.

[162] See *Denmark* ACCC/C/2006/18, ECE/MP.PP/2008/5/Add.4 (29 April 2008), para. 28; *European Union* ACCC/C/2008/32 (Part I), ECE/MP.PP/C.1/2011/4/Add.1 (May 2011), para. 77.

broadly understood[163] and access to justice must be effective, which includes a dimension of affordability.[164]

An example of the operation of such rights in an energy context has been provided earlier in relation to the Hinkley Point C project in the United Kingdom (see Section 3.3.3.1 of this chapter).

3.3.3.2.2 Procedural Dimensions of General Human Rights Beyond specific instruments such as the Aarhus Convention or the Escazú Agreement, procedural dimensions of general human rights have been distilled by regional human rights bodies through interpretation in a number of cases.

The case law of the European Court of Human Rights (ECtHR) has made a substantial contribution to this expansion.[165] In some cases, the ECtHR has relied on the Aarhus Convention to buttress its procedural interpretation of substantive human rights. For example, in *Tătar v. Romania*, the applicants claimed that the operations of a gold mine and the passivity of the competent authorities encroached upon their right to private and family life (Article 8 of the ECHR). The ECtHR noted in this regard that it had to determine whether the approval of the activity had been preceded by appropriate studies of the relevant risks, and whether the public had been granted access to them.[166] Subsequently, it considered that Article 8 included the right of access to environmental information and referred expressly to the Aarhus Convention as evidence of the positive obligations of States with respect

[163] See *Austria* ACCC/C/2011/63, ECE/MP.PP/C.1/2014/3 (13 January 2014), para. 52.

[164] See *United Kingdom* ACCC/C/2008/27, ECE/MP.PP/C.1/2010/6/Add.2 (November 2010), para. 44.

[165] See e.g. *Guerra and others v. Italy*, ECtHR Application No. 116/1996/735/932, Judgment (19 February 1998), para. 60; *Oneryildiz v. Turkey*, ECtHR Application No. 48939/99, Judgment (30 November 2004), paras. 91–96; *L'Erablière A.S.B.L. v. Belgium*, ECtHR Application No. 49230/07, Judgment (24 February 2009), paras. 24–30; *Taşkin and others v. Turkey*, ECtHR Application No. 46117/99, Judgment (30 March 2005), paras. 118–125; *Tătar v. Romania*, ECtHR Application No. 67021/01, Judgment (6 July 2009) [*Tătar v. Romania*], paras. 96–97 and 116–125; *Ivan Atanasov v. Bulgaria*, ECtHR Application No. 12853/03, Judgment (11 April 2011), para. 78; *Vilnes and others v. Norway*, ECtHR Application No. 52806/09, Judgment (5 December 2013), paras. 235–244; *Brincat and others v. Malta*, ECtHR Application Nos. 60908/11, 62110/11, 62129/11, 62312/11, and 62338/11, Judgment (24 July 2014), para. 102; *Özel and others v. Turkey*, ECtHR Applications nos 14350/05, 15245/05, and 16051/05, Judgment (17 November 2015), paras. 170–172, 187–190; *Smaltini v. Italy*, ECtHR Application No. 43961/09, Decision (admissibility) (24 March 2015), paras. 51–54.

[166] *Tătar v. Romania*, para. 101 (our translation from the French).

to environmental information.[167] *In casu*, the Romanian authorities had failed to provide sufficient access, which amounted to a violation of Article 8.

A similar factual configuration was addressed by the ECtHR in *Taşkin v. Turkey*. Of note, however, whereas Romania is a party to the Aarhus Convention, Turkey is not. The Court referred nevertheless to the Aarhus Convention as a 'relevant international text'.[168] The statement of the procedural dimensions of Article 8 deserves reproduction in extenso:

> The Court reiterates that, according to its settled case-law, whilst Article 8 contains no explicit procedural requirements, the decision-making process leading to measures of interference must be fair and such as to afford due respect for the interests of the individual as safeguarded by Article 8. [. . .] Where a State must determine complex issues of environmental and economic policy, the decision-making process must firstly involve appropriate investigations and studies in order to allow them to predict and evaluate in advance the effects of those activities which might damage the environment and infringe individuals' rights and to enable them to strike a fair balance between the various conflicting interests at stake. [. . .] The importance of public access to the conclusions of such studies and to information which would enable members of the public to assess the danger to which they are exposed is beyond question. [. . .] Lastly, the individuals concerned must also be able to appeal to the courts against any decision, act or omission where they consider that their interests or their comments have not been given sufficient weight in the decision-making process.[169]

On the facts, the failure of the government to timely comply with the decisions of domestic courts, and a decision of Turkey's Council of Ministers to continue the production at the gold mine, which was not made public, amounted to a violation of Article 8. Although neither *Tătar* nor *Taşkin* are about energy activities, they illustrate the procedural dimension of human rights in the context of extractive industries, which is relevant for present purposes.

3.3.3.2.3 Rights of Indigenous and Tribal Peoples The third strand of procedural human rights concerns, specifically, the rights of indigenous and tribal peoples. I have discussed already their 'entitlements' (see

[167] *Tătar v. Romania*, paras. 113–118.

[168] In paras. 98–99, the Court had referred to Principle 10 of the Rio Declaration and to the Aarhus Convention as 'relevant international texts'.

[169] *Taşkin v. Turkey*, paras. 118–119.

Chapter 2). Here, my focus is on certain specific procedural rights with respect to forced relocation and some more general procedural rights arising from their relations to ancestral lands.

Regarding the first, ILO Convention No. 169 requires the consultation and prior informed consent of indigenous peoples as a condition for their 'displacement' or 'relocation'.[170] In the same vein, the UN Declaration on the Rights of Indigenous Peoples states, in Article 10, that '[i]ndigenous peoples shall not be forcibly removed from their lands' and that '[n]o relocation shall take place without the free, prior and informed consent of the indigenous peoples concerned'.[171] In an energy context, hydro-electric projects may lead a government to forcibly relocate an indigenous or tribal people from their ancestral lands in violation of their rights as well as of the Performance Requirements of funding agencies.[172]

More generally, general human rights have been interpreted to provide some procedural safeguards to indigenous and tribal peoples. In the case law of the Inter-American Court of Human Rights (ICtHR), the right to property has been subject to a number of procedural restrictions, including the requirement to ensure (1) sufficient participation from the relevant community, (2) appropriate benefit sharing of the fruits of the activity and (3) the conduct of a prior environmental and social assessment.[173] In a similar vein, the African Commission on Human and Peoples' Rights observed, in the *Ogoni case*, which concerned the oil exploration and exploitation in the Niger Delta, that the rights arising from the African Charter included a procedural dimension, particularly regarding environmental impact assessment and public participation.[174]

3.3.4 Substantive Requirements

3.3.4.1 Protection of the Marine Environment The protection of the marine environment is a vast area of international regulation, which

[170] Convention (No. 169) concerning Indigenous and Tribal Peoples in Independent Countries, 27 June 1989, 28 ILM 1382 (1989) [ILO Convention 169], Articles 16(2) and 6.

[171] See UNDRIP, Annex, Articles 10 and 19.

[172] See Section 3.3.3.1 of this chapter.

[173] See *Saramaka People v. Suriname*, ICtHR Series C No. 172, Judgment (28 November 2007), paras. 125–130; *Indigenous community Yakye Axa v. Paraguay*, ICtHR Series C No. 125 (17 June 2005), para. 145; *Kaliña and Lokono Peoples v. Suriname*, ICtHR Case No. 12.639 (Merits, Reparations and Costs), Judgment (25 November 2015), para. 155.

[174] *Social and Economic Rights Action Center (SERAC) and others v. Nigeria*, African Commission Application No. 155/96 (2001–2002), para. 53.

addresses both general and energy-specific aspects. For present purposes, it is useful to distinguish three main layers: general duties; regulation of specific sources of pollution; and regulation of certain regional seas. This section provides only a brief overview of this vast field, focussing on those aspects that are most clearly connected with the negative externalities of energy transactions.

3.3.4.1.1 General Duties Regarding the first layer, the UNCLOS includes a Part XII fully devoted to the 'Protection and preservation of the marine environment'. The opening provision, Article 192, states the general duty 'to protect and preserve the marine environment'. This duty reflects customary international law,[175] and it is applicable to all maritime spaces, including disputed areas and internal waters.[176]

This is particularly relevant for energy activities in the seabed and subsoil, both within and beyond national jurisdiction. The duty involves a requirement of due diligence, as laid out in customary international law.[177] States must take proactive measures to protect and preserve the marine environment and to ensure that such measures are effectively enforced,[178] although the mere occurrence of harm is insufficient for the duty to be breached.[179] Article 194 of the UNCLOS further specifies the duties of States with respect to pollution of the marine environment. It first restates the prevention principle[180] and then specifies which measures may be taken[181] and within which limits. Such measures must not amount to '*unjustifiable interference* with activities carried out by other States in the exercise of their rights and in pursuance of their duties in conformity with this Convention'.[182]

[175] *South China Sea Arbitration*, para. 941.

[176] *Ghana/Côte d'Ivoire – Provisional measures*, paras. 68–73; *IUU Advisory Opinion*, paras. 111, 120; *South China Sea Arbitration*, paras. 927 and 940; *Ukraine v. Russia*, para. 295.

[177] *South China Sea Arbitration*, para. 941.

[178] *South China Sea Arbitration*, paras. 944 and 964. See also *Pulp Mills*, para. 197; *Responsibilities in the Area*, para. 117; *IUU Advisory Opinion*, para. 131;

[179] *South China Sea Arbitration*, para. 974. See further *Pulp Mills*, para. 187; *Responsibilities in the Area*, para. 110; *IUU Advisory Opinion*, para. 129.

[180] UNCLOS, Article 194(2).

[181] UNCLOS, Article 194(3) and (5).

[182] UNCLOS, Article 194(4) (emphasis added). See also *In the matter of the Chagos Marine Protected Area Arbitration before an Arbitral Tribunal constituted under Annex VII of the United Nations Convention on the Law of the Sea (Mauritius v. UK)*, Award (18 March 2015) [*Chagos Island Arbitration*], para. 540, where the arbitral tribunal 'functionally' equated Articles 2(3), 56(2) and 194(4) and reasoned that the creation of a

Echoing the situation in customary international environmental law, the general duty of Article 192 is extended through procedural obligations of cooperation[183] as well as monitoring and assessment.[184] Both extensions reflect customary international law.[185]

3.3.4.1.2 Sources of Pollution Moving to the second layer, in addition to the general duty discussed in the previous paragraph, with its extensions, Part XII of UNCLOS specifically regulates certain sources of pollution of the marine environment. Three of them are particularly relevant for energy.

The first concerns pollution from vessels.[186] The basic duty is stated in Article 211(2) of the UNCLOS:

> States shall adopt laws and regulations for the prevention, reduction and control of pollution of the marine environment from vessels flying their flag or of their registry. Such laws and regulations shall at least have the same effect as that of generally accepted international rules and standards established through the competent international organization or general diplomatic conference.

Vessel-source pollution results from the normal operation of ships, including oil tankers, used for the transportation of goods as well as from the accidents that may occur in this context.[187] The matter is regulated at the global level by the 1973 International Convention for the Prevention of Pollution from Ships and its Protocol of 1978 (known as 'MARPOL'),[188] the adoption of which was prompted by the grounding

marine protected area by the United Kingdom without appropriate consultation of Mauritius encroached on Mauritius' fishing rights in breach of Article 194(4). However, the measure was not in violation of the rights – specifically as regards oil prospection and exploitation – resulting from the Lancaster undertakings because such rights were 'prospective' and Mauritius had not carried out, effectively, any activities the basis of such rights.

183 UNCLOS, Part XII, section 2, Articles 197–201.

184 UNCLOS, Part XII, section 4, Articles 204–206.

185 *South China Sea Arbitration*, paras. 946–948.

186 UNCLOS, Articles 211 and 217–221.

187 See in general, A. K.-J. Tan, *Vessel-Source Marine Pollution* (Cambridge: Cambridge University Press, 2006).

188 See J. Kindt, 'Vessel Source Pollution and the Law of the Sea' (1984) 17 *Vanderbilt Journal of Transnational Law* 287; M. Fitzmaurice, 'The International Convention for the Prevention of Pollution from Ships (MARPOL)', in D. Attard, M. Fitzmaurice, and N. A. Martinez Gutierrez (eds.), *The IMLI Manual on International Maritime Law. Vol. I: The Law of the Sea* (Oxford: Oxford University Press, 2014), pp. 33–77. The

of the Liberian tanker Torrey Canyon off the British coast. MARPOL governs 'discharges'[189] of 'harmful substances'[190] by 'ships'.[191] The term 'ship' encompasses vessels but also fixed or floating platforms flying the flag or operated by a State Party to the Convention,[192] except for ships assigned to governmental purposes.[193] The term 'discharge' means 'any release howsoever caused from a ship and includes any escape, disposal, spilling, leaking, pumping, emitting or emptying'[194] but it expressly excludes 'dumping' and pollution from the 'exploration, exploitation and associated off-shore processing of sea-bed mineral resources', which will be discussed later.[195] MARPOL includes six annexes containing regulations to prevent or reduce discharges,[196] the first two of which (I: Oil; II: Noxious liquid substances) are mandatory. With respect to the prevention of oil pollution, MARPOL introduces restrictions and technical requirements for (1) operational discharges, which are tightly regulated and subject to a record keeping system (Oil Record Book),[197] (2) the design (e.g. segregated ballast tanks and double-hull) and

1978 Protocol facilitated the entry into force of the Convention by allowing for more time for the implementation of Annex II of the Convention.

189 MARPOL, Article 2(3).

190 MARPOL, Article 2(2).

191 MARPOL, Article 2(4).

192 MARPOL, Article 3(1).

193 MARPOL, Article 3(3).

194 MARPOL, Article 2(3)(a).

195 MARPOL, Article 3(3)(b)(i)–(ii).

196 Annex I (Regulations for the Prevention of Pollution by Oil); Annex II (Regulations for the Control of Pollution by Noxious Liquid Substances in Bulk); Annex III (Regulations for the Prevention of Pollution by Harmful Substances Carried at Sea in Packaged Form); Annex IV (Regulations for the Prevention of Pollution by Sewage from Ships); Annex V (Regulations for the Control of Pollution by Garbage from Ships); Annex VI (Regulations for the Prevention of Air Pollution from Ships).

197 MARPOL, Annex I, Regulations 9–11 (prohibition of discharges and exceptions) and 17 and 36 (Oil Record Book). Following the oil spill caused by the *Prestige*, the EU adopted Directive 2005/35/EC, which introduced in Articles 4 and 5 a liability regime for accidental discharges stricter than the one in Regulations 9 and 11(b) of Annex I (and some of Annex II). Some associations of tanker owners challenged the implementation of the Directive before UK courts, which requested a preliminary ruling from the European Court of Justice. In *International Association of Independent Tanker Owners (Intertanko) and others v. Secretary of State for Transport*, ECJ (Grand Chamber), Case C-308/06, Judgment (3 June 2008), the ECJ's Grand Chamber ruled that neither the provisions of the UNCLOS nor those of the MARPOL could be directly relied upon by a private person to challenge the validity of an EU act (at para. 64).

equipment of tankers,[198] (3) regular inspections certified by an 'International Oil Pollution Prevention Certificate',[199] (4) the development of emergency plans (shipboard oil pollution plans or SOPEP) for all ships,[200] (5) the designation of certain specific areas (Special Areas[201] and Particularly Sensitive Sea Areas[202]) where discharges are subject to stricter requirements and (6) the development of 'Reception Facilities' to handle oil residues and oily mixtures.[203] The enforcement of these requirements relies on the International Maritime Organization (IMO) but also on the UNCLOS. Articles 217 to 220 of the UNCLOS distribute enforcement powers across the flag, coastal and port States to ensure the respect of 'applicable international rules and standards' (i.e. MARPOL).

The second source is dumping. Article 5(a) of UNCLOS defines dumping as the 'deliberate disposal of wastes or other matter from vessels, aircraft, platforms or other man-made structures at sea' or of such vessels, aircraft, platforms or other man-made structures as such. Since the beginning of its international regulation, the practice was closely linked to the disposal of radioactive waste. For this reason, in 1961, the International Atomic Energy Agency (IAEA) adopted a set of safety standards to regulate this issue. A decade later, a global framework was developed in the form of the 'London Convention', which was subsequently amended several times, most notably in 1996 with the adoption of the London Protocol.[204] Article 210(6) of the UNCLOS expressly requires that the laws, regulations and measures adopted by States to govern dumping be 'no less effective [. . .] than the global rules and standards'. The approach of the London Convention is relatively simple: it requires State parties to prohibit or restrict the dumping of certain wastes on the basis of their level of harm, as reflected in three annexes. The definition of dumping in Article 3(1)(a) excludes the

[198] MARPOL, Annex I, Regulations 12–14 and 18–33. Regulation 39 provides for special requirements for fixed and floating platforms (e.g. drilling rigs).

[199] MARPOL, Annex I, Regulations 7 to 10.

[200] MARPOL, Annex I, Regulation 37.

[201] MARPOL, Annex I, Regulations 15 (B) and 34 (B).

[202] IMO Resolution A.982(24), 'Revised guidelines for the designation and protection of Particularly Sensitive Sea Areas (PSSAs)' (1 December 2005).

[203] MARPOL, Annex I, Regulation 38.

[204] Convention on the Prevention of Marine Pollution by Dumping of Wastes and Other Matter, 29 December 1972 [London Convention], subsequently modified by the Protocol of 7 November 1996 to the Convention of 1972 on the Prevention of Marine Pollution by Dumping of Wastes and Other Matter, 7 November 1996, 1046 UNTS 120 [London Protocol].

operational discharges regulated by MARPOL[205] and the disposal of wastes from seabed activities.[206] Dumping at 'sea' encompasses all maritime areas of State parties except for internal waters.[207] States are required to prohibit the dumping at sea of wastes and other materials listed in Annex I (e.g. crude oil, fuel oil, cadmium and cadmium compounds, high-level radioactive waste),[208] and they must subject to permitting procedures that of substances listed in Annex II (e.g. radioactive waste not included in Annex I)[209] and III (restrictions by quantity and/or place of disposal).[210] In 1996, the centre of gravity of this approach changed with the adoption of the London Protocol. Under the London Protocol, which replaces the Convention for the States Parties to both instruments[211] and is also open to other States,[212] States are required to prohibit the dumping and incineration at sea[213] of any substances except for those listed in Annex I (which include 'vessels and platforms and other man-made structures at sea' but excludes materials with 'levels of radioactivity other than de minimis (exempt) concentrations as defined by the IAEA'), whose dumping or incineration at sea must be subject to a permit.[214] In 2006, Annex I of the Protocol was amended to include carbon dioxide for subsoil storage. This amendment, which entered into force in 2007,[215] is intended to facilitate carbon capture and sequestration by enabling storage in depleted wells in the ocean subsoil.

The third source concerns the exploration and exploitation of seabed mineral resources, such as hydrocarbons. I have referred earlier to the rules applicable in the Area, but the bulk of this exploration and exploitation takes place in areas subject to national jurisdiction (territorial sea, exclusive economic zone and continental shelf). The general duties to

[205] London Convention, Article III(1)(b).
[206] London Convention, Article III(1)(b) and (c).
[207] London Convention, Article III(3). Under the London Protocol, 'at sea' includes 'the seabed and subsoil' of marine spaces (London Protocol, Art. 1(7)). Moreover, Parties must either extend the application of the Protocol to internal waters or introduce an equivalent domestic system covering dumping in internal waters (Art. 7(2)).
[208] London Convention, Article IV(1)(a).
[209] London Convention, Article IV(1)(b).
[210] London Convention, Article IV(1)(c).
[211] London Protocol, Article 23.
[212] London Protocol, Article 24(1).
[213] London Protocol, Article 5.
[214] London Protocol, Article 4(1).
[215] London Protocol, Article 6 (on export of waste and other matter) was amended in 2009 to allow exports of carbon dioxide to non-Parties for the purpose of dumping, but this amendment has not entered into force yet.

protect and preserve the marine environment are fully applicable in these areas. In addition, Article 208(1) states indeed that:

> Coastal States shall adopt laws and regulations to prevent, reduce and control pollution of the marine environment arising from or in connection with seabed activities subject to their jurisdiction and from artificial islands, installations and structures under their jurisdiction.

Paragraph 3 of this provision adds that '[s]uch laws, regulations and measures shall be no less effective than international rules, standards and recommended practices and procedures'. There is no global treaty comparable to MARPOL on this issue, but the general duties stated in Articles 192 and 194 remain applicable. Moreover, guidelines have been issued on more specific issues. One important area concerns the abandonment and disposal of installations and pipelines. Article 60(3) of the UNCLOS states that:

> Any installations or structures which are abandoned or disused shall be removed to ensure safety of navigation, taking into account any generally accepted international standards established in this regard by the competent international organization. Such removal shall also have due regard to fishing, the protection of the marine environment and the rights and duties of other States. Appropriate publicity shall be given to the depth, position, and dimensions of any installations or structures not entirely removed.

In 1989, the IMO developed a set of 'Guidelines and Standards for the Removal of Offshore Installations and Structures on the Continental Shelf and in the Exclusive Economic Zone'.[216] Section 1.1 of the guidelines state the principle that such installations 'are required to be removed, except where non-removal or partial removal is consistent with' the parameters set in the guidelines. Lightweight installations in shallow waters (section 3.1) and installations emplaced on or after 1 January 1998 (section 3.2) must be removed, although this requirement suffers some limited exceptions (sections 3.4(1) and 3.5). Removal of other installations is left for the coastal State to decide, on a case-by-case basis, in the light of six main considerations (section 2.1), namely safety of navigation, rate of deterioration of the material, effect on the marine environment, risk that the material will shift from its position, the cost,

[216] IMO Resolution A.672 (16), 'Guidelines and Standards for the Removal of Offshore Installations and Structures on the Continental Shelf and in the Exclusive Economic Zone' (19 October 1989).

feasibility and risks involved in the removal, the possibility of new uses or other 'reasonable justification' not to remove.[217]

The many complexities involved in determining the fate of disused oil installations can be illustrated by the Brent Spar, a storage installation in the North Sea owned by Shell. Shell evaluated several options and retained decommissioning by deep water disposal. Greenpeace opposed the move and organised a powerful campaign against Shell, which eventually conceded and towed the structure to Norway for dismantling in a shallow water fjord. It was later shown, however, that Greenpeace had, in part, overstated the risks posed by the decommissioning.[218]

3.3.4.1.3 Regional Seas Instruments Matters of abandonment and dumping have also been addressed in some regional seas instruments, which can serve to illustrate the important role of the third layer of regulation.

In 1974, following a recommendation adopted at the Stockholm Conference on the Human Environment, the UN Environment Programme established the 'Regional Seas Programme' (RSP).[219] The RSP consists of thirteen action plans and treaty-regimes on various marine regions (the Mediterranean Sea, the Kuwaiti regional action plan, West Africa, the Pacific South-East region, the Red Sea and Gulf of Aden, the Caribbean, East Africa, the Pacific Southwest region, the Black Sea), which together with the frameworks applicable to five other regional seas (Arctic, Antarctica, Baltic, Caspian Sea and North-East Atlantic), add a comprehensive regional layer of regulation of marine pollution. This layer is expressly contemplated and relied upon by the UNCLOS. Articles 208(5) (on pollution from seabed activities) and 210(4) (on dumping) call for the establishment of 'global and regional rules, standards and recommended practices and procedures' to tackle pollution.

[217] For an overview of practice in the implementation of these Guidelines in the different continents see A. Scarborough Bull, M. S. Love, 'Worldwide oil and gas platform decommissioning: A review of practices and reefing options' (2019) 168 *Ocean and Coastal Management* 274, at 286–288.

[218] See M. Huxham and D. Sumner, 'Emotion, Science and Rationality: The Case of the "Brent Spar"' (1999) 8 *Environmental Values* 349.

[219] UNEP, Report of the Governing Council on the Work of Its First Session (12–22 June 1973), New York, Decision 1(I), section III, para. 12(e): Report of the Governing Council on the Work of its Second Session (11–22 March 1974), New York, Decision 8 (II), section A I, chapter 4.

Three regional frameworks specifically address the handling of installations no longer in use.[220]

Within the Mediterranean Sea context,[221] the 1994 Offshore Protocol[222] requires State parties to prescribe that any application for authorisation of a project must include 'plans for removal of installations as specified in Article 20'.[223] In turn, Article 20 requires the removal of disused and abandoned installations (Article 20(1)). By contrast, the competent authority can either require the removal or the cleaning and abandonment (or burying) of disused pipelines (Article 20(2)). If the operator fails to act, the authority is required to undertake the relevant works itself 'at the operator's expense' (Article 20(6)).

In the Baltic Sea context, the 1992 Helsinki Convention[224] includes an Annex VI on the 'Prevention of pollution from offshore activities'. Pursuant to Regulation 8 of Annex VI, States Parties: 'shall ensure that abandoned, disused offshore units and accidentally wrecked offshore units are entirely removed and brought ashore under the responsibility of the owner and that disused drilling wells are plugged'. Dumping, including of 'man-made structures', is prohibited by Article 11, and no clear exception applies to the dumping of energy installations. Article 11 (4) reserves certain cases of force majeure, under restrictive conditions that would be difficult to meet in normal energy operations.

Finally, the 1992 OSPAR Convention[225] governs an area of the North-East Atlantic of significant importance for both fossil fuel extraction and

[220] See S. Trevisanut, 'Decommissioning of Offshore Installations: a Fragmented and Ineffective International Regulatory Framework', in C. Banet (ed.), *The Law of the Seabed* (Leiden/Boston: Brill Nijhoff, 2020), pp. 431–453, on which my discussion of regional instruments relies.

[221] Convention for the Protection of the Mediterranean Sea against Pollution, 16 February 1976, as amended and later becoming the Convention for the Protection of the Marine Environment and the Mediterranean Coastal Environment, 10 June 1995 ('Barcelona Convention'), available at: www.ecolex.org/ (TRE-001284).

[222] Protocol for the Protection of the Mediterranean Sea against Pollution Resulting from Exploration and Exploitation of the Continental Shelf and the Seabed and its Subsoil, 14 October 1994, available at: www.ecolex.org/ (TRE-001206). The Protocol entered into force on 24 March 2011, and it currently binds seven States (including Libya and Syria) and the EU.

[223] Offshore Protocol, Article 5(g).

[224] Convention on the Protection of the Marine Environment of the Baltic Sea Area, 9 April 1992, available on www.ecolex.org/ (TRE-001153).

[225] Convention for the Protection of the Marine Environment of the North-East Atlantic, 22 September 1992, 2354 UNTS 67.

offshore renewable energy generation. Annex III is devoted to the 'Prevention and elimination of pollution from offshore sources'. One salient feature of this annex is stated in Article 5(1), according to which:

> No disused offshore installation or disused offshore pipeline shall be dumped and no disused offshore installation shall be left wholly or partly in place in the maritime area without a permit issued by the competent authority of the relevant Contracting Party on a case-by-case basis.

The focus is clearly on hydrocarbon-related activities. Indeed, 'offshore installations' and 'offshore pipelines' are defined, in Article 1(l) and (m) of the Convention by reference to 'offshore activities', in turn defined in Article 1(j) as 'activities carried out in the maritime area for the purposes of the exploration, appraisal or exploitation of liquid and gaseous hydrocarbons'. The general system of Article 5 of Annex III applies to both installations and pipelines. Dumping and abandonment are in principle prohibited subject to a case-by-case permit. However, a Party may not grant a permit if the installation or pipeline contains harmful substances (Article 5(2)) and, for installations and pipelines emplaced after 1 January 1998, notification and consultation (through the OSPAR Commission) of other State parties is required.

In July 1998, the Parties adopted a 'Decision on the Disposal of Disused Offshore Installations'.[226] This decision does not apply to parts of installations located below the seabed surface or used as anchor[227] or to pipelines (which remain governed by Annex III alone). The approach remains similar to Annex III, i.e. dumping or abandonment is prohibited unless a derogation is granted by the competent authority subject to certain conditions.[228] This is possible for the footing of steel installations or for concrete installation of a category listed in Annex I to the Decision, with permits for other installation remaining subject to a higher threshold. The assessment of applications must follow a protocol described in Annex II to the Decision and other contracting parties must be consulted before the permit is granted in accordance with Annex III to the Decision. This is a sophisticated system, which governs an area highly

[226] OSPAR Decision 98/3 on the Disposal of Disused Offshore Installation, Sintra, Portugal (22–23 July 1998) [Decision 98/3].

[227] Decision 98/3, section 1(c)–(d).

[228] Decision 98/3, sections 2 and 3.

populated with installations, striking a balance between different considerations and affording some flexibility to reflect special circumstances.

3.3.4.2 Regulation of Air Pollution The regulation of air pollution has been briefly addressed under the cost internalisation stage. However, the bulk of the regulation focusses on the prevention of harm reaching a certain threshold. Energy transactions, such as the provision of thermal services (e.g. indoor heating or cooking), transportation and electricity generation may have significant consequences on air pollution. Only a portion of such pollution is governed by international law, mainly due to its (long-range) transboundary effects. The two main instruments addressing the international dimensions of air pollution are Annex VI of MARPOL (for air pollution from ships) and the system of the 1979 Convention on Long-Range Transboundary Air Pollution (LRTAP Convention) with its eight protocols.

3.3.4.2.1 Annex VI of MARPOL This annex was introduced in 1997[229] and significantly revised thereafter, most notably in 2008 and 2021.[230]

From the perspective of energy, Annex VI limits the emissions of sulphur oxide and nitrogen oxide from ship exhausts and those of volatile organic compounds (VOCs) from tanker activities. The main regulatory techniques used are technology and performance standards. Under Regulation 13, only diesel ship engines which emit no more than a certain threshold of NO_x are permitted. A NO_x Technical Code adopted in 1997 and subsequently amended further elaborates on engine testing and certification.[231] Similarly, Regulations 14 (directed to ship owners) and 18 (directed to fuel oil suppliers) require fuel oil used on board a ship

[229] Protocol of 1997 to amend the International Convention for the Prevention of Pollution from Ships of 2 November 1973, as modified by the Protocol of 17 February 1978, 26 September 1997, Article 2.

[230] Resolution MEPC.176(58), Amendments to the Annex of the Protocol of 1997 to amend the International Convention for the Prevention of Pollution from Ships, 1973, as modified by the Protocol of 1978 relating there to (10 October 2008); Resolution MEPC.328(76), 2021 Revised MARPOL Annex VI (17 June 2021).

[231] Resolution MEPC.177(58), Amendments to the Technical Code on Control of Emission of Nitrogen Oxides from Marine Diesel Engines, NO_x Technical Code 2008 (10 October 2008); MEPC.317(74), Electronic Record Books and Certification requirements for SCR systems (17 May 2019).

to have a sulphur content below a certain threshold. Regulation 15 governs the emissions of VOCs, and it requires the use of certain VOC emission control systems (so-called VECS) in ports and terminals[232] and of VOC Management Plans in oil tankers.[233] In addition, Regulations 13 and 14 introduced emission control areas (ECAs) where the emission of pollutants (SO_x, NO_x and particulate matter) must be further limited.

3.3.4.2.2 The LRTAP Convention Regime The LRTAP Convention was adopted in 1979 under the aegis of the UN Economic Commission for Europe.[234] At the time, it was seen as a response to the growing problem of 'acid rain' (acidification) suffered by some countries as a result of the emissions of sulphur dioxide from coal-fired power plants located in other countries. The Convention was designed as a framework instrument, which defines its object ('air pollution'[235]), sets broad principles (Articles 2 to 6, which essentially require the adoption by each State of measures to limit long-range transboundary air pollution and cooperation with other States) and, most importantly, it establishes institutions through which more specific obligations were negotiated and adopted over time.

In the two decades since the adoption of the Convention, eight protocols were adopted. One strengthened the European Monitoring and Evaluation Programme (EMEP),[236] which monitors air pollution. Six others focussed on the regulation of specific pollutants that are directly linked to energy activities (thermal, transportation and electricity

232 These must be consistent with MSC/Circ.585 'Standards for vapour emission control systems'.

233 These must be consistent with resolution MEPC.185(59) and circular MEPC.1/Circ.680.

234 Convention on Long-Range Transboundary Air Pollution, adopted in Geneva on 13 November 1979, 1302 UNTS 217 [LRTAP Convention]. See A. Byrne, 'The 1979 Convention on Long-Range Transboundary Air Pollution: Assessing its Effectiveness as a Multilateral Environmental Regime after 35 Years' (2015) 4 *Transnational Environmental Law* 37.

235 LRTAP Convention, Article 1: 'the introduction by man, directly or indirectly, of substances or energy into the air resulting in deleterious effects of such a nature as to endanger human health, harm living resources and ecosystems and material property and impair or interfere with amenities and other legitimate uses of the environment'.

236 Protocol to the 1979 Convention on Long-Range Transboundary Air Pollution on the long-term Financing of the Cooperative Programme for Monitoring and Evaluation of the Long-Range Transport of Air Pollutants in Europe ('EMEP'), 28 September 1984, 1491 UNTS 167.

services), namely sulphur,[237] NO_x,[238] VOCs,[239] heavy metals[240] and persistent organic pollutants.[241] The remaining protocol, adopted at Gothenburg in 1999,[242] is said to be 'multi-pollutant-multi-effect' as it focusses on several problems (acidification, eutrophication and tropospheric ozone) and a range of pollutants that cause them.

Over time, the regulatory techniques used in these instruments have become increasingly complex, from a crude target requiring the same percentage reduction of sulphur from all States to highly differentiated approaches which introduce significant flexibility in a system that is otherwise geared towards a certain degree of harmonisation.

3.3.4.3 Regulation of Climate Change I made reference to the international regulation of climate change earlier in this chapter in connection with cost internalisation mechanisms. Climate change as a regulatory object is complex and goes well beyond the mitigation of greenhouse gases emitted from processes based on the burning of fossil fuels. For this reason, the international regulation of climate change is found in a wide body of instruments, including the UN Framework Convention on Climate Change,[243] the Kyoto Protocol,[244] the Paris Agreement,[245] the decisions and guidelines adopted by their institutions, but also the instruments governing air pollution, protecting the marine environment and, more generally, protecting forests and other biomes.[246] For present

[237] Protocol to the 1979 Convention on Long-Range Transboundary Air Pollution on the Reduction of Sulphur Emissions or their Transboundary Fluxes by at Least 30 Per Cent, 8 July 1985, 1480 UNTS 215; Protocol to the 1979 Convention on Long-Range Transboundary Air Pollution on the Reduction of Sulphur Emissions, 14 June 1994, 2030 UNTS 122.

[238] Protocol to the 1979 Convention on Long-Range Transboundary Air Pollution Concerning the Control of Emissions of Nitrogen Oxides or their Transboundary Fluxes, 31 October 1988, 28 ILM 212, 216.

[239] Protocol to the 1979 Convention on Long-Range Transboundary Air Pollution Concerning the Control of Emissions of Volatile Organic Compounds or their Transboundary Fluxes, 18 November 1991, 31 ILM 573.

[240] Protocol to the 1979 Convention on Long-Range Transboundary Air Pollution on Heavy Metals, 24 June 1998, 2237 UNTS 4.

[241] Protocol to the 1979 Convention on Long-Range Transboundary Air Pollution on Persistent Organic Pollutants (POPs), 24 June 1998, 2230 UNTS 79.

[242] Protocol to the 1979 Convention on Long-Range Transboundary Air Pollution on the Reduction of Acidification, Eutrophication and Ground-Level Ozone, 30 November 1999, Document of the Economic and Social Council EB.AIR/1999/1.

[243] UNFCCC.

[244] Kyoto Protocol.

[245] Paris Agreement.

[246] See D. Bodansky, J. Brunnée, L. Rajamani, *International Climate Change Law* (Oxford: Oxford University Press, 2017), chapter 8, discussing inter alia the rules under Annex VI

purposes, the discussion must focus on the aspects of such regulation more directly focussed on energy and, among them, on those which aim to prevent non-tolerated harm from occurring (rather than merely internalising the costs of emissions, as discussed earlier).

3.3.4.3.1 The UNFCCC As a general matter, the substantive mitigation obligations set by the UNFCCC (Article 4) are of a due diligence nature (obligation of means), whereas those under the Kyoto Protocol required achieving certain quantified emission-reduction targets (Articles 2(1), 3(1) and Annex B) and those under the Paris Agreement are mainly – but not only – procedural in nature (Article 4(2)). This means that no State is specifically required to take measures relating to the energy sector, although this sector will, in most cases, be responsible for a substantial part of emissions of greenhouse gases.

The absence of a requirement to adopt a specific measure (e.g. emission standards and a licensing procedure, or energy efficiency standards for buildings or engines, or mandates targeting a certain amount of electricity to be produced from renewable sources) under the UNFCCC, the Kyoto Protocol or the Paris Agreement must not be equated, however, with the absence of a basis to do. Specifically, the operation of the broad clause in Article 4(1) of the UNFCCC according to which '[a]ll Parties [. . .] shall: [. . .] (b) [f]ormulate, implement, publish and regularly update national and, where appropriate, regional programmes containing measures to mitigate climate change' is not different in nature from the broad duty of Article 192 of the UNCLOS. Unlike Article 192, it is qualified by the need to 'tak[e] into account [the Parties'] common but differentiated responsibilities and their specific national and regional development priorities, objectives and circumstances'. But that qualification, however important, does not change the due diligence nature of the obligation.

The duty is more clearly stated for Annex I countries, each of which 'shall adopt national policies and take corresponding measures on the mitigation of climate change' (Article 4(2)). The measures to be adopted are for each State to decide, but they rest on each State's broad duty to take measures.

3.3.4.3.2 The Kyoto Protocol The Kyoto Protocol contains a broad duty for Annex I countries (Article 2(1)) according to which each such State 'shall: (a) [i]mplement and/or further elaborate policies and measures in accordance with its national circumstances'.

of the MARPOL, the 'Kigali Amendment' to the 1987 Montreal Protocol on Substances that Deplete the Ozone Layer, 16 September 1987, 1522 UNTS 29, and the regulation of 'black carbon' under several frameworks.

During the negotiations of Article 2, two main views were expressed, one calling for the identification of specific measures in some sectors and the other privileging wider freedom of action.[247] The latter view prevailed but some measures were nevertheless mentioned as suggestions, including the '(i) [e]nhancement of energy efficiency in relevant sectors of the national economy', '(iv) [r]esearch on, and promotion, development and increased use of, new and renewable forms of energy', '(vii) [m]easures to limit and/or reduce emissions of greenhouse gases [. . .] in the transport sector' and '(viii) [l]imitation and/or reduction [. . .] in the production, transport and distribution of energy'.

Most importantly, through such measures, Annex I Parties 'shall, individually or jointly, ensure that their aggregate anthropogenic carbon dioxide equivalent emissions [. . .] do not exceed their assigned amounts' (Article 3(1)). None of the aforementioned measures is required, but their adoption is expressly permitted by Article 2(1).

3.3.4.3.3 The Paris Agreement The Paris Agreement does not contain an equivalent quantified duty. The focus of its mitigation system is on the procedural requirement to notify increasingly ambitious nationally determined contributions at least every five years. Yet, the drafting of the main provision on mitigation, namely Article 4(2), is subtle and harbours potentialities that will materialise in time, as the agreement is tested in litigation. Article 4(2) states that: 'Each Party shall prepare, communicate and maintain successive nationally determined contributions that it intends to achieve. Parties shall pursue domestic mitigation measures, with the aim of achieving the objectives of such contributions'.

The first clause of this provision is of a procedural nature. It requires 'each Party', thus making clear that this is an individual obligation, to 'prepare, communicate and maintain' NDCs. The second clause has two main aspects. On one hand, '[p]arties shall pursue domestic mitigation measures'. This is a broad obligation of due diligence. On the other, the clause refers to the 'the aim of achieving the objectives of such contributions'. What this formulation hides is that Parties are not required, by virtue of the Paris Agreement, to meet the specific content of the NDC they set. They are required to prepare, communicate and maintain NDCs (procedure) and to pursue domestic mitigation measures (due diligence), but abiding by the specific measures they communicate is only an 'aim'.

[247] Bodansky, Brunnée, Rajamani, *International Climate Change Law*, at 171.

However, a party may be required under domestic or European law to abide by a specific measure or even as a result of a unilateral act, depending on the circumstances in which it emits its NDC.

3.3.4.3.4 Domestic Climate Change Laws Given the approach followed by these three climate change instruments, one must look at the domestic or regional level to understand the main forms taken by climate policies.[248]

Some States have adopted comprehensive instruments covering mitigation and adaptation.[249] Such is the case of Brazil,[250] China,[251] Fiji,[252] India,[253] Mexico,[254] New Zealand,[255] South Korea,[256] or the United Kingdom.[257] Other States have instead relied on existing instruments on related problems (energy or air pollution),[258] or on general environmental statutes,[259] or on mere executive regulations.[260]

248 This sub-section is based on J. Gundlach, M. Gerrard, 'Climate Change and Energy Transition Policies', in E. Lees, J. E. Viñuales (eds.), *The Oxford Handbook of Comparative Environmental Law* (Oxford: Oxford University Press, 2019), pp. 531–577.

249 Out of the 99 countries surveyed in a 2015 study, 82 have framework laws on climate change, with 58 of these laws addressing both mitigation and adaptation. See Nachmany, M., et al., *2015 Global Climate Legislation Study*, 13.

250 Brazil: *Law no. 12.187 establishing a National Policy on Climate Change* (2009) and implementing *Decree no. 7390* (2010).

251 China: National Development and Reform Commission, *National Climate Change Programme* (2007-) and *12th Five-Year Plan for National Economic and Social Development (2011–2015)* (2011)

252 Fiji: *National Climate Change Policy* (2012).

253 India: Prime Minister's National Council on Climate Change, *National Action Plan on Climate Change* (2008).

254 Mexico: *General Law on Climate Change* (2012, subs. amended).

255 New Zealand: *Climate Change Response Act* (2002); *Resource Management (Energy and Climate Change) Amendment Act* (2004).

256 South Korea: *Framework Act on Low Carbon and Green Growth, Act no. 9931* (2010).

257 United Kingdom: *Climate Change Act*, c. 27 (2008).

258 See e.g. Malaysia: *Renewable Energy Act, Act 725* (2011); United States: *Clean Air Act* (1970, as subs. amended), *Energy Independence and Security Act* (2007), *FY2008 Consolidated Appropriations Act* (2008).

259 See e.g. Argentina: *General Environment Act, Ley N° 25.675* (2002) (establishing an environmental agency), *Decree no 2213/2002* (designating this agency as the implementing authority for the UNFCCC), and Federal Council for the Environment, *Resolution no 166 of 1 April 2009* (making this agency responsible for compliance with climate change treaties); Canada: where there was an initiative to bring greenhouse gases under the framework of the *Canadian Environmental Policy Act* (1999). The initiative to amend the CEPA failed but regulations – adopted under CEPA – covering greenhouse gases have been issued since 2010, including for emissions from both stationary (SOR/2012–167) and mobile sources (SOR/2010–201, SOR/2014–207).

260 See e.g. Malaysia: *National Policy on Climate Change* (Ministry of Natural Resources and Environment Malaysia, 2010).

The types of techniques included in these different instruments show some convergence in the area of mitigation and less so in the area of adaptation.[261] Mitigation techniques usually include (1) targets, (2) market instruments, (3) information-based techniques and (4) command-and-control regulation. The latter two illustrate the preventive approach. Information-based techniques may take the form of labelling (to harness consumer pressure)[262] or corporate disclosures (to harness market discipline).[263] Command-and-control regulation typically involves the introduction of technology and performance standards and control through licensing and inspection of stationary sources.[264] Mobile sources are also regulated on the basis of technology/performance standards on vehicle design, as a condition for their commercialisation[265] or through indirect taxes on fuel (a cost internalisation measure).[266]

These domestic measures change over time, reflecting political shifts and other circumstances, but they are mentioned here as

[261] See e.g. Peru: *Climate Change Framework Law, Law no. 30754* (2018), which addresses an issue such as climate-induced migration, which is central but rarely addressed.

[262] See e.g. EU: Directive 1999/94/EC relating to the availability of consumer information on fuel economy and CO_2 emissions in respect of the marketing of new passenger cars (1999), Directive 2010/30/EU and Regulation 2017/1369 on the indication by labelling and standard product information of the consumption of energy and other resources by energy-related products (2010). See generally Australian Department of Industry, *Energy Standards and Labelling Programs Throughout the World in 2013* (Canberra: Australian Department of Industry, May 2014).

[263] See e.g. France: *Law no 2015-992 on Energy Transition for Green Growth Law* (2015), Art 173 and *Decree no 2015-1850 adopted pursuant to Article L. 533-22-1 of the Monetary and Financial Code* (2015); EU: Council Directive 2014/95 amending Council Directive 2013/34/EU regarding disclosure of non-financial and diversity information by certain large undertakings and groups (2014); United States: Securities and Exchange Commission, *Commission Guidance Regarding Disclosure Related to Climate Change*, 75 Fed. Reg. 6290, 6294 (9 February 2010). See generally the recommendations issued by the Financial Stability Board, Task Force on Climate-related Financial Disclosures, *Phase 1 Report* (31 March 2016).

[264] See United States: *Clean Air Act* (1970). Titles I and V focus on stationary sources and permitting, including an air quality system. See also EPA, *Standards of Performance for Greenhouse Gas Emissions from New, Modified, and Reconstructed Stationary Sources: Electric Utility Generating Units*, 80 Fed. Reg. 64509 (23 October 2015); *Carbon Pollution Emission Guidelines for Existing Stationary Sources: Electric Utility Generating Units*, 80 Fed. Reg. 64,662 (23 October 2015).

[265] See *ibid.*, title II focusing on moving sources. See also EPA & National Transportation Highway Safety Administration, *Light-Duty Vehicle Greenhouse Gas Emission Standards and Corporate Average Fuel Economy Standards, Final Rule*, 75 Fed. Reg. 25324 (7 May 2010); EU: Directive 2009/33/EC on the promotion of clean and energy-efficient road transport vehicles (2009).

[266] See e.g. Mexico (*Special Taxes on Production and Services Act* (1980, as amended in 2013).

illustrations of the types of preventive measures that have adopted to tackle climate change.

3.3.4.4 Area-Based Management Techniques Prevention of environmental harm can also be secured by granting enhanced protection to certain areas. I referred earlier to certain areas designated under MARPOL Annexes I and VI. But area-based management techniques (ABMTs) are much more generally used for the conservation of nature without any specific reference to energy activities. Some major environmental treaties, such as the Ramsar Convention,[267] the World Heritage Convention,[268] the Madrid Protocol on the Antarctic Environment[269] as well as a dense network of regional nature conservation conventions[270] rely on ABMTs as a way of preserving certain areas from economic activities, such as extractive industries.

3.3.4.4.1 The Antarctic Environment The moratorium on mineral resource extraction in Antarctica is one of the most prominent examples of this approach. A negotiation process launched in the early 1970s led to the adoption in 1988 of the Wellington Convention which enabled the prospection, exploration and exploitation of the mineral resources of the Antarctic continent.[271] But this regime, itself restrictive, came under much criticism and was never ratified.

Instead, a Protocol additional to the 1959 Antarctic Treaty[272] was adopted in 1991, the Madrid Protocol, which prohibits (Article 7) any activities involving mineral resources except for scientific research. The

[267] Ramsar Convention.

[268] WHC.

[269] Protocol to the Antarctic Treaty on Environmental Protection, 4 October 1991, 30 ILM 1455 [Madrid Protocol].

[270] Convention on Nature Protection and Wild Life Preservation in the Western Hemisphere, 12 October 1940, 56 Stat. 1354 [Western Hemisphere Convention]; African Convention on the Conservation of Nature and Natural Resources, 15 September 1968, amended 11 July 2003, 1001 UNTS 3 [African Conservation Convention], available at: www.ecolex.org/ (TRE-001395); Convention on the Conservation of European Wildlife and Natural Habitats, 19 September 1979, ETS No. 104 [Bern Convention]; ASEAN Agreement on the Conservation of Nature and Natural Resources, 9 July 1985, 15 EPL 64 [Kuala Lumpur Agreement]; Convention on the Conservation of Nature in the South Pacific, 12 June 1976, available at: www.ecolex.org/ (TRE-000540) [Apia Convention].

[271] Convention on the Regulation of Antarctic Mineral Resource Activities, 2 June 1988 [Wellington Convention].

[272] Antarctic Treaty, 1 December 1959, 402 UNTS 71.

moratorium on all mining activities applies from the entry into force of the Protocol (1998) and extends until 2048 (Article 25(2)). During this period, amendment of the Protocol requires unanimity of all the Consultative Parties of the Antarctic Treaty System (Article 25(1)) and, in addition, the prohibition of mineral resource activities is to continue beyond 2048 unless a binding regime with some pre-determined safeguards (Article 25(5)).

Although Article 7 does not define the area in which the prohibition applies, the Protocol governs activities in the 'Antarctic Treaty area', which is defined in Article 1(b) by reference to Article VI of the Antarctic Treaty, i.e. south of the 60° south latitude. That creates an overlap with the sovereign rights over the exclusive economic zone and the continental shelf projected by certain islands, such as Kerguelen and Crozet. However, given the costs of extraction and the low-carbon transition, the overlap has limited practical relevance from an energy perspective.

3.3.4.4.2 The World Heritage Convention Another major illustration of how ABMTs can limit energy activities, as well as of the many difficulties that arise in such context, is provided by the World Heritage Convention.

A 2015 study comparing World Heritage Sites with commercial mining operations and concessions, and oil and gas operations, infrastructure and concessions found, among others, that 21.74 per cent (40 out 184 World Heritage Sites reviewed) contained oil and gas concessions.[273] This overlap is inconsistent with the obligations arising from the World Heritage Convention, and it illustrates the tensions that may arise from the use of ABMTs.

The Convention protects both cultural monuments and parts of the natural environment of 'outstanding universal value'. States make nominations for inclusion of a 'site' in the World Heritage List envisioned in Article 11(2) of the Convention. This list includes more than a thousand sites. For all sites of outstanding universal value, whether listed or not,[274]

[273] WWF-UK, *A global assessment of extractive activity within natural World Heritage sites* (2015).

[274] M. Bowman, P. Davies and C. Redgwell, *Lyster's International Wildlife Law* (Cambridge: Cambridge University Press, 2nd ed. 2010), at. 454 (and cited references). See also F. Francioni and F. Lenzerini, 'The Destruction of the Buddhas of Bamiyan and International Law' (2003) 14 *European Journal of International Law* 619, 631.

States Parties are required to take measures to ensure 'the identification, protection, conservation, presentation and transmission to future generations of the cultural and natural heritage referred to in Articles 1 and 2 and situated on its territory' (Article 4).[275] They also undertake to cooperate with each other in various ways,[276] including the duty 'not to take any deliberate measures which might damage directly or indirectly the cultural and natural heritage [. . .] situated on the territory of other States Parties to this Convention' (Article 6(3)).

In addition, Article 6(2) states a duty of assistance applicable only to listed sites. In some cases, the World Heritage Committee (without the consent of the territorial State) may move a site from the regular list to a 'List of World Heritage in Danger', if the site is:

> threatened by serious and specific dangers, such as the threat of disappearance caused by accelerated deterioration, large-scale public or private projects or rapid urban or tourist development projects; destruction caused by changes in the use or ownership of the land; major alterations due to unknown causes; abandonment for any reason whatsoever; the outbreak or the threat of an armed conflict; calamities and cataclysms; serious fires, earthquakes, landslides; volcanic eruptions; changes in water level, floods and tidal waves (Article 11(4)).[277]

This list contains fewer than a hundred sites but inclusion in it attracts significant public attention and has sometimes generated tensions with the territorial State.

In some rare cases, sites have been removed from the list of World Heritage as a result of the lack of appropriate protections afforded by the territorial State. One example is the Arabian Oryx Sanctuary site, in Oman. The site was listed in 1994 and delisted in 2007, after Oman had allowed oil and gas exploration and extraction within the boundaries of the initially defined site, which in the meantime it had redefined without the agreement of the World Heritage Committee.[278] Similar tensions have arisen in the Virunga National Park, in the Democratic Republic of Congo. The VNP was listed in 1979 and, in 1994, it was moved to the list of World Heritage in Danger due to the turmoil in the

[275] See also WHC, Article 5 (listing specific measures that States are urged to adopt).
[276] See WHC, Articles 6(1) and 8–14.
[277] Operational Guidelines for the Implementation of the World Heritage Convention, 10 July 2019, WHC.19/01 [Operational Guidelines], para. 177.
[278] See S. D. Turner, *World Heritage Sites and the extractive industries* (20 June 2012), pp. 15–17.

African Great Lakes region. In 2009, reports of oil and gas exploration concessions reached the World Heritage Committee, which sent a mission. Following intensive civil society campaigning, the London-listed multinational oil company active in the site withdrew its operations.[279]

3.3.4.5 Human Rights and Resulting Obligations for States and Operators The prevention of harm to human rights and the environment can be achieved through the formulation or reinterpretation of duties arising for both States and private operators from the recognition of human rights. Aside from the procedural human rights discussed earlier, substantive human rights have been interpreted in such a way as to create three types of obligations for States,[280] namely to respect the human rights of individuals and groups under their jurisdiction, to protect such individuals and groups from deprivation of their human rights by third parties (e.g. private operators), and to fulfil human rights by creating the conditions enabling their full enjoyment. Given that such obligations arise from all substantive human rights, they offer a suitable angle to understand how such rights can be relied on to prevent non-tolerated harm. Specifically, the obligation to protect from deprivation is akin to a positive duty of due diligence to adopt measures to regulate operators and effectively oversee their enforcement.

Beyond the obligations of States, some more recent developments have resulted in the increasing recognition of human rights- and environment-related duties for private operators. In addition to different sets of international guidelines, whether directly targeting private operators (e.g. the OECD Guidelines on Multinational Enterprises,[281] the UN Principles on Business and Human Rights,[282] or the ILO's Tripartite

[279] See Turner, *World Heritage Sites*, at 22–24, and Joint Statement by SOCO International PLC ('SOCO') and WWF (11 June 2014).

[280] See *Report on the Right to Adequate Food as a Human Right. Final Report presented by the Special Rapporteur Asbjørn Eide*, 7 July 1987, UN Doc. E/CN.4/Sub.2/1987/23 (1987), paras. 66–69; Committee on Economic, Social and Cultural Rights, *General comment No. 12: The Right to Adequate Food (Art. 11)*, 12 May 1999, UN Doc. E/C.12/1999/5 (1999), para. 15; Human Rights Committee, *General Comment No. 6: Article 6 (Right to life)*, 30 April 1982, UN Doc. HRI/GEN/1/Rev.9 (Vol. I), paras. 3–5.

[281] OECD, Guidelines for Multinational Enterprises, Annex I to the Declaration on International Investment and Multinational Enterprises, 25 May 2011 [OECD Guidelines].

[282] Guiding Principles on Business and Human Rights: Implementing the United Nations 'Protect, Respect and Remedy' Framework, HRC Resolution 17/4 (16 June 2011) [UN Guiding Principles].

Declaration of Principles concerning Multinational Enterprises and Social Policy[283]) or weighing on them through their financial intermediaries (e.g. the IFC Performance Standards[284] and other 'Socially Responsible Investment' guidelines[285]), such duties have been asserted in transnational litigation under a range of statutes and common law theories, sometimes expressly asserting human rights and some other times relying on domestic law concepts (e.g. the existence of a duty of care). This section briefly surveys the duties of States and operators under both levels of instruments.

3.3.4.5.1 States as Duty-Bearers Many different substantive human rights, whether recognised in global treaties, mainly the two 1966 International Covenants[286] or in regional human rights treaties, mainly the European[287] and American Conventions[288] and the African Charter,[289] require States to regulate energy operations so as to prevent their encroachment on human rights.

Although the specific requirements of this duty will not be the same under different human rights, the overall duty as such presents a recognisable common core. This core can be summarised by reference to the judgment of the ICtHR in *Velásquez Rodríguez v. Honduras*:

> An illegal act which violates human rights and which is initially not directly imputable to a State (for example, because it is the act of a private person or because the person responsible has not been identified) can lead to international responsibility of the State, not because of the act itself, but because of the lack of due diligence to prevent the violation or to respond to it as required by the Convention.[290]

[283] International Labour Organization, Tripartite Declaration of Principles concerning Multinational Enterprises and Social Policy, 5th ed. (2017) [ILO MNE Declaration].

[284] IFC Performance Standards.

[285] See B. Richardson, *Socially Responsible Investment Law* (Oxford: Oxford University Press, 2008).

[286] ICESCR; ICCPR.

[287] ECHR.

[288] ACHR.

[289] African Charter on Human and Peoples' Rights, 27 June 1981, 21 ILM 58 (1982) [African Charter].

[290] *Velásquez Rodríguez v. Honduras* (Merits), ICtHR Series C No. 4 (29 July 1988), para. 172.

The doctrine of 'positive obligations' has been recognised by several human rights bodies,[291] including by the ECtHR,[292] the Human Rights Committee[293] and the African Commission.[294]

In the specific context of economic activities encroaching on human rights, typically by extractive and heavy industries, several cases have charted the scope and operation of the State's duty to protect from deprivation. In the European context, the ECtHR has relied on the rights to private and family life (Article 8) to require States to proactively take measures to protect individuals from waste treatment operations[295] or extractive and heavy industries.[296] In the American context, the ICtHR has developed a substantial body of case law on the protection of indigenous and tribal peoples against extractive industries (e.g. logging, oil and other concessions) under the right to property (Article 21).[297] The Human Rights Committee addressed some communications concerning

[291] For a survey of the relevant case law see S. Krahenmann, *Positive Obligations in Human Rights Treaties* (Geneva: Graduate Institute of International and Development Studies, 2012), pp. 9–37.

[292] *Case 'relating to certain aspects of the laws on the use of languages in education in Belgium' v. Belgium*, ECtHR Applications No. 1474/62; 1677/62; 1691/62; 1769/63; 1994/63; 2126/64, Judgment (23 July 1968); *Siliadin v. France*, Application No. 73316/01, Judgment (26 June 2005), paras. 77–89. See C. Madeleine, *La technique des obligations positives en droit de la Convention européenne des droits de l'Homme* (Paris: Dalloz, 2014), pp. 37–77 (explaining the origins of the doctrine in German jurisprudence).

[293] HRC, General Comment No. 31: The Nature of the General Legal Obligation Imposed on States Parties to the Covenant, CCPR/C/21/Rev.1/Add. 13, 26 May 2004, para. 8 'the positive obligations on States Parties to ensure Covenant rights will only be fully discharged if individuals are protected by the State, not just against violations of Covenant rights by its agents, but also against acts committed by private persons or entities that would impair the enjoyment of Covenant rights in so far as they are amenable to application between private persons or entities'.

[294] *Ogoni case*, para. 57.

[295] *Lopez Ostra v. Spain*, ECtHR Application No. 16798/90, Judgment (9 December 1994), paras. 51–58.

[296] *Tatar v. Romania*, paras. 85–88; *Apanasewicz v. Poland*, ECtHR Application No. 6854/07, Judgment (3 May 2011), paras. 93–104.

[297] The leading case is *Awas Tingni v. Nicaragua*. See further *Indigenous community Yakye Axa v. Paraguay*, ICtHR Series C No. 125 (17 June 2005), para. 137; *Sawhoyamaxa Indigenous Community v. Paraguay*, ICtHR Series C No. 146 (29 March 2006), para. 118; *Indigenous People Kichwa of Sarayaku v. Ecuador*, ICtHR Series C No. 245, Judgment (merits and compensation) (27 June 2012), paras. 145–147; *Case of the Kuna Indigenous People of Madungandí and the Emberá Indigenous People of Bayano and their members v. Panama*, ICtHR Series C No. 284 (Preliminary Objections, Merits, Reparations and Costs), Judgment (14 October 2014), paras. 111–113; *Kaliña and Lokono Peoples v. Suriname*, ICtHR Case No. 12.639 (Merits, Reparations and Costs), Judgment (25 November 2015), para. 122; *Case of the Indigenous Communities of the Lhaka*

oil exploration or stone mining concessions[298] under the right to enjoy one's culture (Article 27). Finally, the African Commission has addressed the matter under several individual and collective rights and in the specific context of oil extraction activities.[299]

Underlying these cases is a broad conception, rarely fleshed out in great conceptual detail, according to which States must both adopt appropriate measures to regulate operators and proactively and diligently enforce them. It is not a doctrine of strict liability but one of due diligence, akin to the one I have referred to earlier in connection with environmental protection.

3.3.4.5.2 Private Operators as Duty-Bearers Regarding private operators, such as multinational enterprises and their subsidiaries, the duties arising from human rights can be applicable to them through five main routes.

First, human rights law may be applicable as such by virtue of a specific statute or other domestic basis. One prominent example is the US Alien Tort Claims Act (ATCA) according to which: 'the district courts [Federal US Courts] shall have original jurisdiction of any civil action by an alien for a tort only, committed in violation of the law of nations or a treaty of the United States'.[300] This act, adopted in 1789, remained dormant until its rediscovery in the early 1980s in *Filártiga v. Peña-Irala*.[301] In subsequent cases, the scope of this act was further specified, including with respect to what type of international rules are actionable under it as well as the (limited) extent to which a new cause action (other than those historically contemplated by the act) can be heard by federal courts.[302] However, in 2013, the operation of the ATCA to hold multinational companies liable for events abroad was severely restricted by the US Supreme Court in *Kiobel v. Royal Dutch Petroleum* on the basis of a presumption against the extraterritorial application of

Honhat Association (Our Land) v. Argentina, ICtHR Case, Judgment (6 February 2020), paras. 92–98.

[298] See *Bernard Ominayak and the Lubicon Lake Band v. Canada*, HRC Communication No. 167/1984 (26 March 1990); *Ilmari Länsman and others v. Finland*, HRC Communication No. 511/1992 (8 November 1995).

[299] See *Ogoni case*.

[300] Alien Tort Claims Act, 28 USC § 1350.

[301] *Filártiga v. Peña-Irala*, 630 F.2d 876 (2n Circ. 1980).

[302] *Sosa v. Alvarez-Machain*, 542 US 692.

the act.[303] Another example is provided by *Nevsun v. Araya*,[304] where the Supreme Court of Canada recognised that a claim for violation of international human rights law (specifically customary international law) may potentially be asserted against a corporation (*in casu* an investor active in the extractive industries). The court noted, indeed, that it is 'not "plain and obvious" that corporations today enjoy a blanket exclusion under customary international law from direct liability for violations of "obligatory, definable, and universal norms of international law"'.[305] Then it recognised that the specific grounds for the claim were not yet clear and left them for the trial judge to examine:

> The mechanism for how these claims should proceed is a novel question that must be left to the trial judge. The claims may well be allowed to proceed based on the recognition of new nominate torts, but this is not necessarily the only possible route to resolving the Eritrean workers' claims. A compelling argument can also be made, based on their pleadings, for a direct approach recognizing that since customary international law is part of Canadian common law, a breach by a Canadian company can theoretically be directly remedied based on a breach of customary international law.[306]

The court did not discuss the merits of the claim, but the decision signals the possibility of a direct cause of action against a corporation for violation of international law. The risk was sufficient for the company to seek a settlement with the plaintiffs, which was reached in late 2020. A third example is provided by *Urbaser v. Argentina*,[307] a case decided by an investment tribunal under the Argentina-Spain BIT. Argentina brought a counterclaim against the investor for violation of human rights (specifically the human right to water). The tribunal asserted jurisdiction over the claim but rejected it on the merits.[308]

The second route is through the enforcement not of human rights treaties as such but of guidelines and standards designed to govern the activities of multinational enterprises. Two major examples are the

[303] *Kiobel v. Royal Dutch Petroleum*, 569 US 108 (2013).
[304] *Nevsun Resources Ltd. v. Araya*, 2020 SCC 5.
[305] *Nevsun v. Araya*, para. 113.
[306] *Nevsun v. Araya*, para. 127.
[307] *Urbaser S.A. and Consorcio de Aguas Bilbao Biskaia, Bilbao Biskaia Ur Partzuergoa v. Argentine Republic*, Award (8 December 2016).
[308] *Urbaser v. Argentina*, paras. 1143–1155, 1182–1210. See further *David R. Aven and Others v. Republic of Costa Rica*, ICSID Case No. UNCT/15/3, Award (18 September 2018), para. 738.

aforementioned OECD Guidelines on Multinational Enterprises and the UN Principles on Business and Human Rights.[309] The first is a broad set of guidelines covering human rights, environmental protection, labour standards and anti-corruption standards, whereas the second is based on three main duties: the duty of States to protect from deprivation, the duty of business enterprises as such to respect human rights, and the duty of States to offer adequate remedies.[310] So far, the implementation of this type of standards through court proceedings has remained elusive,[311] although there are indications that this situation is ripe for change. In a ground-breaking decision of a Hague district court, in *Milieudefensie and others v. Royal Dutch Shell*, the court specifically relied on soft-law instruments, including the UN Principles on Business and Human Rights, to interpret a domestic law standard of care and apply it to a company with far reaching results.[312] There are also certain soft-control mechanisms that can serve an analogous purpose. By way of illustration, a group affected by the activities of a multinational company subject to the OECD Guidelines may bring a complaint before the national contact point (NCP) established under such guidelines in the home country of the company. Numerous complaints have been brought over the years. In the case of oil activities in Virunga National Park, mentioned earlier in this chapter, a complaint was brought against the economic operator, SOCO International Plc, before the UK NCP.[313] Regarding the UN Principles on Business and Human Rights, they have significantly

[309] OECD Guidelines. See generally R. Lindsay, R. McCorquodale, L. Blecher, J. Bonnitcha, A. Crockett and A. Sheppard, 'Human rights responsibilities in the oil and gas sector: applying the UN Guiding Principles' (2013) 6 *Journal of World Energy Law and Business* 2.

[310] UN Guiding Principles.

[311] See e.g. *Kadie Kalma & Ors. v. African Minerals Ltd And Ors* [2020] EWCA Civ 144, at 150-151 (where Lord J. Coulson, delivering the opinion of the Court of Appeal of England & Wales noted, with respect to the argument of the claimants that it had to apply the UN Principles on Security and Human Rights as part of the respondent's duty of care, 'Again, I disagree. Those standards are general in nature and are primarily concerned with the need for liaison with the local community and the like [. . .] there is nothing in the Voluntary Principles which make companies operating abroad generally liable for the unlawful acts of the police forces of the host countries in which they are operating').

[312] *Milieudefensie et al v. Royal Dutch Shell*, District Court of The Hague, Judgment (26 May 2021) [*Milieudefensie v. RDS*], at para. 4.4.2.

[313] UK National Contact Point, *Final Statement following agreement reached in complaint from WWF International against SOCO International plc* (July 2014) (recording the agreement reached by the parties).

contributed to raise awareness among in-house counsel of the need to take human rights seriously in business activities, particularly in overseas operations. Yet, it remains unclear whether human rights are a mere matter of corporate social responsibility or, rather, have hardened to become a matter of compliance alongside anti-corruption and money laundering standards. A 2019 survey of forty businesses (mostly multinational companies, including 27 per cent from the energy sector) concluded that close to 70 per cent of them consider that there is not sufficient legal certainty as to their human rights obligations.[314]

The third route concerns the recognition of a 'duty of care' of parent companies to ensure that their subsidiaries operating abroad abide by certain minimum standards with respect to human rights. Such duty has been recognised in France, the Netherlands and the UK.[315] The situation is constantly evolving, and it is difficult to take a snapshot of such a dynamic process. In France, a statutory 'devoir de vigilance' imposed on parent companies has been recognised as a manifestation of the 'social responsibility' of companies.[316] In the Netherlands, after an initial indication provided by a January 2021 decision of the Court of Appeals of The Hague in a claim against Shell and its Nigerian subsidiary,[317] the Rubicon was crossed in the aforementioned case *Milieudefensie v. Royal Dutch Shell*. In this case, the Hague district court applied the standard of care of the Dutch civil code (Book 6, Section 162), interpreted in the light of a range of human rights and environmental standards, to require Royal Dutch Shell to reduce its emissions of greenhouse gases and those arising from its products (Scopes 1, 2 and 3), by 45% as compared to 2019, within ten years (by 2030).[318] In the UK, in *Chandler v. Cape*, the Court of Appeal of England & Wales recognised, on the basis of a test

[314] I. Pietropaoli et al, *A UK Failure to Prevent Mechanism for Corporate Human Rights Harms* (BIICL, 2019).

[315] See generally C. Bright et al, *Final Report: Study on due diligence requirements through the supply chain: Final report* (Brussels: European Commission, January 2020); L. F. H. Enneking, *Foreign direct liability and beyond: exploring the role of tort law in promoting international corporate social responsibility and accountability* (The Hague: Eleven, 2012).

[316] See *Association Notre Affaire à tous et al v. S.A. Total*, Tribunal judiciaire de Nanterre, Ordonnance de mise en état (11 February 2021), N° RG 20/00915 - N° Portalis DB3R-W-B7E-VQFM, at 10.

[317] See ECLI:NL:GHDHA:2021:132; ECLI:NL:GHDHA:2021:133; ECLI:NL:GHDHA:2021:134 (in Dutch only).

[318] *Milieudefensie v. RDS*, at 4.1.4.

developed in a previous case,[319] that under certain circumstances the parent company owed a duty of care to the employees of its subsidiary.[320] The existence of such a duty, in appropriate factual circumstances, was confirmed by the UK Supreme Court in *Vedanta v. Lungowe* decision of April 2019.[321] The claim was filed by a large number of Zambian villagers against Vedanta and its Zambian subsidiary (KCM), for the harm caused by a copper mine operated by the latter. The key question was whether 'Vedanta sufficiently intervened in the management of the Mine owned by its subsidiary KCM to have incurred, itself (rather than by vicarious liability), a common law duty of care to the claimants'.[322] The Court quoted, with approval, the statement in *AAA v. Unilever*[323] that the foundations of the duty of care lied in the general principles of tort law:

> There is no special doctrine in the law of tort of legal responsibility on the part of a parent company in relation to the activities of its subsidiary, vis-à-vis persons affected by those activities. [. . .] A parent company will only be found to be subject to a duty of care in relation to an activity of its subsidiary if ordinary, general principles of the law of tort regarding the imposition of a duty of care on the part of the parent in favour of a claimant are satisfied in the particular case. The legal principles are the same as would apply in relation to the question whether any third party (such as a consultant giving advice to the subsidiary) was subject to a duty of care in tort owed to a claimant dealing with the subsidiary. Helpful guidance as to relevant considerations was given in *Chandler v. Cape plc*; but that case did not lay down a separate test, distinct from general principle for the imposition of a duty of care in relation to a parent company. [. . .] Although the legal principles are the same, it may be that on the facts of a particular case a parent company, having greater scope to intervene in the affairs of its subsidiary than another third party might

[319] *Caparo Industries Plc v. Dickman* [1990] 2 AC 605. The duty of care of the parent company has also been recognised in The Netherlands in a decision of the Court of Appeals of The Hague, rendered on 29 January 2021, in a claim brought by Friends of the Earth Netherlands/Milieudefensie and four Nigerians against Shell and its Nigerian subsidiary. See ECLI:NL:GHDHA:2021:132; ECLI:NL:GHDHA:2021:133; ECLI:NL:GHDHA:2021:134 (in Dutch only). In France, the statutory 'devoir de vigilance' imposed on parent companies has also been recognised as a manifestation of the 'social responsibility' of companies. See *Association Notre Affaire à tous et al. v. S.A. Total*, Tribunal judiciaire de Nanterre, Ordonnance de mise en état (11 February 2021), N° RG 20/00915 – N° Portalis DB3R-W-B7E-VQFM, at 10.

[320] *Chandler v. Cape*, [2012] EWCA Civ. 525, para. 80.

[321] *Vedanta Resources PLC v. Lungowe* [2019] UKSC 20.

[322] *Vedanta v. Lungowe*, para. 44.

[323] *AAA v. Unilever plc* [2018] EWCA Civ 1532, para. 36.

> have, has taken action of a kind which is capable of meeting the relevant test for imposition of a duty of care in respect of the parent.[324]

It then recalled the reasoning of the trial judge and the Court of Appeal and concluded that there was no error of law vitiating the assessment. More recently, in *Okpabi v. Shell*, the UK Supreme Court relied on Vedanta to reverse a judgment of the Court of Appeal and recognise that Shell, as a parent company, could have a duty of care encompassing the polluting activities of its subsidiary in Nigeria (an oil pipeline operator) and, as a result, the claims brought by a collective of thousands of affected Nigerian villagers could be tried before UK courts.[325]

The *Vedanta* case is also important to illustrate a fourth route, namely the implementation of international standards in the corporate and group policies of multinational companies. In *Vedanta*, the respondent argued that: 'a parent could never incur a duty of care in respect of the activities of a particular subsidiary merely by laying down group-wide policies and guidelines, and expecting the management of each subsidiary to comply with them'.[326] The UK Supreme Court rejected this argument and observed that there are several channels through which such policies could give rise to a duty of care, such as when they 'contain systemic errors which, when implemented as of course by a particular subsidiary, then cause harm to third parties'[327] or when 'the parent does not merely proclaim them, but takes active steps, by training, supervision and enforcement, to see that they are implemented by relevant subsidiaries' or, still, 'if, in published materials, it holds itself out as exercising that degree of supervision and control of its subsidiaries, even if it does not in fact do so'.[328] These are examples of factual circumstances which could give rise to a duty of care, but their focus on group policies and the increasing adoption of such policies by multinational companies to reflect international guidelines make these examples particularly relevant.

The fifth route has already been mentioned in connection with procedural rights, namely the guidelines and standards applicable to the activities of the financiers of multinational corporations. Such guidelines

[324] *Vedanta v. Lungowe*, para. 50.

[325] *Okpabi and others (Appellants) v. Royal Dutch Shell plc and another (Respondents)*, UK Supreme Court, Judgment (12 February 2021), [2021] UKSC 3, paras. 141–152, 153–159.

[326] *Vedanta v. Lungowe*, para. 52.

[327] *Vedanta v. Lungowe*, para. 52.

[328] *Vedanta v. Lungowe*, para. 53.

contain both procedural and substantive standards of conduct for financiers, typically based on environmental and human rights standards. Their implementation can rely, as noted earlier, on a range of inspection panels and compliance offices both at the international and the domestic levels. An example of the latter is given by the Camisea Gas Project in Peru, where the US Export-Import Bank refused to finance a project led by Hunt Oil and PlusPetrol because of the impact of the proposed venture on both indigenous peoples (of the Nahua–Kugapakori Reserve) and the environment (the Paracas National Marine Reserve).[329]

Although the great majority of the examples discussed concern the extractive industries, the obligations arising from substantive human rights are sector-neutral and they also apply to the activities relating to the generation of renewable energy. This is not always the case of rules regulating negative externalities, which, in some cases, apply to hydrocarbons or even oil specifically.

3.4 Response to Harmful Events

3.4.1 Overview

In the event non-tolerated harm occurs, a range of international rules, mostly of treaty law but also of customary international law (reflected in Principle 18 of the Rio Declaration), come into play to organise the response and, more specifically, to contain the harm.[330]

There are two interlocked layers of rules at the global and the regional level. They were developed under the aegis of the IMO and prompted by the occurrence of major oil spills, starting with the grounding in 1969 of the Liberian tanker Torrey Canyon off the coast of Cornwall. Subsequently, the Chernobyl accident led to the adoption of two treaties on notification and assistance in case of nuclear accident, which will be discussed in Chapter 6.

[329] See C. Redgwell, 'International Regulation of Energy Activities', in M. M. Roggenkamp et al. (eds.), *Energy Law in Europe: National, EU and International Regulation* (Oxford: Oxford University Press, 3rd ed. 2016), pp. 13–136, at para. 2.226.

[330] See generally G. Gonzalez and F. Hébert, 'Conventions Relating to Pollution Incident Preparedness, Response, and Cooperation', in D. Attard, M. Fitzmaurice, N. Martinez, R. Hamza (eds.), *The IMLI Manual on International Maritime Law*, vol. III (Oxford: Oxford University Press, 2016), pp. 195–260, on which my discussion is based.

3.4.2 Instruments with a Global Scope

At the global level, following the Torrey Canyon incident, the 1969 Intervention Convention[331] was adopted under the aegis of the IMO. This instrument, in force since 1975, regulates the extent and limits of the measures that a State Party, normally the coastal State, may adopt to 'prevent, mitigate or eliminate grave and imminent danger to their coastline or related interest from pollution or threat of pollution of the sea by oil' and this 'following upon a maritime casualty or acts related to such a casualty' (Article I(1)). 'Maritime casualty' is defined in Article II (1) as: 'a collision of ships, stranding or other incident of navigation, or other occurrence on board a ship or external to it resulting in material damage or imminent threat of material damage to a ship or cargo'. The 'right to take measures' under Article 1(1) is subject to a number of limitations provided for in Articles III and V, mainly the need to notify the relevant parties and engage in consultations, and to remain within proportionality and reasonableness bounds. If the measures taken cause harm to others, then the relevant State is 'obliged to pay compensation to the extent of the damage caused by the measures which exceed those reasonably necessary to achieve the end mentioned in Article I' (Article VI). This regime was subsequently extended to marine pollution for substances other than oil.[332]

The system designed by the Intervention Convention was, however, insufficient to coordinate action in case of maritime casualties from oil. In 1968, the IMO adopted three resolutions encouraging States to adopt appropriate measures at the domestic level,[333] cooperate at the regional level[334] and exchange information and knowledge.[335] This led to several regional developments, which will be briefly referred to later. In addition, during the 1970s, the MARPOL Convention was adopted with a view to regulate operational and accidental discharges of oil and other noxious liquid substances. The UNCLOS provided a further legal basis for

[331] International Convention Relating to Intervention on the High Seas in Cases of Oil Pollution Casualties, 29 November 1969, 970 UNTS 211 [Intervention Convention].

[332] Protocol relating to Intervention on the High Seas in Cases of Marine Pollution by Substances other than Oil, 2 November 1973, 1313 UNTS 4.

[333] Resolution A.148 (ES.IV), National Arrangements for Dealing with Significant Spillages of Oil.

[334] Resolution A.149 (ES.IV), Regional Co-operation in Dealing with Significant Spillages of Oil.

[335] Resolution A.150 (ES.IV), Research and Exchange of Information on Methods for Disposal of Oil in Cases of Significant Spillages.

response action in its Articles 198 (notification of imminent or actual damage) and 199 (contingency plans against pollution). But it was not until November 1990, following the incident of the Exxon Valdez, which released some 37,000 metric tonnes of crude oil over a pristine area of Alaska, that a specific treaty on response was adopted, the OPRC Convention, in force since 1995.[336]

The OPRC Convention aims to organise the response to oil spills on the basis of two main clusters of obligations: vertical and horizontal. Regarding the vertical, States are required 'to take all appropriate measures [. . .] to prepare for and respond to an oil pollution incident' (Article 1(1)), which includes the establishment of a national system with a contingency plan, appropriately designated authorities, some minimal pre-positioned equipment and trained staff (Article 6), oil pollution emergency plans in offshore units, sea ports and oil handling facilities under the jurisdiction of the State (Article 3), and reporting obligations regarding oil pollution incidents (Article 4). With respect to horizontal obligations, States Parties must notify relevant Parties and the IMO in case of an oil pollution incident (Article 5) and, more generally, cooperate with and assist each other in preparing for and responding to the incident (Articles 7 to 10). Like the Intervention Convention, the OPRC Convention was subsequently extended to pollution incidents by hazardous and noxious substances.[337] Of note, Articles 10 and 11 of the OPRC Convention expressly contemplate the possibility of concluding new agreements on preparedness and response as well as the need to respect existing ones.

3.4.3 Instruments with a Regional Scope

At the regional level, in 1969, an Agreement for Cooperation in Dealing with Pollution of the North Sea by Oil and Other Harmful Substances, known as the 'Bonn Agreement',[338] was adopted following the recommendations made by the IMO. Throughout the 1970s, two other regional instruments were adopted on preparedness and response in the context

[336] International Convention on Oil Pollution, Preparedness, Response and Co-operation, 30 November 1990 [OPRC Convention].

[337] Protocol on Preparedness, Response and Co-operation to Pollution Incidents by Hazardous and Noxious Substances, 2000 (OPRC-HNS Protocol).

[338] Agreement for Cooperation in Dealing with Pollution of the North Sea by Oil and Other Harmful Substances, 13 September 1983.

of the Mediterranean[339] and the Gulf countries (known as the 'ROPME Sea Area').[340] These instruments were subsequently updated and, in one case, replaced with a new one, and other protocols were adopted in respect of other regional seas. The discussion of these regional instruments is beyond the scope of this chapter,[341] but it should be mentioned that the three initial ones served as a basis for the design of the OPRC Convention.

3.5 *Reparation of Harmful Consequences*

3.5.1 Overview

At the stage of reparation, the breach of a norm aimed at preventing the occurrence of harm has to be ascertained and its consequences determined and allocated. The applicable rules are derived from the general international law of State responsibility and the special rules applicable to breaches of certain norms of conduct (e.g. a human rights treaty).

In addition, there are rules which anticipate the occurrence of non-tolerated harm but organise its reparation without the need to ascertain a breach of a norm of conduct. These systems of civil liability are exclusively based on treaties, as there is no such basis in general international law, and they concern damage caused by oil pollution incidents and nuclear accidents. Liability is imposed on economic operators.

3.5.2 State Responsibility

The rules of general international law on the responsibility of States for internationally wrongful act are applicable to a larger or narrower extent (depending on the existence of special treaty rules) to the determination of the consequences of breaching a primary norm of conduct, such as the many norms discussed earlier on the protection of human rights and the environment. For present purposes, only two aspects of such rules need to be recalled, namely the rules determining the 'consequences' arising

[339] The Protocol concerning Co-operation in Combating Pollution of the Mediterranean Sea by Oil and other Harmful Substances in Cases of Emergency to the Barcelona Convention, 16 February 1976, subsequently replaced with the Protocol Concerning Cooperation in Preventing Pollution from Ships and, in Cases of Emergency, combating Pollution of the Mediterranean Sea, 25 January 2002.

[340] Protocol concerning regional cooperation in combating pollution by oil and other harmful substances in cases of emergency, 24 April 1978.

[341] For a detailed discussion see Gonzales/Hébert, *Conventions*, at 204–234.

from a 'breach' of a primary norm, and their operation in the relevant judicial practice.

3.5.2.1 Consequences of 'Breach' Regarding the first aspect, although there was much discussion starting in the 1960s on the development of a system of liability of States for harm caused by lawful activities,[342] no such general system could be adopted. Instead, States were encouraged by the recognition of the polluter-pays principle to adopt measures to require polluters to internalise the cost of tolerated (i.e. lawful) negative externalities (see Section 3.2). In addition, certain treaty systems laid down a system of no-fault liability arising for economic operators from oil pollution damage and nuclear accidents (States are only concerned in their possible capacity as economic operators) (see Section 3.5.3).

The work of the UN International Law Commission initially aimed to develop a system of no-fault liability for States was split into two tracks, one leading to a set of draft articles clarifying the contours and implications of the prevention principle (ILC Prevention Articles)[343] or, in other words, focussing on a set of primary norms of conduct, and the other leading to some broad principles on the allocation of loss, which are intended to guide States when they set up civil liability systems for economic operators.[344] Thus, under international law, States are only required to repair non-tolerated harm caused in 'breach' of a primary norm of conduct. The ILC Prevention Articles clarified, however, the level of diligence that must be displayed by States in certain contexts, sometimes called ultra-hazardous activities (e.g. nuclear energy generation), in order not be in breach of the prevention principle and its procedural extensions. Specifically, the mere creation of 'risk' may, under some circumstances, amount to a breach. I discussed the content and operation of the prevention principle earlier in this chapter (see Section 3.3.2). For present purposes, it suffices to stress that reparation by States

342 See W. Jenks, 'Liability for Hazardous Activities' (1966) 117 *RCADI* 102; L. F. E. Goldie, 'Liability for Damage and the Progressive Development of International Law' (1965) 14 *International and Comparative Law Quarterly* 1189; P.-M. Dupuy, *La responsabilité internationale des Etats pour les dommages d'origine technologique et industrielle* (Paris: Pédone, 1976); T. Scovazzi, 'State Responsibility for Environmental Harm' (2001) 12 *Yearbook of International Environmental Law* 43.

343 ILC Prevention Articles.

344 Draft Principles on the Allocation of Loss in case of Transboundary Harm from Hazardous Activities, GA Res. 61/36, UN Doc. A/RES/61/36 [ILC Principles on Loss].

is organised by the international law State responsibility for internationally wrongful act, which requires 'breach'.[345]

The ILC Articles on State Responsibility define the content of State responsibility, i.e. the general consequences of breach, in its Part II. There are ordinary consequences and aggravated (additional) ones (in case of serious breaches of a peremptory norm of international law[346]). That latter point must be noted because some of the primary norms introduced earlier, particularly certain fundamental rules protection human rights, such as the prohibition of slavery, racial discrimination, genocide and torture, as well as the right of peoples to self-determination (which confers an entitlement rather than mere protection against externalities) are widely considered to be peremptory norms (*jus cogens*).[347] Moreover, other peremptory norms, such as the prohibition of the use of force, may also be relevant for energy disputes.[348]

Ordinary consequences are of two types, cessation of the breach (Article 30(a)) (with assurances of non-repetition, Article 30(b)) and reparation of its consequences through restitution (Article 35), compensation (Articles 36 and 38) and/or satisfaction (Article 37). Aggravated consequences, in case of serious breaches of peremptory norms (Article 40) involve the duties for third States not to recognise the situation created by the breach, not to assist the breaching State and to cooperate with other States to bring the breach to an end (Article 41).

The distinction has, in addition, implications for which State can invoke the responsibility of the breaching State. Articles 42 and 48 of the ILC Articles introduce a distinction between 'injured States' and 'States other than the injured State'. In case of breach of a peremptory norm (as well as of certain other norms, e.g. obligations *erga omnes* and *erga omnes partes*) a State other than the injured State would be entitled, according to Article 48, to invoke the responsibility of the breaching State.

345 Responsibility of States for Internationally Wrongful Acts, GA Res. 56/83, UN Doc. A/RES/56/83, 12 December 2001 [ILC State Responsibility Articles], Article 2(b).

346 ILC State Responsibility Articles, Article 41.

347 See Draft Conclusion 23 of the Draft Articles on Peremptory of General International Law (*Jus Cogens*), *Report of the International Law Commission*, Seventy-First Session General Assembly Official Records (A/74/10), chapter V.

348 See *Ukraine v. Russia*. See also *Oil Platforms (Islamic Republic of Iran v. United States of America)*, Judgment, ICJ Reports 2003, p. 161.

3.5.2.2 Operation in Judicial Practice Judicial and quasi-judicial practice have clarified the operation of these broad rules. In *Costa Rica/ Nicaragua*,[349] the ICJ addressed the arguments of both parties with respect to the measures of compensation applicable to the assessment of environmental damage to a wetland protected under the 1971 Ramsar Convention. Nicaragua relied on the practice of environmental damage quantification of the UN Compensation Commission, which handled the claims arising from the 1990–1991 Gulf War. It did so to downplay or exclude the relevance of ecosystem services, i.e. the services performed by the normal operation of natural systems and which are disrupted by human interference, in the quantification of environmental damage, and to limit such quantification to 'restoration' and 'replacement' costs. By contrast, Costa Rica specifically referred to the need to compensate for the loss of ecosystem services, whose value went beyond restoration and replacement costs and included ecosystem services with no commercial value.

In its judgment on compensation, the Court premised its analysis on the legal principle stated by its predecessor in the *Factory at Chorzow* case that 'reparation must, as far as possible, wipe out all the consequences of the illegal act and reestablish the situation which would, in all probability, have existed if that act had not been committed'.[350] It then recalled that 'compensation may be an appropriate form of reparation, particularly in those cases where restitution is materially impossible or unduly burdensome' and that 'compensation should not, however, have a punitive or exemplary character'.[351] Of particular note, the Court observed that:

> In cases of alleged environmental damage, particular issues may arise with respect to the existence of damage and causation. The damage may be due to several concurrent causes, or the state of science regarding the causal link between the wrongful act and the damage may be uncertain. These are difficulties that must be addressed as and when they arise in light of the facts of the case at hand and the evidence presented to the Court. Ultimately, it is for the Court to decide whether there is a sufficient causal nexus between the wrongful act and the injury suffered [. . .] the absence

349 *Certain Activities Carried Out by Nicaragua in the Border Area (Costa Rica v. Nicaragua)*, Compensation, Judgment, ICJ Reports 2018, p. 15 [*Costa Rica/ Nicaragua – Compensation*].

350 *Costa Rica/Nicaragua – Compensation*, para. 29, referring to *Factory at Chorzow*, Merits, Judgment No. 13, 1928, PCIJ, Series A, No. 17, p. 47.

351 *Costa Rica/Nicaragua – Compensation*, para. 31.

> of adequate evidence as to the extent of material damage will not, in all situations, preclude an award of compensation for that damage.[352]

The Court then went on to recognise that 'damage to the environment, and the consequent impairment or loss of the ability of the environment to provide goods and services, is compensable under international law'[353] and defined its scope as follows:

> Such compensation may include indemnification for the impairment or loss of environmental goods and services in the period prior to recovery and payment for the restoration of the damaged environment. [...] Payment for restoration accounts for the fact that natural recovery may not always suffice to return an environment to the state in which it was before the damage occurred. In such instances, active restoration measures may be required in order to return the environment to its prior condition, in so far as that is possible.[354]

With respect to the methodology to assess the damage, the Court neither endorsed nor excluded the methodologies proposed by the parties. It justified its approach by reference to two considerations:

> first, international law does not prescribe any specific method of valuation for the purposes of compensation for environmental damage; secondly, it is necessary, in the view of the Court, to take into account the specific circumstances and characteristics of each case.[355]

All in all, the principles that apply to the assessment of compensation due for environmental damage are not different from the general rules but their application, particularly as regards the existence of damage, causation and quantification, must reflect the specificities of environmental damage.

With respect to serious breaches of peremptory norms, the matter has arisen indirectly before international tribunals, although not specifically in the context of reparation. In *Ukraine v. Russia*, Ukraine claimed that an objection to jurisdiction raised by Russia (contending that that the tribunal had no jurisdiction under the UNCLOS to decide a sovereignty dispute) was inadmissible because the area in question had been annexed by Russia in violation of the prohibition of the use of force and the UN

[352] *Costa Rica/Nicaragua – Compensation*, paras. 34–35 (referring to the Trail Smelter arbitration).

[353] *Costa Rica/Nicaragua – Compensation*, para. 42.

[354] *Costa Rica/Nicaragua – Compensation*, paras. 42–43.

[355] *Costa Rica/Nicaragua – Compensation*, para. 52.

General Assembly had expressly called other States not to recognise or render assistance.[356] The tribunal recognised the existence of an obligation of non-recognition reflected in Article 41 of the ILC Articles on State Responsibility.[357] But it then considered that the characterisation of the situation by the UN General Assembly could not be taken as a given and, as a result, the tribunal would have to settle a dispute (over the annexation by Russia of the relevant area) for which it had no jurisdiction.[358] It referred, in reaching this conclusion, to a prior decision of the ICJ in an energy-related dispute, namely the *East Timor* case.[359] In that case, which preceded the ILC Articles (including the text adopted in first reading), Portugal had argued that Australia's dealings with Indonesia (regarding the energy resources in the Timor Sea) were inconsistent with the status of East Timor as a non-self-governing territory and of Portugal as the administrating power. The Court rejected the argument stating that the resolutions of the UN General Assembly on which Portugal had relied could not be taken as 'givens'.[360] This is problematic because, although the obligation of non-recognition is endorsed, its application is rendered extremely difficult. In practice, the matter is left entirely to the specific circumstances of the case. It would appear that a legal situation authoritatively described by the ICJ (rather than a UN political organ) could nevertheless be relied upon by a third tribunal.[361]

3.5.3 Civil Liability

3.5.3.1 Compensation of Oil Spills: Overview of the System Systems of no-fault liability of economic operators were developed since the 1960s, first with respect to nuclear accidents and then for incidents of

356 *Ukraine v. Russia*, paras. 167–182.
357 *Ukraine v. Russia*, paras. 168–170.
358 *Ukraine v. Russia*, para. 176.
359 *East Timor Case (Portugal v. Australia)*, Judgment, ICJ Reports 1995, p. 90 at p. 104.
360 *East Timor*, para. 32.
361 See *Dispute concerning delimitation of the maritime boundary between Mauritius and Maldives in the Indian Ocean (Mauritius/Maldives)*, ITLOS Case No. 28, Preliminary Objections, Judgment (28 January 2021), paras. 168–175, 188–192, 202–206, 246–247 (referring to the determinations made by the ICJ in Legal Consequences of the Separation of the Chagos Archipelago from Mauritius in 1965, Advisory Opinion, ICJ Reports 2019, p. 95, and stating on that basis that 'it is inconceivable that the United Kingdom, whose administration over the Chagos Archipelago constitutes a wrongful act of a continuing character and thus must be brought to an end as rapidly as possible, and yet who has failed to do so, can have any legal interests in permanently disposing of maritime zones around the Chagos Archipelago by delimitation').

oil pollution arising from maritime transport. Both systems follow a largely similar structure. In this section, I introduce the treaties governing liability for oil pollution developed in 1969 (CLC/69) and 1971 (FUND/71), later expanded and largely replaced, most notably in 1992 (CLC/92 and FUND/92), 2001 (BUNKERS) and 2003 (FUND/2003). The rules applicable to compensation of the consequences of nuclear accidents will be examined in Chapter 5.

Resort to strict liability in these systems must not be misunderstood. It is based on the underlying assumption that the regulated activities are desirable and must be allowed to continue (hence the 'no-fault' liability), subject to a regime that caps the exposure of the economic operator and ensures compensation of the victim through a range of means. The harm is non-tolerated, in that it has to be compensated, but the obligation of compensation is not premised on a breach of a duty, much like in context of cost internalisation. Unlike cost internalisation, however, negligence of the economic operator turns the capped no-fault liability into fault-based liability with unlimited exposure.

The compensation system for oil pollution incidents is based, mainly, on the CLC/92[362] and FUND/92,[363] supplemented by BUNKERS (for spills of bunker oil from ships other than tankers) and FUND/2003 (for a minority of States Parties to FUND/92 who are also parties to FUND/2003). The system can be briefly characterised by reference to five main components:[364] (1) coverage of the system; (2) strict liability and channelling of claims to the ship owner; (3) requirement to take out insurance; (4) additional layers of compensation; (5) non-discriminatory access to compensation procedures.

3.5.3.2 Scope of Application The first component concerns the scope of application of the system. Geographically, the 1992/2003 system was

[362] The CLC/69 is still in force for a minority of States which did not become a party to CLC/92.

[363] FUND/71 ceased to be in force in 2002 and the Fund established by it was wound up in 2014.

[364] See also ILC Principles of Loss, Articles 4, 6 and 7. For analysis see generally *Survey of Liability Regimes relevant to the Topic of International Liability for Injurious Consequences arising out of Acts not prohibited by International Law*, 24 June 2004, UN Doc. A/CN.4/543 [Study of the Secretariat]; M. Jacobsson, 'Liability and Compensation for Ship-Source Pollution', in D. Attard, M. Fitzmaurice, N. Martinez, R. Hamza (eds.), *The IMLI Manual on International Maritime Law*, vol. III (Oxford: Oxford University Press, 2016), pp. 285–342; International Oil Pollution Compensation Funds, *Claims Manual* (London: IOPC Funds, 2019).

extended (as compared to the 69/71 system) to cover pollution damage occurring in the territory (including inland waters if the vessel in question qualifies as a 'ship') but also the exclusive economic zone or equivalent area of States Parties.[365]

The definition of 'ships' was also extended in the 1992/2003 system to cover 'any seagoing vessel and any seaborne craft of any type whatsoever constructed or adapted for the carriage of oil in bulk as cargo'.[366] The scope of the vessels and other craft covered has raised many difficulties in practice, which the institutions of the IOPC Funds have addressed through a range of views and statements. Generally speaking, the system applies to oil tankers (during carriage of oil or of other cargoes or during 'any voyage' following oil carriage) and to floating production, storage and offloading units (FPSOs) (only when they carry oil like cargo outside their ordinary production site) but not to vessels other than tankers, dry cargo ships, and passenger ships.[367]

With respect to 'oil', it is defined as 'any persistent hydrocarbon mineral oil such as crude oil, fuel oil, heavy diesel oil and lubricating oil'.[368] The key characteristics are 'persistence', which excludes spills of non-persistent oil (e.g. gasoline, light diesel oil or kerosene) from the scope of the system, and 'minerality', which also excludes non-mineral oils (e.g. whale oil or palm oil) from the system. The spill of persistent oil from a covered ship could result from its cargo or from its bunker (to power its engine). A loophole in the coverage of bunker oil spills from ships which are not covered tankers was closed with the adoption of BUNKERS, which applies to a wider category of ships (including those covered under the CLC)[369] and oils (including non-persistent oils of mineral origin). Bunker oil is defined by its purpose (the operation and propulsion of the ship).[370]

The type of damage covered is broadly defined in Article I(6)(a) as including 'loss or damage caused outside the ship by contamination

[365] CLC/92, Article II.

[366] CLC/92, Article I(1).

[367] Useful guidance on what is covered by the term 'ship' has been summarised in a set of guidelines adopted in October 2015 by the IOPC Fund's Administrative Council. See IOPC Funds, *Guidance for Member States. Consideration of the definition of 'ship'* (2016 edition, IOPC/OCT15/11/1, paragraph 4.3.23). The Guidance expressly states, however, that it should not be seen as authoritative interpretation of the relevant conventions.

[368] CLC/92, Article I(5).

[369] BUNKERS, Article 1(1).

[370] BUNKERS, Article 1(5).

resulting from the escape or discharge of oil from the ship'. Of note, the compensation of environmental damage is specifically limited by this provision 'to costs of reasonable measures of reinstatement actually undertaken or to be undertaken'. The cost of 'preventive measures', wherever they are taken (i.e. even beyond the geographical scope of application of the system), and the loss caused by them is also compensable when they are 'reasonable'. Such measures must respond to an 'incident' which causes pollution damage or creates an imminent risk thereof.[371]

3.5.3.3 Strict Liability and Channelling of Claims The second component requires the definition of several aspects: the identification of the liable entity, the nature of the liability, any potential grounds of exemption and the exposure caps.

In the oil pollution regime, the liable entity is the ship owner,[372] which has direct control over the regulated activity (the transportation of oil). Importantly, liability is channelled to the ship owner, which means that victims do not need to investigate which specific entities are liable. All claims can be brought against the ship owner only (or its insurer), and only under the regime of the Convention.[373] Yet, from the perspective of economic reality, compensation is predominantly borne by the oil industry as the beneficiary of the activity (see Section 3.5.3.5). When the damage is caused by several contributing entities, these are jointly and severally liable.[374]

The nature of the ship owner's liability is strict or objective, i.e. it arises irrespective of fault, although certain intervening causes (e.g. damage results from war or it is wholly caused intentionally by a third party or, still, it is wholly caused by the negligence of public authorities in maintaining navigational aids) constitute grounds for exemption.[375]

The extent of the strict liability of the ship owner is capped.[376] This cap is necessary to limit exposure and thereby enable the pursuit of the

[371] CLC/92, Article I(8).

[372] CLC/92, Articles I(3), III(1) and (4).

[373] CLC/92, Article III(4) (the exclusion of entities other than the ship owner was addressed in the claims arising from Erika incident. See TGI, 11[e] Chambre, 4[e] section, Jugement du 16 janvier 2008, No. 9934895010; CA Pole 4, Chambre 11 E, Arrêt du 30 mars 2010; Cour de Cassation, Chambre criminelle, Arrêt n° 3439 du 25 septembre 2012. The ship owner may be able to reclaim from other parties, as contemplated in Article III(5).

[374] CLC/92, Article IV.

[375] CLC/92, Article III(2)–(3).

[376] Under CLC/92, the applicable cap is related to the tonnage of the ship, and it can go up to a maximum amount of 89,770,000 Special Drawing Rights (approx. EUR 111 million), see Article V(I) and Resolution: Adoption of amendments of the limitation amounts in

activity, but it must be sufficiently high both to incentivise diligence and to cover a sufficient portion of the damage. The cap does not apply when the damage is due to intentional or reckless conduct.[377]

3.5.3.4 Insurance The third component aims to remove a practical difficulty, namely the insolvency of the ship owner, by requiring it to take out insurance for the amount of its financial exposure.[378]

Insurance and strict liability are closely linked because the ship owner can only benefit from the limitation to its exposure if it constitutes a 'limitation fund', i.e. it deposits the amount of its exposure in an account or otherwise provides a bond. In turn, the limitation fund may be constituted by the insurer. In practice, insurance is provided by 'Protection & Indemnity Clubs' (P&I Clubs), which are associations of ship owners for the purpose of mutualising risks. The injured parties can bring a direct action against the insurer, which can rely on most of the grounds for exemption available to the ship owner.[379]

Collaboration between P&I Clubs and the International Oil Pollution Compensation Funds established by FUND/71, FUND/92 and FUND/2003 ('IOPC Funds') to provide an additional layer of compensation has been instrumental in ensuring the practical operation of the system.

3.5.3.5 Additional Compensation The fourth component of the system concerns compensation of amounts not covered by the ship owner or its insurer. This may be the case due to insolvency of the liable entity, or because of the availability of a ground for exemption of liability or simply because the damage exceeds the cap.[380]

The IOPC Funds will then step in to provide an additional and much larger layer of compensation, which is also capped.[381] The injured parties

the Protocol of 1992 to amend the International Convention on Civil Liability for Oil Pollution Damage, 18 October 2000, Annex. CLC/92 conditions this limitation of liability by the responsible entity to the constitution of a limitation fund or the posting of a financial security, Article V(3).

377 See CLC/92, Art. V(2).

378 See CLC/92, Art. VII(1).

379 CLC/92, Article VII(8).

380 FUND/92, Article 4.

381 FUND/92, Article 4(4)(a)–(c). The ordinary cap is 203,000,000 Special Drawing Rights (approx. EUR 252 million) but it can be raised up to 300,740,000 Special Drawing Rights (approx. EUR 373 million). Under FUND/2003, compensation can reach up to 750,000,000 Special Drawing Rights (approx. EUR 929 million).

can present a claim to the relevant fund.[382] The IOPC Funds sometimes process these claims even before the extent of liability of the ship owner has been determined in court proceedings, which may take several years, and then, as the case may be, bring a reimbursement claim against it.

BUNKERS does not have this additional layer of compensation. Its compensation system is therefore based entirely on the liability of the ship owner and its insurer.

3.5.3.6 Non-Discrimination The fifth component aims to avoid discrimination between victims located in different affected countries. Article IX(1) of the CLC/92 determines which courts are competent to entertain claims, those of the State(s) where the damage occurred or preventive measures have been taken. Non-discrimination is implicit in the requirement, in Article IX(2), for each State part to ensure that its courts 'possess the necessary jurisdiction to entertain such actions for compensation'. Moreover, Article X facilitates the recognition and enforceability in State parties of foreign judgments rendered by the competent courts, thereby granting an additional measure of harmonisation and hence non-discrimination.

[382] FUND/92, Article 4(2).

4

Ad Hoc Approach

Joint Development of Hydrocarbons

I Overview

Energy has traditionally been governed in international law by bespoke frameworks, typically in the form of an overarching treaty which operates as the umbrella for a hybrid regime combining elements of international and domestic law, including contractual arrangements. The focus of this ad hoc governance is, as a rule, a specific deposit of hydrocarbons (including areas disputed by two or more States) or a specific project, whether for the exploitation of part of a hydrocarbon deposit, for the generation of electricity from a shared watercourse or for the development/operation of key energy-related infrastructures, most notably pipelines or electricity transmission lines.

From a legal standpoint, ad hoc governance presupposes the powers, enablers and limitations examined under the foundational approach. For example, a joint development agreement (JDA) between two States to exploit the resources of a disputed area takes as a starting point the existence of competing claims based on the rules that were discussed in Chapter 2. Moreover, such an agreement will not operate in a vacuum. The rules discussed in Chapters 2 and 3 remain generally applicable if the matter falls within their scope. Although the instruments through which an ad hoc framework is established for a deposit or project sometimes claim some measure of insulation from overarching laws, the latter remain applicable in accordance with the special and general conflict rules (particularly the *lex specialis* principle) to an extent to be determined on a case-by-case basis.

This 'artificial gap'[1] results from a deliberate preference of a majority of States to address energy projects through bespoke frameworks. Such

[1] See D. M. Ong, 'The Contribution of State-Multinational Corporation "Transnational" Investment Agreements to International Environmental Law' (2006) 17 *Yearbook of International Environmental Law* 205.

preference came to light during the work of the UN International Law Commission (ILC) on shared oil and gas (see Section 3.2). This work, which stemmed from a wider project also including aquifers, aimed to develop generally applicable principles for the governance of shared oil and gas resources. After the portion of the work on aquifers was completed, the work on hydrocarbons had to be abandoned due to the reluctance of most States to see their transactional discretion affected. Yet, even when claimed, such discretion is not unfettered, as it is subject to all the non-specific applicable rules discussed under the foundational approach.

In this chapter, after a brief introduction to the main features of ad hoc approaches to governance, I begin the examination of this approach by focussing on its most representative illustration, namely the joint development of hydrocarbons. Four other major applications of the ad hoc approach, that is the construction and operation of hydroelectric dams, pipelines, electricity transmission lines and offshore wind energy projects, are examined in Chapter 5.

II Ad Hoc Governance of Energy Deposits/Projects

To understand the ad hoc approach, two main dimensions must be clarified: the defining features shared by the frameworks developed for each case and the interactions between such frameworks and the rules encompassed by the foundational approach, that is the wider body of international law. They are briefly described in general terms; their concrete manifestations will be discussed when presenting the main areas where the approach has found expression.

2.1 Introduction

Ad hoc governance of energy is characterised by *four main features*: (1) the framework is tailored to a specific deposit or project; (2) it is hybrid in nature, combining elements of international and domestic law; (3) it is either bilateral or narrowly plurilateral, as it concerns only those States that enjoy legal entitlements over the deposit/project; and (4) it seeks to achieve some degree of insulation from the generally applicable international and domestic law.

The first feature concerns the specific target of the regulatory framework. Ad hoc governance is specific not only because it is expressly concerned with energy as a legal object but, more characteristically, because it is tailored to the needs of a specific deposit or project. For example, when the legal entitlements over the area where the resources are located are disputed, the framework will typically supplement the vacuum with a clause stating that both parties recognise that the activities do not modify the territorial or maritime status of the area, which remains to be settled. When there is dispute over the area, the framework will still have to organise a wide range of matters specifically concerning the project or projects to be developed (e.g. modalities of exploration and exploitation, taxation, costs and access to infrastructure).

The second feature flows, precisely, from the need to organise a number of project-specific aspects, which will directly concern public and private entities engaged in the production, services and finance of the project. Thus, ad hoc governance typically goes beyond agreements between participating States (e.g. joint development agreements or intergovernmental pipeline agreements) and regulates, through a variety of instruments, the specific situation of other participating entities, such as their ownership structure, their access to licences in the project area, the duties applicable to the equipment brought in to build the necessary infrastructure, the broader tax situation and many other rights and obligations that place them under a bespoke regime arising from participation in the project. The nature of the instruments organising this framework is not limited to treaties in the meaning of international law.[2] It includes a range of memoranda or records of understanding between regulatory authorities, a substantial layer of contractual instruments (including host government agreements), application of both private law (to which the contracts are subject, employment contracts for key staff, land rights) and public law (regarding taxation; customs duties; or operational, construction and environmental permits etc.) and so on. Each project will present its own specificities, but the framework cuts much deeper into domestic law than the sole umbrella treaty.

The deposit/project-based nature of the framework tends to limit the number of participating States to those with direct entitlements (or claims) over the area. Often, the ad hoc frameworks are bilateral or trilateral, involving the States concerned by a transboundary hydrocarbon deposit or watercourse or pipeline. The tailored character and the depth of the regulation make broader membership very difficult and also distinguish instruments of a foundational character, such as the Energy

[2] VCLT, Article 1(a).

Charter Treaty, which is specific to energy (but not deposit/project based) and has a wide and expanding membership, from instruments of an ad hoc character, which by definition concern only a few States.

The fourth feature is the attempt not only to develop a bespoke framework but to insulate it from the otherwise generally applicable law. This broad aim can only be inferred from the detail of the relevant frameworks. For example, imports of equipment relating to the project may be subject to lower or no customs duties or to different processes, which, depending on how the origin of the equipment is defined, can raise inconsistencies with trade law. Similarly, the social and environmental standards incorporated in the framework, even when both State parties agree to them, may be lower than international standards (e.g. the IFC Performance Standards or, more generally, Article 192 of the UNCLOS or customary international environmental law).[3]

States have expressed great reluctance towards subjecting the governance of shared hydrocarbon resources to general principles (see Section 3.2). In other cases, the overarching treaty makes no reference to environmental or human rights standards, which have to be read into the text of the treaty by means of systemic integration. The main difficulty that arises in this context concerns the articulation between the general law (brought into focus by the foundational approach) and the special law (the ad hoc framework).

2.2 Normative Interactions

Normative interactions take place between different regulatory layers at different analytical levels (e.g. treaty and custom; general treaties and special treaties; specific norms, whether customary or treaty based; international vs. domestic norms; international or domestic norms vs. contractual arrangements; different contractual arrangements or provisions). Here, my purpose is to clarify the articulation between the rules that were presented under the foundational approach and those arising from an ad hoc framework.

It is important to emphasise that neither the foundational nor the ad hoc approach has any legal existence as such. Thus, the analysis concerns relations between specific rules, not approaches or – as became misleadingly frequent in certain circles – 'branches' or 'regimes'. The inclusion of

[3] See Chapter 3.

a rule in a given treaty may have implications for its relations with other norms (e.g. if a treaty is deemed to be *lex specialis* with respect to another treaty or a customary norm), but such implications, if at all relevant, are only one aspect of the analysis. Even when a norm is given priority over another norm as a result of one or more considerations, such as specificity, that does not necessarily exclude the application of the latter in toto. As the International Court of Justice observed in its advisory opinion on the *Legality of Nuclear Weapons*, both norms may apply together, with the *lex specialis* modulating the meaning of the *lex generalis*.[4]

The analysis of interactions must follow, at a minimum, three main analytical steps: (1) identifying the relevant analytical level (norms, treaty sections, treaties, systems of legally linked treaties), (2) determining the relevant considerations giving priority to one level over the other (special conflict rules in the relevant instruments and general rules, such as *lex superior*, *lex posterior*, *lex specialis* and/or interpretation techniques), and (3) determining the appropriate articulation between the relevant levels (exclusion in toto or combined application in a variety of forms). These steps normally make part of an integrated analysis, which must be conducted on a case-by-case basis. One illustration may be useful to show the complexities of the exercise.

Article 3(1) of the Intergovernmental Agreement concerning the Nabucco Pipeline Project (Austria, Bulgaria, Hungary, Romania and Turkey) provides that

> the Agreement shall not affect any treaty rights and obligations of the States Parties, including those deriving from the Energy Charter Treaty to which the States Parties are all party, and from the Treaties establishing the European Union for the Republic of Austria, the Republic of Bulgaria, the Republic of Hungary, and Romania.[5]

The subordination of the Nabucco IGA to other agreements illustrates a broader trend in pipeline agreements.[6] By contrast, the BTC Pipeline

[4] *Legality of the Threat or Use of Nuclear Weapons*, Advisory Opinion, ICJ Reports 1996, p. 226, para. 25.

[5] Nabucco IGA, reproduced in R. Leal-Arcas, *Energy Transit Activities: Collection of Intergovernmental Agreements on Oil and Gas Transit Pipelines and Commentary* (Energy Charter Secretariat, 2015) [*ECT Collection*], Annex I. This project was eventually abandoned, but the text of the agreement remains a useful example.

[6] See Energy Charter Secretariat, *Intergovernmental Agreements and Host Government Agreements on Oil and Gas Pipelines: A Comparison* (Energy Charter Secretariat, 2015) [*ECT Comparison*], at 47–48 (referring to several other examples).

(Azerbaijan, Georgia, Turkey)[7] includes a clause (Article III(6)) whereby each State Party

> represents and warrants that ... [it] is not a party to any domestic or international agreement or commitment or lawfully bound to observe or enforce any domestic law or regulation, or international agreement or treaty, that conflicts with, impairs or interferes with this Agreement or limits, abridges or adversely affects the State's ability to implement this Agreement or enter into and implement any other applicable Project Agreement.

Neither of these two clauses clearly settles the matter in case of normative conflict, hence additional considerations (mainly treaty interpretation rules) are necessary.

The BTC IGA clause seems to give priority to the agreement over other international and domestic law (a manifestation of the attempted insulation of the framework), but its operation is unclear. In case a conflict arises, the clause may be breached, but that does not mean that the BTC IGA would pre-empt the application of the other agreement. Moreover, a combined interpretation of the agreements at stake may lead to the conclusion that, when properly interpreted, the other instrument neither 'conflicts with, impairs or interferes with' the BTC IGA nor 'limits, abridges or adversely affects' its application, and therefore the clause is not breached. Furthermore, the clause cannot derogate from the continued application of a *lex superior* (e.g. the UN Charter, under Article 103, or peremptory norms in relation to self-determination and human rights). In the three hypotheses, the situation would remain governed by the alternative rule or instrument, with the caveat that, under the first hypothesis, Article III(6) would be breached, hence raising the possibility of compensation.

With regard to the clause in the Nabucco IGA, despite its apparent clarity, it may also give rise to significant ambiguities, most notably in case of conflicts between the ECT and EU law, which, as a growing body of investment awards suggests, are far from settled.[8] In addition, the reference to the ECT triggers other special conflict clauses, such as Article 7(8) of the ECT, which requires a certain articulation of the rules applicable under the GATT and those under the ECT. As discussed in

[7] BTC IGA, Articles III(6)–(7), in *ECT Collection*, Annex II.

[8] See J. R. Basedow, 'The Achmea Judgment and the Applicability of the Energy Charter Treaty in Intra-EU Investment Arbitration' (2019) 23 *Journal of International Economic Law* 271.

Chapter 2, Article 7(8) of the ECT gives priority to the rules on transit set in the GATT (Article V). But such rules are less specific (particularly for network-bound transit) than those of Article 7 of the ECT. Thus, the conflict rule must be understood as treating Article V of the GATT as a 'floor' but not a 'ceiling'. To the extent that Article 7 of the ECT offers WTO-plus treatment, the provision continues to govern the relevant transaction. However, there are aspects of transit which are not specifically governed by either the GATT or the ECT, such as transit infrastructure development and access. As a result, if third-party access is specifically regulated by an ad hoc agreement, such as the Nabucco IGA (Article 3(3)), the relevant provisions govern this aspect despite the 'floors' set by both the ECT and the GATT.

Thus, overall, what can be broadly referred to as the interactions between the rules of the foundational approach and those of the ad hoc approach must be addressed, at a technical level, through a three-step approach on a case-by-case basis. As a general matter, however, ad hoc frameworks remain governed by the general rules encompassed by the foundational approach.

III Joint Development of Hydrocarbons

3.1 *Introduction*

The need for 'joint' development of hydrocarbon deposits stems from three important factors.

The first is the broader context of the historical assertion of entitlements over such resources. For those deposits clearly located within the territory of a State, the main challenge concerned not only the assertion of full and unconstrained entitlements over energy resources (see Chapter 2) but also the technological and commercial ability to exploit them. That explains the main objectives pursued over time by the Organization of the Petroleum Exporting Countries (OPEC), which in the first years after its establishment in 1960 sought to clarify the 'permanent' nature of State sovereignty over energy resources and to move from the concession model to the production-sharing one. Later, some of its members realised that they could wield oil production levels as a weapon to have their voices heard in international affairs.[9] Eventually, with the increasing experience gained over the years, the

[9] On the development of the OPEC, see Chapter 7.

model was replaced by one where national oil companies (NOCs) hold the majority of fossil fuel reserves, which are exploited in partnership with international oil companies (IOCs), or treat the latter as simple service providers.

The second factor concerns the location of hydrocarbon resources in areas which were only subject to the powers of States well into the second half of the twentieth century, mainly between 1958 and 1982.[10] That led to competing claims over areas potentially rich in offshore oil and gas resources, which require for their exploitation delimitation and/or an agreement on how to exploit the relevant resources in the disputed area. In other words, the new entitlements conferred on States in the form of territorial sovereignty (within twelve nautical miles from the baselines) or sovereign rights over the resources located in their continental shelf and exclusive economic zones brought with them delimitation disputes and the need to manage them, provisionally, to enable the exploitation (or to avoid the unilateral exploitation) of resources located therein, hence the need for 'joint' exploitation. Importantly, even when the relevant areas had been fully delimited, the 'joint' exploitation of hydrocarbon resources straddling the jurisdiction of two or more States was also necessary for geophysical reasons.

The latter provides the third reason why 'joint' development became important. Drilling in a section of a deposit (onshore or offshore) will normally change the pressure within the hydrocarbon field, thus affecting the ability of other States to exploit it. This is because the recovery mechanism of conventional hydrocarbon deposits is based on the existing pressure within the field, which, when drilled, releases the resource. Drilling changes the pressure and therefore the possibility and cost of draining the reservoir, hence the expression used by M. W. Mouton in his 'Hague Lectures on the Continental Shelf': 'never two straws in one glass'.[11] It is possible to re-inject gas to recover more of the oil or, in non-conventional hydrocarbon fields, to inject water with chemicals and drill the reservoir horizontally (rather than vertically) to release the hydrocarbons trapped in the rocks, but these methods are

[10] The first offshore joint development agreement was signed in 1958 (Bahrain–Saudi Arabia Frontier Agreement), at a time when the negotiation of the Geneva Convention on the Continental Shelf had crystallised the legal recognition of this area and the ensuring rights of coastal States. See CCS, Articles 1 and 2.

[11] M. W. Mouton, 'The Continental Shelf' (1954) 85 *RCADI* 343, at 421, referred to by V. Becker-Weinberg, *Joint Development of Hydrocarbon Deposits in the Law of the Sea* (Berlin: Springer, 2014), at 9.

more expensive. As a result, the exploitation of a cross-border or disputed field may have to be 'unitised' to avoid inefficiencies and costs in the development process. This is done for economic reasons, which are themselves based on the geophysical characteristics of the field and lead to the conclusion that the most efficient approach to jointly developing a field is to unitise production. In a context where the land or maritime area boundary is set, the alternative would be more costly and inefficient. In a context where the area is disputed, the State unilaterally exploiting the deposit will normally (although that is a factual matter to be established empirically) cause significant harm to the other State possessing or claiming entitlements over the deposit.

The literature on JDAs is vast, and it has long embodied what most scholars and practitioners understand to be the international law of energy, namely a combination treaty and contractual practice focussing on oil and gas, with aspects of maritime delimitation and investment protection. Within this body of literature, a number of strands can be identified dealing, respectively, with JDAs as a growing State practice,[12] the main terms of the relevant agreements (treaties and related contracts),[13] certain specific topics (e.g. the purported emergence of a '*lex*

[12] See Becker-Weinberg, *Joint Development*; N. Bankes, 'Recent Framework Agreements for the Recognition and Development of Transboundary Hydrocarbon Resources' (2014) 29 *IJMCL* 666; C. Scholfield, 'Blurring the Lines: Maritime Joint Development and the Cooperative Management of Ocean Resources' (2008) 7 *Issues Legal Scholarship* 1; A. E. Bastida, A. Ifesi-Okoye, S. Mahmud, J. Ross, T. Walde, 'Cross-Border Unitization and Joint Development Agreements: An International Law Perspective' (2007) 29 *Houston International Law Journal* 355; D. Ong, 'Joint Development of Common Offshore Oil and Gas Deposits: "Mere" State Practice or Customary International Law?' (1999) 93 *AJIL* 771; I. Townsend-Gault, W. G. Stoermont, 'Offshore Petroleum Joint Development Arrangements: Functional Instrument? Compromise? Obligation?', in G. H. Blake et al. (eds.), *The Peaceful Management of Transboundary Resources* (Berlin: Springer, 1995), at 51–76; R. Lagoni, 'Interim Measures Pending Maritime Delimitation Agreements' (1984) 78 *AJIL* 345; R. Lagoni, 'Oil and Gas across National Frontiers' (1979) 73 *AJIL* 215; W. Onorato, 'Apportionment of an International Common Petroleum Deposit' (1968) 17 *ICLQ* 85; W. Onorato, 'Apportionment of an International Common Petroleum Deposit' (1977) 26 *ICLQ* 324.

[13] See T. Martin, J. Jay Park, 'Global Petroleum Industry Model Contracts Revisited: Higher, Faster, Stronger' (2010) 3 *JWELB* 4; C. Duval et al., *International Petroleum Exploration and Exploitation Agreements: Legal, Economic and Policy Aspects*, 2nd ed. (New York: Barrows, 2009); A. Jennings, *Oil and Gas Exploration Contracts*, 2nd ed. (London: Sweet & Maxwell, 2008); J. Lang Weaver, D. Asmus, 'Unitizing Oil and Gas Fields around the World: A Comparative Analysis of National Laws and Private Contracts' (2006) 28 *Houston Journal of International Law* 3; E. E. Smith, J. S. Dzienkowski, O. L. Anderson, G. B. Conine, J. S. Lowe, B. M. Kramer, *International Petroleum*

petrolea' or the link with maritime delimitation disputes)[14] and certain specific disputes or areas.[15] In the next sections, I first discuss the aborted

Transactions, 2nd ed. (Westminster: Rocky Mountain, 2000); B. Taverne, *Co-operative Agreements in the Extractive Petroleum Industry* (The Hague: Kluwer, 1996); Z. Gao, *International Petroleum Contracts: Current Trends and New Directions* (London: Graham & Trotman, 1994); D. Johnston, *International Petroleum Fiscal Systems and Production Sharing Contracts* (Tulsa: PennWell, 1994); H. Fox (ed.), *Joint Development of Offshore Oil and Gas*, vols. I and II (London: BIICL, 1989–1990).

[14] On the '*lex petrolea*' argument: K. Talus et al., 'Lex Petrolea and the Internationalization of Petroleum Agreements: Focus on Host Government Contracts' (2012) 5 *JWELB* 181; T. C. C. Childs, 'Update on Lex Petrolea: The Continuing Development of Customary Law Relating to International Oil and Gas Exploration and Production' (2011) 4 *JWELB* 214; R. D. Bishop, 'International Arbitration of Petroleum Disputes: The Development of a Lex Petrolea' (1998) XXIII *Yearbook of Commercial Arbitration* 113. On delimitation: British Institute of International and Comparative Law, *Report on the Obligations of States under Articles 74(3) and 83(3) of UNCLOS in Respect of Undelimited Maritime Areas* (London: BIICL, 2016); G. Burn et al., 'Legal Issues in Cross-Border Resource Development' (2015) 8 *JWELB* 154; P. M. Blyschak, 'Offshore Oil and Gas Projects amid Maritime Border Disputes: Applicable Law' (2013) 6 *JWELB* 210; M. Miyoshi, 'The Joint Development of Offshore Oil and Gas in Relation to Maritime Boundary Delimitation' (1999) 2 *Maritime Briefings*, no. 5; G. H. Blake et al. (eds.), *Boundaries and Energy: Problems and Prospects* (The Hague: Kluwer, 1998).

[15] See J. Onele, 'Revisiting Unilateral Exploitation of Mineral Resources in Disputed Water under United Nations Convention on the Law of the Sea: Any New Matter Arising?' (2019) 10 *JIDS* 160; Huaigao Qi, 'Joint Development in the South China Sea: China's Incentives and Policy Choices' (2019) 8 *Journal of Contemporary East Asia Studies* 220; I. Fodchenko, 'Legal Aspects of the Russian–Norwegian Model for Cross-Border Unitization in the Barents Sea and Arctic Ocean' (2018) 49 *Ocean Development & International Law* 262; N. Bankes, 'The Regime for Transboundary Hydrocarbon Deposits in the Maritime Delimitation Treaties and Other Related Agreements of Arctic Coastal States' (2016) 47 *Ocean Development & International Law* 141; R. Beckman, I. Townsend-Gault, C. Schofield, T. Davenport, L. Bernard (eds.), *Beyond Territorial Disputes in the South China Sea* (Cheltenham: Edward Elgar, 2013); R. Colmenter, D. Enriquez (eds.), *International Oil and Gas Transactions in Latin America* (Mexico DF: ITAM, 2011); K. Noussia, 'On International Arbitrations for the Settlement of Boundary Maritime Delimitation Disputes and Disputes from Joint Development Agreements for the Exploitation of Offshore Natural Resources' (2010) 25 *IJMCL* 63; P. de Vareilles Sommieres, A. Fekini, 'Les nouveaux contrats internationaux d'exploration et de partage de production pétrolière en Libye: Problèmes choisis (2eme partie)' (2009) *JDI* 97; P. de Vareilles Sommières, A. Fekini, 'Les nouveaux contrats internationaux d'exploration et de partage de production pétrolière en Libye: Problèmes choisis (1ere partie)' (2008) *JDI* 3; G. Oduntan, 'The Emergent Legal Regime for Exploration of Hydrocarbons in the Gulf of Guinea: Imperative Considerations for Participating States and Multinationals' (2008) 57 *ICLQ* 253; L. E. Rodriguez-Rivera, 'Joint Development Zones and Other Cooperative Management Efforts Related to Transboundary Maritime Resources: A Caribbean and Latin American Model for Peaceful Resolution of Maritime Boundary Disputes' (2008) 7 *Issues Legal Scholarship* 1; C. Schofield, 'Unlocking the Seabed Resources of the Gulf of

attempt by the ILC to codify the principles applicable to shared oil and gas resources; I then survey the main types of JDAs as they developed over time as well as the overarching principles on which they rest.

3.2 The Aborted Work of the International Law Commission

The codification of the principles applicable to 'shared natural resources' was a by-product of the earlier work of the ILC on the topic of non-navigational uses of international watercourses. This work, which led to the adoption of the 1997 New York Convention on the Non-Navigational Uses of International Watercourses,[16] had excluded confined groundwater from its remit, despite the efforts from the last Special Rapporteur, Rosenstock, to expand the scope of the draft.

In 2000, however, the topic of 'shared natural resources' was inscribed in the list of topics of the ILC for the following quinquennium on the basis of a syllabus prepared by Rosenstock which covered, under the expression 'shared natural resources', shared deposits of both groundwater as well as oil and gas.[17] On this basis, work on the topic was formally undertaken in 2002, with Chusei Yamada appointed as Special Rapporteur.[18] Since the beginning, the focus was on transboundary groundwater, with the understanding that oil and gas would be considered later.[19] But already at this early stage, some doubts about the feasibility of a codification project on shared oil and gas were expressed.[20] Work on 'Transboundary Aquifers' progressed well and a first draft was adopted and circulated for State comment. That reopened the question of what to do with oil and gas. After some initial doubts regarding the

Thailand' (2007) 29 *Contemporary Southeast Asia* 286; P. Cameron, 'The Rules of Engagement: Developing Cross-Border Petroleum Deposits in the North Sea and the Caribbean' (2006) 55 *ICLQ* 559; D. Ong, 'Thailand/Malaysia' (1991) 6 *International Journal of Estuarine and Coastal Law* 57; W. Onorato, 'Joint Development in the International Petroleum Sector: The Yemeni Variant' (1990) 39 *ICLQ* 653; J. C. Woodliffe, 'The International Unitization of an Offshore Gas Field' (1977) 26 *ICLQ* 338.

[16] United Nations Convention on the Law of the Non-Navigational Uses of International Watercourses, 21 May 1997, 36 ILM 700 [UN Watercourses Convention].

[17] General Assembly Official Records (GAOR), Fifty-fifth Session, Supplement No. 10 (A/55/10), annex, section 3.

[18] GAOR, *Fifty-seventh Session, Supplement No. 10* (A/57/10); chapter X.A.1, paras. 518–519.

[19] *Shared natural resources: first report on outlines, by Mr. Chusei Yamada, Special Rapporteur*, 30 April 2003, A//CN.4/533, para. 18.

[20] ILC Report (2003), chapter IX, para. 388.

relations between the work on groundwater and that on oil and gas,[21] it became increasingly clear both in the ILC and at the level of the Sixth (Legal) Committee of the UN General Assembly that the second reading of the Draft Articles on Transboundary Aquifers would proceed independently.[22] The latter were adopted in second reading in 2008.[23]

In the meantime, the ILC had started to convene, since May 2007, a Working Group on Shared Natural Resources under the chairmanship of Enrique Candiotti, which, in addition to discuss the work on groundwater also took the initiative to prepare a questionnaire to be sent to States to compile their practice on the management of shared oil and gas resources. The number of responses that this questionnaire elicited remained limited. As late as 2010, there were still fewer than forty responses, although some States made oral statements.[24] Between 2007 and 2010, when work on the topic was formally 'discontinued', the majority of the feedback received by States made it increasingly clear that there was great reluctance to allow the ILC to embark on the codification of principles governing shared oil and gas resources. For present purposes, it is the justification given by States to resist such codification efforts that is of particular interest.

[21] ILC Report (2007), chapter V, paras. 169–173.

[22] Fourth report on shared natural resources: transboundary groundwaters by Mr. Chusei Yamada, Special Rapporteur, 6 March 2007, A/CN.4/580; GAOR, Sixty-second Session, Supplement No. 10 (A/62/10), para. 177. There was wide support for this approach from State delegations at the Sixth Committee, including: Nordic countries, A/C.6/62/SR.22, para. 31; India, A/C.6/62/SR.22, para. 38; Argentina, A/C.6/62/SR.22, para. 57; Guatemala, A/C.6/62/SR.22, para. 72; United States of America, A/C.6/62/SR.22, para. 88; Malaysia, A/C.6/62/SR.23, para. 8; Canada, A/C.6/62/SR.23, para. 18; Hungary, A/C.6/62/SR.23, para. 39; Romania, A/C.6/62/SR.24, para. 18; Mexico, A/C.6/62/SR.24, para. 10; Democratic Republic of the Congo, A/C.6/62/SR.24, para. 30; Greece, A/C.6/62/SR.24, para. 41; Cuba, A/C.6/62/SR.24, para. 68; Russian Federation, A/C.6/62/SR.24, para. 81; Japan, A/C.6/62/SR.24, para. 91; Syrian Arab Republic, A/C.6/62/SR.24, para. 93; Portugal, A/C.6/62/SR.24, para. 104; Israel, A/C.6/62/SR.24, para. 109; Brazil, A/C.6/62/SR.24, para. 110; New Zealand, A/C.6/62/SR.25, para. 14; Indonesia, A/C.6/62/SR.25, para. 33; Islamic Republic of Iran, A/C.6/62/SR.25, para. 44; Thailand, A/C.6/62/SR.25, para. 56; Venezuela, A/C.6/62/SR.25, para. 62; Turkey, A/C.6/62/SR.25, para. 65; Poland, A/C.6/62/SR.26, para. 18. Summarised in Report on shared natural resources: transboundary aquifers, by Chusei Yamada, Special Rapporteur, 21 February 2008, A/CN.4/591 [Yamada's Fifth Report], para. 5.

[23] ILC Report (2008), chapter VI, paras. 46–47.

[24] See *Shared natural resources. Comments and observations received from Governments*, 29 January 2009, A/CN.4/607 (summarising responses from 17 States), and *Shared natural resources. Comments and observations received from Governments*, 7 July 2010, A/CN.4/633 (summarising responses from 19 additional States).

The main reasons are summarised in three reports, two by C. Yamada of 2008[25] and 2009[26] and a third one by S. Murase of 2010.[27] In the first, the reasons identified are mobilised to confirm the independent pursuit of work on transboundary aquifers, and they therefore highlight the differences between the two strands of work,[28] whereas the second and the third reports focus specifically on the feasibility of work on oil and gas as such. Yamada's 2009 'informal paper' took note of the relatively few responses to the ILC questionnaire received from States (only eighteen at that point), which highlighted the bilateral and hybrid nature of the arrangements in place as well as the importance of keeping matters of delimitation solely for the States concerned (para. 6). The paper concluded that, in the absence of consensus among States, the ILC should conduct further studies before deciding whether to proceed or not with the codification process on oil and gas (para. 8). Following Yamada's resignation from the ILC in 2009, the Working Group on Shared Natural Resources entrusted Shinya Murase with the drafting of a study on the feasibility of future work on oil and gas. Murase's study took into account a total of forty-six statements from States, thirty-nine in the form of responses to the ILC questionnaire (including nineteen addressing the question of feasibility) and the rest in the form of oral statements before the Sixth Committee. The study confirmed that the majority of States expressed the view that the ILC should not embark on the codification of this topic. The reasons given by these States are summarised in paragraph 5 of Murase's study:

> The reasons cited by those States, while varying considerably, included the following points: (a) the question of oil and gas is essentially different from that of groundwater; (b) the issue is closely intertwined with the bilateral interests of the States involved; (c) it cannot be separated from boundary delimitation; (d) it is not suitable for codification; and (e) it involves political sensitivity and technical difficulty. Naturally, some of those reasons are closely interrelated, but they are referred to here for the sake of convenience, with a view to highlighting a general trend in the views of States.

25 Yamada's Fifth Report.

26 *Shared natural resources. Paper on oil and gas prepared by Mr. Chusei Yamada, Special Rapporteur on shared natural resources*, 18 February 2009, A/CN.4/608 [Yamada's Informal Paper].

27 *Shared natural resources: feasibility of future work on oil and gas. Paper prepared by Shinya Murase*, 9 March 2010, A/CN.4/621 [Murase's Report].

28 Yamada's Fifth Report, paras. 4–6.

On this basis, the study recommended that 'the Working Group decide [...] that the topic of oil and gas will not be pursued any further' (para. 17). The Working Group followed this recommendation,[29] which was largely welcomed by States in the Sixth Committee.[30]

As discussed in the next sections, the prevailing ad hocism in the governance of energy has long and deep roots. Yet, as noted earlier, the preference for ad hoc frameworks builds upon and remains subject to the general rules discussed under the foundational approach. Even with respect to maritime delimitation, which was and remains a particularly delicate issue, the overarching rules governing the matter result from the UNCLOS and customary international law (see Chapter 2).

3.3 Structure and Content of JDAs

3.3.1 Types

From a descriptive perspective, an initial distinction can be introduced between three types of agreements relevant for the joint development of hydrocarbon resources, namely boundary and delimitation agreements, JDAs, and unitisation agreements. Boundary and delimitation agreements concern the terrestrial and maritime boundaries between the territories and maritime spaces of two or more States. Delimitation agreements on maritime spaces may include a 'mineral resources clause' governing the rights and duties of States regarding mineral resources straddling the boundary, whether these are known or discovered in the future. JDAs, whether they concern onshore[31] or offshore resources, can be seen as a fuller elaboration of such mineral resources clauses, with the three important caveats that (1) they expressly require the 'joint' development of transboundary resources (whereas 'mineral resources clauses'

[29] ILC Report (2010), chapter XII, para. 384.

[30] Report of the International Law Commission on the work of its sixty-second session (2010). Topical summary of the discussion held in the Sixth Committee of the General Assembly during its sixty-fifth session, prepared by the Secretariat, 19 January 2011, A/CN.4/638, paras. 124–129.

[31] For an example of a JDA set concerning onshore resources see the Agreement concerning the principles of geological co-operation between the Czechoslovak Republic and the Republic of Austria, 23 January 1960, 495 UNTS 99; Agreement between the Government of the Czechoslovak Republic and the Austrian Federal Government concerning the working of common deposits of natural gas and petroleum, 23 January 1960, 495 UNTS 125.

may be limited to mere duties of information sharing, cooperation and mutual restraint), (2) they normally specify the area which is to be jointly developed and (3) they do not require prior delimitation. The latter point must be stressed. JDAs are often used as an instrument to develop hydrocarbon resources in a disputed area. Unitisation agreements are a way of implementing JDAs which treats the entire hydrocarbon field as a single unit for efficiency purposes. Unitisation is a way of jointly developing transboundary hydrocarbon deposits to avoid the 'two straws in one glass' problem noted earlier or, in other words, the problems entailed by unilateral exploitation.

A second descriptive approximation to JDAs concerns their nature. Several techniques can and have been used in practice to organise the joint exploitation of transboundary hydrocarbons, including treaties under international law but also a range of other instruments which may not qualify as treaties (e.g. contracts, memoranda or records of understanding, letters of intent). Articles 74(3) and 83(3) of the UNCLOS expressly require States, pending delimitation of their EEZ and continental shelves, to 'make every effort to enter into provisional arrangements of a practical nature', which 'shall be without prejudice to the final delimitation'. The nature of this obligation to 'make every effort' will be discussed in Section 3.4. For now, it suffices to make two observations. First, there are several examples of areas jointly developed despite the absence of delimitation.[32] Secondly, depending on the circumstances, such provisional arrangements may be binding under international law or under domestic law or not binding. They may amount to 'treaties' or not. The key consideration is that, as expressly stated in Articles 74(3) and 83(3), they 'shall be without prejudice to the final delimitation'. The 'provisional' and 'practical' nature of such 'arrangements' may, in addition, be relevant when entered into by States that do not recognise each other as such, although placing the exercise under Articles 74 and 83 would amount to a form of implicit recognition (i.e. that the other entity is a State because it is entitled to an EEZ and a continental shelf).

A third type of characterisation of JDAs concern the overall architecture that they establish for the joint development of the relevant resources. One commentator usefully distinguishes three main models

[32] See Miyoshi, *Joint Development of Offshore Oil and Gas*, at 6–27.

of JDAs on the basis of the degree of cooperation and institutionalisation.[33] The first and most rudimentary model entrusts the development of the transboundary or disputed deposit to one of the States and allocates the proceeds between the two States involved, after deduction of the cost of the first State. This is the model followed by the very first offshore JDA, between Saudi Arabia and Bahrain,[34] as well as by some subsequent JDAs in this area. For example, the 1969 Qatar–UAE Agreement[35] confers equal rights of ownership to each State over the straddling al-Bunduq oil field, despite the fact that most of the field is located (according to the delimitation line agreed by the parties) on the UAE's side. The development of the field is in the hands of an Abu Dhabi company under terms defined by a concession granted by Abu Dhabi, but 'all revenues, profits and other benefits' are shared equally between the two States.[36] Of note, this is both a delimitation and a JDA, but the detail of how the development is to be conducted is delegated to domestic law (the terms of the concession granted by the ruler of Abu Dhabi).

Another model of JDA embodies a higher degree of cooperation. It organises the development of the transboundary or disputed deposit jointly by three main means: (1) the designation of a joint development zone, including sub-zones; (2) development of each sub-zone by joint ventures between designated companies; and (3) the need for both States to approve the agreement whereby the development by each joint venture of a sub-zone is authorised and organised. There are several examples of this approach, whether in Europe,[37] Latin America and the Caribbean,[38]

[33] See Ong, *Joint Development of Common Offshore Oil and Gas Deposits*, at 787–792. The discussion on these models relies on Ong.

[34] Bahrain-Saudi Arabia Frontier Agreement.

[35] Agreement between Qatar and Abu Dhabi on the settlement of maritime boundaries and ownership of islands (with declarations and map), 20 March 1969 [Qatar/Abu Dhabi Agreement], available at: www.un.org/Depts/los/LEGISLATIONANDTREATIES/.

[36] Qatar/Abu Dhabi Agreement, sections (6) and (7).

[37] See e.g. the Convention between France and Spain on the delimitation of the territorial sea and the contiguous zone in the Bay of Biscay (Golfe de Gascogne/Golfo de Vizcaya) (with map), 29 January 1974 [Bay of Biscay Convention], available at: www.un.org/Depts/los/LEGISLATIONANDTREATIES/.

[38] See e.g. Maritime treaty between Jamaica and the Republic of Colombia (with chart), 12 November 1993 [Colombia–Jamaica Agreement], available at: www.un.org/Depts/los/LEGISLATIONANDTREATIES/.

Asia[39] or the Middle East.[40] By way of illustration, the 1974 Japan–Korea Agreement defines the joint development zone (Article II) and its sub-zones (Article III), which are to be developed jointly by 'concessionaires' designated by each State under an 'operating agreement', which must be approved by both parties (Article V). Concessionaires of each party are each entitled 'to an equal share of natural resources extracted in the Joint Development Zone' and they shall also share expenses in 'equal proportions' (Article IX). In this model, a joint commission is established but it is only a liaison organ, without regulatory and licensing powers.

That is the main difference with the third model of JDA, which is characterised by the establishment of a common authority with legal personality, which issues exploration and exploitation licences, enters into contractual arrangements with companies, and also enjoys some regulatory powers. Again, there are several examples of this approach, such as the joint authorities established by agreements between Sudan and Saudi Arabia,[41] Malaysia and Thailand,[42] Timor-Leste and Australia (for the Greater Sunrise field)[43] or Guinea-Bissau and Senegal.[44] The

[39] See e.g. Agreement Between Japan and the Republic of Korea concerning joint development of the southern part of the continental shelf adjacent to the two countries (with map, appendix, agreed minutes and exchange of notes), 30 January 1974 [Japan–Korea Agreement], available at: www.un.org/Depts/los/LEGISLATIONANDTREATIES/.

[40] See e.g. Agreement between the Kingdom of Saudi Arabia and the State of Kuwait concerning the submerged area adjacent to the divided zone, 2 July 2000, available at: www.un.org/Depts/los/LEGISLATIONANDTREATIES/.

[41] Agreement between Sudan and Saudi Arabia relating to the joint exploitation of the natural resources of the seabed and sub-soil of the Red Sea in the Common Zone, 16 May 1974, reproduced in J. N. Moore (ed.), *International and United States Documents on Oceans Law and Policy* (New York: S. Hein, 1986), pp. 198–200.

[42] Memorandum of Understanding Between Malaysia and the Kingdom of Thailand on the Establishment of the Joint Authority for the Exploitation of the Resources of the Sea Bed in a Defined Area of the Continental Shelf of the two Countries in the Gulf of Thailand, 21 February 1979 [Malaysia–Thailand MOU], which was followed by the Agreement Between the Government of Malaysia and the Government of the Kingdom of Thailand on the Constitution and Other Matters Relating to the Establishment of the Malaysia–Thailand Joint Authority, 30 May 1990 [Malaysia–Thailand Agreement], both reproduced in Ong, *Thailand/Malaysia*, Appendices I and II.

[43] Maritime Boundary Treaty signed by the Parties on 6 March 2018 [Australia–Timor-Leste Boundary Treaty] (Annex B). This treaty appears as Annex 28 to the Conciliation Commission Report: *Conciliation Between the Democratic Republic of Timor-Leste and the Commonwealth of Australia*, Report and Recommendations of the Compulsory Conciliation Commission Between Timor-Leste and Australia on the Timor Sea (9 May 2018).

[44] Management and Co-operation Agreement between the Government of the Republic of Senegal and the Government of the Republic of Guinea-Bissau, 14 October 1993 [Guinea-

latter defines a maritime area of joint exploitation (Article 1 of the Agreement) with an unequal allocation of the resources of the continental shelf (Article 2 allocates 85 per cent to Senegal and 15 per cent to Guinea-Bissau, with the possibility of revision for newly discovered resources). Pursuant to Article 4, the parties agree to establish 'an international Agency to exploit the Area' and Article 5 adds that, upon its establishment, 'the Agency shall succeed Guinea-Bissau and Senegal in the rights and obligations deriving from the Agreements concluded by each State and relating to the exploitation of the resources in the Area'. This provision gives a clear sense of the difference between the second and the third model. The agency was effectively established by a Protocol of 1995. The joint development architecture is not limited to hydrocarbons and covers fisheries too (the allocation for fisheries is 50/50). The Protocol characterises the agency as 'an international organization responsible for managing the resources of the Area, directly through the Enterprise or its subsidiaries or through other companies' (Article 4), with the attendant privileges and immunities (Article 8), and it confers upon it 'exclusive rights to mining and petroleum titles [. . .] in the Area'. The actual exploration and exploitation operations are delegated to an 'Enterprise' owned at 51 per cent by both States (67.5 per cent by Senegal and 32.5 per cent by Guinea-Bissau)(Article 14), which can enter into mineral or petroleum exploitation contracts with other 'companies'. These companies pay a range of royalties, taxes and resource shares to the enterprise (Article 15(a)).

Despite their variety, JDAs present a number of recurrent legal issues. The most salient ones are briefly analysed in the following section.

3.3.2 Recurrent Issues

3.3.2.1 Contractual Forms The umbrella provided by JDAs has to be specified through a layer of contractual instruments with operators, which may be public or private companies, national or foreign, operating through voluntary or compulsory joint ventures. Over time, three main contractual forms have developed to structure operations.[45]

Bissau–Senegal Agreement], followed by a Protocol of Agreement relating to the organization and operation of the Agency for Management and Co-operation, 12 June 1995 [Guinea-Bissau–Senegal Protocol] [together Guinea-Bissau–Senegal Agreement and Protocol], available at: www.un.org/Depts/los/LEGISLATIONANDTREATIES/.

[45] For a short historical overview of contractual forms see K. Bindemann, *Production Sharing Agreements: An Economic Analysis*, Oxford Institute for Energy Studies, WPM 25 (October 1999), at 9–11. For more detailed treatments see P. Cameron, *International*

The first and oldest form is the granting of concessions, defined in administrative acts and concession contracts.[46] Under this form, the operator (in most cases one of the oil 'majors' or a consortium thereof) provides the capital, technology and know-how, and assumes the risk, but it owns the resources it recovers and keeps control of the venture (including the level of production). In exchange, it pays the State 'royalties', taxes and some other benefits (e.g. bonus payments). This form was prevailing in the early days of hydrocarbon development in the Middle East, as a result of the capital, technology and know-how gap. It was also linked, particularly as regards the ownership of resources, to the history of colonialism. The 'permanent sovereignty' movement that developed in the 1950s and found concrete expression with the adoption of the UN General Assembly Resolution 1803 (XVII) of 1962[47] was largely aimed to re-assert full ownership over the resources under the control of foreign companies as a result of concessions. At present, a milder version of concessions is still in use in countries such as Norway or the United Kingdom, in the form of 'licence' and 'royalty/tax' agreements. The relevant companies are granted an exclusive licence to explore and exploit the resources in a given block in exchange for the payment of royalties and taxes on their income.

This movement led to the second form of contractual arrangement, namely that of production-sharing agreements (PSAs).[48] Under a PSA model, a company or a consortium thereof undertakes to finance and conduct the hydrocarbon exploration and exploitation activities. The resources are owned by the host State but the company receives – as payment – a share of what it recovers, first to cover its costs ('cost oil') up to a certain agreed ceiling ('cost stop'), and then to partake in the 'profit oil'. This contractual form developed from the practice of Indonesia but later spread to other areas in Asia, the Middle East, Latin America and Africa, as a result of the disaffection in which concessions had fallen by then. Conceptually, the transition from concessions to PSAs marks the assertion of ownership, indeed the permanent sovereignty, over natural resources.

Energy Investment Law (Oxford: Oxford University Press, 2010), at 38–43. The brief discussion of contractual forms follows these two accounts.

[46] See Smith et al, *International Petroleum Transactions*, at 411–447.

[47] UN General Assembly Resolution 1803 (XVII) on 'Permanent sovereignty over natural resources', 14 December 1962, UN Doc. A/RES/1803/XVII.

[48] See Smith et al, *International Petroleum Transactions*, at 448–462.

The final step in what could be seen as a process of 'de-equitising' foreign companies has been made by the move to service contracts.[49] Under this contractual form, the foreign company or consortium thereof undertakes the exploration and possible exploitation for a fee, rather than for a share of the recovered oil. It thus provides a 'service' in exchange for a specified payment, the 'fee'. Unlike under a PSA, the company has no equity position in the venture. This contractual form is also known as 'risk-services' agreements. An early version of such form was in use in the practice of Mexico (PEMEX) and Argentina (YPF), but it mostly developed from the practice of Iran and Iraq.

The companies operating under these contractual arrangements can be a foreign investor or consortium thereof or a joint venture between international and national oil companies. This specific structure can have important distributional implications to the extent that the State assumes, through its equity or participation, a significant part of the risk of the venture.

3.3.2.2 Pre-Existing rights One complex issue arises when States grant exploration and exploitation rights to foreign companies on an area which is disputed and which, subsequently, is delimitated by agreement and/or becomes subject to a JDA.[50] This situation can be made even more complex if the transition unfolds in a decolonisation context, as in the case of East Timor. Given the massive amounts of investment required to develop a field, the key question is whether the initial rights granted by the State are protected.

The answer to this question is highly fact-sensitive. One illustration is given by the licenses granted by Thailand prior to the 1979 agreement with Malaysia.[51] Thailand initially sought to be released from the concession granted to a consortium led by Triton, a US company, but eventually accommodated the situation of the latter as the preferred operator for the block in question. Of note, Malaysia consented to this 'grandfathering' approach going as far as letting Triton proceed under the terms of the concession initially conferred by Thailand rather than

[49] See Smith et al, *International Petroleum Transactions*, at 480–493.

[50] See Becker-Weinberg, *Joint Development*, at 128–129; I. Townsend-Gault, 'The impact of a joint development zone on previously granted interests' in Fox, *Joint Development of Offshore Oil and Gas*, vol. 2, pp. 174–184. The discussion of this issue follows these two accounts.

[51] Malaysia/Thailand MOU.

requiring it to enter into a compulsory joint venture agreement with Petronas (Malaysia's national oil company) and subjecting the operation to a PSA. Thus, the situation of Triton was not simply brought under the new regime of compulsory joint ventures and PSAs but grandfathered in its initial form.

Yet, as noted by one commentator, this outcome does not mean that foreign companies are legally entitled under international law to retain their prior situation. Depending on the circumstances, they may be entitled to claim compensation for the loss suffered as a result of the host State actions, for example, if it can be established that such actions are in breach of domestic law, a contract, a bilateral investment treaty or, possibly, general international law.[52] But even this conclusion may not be straightforward, as the investor may be held to have assumed this risk when it entered the disputed area. As one investment tribunal has noted, although in a different context, investment arbitration is not a substitute for poor business judgement.[53] If an investor accepts the risk of operating in a disputed area, then this is part of its 'commercial', not 'political' risk.

The situation is particularly complex in cases where the block for which the company had received a licence or an interest is subsequently acknowledged to fall under the territory or maritime space of another State in a delimitation treaty. Two illustrations are offered by the 2008 China-Japan 'Principled Consensus' (whereby Japan recognised that a previously disputed area, the Chungxiao oil and gas field, is under the sole jurisdiction of China) and the 2009 Brunei-Malaysia exchange of letters (whereby Malaysia made a similar acknowledgement to the benefit of Brunei).[54] In this situation, the rights received in the first place are void, as only the territorial/coastal State can grant a right or an interest on an area under its jurisdiction. One avenue in such case is to offer a compensatory or substitute block, as Malaysia has done in the

[52] See Chapter 2.

[53] *Maffezini v. Spain*, ICSID Case No. ARB/97/7, Award (13 November 2000), para. 64.

[54] See D. Ong, 'Implications of Recent Southeast Asian State Practice for the international law on offshore joint development', in Beckman et al, *Beyond Territorial Disputes in the South China Sea*, pp. 181–217. The discussion of these cases follows Ong. The Principled Consensus between China and Japan on the East China Sea Issue, of 18 June 2008, is reproduced in Gao Jianjun, 'A Note on the 2008 Cooperation Consensus Between China and Japan in the East China Sea' (2009) 40 *Ocean Development & International Law* 291, Appendix 1. The Brunei/Malaysia exchange of letters took place on 16 March 2009, but the text is not public. See Ministry of Foreign Affairs of Malaysia (Wisma Putra), Press Statement (3 May 2010).

aforementioned case. Another avenue is to specifically address the situation of right- or interest-holders in the arrangement or even in the process leading to it. An example is section III of the China-Japan Principled consensus, which states that:

> Chinese enterprises welcome the participation of Japanese legal person [sic] in the development of the existing oil and gas field in Chunxiao in accordance with the relevant laws of China governing cooperation with foreign enterprises in the exploration and exploitation of offshore petroleum resources.

Another example is the conciliation procedure that led to the 2018 delimitation treaty between Australia and Timor-Leste, Annex D of which specifically addresses pre-existing rights under previous treaties and contracts.[55]

3.3.2.3 Taxation, Costs and Revenues Taxation, costs and revenues are a very important aspect of JDAs but also one that varies significantly from one agreement to another.[56] Agreements differ as to the level of detail, the specific allocation of the costs and benefits, the nature of the applicable taxes, any tax exemptions, and other related aspects. A key difficulty when the area is not delimited concerns the determination of the applicable taxation power. Indeed, when a boundary is set, taxation powers with respect to hydrocarbon development activities are based either on territorial sovereignty or on the functional jurisdiction conferred by the UNCLOS on the coastal State (see Chapter 2). By contrast, when no boundary is set, the matter has to be addressed through a JDA or other related arrangements or, absent that, will fall back on the unilateral exercise of claimed jurisdiction by each State (typically the State issuing the exploration/exploitation licence). Given the significant variation in the practice of States, it is useful to review some illustrations of agreements which address these matters in some detail.

The 1990 agreement between Malaysia and Thailand[57] has two main chapters dealing with 'Financial provisions' (chapter III) and 'Customs and excise, and taxation' (chapter VI). The basic principle is that '[a]ll costs incurred and benefits derived by the Joint Authority from activities carried out in the Joint Development Area shall be equally borne and

[55] Australia/Timor-Leste Boundary Treaty, Annex D (Transitional Provisions).
[56] See Becker-Weinberg, *Joint Development*, at 129–132.
[57] Malaysia/Thailand Agreement.

shared by the Governments' (Article 9(1)). Article 16 governs a number of custom duties, giving favourable treatment to the 'profit oil' sold by the contractor beyond the territories of Malaysia or Thailand as well as setting reduced duties and tax rates for goods used in the joint development zone. Article 17 governs the taxation of income of 'any person who holds the right to explore and exploit any petroleum in the Joint Development Area under a contract awarded by the Joint Authority'. It gives a tax advantage to such companies in the form of a tax exemption, for the first 8 years, and a reduced rate thereafter (10 per cent for the following 7 years and 20 per cent after that) (Article 17(1)(a)).

Another example is provided by the 1993 agreement between Guinea-Bissau and Senegal,[58] which, as mentioned earlier in this chapter, gives Senegal 85 per cent and Guinea-Bissau 15 per cent of the known mineral resources from the continental shelf, and leaves the shares of any newly discovered resources for subsequent negotiation (Article 2). Expenditures already incurred from 'State funds' (hence not by private parties) for petroleum prospecting are to be reimbursed to each State 'in proportion to the size of its share' (Article 3). The 1995 Protocol to this Agreement[59] entrusts, as already noted, the development of relevant area to an agency, which does so through an 'enterprise'. This 'enterprise' may itself carry out development activities or act through other companies. The capital of the enterprise is allocated as follows: 67.5 per cent to Senegal and 32.5 per cent to Guinea-Bissau. Fifty-one per cent of the shares are non-transferable shares (A shares) allocated to the two States, whereas 49 per cent are 'B shares' transferable to the private sector (Article 14). The agency charges several taxes and duties on mining and petroleum: an 'area tax', 'ad valorem royalties on mineral production', 'royalties on petroleum production', income taxes on enterprises exploiting resources in the area, a petroleum levy, and the share of the agency's sales of petroleum products (Article 15(a)).

A third, more recent, example is provided by the 'Special Regime' applicable to the Greater Sunrise field in accordance with Article 7 and Annex B of the 2018 Australia and Timor-Leste agreement.[60] Article 2 of the Annex states that both Australia and Timor-Leste 'have title to all Petroleum produced in the Greater Sunrise Fields'. It then envisages two possible distributions depending on the completion of a pipeline project

[58] Guinea-Bissau/Senegal Agreement.
[59] Guinea-Bissau/Senegal Protocol.
[60] Australia/Timor-Leste Boundary Treaty.

(which can lead to either Timor-Leste or Australia, with the resulting additional profits from its exploitation). If the pipeline links the field with Timor-Leste, the distribution of upstream petroleum will be made according to a ratio of 70 per cent for Timor-Leste and 30 per cent to Australia (Article 2(2)(a)). If, instead, the pipeline links the field with Australia, Timor-Leste will receive 80 per cent and Australia 20 per cent (Article 2(2)(b)). The distribution thus takes into account the profits arising from the pipeline route. Pursuant to Article 3(2) of Annex B, '[t]he application of the Parties' taxation law shall be specified in the fiscal regime as agreed between the Parties and the Greater Sunrise Contractor' under two previous agreements. Thus, the pre-existing taxation regime for the Greater Sunrise Contractor is also specifically addressed by the agreement.

3.3.2.4 Negative Externalities In Chapter 3, I discussed the wide range of rules of international law relevant for what can be seen as the 'negative externalities' of international energy transactions. Recalling the distinction made there between 'special' and 'general' rules, the clauses included in delimitation treaties and JDAs regarding the protection of other goals, particularly the marine environment in offshore petroleum operations,[61] can be seen as 'special' rules. One peculiarity of such clauses is that they may or may not reflect international standards fully. They are a key area in the articulation between the rules of the foundational approach and those of the ad hoc approach.

For decades, the protection of the environment was seen as a matter of 'lesser importance' and ancillary to the core transaction organised by the JDA. Writing in 1989, a working group convened by the British Institute of International and Comparative Law to develop a model JDA observed that:

> [m]atters of lesser importance, but topics on which the Working Group felt that the agreement of the State Parties was necessary if the joint development was to be effective [...] cover the delimitation of the

[61] For one detailed study of treaty practice see D. Ong, 'The Progressive Integration of Environmental Protection within Offshore Joint Development Agreements', in M. Fitzmaurice, M. Szuniewicz (eds.), *Exploitation of Natural Resources in the 21st Century* (The Hague: Kluwer, 2003), pp. 113–141. See also C. A. Low, 'Marine Environmental Protection in Joint Development Agreements' (2012) 30 *Journal of Energy and Natural Resources Law* 45. The discussion in this section follows these two accounts.

> Zone, the definition of resources to be included ... and measures of protection of the marine environment.[62]

This statement accurately reflected the situation prevailing at the time. Since then, environmental protection has gained significant momentum, both as a matter of cost internalisation and prevention. The growing importance of environmental protection finds expression, in practice, in two main ways.

First, the quest for efficiency and cost reduction in the oil industry led to the successive use of certain technologies, from an initial stage characterised by a produce-consume-dispose (PCD) approach, through to the use of waste management technology (WMT), to environmental control technology (EnvCT).[63] Under the PCD approach, waste is a normal part of the production process and the costs it generates for the environment and society are not the responsibility of the producer. Such was the prevailing approach for a long time, until the environmental movement more aggressively denounced the environmental and social impact of hydrocarbon development. Between the late 1980s and the early 1990s, the growing recognition of such impact led to a paradigm change from the PCD to WMT approach. The latter is emblematic of the distinction between transactions and externalities. Under WMT, waste generation continues to be seen as a necessary part of the production process (the 'transaction'), which remains fundamentally unchanged. But the waste generated (the 'externality') needs to be managed. As noted by one commentator, the WMT was founded on three debatable assumptions, namely that (1) the only way to protect the environment is to manage the waste generated, (2) waste has no value and (3) waste is not part of the oilfield process.[64] Instead of targeting the very processes through which oil is produced and waste is generated, the focus is on the clean-up and management of whatever waste is generated. It is only once the high costs of managing and disposing the waste became increasingly clear that the prevention of environmental harm moved from the mere externality level to that of the organisation of the transaction. Over time, the inertia that had left the production processes intact and just added a layer of waste management gave way to a reconsideration of the processes themselves

[62] Fox, *Joint Development*, at 16.

[63] See A. K. Wojtanowicz, 'Environmental control technology in petroleum drilling and production', in S. T. Orszulik (ed.), *Environmental Technology in the Oil Industry* (London: Blackie, 1997), pp. 73–180.

[64] Wojtanowicz, *Environmental control technology*, at 29.

in order to reduce waste, and hence costs. Under the EnvCT approach, (1) the purpose of petroleum engineering is not to protect the environment but to maximise production while minimising its impact on the environment, (2) introducing environmental constraints in the very production process minimises exposure to regulatory risks, (3) waste streams can be managed by the operator as part of the production process itself.[65] It is interesting to note that, under this approach, cost internalisation is achieved by regulation (not market mechanisms). Such regulation provides a strong incentive for producers not to merely manage the waste they generate but to change their production process to minimise such generation. Thus, regulation can move environmental protection from the margins to the core the transaction. The level of detail required by such regulation is normally not found in JDAs themselves but in domestic law. Yet, JDAs often allocate regulatory authority among the States involved.

The second way in which environmental protection has found expression in practice is the inclusion of specific environmental clauses in JDAs. Unsurprisingly, such clauses only started to feature in agreements concluded in the 1970s, that is, after the 1972 Stockholm Conference on the Human Environment.[66] Early examples the 1974 Japan–Korea Agreement,[67] the 1977 Norway/United Kingdom Agreement on the Frigg Field[68] or the 1979 Malaysia-Thailand MOU.[69] Another 'wave' of environmental provisions was possibly catalysed by the 1992 Rio Conference on Environment and Development, although some agreements of the 1980s also included such clauses.[70] Some representative examples include the 1993–1995 Guinea-Bissau–Senegal Agreement and Protocol[71] or the 1993 Colombia–Jamaica Agreement.[72] More recent and sophisticated examples include treaties signed over the 2000s, such as the

65 Wojtanowicz, *Environmental control technology*, at 29.

66 See Ong, *Transnational Investment Agreements.*

67 Japan/Korean Agreement, Article XX.

68 Agreement between the Government of the United Kingdom of Great Britain and Northern Ireland and the Government of the Kingdom of Norway relating to the exploitation of the Frigg Field Reservoir and the transmission of gas therefrom to the United Kingdom, 10 May 1976, 1977 Great Britain TS 113 [Norway–UK Frigg Agreement], Article 23.

69 Malaysia–Thailand MOU, Article IV.

70 Agreement on the Continental Shelf between Iceland and Jan Mayen (Iceland/Norway), 22 October 1981, 21 ILM (1982) 1222 [Iceland–Norway Agreement], Articles 5, 6 and 9.

71 Guinea-Bissau–Senegal Protocol, Articles 5(c), 11(4), and 23.

72 Colombia/Jamaica Agreement, Articles 3(2)(d) and (e), 3(3), 4(1).

2001 Nigeria–São Tomé e Príncipe Agreement,[73] the 2002 Timor Sea Treaty[74] or the 2003 Barbados–Guyana Agreement.[75] The nature of the environmental provisions in these agreements varies. Some merely provide for cooperation between the two States to protect and preserve the marine environment.[76] Others go a step further and expressly allocate regulatory authority[77] or even envision the development of common standards.[78] Others, still, provide for inspection[79] and dispute settlement procedures concerning environmental matters.[80] In some cases, an agency established by the treaty to manage the relevant area is given regulatory (rule-making) powers over environmental matters.[81] The operation of such provisions unfolds within the broader context of the applicable rules of international law, including the UNCLOS, sectoral instruments (e.g. MARPOL) and regional instruments. Moreover, the broader body of international rules protecting the environment (see Chapter 3) remains applicable to an extent that will be determined in each case, in accordance with the methodology introduced earlier in this chapter (see Section 2.2).

3.3.2.5 Applicable Law and Dispute Settlement Like other terms of JDAs, questions of applicable and dispute settlement vary significantly from one agreement to the other.[82] What can be usefully noted in a brief

[73] Treaty between the Federal Republic of Nigeria and the Democratic Republic of São Tomé e Príncipe on the Joint Development of Petroleum and other Resources, in respect of Areas of the Exclusive Economic Zone of the two States, 21 February 2001 [Nigeria–São Tomé e Príncipe Agreement], Articles 30(5) and 38.

[74] Timor Sea Treaty Between the Government of East Timor and the Government of Australia, 20 May 2002, 2258 UNTS 3 (2005) [Timor Sea Treaty], Articles 10 and 12.

[75] Exclusive Economic Zone Co-operation Treaty Between the State of Barbados and the Republic of Guyana Concerning the Exercise of Jurisdiction in Their Exclusive Economic Zones in the Area of Bilateral Overlap Within Each of their Outer Limits and Beyond the Outer Limits of the Exclusive Economic Zones of Other States, 2 December 2003, 2277 UNTS 202 [Barbados–Guyana Agreement], Article 8.

[76] Japan/Korean Agreement, Article XX; Barbados–Guyana Agreement, Article 8.

[77] Malaysia-Thailand MOU, Article IV(1); Iceland/Norway Agreement, Articles 5 and 6.

[78] Norway/UK Frigg Agreement, Articles 17(1) (regarding pipelines) and 23.

[79] Nigeria/São Tomé e Príncipe Agreement, Article 30(5).

[80] Iceland/Norway Agreement, Article 9.

[81] Guinea-Bissau/Senegal Protocol, Articles 5(c), article 11(4), and 23; Colombia/Jamaica Agreement, Articles 3(2)(d) and (e), 3(3), 4(1).

[82] Becker-Weinberg, *Joint Development*, at 137–140; M. Ross, 'Dispute Management and Resolution', in G. Gordon, J. Paterson (eds.), *Oil and Gas Law. Current Practice and Emerging Trends* (Dundee: Dundee University Press, 2007), pp. 431–460.

survey of the practice is the complexity of the applicable law and the variety of dispute settlement methods used.

On the first issue, the complexity derives from the hybrid nature (involving States and private parties) of these agreements and the fact that they may not specify the governing law in case of dispute. Whereas it can be safely assumed that all the agreements that qualify as a 'treaty' under international law are governed by international law, first and foremost by the terms of the agreement itself as well as by other applicable norms (e.g. the UNCLOS), it is not always clear whether an agreement is a 'treaty' (see Section 3.3.2.6). Moreover, even when the nature of the agreement as a treaty is not in dispute, the law applicable to different aspects of the activities governed by the treaty may be complex. An apposite illustration is provided by the 1993 Nigeria–São Tomé e Príncipe Agreement.[83] Article 1(1) states that '"applicable law" means this Treaty, and the principles and rules of law applicable in the Zone by virtue of this Treaty'. Some special rules enacted by the Authority established by the treaty, such as a 'regulatory and tax regime' (Article 21(1)) are 'the applicable law relating to the exploration for and exploitation of petroleum in the Zone'. The Authority is also charged with the development of 'regulatory and tax regimes applicable to non-petroleum development activities within the Zone' (Article 33). And, in the absence of the latter regime 'the States Parties shall apply the provisions of their own laws relating to the exclusive economic zone to the activity of their own nationals in the Zone, but shall refrain from applying those laws to the conduct of persons who are nationals of the other State Party' (Article 34). Moreover, the Authority 'shall propose to the Council for immediate adoption as part of the applicable law, to the extent that the private law of the zone is not determined by or pursuant to other parts of this Treaty, the private law of one of the States Parties' (Article 39). The determination of the applicable criminal law is even more complex. According to Article 40, paragraphs 1 and 2:

> [. . .] a national or permanent resident of a State Party shall be subject to the criminal law of that State Party in respect of acts or omissions occurring in the Zone provided that a permanent resident of a State Party who is a national of the other State Party shall be subject to the

[83] See also the distinctions regarding the applicable law made in Article 24 of the Guinea-Bissau/Senegal Protocol.

> criminal law of the latter State Party. A national of both States Parties shall be subject to the criminal law of both [...]
>
> A national of a third State, not being a permanent resident of either State Party, shall be subject to the criminal law of both States Parties in respect of acts or omissions occurring in the Zone. Such a person shall not be subject to criminal proceedings under the law of one State Party if he or she has already been tried and discharged or acquitted by a competent tribunal or already undergone punishment for the same act or omission under the law of the other State Party.

The 'applicable law' may change over time upon the recommendation of the Authority (Article 44) and, in case of dispute, the applicable law will likely differ (it is not specified) depending on whether the dispute is between the Authority and private interests (Article 47) or between States Parties (Article 48).

As regards dispute settlement, practice shows a wide variety of approaches. Some agreements confine dispute settlement to negotiation. For example, the 1979 Malaysia/Thailand MOU provides, in Article VII, that '[a]ny difference or dispute arising out of the interpretation or implementation of the provisions of this Memorandum shall be settled peacefully by consultation or negotiations between the Parties'. The 1990 Malaysia–Thailand Agreement merely added a political layer. According to Article 21, if no settlement is reached within 3 months, either government may refer the matter to the Prime Ministers of both countries, who shall 'jointly decide' on the mode of settlement. By contrast, other agreements rely on third-party dispute settlement. The 1981 Iceland–Norway Agreement provides for a conciliation procedure specifically for disputes between the parties over the level of protection offered by the safety and environmental regulations adopted and implemented by each party in their portion of the joint area (Article 9). Other agreements, both old and new, provide for arbitration procedures. Such is the case, for example, of the Norway–United Kingdom Frigg Agreement,[84] the Japan–Korea Agreement,[85] the Nigeria–São Tomé e Príncipe Agreement[86] or the Guinea-Bissau–Senegal Protocol.[87] Yet other agreements provide for a multiple approach, whereby the case

[84] Norway/UK Frigg Agreement, Article 28(2).

[85] Japan/Korea Agreement, Article XXVI(2).

[86] Nigeria/São Tomé e Príncipe Agreement, Article 49(2).

[87] Guinea-Bissau/Senegal Protocol, Article 25(2) (arbitration of disputes between the Agency and one of the contracting States).

may be referred to conciliation or arbitration[88] or to arbitration or the International Court of Justice.[89]

3.3.2.6 JDAs and the Law of Treaties: Selected Issues The peculiar context in which JDAs intervene, a disputed area with overlapping claims, and the range of actors involved, including States but also newly established agencies and private contractors, raise some complex questions of treaty law. In this section, I briefly survey three of them, namely the nature of the agreements forming the JDA regime, the implications for third States which are not parties to the cooperative arrangement, and some peculiarities relating to State succession to treaties.

3.3.2.6.1 Nature of Agreements Embodying the JDA Regime Regarding the first question, the nature of agreements varies not only from case to case but also within a single project.

For undelimited portions of the EEZ and the continental shelf, Articles 74(3) and 83(3) of the UNCLOS expressly envisage the possibility that States may enter into 'provisional arrangements of a practice nature'. Yet, the characterisation of an instrument as a 'provisional arrangement of a practical nature' does not prevent it from being a treaty under the law of treaties. This is because, under international law, for an agreement to be a treaty, no specific form is required. The main precedent on this issue is the ICJ's first decision on jurisdiction and admissibility in the case between *Qatar and Bahrain*,[90] where the Court observed that the concept of treaty in international law, reflected in Article 2(1)(a) of the VCLT, is not subject to any specific form (other than the written form) or designation.[91] Recalling a prior decision rendered in the *Aegean Sea Continental Shelf* case,[92] the Court emphasised that it 'must have regard above all to [the text's] actual terms and to the particular circumstances in which it was drawn up'.[93] There are examples of 'provisional

88 Australia/Timor-Leste Boundary Treaty, Article 12(1)–(2) (Conciliation) and (3)–(4) (Arbitration).

89 Guinea-Bissau/Senegal Agreement, Article 9.

90 *Maritime Delimitation and Territorial Questions between Qatar and Bahrain*, Jurisdiction and Admissibility, Judgment, ICJ Reports 1994 [*Qatar/Bahrain*], p. 112.

91 *Qatar/Bahrain*, para. 23.

92 *Aegean Sea Continental Shelf*, Judgment, ICJ Reports 1978, p. 39 [*Aegean Sea Continental Shelf*], para. 96.

93 *Qatar/Bahrain*, para. 23.

arrangements' that certainly fall, by their very terms, under the definition of treaty. For example, Article 2(a) of the Timor Sea Treaty provides:

> This Treaty gives effect to international law as reflected in the United Nations Convention on the Law of the Sea done at Montego Bay on 10 December 1982 which under Article 83 requires States with opposite or adjacent coasts to make every effort to enter into provisional arrangements of a practical nature pending agreement on the final delimitation of the continental shelf between them in a manner consistent with international law. This Treaty is intended to adhere to such obligation.

In the same vein, registration of the agreement with the UN Secretary-General is not a requirement for an agreement to be a binding treaty under the law of treaties. In *Qatar/Bahrain*, the 1987 Exchanges of Letters had not been registered by Qatar – yet both parties and the Court considered it a treaty – and Qatar's notification of the 1990 Minutes was opposed by Bahrain – yet the Court concluded that it was a treaty.[94] In practice, States do not always notify their JDAs or at least not certain parts of a JDA's constellation, such as MOUs. But that does not exclude *a priori* their treaty nature.

By contrast, there are other examples that in all likelihood would not meet the definition of treaty, not only under the Vienna Convention (which applies only to treaties between States) but also under customary law. Such is the case of agreements concluded by contractors with host States (so-called host state agreements) or with the agency established by a JDA. The determination of the law applicable to such relations is complex and, whereas parts of the relationship may be subject to international law (e.g. the JDA itself), some others will be subject to domestic law or to regulations specifically enacted by the relevant agency (see Section 3.3.2.5).

3.3.2.6.2 Implications for Third Parties The second question is also addressed in the VCLT and concerns the situation of third States. Article 34 states the general principle that a 'treaty does not create either obligations or rights for a third State without its consent'. Thus, a delimitation treaty or a JDA (with or without previous delimitation) between two States regarding an area claimed by three States cannot be opposed to the third one.

[94] *Qatar/Bahrain*, para. 29.

It is, however, important for the third State to formally protest against such disregard of its claims to avoid acquiescing to the exercise of powers by other States over the area.[95] One example concerns Portugal's protest, in its capacity of administrating power of East Timor, against the 1989 Timor Gap Treaty between Indonesia (which had occupied East Timor) and Australia.[96] Portugal brought a claim against Australia before the ICJ requesting inter alia that the Court order Australia to refrain from negotiating, signing or ratifying any agreements concerning the delimitation or the exploitation of the area.[97] But the Court declared the claim inadmissible because Indonesia, a necessary party, had not consented to its jurisdiction.[98] An additional source of complexity came from the operation of the right to self-determination of the East Timor people, which is a peremptory norm. The Court recognised only the *erga omnes* character of the obligations flowing from such right, hence opposable to both Australia and Indonesia,[99] but it did not take position on the merits.

In some cases, the 'without prejudice' clauses included JDAs, which are intended to reserve the entitlements of each party, expressly address the situation of third States. For example, Article 6(1) of the Australia/Timor-Leste Boundary Treaty provides that '[n]othing in this Treaty shall be interpreted as prejudicing negotiations with third States with regard to delimitation of the exclusive economic zone and the continental shelf in the Timor Sea'. Article 45 of the Nigeria–São Tomé e Príncipe Agreement provides that: '[i]n the exercise of their rights and powers under this Treaty, the States Parties shall take into account the rights and freedoms of other States in respect of the Zone as provided under generally accepted principles of international law' (Article 45(1)). This provision reserves the freedoms recognised to third States over the EEZ and the continental shelf (e.g. navigation, right of immersion).

95 See e.g. See e.g. *Temple of Preah Vihear (Cambodia v. Thailand)*, Judgment, ICJ Reports 1962, p. 6, at 30–31; *Sovereignty over Pulau Ligitan and Pulau Sipadan (Indonesia/Malaysia)*, Judgment, ICJ Reports 2002, p. 625, paras. 120–122.

96 Treaty between Australia and the Republic of Indonesia on the zone of cooperation in an area between the Indonesian province of East Timor and Northern Australia, 9 December 1989, 29 ILM (1990) 469.

97 *East Timor Case*, para. 10.

98 *East Timor Case*, paras. 33–35.

99 *East Timor Case*, para. 29.

3.3.2.6.3 State Succession to Treaties A third issue concerns State succession to treaties. This is because JDAs were often adopted in the context of decolonisation and of recognition of new maritime areas.

The Vienna Convention on State Succession to Treaties creates a regime whereby State succession proceeds within certain bounds. Article 13 provides an overarching principle according to which '[n]-othing in the present Convention shall affect the principle of international law affirming the permanent sovereignty of every people and every State over its natural wealth and resources'. As a result, a JDA established by a colonial power before the exercise by a people of its right to self-determination, if inconsistent with the permanent sovereignty principle, would not be limited by other rules of the Convention that aim to maintain the territorial situation prior to self-determination.

For boundaries established by a prior treaty, the principle of stability of boundaries (reflected in Article 11(a)) and the principle of *uti possidetis juris*[100] converge and, except in case of unlawful dismemberment of the colonial territory,[101] there would be no *a priori* inconsistency with the permanent sovereignty principle. It is, however, less clear whether some related aspects, such as a 'unitisation', taxation, access or approvals, established either in a boundary treaty or in JDA (without delimitation), would be consistent with the permanent sovereignty principle. Aside from the boundary line itself, such aspects could be deemed to 'relate to the regime of the boundary' or 'attach to the territory' and therefore covered by Article 11(b) or Article 12.

A key issue in this context concerns the protection of pre-existing rights of contractors granted in or under the previous treaty. That issue arises in the relations between contractors and host States (see Section 3.3.2.2) as well as inter-State relations. In practice, given that the Vienna Convention regime is only suppletive, the matter should be addressed through subsequent agreements. Here again, the situation of the Timor Sea provides an illustration. The system of treaties between Australia and Indonesia, as it concerns the self-determination and permanent

[100] See *Frontier Dispute (Burkina Faso/Mali)*, Judgment, ICJ Reports 1986, p. 554, para. 20; *Land, Island and Maritime Frontier Dispute (El Salvador/Honduras; Nicaragua intervening)*, Judgment, ICJ Reports 1992, p. 351, paras. 40–43; *In the matter of an arbitration under the Arbitration Agreement between the Government of the Republic of Croatia and the Government of the Republic of Slovenia, signed on 4 November 2009*, PCA Case No. 2012–04, Final Award (29 June 2017), para. 262.

[101] See *Legal Consequences of the Separation of the Chagos Archipelago from Mauritius in 1965*, Advisory Opinion, ICJ Reports 2019, p. 95, para. 160.

sovereignty of East Timorese people, was revisited through subsequent agreements between Timor-Leste and Australia.

3.4 Overarching Principles Applicable to Straddling/Disputed Hydrocarbon Deposits

3.4.1 Preliminary Observations

The legal context within which JDAs operate and on which they rely for their operation is given by the wide body of rules examined as part of the foundational approach. Due to the matters they address, such rules entertain different degrees of proximity with the JDA framework. For offshore operations, the UNCLOS and other related instruments are particularly relevant to determine matters such as the status of artificial islands, installations and structures, drilling, pipelines, tankers, and many other matters that are not governed by JDAs, precisely because they are left to the general law.

Within this broader body of rules, certain principles discussed in previous chapters govern the rights and duties of States with respect to straddling/disputed hydrocarbon deposits. Such principles are of particular relevance to assess the legality of 'unilateral action', i.e. in the absence of an agreement on how to proceed (whether it delimits the area or not). But they remain relevant in cases where there is an agreement on how to proceed, as they may guide the interpretation of a treaty or supplement its terms in matters not addressed by it. They operate as the 'proximate' legal context of JDAs.

The sources from which such principles are derived have all been introduced in my examination of the foundational model. As such, the principles are all intended to constrain the unilateral action of one State in order to safeguard the rights (or claims) of other States. Unilateral action is not entirely precluded, but it is subject to certain parameters. Overall, these principles can be summarised as follows: (1) obligation of 'mutual restraint', (2) duty to cooperate, further extended through procedural duties of (3) notification, (4) consultation and (5) information sharing, with overall limitations (6) to protect the interest of other States (no harm) and (7) to protect the environment, irrespective of its location (prevention). These principles do not preclude, as noted earlier, the application of other rules (e.g. human rights). They are singled out here for analytical purposes only. For presentation purposes, it is useful to group them under three headings: mutual restraint, cooperation (including notification, consultation, and information sharing), and prevention of harm (to other States and the environment).

3.4.2 Unilateral Exploitation and Mutual Restraint

The obligation of mutual restraint in the exploitation of a straddling hydrocarbon deposit (whether disputed or transboundary) can be better understood in the light of its historical context.[102] The 'rule of capture', as it came to be applied in the domestic order of the United States to groundwater deposits straddling two or more properties and later on to hydrocarbons in a similar context, was derived from the idea that wild animals crossing property boundaries can be captured and appropriated freely by the owner of the land. In the context of hydrocarbons, that had the unwanted effect that drilling by the owner of one of the plots would change the pressure in the entire hydrocarbon deposit and thereby make more onerous the extraction by the owners of the other plots. Moreover, drilling at several points, as incentivised by the 'rule of capture', would also change the pressure conditions of the deposit in such a way that less oil would be recoverable overall. Over time, governments started to adopt so-called conservation measures, namely measures to make oil extraction more efficient. Two such measures were the compulsory 'unitisation' of the extraction operations and/or the compulsory 'pooling' of several plots before extraction could be authorised. Whereas such measures can be adopted by law or regulation at the domestic level, doing so in an international legal system based on sovereign States is much more challenging. States may agree, on a voluntary basis, to coordinate their hydrocarbon development activities, but in the present state of international law, they are not required to do so. This conclusion is important for the understanding of both the obligation of 'mutual restraint' and the duty to cooperate (see Section 3.4.3).

In the context of offshore hydrocarbon deposits, the obligation of mutual restraint has been derived from Articles 74(3) and 83(3) of the UNCLOS.[103] In *Guyana/Suriname*, an arbitral tribunal interpreted these provisions as permitting two types of activities, those proceeding under an agreement ('a provisional arrangement of a practical nature') and

[102] See Becker-Weinberg, *Joint Development*, at 10–18.

[103] Even before the adoption of the UNCLOS, the obligation of mutual restraint enjoyed doctrinal support, although with variations as to its exact implications. See Onorato, *Apportionment (1977)*, at 327; Lagoni, *Interim Measures*, at 362.

certain 'unilateral acts'.[104] The latter are only permitted if they do not 'jeopardiz[e] or hampe[r] the reaching of a final agreement on the delimitation of the maritime boundary'.[105] This category of unilateral acts encompasses 'unilateral acts which do not cause a physical change to the marine environment'.[106] The effect of an act on the marine environment necessarily depends on the way in which it is conducted or, in other words, on the technologies used and the circumstances of the act. Under present conditions, certain forms of exploration (e.g. seismic exploration) seem consistent with this obligation of restraint because they do not 'cause physical change to the marine environment', whereas other activities, such as exploitation of oil and gas, are in principle inconsistent because they do adversely change the physical conditions of the deposit. It is therefore important to understand the purpose pursued by the obligation of 'mutual restraint', namely to preserve the rights of the other State in the peculiar context of hydrocarbon deposits, rather than defining an abstract dividing line between what is permitted and what is not.[107] In a different physical context, such as international watercourses or transboundary aquifers, the level of restraint may not be as high because the straddling resources can be 'reasonably and equitably utilised' through unilateral action. Such action is also subject to constraints (see Chapters 2 and 5), but the scope of unilateral action is less restrictive in this context.

This rationale for the obligation of 'mutual restraint' finds support in other decisions. In *the Aegean Sea Continental Shelf* case,[108] the ICJ emphasised the limited effects of the seismic exploration conducted by Turkey, their transitory nature, and the absence of appropriation of the resources in the disputed area to reject Greece's request for provisional measures.[109] This decision highlights that activities such as seismic

[104] *In the matter of an arbitration between Guyana and Suriname*, PCA Case 2004/04, Award (17 September 2007) [*Guyana/Suriname*], para. 466.

[105] *Guyana/Suriname*, para. 466.

[106] *Guyana/Suriname*, para. 467.

[107] *Dispute Concerning Delimitation of the Maritime Boundary between Ghana and Côte d'Ivoire in the Atlantic Ocean (Ghana/Côte d'Ivoire),* ITLOS Case No. 23, Judgment (23 September 2017) [*Ghana/Côte d'Ivoire – Judgment*], Separate Opinion of Judge Paik, paras. 7 and 9–10 (discussing mutual restraint in the specific context of Article 83(3) of the UNCLOS, rather than at the level of customary international law). However, in the circumstances of the case, Judge Paik concluded that Ghana's hydrocarbon exploitation in the disputed area had violated Article 83(3) (at paras. 16–17).

[108] *Aegean Sea Continental Shelf.*

[109] *Aegean Sea Continental Shelf*, para. 30.

exploration are not lawful as such. What matters is 'how' they are conducted or, more specifically, with what consequences. It was the combination of circumstances (mere exploration, transitory character, no appropriation) that kept Turkey's actions within acceptable bounds. Most importantly, although the decision of the Court was rendered on a request for provisional measures, its assessment of the situation provides guidance beyond the specific wording of Articles 74(3) and 83(3) of the UNCLOS, which had not been adopted yet. Thus, it provides guidance for situations (e.g. onshore resources or deposits straddling a set boundary) where the latter provisions would not apply.

However, under Articles 74(3) and 83(3) of the UNCLOS, the case law has moved in a different direction admitting the possibility of lawful unilateral exploitation activities of a disputed area. As noted in Chapter 2, in *Ghana/Côte d'Ivoire*, a Special Chamber of the ITLOS considered that exploration activities in the disputed area could suffice, under certain circumstances, to 'create a risk of irreversible prejudice to the rights of Côte d'Ivoire'.[110] Yet, at the level of merits, the Special Chamber admitted that unilateral exploitation activities in the disputed area had been lawful under the circumstances of the case and, therefore, they did not engage Ghana's international responsibility.[111] Thus, mutual restraint does not mean total restraint; and the line between lawful and unlawful activities does not overlap entirely with that between exploration and exploitation. Specifically, on the issue of Ghana's unilateral exploitation activities in the disputed area, the Chamber concluded that they did not amount to a violation of the exclusive sovereign rights of *Côte d'Ivoire*:

> in a case of overlap both States concerned have an entitlement to the relevant continental shelf on the basis of their relevant coasts. Only a decision on delimitation establishes which part of the continental shelf

[110] *Dispute Concerning Delimitation of the Maritime Boundary between Ghana and Côte d'Ivoire in the Atlantic Ocean (Ghana/Côte d'Ivoire)*, ITLOS Case No. 23, Order (25 April 2015) [*Ghana/Côte d'Ivoire – Provisional measures*], paras. 95–96.

[111] *Ghana/Côte d'Ivoire – Judgment*, paras. 589–592, 633. See the criticism by Judge Paik, who after distinguishing the purpose of preserving the rights of the parties in a dispute and that of reaching an agreement, concluded that, on the facts, the hydrocarbon exploitation conduct of Ghana in the dispute area was in breach of Article 83(3) of the UNCLOS and could not be justified either by the suspension of activities following a provisional measures order or by the fact that the exploitation area was eventually adjudicated to Ghana. See *Ghana/Côte d'Ivoire – Judgment*, Separate Opinion of Judge Paik, paras. 9, 16–17.

> under dispute appertains to which of the claiming States. This means that the relevant judgment gives one entitlement priority over the other. Such a decision accordingly has a constitutive nature and cannot be qualified as merely declaratory [...] the consequence of the above is that maritime activities undertaken by a State in an area of the continental shelf which has been attributed to another State by an international judgment cannot be considered to be in violation of the sovereign rights of the latter if those activities were carried out before the judgment was delivered and if the area concerned was the subject of claims made in good faith by both States.[112]

As for the argument that such exploitation activities were in violation of Article 83(3) of the UNCLOS (specifically to 'make every effort [...] not to jeopardize or hamper the reaching of the final agreement'), the Chamber rejected the argument on two grounds. First, Ghana had suspended new drilling following the Chamber's order on provisional measures. Second, the areas where exploitation had taken place were eventually attributed to Ghana.[113] Thus, the reasoning seems to rest on the 'constitutive' nature of a delimitation judgment, which in turns makes the legality or illegality of operations entirely dependent on the final outcome, if one is ever reached.

In the absence of either a JDA or a prospect of judicial delimitation, the boundary between unilateral exploitation and required restraint becomes even more blurred. This is not only because, as in previous cases, the assessment of when the line is crossed depends on the specific activities, their location, and the scope of the overlapping claims, but, much more problematically, because there is little incentive for a State to exercise restraint. After all, lack of restraint would be condoned whether the area where the State conducts its exploration is attributed to it or not, in the latter case because the judgment is 'constitutive'. This controversial implication of the reasoning of the Special Chamber was emphasised by judge Paik in his separate opinion. He noted indeed that '[n]ow States may see less reason to exercise restraint in the disputed maritime area'.[114]

[112] *Ghana/Côte d'Ivoire – Judgment*, paras. 591–592. The Chamber referred in this regard to *Territorial and Maritime Dispute (Nicaragua v. Colombia), Judgment, I.C.J. Reports 2012*, p. 624, para. 250.

[113] Judge Paik dismissed these two reasons as unpersuasive because there was evidence that, as a result of the exploitation activities it had authorised, Ghana would have had little margin to negotiate a delimitation agreement, hence the activities had hampered this possibility. See *Ghana/Côte d'Ivoire – Judgment*, Separate Opinion of Judge Paik, paras. 15–17.

[114] *Ghana/Côte d'Ivoire – Judgment*, Separate Opinion of Judge Paik, para. 18.

The situation is therefore highly unsatisfactory. Hence the need for cooperation as well as for the activities to remain with certain parameters.

3.4.3 Duty to Cooperate (Notification, Consultation and Information Exchange)

The duty to cooperate has deep roots in international law, and it has been recognised in several contexts, including but not limited to delimitation or energy matters.[115] When it comes to the development of disputed/straddling hydrocarbon resources, the duty to cooperate rests on the additional rationale dictated by the geophysical aspects of hydrocarbon deposits. What in a domestic context was called (oil) conservation measures has no clear equivalent in international law. Yet, some authors have argued that the very need to exploit disputed/straddling hydrocarbons in a manner which does not cause harm to the other State and which is economically efficient calls for the emergence of a specific obligation to cooperate requiring the adoption of JDAs.[116]

Although such argument may find support in the frequent conclusion of delimitation agreements with mineral resources clauses and joint development regimes, the adoption of treaties could well signal precisely the absence of a customary norm. Moreover, the responses of States to the ILC attempts to codify principles for shared oil and gas resources strongly suggest that a majority of States do not see themselves as bound by an obligation to conclude certain types of agreements or provisional

[115] See *Tacna Arica arbitration*, 19 AJIL 393, 398 (1925); *Railway Traffic between Lithuania and Poland*, 1931 PCIJ Series A/B No. 42, at 108; *Lake Lanoux Arbitration (Spain* v. *France)*, Award of 16 November 1957, RIAA, vol. XII, pp. 281ff.; *North Sea Continental Shelf (Federal Republic of Germany/Denmark; Federal Republic of Germany/Netherlands)*, Judgment, ICJ Reports 1969, p. 47 [*North Sea Continental Shelf*], para. 85; *Nuclear Tests (Australia v. France) (New Zealand v. France)*, Judgments, ICJ Reports 1974, p. 268, paras. 46 and 49; *The MOX Plant Case, Ireland v. United Kingdom of Great Britain and Northern Ireland*, Provisional Measures, ITLOS Case No. 10, Order (3 December 2001), para. 82; *Land Reclamation in and around the Straits of Johor (Malaysia v. Singapore)*, ITLOS Case No. 12, Order (10 September 2003), para. 92; *Ghana/Côte d'Ivoire – Provisional measures*, para. 73; *Pulp Mills on the River Uruguay (Argentina* v. *Uruguay)*, Judgment, ICJ Reports 2010, p. 14, paras. 77, 102, 144–146; *Request for an Advisory Opinion Submitted by the Sub-Regional Fisheries Commission (SRFC)*, Advisory Opinion of 2 April 2015, ITLOS Case No. 21, para. 140; *Certain Activities Carried Out by Nicaragua in the Border Area (Costa Rica v. Nicaragua) and Construction of a Road in Costa Rica along the San Juan River (Nicaragua v. Costa Rica)*, Judgment, ICJ Reports 2015, p. 665 [*Costa Rica/Nicaragua – Judgment*], para. 106.

[116] For a discussion see Ong, *Joint Development of Common Offshore Oil and Gas Deposits.*

arrangements. Furthermore, in the absence of a specific treaty obligation, the duty to cooperate in international law does not require a certain outcome, such as a JDA; only cooperation in good faith through the channels chosen by the parties in their discretion and without an obligation to achieve a specific result.[117] It is also for this reason that some of the implications of the duty to cooperate in good faith are of a procedural nature, namely notification, consultation and exchange of information. These three procedural steps do not exhaust the content and requirements of the duty to cooperate in good faith. Instead, they are extensions of it, which, at the same, are actionable on a stand-alone basis. That means that a State can require another State not merely to broadly cooperate in good faith but to perform certain procedural steps, in the absence of which the first State may be in breach of the stand-alone duty to notify (or the other two duties). Due to the broad and deep roots of the duty to cooperate, its sources and those of its procedural extensions are diverse. In the context of offshore hydrocarbon deposits, they stem from the UNCLOS and general international law. In most cases, the two sources are discussed together.

The UNCLOS includes many provisions relevant to cooperation, notification, consultation and information exchange.[118] Particular attention has been paid in the case law to Articles 74(3) and 83(3), which state similar obligations for the EEZ and the continental shelf, and Article 83 (1) (also relevant for the similarly worded Article 74(1)), which states a broader duty to cooperate in the delimitation of the continental shelf (the EEZ). However, the focus of the discussion here should not be delimitation in general but the implications of these duties for the development of offshore hydrocarbons in the absence of an agreement.

In *Ghana/Côte d'Ivoire*, the Special Chamber addressed Côte d'Ivoire's argument that Ghana had not negotiated in good faith, as required by Article 83(1) of the UNCLOS, particularly because it had sought to preserve the status quo (including the ongoing hydrocarbon development activities) and initially closed off the judicial route for settlement. The Chamber rejected the argument noting that:

[117] *Railway Traffic case*, at 116; *North Sea Continental Shelf*, at 48; *Land and Maritime Boundary between Cameroon and Nigeria (Cameroon v. Nigeria: Equatorial Guinea intervening)*, Judgment, ICJ Reports 2002, p. 303, para. 244; *Ghana/Cote d'Ivoire – Judgment*, para. 604; *Obligation to Negotiate Access to the Pacific Ocean (Bolivia v. Chile)*, Judgment, ICJ Reports 2018, p. 507, paras. 86–87.

[118] See e.g. UNCLOS, Articles 63(3), 64(1), 65, 66(2) and (4), 69(3), 74(3), 83(3), 100, 117, 118, 119, 123, 194(1), 197, 200, 242, 266, 270 and 273.

> the obligation to negotiate in good faith is an obligation of conduct and not one of result. Therefore, a violation of this obligation cannot be based only upon the result expected by one side not being achieved. [. . .] The fact that Ghana tried to preserve the *status quo* as it saw it is, in the view of the Special Chamber, not a violation of an obligation to negotiate in good faith. Equally, the fact that Ghana initially closed off the avenue for a judicial settlement is not contrary to the obligation to negotiate in good faith.[119]

Regarding Articles 74(3) and 83(3), in *Guyana/Suriname*, the tribunal construed these provisions as including two obligations[120] that 'simultaneously attempt to promote and limit activities in a disputed maritime area':

> The first obligation is that, pending a final delimitation, States Parties are required to make 'every effort to enter into provisional arrangements of a practical nature'. The second is that the States Parties must, during that period, make 'every effort . . . not to jeopardize or hamper the reaching of the final agreement'.[121]

For present purposes, the tribunal's understanding of these two obligations must be analysed from the perspective of the legal regime governing hydrocarbon development in the absence of both delimitation and 'provisional arrangements'.

The duty to make '*every effort . . . to enter into provisional arrangements*' was construed as a 'duty to negotiate in good faith', but the tribunal stopped short from requiring a specific result.[122] Yet, and significantly, it found that Suriname had breached this duty because, despite an initial agreement to meet and discuss modalities for joint development, Suriname had not sent a delegation and, thereafter, it had repeatedly failed to respond to Guyana's openings. Of particular significance was the harder stance taken by Suriname once exploratory drilling operations authorised by Guyana had become public and widely known. At that point, according to the tribunal, Suriname's duty 'became particularly pressing and relevant'. Yet:

> Instead of attempting to engage Guyana in a spirit of understanding and cooperation as required by the Convention, Suriname opted for a harder stance. Even though Guyana attempted to engage it in a dialogue which

[119] *Ghana/Côte d'Ivoire – Judgment*, para. 604.
[120] See also *Ghana/Cote d'Ivoire – Judgment*, para. 626.
[121] *Guyana/Suriname*, para. 459.
[122] *Guyana/Suriname*, paras. 461–464.

> may have led to a satisfactory solution for both Parties, Suriname resorted to self-help in threatening the CGX rig, in violation of the Convention. In order to satisfy its obligation to make every effort to reach provisional arrangements, Suriname would have actively had to attempt to bring Guyana to the negotiating table, or, at a minimum, have accepted Guyana's last minute 2 June 2000 invitation and negotiated in good faith. It notably could have insisted on the immediate cessation of CGX's exploratory drilling as a condition to participating in further talks. However, as Suriname did not opt for either of these courses of action, it failed, in the build-up to the CGX incident, in its duties under Articles 74(3) and 83(3) of the Convention.[123]

Thus, this obligation of 'means' is not meaningless. It can indeed be breached under certain circumstances. The assessment heavily depends on the factual circumstances. In *Ghana/Côte d'Ivoire*, the Special Chamber reasoned that a party (Côte d'Ivoire) who would have been expected, in the light of the circumstances (Ghana's activities in the disputed area), to take the initiative of the negotiations, and who failed to do so, cannot claim that the other party violated its duty to make 'every effort . . . to enter into provisional arrangements'.[124]

As for the duty to make '*every effort . . . not to jeopardize or hamper the reaching of the final agreement*', the tribunal in *Guyana/Suriname* stated that 'this obligation was not intended to preclude all activities in a disputed maritime area' and then made the distinction, discussed in the previous section, between activities that 'lead to a permanent physical change . . . and those that do not'.[125] The overall conclusion was that '[i]t should not be permissible for a party to a dispute to undertake any unilateral activity that might affect the other party's rights in a permanent manner'.[126] From the perspective of cooperation, the reason for such a 'restraint' rule is that permanent change is deemed to compromise the reaching of a final agreement. The tribunal in *Guyana/Suriname* found that some exploratory activity which does not cause permanent change to the disputed area remains within the bounds of what is permissible under this duty.[127] What matters then is the effect of the activity (or lack thereof) on the physical environment. The interference with the possibility of reaching agreement is presumed. Yet, the tribunal also concluded

[123] *Guyana/Suriname*, para. 476.
[124] *Ghana/Cote d'Ivoire – Judgment*, para. 628.
[125] *Guyana/Suriname*, paras. 465, 467.
[126] *Guyana/Suriname*, para. 470.
[127] *Guyana/Suriname*, para. 481.

that activities which do not cause permanent change of the physical environment can be sufficient to 'jeopardize or hamper' the reaching of an agreement. Such was the case of the threat of force (by Suriname).[128] What remains to be determined is whether activities that do cause permanent change may nevertheless be permissible because, in the light of the circumstances, they do not 'jeopardize or hamper' the reaching of an agreement. In other words, the question is whether the presumption may be rebutted. The conclusion of the Chamber in *Ghana/Côte d'Ivoire*, discussed in the previous section, suggests that this is indeed possible. As noted earlier, in this case, Ghana had conducted exploitation operations in the disputed area and, yet, the Chamber concluded that Ghana had not breached Article 83(3) of the UNCLOS.[129]

The procedural extensions of the duty to cooperate, i.e. *notification, consultation, and information sharing*, are implications of cooperation in good faith. But not any conceptual implication of the duty to cooperate has crystallised into a stand-alone duty. This is why cooperation means more than notification, consultation, and information sharing, but these three duties are individually recognised as actionable (whereas other potential duties flowing from cooperation are not necessarily so). These two aspects – conceptual relation and individual recognition – of the procedural extensions must be briefly discussed.

Regarding the first aspect, official notification is a preliminary and necessary step towards cooperation. The notification may concern the conduct of activities in the disputed/straddling area or the possible existence of hydrocarbon deposits or, more generally, other steps relating to delimitation. Notification is intended to open a channel for cooperation, i.e. to enter into consultations, not to merely place the other country before a 'fait accompli'. As part of consultations, the sharing of certain information (e.g. if a party has reason to believe that there are hydrocarbon deposits in the disputed area or the nature of the activities envisaged) is required by good faith. Indeed, cooperation about the development of a disputed or straddling area would fall below the threshold of good faith if a party does not share some critical information (e.g. the proved or suspected existence of natural resources). The question, of course, is how much information is to be shared. There is a line to be drawn between the deliberate concealment of critical information,

[128] *Guyana/Suriname*, para. 484.
[129] *Ghana/Cote d'Ivoire – Judgment*, paras. 631–634.

which is inconsistent with good faith,[130] and the full disclosure of information, which would not be reasonable, not only for security reasons[131] but also more generally.[132] Some, not all information is to be shared to meet good faith demands, but it is reasonable to expect that States will negotiate at arms-length.

With respect to the recognition of these procedural duties, as such, the sources are quite diverse including the UNCLOS,[133] some cases that single out these duties in a variety of contexts,[134] and a number of codification instruments.[135] Specific procedural duties are often included in agreements between the parties, but in the absence of such instruments these duties remain applicable. Article 283(1) of the UNCLOS provides, in the general context of dispute settlement procedures, that: 'When a dispute arises between States Parties concerning the interpretation or application of this Convention, the parties to the dispute shall proceed expeditiously to an exchange of views regarding its settlement by negotiation or other peaceful means'. This general obligation concerns the 'settlement by negotiation or other peaceful means'. Article 242(2), which concerns marine scientific research, provides that:

> without prejudice to the rights and duties of States under this Convention, a State, in the application of this Part, shall provide, as appropriate, other States with a reasonable opportunity to obtain from it, or with its cooperation, information necessary to prevent and control damage to the health and safety of persons and to the marine environment.

130 UNCLOS, Article 300.

131 UNCLOS, Article 302.

132 In a different context, the ICJ in *Pulp Mills* referred to the 'fullest possible information' which is necessary to 'enabl[e] [the parties] to assess the plan's impact' on the shared resource. *Pulp Mills*, para. 113.

133 See e.g. UNCLOS, Articles 74(3), 83(3), 198, 200, 242(2), 248, 250, 266, 283, 300 and 302 of UNCLOS.

134 See e.g. *Corfu Channel* case *(UK v. Albania)*, ICJ Reports 1949, p. 4, at 22; *Second stage of the proceedings between Eritrea and Yemen (Maritime Delimitation)*, 17 December 1999, XXII RIAA 335–410 [*Eritrea/Yemen*], para. 86; *Pulp Mills*, paras. 75–77, 110, 113–115, 120, 144–147; *Costa Rica/Nicaragua*, paras. 106–110; *South China Sea Arbitration*, paras. 946–948.

135 Rio Declaration on Environment and Development, 13 June 1992, UN Doc. A/CONF.151/26. Rev.1 [Rio Declaration], Principles 18 and 19; Draft Articles on the Prevention of Transboundary Harm from Hazardous Activities, text and commentaries reproduced in *Yearbook of the International Law Commission*, 2001, vol. II, Part Two [ILC Prevention Articles], Articles 8 and 9.

Yet, the provision does not focus on hydrocarbon resources as such. The same applies to other sources, such as principles 19 and 18 of the Rio Declaration on Environment and Development or Articles 8 and 9 of the ILC Prevention Articles.

For a statement of these duties in the specific context of hydrocarbon deposits straddling a maritime boundary, one must turn to the award in the *Eritrea/Yemen* delimitation case, where the tribunal stated that:

> the Parties are bound *to inform one another and to consult one another on any oil and gas and other mineral resources that may be discovered that straddle the single maritime boundary between them or that lie its immediate vicinity*. Moreover, the historical connection between the peoples concerned, and the friendly relations of the Parties that have been restored since the Tribunal's rendering of its Award on Sovereignty, together with the body of State practice in the exploitation of resources that straddle maritime boundaries, import that Eritrea and Yemen should give every consideration to the shared or joint or unitised exploitation of any such resources.[136]

In a different – although comparable – context, the ICJ noted in the *Pulp Mills* case that:

> the *procedural obligations of informing, notifying and negotiating constitute an appropriate means*, accepted by the Parties, of achieving the objective which they set themselves in Article 1 of the 1975 Statute. *These obligations are all the more vital when a shared resource is at issue*, as in the case of the River Uruguay, which can only be protected through close and continuous co-operation between the riparian States.[137]

The Court made this statement under the applicable treaty but, later on, when addressing a disputed issue relating to the content of the obligation to inform, the Court grounded its interpretation on customary law, specifically on the general duty of prevention in both an environmental and a non-environmental context.[138]

On this basis, the Court explained that the obligation to inform (the relevant river commission) 'allows for the initiation of co-operation between the Parties which is necessary in order to fulfil the obligation of prevention'.[139] Moreover, referring to a prior case on criminal

[136] *Eritrea/Yemen*, para. 86 (emphasis added).
[137] *Pulp Mills*, para. 81 (emphasis added).
[138] *Pulp Mills*, para. 101.
[139] *Pulp Mills*, para. 102.

assistance,[140] the Court specified that the obligation to inform is not fulfilled by the mere fact that the information is public. It requires that the party undertaking the works officially informs the potentially affected party.[141] Subsequently, the Court recalled that: '[t]he obligation to notify is therefore an essential part of the process leading the parties to consult in order to assess the risks of the plan and to negotiate possible changes which may eliminate those risks or minimize their effects'.[142]

Regarding the parameters of the obligation of consultation, they are dictated by good faith. One useful characterisation was made by the arbitral tribunal in the *Lac Lanoux* case, which concerned the use of a shared watercourse. According to the tribunal:

> The upstream State has, under the rules of good faith, the obligation to take into account the different interests in presence, to attempt to satisfy them as far as that is compatible with the pursuit of its own interests and to show, in this respect, a genuine will to conciliate the interests of the other riparian State with those of its own. It is difficult to assess whether such an obligation has been fulfilled. But the judge can, without substituting itself to the Parties, conduct this assessment on the basis of the circumstances of the negotiations.[143]

As noted earlier, such an obligation to consult in good faith can indeed be breached, as suggested by the *Guyana/Suriname* case, where the tribunal concluded that Suriname had behaved in a dismissive and hostile manner inconsistent with its obligations under the UNCLOS.

3.4.4 Prevention of Harm (No Harm and Prevention of Environmental Harm)

'No harm' and the 'prevention of significant environmental harm' are often discussed together and incorrectly amalgamated. There is certainly a historical and conceptual link between them to the extent that the prevention principle was derived from the no harm principle.[144] More generally, both principles are derived from the broader duty of due diligence, first recognised in the *Alabama* case,[145] which has a general

[140] *Certain Questions of Mutual Assistance in Criminal Matters (Djibouti v. France)*, ICJ Reports 2008, p. 231, para. 150.

[141] *Pulp Mills*, para. 110.

[142] *Pulp Mills*, para. 115.

[143] *Lake Lanoux Arbitration (Spain/France)* (1957) 12 RIAA 281, para. 22.

[144] *Pulp Mills*, para. 101.

[145] *Alabama claims of the United States of America against Great Britain*, Decision of 14 September 1872, RIAA vol. XXIX, 125–134.

scope of application (not limited to the environment). But there are also important differences in what each principle protects and in their respective spatial scope of application, among others.

For present purposes, these differences can be stated succinctly (see also Chapter 3). First, whereas no harm is intended to protect the interests (indeed the implications of the sovereignty) of other States, whether environmental, social, economic, political or others, the prevention principle aims to protect the environment as such. Secondly, precisely because of this different focus, the scope of application of each principle is not the same. No harm only applies to conduct that may affect the interests (as an injured party, to use the terminology of Article 42 of the ILC Articles on State Responsibility[146]) of another State, whereas the prevention principle applies to conduct that may affect the environment, irrespective of its location,[147] i.e. that of another State, but also that beyond national jurisdiction, that of a dispute area or even that located in the State of origin itself. Unlike no harm, the prevention principle creates obligations *erga omnes*, the respect of which can be invoked by both 'injured States' and States 'other than the injured State' (to paraphrase Articles 42 and 48 of the ILC Articles on State Responsibility).[148] Their assimilation stems from the fact that, as far as environmental protection is concerned (but not other forms of harm), the prevention principle includes no harm as one of its components.[149]

The most prominent judicial recognitions of the *no harm principle*, as such, are the arbitral award of the tribunal in the *Trail Smelter* case, an environmental dispute *avant la lettre*,[150] and the judgment of the ICJ in

[146] Responsibility of States for Internationally Wrongful Acts, draft articles and commentaries, *Yearbook of the International Law Commission*, 2001, vol. II (Part Two).

[147] See *Legality of Nuclear Weapons*, para. 29; *Ghana/Côte d'Ivoire – Provisional measures*, paras. 68–73; *Request for an Advisory Opinion Submitted by the Sub-Regional Fisheries Commission (SRFC)*, Advisory Opinion (2 April 2015), ITLOS Case No. 21 [*IUU Advisory Opinion*], paras. 111, 120; *South China Sea Arbitration*, paras. 927 and 940; *Dispute Concerning Coastal State Rights in the Black Sea, Sea of Azov, and Kerch Strait (Ukraine v. Russian Federation)*, PCA Case No. 2017–06, Award concerning the preliminary objections of the Russian Federation (21 February 2020), para. 295.

[148] *Responsibilities and Obligations of States sponsoring Persons and Entities with respect to Activities in the Area*, Case No. 17, ITLOS (Seabed Dispute Chamber), Advisory Opinion (1 February 2011), para. 180.

[149] See L.-A. Duvic-Paoli, J. E. Viñuales, 'Prevention of Environmental Harm', in J. E. Viñuales, *The UN Friendly Relations Declaration at 50: An Assessment of the Fundamental Principles of International Law* (Cambridge: Cambridge University Press, 2020), pp. 283–313.

[150] *Trail Smelter Arbitration*, RIAA, vol. III, pp. 1905–1982.

the *Corfu Channel* case. In *Trail Smelter*, the tribunal famously derived a principle from American and international law according to which: 'no State has the right to use or permit the use of its territory in such a manner as to cause injury by fumes in or to the territory of another or the properties or persons therein, when the case is of serious consequence and the injury is established by clear and convincing evidence'.[151] In the *Corfu Channel* case, the Court based its conclusions on 'certain general and well-recognized principles, namely [. . .] every State's obligation not to allow knowingly its territory to be used for acts contrary to the rights of other States'.[152] In these cases, there is no doubt that the illegality of the conduct comes from the fact that it affects the interests of other States. This was confirmed by the ICJ in the *Nuclear Tests* case, where New Zealand's request for provisional measures was granted only on the grounds that France's activities affected New Zealand as such, not in its capacity of member of the international community.[153]

In the context of hydrocarbon development, these are the conceptual roots of the rule identified by the tribunal in *Guyana/Suriname* according to which: '[i]t should not be permissible for a party to a dispute to undertake any unilateral activity that might affect the other party's rights in a permanent manner'.[154] Yet, 'permanence' cannot be equated with the 'significance' threshold required for the no harm principle to be breached.[155] Thus, in this specific context, a distinction could be made between 'permanent' effects, which normally constitute a violation of the obligation of mutual restraint, and 'significant' harm, which would breach the no harm principle. This distinction is important because in cases of disputed hydrocarbon deposits, causing permanent physical change could be unlawful (see Section 3.4.2 for a more detailed

[151] *Trail Smelter Arbitration*, at 1965.

[152] *Corfu Channel Case*, at 22.

[153] *Nuclear Tests (New Zealand* v. *France)*, Request for the Indication of Interim Measures of Protection, Order (22 June 1973), ICJ Reports 1973, p. 135, paras. 31–32.

[154] *Guyana/Suriname*, para. 470.

[155] See *Iron Rhine arbitration*, para. 222; *Pulp Mills*, para. 101; *In the matter of the Indus Waters Kishenganga Arbitration before the Court of Arbitration constituted in accordance with the Indus Waters Treaty 1960 between the Government of India and the Government of Pakistan signed on 19 September 1960 (Islamic Republic of Pakistan v. Republic of India)*, PCA, Partial Award (18 February 2013), para. 451, and Final Award (20 December 2013), para. 112. Draft Articles on the Prevention of Transboundary Harm from Hazardous Activities, text and commentaries reproduced in *Yearbook of the International Law Commission*, 2001, vol. II, Part Two, commentary to Article 2, para. 4.

discussion) even if the effect is not significant. Moreover, the 'permanence' and 'significance' in this context do not necessarily concern the environment as such. The specific geophysical characteristics of hydrocarbon deposits may be such that drilling on one side of the disputed or transboundary deposit may amount to significant harm of the other State (e.g. change recoverability of the resource or increase its cost or, in the context of a disputed resource, extract hydrocarbons claimed by the other State), but the legal thresholds are clearly distinct. 'Permanent' change is a lower threshold than 'significant' harm.

The prevention principle has been discussed in some detail in Chapter 3, as it is one of the most important norms regulating the negative externalities of energy transactions. For present purposes, it will suffice to recall two specific illustrations in the context of disputed hydrocarbon resources in which the application of the prevention principle was confirmed.[156] The first concerns the *Ghana/Cote d'Ivoire* case, where the ITLOS issued an order on provisional measures requiring the Parties to continue to apply the prevention principle, despite the existence of a dispute.[157] The second arises from the dispute between *Russia and Ukraine* relating to the maritime area around Crimea, where Russia is conducting several economic activities, including some related to hydrocarbon resources. In a decision on jurisdiction and admissibility, an arbitral tribunal recalled that 'the obligation to protect and preserve the marine environment under Article 192 applies to "all maritime areas". Such areas, in the Arbitral Tribunal's view, undoubtedly include internal waters'.[158] This statement further clarifies the distinction between 'no harm' and prevention. Whereas prevention is clearly a principle regulative of negative externalities, no harm concerns both such externalities and the allocation of the use of a certain shared resource.

[156] For two confirmations of the same point in the context of biological resources see *IUU Advisory Opinion*, paras. 111, 120; *South China Sea Arbitration*, paras. 927 and 940.

[157] *Ghana/Côte d'Ivoire – Provisional measures*, paras. 68–73, and operative para. 1(d).

[158] *Ukraine v. Russia*, para. 295.

5

Ad Hoc Approach

Hydroelectricity, Offshore Wind, Pipelines and Electricity Transmission Lines

I Overview

The ad hoc approach is often found beyond the joint development of hydrocarbons discussed in Chapter 4, most commonly in relation to hydroelectric projects in international watercourses and for onshore or offshore pipelines. In addition, it is increasingly used for offshore wind farms and for electricity transmission lines. Whether it is for the exploitation of certain resources (e.g. hydrocarbons, the flow of a shared watercourse, the winds in certain areas) or for the development of fixed transmission infrastructure (pipelines and networks) across boundaries, or for combinations thereof (e.g. an offshore structure with pipelines or transmission lines carrying the resource or the product inland), the ad hoc approach is particularly apposite to organise the specificities of such projects. The transfer of nuclear materials or technology also relies on bilateral agreements, often called nuclear cooperation agreements, but these intervene within a more structured context of nuclear energy governance (see Chapter 6).

The needs vary from one type of project to another, and indeed across projects of the same type, but the articulation between the ad hoc rules and the foundational rules remains a useful analytical prism to understand how international law governs such projects. As for the 'proximate' legal context of each type of project, there are only well-defined and consolidated principles on the use of international watercourses. The other types of projects have a more composite and less settled proximate context, including the principles governing transit or the broad powers conferred on States to develop and manage their resources.

In this chapter, I first discuss the applications relating to the exploitation of resources, hydroelectricity and offshore wind power, and then those relating to fixed transmission infrastructures, pipelines and electricity transmission lines. The latter capture also the international aspects of certain domestic projects relying on solar energy which, due to the technological challenges involved in storing the electricity thus produced, can benefit from wider cross-border distribution networks. The increasing variety of applications of the ad hoc approach, particularly in the context of modern renewable energies and electrification, can be seen as a manifestation of the ongoing energy transition. From the analytical perspective used in this book, such applications illustrate the ad hoc legal organisation of new transactions, enabled by the transition. Only a brief discussion of each application is provided, and it relies on a similar analytical order. Further details can be found in the literature referenced in each section.

II Hydroelectric Projects in International Watercourses

2.1 Ad Hoc Governance of Hydroelectric Projects

Hydropower has long been and remains the main source of renewable electricity generation. In 2018, it accounted for 16 per cent of global electricity generation.[1] Moreover, 'pump storage hydropower' (PSH) is an important means of storing electricity (using the excess electricity available at a given point in time to pump water into a reservoir, which can then be released to generate electricity at a chosen time), and it is expected to expand.[2] According to the International Commission on Large Dams (ICOLD), a professional association founded in 1928, as of 2019, there were 57,985 large dams, understood as dams with a height of fifteen metres or more or between five and fifteen metres impounding more than 3 million cubic metres of water.[3] Whether a dam is single-purpose or multi-purpose, the main purpose remains irrigation, with hydropower coming second for single-purpose dams and third (after flood management) for multi-purpose ones. Dams have far-reaching environmental consequences and, for decades, they have been the target of environmental campaigning. The fact that they can generate electricity without large emissions of greenhouse gases and their potential as PSH have, however, tempered to some extent – without removing altogether – their negative perception.

[1] IEA, *World Energy Outlook 2019* (Paris: IEA, 2019), at 264.
[2] IEA, *Renewables 2019. Analysis and Forecast to 2024* (Paris: IEA, 2019), at 19.
[3] ICOLD, General Synthesis, available at: www.icold-cigb.org/.

From a legal standpoint, the resource governed by the ad hoc framework in the context of hydroelectricity is an international watercourse (a watercourse crossing or marking the boundary between two States) or a tributary thereof. Boundary delimitation is less of an issue in this context because, unlike the EEZ and the continental shelf, the powers of States over international watercourses were not newly defined. The main target are the uses of the watercourse and, for present purposes, its use for the generation of hydroelectricity.

Due to their importance, the possibly competing uses of international watercourses have received significant attention both in the literature[4] and in practice, either through the adoption of watercourse-specific agreements[5] or, increasingly, through efforts to develop and codify principles. Over time, the Institut de Droit International (IDI),[6] the International Law Association (ILA),[7] the UN Economic Commission

[4] See S. McCaffrey, *The Law of International Watercourses* (Oxford: Oxford University Press, 3rd ed. 2019); L. Boisson de Chazournes, M. M. Mbengue, M. Tignino, K. Sangbana, J. Rudall (eds.), *The UN Convention on the Non-Navigational Uses of International Watercoures. A Commentary* (Oxford: Oxford University Press, 2018); A. Tanzi, O. McIntyre, A. Kolliopoulos, A. Rieu-Clarke, R. Kinna (eds.), *The UNECE Water Convention on the Protection and Use of Transboundary Watercourse and International Lakes* (The Hague: Brill, 2014); L. Boisson de Chazournes, *Fresh Water in International Law* (Oxford: Oxford University Press, 2013), pp. 65–77; E. Brown Weiss, 'The Evolution of International Water Law' (2009) 331 *RCADI* 167; I. Kaya, *Equitable Utilization: The Law of Non-Navigational Uses of International Watercourses* (Aldershot: Ashgate, 2003); A. Tanzi, M. Arcari, *The United Nations Convention on the Law of International Watercourses* (The Hague: Kluwer, 2001); J. Bruhacs, *The Law of Non-Navigational Uses of International Watercourses* (Dordrecht: Martinus Nijhoff, 1993); L. Caflisch, 'Règles générales du droit des cours d'eau internationaux' (1989) 219 *RCADI* 13; R. Zacklin, L. Caflisch (eds.), *The Legal Regime of International Rivers and Lakes – Le regime juridique des fleuves et des lacs internationaux* (The Hague: Martinus Nijhoff, 1981); J. A. Barberis, *Los Recursos Naturales Compartidos entre Estados y el Derecho Internacional* (Madrid: Tecnos, 1979).

[5] For two databases compiling relevant agreements see: International Freshwater Treaties Database at Oregon State University: https://transboundarywaters.science.oregonstate.edu/content/international-freshwater-treaties-database; and T. Morgandi, 'Bilateral State Practice Concerning Energy Activities in International Law': www.energybilaterals.org/ (November 2017) developed at the Cambridge Centre for Environment, Energy and Natural Resources Governance (C-EENRG), which contains 34 hydropower agreements.

[6] See particularly 'Utilization of Non-Maritime International Waters (Except for Navigation)', Salzburg, 1961 [Salzburg Resolution].

[7] See particularly the 'Helsinki Rules on the Uses of the Waters of International Rivers', adopted at the fifty-second conference of the ILA in August 1966 [Helsinki Rules]; 'Articles on the Regulation of the Flow of Water of International Watercourses', adopted at the fifty-ninth conference of the ILA in 1980 [Belgrade Articles]; 'Seoul Complementary Rules', adopted at the sixty-second Conference of the ILA in 1986 [Seoul Rules]; 'Berlin

for Europe (UNECE),[8] and the International Law Commission (ILC)[9] all contributed to a process of distillation of such principles, which culminated with the adoption in 1997 of the New York Convention on the Non-Navigational Uses of International Watercourses.[10] The New York Convention is not the only framework convention on this matter. A major regional effort developed in the context of the UNECE is the 1992 Helsinki Convention on the Protection and Use of Transboundary Watercourses and International Lakes.[11] An amendment adopted in 2003, in force since 2013, allows any State member of the UN to become a party to the Convention. These two treaties and the many codification efforts that came before them address a wide range of uses, of which hydroelectricity is but one among many others.[12] This is due to the fact that competition for the use of an international watercourse may involve different uses, such as irrigation, hydroelectricity, human consumption, 'instream' or environmental uses and, of course, navigation for a variety of purposes.

As a result, the ad hoc approach, as it applies to hydroelectricity generation, has some features that distinguish it from hydrocarbon development. First, given that the legal principles developed much earlier, and in a context less marked by maritime boundary

Rules on Water Resources', adopted by the ILA on 21 August 2004 [Berlin Rules]. On this work see generally See S. Bogdanovic, *International Law of Water Resources: Contribution of the International Law Association (1954–2000)* (London: Kluwer Law International, 2001).

8 See Convention on the Protection and Use of Transboundary Watercourses and International Lakes, 18 March 1992, 1936 UNTS 269 [Helsinki Convention]; Protocol on Water and Health to the 1992 Convention on the Protection and Use of Transboundary Watercourses and International Lakes, 17 June 1999, 2331 UNTS 202 [Protocol on Water and Health].

9 See particularly 'Draft articles on the law of non-navigational uses of international watercourses and commentaries thereto and resolution on transboundary confined groundwater', *Yearbook of the International Law Commission*, 1994, vol. II, Part Two; United Nations Convention on the Law of the Non-Navigational Uses of International Watercourses, 21 May 1997, 36 ILM 700 [1997 New York Convention]; 'Draft Articles on the Law of Transboundary Aquifers', 11 December 2008, GA Res. 63/124, UN Doc. A/RES/63/124 [ILC Aquifers Draft]. On this work see generally McCaffrey, *The Law of International Watercourses*; Boisson de Chazournes et al, *The UN Convention;* Tanzi/Arcari, *The United Nations Convention.*

10 1997 New York Convention.

11 Helsinki Convention.

12 A more specific instrument was adopted in the 1920s, but it has only a very limited membership. See Convention relating to the Development of Hydraulic Power affecting more than one State, 9 December 1923, 35 LNTS 75.

delimitation, the principles are more settled and, by now, they are part of customary international law (see Section 2.3). Secondly, the uses of the international watercourse may or may not be 'joint' uses. In many cases, it is a unilateral use (e.g. dams or water diversions or excessive extraction for irrigation) by the upstream State, with significant effects on the ability of the downstream State to use the watercourse, which calls for the development of rules. Thirdly, although hydroelectric projects on international watercourses are subject to a 'proximate' legal context (see Section 2.3), in addition to the other rules encompassed by the foundational approach, their ad hoc governance has been watercourse- or project-specific. Yet, these specific agreements concern a variety of possible uses of the watercourses, not only energy-related exploitation.

In the following sections, I first discuss the structure and content of those agreements that are specifically relevant for the ad hoc governance of hydroelectric projects and then survey the main principles that come into play in the absence of an agreement or to clarify/supplement the terms of an agreement.

2.2 Structure and Content of the Agreements

2.2.1 Overview

Most of the literature on the international legal aspects of hydroelectric projects focusses on general aspects, such as the application of broad principles[13] or of certain rules of trade, investment and environmental

[13] See C. Leb, *Cooperation in the Law of Transboundary Water Resources* (Cambridge: Cambridge University Press, 2013); L. Boisson de Chazournes, *Fresh Water in International Law* (Oxford: Oxford University Press, 2014), pp. 65–77; E. Brown Weiss, 'The Evolution of International Water Law' (2009) 331 *RCADI*, pp. 183–230; A. D. Tarlock, P. Wouters, 'Are Shared Benefits of International Waters an Equitable Apportionment' (2007) 18 *Colorado Journal of International Environmental Law and Policy* 523; J. A. Barberis, 'Bilan de recherches de la section de langue française du Centre d'Étude et de Recherche de l'Académie', in J. A. Barberis, R. D. Hayton (eds.), *Droits et obligations des pays riverains des fleuves internationaux* (Leiden: Martinus Nijhoff, 1990), pp. 15–57, at 41–47; L. Caflisch, 'Règles générales du droit des cours d'eau internationaux' (1989) 219 *RCADI* pp. 133–162; M. L. Michael, 'The Allocation of Waters of International Rivers' (1974) 7 *Natural Resources Law* 45; G. Sauser-Hall, 'L'utilisation industrielle des fleuves internationaux' (1953) 83 *RCADI* 465.

protection to such projects[14] or, still, on specific projects or disputes arising from such projects.[15]

Between these two poles of the spectrum, one study by M. Happold stands out for its comparative review of a significant number of agreements specifically related to hydroelectricity.[16] This section follows this study and the agreements reviewed in it as the backbone of the discussion, adding when necessary some extensions. It examines *tour à tour* five main questions: models of cooperation; sharing formulae; territorial aspects; negative externalities; and dispute settlement.[17]

[14] See A. Tanzi, 'International Law and Foreign Investment in Hydroelectric Industry: A Multidimensional Analysis' (2016) 18 *International Community Law Review* 183; A. Rieu-Clarke, 'Transboundary Hydropower Projects Seen Through the Lens of Three International Legal Regimes – Foreign Investment, Environmental Protection and Human Rights' (2015) 3 *International Journal of Water Governance* 27; J. E. Viñuales, 'Access to Water in Foreign Investment Disputes' (2009) 21 *Georgetown International Environmental Law Review* 733; K. S. Clemons, 'Hydroelectric Dams: Transboundary Environmental Effects and International Law' (2008–2009) 36 *Florida State University Law Review* 487.

[15] See e.g. S. McCaffrey, *The Law of International Watercourses* (Oxford: Oxford University Press, 3rd ed. 2019), pp. 302–406 (reviewing examples of watercourse-specific governance in several regions, but without a focus on hydropower); L. del Castillo Laborde (ed.), *La contaminación fluvial en el Derecho Internacional. Casos recientes en la práctica Sudamericana* (Buenos Aires: La Ley, 2013); M. M. Mbengue, 'The Senegal River Legal Regime and its Contribution to the Development of the Law of International Watercourses in Africa', in L. Boisson de Chazournes, C. Leb, and M. Tignino (eds), *International Law and Freshwater: The Multiple Challenges* (Cheltenham: Elgar, 2012), pp. 217–236; N. A. Zawahri, 'India, Pakistan and Cooperation along the Indus River System' (2009) 11 *Water Policy* 1; F. Molle, T. Foran, M. Kakonen (eds.), *Contested Waterscapes in the Mekong Region – Hydropower, Livelihoods and Governance* (London: Earthscan, 2009); S. M. A. Salman, K. Uprety, 'Hydro-Politics in South Asia: A Comparative Analysis of the Mahakali and Ganges Treaties' (1999) 39 *Natural Resources Journal* 295; S. P. Subedi, 'Hydro-Diplomacy in South Asia: The Conclusion of the Mahakali and Ganges River Treaties' (1999) 93 *AJIL* 953; F. O. Boadu, 'Relational Characteristics of Transboundary Water Treaties: Lesotho's Water Transfer Treaty with the Republic of South Africa' (1996) 38 *Natural Resources Journal* 381; J. A. Barberis, 'L'exploitation hydroélectrique du Parana et l'accord triparti de 1979' (1986) 32 *AFDI* 779.

[16] See M. Happold, 'Dams and International Law', in L. Boisson de Chazournes and S. Salman eds, *Les ressources en eau et le droit international/Water Resources and International Law* (The Hague: Martinus Nijhoff, 2005), pp. 577–604. The agreements can be retrieved either in the databases mentioned in n. 5 or on three other databases: that of the International Water Law Project (www.internationalwaterlaw.org/) or the legislative series of the FAO and the UN: FAO, *Treaties concerning the Non-Navigational Uses of International Watercourse* (Study 50: Europe; Study 55: Asia) [FAO Compilation] and UN, *Legislative Texts and Treaty Provisions Concerning the Utilization of International Rivers for other Purposes than Navigation*, United Nations Legislative Series, No. 12, UN, New York, https://doi.org/10.18356/212db78e-en-fr [UN Compilation].

[17] Happold, *Dams*, at 583.

2.2.2 Models of Cooperation

The patterns of cooperation that can be extracted from State practice are broadly comparable to the 'models' reviewed in the context of hydrocarbons. The nature of the shared resource is, of course, reflected in the modalities of cooperation.

Under the first modality, only one State (or State-licensed utility) builds and operates the hydropower project, either for its own benefit (with some restrictions and compensation owed to the other State) or on behalf of both States. Noteworthy examples of this first modality include, among others,[18] the Kaitakoski project (USSR/Norway/Finland),[19] the Kosi project (India/Nepal),[20] and the Owen Falls Dam (Egypt/Uganda).[21]

The second modality concerns common projects where each State (or one or more delegated agencies) builds a part in its territory (e.g. the upstream State builds the dam/reservoir and the downstream State the hydropower plant) and the works and operation are coordinated by a

18 For other examples see Convention entre la République fédérale d'Allemagne et la République française sur l'aménagement du cours supérieur du Rhin entre Bàie et Strasbourg et protocole annexé à la convention, 27 October 1956, in UN Compilation, p. 660; Convention entre le Gouvernement de la République française et le Gouvernement espagnol relative a l'aménagement du cours supérieur de la Garonne, 29 July 1963, JORF of 29 May 1964, p. 4571 [Garonne Agreement]; Convention pour le règlement des rapports entre la Suisse et la France au sujet de certaines clauses du regime juridique de la future derivation du Rhin à Kembs, 27 August 1926, in UN Compilation, p. 710 [Rhine–Kembs Agreement].

19 Agreement between the Government of the Union of Soviet Socialist Republics, the Government of Norway and the Government of Finland concerning the regulation of Lake Inari by means of the Kaitakoski hydroelectric power station and dam, 29 April 1959, 346 UNTS 192/167 [Kaitakoski Agreement]; Additional Protocol between the Union of Soviet Socialist Republics and Finland concerning compensation for loss and damage and for the works to be carried out by Finland in connection with the implementation of the Agreement of 29 April 1959 between the Government of the Union of Soviet Socialist Republics, the Government of Finland and the Government of Norway concerning the regulation of Lake Inari by means of the Kaitakoski hydroelectric power station and dam, on 29 April 1959, 346 UNTS 212 [Kaitakoski Protocol].

20 Agreement between the Government of India and the Government of Nepal on the Kosi project, 25 April 1954, in UN Compilation, p. 290. See also the Amended Agreement between His Majesty's Government of Nepal and the Government of India concerning the Kosi project, 19 December 1966 [Kosi Project Agreement], available at: www.internationalwaterlaw.org/.

21 Exchange of notes constituting an agreement between the Government of the United Kingdom of Great Britain and Northern Ireland and the Government of Egypt regarding the construction of the Owen Falls Dam, 30 and 31 May 1949, in UN Compilation, p. 108.

joint commission. Major illustrations include, among other examples,[22] the Columbia River Treaty (Canada/United States),[23] the Lesotho Highlands Water Project Treaty (Lesotho/South Africa)[24] or the treaty relating to the Uruguay and Pepiri-Guaçu Rivers (Argentina/Brazil).[25]

The third modality is structured around a single newly created or authorised entity which carries out the construction and operation of the project on behalf of the two States sharing the watercourse. Such entity can be an international authority, as in the case of the Itaipú 'binational entity' (Brazil/Paraguay),[26] the Yacyretá 'binational entity' (Argentina/Paraguay),[27] the Zambezi River Authority (Zambia/Zimbabwe)[28] or the Komati Basin River Authority (Swaziland/South

[22] See e.g. Convention between the Government of the Socialist Federal Republic of Yugoslavia and the Government of the Romanian People's Republic concerning the execution of works for the Iron Gates water power and navigation system on the river Danube, 30 November 1963, 559 UNTS 364 [Iron Gates Agreement]; Agreement between the Government of the Socialist Republic of Romania and the Government of the Union of Soviet Socialist Republics on the joint construction of the Stinca–Costesti hydraulic engineering scheme on the River Prut and the establishment of the conditions of its operation (with protocol), 16 December 1971, 890 UNTS 3 [Stinca–Costesti Agreement]; Convention entre la Suisse et l'Italie relative à l'aménagement hydraulique du torrent Breggia à la frontière italo - suisse, 23 June 1972; Treaty between the United States of America and Mexico relating to the utilization of the waters of the Colorado and Tijuana Rivers, and of the Rio Grande (Rio Bravo) from Fort Quitman, Texas, to the Gulf of Mexico, and supplementary protocol, 14 November 1944, 3 UNTS 313 [1944 United States–Mexico Agreement].

[23] Treaty between Canada and the United States of America relating to cooperative development of the water resources of the Columbia River basin, 17 January 1961, 592 UNTS 272 [Columbia River Treaty].

[24] Treaty on the Lesotho Highlands Water Project between the Government of the Kingdom of Lesotho and the Government of the Republic of South Africa, 24 October 1986, available at: www.ecolex.org (TRE-152232) [Lesotho Highlands Agreement].

[25] Treaty between the Government of the Federative Republic of Brazil and the Government of the Argentine Republic for developing the shared water resources of the frontier sections of the Uruguay River and its tributary, the Pepiri-Guaçu (Pepirí-Guazú) River, 17 May 1980, 1333 UNTS 62 [Uruguay River Agreement].

[26] Treaty between the Federative Republic of Brazil and the Republic of Paraguay concerning the hydroelectric utilization of the water of the Paraná River owned in condominium by the two countries, from and including the Salto Grande de Sete Quedas or Salto del Guaira, to the mouth of the Iguazú River, 26 April 1973, 923 UNTS 57 [Itaipú Agreement].

[27] Treaty of Yacyretá between the Republic of Paraguay and the Argentine Republic, 3 December 1973, 13 UNTS 80 [Treaty of Yacyretá].

[28] Agreement relating to the Central African Power Corporation, 25 November 1963 and Agreement between the Republic of Zimbabwe and the Republic of Zambia concerning the utilization of the Zambezi River, 28 July 1987 [Zambezi River Agreement], FAO Compilation - Africa, pp. 271 and 273.

Africa),[29] or a concessionaire subject to the domestic law of one of the watercourse States, as it has been common practice in Europe.[30] The ICJ has recognised that international authorities thus created can be international organisations endowed with international legal personality.[31]

2.2.3 Sharing Formulae

The sharing formulae tend to be case-specific, particularly because many projects are multipurpose (e.g. flood management, hydropower, water transfers) and, even when they are not, watercourse States need the water for several purposes.

Some early treaties distribute the hydropower generating power itself proportionally to the shores/lands under their sovereignty[32] or the generating power under their control that is relinquished as a result of the project.[33] The extent of the respective rights over the

[29] Treaty on the development and utilization of the water resources of the Komati River Basin between the Government of the Kingdom of Swaziland and the Government of the Republic of South Africa, 13 March 1992 [Komati Agreement], FAO Compilation – Africa, p. 266.

[30] See e.g. Convention entre la France et la Suisse pour l'aménagement de la puissance hydraulique du Rhône entre l'usine projetée de la Plaine et un point à déterminer en amont du pont de Pougny-Chancy, 4 October 1913, in UN Compilation, p. 70 [Rhône Agreement]; Convention entre la France et la Suisse concernant la concession de la chute du Chatelot sur le Doubs, signed at Paris, 19 November 1930, in UN Compilation, p. 713; Accord entre la Suisse et l'Italie au sujet de la concession de forces hydrauliques du Reno di Lei, avec protocole additionel, 18 June 1949, in UN Compilation, p. 846 [Reno di Lei Agreement]; Agreement between the Federal Government of the Republic of Austria and the Free State of Bavaria concerning the Österreichisch-Bayerische Kraftwerke AG (Austrian Bavarian Hydroelectric Company) concluded on 16 October 1950, in UN Compilation, p. 470 [Österreichisch–Bayerische Kraftwerke Agreement]; Agreement between the Government of Republic of Austria and the Government of the Federal Republic of Germany and of the Free State of Bavaria concerning the Donaukraftwerk-Jochenstein-Aktiengellschaft (Danube Power-Plant and Jochenstein Joint-Stock Company) concluded on 13 February 1952, in UN Compilation, p. 476; Convention entre la Confédération suisse et la République italienne au sujet de l'utilisation de la force hydraulique du Spöl et protocole additionnel, 27 May 1957, in UN Compilation, p. 859 [Spöl Agreement]; Convention entre la République française et la Confédération suisse au sujet de l'aménagement hydroélectrique d'Emosson (avec modification), 23 August 1963, in FAO Compilation – Europe, p. 333 [Emosson Agreement]; Convention entre la République française et la République fédérale d'Allemagne au sujet de l'aménagement du Rhin entre Strasbourg–Kehl et Lauterbourg–Neuburgweier, 4 July 1969, in FAO Compilation – Europe, p. 239 [Rhine–Strasbourg–Lauterbourg Agreement].

[31] *Pulp Mills on the River Uruguay (Argentina* v. *Uruguay)*, Judgment, ICJ Reports 2010, p. 14, paras. 86–89.

[32] See e.g. Rhône Agreement, Article 5.

[33] See e.g. Rhine/Kembs Agreement, Article 2; Reno di Lei Agreement, Article 5; Spöl Agreement, Article 4; Emosson Agreement, Article 5; Garonne Agreement, Article 4.

waters[34] or the expenses borne by each State[35] are also used as criteria to allocate the benefits. Such benefits can be defined in terms of entitlements to a share of the electricity generated[36] but also in other forms (e.g. payments or water quantities). This is, again, because watercourses and dams can be used for a range of purposes, hydropower being only one of them, and what is shared, and the possible entitlements and compensatory arrangements, are also diverse.

By way of illustration, under the Columbia River Treaty, Canada agreed, as the upstream State, to regulate the flow of the river through the construction of a number of dams and reservoirs (Articles II and IV). In exchange, it has an entitlement to 50 per cent of the electricity produced (Article V(1)) by the hydropower plant built and operated by the United States, the downstream State (Article III). The treaty provides that Canada may sell this electricity in the United States (Article VIII(1)–(2)). Moreover, Canada receives payments from the United States for flood control services (Article VI).

2.2.4 Territorial Implications

By their nature and specificities, agreements establishing a regime for the use of a shared watercourse may have peculiar territorial implications, because they entail an exchange of territories,[37] or they make available certain portions of territory to the other State,[38] or they attach to a

[34] See e.g. 1944 United States–Mexico Agreement, Article 7; The Indus Waters Treaty concluded between India and Pakistan, 19 September 1960, in UN Compilation, p. 300 [Indus Water Treaty], Article 3 and Annexure D. A specific dispute concerning the distribution of the water flow for a several purposes, including hydropower, under the Indus Water Treaty was heard by an arbitral tribunal. See *Indus Waters Kinshenganga Arbitration (Pakistan v. India),* PCA, Partial Award, 18 February 2013 [*Indus Waters Kishenganga – Partial Award*]; *Indus Waters Kinshenganga Arbitration (Pakistan v. India),* PCA, Final Award, 20 December 2013) [*Indus Waters Kishenganga – Final Award*]. See also Rhine/Strasbourg/Lauterbourg Agreement, Article 7(1); Itaipú Agreement, Articles I and XIII; River Uruguay Agreement, Articles I and IV(2)(b); Zambezi River Agreement, Article 23.

[35] See e.g. 1944 United States–Mexico Agreement, Article 7; Stinca-Costesti Agreement, Article 4.

[36] See e.g. Treaty of Yacyretá, Article XIII.

[37] See e.g. Emosson Agreement, Article 24; Iron Gates Agreement, Article 9, and the Exchange of letters constituting an agreement between the Romanian People's Republic and the Socialist Federal Republic of Yugoslavia concerning the adjustment of the frontier on the Danube, 30 November 1963, in FAO Compilation – Europe, p. 522, Article 9; Stinca-Costesti Agreement, Article 9.

[38] See e.g. State treaty between the Grand Duchy of Luxembourg and the Land Rhineland-Palatinate in the Federal Republic of Germany concerning the construction of a hydro-electric power-plant on the Sauer (Sure) at Rosport/Ralingen, 25 April 1950, in UN

portion of the territory (propter rem) in case of State succession,[39] or – due to such possible implications – they seek to reserve the territorial situation prior to the agreement.[40] Thus, the territorial implications of such treaties are not merely factual (e.g. the flooding of vast areas of the upstream State where the reservoir is build and the monetary or in-kind compensation by the downstream for such loss of land) but legal, both under international and domestic law (when ownership of land – but not sovereignty – is transferred).

A special difficulty arises in the context of State succession to treaties. Treaties with a territorial character – particularly those that fix a boundary – are deemed to bind successor States in some respects.[41] Yet, watercourse agreements do not necessarily carry such effects or, at least, not in all respects. In its work of the law of State succession to treaties, the ILC observed that '[t]reaties concerning water rights or navigation on rivers are commonly regarded as candidates for inclusion in the category of territorial treaties'.[42] This statement was cited with assent by the ICJ in the *Gabčíkovo-Nagymaros Project* case by reference to the succession of Slovakia to the 1977 Treaty concluded by Czechoslovakia with Hungary relating to the building of a system of dams for hydroelectric power.[43] In this case, the Court confirmed that Article 12 of the Vienna Convention on State Succession to Treaties reflects customary international law and that the 1977 Treaty was indeed a territorial treaty binding on the successor State.

Yet, the binding character of prior agreements in this area remains highly contested, particularly in a decolonisation context, as suggested by the different positions – acknowledged by the ILC – taken by the States of the Nile Basin.[44] The position that better reflects most – but not all –

Compilation, p. 721; Kosi Project Agreement, Article 5; Agreement between Nepal and India on the Gandak Project, 4 December 1959, in UN Compilation, p. 295, Article 6; Treaty concerning the integrated development of the Mahakali River, 12 February 1996 (India-Nepal), 36 1LM 531 (1996) [Mahakali River Agreement], Article 2(1).

39 See ILC Draft Articles on State Succession to Treaties, commentary ad articles 11 and 12, paras. 26–28.

40 See e.g. Itaipú Agreement, Article VII; Uruguay River Agreement, Article VIII; Österreichisch-Bayerische Kraftwerke Agreement, Article 24.

41 VCST, Articles 11 (boundary regimes) and 12 (other territorial regimes).

42 Draft Articles on State Succession to Treaties, texts and commentaries reproduced in *Yearbook of the International Law Commission*, 1974, vol. II, Part One [ILC Draft on Succession to Treaties], commentary to Articles 11 and 12, para. 26.

43 *Gabčíkovo-Nagymaros Project (Hungary v. Slovakia)*, Judgment, ICJ Reports 1997, p. 7 [*Gabčíkovo-Nagymaros Project*], para. 123.

44 See ILC Draft on Succession to Treaties, commentary ad articles 11 and 12, para. 27. For two overviews and contrasting positions, with specific reference to the emergence of

authorities and practice is that, if the agreement in question creates a territorial regime (e.g. it sets a boundary, navigational rights, a joint hydroelectric project), the rule codified in Article 12 makes the treaty binding on the successor State.[45] However, in the context of decolonisation, a more nuanced solution would prevail due to the principle of tabula rasa. In such a context, a boundary regime would be preserved due to the convergence of the stability of boundaries and the *uti possidetis* principle, but other aspects, such as restrictions on the use of the waters would not be binding on the successor State without its consent. Any doubt that may exist with regard to the latter conclusion would be confined to situations where the previous agreement is not inconsistent with the principle of permanent sovereignty over natural resources. In case of inconsistency, the latter principle – as a corollary of the right to self-determination, which is a peremptory norm – would either exclude the succession to that treaty or prevail over it.

2.2.5 Adverse Effects (Negative Externalities)

One important issue arising from hydropower projects concerns their adverse effects on the affected population and the environment. Building dams requires flooding large areas, which in turn amounts to a direct (formal) or indirect expropriation of the relevant lands, the displacement of the affected population, and a major interference with ecological processes.

Reference to such matters in the text of the agreements is relatively rare, with most recent agreements paying more attention to these issues. Aside from provisions relating to other affected resources (fish stocks) or human interests (public health and irrigation), which appear in early treaties,[46] explicit reference to the safeguards governing the expropriation of the relevant lands,[47] respect for human rights[48] and protection of the

South Sudan, see M. S. Helal, 'Inheriting International Rivers: State Succession to Territorial Obligations, South Sudan, and the 1959 Nile Waters Agreement' (2013) 27 *Emory International Law Review* 907; A. C. Worku, 'State Succession in International Transboundary Water Obligations: South Sudan and the Nile Water Agreements' (2016) 10 *Mizan Law Review* 100.

45 *Gabčíkovo-Nagymaros Project*, para. 123.

46 See e.g. Rhône Agreement, Article 9; Emosson Agreement, Article 3; Treaty of Yacyretá, Article XVIII(i).

47 See e.g. Zambezi River Agreement, Articles 20 and 24.

48 See e.g. Lesotho Highlands Agreement, Articles 7(18) and 15; Komati Agreement, Articles 5 and 15.

environment[49] are found only in treaties concluded from the late 1970s onwards. For this reason, the articulation between the rules of the ad hoc framework and those discussed under the foundational approach are particularly important in this context. The application of the latter, which include customary and treaty-based environmental and human rights standards as well as performance standards for multilateral lending institutions (see Chapter 3), raises two main issues.

The first concerns whether and how such other rules apply when the watercourse treaty is silent on such matters. The question was specifically addressed in the *Indus Water Kishenganga* case, in the context of the 1960 Indus Water Treaty, which does not expressly regulate environmental protection. The arbitral tribunal applied nevertheless the principle of prevention of environmental harm, while at the same time preserving the water allocation effected by the treaty in favour of India.[50]

The second issue concerns the possibility for a watercourse agreement to displace or limit the application of such more general norms. In *Indus Water Kishenganga*, the tribunal admitted that such norms may be displaced or derogated from by agreement of the parties, at least to some extent, but this possibility would not apply when the relevant norms exclude it. Aside from well-recognised peremptory norms, such as the right to self-determination, the prohibition of racial discrimination, slavery, torture or genocide, one important practical question concerns the requirement of prior informed consent before an indigenous or tribal people can be displaced from its ancestral land.[51] By way of illustration, the compensatory arrangements envisioned in the Lesotho Highlands[52] and Komati Agreements[53] for displaced populations may be inconsistent with the rights of indigenous and tribal peoples recognised and largely codified in the 1989 ILO Convention No. 169 and the 2007 UN Declaration on the Rights of Indigenous Peoples. Whether or not the requirement of consent is part of *jus cogens*, it may prevail over a watercourse agreement through the application of basic conflict of norm

[49] See e.g. Agreement on Parana River projects (Argentina–Brazil–Paraguay), 19 October 1979, 19 ILM 615 (1980), Article 5(j); Uruguay River Agreement, Article 1; Lesotho Highlands Agreement, Article 15; Komati Agreement, Article 13.

[50] *Indus Waters Kishenganga – Partial Award*, paras. 445–454; *Indus Waters Kishenganga – Final Award*, paras. 112–116.

[51] Convention (No. 169) concerning Indigenous and Tribal Peoples in Independent Countries, 27 June 1989, 28 ILM 1382 (1989) [ILO Convention 169], Articles 16(2) and 6; UNDRIP, Annex, Articles 10 and 19.

[52] Lesotho Highlands Agreement, Article 7(18).

[53] Komati Agreement, Article 15.

rules (e.g. *lex superior*, *lex posterior*, *lex specialis*) or modulate the understanding of the relevant provision.

2.2.6 Dispute Settlement Mechanisms

The fifth main question concerns the dispute settlement mechanisms contemplated in the relevant agreements. As a general matter, the agreements provide for a sequence which begins with non-legalised means, whether negotiation (when no joint commission is set up) or discussion within the joint technical body created by the agreement,[54] and continue with legalised means, arbitration or submission to the ICJ.[55] The latter have been rarely used.

One example is the *Indus Water Kishenganga* arbitration, which was based on Article IX of the Indus Water Treaty. The few other disputes relating to hydroelectric projects, which have been decided by international courts and tribunals, have instead been based on special agreements (*compromis*) to submit the dispute to an arbitration tribunal, as in the *Lac Lanoux* case,[56] or the ICJ, as in the *Gabcikovo-Nagymaros* case.[57] The very rare submission of such disputes to judicial bodies can be explained by the need for continued cooperation between the riparian States, particularly with regard to jointly beneficial hydroelectric projects. In the three cases mentioned, the project was not jointly beneficial and/or it was not completed and/or it intervened in an already conflictual relation between riparian States.

2.3 Overarching Principles

2.3.1 Overview

Unlike the aborted work on the principles for shared oil and gas resources, the codification of the principles relating to the non-navigational uses of international watercourses was highly successful,

54 See e.g. 1944 United States–Mexico Agreement, Article 24(d); Indus Water Treaty, Article IX(1); Iron Gates, Article 21(1); Columbia River Treaty, Article XVI(1); Stinca-Costesti Agreement, Article 17; Lesotho Highlands Agreement, Article 16(4).

55 See e.g. Indus Water Treaty, Article IX; Reno di Lei Agreement, Article 13; Spöl Agreement, Article 18; Columbia River Treaty, Article XVI(2); Emosson Agreement, Article 21; Iron Gates, Article 21(3); Lesotho Highlands Agreement, Article 16(8); Komati Agreement, Article 16.

56 *Lake Lanoux Arbitration (Spain/France)* (1957) 12 RIAA 281 [*Lake Lanoux*]. This case was based on a compromis d'arbitrage signed on 19 November 1956.

57 *Gabčíkovo-Nagymaros Project.* This case was submitted to the ICJ by a Special Agreement signed on 7 April 1993.

leading to the adoption of the 1997 New York Convention, which reflects the state of customary international law.[58] The four main principles formulated in this instrument constitute the proximate legal context of international watercourse agreements for a range of questions, including hydropower. These principles have been briefly introduced in Chapter 2 in connection with the rules allocating powers over energy. Given their importance as the proximate legal context of hydropower projects, they are further discussed here.

In general international law, the rights and duties of States regarding the use of a shared watercourse stem from the existence of a 'community of interest' among riparian States. This concept was first developed by the Permanent Court of International Justice (PCIJ) in the context of navigational uses, in *Territorial Jurisdiction of the International Commission of the River Oder*.[59] It was then transposed by the ICJ in the *Gabčíkovo-Nagymaros* case, where the Court equated it with the principle of equitable and reasonable utilisation.[60] Thus, it is the community of interest arising from the shared character of the watercourse which requires some degree of restraint from riparian States, while at the same time recognising the principle that watercourses can indeed be used. The broad principles that define the rights and duties of States in such a context are four: (1) equitable and reasonable utilisation; (2) no harm, (3) the duty to cooperate and (4) the duty to protect and preserve the environment.

2.3.2 Equitable and Reasonable Utilisation

The principle of equitable and reasonable utilisation and participation is codified in Article 5 of the 1997 New York Convention. It states that '[w]atercourse States shall in their respective territories utilize an international watercourse in an equitable and reasonable manner'.[61]

Article 6(1) of the Convention lists some non-exhaustive criteria on the basis of which the equitable and reasonable character of the watercourse use is to be determined. These include, among several others, current and potential uses (letter (e)), effects of the use (letter (d)), and the social and economic needs of the watercourse States (letter (b)).

[58] See *Gabčíkovo-Nagymaros Project*, para. 85, and the codification works referred to in n. 6, 7 and 9.

[59] *Case relating to the territorial jurisdiction of the International Commission on the River Oder*, PCIJ Series A No. 23, Judgment (10 September 1929), p. 27.

[60] *Gabčíkovo-Nagymaros Project*, para. 85.

[61] 1997 New York Convention, Article 5. See also Salzburg Resolution, Article 3; Helsinki Rules, Article IV; Helsinki Convention, Article 2(2)(b); Berlin Rules, Article 12; *Gabčíkovo-Nagymaros Project*, para. 78.

Importantly, contrary to domestic law, no 'rule of capture' or 'seniority' of water rights based on prior use is recognised under international law.

Even when a State started to use a watercourse first, if such use goes beyond what is acceptable under the 'equitable and reasonable' standard, it is inconsistent with the principle. States remain free to negotiate allocations which favour one State or give legal expression to prior uses (e.g. Egypt's share under the 1929 and 1959 Nile Treaties and India's share under the Indus Water Treaty), but such allocations may not be consistent with the principle of equitable and reasonable utilisation in the absence of a specific agreement.

2.3.3 No Harm

The 'effects' criterion in Article 6(1) is only one consideration among others in determining the equitable and reasonable character of a use. Yet, if the adverse effect crosses a threshold of 'significance', the use would be contrary to the no harm principle (Article 7(1)), irrespective of the assessment under other criteria. One must say 'would be' rather than 'is' because the no harm principle is understood as a due diligence duty, which is only breached in case of 'fault' and not by the mere occurrence of 'harm' (strict liability).

This leads to two clarifications. First, harm below the threshold of significance remains permissible if the overall assessment makes the use equitable and reasonable. Second, the no harm principle remains applicable as a constant duty of due diligence with certain practically important implications. One is that, even when significant harm has occurred without any negligence from the State of the activity, this State is required to intervene to eliminate or mitigate the harm, or to consider the possibility of compensating the affected State.[62] Another is that due diligence must be exercised to prevent harm from becoming significant. The State of origin is thus under this duty when adopting measures to assess and prevent harm even below the threshold of significance.

2.3.4 Duty to Cooperate

The difficulties involved in ascertaining references to what is 'equitable and reasonable' or what level of diligence meets the standard of 'due' diligence or, still, what level of harm is 'significant', makes process all the more important. In the context of shared watercourses, the duty to cooperate finds expression in Articles 8(2), 9 (regular exchange of

[62] 1997 New York Convention, Article 7(2).

information) and 11 to 18 (notification and consultation) of the 1997 New York Convention.[63]

As noted in Section 2.2.2, cooperative frameworks are often adopted at the level of a watercourse or a specific project therein. Such ad hoc agreements can embody different degrees of cooperation, from basic compensatory measures, to coordinated projects, to the creation of a stand-alone entity to manage the project. The principles formulated in the 1997 New York Convention are only intended to provide an overall context, which States are free to adjust and specify by agreement. Article 3(1) of this Convention expressly reserves prior agreements, and Articles 3 and 4 contemplate the possibility that newly concluded watercourse agreements depart from the principles of the Convention (Article 3(3)–(4)). The expectations under the 1997 New York Convention are more limited in this respect than those under the 1992 Helsinki Convention, which expressly requires riparian States to 'enter into bilateral or multilateral agreements or other arrangements, where these do not yet exist, or adapt existing ones, where necessary to eliminate the contradictions with the basic principles of this Convention' (Article 9(1)).

Under general international law, which – as suggested by the ICJ in *Pulp Mills*[64] – may be applied together with a watercourse agreement (to clarify or supplement it), the scope of the duty to cooperate is defined by the principle of good faith. In the absence of a specific agreement, the consent of the downstream or affected State is not a requirement for the pursuit of an activity, but the State of origin of the activity must give sufficient prior notice and allow for a reasonable waiting period before undertaking such activities.[65] In case of disagreement, States are required to enter into consultations in good faith[66] and, while these consultations last, the State of origin is expected not to approve the activities.[67]

63 See also Helsinki Convention, Articles 9, 11 and 12. On this topic see C. Leb, *Cooperation in the Law of Transboundary Water Resources* (Cambridge: Cambridge University Press, 2015).

64 *Pulp Mills*, paras. 101–102 and 144–147. See also *Indus Water Kishenganga – Partial Award*, paras. 448–450.

65 See *Pulp Mills*, para. 120. See also, for World Bank supported projects, the notification requirement stated in World Bank, Operational Policy (OP) 7.50: Projects on International Waterways (March 2012), para. 4 ('The Bank ensures that the international aspects of a project on an international waterway are dealt with at the earliest possible opportunity. If such a project is proposed, the Bank requires the beneficiary state, if it has not already done so, formally to notify the other riparians of the proposed project and its Project/Program Details'). This requirement has some exceptions, stated in para. 7 (e.g. for resource surveys or feasibility studies).

66 *Lake Lanoux*, para. 22.

67 See 1997 New York Convention, Article 19; *Pulp Mills*, para. 144.

2.3.5 Duty to Protect and Preserve the Environment of the Watercourse

Finally, regarding the duty to protect and preserve the environment of the watercourse, as discussed in Chapter 4 in connection with hydrocarbon resources, it is related to but clearly distinct from the no harm principle.

Article 20 of the 1997 New York Convention requires States to 'protect and preserve the ecosystems of international watercourses'.[68] The terms used in this provision recall the general duty stated in Article 192 of the UNCLOS to 'protect and preserve the marine environment'.[69] This similarity is worth-noting because it signals the relevance of the case law on Article 192 for the context of watercourses. The duty stated in Article 20 of the New York Convention, much like the one stated in Article 192 of the UNCLOS, are expressions of the broader duty of due diligence and of the principle of prevention of significant environmental harm. The principles discussed in Chapter 3 are therefore fully applicable. Their grounding in customary international law has been repeatedly recognised, including in cases specifically dealing with the use of international watercourses.[70]

Another noteworthy issue is the application of the duty even in cases where there is a watercourse agreement which is silent on the matter.[71] In such cases, although the parties can agree to limit the amount of water available for 'instream' or environmental protection purposes, the agreement must nevertheless take into account such protection to all the extent possible.[72]

The four principles examined so far provide the proximate legal context of ad hoc frameworks governing hydroelectricity projects but, as for joint development agreements, the rights and duties of riparian States remain more generally governed by the rules examined under the foundational model. That is particularly important for the regulation of negative externalities, such as environmental and human rights protection.

III Offshore Wind Power

3.1 Ad Hoc Governance of Offshore Wind Projects

Offshore winds are a resource for the generation of electricity of growing importance. Although its contribution to the global supply of electricity

[68] See also Helsinki Convention, Articles 2(2) and 3 and Annexes I–III.
[69] UNCLOS, Article 192.
[70] See *Pulp Mills*, para. 101; *Indus Water Kishenganga*, paras. 448–450; *Costa Rica/Nicaragua*, para. 104.
[71] *Indus Water Kishenganga – Partial Award*, paras. 448–450.
[72] *Indus Waters Kishenganga – Final Award*, para. 111.

is still small (0.3 per cent in 2018), it has the second highest annual deployment rate (an increase of close to 30 per cent per year between 2010 and 2018) after solar photovoltaics.[73] The development of offshore wind power has been spearheaded by European countries, particularly Denmark, Germany and the United Kingdom. The winds in the North Sea offer a potential 635 GW of electricity if fully exploited. So far, this potential is only beginning to be put to use, with an estimated installed capacity of 90 GW by 2030.[74] In Asia, China, Japan, Korea, Taiwan and Vietnam, offshore wind power is also growing. In 2019, the overall investment of the latter countries in new offshore wind capacity was almost twice as much (approximately USD 10 billion) the amounts invested in Europe (approximately USD 5.5 billion).[75]

From the perspective of international law, the literature on ad hoc frameworks is still limited,[76] but it includes a full monographic study of the main ongoing experiment, i.e. the development of a transnational offshore grid connecting multi-jurisdictional clusters of wind farms in the North Seas,[77] and a detailed non-legal report recommending certain measures – Hybrid Asset Networks Support Agreements (HANSAs), Memoranda of Understanding (MoUs) or voluntary cooperation – which can be used to reduce the legal complexity of such projects.[78] The resource, as such, is provided by the electricity generating potential of offshore winds. Much like for hydropower, such potential is a flow (not a stock,

[73] IEA, *World Energy Outlook 2019* (2019), chapter 14.

[74] See WindEurope. 2017. *Unleashing Europe's offshore wind potential.* https://windeurope.org/wp-content/uploads/files/about-wind/reports/Unleashing-Europes-offshore-wind-potential.pdf; U. Weichenhain et al, *Hybrid Projects: How to reduce costs and space of Offshore Developments. North Sea Offshore Energy Clusters study* (20 May 2019) [Hybrid Projects Study], at 1; J. Gorenstein Dedecca, R. A. Hakvoort. 2017. *A review of the North Seas offshore grid modelling: Current and future research.* https://doi.org/10.1016/j.rser.2016.01.112.

[75] Renewables Consulting Group, *Global Offshore Wind: Annual Market Report* (2019).

[76] See H. K. Muller, M. Roggenkamp, 'Regulating Offshore Energy Sources in the North Sea-Reinventing the Wheel or a Need for More Coordination?' (2014) 29 *IJMCL* 716; R. Long, 'Harnessing Offshore Wind Energy: Legal Challenges and Policy Conundrums in the European Union' (2014) 29 *IJMCL* 690; T. Scovazzi, I. Tani, 'Off-Shore Wind Energy Development in International Law', in J. Ebbesson et al. (eds.), *International Law and Changing Perceptions of Security. Liber Amicorum Said Mahmoudi* (Leiden: Martinus Nijhoff, 2014), pp. 244–258; V. Roeben, 'Governing Shared Offshore Electricity Infrastructure in the Northern Seas' (2013) 62 *ICLQ* 839 [Roeben, *Shared offshore electricity*].

[77] H. K. Muller, *A Legal Framework for a Transnational Offshore Grid in the North Sea* (Antwerp: Intersentia, 2016). This book is based on a doctoral dissertation defended in September 2015 at the University of Groningen.

[78] See *Hybrid Projects Study.*

as fossil fuels) that can be put to profitable uses at different geographical points. Yet, like hydrocarbon development, the activities take place offshore in maritime areas which may be fully delimited or not and which, in all events, have to accommodate other uses of the seas, such as navigation and fishing. Moreover, storage challenges make it necessary for different wind power projects to be connected to inland grids, which brings a range of economic and regulatory challenges, including connections to 'national' grids, even if they are farther than the grids of other countries or the possible replication of connecting infrastructures, instead of cost-sharing and economies of scale. These could be addressed by cooperative approaches among States, whether bilateral or multilateral.

One ambitious approach is the clustering of wind farms in one or more specific areas and the development of joint connecting infrastructure (offshore hubs connected to inland grids through high-voltage direct current infrastructure or HVDC). But that raises complex legal questions relating to the allocation of regulatory matters (planning, oversight, environmental requirements), market aspects (allocation of development blocks) and subsidies (which country pays which renewable energy subsidies to which entity or how the overall cost is apportioned).

Because such legal complexities need to be clarified for the necessary amounts of long-term investment to be secured, ad hoc approaches can be used to formalise, in legal terms, the political commitments and understandings of the relevant public authorities. Yet, offshore wind projects present their own specificities, most notably arising from (1) the nature of the energy generating process (which may be an isolated offshore wind farm or one or more clusters thereof, under the same or several jurisdictions) and (2) the nature (cross-border or not), design (farm/cluster to inland grid, to hub or to cross-border interconnector) and regime (as cables and/or infrastructures and according to the maritime area) governing the connecting infrastructure.

In the following sections, I discuss two approaches to offshore wind development, the so-called conventional projects (wind farms operated separately from transmission and connected to one national grid) and 'hybrid projects' (joint wind farm/transmission projects and pluri-State connecting infrastructure). After a brief introduction of the North Seas Energy Cooperation Initiative, which provides the political background of offshore wind development in this area, the main features of conventional and hybrid projects are discussed (3.2). The 'proximate' international legal context of these projects is then recalled, focussing on the regime of marine renewable energy, cables and infrastructures (3.3).

3.2 The Structure of Offshore Wind Projects

3.2.1 The North Seas Cooperation Initiative

In 2009, several European countries (Belgium, Denmark, France, Germany, Ireland, Luxembourg, Norway, The Netherlands, the United Kingdom – then in the EU – and Sweden), as well as the EU Commissioner for Energy, signed a political declaration launching the 'North Seas Countries' Offshore Grid Initiative' (NSCOGI),[79] followed in 2010 by a memorandum of understanding (establishing three intergovernmental working groups on grid scenarios, market access and regulation, and planning and process, respectively)[80] and, in 2016, by a wider political declaration on energy cooperation between the North Seas Countries.[81] The latter brought these processes under the umbrella of a 'North Seas Energy Cooperation' initiative, which has since been strengthened from an institutional perspective.[82]

The aims and terms of these instruments are presented as devoid of any legally binding character.[83] That means, as one observer puts it, that they 'establis[h] a regional governance structure aimed at the coordinated exercise by the participating states of their UNCLOS rights with respect to cable laying, installations and marine renewable energy'.[84] The legal formalisation of such coordination, under the umbrella of the North Sea Energy Cooperation Initiative, is the main reason requiring an ad hoc framework in this context.

Significantly, the coordination is not limited to the exercise of powers under international law but also under EU and domestic law.[85] The components to be coordinated can only be understood by reference to the structure of offshore wind projects.

[79] North Seas Countries' Offshore Grid Initiative, 7 December 2009, available at: www.benelux.int [NSCOGI Declaration].

[80] The North Seas Countries' Offshore Grid Initiative, 'Memorandum of Understanding' (10 December 2010) [NSCOGI MoU].

[81] Political Declaration on energy cooperation between the North Seas Countries, available at: https://ec.europa.eu/energy/ [Political Declaration]. Although the United Kingdom's withdrawal from the EU did not technically affected the United Kingdom's participation in this initiative, in 2020, the United Kingdom departed from it.

[82] See Political Declaration, Annex II.

[83] See NSCOGI MoU, p. 3; Political Declaration, p. 3.

[84] Roeben, *Shared offshore electricity*, at 858.

[85] For a detailed analysis of these two dimensions see Muller, *Dissertation*, which is largely focused on the EU law regime as well as those of four countries, The Netherlands, Denmark, the United Kingdom and Germany (see chapter 4).

3.2.2 'Conventional' and 'Hybrid' Offshore Wind Projects

As a general matter, there are two main types of projects, often referred to as 'conventional' and 'hybrid' projects.

Conventional projects are characterised by two main features: (i) electricity generation and transmission assets are developed, organised and operated as separate entities; (ii) transmission assets connect electricity generation assets to one 'national' grid, namely the grid of the State under whose jurisdiction the electricity generation activities unfold. An example would be an offshore wind farm (developed and operated as a separate entity) located in Germany's territorial sea or EEZ, which is connected by transmission infrastructure (developed and operated as a separate entity) to the German grid. Aside from the many requirements to which conventional projects are subject under the relevant domestic and EU law, from the perspective of the international law, the situation does not raise major complexities. The coastal State regulates and profits from the relevant activities, which are conducted under its sovereignty (in the territorial sea) or its 'sovereign rights' over the conduct in its exclusive economic zone (EEZ) of 'other activities for the economic exploitation and exploration of the zone, such as the production of energy from the water, currents and winds'.[86] The specific features of the project must take into account the rights of other States – particularly regarding navigation – in the EEZ, but that does not call for an ad hoc approach; quite the opposite, as discussed in Section 3.3.

By contrast, hybrid projects involve much more legal complexity at the domestic, EU and international levels. These projects are characterised by (1) their combination of offshore generation and transmission assets at the development, organisation and operational levels and (2) their cross-border/transnational basis. A basic example would be the joint development and operation of generation and transmission assets, whereby the generation takes place in Germany's territorial sea or EEZ and the transmission connects the windfarm to the Dutch electricity grid. This is only a basic form of hybrid cross-border projects.

Hybrid projects can take several forms, which leads to 'sub-types' of hybrid projects. Depending on the criteria used to classify them, there will be a different number of sub-types. A study of hybrid projects commissioned by the European Commission identifies five 'sub-types' of hybrid project:[87] (1) a 'combined grid solution' connecting two

[86] UNCLOS, Article 56(1)(a).
[87] See *Hybrid Projects Study*, at 2.

conventional offshore projects, each individually connected to the grid in their own countries;[88] (2) a 'modular grid' connecting several farms located under different jurisdictions by means of a single export cable system;[89] (3) an 'interconnector tie-in' connecting one or more offshore farms to an interconnector, which itself connects to the grids of two jurisdictions;[90] (4) an 'offshore hub', with several offshore wind farms, located under different jurisdictions, connected to the hub, which is itself connected to the grids of two or more countries;[91] and (5) a 'neighbour offshore wind farm', namely a farm located under the jurisdiction of a State but connected to the grid of another State, whose shore is closer.[92]

This taxonomy focusses only on hybrid projects (with the cross-border component) and relies heavily on criteria of cost-effectiveness. It identifies eighteen potential projects which are at an early level of development or construction and compares the economic costs/benefits and regulatory challenges of such projects under two modalities, i.e. as conventional projects and as hybrid projects. For five of these, the study concludes that the 'hybrid' modality is significantly more beneficial than the reference 'conventional' modality, mainly due to cost reductions relating to cable distance, converter stations and maintenance and operation costs. It also finds that hybrid projects face significant legal challenges, due their regulatory complexity. It proposes to reduce such complexity by means of ad hoc legal frameworks in the form of the above-mentioned HANSAs, but given the

[88] An example is provided by the Kriegers Flak transmission project between Denmark and Germany. On this project see Hybrid Projects Study, at 2–3, and https://en.energinet.dk/Infrastructure-Projects/Projektliste/KriegersFlakCGS.

[89] The Hybrid Projects Study gives, as an example, the Modular Offshore Grid in Belgium, which connects nine offshore wind farms to the Belgian grid. In this case, however, there is no crossborder dimension because the farms are all located under Belgian jurisdiction. But if one (or more of them) was located under the jurisdiction of a different country, then it would be a clear illustration.

[90] According to the Hybrid Projects Study, there is no example of such a project at present. But the COBRA Cable project discussed in the study provides a close illustration. Under this project, an offshore wind farm located under German jurisdiction will be connected to the COBRA Cable Interconnector, which connects the Dutch and Danish grids. On this project see *Hybrid Projects Study*, at 144–170.

[91] An example is the proposed North Sea Wind Power Hub, under which offshore wind farms located in the Dutch, German and Danish EEZs are connected to the Dutch, German and Western Danish grids via a hub. On this example, its economic advantages and the barriers it faces see *Hybrid Projects Study*, at 114–144. See further the website of teh North Sea Wind Power Hub consortium: https://northseawindpowerhub.eu/project/.

[92] According to the *Hybrid Projects Study*, there is no example of such a project at present, but the study examines the possibility of connecting an offshore wind far under German jurisdiction to the Dutch grid only. See *Hybrid Projects Study*, 173–195.

limited practice, no standard approach or content has emerged for such agreements yet.

Another classification proposed in the literature encompasses both conventional and hybrid projects, which are organised in four main 'options', with some 'sub-options'.[93] The first option encompasses the 'radial connection' of an offshore wind farm to its national grid (what was earlier referred to as a 'conventional project') (sub-option 1(a)) or the radial connection, via an interconnector, of the grids of two countries (sub-option 1(b)). The second option concerns cases where several offshore wind farms are 'clustered via offshore hubs', namely they are connected to an offshore hub which collects and converts the electricity from different farms into HVDC for transmission to the onshore grid. This option can have a cross-border component (e.g. when the cluster brings together farms located under different jurisdictions) or not (e.g. when all the farms and the hub are under the same jurisdiction). The third option concerns the connection of one or more offshore windfarms to two or more onshore grids. This option admits several sub-options depending on whether one (option 3(a)) or more farms (option 3(b)) are connected to two onshore grids or on whether the connection of one (option 3(c)) or more farms (option 3(d)) is effected through 'teeing into', i.e. linking to, an interconnector cable. The fourth and most complex option is a 'meshed offshore grid' whereby hubs collecting the electricity from different clusters located in different jurisdictions are connected with each other and with the different onshore grids creating a pattern similar to an offshore 'mesh'.

At present, many of these options, particularly the most ambitious ones, are only theoretical. Most existing developments are conventional ones, with some hybrid projects being either planned or quite advanced, as the Kriegers Flak one. However, this classification is useful for present purposes not only in its wider coverage but also because it is specifically developed from the perspective of legal analysis. Whether there is an ad hoc framework agreement or not, some key legal questions remain governed by the 'proximate context' of such projects, which is found in the UNCLOS, as discussed next.

3.3 *Overarching Principles*

3.3.1 Overview

Beyond the complexities of offshore wind energy projects that call for an ad hoc approach, such as the allocation of regulatory powers over undelimited areas or the allocation of costs/benefits relating to project

[93] Muller, *Dissertation*, 10–13.

development, there are rules that deal with the 'proximate context' of such projects. Analytically, these rules have been introduced under the foundational approach when examining the powers of States over maritime areas.

Whereas projects located within the territorial waters of a single States do not raise any special complexity, projects in the EEZ (where the coastal State has only 'sovereign rights') and/or with cross-border dimensions raise some specific issues relating to the application of the general rules provided in the UNCLOS.

3.3.2 The Principles Embodied in Article 56 of the UNCLOS

In the context of activities in the EEZ, Article 56 of the UNCLOS, entitled 'Rights, jurisdiction and duties of the coastal State in the exclusive economic zone', is the pivotal provision:

> 1. In the exclusive economic zone, the coastal State has:
>
> (a) sovereign rights for the purpose of exploring and exploiting, conserving and managing the natural resources, whether living or non-living, of the waters superjacent to the seabed and of the seabed and its subsoil, and with regard to other activities for the economic exploitation and exploration of the zone, such as the production of energy from the water, currents and winds;
> (b) jurisdiction as provided for in the relevant provisions of this Convention with regard to:
>   (i) the establishment and use of artificial islands, installations and structures;
>   (ii) marine scientific research;
>   (iii) the protection and preservation of the marine environment;
> (c) other rights and duties provided for in this Convention.
>
> 2. In exercising its rights and performing its duties under this Convention in the exclusive economic zone, the coastal State shall have due regard to the rights and duties of other States and shall act in a manner compatible with the provisions of this Convention.
> 3. The rights set out in this article with respect to the seabed and subsoil shall be exercised in accordance with Part VI.

Within this provision, four main components can be identified. The first is, as noted earlier, a clear allocation of 'sovereign rights' to the coastal State over 'other activities for the economic exploitation and exploration of the zone, such as the production of energy from the water, currents and winds' (56(1)(a)).

The second is the assertion of the jurisdictional powers of the coastal State over certain matters, including 'the establishment and use of artificial islands, installations and structures' (56(1)(b)(i)) and 'the protection and preservation of the marine environment' (56(1)(b)(ii)). This confers both powers and duties. Powers over 'artificial islands' and 'installations and structures' are further specified in Article 60, which makes a difference between the exclusive right of the coastal State to construct, authorise and regulate the construction and operation of 'artificial islands', irrespective of their purpose, and this same right with respect to 'installations and structures'. In the latter case, the coastal State only enjoys this right if the installations and structures pursue certain purposes (mainly 'economic purposes', Article 60(1)(b)) or may interfere with other rights of the coastal State in its EEZ. That raises the question of the characterisation of offshore generation and transmission assets, on which I will comment later (see Section 3.3.3). As for duties, Article 56(1)(b)(ii) brings to bear Part XII of the UNCLOS specifically in the context of the EEZ.

The third component further clarifies the powers of the coastal State over the seabed and subsoil of the EEZ, which must be exercised in accordance with the rules set for the continental shelf in Part VI. Among the latter, Article 79 is particularly relevant, as it defines the powers of coastal States and other States over the laying and regulation of cables. In essence, coastal States can impose conditions on cables entering their territory (reaching the onshore grid) or, even when this is not the case, they have the right to regulate cables 'constructed or used in connection' with the exploitation of their continental shelf or the operation of artificial islands, installations and structures under their jurisdiction.

Finally, Article 56(2) reserves the rights of other States through the formulation of coastal State's duty of 'due regard', which is particularly relevant for other States freedom of navigation in the EEZ.[94]

3.3.3 Application to Offshore Wind Projects

When these broad principles are applied to offshore wind projects, several questions may arise depending on the structuring of the project.

One is a question of characterisation, which has two aspects: what object is to be characterised and how it should be characterised. Regarding the object, one could distinguish the electricity generation assets (the offshore wind farm) from the transmission assets (the connecting infrastructure) and treat each as a single object. Conversely, one could treat the entire 'hybrid' project, including both generation and transmission assets, as a single object. This distinction has implications for the characterisation of the object. Considered separately, the generation assets (the wind farm

[94] UNCLOS, Article 58(1), referring to the freedom of navigation in the high seas (Article 87) and Article 60(3)–(7) governing the requirement of due notice on the construction of artificial islands, installations and structure and the establishment of safety zones.

itself or its components) would be 'installations and structures', whereas part of the transmission assets, depending on the project specifications, would be 'cables'. Conversely, considered together (with transmission assets as ancillary to generation assets), the entire object would be characterised as 'installations and structures'.

Different characterisations raise further questions due to the different legal regime applicable to 'installations and structures' and 'cables'. Provided that they pursue an 'economic purpose' or otherwise fall under Article 60(1), 'installations and structures' are under the exclusive jurisdiction of the coastal State. By contrast, the principle governing the laying of 'submarine cables' (e.g. array and export cables) is the freedom of all States. Regulation of such cables by the coastal State is either limited in scope (reasonable measures to exercise its sovereign rights and environmental protection duties[95]) or subject to the requirement that the cable enters the territory of this State (as with interconnectors linking onshore grids) or is 'constructed or used in connection' with the exploitation of its resources or the operation of '[...] installations and structures under [the coastal State] jurisdiction'.

Existing projects, such as conventional projects where the generating assets are in the EEZ and the transmission assets connect the offshore windfarm to the national onshore grid, fall under coastal State jurisdiction. But more sophisticated hybrid projects, developed in an integrated (generation/transmission) and multi-jurisdictional manner, are far more complex to frame. Rather than compartmentalising the object according to the nature of the asset, for such projects, it may be necessary to consider the generation/transmission assets as a single multi-jurisdictional object governed by an ad hoc regime laid out in an agreement, much like for joint development agreements of petroleum or hydropower agreements in shared watercourses.

IV Oil and Gas Pipelines

4.1 *Ad Hoc Governance of Pipelines*

Pipelines are largely used to transport energy resources, mainly oil and gas (and to some extent coal slurry), from producer to consumer countries, often through the territories or maritime spaces of transit countries. They are complex and expensive infrastructures which, due to their cross-border nature, raise several intricate legal issues.[96] Such issues

[95] UNCLOS, Article 79(2).

[96] See generally B. Gayling-Westphal, *Intergovernmental Agreements and Host Government Agreements on Oil and Gas Pipelines – A Comparison* (Energy Charter Secretariat, 2015) [ECT Comparative Study]; R. Leal-Arcas, *Energy Transit Activities: Collection of*

largely depend on the type of pipeline project, which varies significantly depending on whether it is an onshore or a submarine pipeline (the latter are subject to a special regime in international law[97]), the areas (territorial waters or beyond) over which the pipeline is to run (beyond State territory, the freedom to lay pipelines – the right of immersion – is the rule[98]), whether it connects only two States or runs through one or more 'transit' States (in which case the scope of the latter's powers over the construction and trajectory of the pipeline, the status of resources in transit, the operation and regulation of the pipeline, and the uninterrupted flow must be clarified).

As will be discussed in Section 4.3, the rules examined under the foundational approach, particularly in connection with entitlements over spaces, transit and the regulation of negative externalities go some way in clarifying these issues (see Chapters 2 and 3). But they leave several key aspects, such as the allocation of construction costs and profits, the determination of the private entities which can build, operate and/or access the pipeline, the taxes, duties and other requirements/advantages applicable to the project (during construction and operation), among other aspects, to be specified by special agreements. These agreements have been used to facilitate and to some extent insulate such very costly infrastructure projects from the risks that may arise in the long timespan over which pipelines are expected to remain operational and become

Intergovernmental Agreements on Oil and Gas Transit Pipelines and Commentary (Energy Charter Treaty, 2015) [ECT Transit Study]; D. Azaria, *Treaties on Transit of Energy via Pipelines and Countermeasures* (Oxford: Oxford University Press, 2015); M. D. Piri, M. Faure, 'The effectiveness of cross-border pipeline safety and environmental regulations (under international law') (2014) 40 *North Carolina Journal of International Law and Commercial Regulation* 55; E. J. Omonbude, *Cross-Border Oil and Gas Pipelines and the Role of the Transit State: Economics, Challenges and Solutions* (London: Palgrave, 2013); S. Vinogradov, G. Mete, 'Cross-Border Oil and Gas Pipelines in International Law' (2013) 56 *German Yearbook of International Law* 65; C. Redgwell, 'Contractual and Treaty Arrangements Supporting Large European Transboundary Pipeline Projects: Can Adequate Human Rights and Environmental Protection Be Secured?', in M. M. Roggenkamp et al. (eds.), *Energy Networks and the Law: Innovative Solutions in Changing Markets* (Oxford: Oxford University Press, 2012), pp. 102–117; S. Wolf, *Unterseeische Rohrleitungen und Meeresumweltschutz: Eine völkerrechtliche Untersuchung am Beispiel Ostsee* (Berlin: Springer 2012); R. Lagoni, 'Pipelines', *MPEPIL* (April 2011); M. Dulaney, R. Merrick, 'Legal Issues in Cross-Border Oil and Gas Pipelines' (2005) 23 *Journal of Energy & Natural Resources Law* 247; S. Vinogradov, 'Cross-border Pipelines in International Law' (1999) 14 *Natural Resources & Environment* 75.

[97] See D. Nelson, 'Submarine Cables and Pipelines', in R-J Dupuy, D. Vignes (eds), *A Handbook on the New Law of the Sea*, vol. 2 (Leiden: Martinus Nijhoff, 1991), pp. 977–988; M. Roelandt, *La condition juridique des pipelines dans le droit de la mer* (Paris: PUF, 1990).

[98] See UNCLOS, Article 79(1).

profitable. The involvement of private investors and companies in the development of pipelines also requires the signing of other related agreements, both between private parties and host States and between operators themselves. Thus, pipeline agreements display all the hallmarks of the ad hoc approach to energy governance.

Although some bilateral and multilateral pipeline agreements were entered into as early as the 1930s,[99] project-specific agreements only developed from the 1970s onwards as a result of several factors: the increasing consumption of oil, which signalled the oversupply problem faced by many oil producers; the increase in the price of oil (following the 1973 oil crisis), which made the investment worthwhile; the development of offshore petroleum projects, which required transportation of the resource from offshore platforms to the mainland; and consumer countries' efforts to diversify the producer countries from which they sourced their oil and gas. Some agreements from this period include the Ekofisk pipeline (Norway–United Kingdom),[100] the Canada–United States Northern pipeline,[101] or the Kirkuk-Ceyhan pipeline (Iraq–Turkey).[102] Starting in the 1990s, with the disaggregation of the Soviet Union, the same configuration

[99] See Agreement between the Governments of Brazil and Bolivia on the exportation and use of Bolivian petroleum, 25 February 1938, 51 UNTS 256 [Brazil–Bolivia Agreement] (this agreement is not project-specific but lays the ground for possible pipeline projects); Convention on Construction of Oil Pipelines signed by Argentina, Bolivia, Brazil, Paraguay, and Uruguay, 6 February 1941, reproduced in Hudson, *International Legislation* (Washington: Carnegie Endowment, 1949), vol 8, 623 [Oil Pipeline Convention] (this agreement was also intended to lay the ground for possible pipeline projects). A prominent pipeline project from this early period is the Trans-Arabian Pipeline (TAPLINE), built in 1950, which transported Saudi oil to Western consumers for forty years. See D. Little, 'America, TAPLINE and the Arabs' (1990) 64 *Business History Review* 255.

[100] Agreement between the Government of the United Kingdom of Great Britain and Northern Ireland and the Government of the Kingdom of Norway relating to the Transmission of Petroleum by Pipeline from the Ekofisk Field and Neighbouring Areas to the United Kingdom, 22 May 1973 [Ekofisk Agreement]. See also Exchange of Notes between the Government of the United Kingdom of Great Britain and Northern Ireland and the Government of the Kingdom of Norway amending the Agreement relating to the Transmission of Petroleum by Pipeline from the Ekofisk Field and Neighbouring Areas to the United Kingdom, 27 July 1994 [Ekofisk Amendment].

[101] Agreement between the United States of America and Canada on Principles Applicable to a Northern Natural Gas Pipeline, 20 September 1977, 29 UST 3581 [Northern Pipeline Agreement].

[102] Crude Oil Pipeline Agreement between the Government of the Turkish Republic and the Government of the Iraqi Republic, 27 August 1973 [Kirkuk-Ceyhan Agreement]; Crude Oil Pipeline Protocol between the Government of the Turkish Republic and the Government of the Iraqi Republic, 16 May 1976 [Kirkuk-Ceyhan Protocol]; Addendum to the Crude Oil Pipeline Agreement of 27 August 1973 between the Government of the Iraqi Republic and the Government of the Turkish Republic, 30 July 1985 [Kirkuk-Ceyhan Addendum].

of factors that led to the adoption of the Energy Charter Treaty (ECT) also gave renewed impetus to the development of pipeline projects from former Soviet republics to European markets. Numerous agreements were adopted in this context, including the Baku–Tbilisi–Ceyhan (BTC) pipeline (Azerbaijan–Georgia–Turkey),[103] the Caspian Pipeline Consortium (CPC) pipeline (Kazakhstan–Oman–Russia),[104] the South Caucasus Pipeline (SCP) (Azerbaijan–Georgia),[105] the Trans-Anatolian Gas pipeline (Azerbaijan–Turkey),[106] the Trans-Adriatic pipeline project (Albania–Greece–Italy)[107] and the Nord Stream projects (Russia and several European countries, mainly Germany).[108] Production in other regions, whether by traditional or new producers, as well as the important increase in consumption in countries such as India or China also led to the

[103] Agreement among the Azerbaijan Republic, Georgia and the Republic of Turkey relating to the Transportation of Petroleum Via the Territories of the Azerbaijan Republic, Georgia and the Republic of Turkey through the Baku-Tbilisi-Ceyhan Main Export Pipeline, 18 November 1999 [BTC Agreement].

[104] Pipeline Consortium Agreement between the Government of the Republic of Kazakhstan and the Government of the Sultanate of Oman, 17 June 1992, joined by Russia in July 1992 [CPC Agreement], and later reorganised in 1996 by the Agreement on the Establishment of Closed Joint Stock Company 'Caspian Pipeline Consortium-R' and Closed Joint Stock Company 'Caspian Pipeline Consortium-K' and Caspian Pipeline Consortium Restructuring and Shareholders' Agreement among the Government of the Russian Federation, the Government of the Republic of Kazakhstan, the Government of the Sultanate of Oman, Oman Oil Company Ltd. and Chevron Overseas Petroleum Inc., Open Joint Stock Oil Company Lukoil, Mobil Corporation, Open Joint Stock Oil Company Rosneft, Agip SPA, British Gas Exploration and Production Ltd., State Holding Company Munaigaz, Oryx Energy Company and Caspian Pipeline Consortium Ltd, 6 December 1996 [CPC Hybrid Agreement], referred to in Vinogradov/Mete, at 98.

[105] Agreement between Georgia and the Azerbaijan Republic relating to the Transit, Transportation and Sale of Natural Gas in and Beyond the Territories of Georgia and the Azerbaijan Republic through the South Caucasus Pipeline System, 29 September 2009 [SCP Agreement]. See also the previous Agreement between the Azerbaijan Republic and Georgia relating to the Development and Refurbishment of certain existing Petroleum Transportation Facilities, the Development of New Petroleum Transportation Facilities, and the Transportation of Petroleum via such Facilities beyond the Territory of Georgia, 8 March 1996.

[106] Intergovernmental Agreement between the Government of the Republic of Turkey and the Government of the Republic of Azerbajian concerning the Trans Anatolian Natural Gas Pipeline System, 26 June 2012.

[107] Agreement among the Republic of Albania, the Hellenic Republic and the Italian Republic relating to the Trans-Adriatic Pipeline Project, 13 February 2013 [Trans-Adriatic Pipeline Agreement].

[108] The first pipeline project, Nord Stream, is based on contractual arrangements. A projected extension, Nord Stream II, which was still under construction at the time of writing, has raised significant controversy. See V. Jeutner, 'Amendments, annexations, alternatives: Nord Stream 2's contemporary status under EU and international law' (2019) 12 *JWELB* 502.

conclusion of several pipeline agreements during this same period. Examples are found in several regions, including Africa,[109] Asia,[110] Europe,[111] the Americas[112] and the Middle East.[113]

[109] See the Agreement between the Government of the Republic of Chad and the Government of the Republic of Cameroon Relating to the Construction and Operation of a Transportation System of Hydrocarbons by Pipeline, 8 February 1996 [Chad–Cameroon Agreement]; Treaty on the West African Gas Pipeline Project between the Republic of Benin and the Republic of Ghana and the Federal Republic of Nigeria and the Republic of Togo, 31 January 2003 [West African Pipeline Agreement]; Accord intergouvernemental entre la République algérienne démocratique et populaire, la République fédérale du Nigéria et la République du Niger, relatif au projet trans-saharien-gaz-pipeline, 3 July 2009 [Trans-Saharan Pipeline Agreement].

[110] See Gas Pipeline Framework Agreement between the Government of the Islamic Republic of Afghanistan, the Government of the Republic of India, the Government of the Islamic Republic of Pakistan and the Government of Turkmenistan, 11 December 2010 [TAPI Framework Agreement] and related inter-governmental agreement of the same date [TAPI IGA]; See also M. Skalamera, 'Explaining the 2014 Sino–Russian Gas Breakthrough: The Primacy of Domestic Politics' (2018) 70 *Europe-Asia Studies* 90 (discussing the agreement signed in May 2014 which led to the construction of a Russia-China gas pipeline called 'The Power of Siberia'). There are other pipelines from countries in Central Asia to China. See Keun-Wook Paik, 'Sino-Russian Gas and Oil Cooperation: Entering into a New Ear of Strategic Partnership?', *Oxford IES WPM 59* (April 2015).

[111] Northern Europe has seen significant developments. See e.g. Agreement between the Government of the United Kingdom of Great Britain and Northern Ireland and the Government of the Republic of Ireland relating to the Transmission of Natural Gas by Pipeline between the United Kingdom of Great Britain and Northern Ireland and the Republic of Ireland, 30 April 1993 [United Kingdom–Ireland Agreement]; Accord entre le Gouvernement de la République française et le Gouvernement du Royaume de Norvège portant sur le transport par gazoduc de gaz du plateau continental norvégien et d'autres secteurs vers la France, 27 March 1995 [Norway–France Agreement]; Agreement between the Government of the Kingdom of Belgium and the Government of the United Kingdom of Great Britain and Northern Ireland relating to the Transmission of Natural Gas through a Pipeline between the Kingdom of Belgium and the United Kingdom of Great Britain and Northern Ireland, 10 December 1997 [United Kingdom–Belgium Agreement]; Agreement Relating to the Transmission of Natural Gas through a Second Pipeline between the United Kingdom of Great Britain and Northern Ireland and Ireland and through a Connection to the Isle of Man, 24 September 2004 [United Kingdom–Ireland Second Pipeline Agreement].

[112] For a dated but still useful overview of the interconnections in this region see Organización Latinoamericana de Energía (OLADE), *La situación energética en América Latina. Informe Final* (M 545–P 235/01, March 2003), pp. 123–126.

[113] See e.g. Agreement between the Government of the State of Qatar and the Government of the United Arab Emirates relating to the Transmission of Gas by Pipeline between the State of Qatar and the United Arab Emirates, 26 September 2004 [Dolphin Gas Pipeline Agreement]; Framework Agreement between the Republic of Iraq and the Hashemite Kingdom of Jordan to implement a project to transport Iraqi crude oil through the territory of the Kingdom of Jordan to the export terminal port (Aqaba) on the Red Sea coast for export with a parallel gas pipeline, 24 April 2013 [Iraq–Jordan Agreement].

In the next section, the main features regarding the structure and content of these agreements are briefly examined. They can be characterised from four main perspectives.

4.2 Structure and Content of the Agreements

4.2.1 Focus of the Agreement: Relation-Based versus Project-Based Agreements

From this initial perspective, it is possible to distinguish agreements that set broad principles governing the development of energy interconnections, without structuring an identified pipeline project (relation-based agreements), and those which specifically concern one such project (project-based agreements).

Examples of the first category include the 1938 Brazil–Bolivia Agreement, the 1941 Oil Pipeline Convention or the 1977 Canada–United States Transit Pipelines Agreement.[114] Examples of the second category include most of the other agreements mentioned so far, including the 1973 Kirkuk–Ceyhan Agreement between Iraq and Turkey, the 1977 United States–Canada Northern Pipeline Agreement, the 1996 Chad–Cameroon Agreement, the 1999 BTC Agreement between Azerbaijan, Georgia and Turkey, the 2004 United Kingdom–Ireland Second Pipeline Agreement or the 2010 TAPI Framework Agreement between Turkmenistan, Afghanistan, Pakistan and India.

4.2.2 Nature of the Agreements: IGAs, HGAs and Private Agreements

The second perspective concerns the nature of the relevant agreements. As in other examples of the ad hoc approach, the agreements can be intergovernmental ('IGAs'), as the examples mentioned in the previous sub-section, or between private parties (there are usually a large number of such agreements in every project, governing matters such as joint ventures, shareholder agreements, financing, services) or, still, mixed.

The latter include so-called host government agreements (HGAs) between a private constructor or operator of one or more segments of

[114] Agreement between the Government of Canada and the Government of the United States of America concerning transit pipelines, 28 January 1977, 28 UST 7449 [Transit Pipelines Agreement].

the pipeline and the host State[115] as well as hybrid agreements, which bring together both governmental and private parties. An interesting example of the latter category is provided by the agreement concluded between three governments (Russia, Oman and Kazakhstan) and ten companies in the context of the Caspian Pipeline Consortium.[116]

Some IGAs serve as the formal framework of HGAs, which are incorporated by reference as integral appendices. Such is the case of the HGAs concluded by the company, BTC, with Azerbaijan, Georgia and Turkey, which are incorporated in the BTC Agreement.[117]

Also, some major projects do not rely on a treaty framework. For example, the important Nord Stream project that runs from Russia to Germany, through three transit States, with inland and submarine parts (both in the territorial sea and the EEZ) is not based on any ad hoc framework. It relies on the relevant rules of international law (e.g. for submarine pipelines, environmental impact assessments), EU law and domestic law.[118]

4.2.3 Project Structure: 'Connected' versus 'Integrated' Pipelines

The third perspective concerns how the body of agreements relating to a project structure the pipeline. A distinction can be made[119] between so-called 'connected' national pipelines and 'integrated' pipelines.

Under the 'connected' model, each segment of a pipeline located under a different national jurisdiction is treated as a separate asset governed by the applicable domestic law. Some measure of transnational harmonisation is achieved through political declarations and other soft instruments (an approach that has been subsequently used for hybrid offshore wind projects) and/or by contractual arrangements and/or by bilateral agreements between the sponsor government and each relevant State.[120]

115 For an analysis comparing selected IGAs and HGAs to the models developed by the ECT see both ECT Comparative Study and the ECT Transit Study.

116 See CPC Hybrid Agreement.

117 See BTC Agreement, Article II, section 2.

118 On the legal aspects of Nord Stream, see D. Langlet, 'Nord Stream, the Environment and the Law: Disentangling a Multijurisdictional Energy Project' (2014) 59 *Scandinavian Studies in Law* 79.

119 See Vinogradov/Mete, *Cross-Border Oil and Gas Pipelines*, at 94.

120 Such was the case of the South Stream project, now discontinued, for which Russia signed separate bilateral agreements with several countries in Southern Europe (Bulgaria, Serbia, Hungary, Greece, Slovenia, Croatia and Austria). See Azaria, *Treaties on Transit*, at 8 (n. 96, listing the relevant treaties).

A classic example of connected national pipelines is provided by the Kirkuk-Ceyhan pipeline between Iraq and Turkey. Article 1 of the 1973 Kirkuk-Ceyhan Agreement states that '[e]ach of the two sides guarantees to erect, construct, operate, maintain, manage, finance and to provide all other requirements for the part of the Project situated within its territory'. To ensure sufficient coordination, Article 5 provides that the entities nominated by each party 'shall establish a joint committee for the purpose of coordinating all matters pertaining to the Project'. However, the many challenges involved in handling regulatory misalignments between different jurisdictions has supported a trend away from this model and towards an 'integrated' pipeline model.

Under an integrated model, the assets are developed and operated as a single unit, which requires a deeper level of cooperation reflected in the more integrated set of agreements governing the project. The BTC Pipeline offers a good example. The 'MEP Project' is defined in Article 1 as a unity (including the entire life-cycle of the project and its span from Baku, through Tbilisi, to Ceyhan) and the assets, the 'Transportation System', are defined as 'an integrated system necessary for the transportation of Petroleum' from Baku to Ceyhan. As noted earlier, the BTC Agreement incorporates the HGAs concluded with each country. HGAs operate as *lex specialis* with respect to the IGA, as repeatedly stated in several clauses that formulate duties conditioned by a reservation ('except as otherwise specifically provided in the applicable Host Government Agreement').[121]

4.2.4 Basic Contents of Pipeline Agreements

The ad hoc character of pipeline agreements carries the consequence that their specific terms vary significantly. But some broad types of clauses often found in them can be identified by reference to the model IGA and HGA developed by the ECT Secretariat as a 'package', i.e. on the assumption that they would be used in combination.[122] Although it remains unclear the extent to which such models have been followed in State practice, they were developed on the basis of prior practice and therefore can provide some broad guidance.

IGAs are treaties under international law and concern 'horizontal' inter-States issues. Typical terms cover, aside from detailed definitional

[121] See e.g. BTC Agreement, Article V(1) (on taxation).

[122] See Energy Charter Secretariat, *Model Intergovernmental and Host Government Agreements for Cross-border Pipelines* (ECT, 2nd ed. 2007), Introductory note, para. 21.

clauses, the relations between the agreement and international/domestic law, land rights (which must be made available for the pipeline), status of the resource transported in the pipeline, duties relating to transit and the non-interruption of activities, environmental, safety and technical standards, taxes and other duties, non-discrimination standards, and dispute settlement clauses.

By contrast, HGAs are commercial agreements focussing on 'vertical' issues. As such, they are not governed by international law. Their terms may, however, be incorporated in IGAs thereby modulating the rights and duties of States thereunder. Typical examples of such modulation include more favourable duties, taxes, permitting processes, immigration terms etc. that are conducive to the development and exploitation of the pipeline infrastructure.

Specific examples of relevant terms are provided in the next section in order to illustrate how pipeline agreements relate to the broader principles defining their proximate legal context.

4.3 *Overarching Principles*

4.3.1 Overview

The proximate legal context of pipeline agreements has three main components: entitlements over the laying of pipelines through different land and maritime spaces; transit obligations; certain considerations relating to human rights, health, safety and environmental protection. The relevant rules have been discussed in Chapters 2 and 3. This section is only intended to illustrate how they operate in this specific context.

4.3.2 Laying of Pipelines

Regarding the laying of pipelines over the territory of a State (whether the land territory or the territorial sea), it is subject to the authorisation and regulation of that States. By contrast, as discussed in Chapter 2, there is a right to lay 'submarine pipelines' in the EEZ, continental shelf and beyond, the 'right of immersion', subject to certain specific constraints.

Article 79 of the UNCLOS on the scope of such right in the continental shelf is the pivotal provision to which the relevant provisions dealing with the EEZ (Article 58(1)) and the high seas (Article 87(1)(c)) refer. Under Article 79, the laying of the pipeline is not subject to the consent of coastal State, but the delineation of its trajectory is. This permissive rule is subject to two limitations. The coastal State is entitled 'to take reasonable measures' for the enjoyment of its sovereign rights over the resources of the EEZ and the continental shelf or the protection of the marine environment therein, and *a fortiori* the coastal State has the right to authorise and regulate the pipeline when it is 'constructed or used in connection' with the exploitation of its resources or the operation of artificial islands, installations and structures under its jurisdiction. That leaves out situations where the pipeline carries oil and gas 'in transit' from a third State to another third State over the EEZ/continental shelf of a coastal State.

Such was the situation of Estonia in the initial planning of the Nord Stream pipeline. In practice, Estonia managed to block a possible pipeline trajectory through its EEZ by refusing to grant a permit to conduct marine research (to determine environmental implications) in the area.[123] Pursuant to Article 246(2), the conduct of marine scientific research in the EEZ/continental shelf requires the consent of the coastal State. Article 246 of the UNCLOS subjects withdrawal of consent to a subtle set of conditions. In practice, however, the Estonian refusal led to the use of a different pipeline route.

4.3.3 Transit Principles

The example of Estonia in the previous sub-section illustrates the importance of transit States. As discussed in Chapter 2, the general principle stated in the main treaties, such as the GATT[124] (Article V) or the ECT (Article 7) in this regard is (1) the freedom of transit, further modulated by certain supporting principles: (2) non-discrimination on the basis of origin, ownership or destination of the goods in transit, (3) prohibition of imposing customs duties on the goods in transit, (4) reasonableness and proportionality of charges, (5) due diligence in avoiding delays and other obstacles to transit and (6) cooperation in developing adequate infrastructures for transit and/or granting access to them.[125]

These are all treaty-based principles, and they constitute the proximate context of pipeline agreements. The latter rely on, specify and sometimes extend these principles, e.g. providing for the construction of specific

[123] Tallinn, 21 September 2007, no. 60 (Refusal to give consent to conduct marine research), referred to in T. Koivurova and I. Polonen, 'Transboundary Environmental Assessment in the Case of the Baltic Sea Gas Pipeline' (2010) 25 *IJMCL* 151, at 171.

[124] GATT, Annex 1A.

[125] See V. Pogoretskyy, *Freedom of Transit and Access to Gas Pipeline Networks under WTO* (Cambridge: Cambridge University Press, 2017), at 79.

pipelines (or sections thereof), clarifying the status of the resources in transit and/or access rights to infrastructures and their use. For example, under the BTC Agreement, States Parties undertake inter alia to take measures:

> except as specifically provided in the applicable Host Government Agreement, not interrupt or impede the freedom of transit of Petroleum in, across and/or exiting from its Territory through the Facilities and the taking of all measures and actions which may be necessary or required to avoid and prevent the interruption or curtailment of such freedom of transit.[126]

According to Article VII(2) '[e]ach State acknowledges and agrees that all Petroleum transported through the Transportation System shall remain vested in the Project Investors and/or Shippers in accordance with their commercial agreements'.

Another illustration is provided by the TAPI Framework Agreement. Section 15 expressly regulates the access to the use of the pipeline establishing the priority of Turkmen gas:

> [E]ach Party shall have the right, with the consent of the other Parties, to transport or export its own natural gas through the Transport Pipeline under clear commercial terms provided Transport Pipeline capacity permits transport of such additional volumes. However, the Turkmen gas will always have priority for the utilization of the Transport Pipeline to the extent of contract quantities.

Section 18 deals with ownership of transported resources, and section 19 restates the freedom of transit principle.

4.3.4 Interactions between Pipeline Agreements and Their Proximate Context: Human Rights and Environmental Protection

The third component raises one complex issue, which has already been mentioned in Chapter 4, namely the operation of clauses found in IGAs and HGAs governing the relations between the agreement and international/domestic law or stabilising the legal framework/economic bargain. This is the heart of the attempt to 'insulate' the project from rules other than those laid down or filtered by the ad hoc framework.

[126] BTC Agreement, Article II, section 4(iii) on freedom of transit.

A prominent example of such attempts concerns the debate over the environmental and human rights standards of the BTC project.[127] Article II, section 6 states that:

> With respect to this Agreement, each State hereby represents and warrants that, as of its ratification and/or adoption as herein contemplated, the State is not a party to any domestic or international agreement or commitment or lawfully bound to observe or enforce any domestic law or regulation, or international agreement or treaty, that conflicts with, impairs or interferes with this Agreement or limits, abridges or adversely affects the State's ability to implement this Agreement or enter into and implement any other applicable Project Agreement.

This clause gives priority to the IGA over other international obligations, including human rights and environmental norms. The formulation, which is standard practice,[128] is intended to create State responsibility for breach of a representation and warranty in case the State claims that it is bound under international law to adopt a measure interfering with the project. In most cases, an outright conflict could be avoided through a consistent or 'systemic' integration.[129] But should a clear conflict arise, then the clause may render the application of such standards at least arguable. This risk is compounded by the non-interference provision included in the HGAs (Article 5 'Government Guarantees'), according to which the host State commits not to interfere with the operations except when the continued operation 'without corrective action creates an imminent, material threat to public security, health, safety or the environment'. In other words, the State would be relinquishing its ability to act unless there is an emergency. Such commitment runs counter the broader duties to respect, protect and fulfil human rights (see Chapter 3).

The attempted insulation came under much criticism from external observers. In a report, Amnesty International concluded that '[u]nder the present framework of protocols and agreements that circumscribe the project, mechanisms for protecting human rights are being systematically undermined'.[130] The pipeline States and the consortium responded issuing a 'Joint Statement' expressly presented as an integral part of BTC Agreement, which also incorporates the HGAs. The Statement interprets,

[127] See Redgwell, *Contractual and Treaty Arrangements*, at 105–110.

[128] See Model IGA, Article 3, Option 1, section 1.

[129] See VCLT, Article 31(3)(c).

[130] Amnesty International, *Human Rights on the line. The Baku-Tbilisi-Ceyhan Pipeline Project* (May 2003), at 4–5.

indeed modifies the agreements to provide for a 'basement' (a minimum threshold of protection consistent with EU environmental standards as they evolve over time) and a 'ceiling', according to which the stabilisation clauses do not preclude legal challenges relating to health, safety and environmental protection as long as they remain within certain bounds, carefully defined by reference to 'international labour and human rights treaties' binding on the host State. Moreover, a Code of Practice was incorporated into the HGAs to apply international standards to the private entities involved. Furthermore, BTC Co. undertook a 'Human Rights Undertaking' of unclear legal character and BP concluded with Amnesty International a 'Memorandum of Understanding in relation to Human Rights' which preserves the application of new domestic legislation in the fields of human rights.

V Electricity Transmission Lines

5.1 *Ad Hoc Governance of Electricity Transmission Lines*

The discussion in the previous sections is relevant for the understanding of the ad hoc legal frameworks applicable to electricity transmission lines.[131] These transmission infrastructures are key components of hydroelectric and offshore wind projects, which, unlike oil and gas

[131] See generally IEA, *Integrating Power Systems across Borders* (June 2019) [IEA Study]; M. Sanchez Miranda, 'Liberalization at the Speed of Light: International Trade in Electricity and Interconnected Networks' (2018) 21 *JIEL* 67; T. Cottier, I. Espa (eds.), *International Trade in Sustainable Electricity* (Cambridge: Cambridge University Press, 2017); South Asia Regional Initiative for Energy Integration (SARI/EI), *Transmission Service Agreement for Cross-Border Electricity Trade* (IRAD, 2016) [SARI/EI – Model TSA]; SARI/EI, *Power Purchase Agreement for Cross-Border Electricity Trade between Seller (New Hydro Generator) & Procurer* (IRAD, 2016) [SARI/EI – Model PPA]; Energy Charter Secretariat, *Guidelines for the Development of the Market and System Inter-Operability Model Agreement* (ECT) [ECT – IMA]; Energy Charter Secretariat, *Model Intergovernmetal and Host Government Agreements for Cross-Border Electricity Projects* (ECT) [respectively ECT – Report; ECT Model Electricity IGA; ECT Model Electricity HGA]; World Bank, *Building Regional Power Pools: A Toolkit* (2008) [WB Toolkit]; United Nations Department of Economic and Social Affairs, *Multi-Dimensional Issues in International Electric Power Grid Interconnections* (New York, 2006) [UNDESA Report], particularly chapter 4; M. Roggenkamp, F. Boisseleau (eds.), *The Regulation of Power Exchanges in Europe* (Antwerp: Intersentia, 2005); F. Meslier (1999), 'Historical Background and Lessons for the Future', in J. Casazza, G. Loehr (eds), *The Evolution of Electric Power Transmission Under Deregulation* (Piscataway, NJ: IEEE, 1999), pp. 28–31.

exploration and exploitation projects, directly generate a 'product' (electricity), which is then transmitted to the grids of participating countries for eventual distribution and consumption.

Interconnected electricity systems are not a new phenomenon. Throughout the twentieth century, the development of large synchronous alternating current (AC) power grids spanned vast expanses. For example, the Western European interconnection reaches from the United Kingdom and Scandinavia to countries in Eastern Europe to Greece and Italy.[132] But, in the last decades, there have been increasing calls for a higher level of power system integration across borders.[133] Cross-border electricity trading has grown in importance as a result of several factors, including the liberalisation of energy markets in some regions (e.g. the EU), technological developments (such as long-distance high-voltage direct current – HVDC – interconnectors between grids which operate at different frequencies or are otherwise incompatible), the increasing need to share (pool) capacity reserves and infrastructure costs across borders, the integration of greater shares of variable renewable energy sources, and the persisting challenges relating to storing electricity.

There are different degrees and models of cross-border power system integration. One can characterise them from five main angles. First, from the perspective of the degree of integration, a spectrum can be defined[134] from mere *bilateral trade* in electricity (unidirectional[135] or bidirectional[136]), to *multilateral and multidirectional* trade (whether among differentiated[137] or harmonised[138] markets), to *unified or fully*

[132] See UNDESA Report, at 15.

[133] See IEA Study.

[134] IEA Study, at 15–16. The following examples are derived from this study.

[135] For example, Laos' sales of electricity to Thailand or to Malaysia (through Thailand).

[136] For example, trade between the United States (California) and Mexico (Baja California) or between the United States and Canada.

[137] For example, the Southern African Power Pool (SAPP) or the Central American Electrical Interconnection System (Sistema de Interconexión Eléctrica de los Países de América Central (SIEPAC)). On these and other regional initiatives see A. Medinilla, B. Byiers, K. Karaki, *African Power Pools*, ECDPM Discussion Paper No. 244 (February 2019); C. Echeverria et al., *Integración Eléctrica Centroamericana* (IADB, 2017); Y. Wu, F. Kimura, X. Shi (eds.), *Energy Market Integration in East Asia* (London: Routledge, 2014).

[138] For example, the EU's Internal Energy Market. See V. Roeben, *Towards a European Energy Union: European Energy Strategy in International Law* (Cambridge: Cambridge University Press, 2018).

integrated system (whether relying on several institutions[139] or on a single one[140]).

A second and closely related distinction is that between bilateral and multilateral systems. This distinction refers to the number of States involved in electricity trading rather than to the degree of integration. A fully integrated system such as PJM in the United States operates at the domestic level. It is therefore neither bilateral nor multilateral. By contrast, the Nord Pool covers the Nordic (Denmark, Finland, Norway, Sweden), Baltic (Estonia, Latvia, Lithuania), United Kingdom, German, French, Dutch, Belgian and Austrian markets.

The third angle reflects the degree of integration in a different manner, namely how fluid and short-notice cross-border sales of electricity can be. This spectrum ranges from the less ambitious long-term cooperation, where electricity cannot be exchanged in the short term, to much more integrated systems, where 'day-ahead' or even 'intra-day' electricity trade is possible (e.g. Nord Pool).

The fourth angle looks at the nature of the agreements that are used to establish and manage different degrees of integration in cross-border electricity trade. Such agreements could be organised according to the nature of the parties (inter-State, mixed or private) or by their broad focus, namely intergovernmental framework agreements (IGAs), host government agreements (HGAs), inter-utility agreements, power pool agreements, and power purchase agreements.[141]

Finally, the fifth angle concerns the nature of the issues addressed in these agreements and, more specifically, in international agreements involving State parties. These issues typically include (1) cross-border sales/purchases of electricity, (2) the construction or improvement of the transmission infrastructure, (3) 'transit' issues when the infrastructure runs through a 'transit' States, (4) taxes and duties imposed on constructors/operators and (5) access by different electricity generators to the transmission infrastructure (including by those who do not manage it).

In the following paragraphs, I rely on the latter two angles to characterise the types of international agreements used in building and

[139] For example, the Nord Pool. On this important market see H.-A. Bredesen, T. Nilsen, *Power to the People: The First 20 Years of Nordic Power-Market Integration* (Oslo: Nord Pool Spot/Nasdaq OMX, 2013).

[140] For example, the PJM (named after Pennsylvania, New Jersey and Maryland) system which covers all or parts of Delaware, Illinois, Indiana, Kentucky, Maryland, Michigan, New Jersey, North Carolina, Ohio, Pennsylvania, Tennessee, Virginia, West Virginia and the District of Columbia, in the United States.

[141] See Miranda, *Liberalization*, at 76–82.

operating cross-border transmission lines and then briefly discuss their 'proximate context', namely the rules of trade and transit of electricity as a good and transmission as a service.

5.2 *Structure and Content of the Agreements*

5.2.1 Overview

From the perspective of their focus, IGAs and HGAs for electricity transmission projects present many similarities with those used for pipelines. IGAs provide a treaty framework focussing on the development (construction) and operation of the connecting infrastructure and HGAs specify, in a contract between each participating entity and the relevant host government, the terms of the framework agreement and some other aspects. Within this framework, the horizontal relations between participating entities (public or private) as regards the construction and operation of the infrastructure must also be organised, which takes the form of inter-utility agreements, sometimes preceded by a memorandum of understanding. Electricity purchase agreements focus, by contrast, on the sale/purchase itself rather than on developing the infrastructure and setting the rules for its operation.

A clear distinction must be made between the generation of the electricity sold/purchased and the service of transmitting it through the connecting infrastructure. These two activities may be separated or cumulated, depending on whether the market is 'unbundled' or not. The key issue that arises, as for pipelines, is that of access to the infrastructure by generators who do not manage it. In an unbundled market, the entity (called 'Transmission System Operator' or TSO) that owns and manages the infrastructure cannot be at the same time a generator of electricity sold through the infrastructure, so as to avoid anti-competitive practices.

But that does not solve questions of capacity allocation, access, coordination and competition. These matters may be addressed to some extent in the IGAs, HGAs and inter-utility agreements.[142] Yet, given the specificities of connecting different electricity markets which may not be

[142] See e.g. 'Ukraine and Its EU Neighbours Agree to Improve Cross-Border Electricity Trade', press release, 4 April 2019 (stating that, at a meeting of the Energy Community Secretariat, electricity TSOs and energy regulators of Ukraine (Ukrenergo, NEURC) and four neighbouring EU Member States – Hungary (MAVIR, HEO), Romania (Transelectrica, ANRE), Slovakia (SEPS, URSO) and Poland (PSE) – agreed to jointly

aligned, either legally (some unbundled, some not) or technically (grids must be made compatible), questions of market alignment and operation require a dedicated legal framework in the form of a market and system inter-operability agreement. Depending on the degree of integration sought, these agreements may set up an electricity pool across several jurisdictions. In what follows, each category of agreement is discussed by reference to some examples.

5.2.2 Intergovernmental Agreements on Electricity

As noted earlier, IGAs serve as framework agreements for the development of electricity transmission lines[143] or, in their early stages, as brief declarations of intention to this effect.[144]

As a general matter, IGAs in this context have broadly the same components as those applicable to pipelines.[145] States undertake to cooperate in order to facilitate the construction and operation of the transmission infrastructure, they commit not to interfere with it, they recognise the legal status of the electricity transmitted through the facility, they regulate access to the facility and they further provide for environmental and safety standards, taxation terms and non-discrimination.

One aspect to be singled out is the need for both 'market' and 'technical' harmonisation for cross-border electricity trade to be possible, which in turn requires granting 'access' and ensuring some degree of policy coordination. By way of illustration, Article IV(a)–(b) of the India-Nepal IGA addresses these questions by requiring the parties to 'cooperate on the various aspects of policy harmonization for the realization of cross-border interconnections, grid connectivity and power trade'. The type of cooperation envisioned in Article IV(a)–(b) specifically refers to

allocate capacity at their electricity interconnections to improve cross-border electricity trading).

143 See e.g. Agreement between the Government of Nepal and the Government of the Republic of India on Electric Power Trade Cross-Border Transmission Interconnection and Grid Connectivity, 21 October 2014 [India–Nepal IGA].

144 Memorandum of Understanding between the Ministry of Industry, Energy and Tourism in Iceland and the Department for Energy and Climate Change in the United Kingdom on Cooperation in the Energy Sector, 30 May 2012 (this one-page instrument merely notes that '[t]he Participants express their willingness to explore the possibility of developing an electricity interconnection between Iceland and the United Kingdom, including the legal and regulatory issues').

145 See ECT Model Electricity IGA.

cross-border duties and access. On the first, the provision requires 'work [ing] towards removing, and mutually resolving issues relating to, barriers, including tariff, levies, fees, taxes, duties or charges of similar effects, if any, in the cross-border exchange and trading of electricity'. On the second, it requires 'allow[ing] the authorized/licensed electricity producers/buyers/traders of each country to engage in cross-border electricity trading, including that through Power Exchanges, and to seek cross-border transmission access as per the laws of the respective country'.

5.2.3 Host Government Agreements on Electricity

HGAs specify the framework laid out in the IGAs by clarifying the specific terms offered by the host State to one or more project investors as regards the construction and operation of the infrastructure. By their nature and scope, they are much more detailed than IGAs.

As in the case of pipelines, these agreements are not treaties but only contracts subject to a domestic law chosen by the parties, whether the host State's or another one. For this reason, they cannot technically conflict with a treaty, such as the ECT or the GATT. Yet, the treatment accorded to the entities benefitting from the HGA may nevertheless amount to a breach of a treaty or, conversely, the treaty could provide a basis to breach a contractual term. In this regard, under Article 9 of the ECT Model Electricity HGA the host State 'represents and warrants' that the terms of the HGA do not contravene any 'treaty, agreement, decree or order to which [the host government] is a party'.

Also of note is Article 25 on 'access to available capacity', which addresses access to the transmission infrastructure by third parties. Several options are possible, from access negotiated with the infrastructure owners and operators on a case-by-case basis to access automatically granted under the terms of a related market and system inter-operability agreement.

5.2.4 Inter-Utility Agreements

Inter-utility agreements are entered into among participating entities, public or private, in order to coordinate the development and operation of the relevant infrastructure. Key aspects addressed in these agreements are the allocation of responsibility and costs for the development of the relevant infrastructure, its management and, as noted earlier, the issue of access to the infrastructure to trade electricity.

These aspects can be illustrated by reference to the SAPP Inter-Utility Memorandum of December 1994.[146] Article 9.1 on 'ownership' provides that '[u]nless otherwise agreed, each Pool Member [. . .] shall at its own costs, build, operate and maintain its own transmission facilities'. With respect to access, Article 6.1 provides that '[a]ll Electricity Supply Enterprises as defined in Article 3.3 situated in a SADC country as in September 1994 plus Zaire, can become a member of the SAPP'. The provision adds, however, that the addition of an electricity generator is subject to the discretion of the Executive Committee (a body which, according to Article 4.1, comprises the CEOs of the initial utilities), adopting its decisions by a two-thirds majority. Article 10.7 restates the principle that '[t]he Executive Committee shall have the authority to accept new Members into the SAPP as specified in Article 6.1'. The remaining provisions of the SAPP Memorandum are mostly concerned with the administrative bodies established to discharge different functions in the development and management of the system.

5.2.5 Electricity Purchase and Transmission Agreements

Cross-border trade of electricity can take place between interconnected systems in simpler or more complex ways. A sale/purchase of electricity can be structured around agreements covering the sale/purchase itself (the power purchase agreement or PPA)[147] and the transmission service, i.e. the cost of transporting the electricity sold/purchased through the infrastructure (the transmission service agreement or TSA).[148]

These agreements can be more or less comprehensive in their scope. For example, the TSA may include the construction of transmission infrastructure (as in the SARI/EI – Model TSA) or rely on existing infrastructure. The service will be typically billed to the beneficiary (either the seller or the buyer) monthly in the form of a tariff. The PPA itself is entered into between a seller (whether it commits its full generation capacity or only part thereof) and a buyer, who may be an end consumer, a distributor (a company distributing the electricity to end consumers) or a trader (a company selling the electricity to distributors or end consumers).

146 Southern African Power Pool (SAPP) Inter-Utility Memorandum, 7–8 December 1994 [SAPP Inter-Utility Memorandum].

147 See the SARI/EI – Model PPA.

148 See the SARI/EI – Model TSA.

PPAs introduce an element of predictability in the sales of electricity, which is important for investors, particularly when cross-border sales are a substantial part of the seller's revenue. Like the TSAs, PPAs are continuous contracts for a certain period of time under which the buyer pays for the electricity supplied at regular intervals (e.g. monthly) at a set tariff. Both PPAs and TSAs are contractual arrangements governed by a chosen domestic law.

5.2.6 Market Integration

Another way of organising electricity transactions is in the form of a fully integrated market for electricity. The main illustration is provided by Nord Pool, which emerged from the liberalisation of the electricity market in Norway, in 1993, and progressively expanded to Sweden, Finland and Denmark over the next decade, and then beyond (to the Baltic countries and some other European countries).

The structure of this market grew out of a combination of corporate law, contractual arrangements, domestic law and EU law. In essence, the market is managed by a company incorporated in Norway, Nord Pool ASA.[149] Nord Pool managed both the physical (electricity sales/purchases) marketplace and the marketplace for financial instruments based on the underlying spot price of the physical marketplace. In 2001, the physical marketplace was entrusted to a wholly owned subsidiary, Nord Pool Spot AS, which manages two physical marketplaces, the 'day-ahead' market (called Elspot) and the 'intra-day' hour-ahead market (called Elbas). Participation in these markets has progressively expanded from Norway and Sweden to Finland, then Denmark, and subsequently to other countries, including Germany and the Baltic States. Today, it provides day-ahead and intra-day trading services across nine European countries. It also provides clearing (through Nord Pool Clearing ASA) and Consulting (through Nord Pool Consulting). This ad hoc complex structure grew out of historical factors.

An integrated market and system can also be built on the basis of a power pool agreement. The ECT Secretariat has developed guidelines for the structuring of 'Market and System Inter-Operability Model

[149] On the legal foundations of the Nord Pool see O-H. Wasenden, 'The Nordic Electricity Market – A Mature International Market and Power Exchange', in M. Roggenkamp, F. Boisseleau (eds.), *The Regulation of Power Exchanges in Europe* (Antwerp: Intersentia, 2005), chapter 2. This brief account follows the detailed account provided in Wasenden. See also: www.nordpoolgroup.com/About-us/History/

Agreements'.[150] These are complex agreements combining market structural aspects (markets must be liberalised for this level of integration to be possible) as well as a range of institutional, technical and commercial aspects (to enable the electricity exchange across different grids in an organised manner under clear commercial terms). Such agreements are of a contractual nature, although their broad framework may be provided by an IGA.

5.3 *Overarching Principles*

The basic context of the ad hoc frameworks examined in the previous section is broadly similar to that of offshore wind projects and pipelines (see Sections 3.3 and 4.3), although some specificities must be briefly noted.

First, trade in electricity requires clarification of the nature of electricity under trade rules. As discussed in Chapter 2, the electricity sold/purchased in cross-border transactions is a good under both the GATT and EU law.[151] By contrast, transmission of electricity through the relevant infrastructure is a service, which therefore falls, as applicable, under the GATS.[152] Significantly, given the nature of the good and service, the duties and requirements applicable at the border must be applied by the TSO which manages the transmission infrastructure, which also has implications for the nature of its activities and the attribution of its conduct.

Secondly, as for pipelines, the construction and access to the relevant infrastructures is not determined at the level of the proximate context. Even Article 7 of the ECT does not, as such, require transit countries to build the necessary infrastructure or to provide access to third parties. These are matters that are typically left to the ad hoc framework level, i.e. the IGAs extended by HGAs and other contractual arrangements.

Thirdly, transit continues to play a role in the context of transmission lines, but a more limited one. This is because inland cross-border

[150] See ECT – IMA.

[151] See Miranda, *Liberalization*, at 94; *Municipality of Almelo v. NV Energiebedrijf Ijsselmij*, ECJ Case C-393/92, Judgment of 27 April 1994, para. 28 (referring further to *Costa v. ENEL*) and *Commission v. Italy*, Case C-158/94, Judgment of 23 October 1998, para. 17 (confirming Almelo).

[152] A similar distinction between gas and gas transmission was made by the panel in *European Union and its Member States – Certain Measures Relating to the Energy Sector* (Complainant: Russia), Panel Report (10 August 2018), WT/DS476/R, para. 7.338.

infrastructures are in most cases connected to the grids of the jurisdictions that they cross so as to enable electricity trade (rather than mere transit) across all the interconnected jurisdictions.[153] As for infrastructures in maritime spaces, the distinctions discussed in the context of offshore wind projects (see Sections 3.3.2 and 3.3.3) remain relevant. For submarine cables, the issue of transit is less of a problem in light of the right of immersion relating to submarine cables laid in the EEZ.[154]

[153] ECT – Report, para. 25.

[154] See T. Davenport, 'The Installation of Submarine Power Cables under UNCLOS: Legal and Policy Issues' (2013) 56 *German Yearbook of International Law* 107.

6

Centralised Approach

Nuclear Energy

I Overview

In addition to the energy-unspecific regulation covered by the foundational approach and the highly deposit/project-specific regulation embodied in ad hoc approaches, a growing number of institutionalised regimes have been established, with varying degrees of energy-resource specialisation and centralised governance.

In no other area is this approach more prominent than in the international regulation of nuclear energy, mainly as a result of the 'dual use' of nuclear technology, military and peaceful.[1] Centralisation in this context does not mean that everything is managed at the international level. This is certainly not the case, even for nuclear energy. States rarely miss an opportunity to state that the regulation of nuclear activities and its implementation are sovereign prerogatives. But such regulation is internationally induced or 'steered' mainly by one international agency, the International Atomic Energy Agency (IAEA). Even when States enter into bilateral or multilateral agreements relating to matters such as nuclear energy transfers and security, they very often refer to the IAEA standards and sometimes vest specific functions in it (e.g. supervision and inspection under safeguard agreements). Thus, the term 'centralised' is used here to reflect both a high level of institutionalisation and, importantly, a central 'steer', but not a regime exclusively managed at the international level.[2] Some attempts at a quasi-centralised institutionalisation, at least as a way of organising more focussed cooperative efforts, have also been made for other resources,

[1] See J. Schneider, O. Thränert, 'Dual Use: Dealing with Uranium Enrichment', *CCS Analyses in Security Policy*, no. 151 (April 2014).

[2] A possible example of such a regime would be the International Seabed Authority, which is vested with the power to manage the 'Area' under Part XI of UNCLOS.

such as oil, gas and renewables. This chapter focuses on the international law governing nuclear energy. The other examples are surveyed in Chapter 7.

From a legal standpoint, the centralised approach introduced in this chapter by reference to nuclear energy relies on the entitlements, enablers and limitations discussed under the foundational approach (see Chapters 2 and 3). It is also reliant on ad hoc project-specific agreements, mostly of a bilateral nature. One key question that arises in this context concerns the interactions among these different layers of energy governance. The highly technical and specialised nuclear energy regime may give the impression of a 'self-contained regime' that can escape the rules examined in Chapter 3 relating to the protection of human rights and/or the environment. But this conclusion would be legally inaccurate. The analytical process to determine the articulation of different norms remains the one introduced in Chapter 4.

Importantly, however, the goals pursued by the international law of energy may allocate priorities in a manner that changes the boundaries between the organisation of the transaction and the regulation of externalities. Briefly stated, considerations of international security (non-proliferation of nuclear weapons), security (in the narrow sense of security against external threats, rather than security of supply) and safety have played a much greater role than in other contexts. They are deemed of overriding importance and, as a result, the regulations giving expression to them can block or disable, rather than merely mitigate the effects of, the very transaction. In addition, sustainability as a goal of nuclear regulation has significantly grown in importance since the 1980s and, particularly, in the 1990s.

In the following sections, I begin by introducing the main features of the centralised approach in general terms before turning to its clearest illustration, the international law of nuclear energy. The examination of the latter follows two main steps. First, I discuss the 'dual use' of nuclear technology as main historical driver for centralisation. Secondly, I analyse the structure and content of the centralised governance of nuclear energy, paying particular attention to the role of the IAEA.

II Centralised Governance of Energy Resources

As noted in connection with the ad hoc approach, in order to characterise the centralised approach, two main dimensions must be clarified: the defining features shared by the type of institutionalisation efforts encompassed by this approach and the interactions between the rules embodying such efforts and those underpinning them (covered by the foundational approach) or specifically organising transactions (covered by the ad hoc approach).

2.1 Introduction

The centralised governance of energy is characterised by four main features, which are only fully present in the example of nuclear energy governance, from which they are derived. Other possible illustrations of the centralised approach display a sub-set of these four features, typically two or, exceptionally, three, but not all four of them. These four features are (1) the establishment of an international organisation or agency with a steering role, i.e. designed to serve as the epicentre of the efforts to govern a certain energy resource or form of producing energy at the international level; (2) as a result, another feature is that the organisation does not focus on a given project, deposit or activity (e.g. trade, transit or transportation) but on an energy resource or form of producing energy (e.g. nuclear, oil, gas, renewables or hydroelectricity); (3) in order to perform its steering activity, the organisation enjoys some measure of formal or informal normative power; and (4) the scope of the governance framework steered by the organisation is sufficiently comprehensive, encompassing the 'life-cycle' of the relevant form of energy, rather than a specific aspect or activity.

The first feature is the most characteristic one. Yet, the existence of an institution, as such, is not sufficient to distinguish this approach from the foundational or the ad hoc approach, which often rely on institutions too (e.g. the Word Trade Organization,[3] a plurinational entity managing a hydroelectric project,[4] or an agency established by a joint development agreement[5]). What characterises the centralised approach is the establishment of an institution with certain features, in terms of mandate,

[3] Marrakesh Agreement Establishing the World Trade Organization, 15 April 1994, 1867 UNTS 3.

[4] See e.g. the 'binational entity' established by the Treaty of Yacyretá between the Republic of Paraguay and the Argentine Republic, 3 December 1973, 13 UNTS 80, Article 3(1).

[5] See e.g. the Agency established by the Management and Co-operation Agreement between the Government of the Republic of Senegal and the Government of the Republic of Guinea-Bissau, 14 October 1993, to 'exploit the Area' (Article 4), and further organised by the Protocol of Agreement relating to the organization and operation of the Agency for Management and Co-operation, 12 June 1995.

powers and ambit, which allow it to perform a steering function with respect to an energy resource or form of producing energy. The main illustration is the IAEA, established by an Intergovernmental Conference on 23 October 1956.[6] Article I of the Statute establishes 'the Agency', which is vested by Article XV with certain 'privileges and immunities' necessary to perform its functions.[7] Other organisations, such as the Organisation of Petroleum Exporting Countries (OPEC) established in 1960,[8] the International Energy Agency (IEA) established in 1974,[9] or the International Renewable Energy Agency (IRENA) established in 2009,[10] have more limited mandates, powers and/or ambits (see Chapter 7). Thus, the institution embodying this first feature must meet, to certain extent, one or more of the remaining three features.

The second feature concerns the focus of the institution on an energy resource or a form of producing energy. Article II of the IAEA Statute states, in relevant part, that '[t]he Agency shall seek to accelerate and enlarge the contribution of *atomic energy* to peace, health and prosperity throughout the word' (emphasis added). Thus, the focus is on 'atomic energy' in general. Similarly, Article 2(A) of the OPEC Statute concerns the coordination of 'petroleum policies' and Article 2(1) of the IEA Statute focuses on 'oil supplies'. Yet another example is Article II of the IRENA Statute, according to which the agency is to promote 'all forms of renewable energy'. Such a focus clearly differs from that of Article 34 of the Energy Charter Treaty (ECT), which does not vest in the Energy Charter Conference a steering role on any particular energy resource, or from that of the Malaysia-Thailand Joint Authority, established by Article 3(1) of the Malaysia-Thailand MOU of 1979[11] for the purpose

[6] Statute of the International Atomic Energy Agency, 23 October 1956, 276 UNTS 3 [IAEA Statute].

[7] See further the Agreement on the Privileges and Immunities of the IAEA, 1 July 1959, INFCIRC/9/Rev.2 [IAEA Immunities].

[8] Statute of the Organization of Petroleum Exporting Countries (OPEC), 10–14 September 1960. The Statute was adopted at the second conference, held in Caracas in January 1961, Resolution II.6 [OPEC Statute].

[9] Agreement on an International Energy Program, 18 November 1974, 1040 UNTS 272 [IEA Statute].

[10] Statute of the International Renewable Energy Agency (IRENA), 26 January 2009, IRENA/FC/Statute [IRENA Statute].

[11] Memorandum of Understanding Between Malaysia and the Kingdom of Thailand on the Establishment of the Joint Authority for the Exploitation of the Resources of the Sea Bed in a Defined Area of the Continental Shelf of the two Countries in the Gulf of Thailand, 21 February 1979.

of exploring and exploiting the non-living resources in a specifically defined 'overlapping area'.

The third feature relates to the degree of normative power with which the institution is vested to perform its activities. By 'normative power' it is not meant the ability to adopt decisions or perform actions which are binding upon the institution's members but, more generally, the ability to enact normative acts that guide the governance of an energy resource. By way of illustration, Article III(A)(6) of the IAEA Statute expressly authorises the agency 'to establish or adopt [...] standards of safety for protection of health and minimization of danger to life and property'. This is not the only illustration of the normative powers of the agency.[12] The establishment and administration of safeguards against the redirectioning of nuclear energy technology for military purposes, under both the IAEA Statute (Article III(A)(5)) and the 1967 Non-Proliferation Agreement (Article III(1)) provides another major illustration of such power.[13] In other cases, such as the IEA Statute's collective emergency response system mechanism, State members are required to take demand restriction measures in case of reduction of oil supplies under Articles 13, 14 and 17 of the Statute, ascertained by the Secretariat (Articles 19(1) and 23(1)). Yet, this mechanism has never been formally used. In the three instances in which the IEA intervened to tap on Members' oil reserves (1991, 2005 and 2011), it was through the more informal 'coordinated emergency response measures' (CERM) approach.[14] The normative power of the IEA has found further expression through a wider activity of policy guidance through the provision of information and analysis on a range of energy sources. This reorientation is driven by Director-General F. Birol's three-pillar modernisation strategy, endorsed by ministerial declaration in November 2015.[15]

The fourth feature is the ambit covered by the instruments steered or managed by the relevant institution. This ambit is, in turn, characterised

[12] See generally O. Jankowitsch-Prevor, 'The Normative Role of the International Atomic Energy Agency, Legal Basis and Legal Sources', in *International Nuclear Law: History, Evolution and Outlook* (OECD: Nuclear Energy Agency, 2010), pp. 13–30.

[13] NPT.

[14] IEA Governing Board, Decision on Stocks and Supply Disruptions, 11 July 1984, IEA/GB (84)27, Item 2(a) and Annex I.

[15] On the IEA see Chapter 7.

by the focus (on the same energy source) and generally applicable nature (rather than project/deposit-specific) of the instruments. The field thus covered captures most of the life-cycle of the relevant energy source. In the case of nuclear energy, it spans uranium mining, to generation, transportation, and spent fuel/waste management. Thus, the relevant energy-specific instruments cover much of the ground which would otherwise be governed only by the unspecific rules examined under the foundational approach. This chapter analyses these nuclear energy-specific instruments in some detail.

2.2 *Normative Interactions*

In Chapter 1, I cautioned against reifying what I called energy governance 'approaches'. These are mere analytical categories useful to organise one's understanding of the international law of energy. From a legal standpoint, the level of analysis would be at the norm or treaty level or, occasionally, at the level of a sub-section of a treaty or of legally linked treaties. The same caveat applies to the analysis of normative interactions involving the centralised approach. From a strictly legal standpoint, such an approach has no existence. It merely unveils a pattern used in international law to govern certain energy resources or processes.

Thus, the analysis of normative interactions in this context must also follow the three analytical steps introduced in Chapter 4, namely (1) the identification of the relevant analytical level (norms, treaty sections, treaties, systems of legally linked treaties); (2) the determination of the relevant considerations giving priority to one level over the other (special conflict rules in the relevant instruments and general rules such as *lex superior*, *lex posterior*, *lex specialis* and interpretation techniques); and (3) the determination of the appropriate articulation between the relevant levels (exclusion *in toto* or combined application in a variety of forms). When norms and/or treaties organised following a centralised pattern are part of the analytical levels to be taken into account, the very centralisation may entail some specificities not only due to the existence of a wider and more comprehensive framework but also regarding prioritisation and articulation. By way of illustration, the governance of nuclear energy includes important instruments covering the negative externalities, in terms of security, safety and environmental sustainability, of the energy transaction. Unlike the ad hoc approach, which is largely built to insulate a specific project, aspects of nuclear energy can be expressly addressed in environmental treaties[16] or, conversely, they may be expressly excluded from them.[17] Often, they are covered by treaties and standards that focus specifically on nuclear energy[18] and the relations with broader or unspecific environmental and human rights instruments are not expressly addressed.

An illustration of the complex relations that may arise between different legal instruments applicable to nuclear energy is provided by the Hinkley Point C project in the United Kingdom. One of the complaints made by other countries and civil society regarding the way in which the United Kingdom developed this project concerned the lack of public participation in the process leading to the evaluation and approval of the project. In 2013, the matter was brought before the Compliance Committee of the Aarhus Convention[19] by a German citizen, who claimed that the United Kingdom had failed to comply with Article 6 (2), (5) and (7) and the Convention's requirement of non-discrimination (Article 3(9)) as a result of the lack of opportunity for the German public to participate in a transboundary EIA.[20] The Committee examined the communication and made a number of significant findings. First, the 'public concerned' (Article 2(5)) by an ultra-hazardous activity such as HPC included the foreign public, i.e. the German public.[21] The circle of

[16] See e.g. the regulation of dumping of radioactive waste in the Convention on the Prevention of Marine Pollution by Dumping of Wastes and Other Matter, 29 December 1972 [London Convention], subsequently modified by the Protocol of 7 November 1996 to the Convention of 1972 on the Prevention of Marine Pollution by Dumping of Wastes and Other Matter, 7 November 1996, 1046 UNTS 120 [London Protocol]. See also the application of the environmental impact assessment requirements of the Espoo Convention to certain nuclear activities, Convention on Environmental Impact Assessment in a Transboundary Context, 25 February 1991, 1989 UNTS 310 [Espoo Convention], Appendix, paragraph 3.

[17] See e.g. Consolidated text of the International Convention on Liability and Compensation for Damage in Connection with the Carriage of Hazardous and Noxious Substances by Sea, 1996, and the Protocol of 2010 to the Convention, 30 April 2010, www.hnsconvention.org [HNS Convention], Article 4(3)(b) (excluding damage caused by radioactive material from the scope of the HNS Convention).

[18] These will be discussed later in this chapter. For a brief overview see S. Emmerechts, 'Environmental Protection under Nuclear Law: Still a Long Way to Go', in *International Nuclear Law: History, Evolution and Outlook* (OECD: Nuclear Energy Agency, 2010), pp. 121–156, esp. 136ff.

[19] Aarhus Convention on Access to Information, Public Participation in Decision-making and Access to Justice in Environmental Matters, 25 June 1998, 2161 UNTS 447 [Aarhus Convention].

[20] United Kingdom, ACCC/C/2013/91 (19 June 2017) [*UK – HPC – Aarhus*], para. 2.

[21] *UK – HPC – Aarhus*, para. 75.

the public 'having an interest in the environmental decision-making' was widely drawn as including:

> not only members of the public whose legal interests or rights guaranteed under law might be impaired by the proposed activity, but also those who have a mere factual interest (for example, in the case of a proposed activity that may affect a waterway, bird watchers interested in keeping nests intact or anglers interested in keeping waters fishable). It may also include, as is the case in many jurisdictions, persons who have expressed an interest in a given case without having stated any specific reason for their interest.[22]

As for the obligation to notify the public concerned (Article 6(2)), the Committee emphasised that it applied irrespective of whether the proposed activity was formally subject to a transboundary EIA (under another environmental treaty, the Espoo Convention[23]) or not, as long as it may have transboundary environmental impact, and that it was the responsibility of the competent authority of the State of origin.[24] The United Kingdom's failure to ensure that the German public was informed and the lack of a specific provision of UK law targeting this situation amounted to non-compliance with Article 6(2) of the Aarhus Convention.[25] Clearly, then, the mere fact that a project concerns nuclear energy does not place it beyond the reach of general environmental and human rights instruments.

Yet, the incorporation of such other goals within the instruments governing not only the negative externalities but the very formation of the transaction is a distinct feature of the centralised governance of nuclear energy. Its underlying rationale stems from the 'dual use', civil and military, of nuclear technology, as discussed next.

III Centralised Governance of Nuclear Energy

3.1 Introduction

The main distinctive feature of the centralised governance of energy stems from the rationale for centralisation, which is much clearer

[22] *UK – HPC – Aarhus*, para. 74.
[23] Espoo Convention.
[24] *UK – HPC – Aarhus*, paras. 79–81 (referring to Czech Republic, ACCC/C/2012/71, ECE/MP.PP/C.1/2017/3, para. 73).
[25] *UK – HPC – Aarhus*, paras. 83–84.

technologically and historically in the case of nuclear energy than in that of any other resource.

For this reason, the discussion in this section begins with a brief survey of the implications of the 'dual use' of nuclear technology for its emerging governance up until the establishment of the IAEA. Reference to history is not a mere exercise of style but an important reminder that 'centralisation' was present since the very first report considering the expansion of nuclear technology beyond the United States. The subsequent section discusses the structure and content of the international law of nuclear energy. It begins with an examination of the different goals of nuclear energy governance at the international level and their interrelations. This has a very specific reason: the structure of the international law of nuclear energy follows broadly that of its different goals: security, safety and environmental protection. The discussion then covers in some detail the dense body of bilateral agreements relating to the transfer of nuclear fuel and technology as well as to the safeguards imposed on their use, before analysing the main multilateral instruments developed since 1956 until the present day as they concern safety and sustainability.

Describing the international law of nuclear energy as a centralised approach does not mean that it escapes the rules covered under the foundational approach or that it does not rely on project-specific ad hoc agreements; it means that a strong institutional component (in international legal terms) is added with the purpose of steering the wide range of rules and processes developed to govern nuclear energy. For this reason, the IAEA will not be discussed in isolation[26] but in the context of each of the main aspects mentioned above.

3.2 *The Dual Use of Nuclear Energy Technology*

In the months that followed the bombing of the Japanese cities of Hiroshima and Nagasaki, the devastating and tragic effects of nuclear weapons and their strategic implications became an issue of paramount

[26] For two studies on the IAEA, one of a historical nature and the other from the perspective of the law of international organisations see: D. Fischer, *History of the International Atomic Energy Agency: The First Forty Years* (Vienna: IAEA, 1997); P. C. Szasz, *The Law and Practices of the International Atomic Energy Agency* (Vienna: IAEA, 1970), later supplemented by 'Law and Practice of the IAEA 1970–1980'. Despite dating back to the 1970s, Szasz's study is a tour de force and remains an important source of guidance, externally and internally.

importance, in the United States and around the world. The United States, as the sole holder of the weapon and the technology to replicate it, needed to elaborate a strategy on how to use it to its broader advantage. Importantly, at the time, nuclear technology was only mastered for military purposes. Its potential for civil or peaceful uses was still a 'promise', without tested commercial applications, whether for electricity production or for other uses, such as the propulsion of vehicles. Thus, the search for adequate policies was, since the beginning, a search for means to extend a military technology to peaceful purposes without conceding a security advantage or risking proliferation.

In this context, a report presented to US State Secretary J. F. Byrnes in March 1946, known as the 'Acheson-Lilienthal Report' after the then Under-Secretary of State Dean Acheson and public law expert David E. Lilienthal, reached the following conclusion:

> We have concluded unanimously that there is no prospect of security against atomic warfare in a system of international agreements to outlaw such weapons controlled *only* by a system which relies on inspection and similar police-like methods. The reasons supporting this conclusion are *not merely technical*, but primarily the inseparable political, social and organizational problems involved in enforcing agreements between nations each free to develop atomic energy but only pledged not to use it for bombs. National rivalries in the development of atomic energy readily convertible to destructive purposes are at the heart of the difficulty.[27]

Yet, the approach to the 'promotion versus control' dilemma presented as unviable in this report is the one that eventually came to be embodied in the IAEA. It is in this light that we must understand the somewhat rigid narrative of the development of nuclear energy in three main phases, first a short-lived attempted cooperation phase at the level of the UN, followed by one of nuclear secrecy imposed through a stringent government monopoly (specifically of the Atomic Energy Commission or 'AEC') established by the 1946 McMahon Act, later substantially revised to allow for the propaganda and market prospects sought through

[27] *A Report on the International Control of Atomic Energy* (Washington DC: Government Printing Office, 16 March 1946), at 4–5 (italics are original). Lilienthal was the chairman of the Boards of Consultants assembled by Acheson. The Board also included Chester I. Barnard, J. R. Oppenheimer, Ch. A. Thomas, and H. A. Winne. The report is available at: www.cia.gov/library.

US President D. Eisenhower's 'Atoms for Peace' speech at the UN General Assembly in December 1953.[28]

Eisenhower's impulsion to move away from a nuclear secrecy policy that had at least failed as regards the development of nuclear military technology by the Soviet Union was itself the result of a combination of factors. Aside from the emerging arms race with the Soviet Union and the realisation of the unfathomable level of destruction of the new thermonuclear weapons, Eisenhower came under pressure from the industrial sector to break the AEC's monopoly over nuclear technology, and he also wanted to score a decisive point in the propaganda warfare against the Soviet Union. But what he had in mind in the second half of 1953 was the creation of a sort of 'uranium bank', which, under the pretext of diffusing the benefits of nuclear power to the world, would in fact serve to redirect a significant amount of uranium (which at the time was believed to be extremely limited) to peaceful uses and away from military uses. Given the stockpiles amassed by the United States, Eisenhower thought (although he could not rely on this point on specific intelligence) that it had much more than the Russians, which, by matching the contributions made by the United States to the bank, would therefore have far less for their own military programme.[29] Thus, the uranium bank idea was first and foremost about arms control. His speech in December 1953 did not give specific details on the US plan to share nuclear energy with other countries, because no such clear plan existed at the time.[30] The policies subsequently developed led to the amendment of the McMahon Act to enable the sharing of materials and technology and, subsequently, to the establishment of the IAEA. But the main point is the importance of the national security imperative. The 'dual use' of nuclear technology was an

[28] For a comprehensive analysis of the Atoms for Peace initiative see R. G. Hewlett, J. M. Holl, *Atoms for Peace and War 1953–1961. Eisenhower and the Atomic Energy Commission* (Berkeley: University of California Press, 1989). A short examination of the convoluted process leading to this policy is provided by L. Weiss, 'Atoms for Peace' (2003) 59 *Bulletin of the Atomic Scientists* 34 [Weiss, *Atoms for Peace*]. A historical analysis of the nuclear energy policies through which the initiative came to be implemented can be found in M. Drogan, 'The Nuclear Imperative: Atoms for Peace and the Development of US Policy on Exporting Nuclear Power, 1953–1955' (2016) 40 *Diplomatic History* 948.

[29] See Weiss, *Atoms for Peace*, at 39.

[30] See Drogan, *Nuclear Imperative*, at 952–953.

inescapable fact, indeed the defining feature of the different governance approaches explored by the United States since late 1945.

The establishment of the IAEA was an expression of this imperative. The United States was drawn, by internal (its industrial sector) and external pressures (including the race with the USSR and the expectations raised by Eisenhower's 1953 speech), to share nuclear materials and technology for civil purposes and, in designing policies to do so, it found itself facing the very international arrangements that the report of 1946 had envisaged and discarded. The centrepiece of these arrangements was the IAEA and its inspection (safeguards) system, which mirrored the arrangements that had been introduced in its domestic law through the 1954 Atomic Energy Act, namely a system of material and technology transfer to friendly countries by means of bilateral cooperation agreements subject to the approval and inspection of the AEC.[31] Since 1954, Eisenhower had charged Ambassador Morehead Patterson to negotiate, with some key US allies (Australia, Belgium and South Africa, which supplied uranium ore to the United States, and Canada, France, Portugal and the United Kingdom) as well as, bilaterally, with the USSR, the establishment of an international agency. Within Europe, two other initiatives were also launched, one under the aegis of the OECD (then a European offspring of the Marshall Plan) and the other under that of the European Coal and Steel Community.[32] The three initiatives led to systems tackling the 'promotion versus control' dilemma by means of 'safeguards'.

The negotiations leading to the IAEA were initially opposed by the USSR. Then, in July 1955, the Russians asked to join the ongoing multilateral negotiations by the 'Washington Group'. Throughout these negotiations, there were two main views of what the agency should be. One, arising from Eisenhower's initial ideas, saw the agency as a

[31] Weiss, *Atoms for Peace*, at 40–41.

[32] For the OECD context, see the Convention on the Establishment of a Security Control in the Field of Nuclear Energy, 20 December 1954, OECD/LEGAL/0020. This instrument established a security control system managed by the (European) Nuclear Energy Agency aimed to ensure that 'joint undertakings' and 'materials, equipment and services' made available by the NEA 'shall not further any military purpose'. The operation of this system was suspended in 1970 to avoid duplication with those of the IAEA and the Euratom. With respect to the EU context, see the Treaty Establishing the European Atomic Energy Community, 25 March 1957, 298 UNTS 167 (consolidated version in OJ C 203 (7 June 2016) [EURATOM Treaty], chapter 7 ('Safeguards'). The Euratom safeguards system was brought under the umbrellla of the IAEA in 1973.

fissionable materials pool or bank siphoning off part of the Russian stockpiles and thus controlling the arms race; the other, favoured by the United Kingdom and the USSR, saw it as a mere 'broker' or 'clearinghouse'.[33] The latter view prevailed, although the IAEA Statute still reflects the tension.[34] Then, in early 1956, Brazil, Czechoslovakia and India joined the negotiations and, in a period of eight weeks (27 February to 18 April 1956), the main contents of the IAEA Statute were agreed. The Statute was formally adopted on 23 October 1956 at a Conference held at the UN headquarters. Its focus on the 'promotion versus control' dilemma is stated in Article II, according to which the agency 'shall ensure . . . that assistance provided by it or at its request or under its supervision or control is not used in such a way as to further any military purpose'. Article III(A)(5) specifically authorises the agency:

> To establish and administer safeguards designed to ensure that special fissionable and other materials, services, equipment, facilities, and information made available by the Agency or at its request or under its supervision or control are not used in such a way as to further any military purpose; and to apply safeguards, at the request of the parties, to any bilateral or multilateral arrangement, or at the request of a State, to any of that State's activities in the field of atomic energy.

The IAEA safeguards system will be analysed in Section 3.3.2. For now, the main conclusion to be drawn from the foregoing discussion is that the need to centralise the governance of nuclear energy was perceived since the beginning as a result of the dual use of nuclear technology. Although the idea of centralising materials and technology (as organised under the initial AEC system in the United States or as a 'uranium bank') was abandoned in the course of the negotiations, the centralisation of inspection was placed at the heart of the IAEA, and it was later strengthened through a number of international and regional initiatives.

3.3 *The Structure and Content of the Regulation*

3.3.1 Purposes

The most remarkable feature of the purposes pursued by the international law of nuclear energy is the overriding importance given to

[33] See Fischer, *History of the IAEA*, at 34.
[34] See IAEA Statute, Articles IX and XII(B).

matters of security and safety over matters of economic exploitation. Security in this specific context does not mean, as in other energy contexts, security of supply. It means international security, i.e. non-proliferation of nuclear weapons and arms control, and national security, i.e. the physical protection of nuclear materials and technology, broadly understood to encompass facilities, equipment, know-how, services etc. The term 'safety' in the nuclear energy context means, specifically, the protection of the population from accidents and, following an older line of regulation, also the protection from radiological risks.

This overriding importance is the result of the immense destructive power of the nuclear processes (nuclear fission) on which the generation of electricity relies, the insidious health effects of exposure to radioactivity, and the shock and panic caused in public opinion by the tragic bombing of Hiroshima and Nagasaki and subsequent atmospheric tests. The three main accidents that took place in the United States (Three Mile Island, 1979), the USSR (Chernobyl, 1986), and Japan (Fukushima, 2011), have significantly added to the fears raised by nuclear energy and the need for tight regulation. From the perspective of the analytical framework used in this book, the result is that certain externalities are deemed so important that they are not addresses as 'external' or as 'side effects' but as core elements of the transaction. By contrast, other considerations, such as the protection of the environment or the management of radioactive waste, remain addressed as negative 'externalities' by an additional layer of regulation.

This specific prioritisation drives the structure of the international law of nuclear energy. The very transactions whereby nuclear materials and/or technology are transferred – for prosperity purposes – are largely based on ad hoc bilateral agreements, but they are conditioned on a system of safeguards, which is based on both ad hoc and multilateral instruments managed by the IAEA or by other organisations upon delegation from the IAEA. Thus, the 'dual use' of nuclear technology is manifested in the dual nature of the organisation of the transaction, with its elements of transfer and safeguards. Historically, the first multilateral instruments governing nuclear energy introduced and then strengthened this transfer-safeguard structure, first with the adoption of the IAEA Statute, mirrored by instruments at the level of what today corresponds to the OECD (the 1957 Security Control Convention[35]) and the EU (the

[35] Convention on the Establishment of OECD Legal Instruments a Security Control in the Field of Nuclear Energy, 20 December 1957, OECD/LEGAL/0020.

EURATOM Treaty[36]), then by the 1968 Non-Proliferation Treaty[37] and some other instruments of a regional scope,[38] and the 1980 Convention on the Physical Protection of Nuclear Material.[39] Following the terrorist attacks of 11 September 2001 on US soil, the latter instrument was revised[40] and another one was adopted specifically against terrorist attacks, the International Convention for the Suppression of Acts of Nuclear Terrorism.[41]

Safety was also a major consideration since the beginning, and it drove a parallel process of normative development leading to the adoption of several multilateral instruments.[42] These instruments have grown to become the epicentre of nuclear energy governance at the international level. Initially, the IAEA issued a range of standards and other guidance instruments to the attention of national regulators. In the early 1960s, the prospects of large-scale damage resulting from a nuclear accident, as well as the need to cap the exposure of diligent operators, led to the adoption of two systems of civil liability, one under the aegis of the OECD, the 1960 Paris Convention,[43] and the other under the framework of the IAEA, which included socialist States, the 1963 Vienna Convention.[44] Over time, a normative framework for nuclear safety was introduced capturing the entire life-cycle of nuclear energy generation. A useful way to present it is to focus on the regulatory angles discussed in Chapter 3,

[36] EURATOM Treaty.

[37] NPT.

[38] These instruments concern more broadly the issue of denuclearisation and go beyond the sole requirement of States to accept safeguards and inspection. For an overview see S. Szurek, 'De Rarotonga à Bangkok et Pelindaba: Note sur les traités constitutifs de nouvelles zones exemptes d'armes nucléaires' (1996) 42 *AFDI* 164.

[39] Convention on the Physical Protection of Nuclear Material, 3 March 1980, 1458 UNTS 125 [Physical Protection Convention].

[40] For a compilation of documents leading to the amendment see *Amendment to the Convention on the Physical Protection of Nuclear Material* (Vienna: I, IAEA International Law Series No. 2, 2006).

[41] International Convention for the Suppression of Acts of Nuclear Terrorism, 13 April 2005, 2445 UNTS 89 [Nuclear Terrorism Convention].

[42] On the earlier stands of regulation of safety focussing on radiological protection see E. N. Lazo, 'International System of Radiological Protection', in *International Nuclear Law: History, Evolution and Outlook* (OECD: Nuclear Energy Agency, 2010), pp. 105–120.

[43] Convention on Third Party Liability in the Field of Nuclear Energy, 29 July 1960, 956 UNTS 251 [Paris Convention].

[44] Convention on Civil Liability for Nuclear Damage, 21 May 1963, 1063 UNTS 265 [Vienna Convention].

namely prevention, response and reparation.[45] The latter angle remains anchored in the Paris and Vienna liability systems, which have been both expanded and linked.[46] Prevention is by far the most comprehensively regulated.[47] As discussed in this chapter, the relevant instruments include treaties and a vast body of international standards and codes, and they focus on the safety of nuclear power plants, transportation of radioactive materials, and the management of radioactive waste. The organisation of an international response to nuclear accidents became an imperative following the 1986 Chernobyl disaster, which catalysed the adoption of two conventions on notification of nuclear accidents[48] and assistance in case of emergency.[49]

Environmental sustainability as a purpose came along the way, starting in the 1970s. Its regulation is less close to the core of the transaction than security and safety considerations. It rests on some of the instruments relating to safety as well as on a wider body of multilateral environmental agreements that govern one or more aspects of nuclear energy transactions, such as the transport[50] or dumping of radioactive waste[51] or the requirement of an environmental impact assessment.[52] The latter instruments are clearly part of the wider set of instruments that regulate the negative (environmental) externalities of nuclear energy transactions. Many more are also relevant, although they do not expressly mention nuclear energy activities (see Chapter 3).

The foregoing purposes largely dictate the structure and content of the international law of energy. In what follows, I rely on them to examine, first, the transfer-safeguard form of nuclear energy transactions (3.3.2), then the regulation of safety (3.3.3), with a focus on prevention, response and reparation, and finally the integration of environmental

[45] Cost-internalisation has not played a significant role in nuclear regulation due to the nature of the risk that exposure to radiation and nuclear accidents present.

[46] See Section 3.3.3.4 of this chapter.

[47] See Section 3.3.3.2 of this chapter. The main instrument focussing on prevention the Convention on Nuclear Safety, 17 June 1994, 1963 UNTS 293 [Convention on Nuclear Safety].

[48] Convention on Early Notification of a Nuclear Accident, 26 September 1986, 1439 UNTS 275 [Convention on Early Notification].

[49] Convention on Assistance in Case of a Nuclear Accident or Radiological Emergency, 26 September 1986, 1457 UNTS 133 [Convention on Assistance].

[50] International Convention for the Safety of Life at Sea, 1 November 1974, 1185 UNTS 2 [SOLAS Convention].

[51] London Convention and London Protocol.

[52] Espoo Convention.

considerations within this centralised framework (3.3.4). The role of IAEA in these different aspects of the system varies significantly. It will be studied in each context.

3.3.2 Nuclear Transfers and Safeguards

3.3.2.1 Materials and Technology Transfers and Proliferation Risks The development of nuclear energy was largely government-led in the late 1950s and early 1960s. Thereafter, the private sector played a growing role, particularly during the expansion of the industry in the 1970s, followed by a period of consolidation starting in the 1980s, which saw a small number of major global players, mainly in the United States, Canada, Western Europe and Japan and, more recently, Russia, South Korea and increasingly China.[53]

From a market structure perspective, nuclear energy offers a rather complex mosaic of activities where competition among both countries and private companies, often with government support, unfolds. Following an adjusted version of the broad spectrum of energy activities introduced in Chapter 1, four main types of markets can be identified:[54] (1) the front-end of the nuclear fuel cycle, including (i) the supply of uranium ore, (ii) the conversion of uranium ore into uranium oxide, and of the latter into uranium hexafluoride (which can be enriched), (iii) uranium enrichment services (which are extremely sensitive due to proliferation risks) and (iv) fuel fabrication services (although most reactors are pressurised water reactors (PWRs), the fuel must normally be tailored to each power plant); (2) the design, engineering and construction of nuclear power plants and, more specifically, the so-called nuclear island, i.e. the materials, equipment and services specific to a nuclear power plant, by contrast with the 'balance of plant', i.e. components that are not exclusive to nuclear energy plants; (3) the maintenance and upgrading of existing plants, including (i) routine maintenance and inspection services, (ii) refuelling services, (iii) replacement or upgrading of major components (steam generators or reactor pressure vessel heads) and (iv) outage planning, management and efficiency services; and (4) the back-end of the nuclear fuel cycle, including (i) spent fuel reprocessing services (particularly the separation of plutonium, with the associated proliferation risks),

[53] On the structure of the nuclear energy industry see Nuclear Energy Agency, *Market Competition in the Nuclear Industry* (Paris: OECD, 2008), at 23.

[54] This structuring is derived from NEA, *Market Competition*.

(ii) the fabrication of mix oxide (MOX) fuel for use in PWRs and (iii) radioactive waste management and decommissioning services.

Some of these markets present a higher proliferation risk than others, particularly the enrichment of uranium or the separation and provision of plutonium. Such risks were anticipated to some extent, but, as it is often the case, reality has outpaced the mechanisms put in place to manage it. The initial system of transfers of nuclear materials, equipment and services under 'safeguards' designed in the 1950s led to what in hindsight turned out to be a fairly liberal approach. With the strengthening of the global and regional non-proliferation framework, particularly through the 1968 NPT, the need for clarity on certain issues (e.g. transfers to non-nuclear States non-members of the NPT or the definition of certain terms) led in 1974 to a series of unilateral undertakings known as the Zangger Committee undertakings, after the chairman of the Committee which discussed and proposed the relevant guidance.[55] Yet, the 1974 nuclear test by India and adoption of two transfer agreements with recipients which were not parties to the NPT (Brazil and Pakistan), laid bare the inadequacy of the safeguards regime to contain the risks of proliferation. Between 1975 and 1977, a group of nuclear supplier States met in London (the Nuclear Supplier Group (NSG), also known as the 'London Club') and agreed a set of guidelines involving additional controls on the transfer of nuclear materials, equipment and technology under the NPT. Such guidelines were adopted as undertakings, following the formula used by the Zangger Committee, and subsequently recorded as IAEA instrument.[56] Importantly, the United States went further and, under President Carter, it revised section 123 of the 1954 Atomic Energy Act to impose additional controls on nuclear transfers from the United States. Although several 'Section 123 Agreements' have been since concluded with other countries, some commentators have argued that the loss of competitiveness of the US

[55] See Communications Received from Members Regarding the Export of Nuclear Material and of Certain Categories of Equipment and Other Material, 3 September 1974, INFCIRC/209.

[56] See Guidelines for Nuclear Transfers, INFCIRC/254. These guidelines were subsequently developed and revised several times. At present, the NSG has two main sets of guidelines: the Guidelines for Nuclear Transfers, INFCIRC/254, Part 1 (focussing on 'Trigger List Items') and the Guidelines for Transfers of Nuclear-Related Dual-Use Equipment, Materials, Software and Related Technology, INFCIRC/254, Part 2 (focussing on 'Dual-Use Items'), as subsequently revised.

nuclear industry in international markets (to countries such as Russia, South Korea or China) is a direct result of the additional non-proliferation controls required by section 123.[57] In the early 1990s, a series of events called for another overhaul of the non-proliferation system. The collapse of the USSR, the difficulties in verifying the scope of the nuclear research programme in North Korea, South Africa's adhesion to the NPT and the realisation of the scale of Iraq's nuclear programme, which it had managed to develop (relying on dual-use goods and technologies) despite complying with the IAEA safeguards' requirements and inspections, steered further negotiations. This process led to the adoption of the 1995 Wassenaar Arrangement,[58] which focusses on dual use equipment and technology. In the last decade, other efforts to further strengthen the mechanisms against proliferation have led to calls for an increasing multilateralisation of the nuclear fuel, although limited concrete progress has been made on this front.[59]

From a legal standpoint, these two dimensions – transfers and safeguards – are two different sides of the same coin. The IAEA plays a key role in both of them, mostly as a broker, a standard-setter and an inspector. To understand this role, as one of the main manifestations of the centralised architecture of the international law of nuclear energy, it is first necessary to provide an overview of the bilateral agreements that serve as an umbrella for the structuring of such transfers (both in domestic law and in contractual arrangements) and of the safeguards system to which such transfers are subject.

3.3.2.2 Nuclear Cooperation Agreements (NCAs)

3.3.2.2.1 The IAEA as a Broker The IAEA Statute foresaw the agency's role, in connection with transfers, as that of making available, brokering or controlling transfers of information, materials, or technology (broadly understood as equipment, facilities and services) on nuclear energy.

[57] See R. Nephew, *Reconsidering US Nuclear Cooperation Agreements* (New York: SIPA, 2020).

[58] Final Declaration of 20 December 1995 embodying the initial arrangement, reproduced in Wassenaar Arrangement Secretariat, *Wassenaar Arrangement on Export Controls for Conventional Arms and Dual-Use Goods and Technologies. Public Documents, vol. I: Founding Documents* (December 2019).

[59] For an overview, see Y. Yudin, *Multilateralization of the Nuclear Fuel Cycle: Assessing the Existing Proposals* (Geneva: UNIDIR, 2009).

Article III(A)(5), which deals with safeguards, summarises this role by referring to the 'special fissionable and other materials, services, equipment, facilities, and information' which are 'made available by the Agency or its request or under its supervision or control'. The Statute further relies on this understanding of transfers in other provisions. For example, Article III(A)(3) and (4) mention, as functions of the agency, 'to foster the exchange of scientific and technical information on peaceful uses of atomic energy' and 'to encourage the exchange and training of scientists and experts in the field of peaceful uses of atomic energy', and Article VIII is fully devoted to the 'Exchange of information'. Article IX organises in some detail the regime for the 'Supplying of materials' and Article X broadly refers to 'services, equipment and facilities'. These provisions are drafted in soft language, with the opening clause of Article VIII using the expression 'Each member *should* make available [. . .]' (emphasis added) and those of Articles IX and X stating 'Members *may* make available [. . .]' (emphasis added).

Article XI organises the system to be followed in case of a request made to the agency by a Member State (or group thereof) to assist it 'in securing special fissionable and other materials, services, equipment, and facilities necessary for [peaceful purposes]'. In practice, transfers of materials and technology, to summarise the key objects, have been organised through ad hoc agreements between two States, subject to the application of safeguards. With the adoption of the NPT in 1968, such transfers/safeguards became part of the bargain for which non-nuclear-weapon-States (NNWS) renounced to seek nuclear weapons (Articles IV(1) and V), and therefore an expectation.

3.3.2.2.2 Legal Structure of Nuclear Transfers Transfers of nuclear materials and/or technologies are complex transactions, based on different layers of regulation, including treaties (often called 'nuclear cooperation agreements' or 'NCAs'), contracts and domestic law. Here, the focus is mostly on the first layer, although some reference is made to the relevant domestic requirements.

Many States have become suppliers of nuclear materials and/or technology, as suggested by the growing number of members of the Nuclear Suppliers Group. In 1975, when this group first met, there was only a handful of them, whereas today the NSG has forty-six members. However, only some of them can claim to be major players in global nuclear energy-related markets, including the United States, Russia, the United Kingdom, France, Japan, Canada and, increasingly, China and

South Korea.[60] Their practice regarding the structuring of nuclear transfers varies significantly both across countries and over time.[61]

Not every country requires the adoption of a framework NCA as a precondition for a transfer to be possible. For example, unlike the United States, Canada, Australia and Japan, the United Kingdom does not require such a layer as a statutory requirement, although it has in practice adopted a number of NCAs.[62] Perhaps due to such variation, the literature on the international law of energy pays far less attention to NCAs than to the treaties and other instruments relating to security, safety and environmental protection. For present purposes, such practice can be illustrated by reference to some major examples.

3.3.2.2.3 The US Practice: Section 123 Agreements One major illustration is provided by the so-called Section 123 agreements (after Section 123 of the 1954 Atomic Energy Act, as amended in 1978) required by US law as a necessary (but not sufficient) condition to enter into 'significant' nuclear cooperation with other countries.[63]

Significant nuclear cooperation is characterised by reference to the type of nuclear material ('special nuclear material', mainly plutonium and uranium enriched in the isotopes 233 or 235), equipment (reactors and critical parts of reactors) or information ('restricted data', which includes that relating to nuclear weapons, the production of 'special nuclear material' or its use for nuclear energy). If such is the case, then any transfer is conditioned on the prior conclusion of a Section 123 agreement and the application of export licensing requirements for each export of nuclear material, equipment or technology.[64]

[60] See generally NEA, *Market Competition* and Nephew, *Nuclear Cooperation Agreements.*

[61] For some sixty examples of transfer agreements by each of these suppliers see www.energybilaterals.org

[62] See Office for Nuclear Regulation, Nuclear Cooperation Agreements between the United Kingdom and International Partners. Implementation Guidelines for Nuclear Operators, available at: https://assets.publishing.service.gov.uk/.

[63] On the US treaty practice see Congressional Research Service, *Nuclear Cooperation with Other Countries: A Primer* (RS22937, 4 March 2020). The discussion of the US practice is based on this report and the examination of several treaty examples. By contrast, limited forms of nuclear cooperation can proceed with the authorisation of the Secretary of Energy if it is determined that the transfer 'will not be inimical to the interests of the United States'. These are called 'Part 810 Agreements' by reference to title 10 of the Code of Federal Regulations, Part 810.

[64] These export licensing requirements are stated in title 42 of the United States Code, Sections 2155, 2156, 2157.

Section 123 agreements require a special form of congressional approval. They must be submitted to the Foreign Affairs Committee of the House of Representatives and to the Foreign Relations Committee of the Senate, together with a 'Nuclear Proliferation Assessment Statement' from the State Department and a defence and security determination from the President. On content, Section 123a requires such agreements to state the 'terms, conditions, duration, nature and scope of the cooperation'. Agreements typically include detailed definitions of terms used and provisions on the 'scope of cooperation' (wider or narrower), transfer of information, transfer of material, equipment and components, storage and retransfers, coordination of multiple suppliers (when the recipient has granted similar terms to other suppliers), cessation of cooperation and rights of return (of the transfers). In addition, as noted earlier, they also cover security matters, such as regulation of enrichment and reprocessing (ENR), physical protection, prohibition of military uses, and safeguards.

Of particular note, Section 123a also requires the inclusion of nine non-proliferation requirements (unless one or more of them are 'exempted' by the president, under certain conditions), such as a commitment of the recipient country (which is a NNWS) to apply full-scope IAEA safeguards, return any transfers in case of violation of the safeguards, and obtain the consent of the United States (through an additional agreement) prior to enrichment or reprocessing ('ENR') of materials transferred by the United States (or obtained from them). The possibility for a recipient State to conduct ENR has been at the centre of a debate, with some recipients having renounced such possibility. Article 6 of the nuclear cooperation agreement between the United States and the United Arab Emirates[65] states indeed:

> 1. Material transferred pursuant to this Agreement and material used in or produced through the use of material or equipment so transferred shall not be reprocessed unless the Parties agree.
>
> 2. Plutonium transferred pursuant to this Agreement and material used in or produced through the use of material or equipment so transferred shall not be reprocessed unless the Parties agree.

[65] Agreement for Cooperation between the Government of the United States of America and the Government of the United Arab Emirates concerning Peaceful Uses of Nuclear Energy, 21 May 2009 [US–UAE NCA], available at: www.energybilaterals.org/. The ENR requirements in this agreement have been dubbed the 'gold standard', but they are not applied to all countries.

> 3. Plutonium, uranium 233, high enriched uranium and irradiated source or special fissionable material transferred pursuant to this Agreement or used in or produced through the use of material or equipment so transferred shall not be otherwise altered in form or content, except by irradiation or further irradiation, unless the Parties agree.

At the opposite end, some other countries have received a blanket approval to conduct ENR, most notably India. Article 6 of the United States–India nuclear cooperation agreement[66] clearly authorises ENR:

> In keeping with their commitment to full civil nuclear cooperation, both Parties, as they do with other states with advanced nuclear technology, may carry out the following nuclear fuel cycle activities:
>
> i) Within the territorial jurisdiction of either Party, enrichment up to twenty percent in the isotope 235 of uranium transferred pursuant to this Agreement, as well as of uranium used in or produced through the use of equipment so transferred, *may be carried out.*
> ii) Irradiation within the territorial jurisdiction of either Party of plutonium, uranium-233, high enriched uranium and irradiated nuclear material transferred pursuant to this Agreement or used in or produced through the use of non-nuclear material, nuclear material or equipment so transferred *may be carried out.*
> iii) With a view to implementing full civil nuclear cooperation as envisioned in the Joint Statement of the Parties of July 18, 2005, *the Parties grant each other consent to reprocess or otherwise alter* in form or content nuclear material transferred pursuant to this Agreement and nuclear material and by-product material used in or produced through the use of nuclear material, non-nuclear material, or equipment so transferred [. . .]. (emphasis added)

The contrast is stark. Between these two extremes, several intermediate positions are possible. The debate is epitomised by the protracted negotiations between the United States and Saudi Arabia, with the latter resisting attempts by the United States to subject the transfer to conditions similar to those accepted by the UAE.[67]

[66] Agreement for Cooperation between the Government of the United States of America and the Government of India concerning Peaceful Uses of Nuclear Energy, 10 October 2008, available at: www.energybilaterals.org/.

[67] The application of such more stringent conditions to nuclear transfers has been criticised as undermining the US competitiveness in international markets to the benefit of countries such as Russia, China or South Korea, which subject transfers to the less stringent safeguard standards agreed in 1977 by the NSG. See Nephew, *Nuclear Cooperation Agreements.*

3.3.2.2.4 The Practice of Other Major Suppliers Other major suppliers, such as Russia, Japan, France or South Korea have followed different treaty practices on the basis of their own domestic regulations on export control.[68] The areas covered by such agreements are broadly similar, including definitions, scope of cooperation, transfers (of information, materials and technology), retransfers, as well as security concerns (ENR, physical protection, prohibition of military uses, and safeguards), but with sometimes significant variations.

For example, the nuclear cooperation agreement between France and China contemplates the transfer of French technology relating to the 'upstream nuclear fuel cycle' including for the treatment and reprocessing of nuclear materials, subject to modalities of application, including IAEA safeguards, to be defined by a joint working group.[69] Also of note, the two States: 'encourage French and Chinese industrialists to develop their cooperation for the search and exploitation of new uranium resources in third countries, outside the countries having signed the EURATOM treaty, consistent with their respective interests'.[70] In addition, cooperation is also envisaged among the agencies of the two States as regards the drafting of regulations, safety standards, security controls and inspections.[71]

The nuclear cooperation agreement between China and Algeria[72] covers the same broad areas (Article 2) and then identifies the forms that cooperation may take, including information exchange, provision of materials, technology and services, and intellectual property arrangements (Article 3). Article 5 emphasises the framework nature of the

[68] Generally speaking, such requirements are seen as less burdensome and stringent than those of the United States. See J. A. Glasgow et al, *Nuclear Export Controls. A Comparative Analysis of National Regimes for the Control of Nuclear Materials, Components and Technology* (Nuclear Energy Institute, October 2012), at 4.

[69] Examples of such practice include: Accord d'application de l'accord de coopération du 15 mai 1997 entre le Gouvernement de la République française et le Gouvernement de la République Populaire de Chine pour le développement des utilisations pacifiques de l'énergie nucléaire, 26 November 2007, Article 4 [France–China NCA], available at: www.energybilaterals.org/.

[70] France–China NCA, Article 6 (our translation from the French text).

[71] France-China NCA, Article 8.

[72] Accord de coopération entre le Gouvernement de la République algérienne démocratique et populaire et le Gouvernement de la République populaire de Chine pour le développement des utilisations pacifiques de l'énergie nucléaire, 24 March 2008 [China–Algeria NCA], available at: www.energybilaterals.org/.

agreement, stating that the modalities of application of the cooperation envisaged are to be defined in 'distinct and specific agreements' and 'contracts'. Articles 9 and 10 address ENR and retransfer issues by means of a reference to the agreements of the parties with the IAEA, with the additional requirement that retransfers are conditioned on the agreement of both parties.

The agreement between Russia and Brazil[73] follows a similar format, identifying the areas (Article II) and modalities of cooperation (Article III), and relying on a broad transfers clause (Article VII). As regards security and safety, however, it includes a single detailed clause (Article VIII), which refers to the international undertakings of each party under the IAEA and, for Brazil, a regional agreement.[74]

Yet another example is the agreement between South Korea and Brazil,[75] which, after framing the areas (Article III) and forms of cooperation (Article IV), it also contains a broad transfers clause (VIII) and then several clauses relating to security (Article IX on retransfers, Article X on prohibition of military applications, Article XI on safeguards and Article XII on physical protection).

3.3.2.2.5 Regional Agreements In addition to bilateral agreements on nuclear transfers, some regional agreements have also been developed. I referred earlier to the systems established under the aegis of the OCDE and the EU (EURATOM).[76]

The IAEA has also promoted regional cooperation in nuclear matters through the adoption of four regional framework agreements, respect-

[73] Agreement between the Government of the Federative Republic of Brazil and the Government of the Russian Federation for the Cooperation on the Peaceful Uses of Nuclear Energy, 15 September 1994 [Russia–Brazil NCA], available at: www.energybilaterals.org/.

[74] Agreement between the Federative Republic of Brazil, the Republic of Argentina, the Brazilian-Argentinean Agency for Accounting and Control of Nuclear Materials (ABACC) and the International Atomic Energy Agency (IAEA), 13 December 1991, 1828 UNTS No. I-31263.

[75] Acordo entre o Governo da República Federativa do Brasil e o Governo da República da Coréia para. Cooperação nos Usos Pacíficos da Energia Nuclear, 18 January 2001 [Korea–Brazil NCA], available at: www.energybilaterals.org/.

[76] On the specific relations between the Euratom Treaty and the EU Treaties see Swedish Radiation Safety Authority, *The Euratom Treaty v. Treaties of the European Union: limits of competence and interaction* (Report 2011:32, July 2011).

ively, in the Asia-Pacific region,[77] Latin America and the Caribbean,[78] Arab States in Asia[79] and Africa.[80] All these agreements are based on earlier cooperative efforts dating back to as early as 1972. They have a limited duration and can be extended or replaced. Their purpose is the development of 'cooperative projects', submitted by a party and open to the participation of other parties. Their structure is therefore very different from that of bilateral agreements and focusses on the institutionalisation of potential cooperation.

Under their framework, the IAEA (acting through the Department of Technical Cooperation) brokers a supply agreement between supplier and recipient States and enters into a project agreement with the recipient State, which may require the application of safeguards. At the time of writing, there are twelve active technical cooperation projects and one active coordinate research project which have been undertaken on this basis.[81]

3.3.2.3 Safeguards

3.3.2.3.1 Overview The safeguards referred to in NCAs are based on general and specific undertakings made by States under both multilateral and bilateral agreements. This section discusses the basic requirements and main legal bases governing the IAEA safeguards system.[82] The architecture of the system rests on four main elements: (1) the undertaking of States to enter into safeguard agreements with the IAEA, (2) the safeguard agreements themselves with their protocols and subsidiary arrangements, (3) the instruments guiding or providing the contents of

[77] Regional Cooperative Agreement for Research, Development and Training Related to Nuclear Science and Technology for Asia and the Pacific, 18 March 2016, INFCIRC/919 [RCA Agreement]. This agreement replaces a former version adopted in 1987.

[78] Regional Cooperation Agreement for the Promotion of Nuclear Science and Technology in Latin America and the Caribbean, 25 September 1998, INFCIRC/582 [ARCAL Agreement].

[79] Cooperative Agreement for Arab States in Asia for Research, Development and Training related to Nuclear Science and Technology, 19 September 2017, INFCIRC/929 [ARASIA Agreement], replacing a previous version adopted in 12 June 2002.

[80] African Regional Cooperative Agreement for Research, Development and Training related to Nuclear Science and Technology, 20 September 2019, INFCIRC/935 [AFRA Agreement], replacing a previous version adopted on 4 April 1990.

[81] See the relevant section of the IAEA website: www.iaea.org/about/partnerships/regional/cooperative-agreements

[82] See generally L. Rockwood, 'The IAEA Safeguards System', in in *International Nuclear Law: History, Evolution and Outlook* (OECD: Nuclear Energy Agency, 2010), pp. 243–270.

such agreements (whether they are standards incorporated by reference, guidance instruments, model agreements or decision and practices of the IAEA's Board of Governors), and (4) the institution (above all the IAEA) administering the system, particularly the international verification system. I will present them in this order, discussing (2) and (3) together, as the types of safeguards treaties have been driven by the instruments shaping their contents.

3.3.2.3.2 Undertaking to Enter into Safeguard Agreements The initial safeguards system was based on the IAEA Statute. There are several provisions in the Statute stating the objective of safeguards (Article II) and the functions of the agency in this respect (Articles III.A.5, XI.F.4 and XII). Article XII specifically defines three aspects of the IAEA's role, namely the 'rights and responsibilities' of the agency '[w]ith respect to any Agency project, or other arrangement where the Agency is requested by the parties concerned to apply safeguards', the establishment of a staff of inspectors, and the powers and responsibilities of such inspectors, particularly in case of non-compliance by a State with its obligations. Importantly, however, the IAEA Statute does not contain, as such, (i) an undertaking by States Parties to enter into safeguard agreements or, if they do so, (ii) to accept certain specific types of safeguard measures or, from a different perspective, (iii) an undertaking by supplier States not to supply materials or technology unless a safeguards agreement is in place. Thus, the IAEA Statute as such is not sufficient to require States to apply safeguards.

Such a requirement arises from either a specific clause in an NCA (and, for the supplier State, from its own domestic law) (see Section 3.3.2.2) and/or from a global or regional multilateral agreement. Regarding the latter, the main legal basis is Article III.1 of the NPT, according to which each NNWS 'undertakes to accept safeguards, as set forth in an agreement [. . .] with the International Atomic Energy Agency in accordance with the Statute [. . .] and the Agency's safeguards system'. Article III.4 of the NPT further states that NNWS 'shall conclude' agreements with the IAEA 'to meet the requirements of this Article either individually or together with other States'. Thus, undertakings (i) and (ii) above are covered by this provision. As for (iii), Article III.3 of the NPT requires all parties (including both NWS and NNWS) not to provide the relevant materials and technology 'unless the source or special fissionable material shall be subject to the safeguards required by this Article'.

Similar commitments are contained in some multilateral denuclearisation agreements of regional scope, namely Article 13 of the Tlatelcoco Treaty[83] (covering undertakings (i) and (ii)), Articles 4, 8 and Annex II of the Rarotonga Treaty[84] (covering undertakings (i), (ii) and (iii)), Articles 4(3) and 5 of the Treaty of Bangkok[85] (covering undertakings (i), (ii) and (iii)), Article 9 of the Pelindaba Treaty[86] (covering undertakings (i), (ii) and (iii)) and Article 8 of the Semipalatinsk Treaty[87] (covering undertakings (i), (ii) and (iii)). Two other multilateral agreements, of a different nature, provide for an undertaking to apply safeguards and specifically address the relations between the IAEA and a regional agency.[88]

3.3.2.3.3 Structure and Contents of Safeguard Agreements The safeguards agreements entered into as a result of these undertakings vary significantly, although the IAEA has made substantial efforts to expand their scope and stringency as well as to standardise their content.

The initial safeguard agreements were highly tailored to the specific circumstances of the transfer relationship. These are 'item-specific' agreements in that they cover certain specified materials, equipment and facilities identified in an inventory included in the agreement. They are known as INFCIRC/66-type agreements, after the name of the document developed by the IAEA to shape their content: INFCIRC/66/Rev.2. This document was adopted on 16 September 1968, but it builds upon and incorporates previous safeguard documents developed between 1961 and

[83] Treaty for the Prohibition of Nuclear Weapons in Latin America, 14 February 1967, 634 UNTS 281 [Treaty of Tlatelcoco].

[84] South Pacific Nuclear Free Zone Treaty, 6 August 1985, 1445 UNTS 177 [Treaty of Rarotonga].

[85] Treaty on the Southeast Asia Nuclear Weapon-Free Zone, 15 December 1995, INFCIRC/548 [Treaty of Bangkok].

[86] African Nuclear Weapon-Free Zone Treaty, 11 April 1996, 35 ILM 698 (1996) [Treaty of Pelindaba].

[87] Treaty on a Nuclear-Weapon-Free Zone in Central Asia, 8 September 2006, 2212 UNTS 257 [Semipalatinsk Treaty].

[88] See Agreement Between Belgium, Denmark, the Federal Republic of Germany, Ireland, Italy, Luxembourg, the Netherlands, the European Atomic Energy Community and the Agency in Connection with the Treaty on the Non-Proliferation of Nuclear Weapons, 14 September 1973, Article 1 INFCIRC/193; Agreement between the Republic of Argentina, the Federative Republic of Brazil, the Brazilian-Argentine Agency for Accounting and Control of Nuclear Materials and the International Atomic Energy Agency for the Application of Safeguards, 13 December 1991, Article 1, INFCIRC/435.

1966.[89] It includes two annexes, one on 'Provisions for reprocessing plants' (Annex I) and the other on 'Provisions for safeguarded nuclear material in conversion plants and fabrication plants' (Annex II). It also incorporates by reference the so-called Inspectors Document (GC(V)/INF/39, annex), adopted by the IAEA Board of Governors in June 1961.[90] In turn, INFCIRC/66-type agreements incorporate by reference the safeguards system described in INFCIRC/66/Rev.2. In addition, over time, the IAEA Board has adopted a number of decisions and practices to clarify and expand the coverage of these agreements.[91] Although this type of agreements has not disappeared, with the adoption of the NPT and the other aforementioned treaties, their relevance has been greatly reduced, with their scope of application essentially limited to States which are not parties to the NPT.

Following the NPT, the IAEA undertook work on a new and more comprehensive safeguards system. A Committee established by the Board in 1970 developed a document to guide and standardise the content of the safeguards agreements to be concluded by NNWS with the IAEA under Article III of the NPT. This document, adopted in 1972 and entitled 'The Structure and Content of Agreements between the Agency and States Required in connection with the Treaty on the Non-Proliferation of Nuclear Weapons', is known as INFCIRC/153 (Corr.). There are significant differences in both scope and operation between the safeguard agreements shaped by this document and the previous category. First and foremost, the new agreements are not 'item-specific' but 'full-scale' or 'comprehensive safeguards agreements' (CSAs). They apply to all materials and all activities and facilities of the relevant State, rather than to specifically agreed items. Moreover, INFCIRC/153 (Corr.) was not intended as a document to be incorporated by reference in the text of the safeguards agreement but as guidance on the content. In fact, in 1974, the IAEA adopted a model CSA based on INFCIRC/153 (Corr.).[92] The approach of INFCIRC/153 (Corr.) has become generalised under the NPT as well as other multilateral non-proliferation agreements. Moreover, it has also shaped agreements between the IAEA and NWS, the so-called voluntary offer agreements (VOAs), as NWS are not subject to the obligation to enter into a safeguards agreement. At present,

[89] See INFCIRC/66/Rev.2, cover page.
[90] INFCIRC/66/Rev.2, para. 76.
[91] See Rockwood, *IAEA Safeguards*, at 255–256.
[92] GOV/INF/276, Annex A.

CSAs are the most frequent type of safeguards agreements. They require the conclusion of subsidiary arrangements between the relevant State and the IAEA for the practical implementation of the provisions of the CSA. Often, CSAs are also supplemented by protocols, as discussed next.

The post-1990 events described earlier in this chapter, particularly the discovery of Iraq's hidden nuclear programme, led to the additional strengthening of the safeguards system, mainly through the development under Programme 93+2 of a Model Additional Protocol[93] to existing CSAs, also known as INFCIRC/540 (Corr.). Under such protocols, which can only be concluded in addition to a safeguards agreement, the IAEA enjoys additional inspection powers ('complementary access') relating to information about the fuel cycle, all buildings on a nuclear site, manufacture and export of sensitive nuclear technologies and/or collection of environmental samples beyond declared locations. Approximately two-thirds of States having concluded CSAs have also entered into Additional Protocols. Of note, Article 8(b) of the Semipalatinsk Treaty requires the conclusion not only of a CSA but also of an Additional Protocol (INFCIRC/540 (Corr.)).

There are also other protocols that may be concluded to limit the scope of application of safeguard measures. These include the so-called Small Quantities Protocols or SQPs,[94] Suspension Protocols giving priority to CSAs over other safeguard agreements,[95] and cooperation protocols organising relations between the IAEA and other agencies.

3.3.2.3.4 International Verification and Inspection System The international verification and inspection system to determine compliance with safeguards agreements is the pillar of the entire system and the main expression of the centralisation embodied by the IAEA.

Article XII.B requires the agency to 'establish a staff of inspectors', who not only have the responsibility to conduct certain verifications and inspections (which have expanded over time) but also, under Article XII.C, to 'report any non-compliance to the Director General [of the

[93] INFCIRC/540: Model Protocol Additional to the Agreements between States and the International Atomic Energy Agency for the Application of Safeguards, 15 May 1997. See also the 'Guidelines and Format for Preparation and Submission of Declarations Pursuant to Articles 2 and 3 of the Model Protocol Additional to Safeguards Agreements' (Services Series 11), May 2004.

[94] GOV/INF/276, Annex A, 22 August 1974, subsequently revised by GOV/INF/276/Mod.1 and Corr.1, 21 February 2006.

[95] See INFCIRC/153 (Corr.), para. 24.

IAEA]', who is required to escalate it to the Board of Governors for it to 'call upon the recipient State or States to remedy forthwith any non-compliance' and to report it to all IAEA members as well as to both the UN Security Council and General Assembly.

In accordance with Article XV.A of the IAEA Statute, '[t]he Agency shall enjoy in the territory of each member such legal capacity and such privileges and immunities as are necessary for the exercise of its functions'. This general provision encompasses both the agency as such and its agents, such as inspectors. It has been implemented through a specific Agreement on the Privileges and Immunities of the Agency, concluded on 1 July 1959,[96] the contents of which are incorporated by reference in safeguards agreements. Importantly, it is generally understood that Article XV.A provides a sufficient basis for such privileges and immunities to be enjoyed by the agency and its officials, including inspectors, even in States Parties to the IAEA Statute which have not accepted the 1959 Agreement.[97] Thus, the 1959 Agreement can be seen as an elaboration, through authentic interpretation, of the IAEA Statute.

With respect to the structure of the control exercised by the IAEA, although there are some variations across types of safeguards treaties, all include two types of controls: States must submit information on the design of the safeguarded facilities and the agency has a right of access to verify such design information (design information verification or 'DIV'); the agency conducts three types of inspections, ad hoc (prior to the conclusion of 'subsidiary arrangements'), routine and special inspections.

Regarding the focus of such verifications and inspections, they have changed over time from an assessment of the 'correctness' of the information declared to that of its 'completeness'.[98] This was mainly due to the realisation that Iraq had been able to develop an undisclosed nuclear programme despite reporting to the IAEA and undergoing verification and inspection. Such shift in focus has required an expansion in the means of verification and inspection, most notably through reliance on other sources of information (e.g. environmental sampling, remote monitoring, satellite imagery) and enhanced inspection rights.

[96] Agreement on the Privileges and Immunities of the Agency, 1 July 1959, INFCIRC/9/Rev.2.

[97] See Rockwood, *IAEA Safeguards*, at 254–255.

[98] See L. Rockwood, L. Johnson, 'Verification of Correctness and Completeness in the Implementation of IAEA Safeguards: The Law and Practice', in J. Black-Branch, D. Fleck (eds), *Nuclear Non-Proliferation in International Law* (The Hague: TMC Asser Press, 2016), vol. II, pp. 57–94.

3.3.2.4 Physical Protection of Nuclear Materials and Facilities

3.3.2.4.1 IEA Guidelines One aspect of security that is frequently addressed in NCAs and IAEA cooperation agreements is the physical protection, i.e. the protection against unauthorised removal and sabotage, of nuclear materials and facilities.[99]

As early as 1972, the IAEA developed a set of guidelines on the 'Physical Protection of Nuclear Materials and Nuclear Facilities', also known as INFCIRC/225, which has been revised five times since then.[100] These guidelines are not binding on States under the IAEA Statute, but they may be so if a State has agreed to implement them in a treaty clause. For example, Article 8(2) of the US–UAE NCA requires each party to 'apply at a minimum measures in accordance with [. . .] the recommendations published in IAEA document INFCIRC/225/Rev.4'.

These recommendations initially focussed on 'materials' but they were subsequently expanded to cover 'facilities'. The structure of INFCIRC/225/Rev.5 focusses on three types of risks: unauthorised removal of nuclear material in use and storage, sabotage of nuclear facilities and nuclear materials in use and storage, and unauthorised removal and sabotage of nuclear material during transport. For each risk, a graded approach is identified requiring increasing levels of protection (more stringent measures) for higher risks.

3.3.2.4.2 Convention on the Physical Protection of Nuclear Material In the mid 1970s, the lack of a general obligation requiring the adoption of physical protection measures led to increasing calls for the development of an international agreement.[101]

On this basis, in 1977, the IAEA Director-General circulated a draft 'Convention on Physical Protection of Nuclear Facilities, Material and Transports' prepared by the United States. In the following two years, the scope of the draft was significantly reduced, on the basis of sovereignty

[99] See generally C. Stoiber, 'Nuclear Security: Legal Aspects of Physical Protection, Combating Illicit Trafficking and Nuclear Terrorism', in *International Nuclear Law: History, Evolution and Outlook* (OECD: Nuclear Energy Agency, 2010), pp. 219–242; M. L. V. Carmona, 'The International Regime on the Physical Protection of Nuclear Material and the Amendment to the Convention on the Physical Protection of Nuclear Material' (2005) 76 *Nuclear Law Bulletin* 29.

[100] Physical Protection of Nuclear Materials and Nuclear Facilities, INFCIRC/225/Rev.5.

[101] See e.g. Resolution of the IAEA General Conference in September 1975 (GC/XIX/RES/328).

concerns, and confined only to international transport of nuclear materials. The Convention on the Physical Protection of Nuclear Material was adopted on 26 October 1979 and opened for signature in March 1980.[102]

The Convention governs three aspects, namely the physical protection of nuclear materials during international transport (and incidental storage), the criminalisation of related offences, and cooperation and information exchange. The Convention reflects the graded approach of INFCIRC/225. Annex II defines three categories of nuclear materials on the basis of the type and quantity of the material. Annex I then defines the 'levels of protection' applicable to each category, from low (applicable to Category III) to high (applicable to Category I, e.g. two kilogrammes or more of plutonium or uranium-233 or five kilogrammes or more of uranium-235).

Following the terrorist attacks on US soil of 11 September 2001, further negotiations led in 2005 to an amendment of the Convention,[103] which entered into force in 2016. The amendment extended the scope of application of the Convention beyond the narrow focus on international transport (and incidental storage) to cover 'nuclear facilities used for peaceful purposes' (Article 2(1)). It introduced, among other things, a new Article 2A, which, in paragraph 3 requires States to 'apply insofar as is reasonable and practicable'[104] twelve 'Fundamental Principles of Physical Protection of Nuclear Material and Nuclear Facilities', which were subsequently also included in the revised INFCIRC/225, thus harmonising the two instruments. These principles include clear statements that the responsibility to ensure physical security rests on the State, that within a State such responsibility has to be clearly allocated, that it must be infused in a security culture and organised according to a graded and layered approach with adequate contingency plans and management of confidential information.

The process triggered by the 11 September events also led to a strengthening of the criminalisation of nuclear terrorism, most notably with the adoption, on 14 September 2005, of an International Convention for the Suppression of Acts of Nuclear Terrorism.[105]

102 Physical Protection Convention.

103 Final Act of the Conference to Consider and Adopt Proposed Amendments to the Convention on the Physical Protection of Nuclear Material, document GOV/INF/2005/10-GC(49)/INF/6. See Amendment to the Convention on the Physical Protection of Nuclear Material, INFCIRC/274/Rev.1/Mod.1 [Physical Protection Convention – Amendment].

104 On the origin of these terms see Carmona, *Physical Protection*, paras. 41 and 59.

105 Nuclear Terrorism Convention.

3.3.3 Nuclear Power and Safety

3.3.3.1 Nature and Scope of the Instruments The IAEA Statute expressly vests in the agency the power to 'establish or adopt . . . standards of safety for protection of health and minimization of danger to life and property (including such standards for labour conditions)' (Article III.A.6). But it does not have an equivalent provision authorising the agency to operate as a 'norm entrepreneur' for the impulsion, negotiation and adoption of multilateral conventions. Such power can only be derived indirectly from Article II, according to which the objective of the agency is to 'seek to accelerate and enlarge the contribution of atomic energy to peace, health and prosperity throughout the world'. This difference has raised some challenges at the IAEA, mostly as a result of the administrative activities devolved to the IAEA Secretariat in some subsequent multilateral conventions.

In practice, the agency has been an important norm entrepreneur, changing the practice of States first through the issuance of 'standards', i.e. non-binding technical guidance instruments, and then serving as the neutral convenor for the adoption of multilateral conventions on different aspects of safety. The IAEA maintains a specific 'Series' of 'safety standards', consisting of three sets of publications, the Safety Fundamentals, the Safety Requirements ('General' and 'Specific'), and the Safety Guides. The relation between them goes from general to specific, with the Safety Fundamentals at the top,[106] then – as of 2020 – fourteen sets of 'Requirements' on matters such as 'Governmental, Legal and Regulatory Framework for Safety',[107] 'Radiation Protection and Safety of Radiation Sources' (also known as 'BSS'),[108] 'Site Evaluation',[109] 'Safety of Nuclear Power Plants',[110] 'Safety of Nuclear

[106] No. SF-1 Fundamental Safety Principles.

[107] GSR Part 1 (Rev. 1) Governmental, Legal and Regulatory Framework for Safety [Governmental, Legal and Regulatory Framework].

[108] GSR Part 3 Radiation Protection and Safety of Radiation Sources: International Basic Safety Standards [BSS].

[109] SSR-1 Site Evaluation for Nuclear Installations [Site Evaluation].

[110] SSR-2/1 (Rev. 1) Safety of Nuclear Power Plants: Design; SSR-2/2 (Rev. 1) [Safety of Nuclear Power Plants: Design]; SSR-2/2 (Rev. 1) Safety of Nuclear Power Plants: Commissioning and Operation [Safety of Nuclear Power Plants: Commissioning and Operation].

Fuel Cycle Facilities',[111] 'Safety of Research Reactors',[112] 'Safe Transport of Radioactive Material',[113] 'Preparedness and Response',[114] 'Decommissioning of Facilities'[115] or the 'Predisposal'[116] and 'Disposal of Radioactive Waste',[117] and finally over fifty 'Safety Guides'. As it is made clear from the scope of these standards, the full life-cycle of nuclear energy, from the fuel cycle to generation and transport to decommissioning and waste management, is covered. Also of note is the fact that IAEA standards not only take into account work done by other bodies,[118] they are sometimes jointly sponsored by several of them, as in the case of the Fundamental Safety Standards.

IAEA Safety standards are developed by a standing body of senior government officials, the Commission on Safety Standards (CSS), with support from the Secretariat.[119] They are not binding as such, but they may become so on the basis of an additional undertaking included in a treaty between the IAEA and a State or between two States, much in the same way as the security standards examined in the previous sections. Moreover, a number of multilateral conventions emerging from previous non-binding standards expressly incorporate their terms. Thus, as discussed next, there is a symbiotic relationship between the standards and the multilateral conventions in the area of nuclear safety. The former generated the latter, and the latter strengthen the former. At the same time, standards present the substantial advantage of being much more easily revised over time. After the Fukushima Daiichi accident, the IAEA Board of Governors and the IAEA General Conference launched an Action Plan on Nuclear Safety, which included an action point entitled 'Review and strengthen IAEA Safety Standards and improve their

[111] SSR-4 Safety of Nuclear Fuel Cycle Facilities.

[112] SSR-3 Safety of Research Reactors.

[113] SSR-6 (Rev. 1) Regulations for the Safe Transport of Radioactive Material (2018 Edition).

[114] GSR Part 7 Preparedness and Response for a Nuclear or Radiological Emergency [Preparedness and Response Standards].

[115] GSR Part 6 Decommissioning of Facilities.

[116] GSR Part 5 Predisposal Management of Radioactive Waste.

[117] SSR-5 Disposal of Radioactive Waste.

[118] Such as International Commission on Radiological Protection (ICRP), the UN Committee on the Effects of Atomic Radiation (UNSCEAR), the OECD Nuclear Energy Agency, Euratom, the UN Food and Agriculture Organization (FAO), the World Health Organization (WHO), the International Maritime Organization (IMO), the UN Environment Programme (UNEP) or the International Labour Office (ILO).

[119] See CSS, Terms of Reference, 17 December 2015, available at: www-ns.iaea.org/downloads/standards/css-tor.pdf.

implementation'.[120] That led to the review of five main standards[121] to account for the lessons of the accident.[122] Such level of reactivity could not be expected for a process that involves the formal amendment of a treaty.[123]

In the following sections, the normative activity relating to the prevention of, response to and reparation of nuclear accidents and radiological risks is discussed by reference to both standards and multilateral conventions. The latter serve as the epicentre of the preventive systems.

3.3.3.2 Prevention: The 1994 Nuclear Safety Convention and 1997 Joint Convention

3.3.3.2.1 Overview Given the scale of the risk arising from the mishandling of nuclear energy processes, the main focus of safety standards as well as of treaty law is on preventing harm from occurring, rather than responding to it or compensating its consequences. Prevention efforts concern the entire life-cycle of nuclear energy processes, and they overlap significantly with instruments focussing on security (see Section 3.3.2) and environmental protection (see Section 3.3.4). Four main areas can be identified from a regulatory perspective: (1) radiological protection, (2) safety of nuclear installations and materials, (3) transport and (4) spent fuel and waste management.

3.3.3.2.2 Radiological Protection Radiological protection or, more specifically, the protection of humans and the environment from the effects of ionising radiation, preceded the development of nuclear energy.[124] It was first institutionalised in 1928, with the creation of the International Commission on Radiological Protection (ICRP)[125] and the

[120] Action Plan on Nuclear Safety, 5 September 2011, GOV/2011/59-GC(55)/14.

[121] Governmental, Legal and Regulatory Framework; GSR Part 4, 2009 Safety Assessment for Facilities and Activities [Assessment of Facilities and Activities]; Safety of Nuclear Power Plants: Design; Safety of Nuclear Power Plants: Commissioning and Operation; and Site Evaluation.

[122] See generally *The Fukushima Daiichi Accident. Report by the Director General*, 2015, GC (59)/14 [IAEA Fukushima Report].

[123] Following the IAEA Action Plan, Switzerland tabled a proposal for the amendment of Article 18 of the Convention on Nuclear Safety in order to strengthen the requirements for new and existing nuclear facilities. But this proposal failed to reach consensus in a 2015 convened to discuss it. The conference only adopted a Vienna Declaration on Nuclear Safety, 9 February 2015, CNS/DC/2015/2/Rev.1.

[124] See generally Lazo, *Radiological Protection*, on which the following discussion is based.

[125] See www.icrp.org/.

instruments and reports developed by this and other relevant bodies, such as the UN Committee on the Effects of Atomic Radiation (UNSCEAR),[126] the OECD Nuclear Energy Agency (NEA) and EURATOM, have influenced the work of the IAEA in this area.

Radiological protection is a useful starting point for a discussion of safety because it highlights that safety concerns go beyond specific incidents with catastrophic consequences (e.g. nuclear accidents) and must be mainstreamed in the regulation of any activity involving ionising radiation, including all activities related to nuclear materials and facilities. For this reason, the relevant regulations have been described as a 'chapeau', i.e. as basic requirements for all nuclear law.[127]

At the global level, the main instruments concerning radiological protection are the 2007 Recommendations of the ICRP (ICRP Publication 103)[128] and the IAEA BSS, whose origins can be traced back to the Health and Safety Measures adopted by the IAEA Board in March 1960.[129] The BSS, as most recently revised in 2011,[130] take into account the 2007 ICRP Recommendations and are intended to implement the Fundamental Safety Principles. They begin with a statement of general principles ('General Requirements for Protection and Safety') and then state specific requirements on the basis of the type of 'exposure' to radiation, 'Planned Exposure' (broadly defined in section 3.1 and including, under letter (c) '[t]he generation of nuclear power'), 'Emergency Exposure' (due to nuclear or radiological emergencies, mostly accidents)[131] and 'Existing Exposure' (due to contamination from residual radioactive material from past events, contaminated commodities and natural sources of radiation).

These requirements vary significantly, but some examples applicable to 'planned exposure' are notification and licensing requirements for covered activities, responsibilities of licensees ('Registrants'), dose limits for occupational and public exposure, safety assessments, monitoring

[126] See www.unscear.org/.

[127] See C. Stoiber, A. Baer, N. Pelzer, W. Tonhauser, *Handbook on Nuclear Law* (Vienna: IAEA, 2003), at 47.

[128] The 2007 Recommendations of the International Commission on Radiological Protection. ICRP Publication 103. Annals ICRP 37 (2–4).

[129] Health and Safety Measures, INFCIRC/18, IAEA, Vienna (1960).

[130] See n. 108.

[131] This section of the BSS concerns mainly 'response' measures.

and verification of compliance, and measures for the prevention and mitigation of accidents.

3.3.3.2.3 Safety of Nuclear Installations and Materials With respect to the safety of nuclear installations and materials,[132] as noted earlier, the relevant regulation partly overlaps with that of security (physical protection).

There is, however, a dense body of IAEA standards focussing specifically on safety. In addition to the Fundamental Safety Principles, these include standards on 'Governmental, Legal and Regulatory Framework for Safety', 'Leadership and Management for Safety',[133] 'Site Evaluation for Nuclear Installations', 'Assessment of Facilities and Activities', 'Safety of Nuclear Power Plants: Design', 'Safety of Nuclear Power Plants: Commissioning and Operation', 'Safety of Nuclear Fuel Cycle Facilities', 'Safety of Research Reactors' and 'Decommissioning of Facilities'. Two important codes of conduct, one on the 'Safety and Security of Radioactive Sources'[134] and the other on the 'Safety of Research Reactors'[135] complete this picture.

But the cornerstone of the system is the Convention on Nuclear Safety (CNS) adopted in June 1994 under the aegis of the IAEA.[136] The process leading to the CNS was prompted not only by the consequences of the Chernobyl accident but also by the run-up to the 1992 Rio Conference on Environment and Development. In this context, the General Conference of the IAEA endorsed the proposal of developing an international agreement on nuclear safety. Two main views on the scope and contents of this agreement were advanced. One which saw the instrument as an encompassing framework convention to be subsequently specified through annexes and protocols; the other aimed for a single instrument,

[132] See generally W. Tonhauser, A. Wetherall, 'The International Legal Framework on Nuclear Safety: Developments, Challenges and Opportunities', in *International Nuclear Law: History, Evolution and Outlook* (OECD: Nuclear Energy Agency, 2010), pp. 157–169.

[133] GSR Part 2 Leadership and Management for Safety.

[134] Code of Conduct on the Safety and Security of Radioactive Sources (Vienna: IAEA, 2004).

[135] Code of Conduct on the Safety of Research Reactors (Vienna: IAEA, 2006).

[136] On this instrument see O. Jankowitsch, 'The Convention on Nuclear Safety' (1994) 54 *Nuclear Law Bulletin* 9; M. Kaminga, 'The IAEA Convention on Nuclear Safety' (1994) 44 *ICLQ* 872; P. Reyners, 'La Convention de 1994 sur la sûreté nucléaire' (1995) 99 *RGDIP* 605; G. Handl, 'The IAEA Nuclear Safety Conventions: an Example of Successful "Treaty Management"?' (2003) 72 *Nuclear Law Bulletin* 7.

limited in its scope to land-based nuclear power plants and in its content to the Fundamental Safety Principles.[137]

The latter view prevailed but the former one found nevertheless expression in the preamble, which refers, in paragraphs (ix) and (x), to the aim to develop other international agreements on nuclear waste and other parts of the fuel cycle. It eventually led to the adoption of the adoption of the Joint Convention,[138] discussed later. A carefully worded compromise is also embodied in paragraph (viii), which commits State parties 'to the application of fundamental safety principles for nuclear installations rather than of detailed safety standards' but adds right after 'that there are internationally formulated safety guidelines which are updated from time to time and so can provide guidance on contemporary means of achieving a high level of safety'.[139]

The CNS applies to 'nuclear installations' (Articles 3 and 2(i)), both new and existing (Article 6). It has two main components. The first is a set of obligations, for which States Parties are required to adopt implementing measures (Article 4), concerning three main areas: legislation and regulation, general safety considerations, and the safety of installations. These obligations are based on the Fundamental Safety Principles. The second, and perhaps most emblematic one, is a peer-review mechanism to secure compliance and implementation. Article 20 organises 'review meetings [...] for the purpose of reviewing the reports submitted pursuant to Article 5'. The underlying rationale is that each State has an individual interest in ensuring nuclear safety in its territory, which offers a stronger incentive for compliance than any international top-down investigative mechanism. For this reason, peer pressure is deemed to be sufficient to support the diligence arising from each State's individual interest.

3.3.3.2.4 Transport of Nuclear and Radioactive Materials Transportation raises important issues not only as regards the 'security' of transported materials, as discussed earlier in this chapter by reference to the

[137] Joint Convention on the Safety of Spent Fuel Management and on the Safety of Radioactive Waste Management, 5 September 1997, available at: www.ecolex.org/ (TRE-001273).

[138] See Jankowitsch, *Convention on Nuclear Safety*, paras. 19–20.

[139] See Jankowitsch, *Convention on Nuclear Safety*, para. 22.

Convention on Physical Protection of Nuclear Materials, but also the 'safety' of the transport operations.[140]

The main instrument regarding the latter is a standard developed by the IAEA as early as 1961, the Regulations for the Safe Transport of Radioactive Materials ('Transport Regulations'), and subsequently revised, lastly in 2018.[141] With the notable exception of the CNS Convention, most other international instruments on nuclear materials, including those on spent fuel and radioactive waste (including the 1997 Joint Convention and the 1990 Code of Practice[142]), notification and assistance in case of emergency and liability for damage, apply directly or indirectly to transport activities.[143] Much like the issue of transit in general, discussed in Chapter 2 of this book, the governance of the transport of nuclear and radioactive materials is a mosaic, relying on the aforementioned core instruments as well as on a wide range of sometimes unspecific instruments and norms, reaching as far as the freedom of navigation and the right of innocent passage.[144]

The Transport Regulations have a broad scope of application defined in section 106 as:

> the transport of *radioactive material* by all modes on land, water, or in the air, including transport that is incidental to the use of the *radioactive material*. Transport comprises all operations and conditions associated with, and involved in, the movement of *radioactive material*'. (emphasis original)

Thus, they apply to radioactive material broadly defined (section 236, with the exclusions mentioned in section 107), present in the consignment (section 211) which is shipped (section 237) from origin to destination, irrespective of the 'mode' of transport (land, water or air). Transport is also broadly defined, including but not limited to the narrower category of 'transboundary' transport or movement, but excluding radioactive material which is moved within an establishment subject to appropriate safety regulations (section 107(b)). They then

[140] See generally O. Jankowitsch-Prevor, 'The International Law of Transport of Nuclear and Radioactive Material', in *International Nuclear Law: History, Evolution and Outlook* (OECD: Nuclear Energy Agency, 2010), pp. 187–218.

[141] See n. 113.

[142] Code of Practice on the Transboundary Movement of Radioactive Waste', 13 November 1990, INFCIRC/386.

[143] Jankowitsch-Prevor, *Transport*, at 188.

[144] See the list in Jankowitsch-Prevor, *Transport*, at 190–194.

formulate detailed requirements for the packaging to be used, the testing of the packaging before the first and in subsequent shipments, their marking, notification, certification and approvals, transport and storage in transit etc.

As other IAEA standards, the Transport Regulations are based on a graded approach, whereby the stringency of the requirements is a function of the level of danger posed by the nature and amount of the relevant materials. Although widely followed, the Transport Regulations are not binding, unless States have made them so by agreement.

3.3.3.2.5 Radioactive Waste and Spent Fuel Management The issue of waste has also been a long-standing cause for concern.[145] Like transport, the relevant international regulation rests on a mosaic of specific and unspecific instruments, including both standards and treaties, most notably the Joint Convention on the Safety of Spent Fuel Management and on the Safety of Radioactive Waste (the 'Joint Convention'), developed under the aegis of the IAEA and adopted in 1997. Radioactive waste is also specifically addressed in a broader body of instruments and conventions[146] but also sometimes expressly excluded from others.[147]

The most commonly accepted definition of 'radioactive waste' was introduced by the IAEA in its 1990 Code of Practice on the Transboundary Movement of Radioactive Waste,[148] in its section II devoted to definitions: 'any material that contains or is contaminated with radionuclides at concentrations or radioactivity levels greater than that "exempt quantities" established by the competent authorities and for

[145] See generally M. Montjoie, *Droit international et gestion des déchets radioactifs* (Paris: LGDJ, 2011).

[146] See e.g. Antarctic Treaty, 1 December 1959, 402 UNTS 71, Article V(1) (prohibiting nuclear explosions and the disposal of radioactive waste); Convention on the Prevention of Marine Pollution by Dumping of Wastes and other Matter, 13 November 1972, 1046 UNTS 138, Article IV(1)(a), Annexes I (para. 6); Protocol to the Convention on the Prevention of Marine Pollution by Dumping of Wastes and Other Matter, 7 November 1996 (1997) 36 ILM 1, Article 4(1)(1) and Annex 1 (para. 3); Bamako Convention on the Ban of the Import into Africa and the Control of Transboundary Movement and Management of Hazardous Wastes within Africa, 30 January 1991, 2101 UNTS 177, Article 2(1)(a) and Annex I.

[147] See Basel Convention on the Control of Transboundary Movements of Hazardous Wastes and Their Disposal, 22 March 1989, 1673 UNTS 57, Article 1(1)(3) (which excluded radioactive waste on the insistence of the United States, which eventually did not become a party to the Convention).

[148] See n. 142.

which no use is foreseen'. Spent fuel for reprocessing was not deemed to be radioactive waste. Only with the adoption of the 1997 Joint Convention[149] was the safety of both spent fuel management and radioactive waste management brought under the scope of a binding international agreement. Yet, spent fuel is only covered if two conditions are met: it results from the operation of civilian nuclear reactors (not military ones) and, when held for reprocessing into new fuel, it is only covered if the relevant State declares reprocessing as part of 'spent fuel management' (Article 3(1)). Also, Article 3(3) expressly excludes spent fuel and radioactive waste 'within military or defence programmes' from the scope of the Convention except when brought under it by the relevant State or when transferred and permanently managed within 'civilian programmes'.

The management of 'spent fuel' and 'radioactive waste' under the Joint Convention rests on the principles of the IAEA Safety Fundamentals, which are recalled in the preamble. In each of these two areas, the Joint Convention applies to existing and new facilities, although the review of the safety standards of existing facilities is worded in soft language (Articles 5 and 12). For each area, chapters 2 and 3 of the Joint Convention begin with a general due diligence requirement to 'take the appropriate steps to ensure that at all stages of [spent fuel/radioactive waste] management individuals, society and the environment are adequately protected against radiological and other hazards' (Articles 4 and 11), followed by provisions on sitting, design and construction, safety assessment and operation of the relevant facilities, as well as on the disposal and institutional measures after closure. Chapter 4 reflects the IAEA Safety Fundamentals regarding the legal and regulatory framework for implementation, radiological protection and response in case of emergency. Of particular note, Article 27 introduces a 'prior informed consent' mechanism for 'transboundary movements' of spent fuel or radioactive waste. Finally, as for the CNS, compliance is approached through a reporting obligation (Article 32) and a 'peer-review' mechanism (Article 30).

[149] See W. Tonhauser, O. Jankowitsch, 'The Joint Convention on the Safety of Spent Fuel Management and on the Safety of Radioactive Waste Management' (1997) 60 *Nuclear Law Bulletin* 9; A. de Kagenek, C. Pinel, 'The Joint Convention on the Safety of Spent Fuel Management and on the Safety of Radioactive Waste Management' (1998) 47 *ICLQ* 409; Handl, *Nuclear Safety Conventions*.

3.3.3.3 Response: The 1986 Early Notification and Assistance Conventions The international legal framework relating to response measures in case of nuclear emergencies is itself a response. Its two main stages of development were triggered by a major accident, first in the United States, with the meltdown of the second reactor of the Three Mile Island Nuclear Power Plant (TMI-2) on 28 March 1979, and then with the accident during a safety test of reactor 4 of the Chernobyl Nuclear Power Plant, in the former USSR, on 26 April 1986. Each accident was followed by regulatory initiatives. After the first, the IAEA adopted two sets of guidelines, the Guidelines for Mutual Emergency Assistance Arrangements in Connection with a Nuclear Accident or Radiological Emergency (INFCIRC/310) and the Guidelines on Reportable Events, Integrated Planning and Information Exchange in a Transboundary Release of Radioactive Materials (INFCIRC/321).[150] After Chernobyl, these instruments served for the negotiation and adoption in record time (in September 1986) of the Convention on Early Notification of a Nuclear Accident,[151] and the Convention on Assistance in Case of a Nuclear Accident or Radiological Emergency.[152]

The Early Notification Convention applies to nuclear accidents from facilities or activities (Article 2) in a State Party that result or may result in a 'release of radioactive material', which in turn result or may result in 'an international transboundary release that could be of radiological safety significance for another State' (Article 1). The key obligations are stated in Article 3, namely to 'notify' States which are or may be 'physically affected' directly or through the IAEA, and to provide available information (specified in Article 5) to minimise the radiological consequences. State parties where the nuclear accident occurs must also 'respond promptly' to requests for further information or consultation (Article 6). To facilitate the process, all parties must designate a national contact point (Article 7). An Emergency Notification and Assistance Technical Operations Manual (ENATOM) has been developed to support national authorities in the implementation of this Convention. The 2007 was revised following the 2011 accident in Fukushima to reflect the lessons learnt from it.[153]

[150] See Preparedness and Response Standards.

[151] Convention on Early Notification of a Nuclear Accident, 26 September 1986, 1439 UNTS 275.

[152] Convention on Assistance in Case of a Nuclear Accident or Radiological Emergency, 26 September 1986, 1457 UNTS 133.

[153] Operations Manual for Incident and Emergency Communication, EPR-IEComm 2012.

As for the Assistance Convention, the system is premised on a duty to cooperate in case of nuclear accident or radiological emergency (Article 1). Importantly, assistance must be requested by a State, whether the State where the emergency occurs or another State (Article 2(1)). And it can be requested from the agency, another international organisation or another State (directly or through the agency). The scope and type of assistance must be specified by the requesting State or with its agreement, who keeps the overall direction and control of the assistance in its territory (Article 3) and may decide to terminate it at any time (Article 11). To facilitate the process, States must identify national contact points (Article 4). The Convention also includes provisions on communications and the confidentiality of information (Article 6), reimbursement of costs (Article 7), facilities for personnel and equipment (Articles 8 and 9) as well as an interesting provision whereby the requesting State assumes responsibility for claims against the assisting State or its agents brought by third parties (Article 10). In order to implement the Assistance Convention, the IAEA established a Response and Assistance Network (RANET) to facilitate the provision of assistance.

The system was tested during the 2011 Fukushima accident. Japan has been a party to both instruments since 1987. Yet, the notification and information system was deficient at the beginning of the crisis, until the IAEA Director-General made an urgent visit to Japan and established additional communication channels in the form of liaison officers. Moreover, Japan did not request assistance under the Assistance Convention and, therefore, this instrument and the RANET were not used. Instead, Japan requested bilateral assistance to other countries. In the aftermath of the accident, the role of the IAEA in responding to nuclear emergencies was expanded, through the IAEA Action Plan on Nuclear Safety, to include the provision of a prognosis of the evolution of the emergency or its possible consequences.[154]

3.3.3.4 Reparation: The IAEA and OECD Liability Systems

3.3.3.4.1 Overview It may seem unintuitive that the very first international agreements[155] that were adopted to regulate nuclear energy are

[154] See IAEA Fukushima Report, at 94–96.

[155] See generally J. Schwartz, 'Liability and Compensation for Third Party Damage resulting from a Nuclear Incident', in *International Nuclear Law: History, Evolution and Outlook* (OECD: Nuclear Energy Agency, 2010), pp. 307–354; N. Pelzer, 'Main Features of the Revised International Regime Governing Nuclear Liability – Progress and Standstill', in

two systems of liability for nuclear accident, one confined to the OECD context (then the OEEC), i.e. the 1960 Paris Convention and its extensions (known as the 'Paris-Brussels' system),[156] and the other with a global scope, under the aegis of the IAEA, i.e. the 1963 Vienna Convention and its extensions.[157]

In order to understand the need for such instruments, one must go back to the period following Eisenhower's 'Atoms for Peace' speech and the race to develop, in the late 1950s, commercial reactors to provide electricity. One major aspect of the initiative to regulate liability was certainly the destructive power of an atomic explosion arising from a nuclear accident and the need to compensate the victims for the damage suffered. Another no less important driver, which explains in part why European States moved first with a liability regime, was the need to limit the financial exposure of companies undertaking the investment to build nuclear power plants in case of mass claims resulting from an accident. The private sector needed legal clarity on its exposure in order to make investments in this sector, and such investments were indispensable to move from the promise to the reality of nuclear power generation. Last but not least, it was also understood that risks arising from nuclear

International Nuclear Law: History, Evolution and Outlook (OECD: Nuclear Energy Agency, 2010), pp. 355–386; *The 1997 Vienna Convention on Civil Liability for Nuclear Damage and the 1997 Convention on Supplementary Compensation for Nuclear Damage – Explanatory Texts*, IAEA International Law Series No. 3 (Revised) (Vienna: IAEA, 2017).

156 Paris Convention. The Paris Convention was supplemented by the Convention Supplementary to the Paris Convention of 29 July 1960, 31 January 1963, 1041 UNTS 358 [Brussels Supplementary Convention]. The two treaties were subsequently amended in 1964, 1982 and 2004, but the 2004 amendments are not yet in force. A number of related decisions, recommendations and interpretations of the Paris and Brussels Conventions have been adopted over time by the OECD Council or the NEA (Steering Committee for Nuclear Energy) to clarify the terms and operation of these instruments.

157 Vienna Convention. The Vienna Convention was amended by a Protocol to amend the Vienna Convention on Civil Liability for Nuclear Damage, 12 September 1997, 2241 UNTS 302, following which there are two systems (the initial one – the 1963 Vienna Convention – and the amended one – the 1997 Protocol). On 12 September 1997, States adopted a Convention on Supplementary Compensation for Nuclear Damage, 12 September 1997, IAEA INFCIRC/567 [Supplementary Vienna Convention], in force since 2015. Importantly, the Supplementary Vienna Convention is a stand-alone agreement in that, under certain conditions (their domestic law regime), a State may become a party even if it is not a party to the 1963 Vienna Convention or the 1997 Protocol. Such is the case of Japan, which joined the Supplementary Vienna Convention in January 2015, as result of Fukushima.

accidents made international collaboration necessary as a result of both their transboundary effects and the scale of resources required for compensation and insurance. In this context, the OECD and the IAEA developed their civil liability regimes.

Despite differences in membership as well as on some specific points,[158] the two regimes are linked[159] and structured in the same manner around the five main components introduced in Chapter 3 in connection with liability for oil pollution damage, namely (1) the coverage of the system; (2) strict liability of and channelling of claims to the operator; (3) requirement to take out insurance; (4) additional layers of compensation; (5) non-discriminatory access to compensation procedures. In the following paragraphs, I only provide a brief overview of these components to illustrate the coverage of nuclear damage in the international law of energy.

3.3.3.4.2 Scope of Application of the Systems Regarding the scope of application of the systems, they concern the liability of operators of nuclear installations (not State responsibility for internationally wrongful act) for 'nuclear incidents'[160] in a 'nuclear installation'[161] or in the course of transport of nuclear material,[162] which have resulted in 'nuclear damage'[163] within the geographical area covered by State parties.[164]

[158] See Schwartz, *Liability and Compensation*, at 323–324.

[159] In the aftermath of the Chernobyl accident, mismatches in the scope of compensation available to victims in different countries led to an attempt to render the entire system, Paris and Vienna together, more attractive through the adoption of a Joint Protocol Relating to the Application of the Vienna Convention and the Paris Convention, 27 September 1988, 1672 UNTS 293 [Joint Protocol]. It must be noted that the USSR was not a party to the Vienna Convention.

[160] Vienna Convention, Articles II.1(a); II.3(a) and (c); II.4; IV.4; IV.5(a); Paris Convention, Articles 3; 5(a), (b) and (d); 1997 Protocol, Articles II.1(a); II.3(a) and (c); II.4; IV.4; IV.5; Vienna Supplementary Convention, Annex, Articles 3.1(a); 3.4; 3.7(a) and (b); 7.1; 7.3; 7.4.

[161] Vienna Convention, Article I.1(j); Paris Convention, Article 1(a)(ii) and 1(b); 1997 Protocol, Articles I.1(j); I.2; I B; Vienna Supplementary Convention, Article II.2; Annex, Arts 1(b); 1.2.

[162] Vienna Convention, Articles II.1(b) and (c); II.2; II.3(b) and (c); II.4; III; IV.4; IV.5(b); Paris Convention, Articles 4, 5(c)–(d); 1997 Protocol, Articles II.1(b) and (c), II.2; II.3(b) and (c), II.4; III; IV.4; IV.6; Vienna Supplementary Convention, Annex, Articles 3.1(b) and (c); 3.2; 3.7(c); 7.2; 7.3; 7.4. See also the Convention relating to Civil Liability in the Field of Maritime Carriage of Nuclear Material (NUCLEAR), 17 December 1971, 974 UNTS 255.

[163] Vienna Convention, Article I(k); Paris Convention, Article 3(a); 1997 Protocol, Article I (k), Vienna Supplementary Convention, Article I(f).

[164] These terms are defined in Article 1 of the Paris Convention and Article I of the Vienna Convention.

The Paris Convention expressly states that it does not apply to incidents or effects occurring in a non-party, although the domestic legislation of a State may extend this application.[165] The Vienna Convention does not contain an express equivalent provision. It is generally accepted that only nuclear incidents occurring in a State Party are covered, and the IAEA Standing Committee on Civil Liability for Nuclear Damage issued a recommendation, early on, followed by State practice, according to which only effects suffered in State parties are covered.[166] By contrast, the 1997 Protocol introduced a provision, Article 1A(1), whereby the amended Vienna Convention applies to 'nuclear damage wherever suffered', although the application in non-parties may be excluded in a party's domestic legislation. Both the Paris and Vienna Conventions apply to nuclear incidents occurring during transport ('carriage') and incidental storage.[167]

The limitations in the spatial application of the two systems were laid bare by the Chernobyl disaster. The USSR was not bound by any civil liability convention and therefore the incident fell beyond the scope of the Paris and Vienna Conventions. Moreover, even if the USSR had been a party to the Vienna Convention, only victims in States Parties to such instrument would have benefited from the compensation system. A similar problem emerged after the Fukushima accident, as Japan was also (until January 2015) a 'non-convention State', i.e. a State with important nuclear installations but not bound by any liability convention.

Following Chernobyl, efforts to extend the scope of application of the systems were made[168] by linking the Paris and Vienna Conventions through a 1988 Joint Protocol[169] and the 1997 Vienna Supplementary Convention (which is expressly intended to supplement both systems[170] and can also operate as a stand-alone instrument[171]). Moreover, as noted earlier, the 1997 Protocol extended the scope of the Vienna Convention for parties to that Protocol. A similar effort was made in 2004 to amend the Paris Convention and the Brussels Supplementary Convention, but such amendments are not yet in force.

165 Paris Convention, Article 2.
166 See Pelzer, *Progress and* Standstill, at 361.
167 Paris Convention, Article 4; Vienna Convention, Article 2(1)(b)–(c).
168 See Pelzer, *Progress and Standstill*, at 361–365.
169 Joint Protocol, Article II.
170 Vienna Supplementary Convention, Article II(1)(a).
171 Vienna Supplementary Convention, Article II(1)(b).

3.3.3.4.3 Strict Liability of the Operator The second component concerns the organisation of a strict liability regime channelled exclusively to the operator of the nuclear installation.[172] The 'operator' is the 'person designated or recognised by the competent public authority as the operator of that installation'.[173]

This is the heart of the system, as it emerged from the compromise between the need to compensate the victims and the effort to incentivise the private sector to invest and develop nuclear power by limiting its exposure. The compromise has two sides. On the one hand, the operator is strictly liable (there is no need to establish fault), and it is the only liable entity (with its insurer) to which all claims must be directed,[174] thereby facilitating the situation of victims to bring their actions. On the other hand, the liability of the operator is capped, so as to shield it from excessive exposure and enable the development of insurance policies to cover such capped amount,[175] and the claims must be brought to an exclusive forum, that of the State where the nuclear incident occurred, with some subtleties.[176] If, instead, claims were allowed in different jurisdictions, there would be no practicable manner of implementing the cap.

This basic compromise has some additional elements. For example, when the nuclear incident engages the liability of more than one operator, the solution has been the establishment of joint and several liability.[177] Moreover, when the damage results from circumstances such as armed conflict, force majeure or the unlawful conduct of a third party, the operator may be exonerated from liability.[178] Furthermore, the possibility to bring a claim is time-barred,[179] for reasons of financial management of the necessary contingency funds.

[172] Paris Convention, Article 3(a); Vienna Convention, Articles I(a)(c) and IV(1).

[173] Paris Convention, Article 1(a)(vi); Vienna Convention, Article I(1)(c).

[174] Vienna Convention, Arts II.5–7; IV.7; Paris Convention, Art. 6; 1997 Protocol, Arts II. 5–7; IV.7; Vienna Supplementary Convention, Annex, Arts 3.8; 3.9; 3.10.

[175] Vienna Convention, Art. V; Paris Convention, Art. 7; 1997 Protocol, Arts V; V A; V D; Vienna Supplementary Convention, Annex, Arts 4; 6; 8.1.

[176] Vienna Convention, Article XI(1)–(3); Paris Convention, Article 13(a)–(c); 1997 Protocol, Article XI(1)–(4); Vienna Supplementary Convention, Article XIII.

[177] Vienna Convention, Article II(3)(a); Paris Convention, Article 5(b).

[178] Vienna Convention, Article IV(1)–(3); Paris Convention, Article 9; 1997 Protocol, Article IV(1)–(3); Vienna Supplementary Convention, Annex, Arts 3.3; 3.5; 3.6.

[179] Vienna Convention, Article VI(1) (10 years); Paris Convention, Article 8(a) (10 years); 1997 Protocol, Article VI(1)(a) (30 years for loss of life and personal injury, and 10 years for other damage); Vienna Supplementary Convention, Article XI(1).

Over time, the inadequacy of the caps set for the liability of the operator when compared to the scale of damage, as shown by Chernobyl and Fukushima (both handled beyond these liability conventions), and the fact that the incentives given to a nascent nuclear industry have no reason to be maintained now that the industry is commercially mature, have led to increases in the available amounts and calls for the elimination of the liability caps.[180] Several countries, including some 'non-convention States' such as Austria, Switzerland and Japan, have even embraced the unlimited liability concept in their domestic laws, although the huge financial exposure of the Japanese government, through its support to TEPCO, the operator of the Fukushima Daiichi nuclear power plant, may lead to a serious reconsideration of this issue.

Without a limitation of liability, the operator cannot expect to secure insurance (the insurer would be unable to define its risk and exposure) and, in practice, the burden of compensating the victims would fall essentially on the State, that is on tax-payers. That would be particularly true when the State cannot afford to see a particular operator go bankrupt, for a range of economic but also safety considerations, if the operator manages other facilities. As noted earlier, in 2015, Japan took the remarkable step of becoming a party to a liability convention, the 1997 Vienna Supplementary Convention.

3.3.3.4.4 Financial Guarantee The third component seeks to cover for the insolvability of the operator of the nuclear installation by requiring it to maintain a financial guarantee of its exposure, up to the amount of the cap. This normally takes the form of an obligation to take out insurance.[181]

This obligation has deep implications. In fact, in the early days of the design of the regimes, it was the commercial viability of insurance products capable of providing back-up to nuclear operators that served as guidance to set the liability caps of the latter. That is yet another illustration of the importance of nuclear power development in the minds of the drafters. Liability regimes were, in many ways, industrial policy measures to favour the emergence of a nuclear power industry.

Today, the capacity of the insurance market would likely allow it to absorb a higher exposure than the one reflected in the liability caps,

[180] See Schwartz, *Liability and Compensation*, at 338–339.

[181] Vienna Convention, Article VII; Paris Convention, Article 10; 1997 Protocol, Art. VII; Vienna Supplementary Convention, Annex, Art. 5.

hence the aforementioned debate about the suitability of such caps. Insurance is only required up to the amount of the cap. Beyond that amount, any additional compensation comes from the State or from State-pooled funds.

3.3.3.4.5 Tiered Compensation The scale of the damage caused by nuclear incidents was, since the early days, deemed to go well beyond the liability caps set on operators of nuclear installations, backed by their insurers. Such was the main motivation for the adoption, as early as 1963, of the Brussels Supplementary Convention and, in 1997, of the Vienna Supplementary Convention. These 'tiered' additional layers of compensation are designed to make up for the failings in the basic regime to compensate for the damage effectively caused.[182]

The 1963 Brussels Supplementary Convention, as amended in 1964 and 1982 (the amendment of 2004 is not yet in force), applies to nuclear incidents falling under the Paris Convention (except when they occur within a State which is not a party to the Brussels Convention).[183] For the compensation of such incidents, it establishes a three-tiered system.[184] The first tier is the financial guarantee provided by the nuclear operator to cover its liability cap.[185] The second tier is provided by the State where the nuclear installation of the liable operator is located, and it covers the difference between the insured liability cap and 175 million 'special drawing rights' (SDRs). The third tier is provided by all States Parties of the Brussels Convention and covers the difference between 175 million and 300 million SDRs. Interestingly, the contribution of each State Party to the third tier is calculated on the basis of a formula that takes into account the power capacity of the reactors located in that State.[186]

As for the Vienna Supplementary Convention, the system is broadly similar, but with some noteworthy innovations. The first tier is supported up to 300 million SDRs by the nuclear operator itself, the State of the nuclear installation or both (according to domestic law).[187] Given that

182 See the discussion in Schwartz, *Liability and Compensation*, at 322–323, 329–332.

183 Brussels Supplementary Convention, Article 2(a).

184 Brussels Supplementary Convention, Article 3.

185 However, the Convention allows the State to place a heavier burden on the operator, including the requirement to provide financial security for the full 300 million SDRs, see Brussels Supplementary Convention, Article 3(3)(1).

186 Brussels Supplementary Convention, Article 12.

187 Vienna Supplementary Convention, Articles III(1)(a)(i) and (2)(a).

the State of the installation bears the financial burden of this tier, it may decide in its domestic law that such funds can be used to compensate damage suffered by victims in a State which is not a party to the Vienna Supplementary Convention. The second tier consists of an international fund based on contributions from all States Parties. The broad allocation of such fund is pre-determined, with 50 per cent pre-allocated to victims in the installation State and the other 50 per cent to transboundary victims in other States Parties (it cannot be used to compensate damage in non-parties).[188]

3.3.3.4.6 Non-Discrimination The fifth component seeks to harmonise the situation of victims in different States affected by the same nuclear incident. The key principle is the requirement of non-discrimination between national and foreign victims bringing claims before the courts with exclusive competence over the consequences of a nuclear incident.[189] Of note, the 1997 Protocol amending the Vienna Convention requires States Parties, when their courts have exclusive jurisdiction over the incident, to enable another State Party to bring a class action before such courts on behalf of its nationals or residents (with their consent).[190]

3.3.4 Environmental Protection

3.3.4.1 Overview Environmental protection was implicit in the safety instruments examined in the previous section.[191] Some early multilateral environmental agreements, such as the 1972 London Convention on Dumping (and then the 1996 Protocol) expressly govern nuclear waste. Others, however, expressly exclude nuclear materials and activities from their scope.[192] From the perspective of the centralised governance of nuclear energy, what must be emphasised is the explicit pursuit of environmental protection as a goal in the legal architecture described earlier.

188 Vienna Supplementary Convention, Articles III(1)(b), (2)(b), IV, V and XI(1)(b).

189 Paris Convention, Article 14 (a) and (c); Vienna Convention, Article XIII; 1997 Protocol, Article XIII; Vienna Supplementary Convention, Art. III.2.

190 1997 Protocol, Article XI.A(a).

191 On the protection of the environment under nuclear law see P. Reyners, 'Le droit nucléaire confronté au droit de l'environnement: autonomie ou complémentarité?' (2007) *Revue québécoise de droit international (Hors-série)* 149; Emmerechts, *Environmental Protection*; A. Al Faruque, *Nuclear Energy Regulation, Risk and the Environment* (London: Routledge, 2019).

192 Basel Convention; HNS Convention.

It was the Chernobyl disaster that made consideration of environmental protection an inescapable goal of nuclear law. From a chronological perspective, the very first nuclear treaty expressly referring to this goal is the 1986 Assistance Convention, which states in Article 1(1) that its goal is to 'facilitate prompt assistance in the event of a nuclear accident or radiological emergency to minimize its consequences and to protect life, property *and the environment* from the effects of radioactive releases' (emphasis added). The 1986 Early Notification Convention does not contain an equivalent provision, but it acknowledges the importance of environmental impacts in its description of the information to be provided in the notification.[193]

Here, my purpose is to survey how environmental sustainability has explicitly gained ground in the international law of nuclear energy. As before, the presentation moves from prevention, to response, to reparation.

3.3.4.2 Prevention of Environmental Harm At the level of prevention, the most notable instrument, which was developed specifically as a contribution to the 1992 Rio Conference on Environment and Development, is the 1994 Convention on Nuclear Safety or CNS. In the aftermath of Chernobyl, it was impossible to ignore the environmental consequences of nuclear accidents.

In the opening paragraph of the preamble, the CNS expressly links safety and environmental protection: '[a]ware of the importance to the international community of ensuring that the use of nuclear energy is safe, well regulated *and environmentally sound*' (emphasis added). Then, Article I(ii) states, as one of the objectives of the CNS 'to establish and maintain effective defences in nuclear installations against potential radiological hazards in order to protect individuals, society *and the environment* from harmful effects of ionizing radiation' (emphasis added). Environmental considerations must be taken into account in the evaluation of the safety of existing nuclear installations (specifically for the timing of their potential shutdown (Article 6)), as well as for the sitting of new ones (Article 17(ii)).

Similarly, the 1997 Joint Convention expressly recalls in paragraph (xv) of its preamble the action plan (Agenda 21)[194] and the Rio

[193] Early Notification Convention, Article 5(1)(f).

[194] Report of the United Nations Conference on Environment and Development, A/CONF.151/26/Rev.1 (Vol. 1), 13 June 1992, Resolution 1, Annex 2: Agenda 21 (Agenda 21), chapter 22.

Declaration[195] adopted at the 1992 Rio Conference on Environment and Development, and it states, in Article 1(ii), as one of its objectives:

> to ensure that during all stages of spent fuel and radioactive waste management there are effective defenses against potential hazards so that individuals, society *and the environment* are protected from harmful effects of ionizing radiation, now and in the future, in such a way that *the needs and aspirations of the present generation are met without compromising the ability of future generations to meet their needs and aspirations.* (emphasis added)

Thereafter, it refers to environmental considerations in describing the general requirements that States must adopt in connection with the safety of spent fuel management (Article 4), specifically as regards the sitting (Article 6(1)(ii)), construction and design (Article 7(i)), assessment of the regulated facilities (Article 8). Similar requirements apply to the safety of radioactive waste management (Article 11), also with respect to the sitting (Article 13(1)(ii)), design and construction (Article 14(i)), assessment (Article 15) and closure (Article 17(iii)) of regulated facilities. More generally, environmental considerations are integrated into the provisions on radiological protection (Article 24).

In the three years between the 1994 CNS and the 1997 Joint Convention, environmental protection thus became much more explicitly integrated into the regulatory system.

3.3.4.3 Response to Emergencies Response to emergencies has been discussed earlier from the perspective of safety (see Section 3.3.3.3). As mentioned before, the Assistance and Early Notification Conventions expressly refer to environmental protection.

Of particular note, the Assistance Convention specifically regulates the possible compensation claims that may arise from the provision of assistance, including for 'damage to the environment' in the requesting State as a result of activities by the assisting State. Under Article 10(2), the requesting State undertakes (1) not to bring legal proceedings against the assisting party, (2) to assume responsibility for dealing with any such proceedings that may be brought by third parties against the assisting party and (3) to hold it harmless in case such proceedings succeed.

[195] Rio Declaration on Environment and Development, 13 June 1992, UN Doc. A/CONF.151/26.

Moreover, the requesting State must compensate the assisting party for certain costs suffered by the latter in the course of providing assistance.

The thrust of the allocative provision is to remove one important disincentive for the provision of assistance in a situation as complex as a nuclear accident or a radiological emergency.

3.3.4.4 Reparation of Environmental Harm The latter point leads to perhaps the most significant reform resulting from Chernobyl, namely an overhaul of the nuclear liability system, in the form of substantial review of the Vienna system, through the 1997 Protocol and the 1997 Vienna Supplementary Convention, and the Paris system, through the 2004 Protocols amending the Paris and Brussels Conventions. As the latter are not yet in force, I will focus on the law in force, from the perspective of the compensation of preventive measures (i.e. response measures to contain or mitigate the effects of a nuclear incident) and compensation of environmental damage (i.e. reparation proper).[196]

Regarding preventive measures, they are now expressly included in the definition of 'nuclear damage' in the 1997 Protocol (Article I(1)(k)(vi) and (n)) and the Vienna Supplementary Convention (Article I(f)(vi) and (h)). Their scope of recovery is circumscribed by parameters (significance of harm and reasonableness) which leave much space for the law and courts of the competent forum.

With respect to compensation of environmental harm, the matter is more complex. In the basic systems of the Paris and Vienna Conventions, such harm may be compensated to the extent that the law of the competent forum includes it within the broad concept of damage to or loss of 'property'.[197] In the post-Chernobyl systems, it is expressly included but in a form that raises difficult questions. The 1997 Protocol specifically includes in the definition of 'nuclear damage' the 'costs of measures of reinstatement of impaired environment, unless such impairment is insignificant, if such measures are actually taken or to be taken, and insofar as not included in sub-paragraph (ii) [i.e. loss or damage to property]' (Article I(1)(k)(iv)). It then defines 'measures of reinstatement' in Article I(1)(m) as:

> any reasonable measures which have been approved by the competent authorities of the State where the measures were taken, and which aim to

[196] See Emmerechts, *Environmental Protection*, at 141–149.

[197] See Paris Convention, Article 3(a)(ii); Vienna Convention, Article I(1)(k).

> reinstate or restore damaged or destroyed components of the environment, or to introduce, where reasonable, the equivalent of these components into the environment. The law of the State where the damage is suffered shall determine who is entitled to take such measures.

Impairment to the environment may also result in other form of recoverable damage recognised by the 1997 Protocol (Article I(k)(v)), namely the 'loss of income deriving from an economic interest in any use or enjoyment of the environment, incurred as a result of a significant impairment of that environment, and insofar as not included in subparagraph (ii)'. A similar approach is followed by the Vienna Supplementary Convention (Article I(f)(iv)–(v) and (g)).

Despite the effort to circumscribe the scope of the measures, and hence of the associated costs, the definition leaves open questions such as the identification of the relevant 'components' and the extent to which they are to be 'reinstated'. That, in turn, has prevented the development of commercially viable insurance products and hence of potential financial guarantees in case of harm. As for 'loss of income' (e.g. of a hotel resort) resulting from a 'significant impairment to the environment', it leaves several matters of scope and judgement to the law and courts of the forum, such as the directness of the link, the significance of the impairment, and the extent of compensation.

In all events, it is the basic tiered system of compensation that is expected to cover the loss now identified under these two heads of damage. Yet, the express inclusion of both preventive measures and reinstatement measures is a clear indication that the response and compensation regimes of nuclear law now see environmental protection as one of their purposes.

7

Centralised Approach

Producer/Consumer, Promotion and Regional Cooperation Organisations

I Overview

As noted in Chapter 6, there is some measure of proto-centralisation beyond the governance of nuclear energy. Proto-centralisation is understood as meeting a sub-set, typically two or three, of the four definitional features of the centralised approach: (1) the establishment of an international organisation or agency with a steering role; (2) a focus on an energy resource or form of producing energy; (3) some measure of formal or informal normative power; and (4) a governance framework with a comprehensive scope steered by the organisation.

The most advanced form of proto-centralisation is found in the organisation of oil producers, under the 1960 Organization of Petroleum Exporting Countries (OPEC), and consumers, under the 1974 International Energy Agency (IEA), as well as their interactions through the International Energy Forum (IEF) which evolved from an informal process in the early 1990s to a formalised one based on the Charter adopted in 2011. Other organisations of a private nature, particularly the New York Mercantile Exchange (NYMEX), the Intercontinental Exchange (ICE) and the Chicago Mercantile Exchange (CME), serve as hubs for the formation of the oil price. The international law governing oil also relies on the unspecific rules discussed under the foundational approach (Chapters 2 and 3) and the highly specific ones examined under the ad hoc approach (Chapter 4). Some significantly more limited measure of proto-centralisation is also found in the context of natural gas, embodied in the Gas Exporting Countries Forum (GECF), a producers' organisation.

Another form of proto-centralisation does not revolve around producers/consumers organisations but seeks to promote knowledge and ultimately the uptake of other forms of energy. The main example is provided by the International Renewable Energy Agency (IRENA), established in 2009.

Finally, there are some organisations established in a regional context, which have a broader focus on energy cooperation. Aside from the EU, which is a peculiar case, less integrated forms of energy cooperation include the ASEAN Energy Cooperation Framework and the Latin American Energy Organization (OLADE).

In this chapter, I discuss these three main forms of proto-centralisation, i.e. producer/consumer, promotion, and regional organisations, by reference to their main illustrations: oil and gas, renewable energies, and energy cooperation in Europe, Asia and Latin America.

II Producer/Consumer Organisations

2.1 Introduction

In Chapter 2, I introduced the Energy Charter Treaty (ECT) as a regional instrument which organises investment, trade and transit in energy, which together with the foundational rules defining and allocating powers over energy, form the main components of international energy transactions. The ECT could also feature in this section as an instrument organising the relations between producer countries (mostly those arising from the former USSR) and consumer countries (mostly from the EU). The grand bargain underpinning the ECT was indeed the alignment of consumer countries' energy security needs and producer countries' market access. From an institutional perspective, however, the ECT operates very differently from the producer-only and consumer-only organisations analysed in this section. First and foremost, the ECT was not designed to advance the interests of one group (producers or consumers) only. Moreover, its institutions display a weak steering role and lack normative power to any significant degree, and its focus is on energy in general, mostly fossil fuels but also, to some extent, nuclear energy and increasingly renewables, given the lack of specificity of the ECT standards.

In contrast, producer and consumer organisations were specifically created to advance or protect the interests of a group of States against another. They are 'partial' organisations by definition, as they exclude those States against which the organisation's activities are expected to be deployed. The two main examples concern oil and gas. The organisations relating to oil are old and well developed. The rise of OPEC since 1960 is closely linked to the rise in international law of the 'Permanent Sovereignty' movement, itself a result of the decolonisation and development processes. The establishment of the IEA in 1974 was, in turn, a direct response to weaponisation of oil supply by the Arab members of OPEC, the Organization of Arab Petroleum Exporting Countries (OAPEC), during the 1973 Arab-Israeli war. With the end of the Cold War, the IEF was increasingly developed and formalised to bring these two groups together. Not every major producer of fossil fuels is part of these organisations. Most notably, the USSR and then Russia remained outside OPEC, although it has sometimes agreed to cut production in deals under the framework of the so-called OPEC+.

In the next sections, my discussion of proto-centralisation through producer/consumer organisation focusses on oil, with only a brief reference to the more embryonic institutionalisation in the area of gas.

2.2 Proto-Centralisation in the International Governance of Oil

2.2.1 The 1960 Organization of Petroleum Exporting Countries (OPEC)

2.2.1.1 Overview The emergence, structure and changing role of the OPEC have been examined in an extensive body of literature.[1] Widely

[1] See D. H. Claes, G. Garavini (eds.), *Handbook of OPEC and the Global Energy Order: Past, Present and Future Challenges* (London: Routledge, 2020); G. Garavini, *The Rise and Fall of OPEC in the Twentieth Century* (Oxford University Press, 2019); F. Parra, *Oil Politics: A Modern History of Petroleum* (London: I.B. Tauris, 2009); D. H. Claes, *The Politics of Oil-Producer Cooperation* (Boulder: Westview Press, 2001); J. Amuzegar, *Managing the Oil Wealth: OPEC's Windfalls and Pitfalls* (London: I.B. Tauris, 1999); L. Lugo, *La singular historia de la OPEP* (Caracas: Ediciones CEPET, 1994); D. Yergin, *The Prize: The Epic Quest for Oil, Money, and Power* (New York: Free Press, 1991); J. Skeet, *OPEC: Twenty-Five Years of Prices and Politics* (Cambridge: Cambridge University Press, 1988); I. Seymour, *OPEC: Instrument of Change* (London: Palgrave Macmillan, 1980); Z. M. Mikdashi, *The Community of Oil Exporting Countries: A Study in Governmental Cooperation* (Ithaca: Cornell University Press, 1972); F. Rouhani, *A History of OPEC* (New York: Praeger, 1971); E. Acosta Hermoso, *Análisis Histórico de la OPEC* (Merida: Universidad de Los Andes, 1969); J. P. Perez Alfonzo, *El Pentágono Petrolero* (Caracas: Ediciones Revista Politica,1967). From the specific perspective of law see L. Moos, 'Organization of Petroleum Exporting Countries (OPEC)' (2011) *MPEPIL*; J. P. Terhechte, *OPEC und europäisches Wettbewerbsrecht: Zugleich ein Beitrag zum Phänomen der Fragmentierung des internationalen Wirtschaftsrechts* (Baden-Baden: Nomos, 2008); L. E. Cuervo, 'OPEC from Myth to Reality' (2008) 30 *Houston Journal of International Law* 433; L. Stoehr, 'OPEC as a Legal Entity' (1979) 3 *Fordham International Law Journal* 91; M. El-Sayed, *L'Organisation des pays exportateurs de pétrole. Etude d'une organisation internationale pour la défense des intérêts privés des Etats* (Paris: LGDJ, 1967).

different perceptions are at play in these accounts, which portray the OPEC in a more positive or negative light, as a champion of developing and newly independent States or an inefficient cartel of authoritarian 'petrostates' where ruling elites deprive their population of basic entitlements.

My purpose here is not to survey the relative accuracy of these and other accounts but only to briefly examine five main aspects of the OPEC as part of a proto-centralised oil governance framework, namely (1) the reasons explaining its emergence, (2) its embeddedness in the wider international legal developments of the time, (3) its structure and powers, (4) its evolving role since the time of its establishment and (5) some legal problems that have emerged from it.

2.2.1.2 The Origins of the OPEC The origins of the OPEC must be sought in a range of factors, most notably the increasing demand for oil in the post-1945 world, but also the growing realisation of its abundance and uneven distribution at the global level as well as, above all, the virtually full control over pricing exercised by the oligopoly formed by the so-called seven sisters, the main international oil companies which controlled the main oil concessions.[2]

From a historical perspective, the idea preceded the decolonisation and development movement. Venezuela, as a major exporter of oil to the United States and the United Kingdom realised that, with the discovery of vast oil reserves in the Persian Gulf extractable at a much lower price, it was critical to enter into some form of coordination agreement with Gulf States to keep production and therefore prices at a stable and satisfactory level. With international companies controlling oil pricing in ways which were opaque and detached from actual production costs, and with the prevailing 'concessions system', whereby home States received benefits only by means of a combination of royalties and taxes depending on the oil price, a change in the overall legal architecture applicable to oil became increasingly pressing. The production and pricing control issues, as economic considerations, were soon exacerbated by the decolonisation and development movements. The Arab nationalism catalysed by the 1956 Suez crisis, in which Egypt's ruler Gamal Abdel Nasser nationalised the Anglo-French Suez Canal company and managed to see off an attempted

[2] A. Sampson, *The Seven Sisters: The Great Oil Companies and the World They Shaped* (New York: Viking, 1975).

intervention from France, the United Kingdom and Israel, further lent momentum to the efforts to control oil resources.[3]

The immediate trigger was a sequence of events between 1959 and 1960. In April 1959, the first Arab Petroleum Congress, held in Cairo, adopted a resolution known as the 'Maadi Pact', named after the Cairo suburb of Maadi, calling on oil majors to consult with producer countries before taking unilateral decisions on pricing.[4] Yet, on 9 April 1960, one of the oil majors (New Jersey Standard) announced a unilateral reduction of the price of Saudi crude oil, i.e. a reduction of the price on which the country's revenues were calculated. This unilateral move caused great exasperation in producer countries. It has been characterised by historians of the OPEC as the 'equivalent to the murder of Archduke Ferdinand in Sarajevo',[5] which catalysed the outbreak of the first world war. In this context, Abd al-Karim Qassim, the new nationalist ruler of Iraq, convened an international conference in Baghdad, with the participation of Iran, Kuwait, Saudi Arabia, and Venezuela, which gave birth to the OPEC.

2.2.1.3 The OPEC and the Permanent Sovereignty Movement From the perspective of international law, the creation of the OPEC was a major stepping-stone in the 'Permanent Sovereignty' movement. As noted in a recent historical account, OPEC was the first 'global South' organisation – to use today's terminology – set up to advance the interests of developing and newly independent countries.[6] The Non-Aligned Movement, established in early September of 1961,[7] and the UN Conference on Trade and Development (UNCTAD), established in 1964,[8] were further manifestations of the effort by an emerging majority of countries to change the rules of the game.

[3] Yergin, *The Prize*, chapter 24.

[4] Garavini, *The Rise and Fall of OPEC*, at 114–115.

[5] Garavini, *The Rise and Fall of OPEC*, at 118, quoting the analogy made by Skeet, *OPEC*, at 6.

[6] Garavini, *The Rise and Fall of OPEC*, at 89.

[7] See J. Dinkel, *The Non-Aligned Movement: Genesis, Organization and Politics (1927–1992)* (Leiden: Brill, 2019).

[8] Proceedings of the United Nations Conference on Trade and Development, Geneva, 23 March–16 June 1964, vol. I, Final Act and Report, E/CONF.46/141, Vol. I. See UNCTAD, *The History of UNCTAD. 1964–1984* (New York: UN, 1984); D. Cordovez, 'The Making of UNCTAD' (1967) 1 *Journal of World Trade Law* 243.

At a more granular level, the tension between oil needs (by consumer countries) and oil pricing (which was in the hands of international oil companies) was visible already in the wording of some early UN General Assembly resolutions. In the early 1950s, the assertion of a right to exploit national resources in the national interest was not as obvious as it may appear today. Schrijver provides an illuminating example concerning the drafting history of what became UN General Assembly Resolution 523 (VI).[9] The draft proposed by Poland stated that 'under-developed countries' have the full right to determine freely the use of their natural resources. The United States opposed this formulation and proposed an amendment adding a reference to 'the interests of an expanding world economy'. The final compromise text, brokered by Egypt, India and Indonesia, referred to both the national interest and that of the world economy.[10] Schrijver notes that, quite remarkably, this resolution states for the first time the 'right' of under-developed countries to determine freely the use of their natural resources and for the first *and last* time the obligation to use such resources not only in their national interest but also to further the expansion of the world economy.[11]

The 1953 UK- and US-sponsored coup in Iran against M. Mossadegh, who had nationalised the Anglo-Iranian Oil Company (AOIC), came as a stark reminder that the free use of national resources remained politically very delicate. Two years earlier, the United Kingdom had filed a claim against Iran before the ICJ to protect AOIC's interests.[12] Yet, over the course of the 1960s, oil majors' control over the pricing of oil was increasingly challenged, as a result of concerted action by oil producers, most notably through the establishment of the OPEC. From a legal standpoint, such challenge found expression in the

[9] 'Integrated economic development and commercial agreements', 12 January 1952, UN Doc. A/RES/523(VI) (Resolution 523 (VI)).

[10] Resolution 523 (VI), first preambular paragraph ('under-developed countries have the right to determine freely the use of their natural resources and that they must utilize such resources in order to be in a better position to further the realization of their plans of economic development in accordance with their national interests, and to further the expansion of the world economy').

[11] See N. Schrijver, *Sovereignty over Natural Resources. Balancing Rights and Duties* (Cambridge: Cambridge University Press, 1997), at 37ff.

[12] The ICJ ordered provisional measures in 1951 but it subsequently declined jurisdiction to hear the claim on the merits. See *Anglo-Iranian Oil Co. case (jurisdiction)*, judgment of 22 July 1952, ICJ Reports I952, p. 93.

adoption of UN General Assembly Resolution 1803 (XVII) on 'Permanent Sovereignty over Natural Resources'.[13]

The tension, as I shall discuss later, lied in the fact that oil majors controlled the price of a wasting (non-renewable) asset and an increase in production had a dual effect, on the one hand pushing the market price downwards (thus depleting oil reserves at low prices) while, on the other hand, increasing the revenues, however inefficiently, of rentier States. This tension explains why OPEC's efforts to achieve both production and pricing control lacked traction, for most of the 1960s, with Iran and Saudi Arabia accepting the rentier position whereas Indonesia and Iraq attempted to gain control over production.

2.2.1.4 Structure and Powers The OPEC is an intergovernmental organisation created by agreement of its five initial members (Founder Members), namely Iraq, Iran, Kuwait, Saudi Arabia and Venezuela,[14] and later joined by several others (called Full Members) accepted by OPEC's Conference.

Overall, it has at the time of writing thirteen members. Over time, some States have suspended/reactivated (and sometimes suspended again) their membership or withdrawn from/rejoined the organisation. Under Article 7.C of the OPEC Statute, membership is open to States meeting two main criteria, which have never been authoritatively defined, namely 'a substantial net export of crude petroleum' and 'fundamentally similar interests to those of Member Countries', and subject to a three-fourths majority vote of Full Members, including all Founder Members. The Statute also allows the possibility of Associate Membership in case a State does not meet the 'substantial net export' criterion, but the 'similar interest' criterion cannot be set aside.

The organisation has three main organs (Article 9): a Conference, a Board of Governors and a Secretariat, originally based in Geneva but moved to Vienna in 1965. The Conference consists of State delegations (normally led by ministers) and it adopts its resolutions by unanimity (Article 11.C). The Statute does not clarify whether resolutions are binding, although, as I will discuss later, there are several indications

[13] 'Permanent sovereignty over natural resources', 14 December 1962, UN Doc. A/RES/1803/XVII (Resolution 1803 (XVII)).

[14] Statute of the Organization of Petroleum Exporting Countries (OPEC), 10–14 September 1960. The Statute was adopted at the second conference, held in Caracas in January 1961, Resolution II.6 (OPEC Statute).

that this is indeed the case. The Statute also contemplates the possibility to convene consultative meetings (Article 35) and establish specialised organs (Article 36).

2.2.1.5 Evolving Practice The role played by the organisation in guiding the policies and practices of oil producer countries is best understood by reference to the actual practice of OPEC, which also unveils the major fault-lines underlying it.

For most of the 1960s, despite the attempts of States such as Iraq, Indonesia and Venezuela to push for a much more assertive OPEC, most OPEC countries tended to accept the drive towards increasing production to satisfy the growing demand for oil around the world. Iran and Saudi Arabia, in particular, preferred to let foreign oil companies increase production under slightly improved terms[15] so as to use the associated revenue in their efforts to modernise their societies.[16]

By the end of the 1960s, however, OPEC managed to get its act together. The catalyst was the anti-Israel and anti-US sentiment generated by the 1967 Six-Day war waged by Israel against Egypt, Jordan and Syria. The massive reaction of the populations of Arab OPEC members and the growing criticism against their leaders led the latter to confront foreign oil companies, largely as a way of leveraging the popular sentiment to consolidate their position. First, a sub-set of OPEC Members established the Organization of Arab Petroleum Exporting Countries (OAPEC) in 1967, which imposed an initial – largely unsuccessful – embargo in 1967 and later took the lead in the major 1973 oil embargo. Within OPEC, in 1968, the organisation adopted a Declaratory Statement of Petroleum Policy in Member States,[17] which was premised on Resolution 1803 (XVII) on 'Permanent Sovereignty over Natural Resources' and called on members to: assume production as much as possible; seek equal 'participation', if necessary through a redefinition of the relationship with foreign oil companies (based on the 'change of circumstances' argument);

[15] A 1964 'Supplementary Agreement' confirmed the concessions while at the same time accepting the principle that royalties would be treated as expenses (rather than merely deducted from income tax), with non-negligible financial implications for producer countries, taking the total government income per barrel from USD 80 to 83 cents. Garavini, *The Rise and Fall of OPEC*, at 154.

[16] See S. Hertog, 'Shaping the Saudi State: Human Agency's Shifting Role in Rentier-State Formation' (2007) 39 *International Journal of Middle East Studies* 539.

[17] OPEC, Resolution XVI. 90: Declaratory Statement of Petroleum Policy in Member States', 24–25 June 1968, *OPEC Official Resolutions and Press Releases 1960–1990*, 61.

ensure 'indexation' of posted prices (on which oil revenues were calculated) to reflect the deteriorating terms of trade (with raw materials losing value relatively to manufactures); and use best available oil conservation practices, potentially paving the way for cuts in production.

The Declaratory Statement inaugurated a decade of successful assertiveness, during which OPEC members managed first to impose new taxation conditions,[18] then 'weaponise' oil supply through the 1973 oil embargo imposed by OAPEC members on Western States supporting Israel in the Yom Kippur War, and then nationalise oil resources around the mid 1970s. This assertiveness was formalised in the Solemn Declaration adopted during the 1975 Algiers Summit,[19] which challenged the recriminations that the ongoing economic crisis had been a result of the oil embargo and declared the willingness of OPEC members to cooperate with consumers, now organised under the umbrella of the IEA. The 1970s ended with a new display of supply control power following the 1979 Iranian Revolution, which deposed the Shah.

The rise of the OPEC's power during the 1970s made, however, its downfall over the 1980s all the more resounding. In early 1986, the price of oil decreased to as little as USD 10 per barrel as a result of a combination of factors, including economic recession, the rise of 'alternative' sources (both non-OPEC oil and other energy sources), and the increase in production by Saudi Arabia to capture back the market from non-OPEC producers as well as to punish higher-cost OPEC producers which had failed to comply with production quotas.[20]

Major fluctuations in the price of oil have remained a feature of world politics since then. The 1990s and 2000s saw a strong increase in prices (with Brent reaching USD 140 per barrel in early June 2008) driven not

[18] OPEC Resolution XXI.120 Calling for Negotiations and Forming Three-Member Negotiating Committee, 9–12 December 1971, I.L.M. vol. 10/2 (March 1971), pp. 240–254; OPEC Resolution XXII.131 Calling for Legislative Measures in the Event No Agreement is Reached with Oil Companies, 3–4 February 1971, I.L.M. vol. 10/2 (March 1971), pp. 240–254. Resolution XXI.120 (1971) agreed to a harmonised increase in the taxation (a minimum tax rate of 55 per cent on net income) and the posted prices across members, and Resolution XXI.131 (1971) called for members to implement these changes through legislative measures and to impose them on oil companies, if necessary, through an embargo. These resolutions were followed by the Tehran Price Agreement of 14 February 1971 with oil companies, in which the latter accepted the new conditions.

[19] OPEC Solemn Declarations (Algiers 1975, Caracas 2000, Riyadh 2007), available at: www.opec.org/.

[20] See D. Basosi, G. Garavini, M. Trentin (eds.), *Counter-Shock. The Oil Counter-Revolution of the 1980s* (London: I.B. Tauris, 2018).

only by specific events, e.g. the 1990–1991 Gulf War and the 2003 US-led invasion of Iraq, but also deeper and longer-term trends, such as the rapid development undergone by China. An attempt to stabilise the price between USD 22–28 per barrel was introduced in 2000 in the form of a price-band mechanism, but by 2005 it had become clear that such mechanism was unrealistic, and it was discontinued.[21] Then, in 2010, in response to what was widely seen as a 'rollercoaster ride' of very high and then very low prices, the Ministerial Conference adopted a new 'Long-Term Strategy',[22] on the occasion of OPEC's fiftieth anniversary. It reaffirmed the overall goal of a 'fair and stable prices' and presented three projections of future oil demand, while referring to – indeed downplaying – non-OPEC production and environmental concerns.

Ironically, these two aspects were bound to become decisive in the subsequent decade, with the 'shale revolution' mostly in the United States[23] and the massive investment in low-carbon technologies driving down oil demand.[24] The two aspects are interlinked to the extent that declining or 'peak' oil demand exacerbates the competition between OPEC and non-OPEC producers for what may remain of the market in the future. Hence the efforts by both groups to establish some form of cooperation on the level of production through the adoption of a Declaration of Cooperation (DoC) on 10 December 2016,[25] followed by a Charter of Cooperation (CoC) signed on 2 July 2019. Yet, cooperation has been difficult, as shown by the 'price war' between Saudi Arabia and Russia in April 2020, triggered by a disagreement on production adjustments.[26]

[21] The suspension of the price-band mechanism at the 134th (Extraordinary) Meeting of the OPEC Conference was dubbed the 'New Realism'. See *OPEC Bulletin*, vol. XXXVI, No. 2 (February 2005).

[22] OPEC Long-Term Strategy, 14 October 2010, available at: www.opec.org/.

[23] See R. Manning, *The Shale Revolution and the New Geopolitics of Energy* (Washington DC: Atlantic Council, 2014).

[24] J.-F. Mercure et al, 'Macroeconomic impact of stranded fossil-fuel assets' (2018) 8 *Nature Climate Change* 588.

[25] Declaration of Cooperation OPEC and non-OPEC, 10 December 2016, adopted at the first OPEC and non-OPEC Ministerial Meeting [DoC]. Under the DoC, the OPEC members agreed to reduce their production by 1,200,000 barrels a day and non-OPEC States agreed to a combined first reduction adjustment of production of 558,000 barrels a day for a specified period, subsequently extended.

[26] J. Yaffa, 'How the Russia–Saudi Oil War Went Awry – for Putin Most of All', *The New Yorker* (15 April 2020).

2.2.1.6 Selected Legal Questions Moving to some of the legal questions that have arisen over time, one concerns the legal characterisation of the instruments (resolutions) whereby production levels are agreed by OPEC Members as well as by OPEC and non-OPEC States under the cooperation framework.

Regarding the former, the OPEC Statute expressly states that resolutions from the (Ministerial) Conference become 'effective' after thirty days or such period of time stated in the resolution (Article 11C). Article 4 speaks of 'sanctions' emerging from the implementation of decisions adopted by the organisation. This is an indication that such decisions display, under the Statute, a binding character. There are three important caveats to this. The first is that resolutions can only be adopted by unanimity, thus effectively subordinating the binding character to the consent of the State. The second is that States may, within a prescribed period, send 'notification to the contrary', i.e. express their lack of consent even after the meeting. Thirdly, although the term 'effective' remains ambiguous, the reference in Article 3 of the OPEC Statute to 'good faith' must itself be understood as emphasising the binding character of treaties, as per the rule codified in Article 26 of the Vienna Convention on the Law of Treaties.[27] Thus, the obligations assumed under the Statute, including those arising from effective resolutions, must be considered binding.[28] Moreover, depending on the circumstances, decisions adopted by unanimity could also constitute 'treaties' under general international law and the Vienna Convention. This said, the terms of a resolution may make some of its provisions expressly voluntary and, in all events, the organisation has no enforcement powers to bring a non-compliant State into compliance.

With respect to production levels agreed under the cooperative framework with non-OPEC countries, these are voluntary in nature but their implementation is monitored by a Joint Ministerial Monitoring Committee (JMMC), consisting of three OPEC (Algeria, Kuwait and Venezuela) and two non-OPEC members (Oman and Russia), with the participation of Saudi Arabia as the OPEC Conference president in 2017.[29]

[27] 'Every treaty in force is binding upon the parties to it and must be performed by them in good faith'

[28] See El-Sayed, *L'Organisation des pays exportateurs de pétrole*, at 136; Stoehr, *OPEC as a Legal Entity*, at 94–95.

[29] Declaration of Cooperation OPEC and non-OPEC, p. 3.

The nature of the production control measures discussed so far has wider implications for trade, investment and anti-trust law. There has been some debate as to whether OPEC production control measures may amount to quantitative restrictions in violation of Article XI of the GATT.[30] Similarly, domestic measures adopted in pursuance of an OPEC resolution would be required by an international treaty and therefore, in case of inconsistency with an investment treaty, the relevant rules of conflict would escape the subordination of domestic law to international law.[31] As for antitrust legal suits, price-setting action by the OPEC has been challenged before US federal courts since 1979, either in cases against the OPEC itself[32] or in proceedings against national oil companies.[33]

2.2.2 The Consumers' Response: The International Energy Agency (IEA)

2.2.2.1 Origins of the IEA In early October 1973, as Israel prepared to celebrate Yom Kippur, a joint Egyptian-Syrian military offensive took Israel forces by surprise making rapid military gains in the North and South. However, over the following days, the odds of battle reversed, partly due to the massive support offered by the United States to Israel. In this context, at a meeting of OPEC Members held on 16–17 October, the Arab members of the OPEC, organised under the OAPEC, decided to cut

[30] See T. Carey, 'Cartel Price Controls vs Free Trade: A Study of Proposals to Challenge OPEC's Influence in the Oil Market through WTO Dispute Settlement' (2009) 24 *American University International Law Review* 783.

[31] VCLT, art 27.

[32] See *International Association of Machinists and Aerospace Workers (IAM) v. Organization of Petroleum Exporting Countries (OPEC)*, US District Court Central District of California (18 September 1979) 477 F Supp 553 (dismissed on the basis of the sovereign immunity doctrine), upheld on appeal but on the basis of the Act of State doctrine. See *International Association of Machinists and Aerospace Workers (IAM) v. Organization of Petroleum Exporting Countries (OPEC)*, US Court of Appeals Ninth Circuit (6 July 1981) 649 F 2d 1354. See also *Prewitt Enterprises Inc v. Organization of Petroleum Exporting Countries*, US District Court Northern District of Alabama (2001) 2001 US Dist Lexis 414; *Prewitt Enterprises Inc v. Organization of Petroleum Exporting Countries*, Court of Appeals Eleventh Circuit (18 December 2003) 353 F 3d 916. For an overview see S. W. Waller, 'Suing OPEC' (2002) 64 *University of Pittsburgh Law Review* 105.

[33] *In re Refined Petroleum Products Antitrust Litigation*, United States District Court, S.D. Texas (9 January 2009), 649 F. Supp. 2d 572 (S.D. Tex. 2009) (dismissed on the basis of the Act of State doctrine), subsequently upheld on appeal in *Spectrum Stores, Inc. v. Citgo Petroleum Corp.*, Fifth Circuit Court of Appeals Fifth Circuit (8 February 2011), 632 F.3d 938.

exports of oil across the world by 5 per cent. Over the following days, a total embargo of oil exports was imposed on the United States and some other countries, such as The Netherlands, Portugal and South Africa. OAPEC production cuts of 25 per cent were also introduced in early November, alongside a segmentation of consumer countries: preferred countries, which would receive shipments at the pre-October levels; neutral countries, which would receive less than their requested quotas; and embargoed countries, such as the United States.[34]

Following what became known as the 'oil crisis', the United States tried to reconstitute and enhance the bargaining power of consumer countries by means of an international initiative, unveiled in a Conference held in Washington in February 1974 and eventually formalised in November 1974. This initiative gave birth to the International Energy Agency (IEA),[35] which was established under the aegis of the OECD[36] to broaden its basis and avoid a US-centred perception. Although the IEA Statute formally entered into force in 1976, it became provisionally applicable right after its adoption in 1974 as a result of Article 68(1).

The proto-centralised governance approach organised around the IEA can be introduced by reference to three main aspects, namely (1) the measures to manage oil supply and demand, (2) other expressions of the

[34] See Garavini, *The Rise and Fall of OPEC*, at 217ff. On the oil crises see further G. J. Ikenberry, *Reasons of State: Oil Politics and the Capacity of American Government* (Ithaca: Cornell University Press, 2015).

[35] Agreement on an International Energy Program, 18 November 1974, 1040 UNTS 272 [IEA Statute], chapter IX. On the legal aspects of the IEA see particularly: R. Scott, *History of the International Energy Agency 1974–1994: The First Twenty Years, vols. I-III* (Paris: IEA, 1994–1995) (volume III provides a compilation of several important legal instruments); C. Bamberger, *History of the International Energy Agency 1974–2004: The First Thirty Years, vol. IV. Supplement to volumes I, II & III* (Paris: IEA, 2004). On the broader governance dimension see T. van den Graaf, 'Obsolete or resurgent? The International Energy Agency in a changing global landscape' (2012) 48 *Energy Policy* 233; A. Florini, 'The International Energy Agency in Global Energy Governance' (2011) 2 *Global Policy* 40; W. L. Kohl, 'Consumer country energy cooperation: the International Energy Agency and the global energy order', in A. Goldthau, J.-M. Witte (eds.), Global Energy Governance: The New Rules of the Game (Washington DC: Brookings Institution Press, 2010), pp. 195–220; T. van den Graaf, D. Lesage, 'The International Energy Agency after 35 years: Reform needs and institutional adaptability' (2009) 4 *The Review of International Organizations* 302; R. O. Keohane, 'The International Energy Agency: State Influence and Transgovernmental Politics' (1978) 32 *International Organization* 929; U. Lantzke, 'The OECD and its International Energy Agency' (1975) 104 *Daedalus* 217.

[36] OECD Council Decision Establishing an International Energy Agency, 18 November 1974, OECD Document C(74)203(Final).

IEA's normative power and (3) the IEA's changing focus as a result of the changing geopolitics of energy.

2.2.2.2 IEA Oil Shortage Management Measures Regarding the first aspect, the main element of the IEA was a collective emergency response system, whereby State members are required to maintain 'emergency reserves sufficient to sustain consumption' for at least ninety days (Article 2(1)–(2)). Compliance with this requirement is monitored by a Standing Group on Emergency Questions (Article 4(1)). In addition, participating States are required to maintain a contingency plan for oil demand restraint so as to be able, if necessary, to reduce their consumption (Article 5(1)). Thus, the IEA is able to intervene on both oil supply (through release and allocation of reserves) and demand (consumption reduction).

Chapter IV of the IEA Statute governs the 'activation' of the mechanism, which follows a reduction of oil supplies (Article 13, 14 and 17) ascertained as such by the Secretariat (Articles 19(1) and 23(1)), which results in an allocation of the reserves across different participant countries governed by chapter III.

Significantly, this mechanism has never been formally used. In three cases, however, the IEA intervened to manage pressures in the oil market arising from the 1991 Gulf War, hurricanes Katrina and Rita in 2005, and the Libyan civil war in 2011. Such interventions were organised around the more informal 'coordinated emergency response measures' (CERM) approach, introduced in 1984 decision of the IEA's Governing Board.[37]

2.2.2.3 The Broader Normative Power of the IEA The normative power of the IEA has found further expression through the power conferred on the Governing Board to adopt both binding decisions (Article 52(1) IEA Statute) and non-binding recommendations (Article 52(2)). Although the Board has made more frequent use of the latter, the former have provided an important basis for the development of the agency.

[37] IEA Governing Board, Decision on Stocks and Supply Disruptions, 11 July 1984, IEA/GB (84)27, Item 2(a) and Annex I. See also the following decisions of the IEA Governing Board: Decision on Preparation for Future Supply Disruptions, 10 December 1981, IEA/GB(81)86, Item 2 and Annex I; Decision Adopting CERM Operations Manual, 13 September 1988, IEA/GB(88)25, Item 2(b)(ii); Decision on Emergency Response Policies, 22 February 1995, IEA/GB(95)11, Item 4 and the Common Explanation of the Decision, 10 March 1995.

One important example is the decision establishing the Programme of Long-Term Co-operation on energy (LTCP).[38] Chapter III, section A of the LTCP provided for the periodic review of the national diversification programmes and policies of participant countries, which has grown over time to become one of the main activities of the IEA. The review is conducted by a Standing Group on Long-Term Co-operation (SLT) established by section II.2(a) of the LTCP, but already contemplated in Article 49(1) of the IEA Statute. As other IEA Standing Groups, the SLT is composed of State representatives, making the review process a peer-review. Importantly, the comparative review of policies over several decades, which now extends beyond IEA's Members, has also allowed the agency to build substantial and highly sought-after expertise.

Since its early days, the IEA has also coordinated a vast programme of technological collaboration through facilitated 'Implementing Agreements', referred today as the Technology Collaboration Programme (TCP). The programme was first introduced in 1976,[39] together with the establishment of a Committee on Energy Research and Technology (CERT).[40] As of 2017, there were close to forty IEA Technology Collaboration Programmes, on matters as diverse as advanced fuel cells, clean energy education and empowerment, district heating and cooling, energy storage, nuclear fusion or geothermal.[41]

Last but not least, the IEA is widely perceived as a data and analysis powerhouse of issues relating to energy and economic development at large, not just oil. Its flagship annual report, the *World Energy Outlook* (WEO), as well as other reports and analytical products, e.g. the *Energy Technology Perspectives*, display a different form of normative effect, akin to that of promotion organisations (see Section III).

[38] IEA Governing Board, Decision adopting the Long-Term Co-operation Programme, 29–30 January 1976, IEA/GB(76)5, Item 2.

[39] IEA Governing Board, Guiding Principles for Co-operation in the Field of Energy Research and Development, 30 January 1976, as amended, Annex II. These Guiding Principles were replaced in April 2003 with a 'Framework for International Energy Technology Co-operation', IEA/GB/C(2003)3, Item 8, and IEA/GB(2003)6/REV2.

[40] IEA Governing Board, Decision on the Establishment of the Committee on Energy Research and Technology (CERT), 20–21 December 1975, initially as the Committee on Energy Research and Development (CRD), IEA/GB(75)94, Item 7 and Annex II.

[41] See the appendix to the FAQs on this programme: https://delegates.iea.org/delegates/media/protected/iaforum/TCPnamesFAQ12Dec17.pdf. For an analysis of the IEA's TCP see T. Hattori, H. Nam, 'Essence of Multilateral Energy Technology Collaboration: A Case Study of the International Energy Agency (IEA) Technology Collaboration Programmes (TCPs)', *KIER Discussion Papers No. 1023* (March 2020).

2.2.2.4 Evolving Practice The focus of the IEA has changed substantially over the last four decades. Designed and operated first and foremost to prevent and manage potential oil supply shocks in consumer countries, i.e. with an energy security purpose, the agency was widely perceived until the early 2000s as lacking credibility to inform the transition from a fossil fuels-based (its main historical focus) to a low-carbon economy. That perception has not entirely dissipated today despite the major efforts made by the IEA to expand its scope of work and collaborations, including a joint IEA/IRENA Renewable Energy Policies and Measures Database.[42]

In a speech delivered in 2009 on the occasion of the thirty-fifth anniversary of the IEA, Henry Kissinger, who as US Secretary of State during the 1973 oil crisis masterminded the system of the agency, observed that the IEA was at a 'critical juncture'.[43] New realities, particularly the growing role of countries such as China and India, as consumers, but also other countries as producers, the increasing challenges involved in producing less readily available fossil fuels, and climate change, all required the IEA to rethink its role.

With the benefit of hindsight, not all of these challenges have the same future relevance. Fears relating to peak oil supply or to increasing cost of less readily available deposits have to some extent subsided, first with the 'shale revolution', which changed the oil supply landscape for geopolitical purposes, and secondly with the growing understanding of a coming peak in fossil fuel demand (not supply).[44] Yet, wider engagement and climate change remain pressing challenges, and the implications of the latter may require the IEA to focus not on oil supply shocks but on the management of demand shocks, price wars potentially driving significant parts of the industry (higher-cost producers, such as the shale sector) to bankruptcy.

Recognising the changing landscape, in November 2015, an IEA Ministerial Meeting endorsed Executive Director F. Birol's three-pillar modernisation strategy, which rests on three 'pillars', namely 'enhanced engagement with major emerging economies, strengthened and

42 See the IEA's Policy Database: www.iea.org/policies/about.

43 Speech by Henry Kissinger at the IEA Ministerial, 14 October 2009.

44 See J.F. Mercure et al, 'Macroeconomic impact of stranded fossil fuel assets' (2018) 8 *Nature Climate Change* 588.

broadened commitment to energy security, and greater focus on clean energy technology, including energy efficiency'.[45]

Despite some significant efforts to expand its country base, such as the introduction of a new status, that of 'Association', for countries of particular interest to the IEA, including China, India, Indonesia, Morocco, Singapore or Thailand, the IEA is far from having reached the degree of representativeness and centrality of an organisation such as the International Atomic Energy Agency. Formally, its normative power remains limited to IEA members, who are mostly energy consumers. Yet, as discussed next, the IEA and the OPEC Member States have increased their interactions through a neutral forum, the International Energy Forum.

2.2.3 Producer–Consumer Dialogue: The International Energy Forum (IEF)

2.2.3.1 Origins of the IEF The establishment of producers-only and consumers-only organisations, and their specific institutional design, did little to dissipate the atmosphere of distrust and confrontation that followed the oil crises of the 1970s. The initiative of the French government to convene, in the mid 1970s, a conference bringing together producers and consumers[46] was a failure, which left the general impression that such cooperation was not possible.

A second window of opportunity was offered by the Gulf War in the early 1990s. The conflict had the effect of removing some 5 million barrels of oil from overall supply raising fears of a new oil crisis. A key consideration was whether OPEC producers should increase production

[45] Summary of the Chair, the Honorable Ernest J. Moniz, Secretary of Energy, IEA Ministerial Meeting, 17–18 November 2015, para. 5.

[46] The Conference on International Economic Co-operation (CIEC) was held in Paris in sessions spanning from 1975 to 1977. Born from divisions within consumer countries, with France favouring engagement with OPEC countries rather than the more confrontational approach taken by the United States through the IEA system, the initiative also generated divisions within oil producers. In the end, a major fault line between the narrow focus on oil favoured by the West and the wider focus on economic and monetary relations sought by producers and a wider range of developing countries, made progress impossible. In the early hours of 3 June 1977, the Conference 'came to a battered and confused end [. . .] [a]n 18-month "dialogue" between the rich North and the poor South, which had begun with much enthusiasm and great hope in Paris, finished on a faint and joyless note', J. Amuzegar, 'A Requiem for the North-South Conference' (1977) 56 *Foreign Affairs* 136. On the CIEC see G. Williams, 'The Conference on International Economic Cooperation (CIEC) 1975–7', in *Third-World Political Organizations* (London: Palgrave Macmillan, 1981), pp. 91–98.

to compensate for the shortfall or IEA members should activate the release of strategic stocks.[47] In this context, France and Venezuela decided to convene a seminar in Paris, in early July 1991, which, as in the 1970s, was opposed by the United States. Yet, gradually, this initial step paved the way for increased interactions between IEA's Executive Director R. Priddle and OPEC Secretary-General R. Lukman.

It took a decade, however, before the heads of these two organisations felt comfortable enough to host a joint press conference. In September 2002, they appeared together at the World Petroleum Congress, held in Rio de Janeiro.[48] By then, there was a more solid basis for cooperation, particularly as regards joint data gathering, and the possibility, raised by Saudi Arabia during the seventh International Energy Forum meeting, to establish a Permanent Secretariat to further institutionalise the forum.[49] This proposal was endorsed in the eighth IEF Meeting, held in Osaka in 2002, and the IEF Secretariat was effectively established in Riyadh, in 2003.[50]

The last step in the construction of the IEF came as a result of the 'rollercoaster ride' undergone by the price of oil between mid 2008 and early 2009. Oil price volatility prompted several producer-consumer States meetings and, eventually, at the twelfth IEF Meeting held in Cancun in March 2010, the closing ministerial declaration approved a project for an 'enhanced IEF framework to sustain and reinforce the commitment of producer and consumer states to the informal dialogue'.[51] The project, appended to the ministerial declaration as Attachment I, recommended the adoption of a 'Charter of the International Energy Forum'. The Charter was effectively adopted on 22 February 2011, at an extraordinary meeting of the IEF.[52]

2.2.3.2 Structure and Powers The Charter clarifies the nature, purposes and organs of the IEF. The IEF is characterised as a 'an intergovernmental arrangement that serves as a neutral facilitator of informal, open, informed and continuing global energy dialogue among its membership of energy producing and energy consuming States, including

[47] IEF, *30 Years of Global Energy Dialogue* (Riyadh: IEF, 2020), at 6.
[48] See the press release IEA/PRESS(02)21.
[49] Bamberger, *History of the IEA*, at 33.
[50] IEF, *30 Years*, at 1.
[51] Cancún Ministerial Declaration, twelfth IEF Meeting, 31 March 2010, para. 4.
[52] International Energy Forum Charter, 22 February 2011, 51 ILM 201 (2012) [IEF Charter].

transit States' (section I.2). The 'objectives' of the IEF are stated in broad aspirational terms (section II), but their core content is market stability and energy security.

The Charter expressly states that it 'does not create any legally binding rights or obligations between or among its members' (section I.3), and implicitly reserves the pre-existing obligations of the latter under the IEA and the OPEC Statutes (section I.4). Membership of the IEF is open to any UN Member State, provided that it notifies its approval of the Charter and its application is accepted by IEF's Executive Board (section III.2). At present, the IEF has seventy-one members, including the traditional producers and consumers, as well as some important countries such as China, India and Russia (but not Brazil), which are not part of either OPEC or the IEA.

The organs of the IEF are listed in section IV.1. In addition to the Secretariat and the Executive Board, the Charter institutionalises the biennial ministerial meetings (section V). Decision-making is to be made by consensus, but when that is not possible decisions can be adopted by a 2/3 majority of parties present and voting (section IV.2). The implications of this clause are limited, however, by the fact that decisions cannot create 'legally binding rights or obligations' (section I.3). But they display certain effects, as illustrated by decisions of the Executive Board approving applications for membership (section VI.1 (b)(i)) or appointing the IEF's Secretary-General (section VI.1(b)(ix)). The Board consists of thirty-one members, out of which twenty-three are permanent and the rest rotate. Permanent members include Saudi Arabia, as host, the eleven largest consumers and the eleven largest producers of oil and gas, according to the latest figures collected by the Secretariat (section VI.2(d)).

In addition, the Charter formalises the connection with the IEA and OPEC Secretariats through an International Support Group (section VIII) and those with the industry through an Industry Advisory Committee (section IX).

2.2.3.3 Evolving Practice Together with the institutionalisation of the producer–consumer dialogue, the IEF Secretariat has traditionally served as a neutral coordinator of the 'Joint Organisations Data Initiative' (JODI), on behalf the IEA, the OPEC, but also of other organisations, such as the GECF, OLADE, the EU Eurostat, APEC and the UN Statistics Division (UNSD).

This initiative, launched in the early 2000s first as the Joint Oil Data Exercise, then renamed as the Joint Oil Data Initiative, then again as the Oil Data Transparency Initiative, and finally as the JODI, has proved to be a powerful confidence building measure over the years and a very useful monthly record of official oil and gas data from both producer and consumer countries. It is intended as an empirical basis to facilitate transparency and market stability, and thereby dissipate distrust and improve decision-making.

The IEA, the OPEC and the IEF also cooperate to host an annual Symposium on Energy Outlooks, which brings together energy experts, oil executives and a range of other stakeholders to discuss issues relating to energy.

Despite the contribution made by the IEF to facilitate relations between producers and consumers, it lacks formal normative power, and its role remains limited to that of a neutral host and broker between two competing groups. In addition, aside from its coordination of the JODI, the IEF also lacks the analytical power and credibility to perform a promotion role akin to that of the IEA.

2.3 Proto-Institutionalisation in the Gas Sector: The Gas Exporter Countries Forum (GECF)

A process of incremental institutionalisation has taken place among some major gas exporting countries leading to the establishment of an intergovernmental organisation, the Gas Exporter Countries Forum (GECF). This process shares some aspects with both the OPEC and the IEF.

Like the process leading to the institutionalisation of the IEF, the GECF began in 2001 in the form of two-track regular meetings, at the ministerial level, involving countries with a similar positioning as gas exporters, and the technical level, through expert meetings bringing together a wider network of gas experts. It was then further institutionalised with the creation of a Liaison Office in 2003 (which later became the GECF's Secretariat, based in Qatar) and then the establishment of an Executive Bureau (which later became the GECF's Executive Board). Finally, like the IEF, an agreement on the functioning of the Gas Exporting Countries Forum (GECF)[53] and a Statute of the GECF were

[53] Agreement on the functioning of the Gas Exporting Countries Forum, 23 December 2008, Qatar Official Gazette, vol. 11, pp. 45ff., 25 November 2009 [GECF Agreement].

adopted at the seventh Ministerial Meeting held in Moscow, in December 2008.[54] The GECF Agreement provides that '[t]he Forum shall have international legal status. It shall have such legal capacity as necessary to exercise its functions and to achieve its purposes'. (Article 1). The GECF Statute identifies, in Article 3(A), that its objective is 'to support the sovereign rights of Member Countries over their natural gas resources and their abilities to independently plan and manage the sustainable, efficient and environmentally conscious development, use and conservation of natural gas resources for the benefit of their peoples'. This objective can only be modified by unanimity.

Unlike the IEF, however, the GECF is a producers' organisation, which makes it similar, from this point of view, to the OPEC. Members of the GECF Agreement include Algeria, Bolivia, Egypt, Equatorial Guinea, Iran, Libya, Nigeria, Qatar, Russia, Trinidad and Tobago, and Venezuela, which together account for some 70 per cent of the world's proven gas reserves, but less than half (46 per cent) of the gas market. Some major gas producers, such as the United States, Australia or Turkmenistan, have remained out of the process. Membership of the GECF can be expanded to '[a]ny gas exporting country sharing the common interests and objectives of the Forum' on the condition that the applicant approves the Statute and that its application is approved by a resolution of the Ministerial Meeting, adopted at a 3/4 majority (Article 6(A)). This majority vote is a departure from the basic rule governing the adoption of resolutions by the Ministerial Meeting, which requires unanimity of members except for procedural decisions, which can be adopted by a simple majority (Article 9(D). Participation as an 'Observer Member' is also possible (Article 6(B)), if approved by a 3/4 majority of the Ministerial Meeting. At present, the following countries are observers: Angola, Azerbaijan, Iraq, Kazakhstan, Malaysia, Norway, Oman, Peru and the United Arab Emirates.

Although the GECF has, quite understandably, been assimilated to the OPEC, the two organisations present some significant differences. The main differences concern the gas market itself and the more embryonic level of institutionalisation, which falls short of enabling the GECF to set production quotas for its members. On the nature of the markets, unlike oil, which has a global market with a largely unified price, the price of gas is regional because a large part of its costs arise from transportation.

[54] The GECF Statute is attached to the GECF Agreement. See Qatar Official Gazette, vol. 11, pp. 45ff., 25 November 2009 [GECF Statute].

Long-distance transportation, when pipelines are unavailable, requires the liquefaction of natural gas to compress it in the form of LNQ. This in turn requires specific technological capabilities as well as suitable carriers and terminals. Moreover, gas is commercialised on the basis of long-term contracts rather than on spot markets. Such contracts are priced by reference to oil prices, but they do not depend to the same extent as oil on short-term demand fluctuations. As a result of these two market features, the ability to affect the price of gas globally through coordinated production action in the short term, in a manner analogous to the oil crises of the 1970s, is much more limited than for oil.[55]

So far, the GECF has played mostly a data gathering and exchange role, rather than attempting a production regulation or price-setting one, for which it has not statutory powers. Its strategic goals, as stated in the 2017 Long-Term Strategy, aim to position the GECF mainly as a promotion organisation, which 'promote[s] natural gas as the fuel of choice', supports information exchange and a common understanding of market conditions, and provides a 'framework for co-operation amongst GECF Member Countries'.[56]

III Promotion Organisations

3.1 *A Complex Institutional Landscape*

The range of institutions, whether organised as intergovernmental organisations or in some other form, which play a role in promoting the development of certain energy sources, products or technologies is daunting. One could say that all the organisations discussed so far in this book have, to a varying degree, some role in energy promotion. From an analytical standpoint, this assertion is, of course, of limited use other than as a warning of the sheer variety and complexity of the institutional landscape. In this introductory section, my purpose is three-fold. First, I clarify the specificities of what I have called 'promotion organisations' so as to somewhat reduce the field of potentially relevant institutions. Secondly, I briefly survey a range of promotion organisations of different natures, including inter-agency and other mixed institutions, which bring

[55] See M. Ratner, 'Gas Exporting Countries Forum (GECF): Cartel Lite?', US Congressional Research Service, IF10939 (2 August 2018).

[56] GECF, The Gas Exporting Countries Forum Long-Term Strategy, Executive Summary, Final, approved by the nineteenth Ministerial Meeting, 4 October 2017, Moscow.

together different types of stakeholders. Thirdly, I single out IRENA as a particularly relevant illustration of an intergovernmental promotion organisation.

Discussions in the literature of global energy governance or the global energy architecture tend to take the form of maps or, in other words, descriptive surveys of the relevant institutions.[57] Each survey has its own focus and hence its own selection of institutions and cartography. My focus in this chapter, and in this book, is on the international law of energy and, specifically, on what I have characterised as a centralised approach, admitting different degrees of centralisation. As noted earlier, a low degree of centralisation, i.e. proto-centralisation, is understood in this context as an institutional arrangement which meets only some of the four definitional features of the centralised approach: (1) an international organisation or agency with a steering role; (2) a focus on an energy resource or form of producing energy; (3) some measure of formal or informal normative power; and (4) a governance framework with a comprehensive scope steered by the organisation. The organisations reviewed in this section meet the first two features. Some enjoy a measure of informal normative power as a result of their knowledge/expertise and/or convening power. Although some of them may be involved in regional or sectoral governance arrangements, none can be said to meet the fourth feature.

Some of the organisations examined earlier, such as the IAEA, the OPEC and the IEA have an important role in promoting specific sources of energy, i.e. nuclear, oil and – increasingly for the IEA – an energy mix. Their promotion role is one part of a wider governance role, with a significant regulatory dimension embodied in their display of normative power. These are intergovernmental organisations, based on a charter or constitutive instrument agreed by States, although they also engage with other stakeholders such as the private sector and expertise reservoirs. If one looks beyond intergovernmental organisations, the landscape of institutions (feature (1)) with a focus on certain energy sources, products or technologies (feature (2)) is diverse and complex. Some institutions have a soft base (e.g. a resolution of an international organisation), a relatively wide scope (energy or sustainable energy) and play an essentially coordinating function. One example is UN-Energy, an inter-agency

[57] For a review article of these bodies of literature see T. van den Graaf, J. Colgan, 'Global energy governance: A review and research agenda' (2016) 2 *Palgrave Communications* 1, doi: https://doi.org/10.1057/palcomms.2015.47

'system-wide collaborative mechanism' established in 2004 by the UN System Chief Executives Board for Coordination (CEB).[58] UN-Energy's activities promotion activities are driven by wider action plans, from the Johannesburg Plan of Implementation, adopted in 2002,[59] to the 2030 Agenda for Sustainable Development, adopted in 2015, particularly SDG 7.[60] The focus on SDG 7 is particularly clear in UN-Energy's Plan of Action 2019–2020, which aims to develop a small number of 'High Impact Targeted Interventions' by each UN-Energy member organisation.[61] A related initiative, launched in 2011 by the then UN Secretary-General Ban Ki-moon, is 'Sustainable Energy for All' or SEforALL,[62] which later became an independent body.[63] SEforALL's promotion activities take mainly the form of 'programmes', 'hubs' and 'accelerators', which operate as multi-stakeholder networks focussing on a theme and/or a region. For example, in 2014, SEforALL established the Global Energy Efficiency Accelerator Platform, which encompasses other more specific energy efficiency-related 'accelerators' focussing on buildings, appliances and equipment, cities, industry, lightning etc. The overall goal of these accelerators is to facilitate the achievement of the efficiency targets under SDG 7. More specific objectives vary from one accelerator to another. By way of illustration, the Buildings Efficiency Accelerator (BEA) has provided a platform whereby twenty-five cities around the world have committed to introduce at least one building efficiency measure, run one demonstration project and record progress, with

[58] The establishment of UN-Energy was a follow-up action to the 2002 World Summit on Sustainable Development. See Annual overview report of the United Nations System Chief Executives Board for Coordination for 2003, 18 May 2004, UN Doc. E/2004/67, para. 13(e).

[59] Plan of Implementation, Report of the World Summit on Sustainable Development at Johannesburg (South Africa), 26 August–4 September 2002, UN Doc. A/CONF.199/20.

[60] Resolution 70/1, 'Transforming our World: The 2030 Agenda for Sustainable Development', 21 October 2015, UN Doc. A/RES/70/1, Sustainable Development Goal 7.

[61] UN-Energy Plan of Action 2019–2020 – Collective Energy Action, para. 2, available at: www.un-energy.org/wp-content/uploads/2020/08/Plan-of-Action-for-UN-Energy.pdf.

[62] A Vision Statement of Ban Ki-moon, Secretary General of the United Nations, Sustainable Energy for All (November 2011), available at: www.seforall.org/sites/default/files/gather-content/SG_Sustainable_Energy_for_All_vision.pdf.

[63] It was established under Austrian law in the form of a Quasi-International Organization (*Quasi-Internationale Organisation*). Federal Law on the Granting of Privileges to Non-Governmental International Organisations, Federal Law Gazette No. 174/1992, as later amended, section 7(2).

technical support from BEA, including resources on matters such as energy codes, retrofits, green building incentives etc.[64]

Aside from UN-Energy and SEforALL, many other institutions with diverse compositions (State or multi-stakeholder partnerships, industry associations etc.) perform a promotion function. This complex landscape includes: REN21,[65] devoted to promote and track the state of renewable energies around the world; the International Partnership for Energy Efficiency Cooperation (IPEEC), an inter-State partnership among some most members of the G20 which between 2009 and 2019 promoted energy efficiency around the world;[66] the Renewable Energy and Energy Efficiency Partnership (REEEP), a quasi-international organisation under Austrian law (like SEforALL) which leverages private finance for renewable energy and efficiency initiatives using targeted injections of public funds;[67] the Clean Energy Ministerial (CEM), a high-level global forum promoting the transition to a global clean energy economy;[68] the International Commission on Large Dams (ICOLD),[69] an organisation founded in 1928 which brings together national committees of engineers and other technical experts from the public and private sectors; the International Hydropower Association (IHA),[70] an industry association of the hydropower sector; the Global Bioenergy Partnership (GBEP), an initiative launched by the G8+5's 2005 meeting held in Gleneagles to 'support wider, cost effective biomass and biofuels deployment';[71] the Society for Solar Energy (ISES),[72] an advocacy organisation created in the 1950s to promote solar energy;[73] or the International Partnership for the Hydrogen Economy (IPHE),[74] a partnership of twenty-one States and

64 See the website of the BEA, available at: www.buildingefficiencyaccelerator.org/resources/.

65 See REN21's website: www.ren21.net/

66 The mandate of IPEEC was terminated in December 2019. See, however, the website of the partnership, which continues to record its activities and resources: https://ipeec.org/

67 See REEEP's website: www.reeep.org/

68 See CEM's website: www.cleanenergyministerial.org/

69 See ICOLD's website: www.icold-cigb.org/GB/icold/icold.asp

70 See IHA's website: www.hydropower.org/

71 See Terms of Reference for the Global Bioenergy Partnership (GBEP), 11 May 2006, available at: www.globalbioenergy.org/aboutgbep/history/en/.

72 See the ISES' website, available at: www.ises.org/home.

73 There is a two-volume account of the history of this little-known organisation: K. W. Böer (ed.), *The Fifty-Year History of the International Solar Energy Society and its National Sections*, vols. 1–2 (Boulder: American Solar Energy Society: 2005).

74 See the IPHE's website, available at: www.iphe.net/.

the EU established in 2003 to promote the development and uptake of fuel cells and hydrogen (FCH) technologies.

Among the many organisations that could be selected to illustrate the governance function of promotion organisations, IRENA is the most suitable one because it is constituted by treaty with a clear steering role and it focusses on specific energy resources, products and technologies. Its role as an expertise reservoir and its growing international profile could endow it, in the future, with some degree of normative power, which it lacks formally. Yet, it is neither tasked nor does it operate in practice as the epicentre of a legal regime.

3.2 The International Renewable Energy Agency (IRENA)

3.2.1 Origins of the IRENA

The establishment of IRENA is a textbook example of 'norm entrepreneurship'. Although international cooperation on 'alternative' or renewable energy sources can be traced back to at least the early 1960s, with more significant developments in the early 1980s, the impulsion that eventually led to the creation of IRENA came from one man, Hermann Scheer.[75]

Scheer was a German politician, affiliated with the Social Democratic Party (SPD), who campaigned for the creation of an international organisation focussing on renewable energy for over two decades,[76] until its formal establishment in January 2009.[77] Through his political

[75] The process leading to the creation of IRENA, including the role of Scheer, are documented in EUROSOLAR/World Council for Renewable Energy (eds.), *The Long Road to IRENA* (Bochum: Ponte Press, 2009). On IRENA in general see T. van de Graaf, 'Fragmentation in Global Energy Governance: Explaining the Creation of IRENA' (2013) 13 *Global Environmental Politics* 14; I. Overland, G. Reischl, 'A place in the Sun? IRENA's position in the global energy governance landscape' (2018) 18 *International Environmental Agreements* 335.

[76] Scheer's vision can be found in a variety of public interventions, most notably one book (*A Solar Manifesto* (London: James & James, 1994)), two memoranda describing the project (the first – Memorandum for the Establishment of an International Solar Energy Agency (ISEA) within the United Nations (1990) – envisioned an entity part of the UN family of organisations, whereas the second – Memorandum for the Establishment of an International Renewable Energy Agency (IRENA) (2000) – more specifically contemplated an 'International Renewable Energy Agency'). Excerpts of these documents are reproduced in EUROSOLAR/WCRE, *The Long Road*, at 9, 20 and 24.

[77] Statute of the International Renewable Energy Agency (IRENA), 26 January 2009, IRENA/FC/Statute. The organisation was physically established in 2011, following a transitional period managed by a Preparatory Commission.

involvement, Scheer managed to secure the support of Germany from 2002 onwards,[78] which further relied on Denmark and Spain as the two other advanced EU countries in the area of renewable energy. However, despite two significant diplomatic efforts, first at the 2002 Johannesburg Summit on Sustainable Development and then at a specifically organised conference in Bonn, in 2004,[79] Germany failed to mobilise a sufficiently broad base of countries to set up the organisation.

Eventually, starting in early 2007, Germany engaged with a range of countries on a bilateral basis to secure support for the establishment of IRENA, which was agreed at a Conference held in Bonn on 26 January 2009. Scheer's justified excitement at this development soon turned into disappointment, after Germany, in an attempt to bid for the seat of the organisation, decided not to push for Scheer's appointment as first director-general. As it turned out, Germany failed to secure the seat (attributed to the United Arab Emirates, in the low-carbon Masdar City, after a major lobbying campaign, including a major financial contribution) and the directorship (secured by France), and it only received the seat of IRENA's Centre of Innovation and Technology.[80] The following year, Scheer passed away at the age of sixty-six.

3.2.2 Structure and Powers

The overarching objective of the agency, as stated in the chapeau of Article II of the IRENA Statute is to 'promote the widespread and increased adoption and the sustainable use of all forms of renewable energy'. The expression 'all forms of renewable energy' is ambiguous. 'Renewable energy', as such, is defined in Article III as 'all forms of energy produced from renewable sources in a sustainable manner, which include, inter alia: 1. bioenergy; 2. geothermal energy; 3. hydropower; 4.

[78] Van de Graaf, *Explaining the Creation of IRENA*, at 22.

[79] The Political Declaration unanimously adopted on 4 June 2004 recorded, in paragraph 9, the agreement of the 154 participating States to 'work within a "global policy network"'. This paragraph gave the impulsion for the establishment of REN21. Of note, however, there is no specific reference to the creation of an agency. In parallel to the intergovernmental conference, Scheer chaired an International Parliamentary Forum at the German Bundestag, on 2 June 2004. The conference report expressly stated that: 'In particular, parliamentarians from around the world voiced their support for the establishment of an International Renewable Energy Agency (IRENA), whose task would be to promote the international transfer of technology and knowledge', EUROSOLAR/WCRE, *The Long Road*, at 70.

[80] Van de Graaf, *Explaining the Creation of IRENA*, at 23–24.

ocean energy, including inter alia tidal, wave and ocean thermal energy; 5. solar energy; and 6. wind energy'. Nuclear energy is neither expressly included not expressly excluded, a matter which was important for France. The promotion role and the focus on certain energy sources, despite the ambiguities, are therefore stated upfront in the IRENA Statute. This is further specified in Article IV, which defines the 'activities' of the agency inter alia 'as a facilitator and catalyst . . . offering support on all matters relating to renewable energy', including the provision of 'relevant policy advice and assistance to its Members upon their request' (Article IV.A(1)(c)).

From an institutional standpoint, the agency is open to States and regional intergovernmental economic integration organisations (i.e. the EU) (Article VI) and it also admits governmental, intergovernmental and even non-governmental observers (Article VII). The three main organs are the Assembly (meeting once a year), the Council (meeting twice a year) and the Secretariat. Voting in the Assembly, which is the highest organ, is governed by a peculiar rule of consensus for substantive decisions, which is deemed achieved if no more than two members of object (Article IX.F). This rule applies, inter alia, to decisions on applications on membership (Article IX.H(1)) but not to other important matters, most notably the appointment of the director-general, which is possible at a 2/3 majority of members present and voting (Article IX.I).

None of the organs has the power to adopt decisions binding of Member States. The Assembly may only 'make recommendations to the Members of the Agency, upon their request' (Article IX.A(3)(b)). The Council's powers as regards Members are limited to 'facilitate[ing] consultations and cooperation among [them]' (Article X.F(1)). As for the Secretariat, although it has no power to adopt measures binding upon Members, it can provide policy advice upon the request of a Member (Article IV.A(1)(c)) and subject to the requirement to inform other Members after the advice has been given (Article IV.C(2)). This power, which is vested in the agency, is allocated to the Secretariat in Article XI.E(6).

The knowledge development and reservoir, combined with the policy advice function, are typical manifestations of the promotion role of IRENA. The other major role is that of a catalyst, a convenor bringing together different stakeholders to facilitate the uptake of renewable energies. This also suggests that the normative power of the agency largely depends on the credibility and authority it commands in this regard.

3.2.3 Evolving Practice

In practice, after a difficult beginning marked by controversies regarding its leadership and budget,[81] IRENA's role as both a catalyst and an adviser is becoming increasingly recognised and sought after.

One indicator is the significant expansion of its membership from the initial 75 signatory States to the 162 Members as of December 2020, with an additional 22 States in the process of accession. Another indicator is provided by its work as both a catalyst and a provider of advice through a range of initiatives, most notably the three regional Clean Energy Corridors (two for Africa[82] and one for Central America[83]), the SIDS (Small Island Development States) Lighthouses Initiative (LHI),[84] the Global Geothermal Alliance (GGA) launched in 2015 at the twenty-first meeting of the UNFCCC's Conference of the Parties,[85] or the softer multi-stakeholder 'IRENA Coalition for Action', launched in January 2014.

Empirical research on the role of IRENA points also to the fact that government representatives attending IRENA meetings come mostly from energy ministries (rather than environment ministries), although the second main constituency are diplomats from foreign affairs ministries.[86] This is relevant because government officials from energy

[81] Van de Graaf, *Explaining the Creation of IRENA*, at 24–25.

[82] The Africa Clean Energy Corridor (ACEC) was launched in 2014 by means of a ministerial communiqué (IRENA Communiqué, Africa Clean Energy Corridor Ministerial, Abu Dhabi, 17 January 2014). Subsequently, IRENA initiated a West Africa Clean Energy Corridor (WACEC), in collaboration with ECOWAS Centre for Renewable Energy and Energy Efficiency (ECREEE), West African Power Pool (WAPP), and ECOWAS Regional Electricity Regulatory Authority (ERERA). The WACEC was endorsed by the ECOWAS Energy Ministerial in December 2016. For a summary of IRENA's role in these two contexts see IRENA, *Scaling up renewable energy deployment in Africa* (January 2019).

[83] The Clean Energy Corridor of Central America (CECCA) was launched in 2015 by means of a Strategic Document (IRENA, Clean Energy Corridor of Central America (CECCA), Strategy) endorsed by the ministers of participating countries.

[84] LHI was launched at the 2014 UN Climate Summit, and it aims to support and accelerate the transition from fossil fuels to a renewable energies-based economy in 36 SIDS from the Atlantic, Indian Ocean and South China Sea, the Caribbean and the Pacific. For a summary of IRENA's role in this context see IRENA, SIDS Lighthouses Initiative. Progress and Way Forward (January 2020).

[85] See Joint Communiqué on the Global Geothermal Alliance, 7 December 2015. The GGA has 46 country Members and 40 non-State partners. For an overview of its work see GGA/IRENA, *Tap into Geothermal Insights and Experience* (January 2020).

[86] Overland/Reischl, *A place in the Sun?*, at 340.

ministries may be expected to have greater impact at the domestic level on energy policy, thus suggesting the possible influence of IRENA through this channel.[87] Yet, very few countries have made substantial voluntary contributions to the IRENA's budget (aside from the UAE, Germany and Norway, which each has specific reasons), which suggests that Members do not yet see IRENA as a service which deserves to be supported through prioritised contributions.[88] As regards references in domestic policy documents to IRENA, although the frequency seems to be increasing steadily, when examined in more detail, such references do not convey the same degree of influence or credibility as those made to the IEA.[89]

Competition between IRENA and the IEA is a long-standing matter, with a former IEA director-general having claimed that the IEA had defused more than once attempts at creating IRENA.[90] Since the establishment of the latter, however, the two organisations have developed a reasonable degree of cooperation, first through the signing of a memorandum of understanding on 9 April 2012[91] and, subsequently, through some data-related initiatives, mainly the joint database of renewable energy policies and measures,[92] as well as publications.[93]

IV Regional Cooperation Organisations

4.1 *Introduction*

A number of regional arrangements of different natures have emerged over time to facilitate cooperation on energy. Including among them the EU is both necessary and inaccurate. It is necessary because the regulation of energy within the EU and in the EU's external action is highly developed at the policy, law and institutional levels. Any account of regional energy cooperation organisations would be expected to refer to

[87] Overland/Reischl, *A place in the Sun?*, at 340.
[88] Overland/Reischl, *A place in the Sun?*, at 341–342.
[89] Overland/Reischl, *A place in the Sun?*, at 344–345.
[90] Van de Graaf, *Explaining the Creation of IRENA*, at 22.
[91] IRENA and IEA Strengthen Cooperation for a Secure and Sustainable Energy Future, IRENA Press release, 9 April 2012.
[92] Available at: www.iea.org/policies?source=IEA%2FIRENA%20Renewables%20Policies%20Database.
[93] See e.g. IRENA/IEA/REN21, *Renewable Energy Policies in a Time of Transition* (2018).

the EU regime. It is inaccurate, however, because the EU integration process goes far beyond energy, despite its origin in three foundational treaties, two of which concerned energy specifically.[94]

Even when seen from the specific energy angle, the EU system is peculiar because it is much more comprehensive and detailed than the most developed example of a centralised approach at the international level, nuclear energy governance around the IAEA. It is therefore misleading to describe it as an example of a 'proto-centralised' approach. Moreover, it has focussed over time on many energy sources and products, most notably coal, nuclear, petroleum, gas and electricity, and renewables. Such a system is unique, and it can only be discussed alongside the far more limited arrangements existing in other regions if this initial observation is emphasised.

With this important caveat in mind, the purpose of this section is to briefly survey some regional arrangements, with varying degrees of institutionalisation and coverage, which seek to facilitate cooperation on energy matters in general or on some specific forms of energy (e.g. renewable energies). Several examples of this regional approach can be provided in Africa (the African Energy Commission (AFREC)),[95] Asia (the Asia-Pacific Energy Cooperation (APEC) Energy Working Group),[96] Europe (the European Renewable Energy Council (EREC))[97] or Latin America (the Latin American Energy Organization (OLADE)).[98]

For the illustrative purposes pursued in this section, it will be sufficient to introduce only two of them, which are based on a treaty and have been in place for several decades, namely the 1973 OLADE and the ASEAN Energy Cooperation Framework, which grew out of earlier cooperation initiatives dating back to the 1970s. Before discussing these two examples, I will briefly examine the history and legal architecture of the EU energy system.

[94] See Treaty establishing the European Coal and Steel Community, 18 April 1951, 261 UNTS 140 [ECSC Treaty]; Treaty establishing the European Atomic Energy Community (Euratom), 25 March 1957, OJ C 327 (26.10.2012), pp. 1–107 [EURATOM Treaty].

[95] See AFREC's website, available at: https://au-afrec.org/.

[96] See the APEC Working Group's website, available at: www.ewg.apec.org/.

[97] Founded in 2000, the EREC was subsequently dissolved by a 2014 decision of its members. Its website remains available in the web archive at: https://web.archive.org/web/20110224075133/http://erec.org/.

[98] See Section 4.3.

4.2 *The EU System of Regional Energy Governance*

4.2.1 Overview

The European integration process had, since its inception, energy as its very core.[99] The 1951 Treaty instituting the European Coal and Steal Community (ECSC)[100] and the 1957 EURATOM Treaty establishing the European Atomic Energy Community[101] were specifically about two energy resources, and the 1957 Treaty establishing the European Economic Community (EEC) applied to energy.[102] Yet, in the early years of the integration process there was significant reluctance to place energy policy as a matter for community law.[103] A major impulsion in this direction came from the 1973 oil crisis. In 1974, the Council adopted a resolution on a 'new energy policy strategy for the Community',[104] followed by several directives and regulations relating to energy security.[105]

This reactive approach gave place, throughout the 1980s, to a focus on the completion of the internal market,[106] including in the energy sector.[107] The starting point was a landscape of national monopolistic

[99] On EU energy law see generally: A. Johnston, G. Block, *EU Energy Law* (Oxford: Oxford University Press, 2012); K. Talus, *EU Energy Law and Policy: A Critical Account* (Oxford: Oxford University Press, 2013); M. Roggenkamp, C. Redgwell, A. Ronne and I. del Guayo (eds.), *Energy Law in Europe* (Oxford: Oxford University Press, 3rd ed. 2016); P. Cameron, R. Heffron (eds.), *Legal Aspects of EU Energy Regulation* (Oxford: Oxford University Press, 2nd ed. 2016). A highly condensed summary of the main aspects of EU energy law is provided in H. Vedder, H., A. Ronne, M. Roggenkamp, I del Guayo, 'EU Energy Law', M. Roggenkamp, C. Redgwell, A. Ronne and I. del Guayo (eds.), *Energy Law in Europe* (Oxford: Oxford University Press, 3rd ed. 2016), pp. 187–366. My account here follows the latter, updated and supplemented as necessary.

[100] The ECSC Treaty was concluded for fifty years and expired on 23 July 2002.

[101] EURATOM Treaty.

[102] Treaty establishing the European Economic Community, 25 March 1957, 298 UNTS 3.

[103] See T. Daintith, L. Hancher, 'The Management of Diversity: Community Law as an Instrument of Energy and other Sectorial Policies' (1984) 4 *Yearbook of European Law* 123.

[104] Council Resolution of 17 September 1974 concerning the new energy policy strategy for the Community.

[105] See e.g. Council Directive 75/339/EEC of 20 May 1975 obliging the Member States to maintain minimum stocks of fossil fuel at thermal power stations; Council Directive 75/404/EEC of 13 February 1975 on the restriction of the use of natural gas in power stations; Directive 75/405/EEC of 14 April 1975 concerning the restriction of the use of petroleum products in power stations.

[106] *Completing the Internal Market. White Paper* from the Commission to the European Council, Milan, 28–29 June 1985, COM (85) 310 final.

[107] The Internal Energy Market (Commission Working Document), Brussels, 2 May 1988, COM (88) 238 final.

entities concentrating energy activities, and the goal was to introduce an increasing level of competition within the sector.[108] Also during the 1980s, the Single European Act[109] introduced a number of amendments to the EEC Treaty of relevance for the subsequent development of the energy architecture in Europe, namely environmental protection (Article 130r, today 192 TFEU) and the 'prudent and rational utilization of natural resources' (Article 130r, today 191 TFEU), paving the way for the development of both renewable energy and efficiency-related instruments.

By the mid 1990s, the security, competition and sustainability dimensions of European energy law and policy had been clearly identified. In 1995, a White Paper from the European Commission expressly called for 'An Energy Policy for the European Union':

> Although the Treaties already provide for an important Community role in the energy field, the Commission has come to the conclusion, on the basis of past experience and in light of energy trends, that it is only within a sound and coherent energy policy framework at Community level, that maximum benefits can be realised from actions at both Community and Member State levels and a full contribution made to other policy objectives.[110]

The 'general framework' within which the energy policy was to be developed was given by four 'key concepts', namely the globalisation of markets (external dimension with particular regard for the dissolution of the USSR and the emergence of energy-relevant countries in the Community of Independent States (CIS)), increasing environmental concerns (particularly CO_2 emissions driving climate change), technology developments (with a focus on the implications of new technologies relating to renewable energies and efficiency for competitiveness, environmental protection and energy security through a diversification of the

[108] The initial focus concerned pricing and network-bound transit: Council Directive 90/377/EEC of 29 June 1990 concerning a Community procedure to improve the transparency of gas and electricity prices charged to industrial end-users; Council Directive 90/547/EEC of 29 October 1990 on the transit of electricity through transmission grids; Council Directive 91/296/EEC of 31 May 1991 on the transit of natural gas through grids.

[109] *Single European Act*, 17 February 1986, 1987 O.J. (L 169) 1.

[110] European Commission, *White Paper – An Energy Policy for the European Union*, Brussels, 13 December 1995, COM(95) 682 Final, para. 10. Earlier that year, the Commission had issued a *Green Paper – For a European Energy Policy*, 11 January 1995, COM(95) 659 Final.

energy mix), and the Community's institutional responsibilities (with a focus on a regulated move to more competitive energy markets).

In what follows, I briefly examine three main aspects of the energy union built between 1990 and 2020: (1) the consolidation of energy policy as a shared competence of the EU and Member States; (2) the four so-called 'packages' adopted in 1996/1998, 2003, 2009 and 2019/2020; and (3) the institutional architecture of EU energy governance. These are three different vantage points on the same overall and interlocked reality but keeping them distinct is useful to understand its main dimensions.

4.2.2 Energy as a Shared Competence

The distribution of competence over energy policy in the EU is complex. For present purposes, it will suffice to note that the adoption of secondary legislation (mainly directives and regulations) on energy matters began decades before the formal conferral of competence in the area of energy to the Union in 2007 by means of the Treaty of Lisbon.[111] Many instruments were adopted before such conferral, mainly on the basis of the Union's (then Community's) competence for the development of the internal market (now Articles 4(2)(a) and 114 TFEU), environmental protection (now Articles 4(2)(e) and 192 TFEU) and the prudent and rational utilisation of natural resources (now Article 191 TFEU).

Following the entry into force of the Treaty of Lisbon, shared competence over energy has been expressly conferred in Articles 4(2)(i) and 194 TFEU. Articles 4(2)(h) and 170 TFEU further confer on the Union a shared competence on trans-European networks, a matter which had been introduced already in 1992 by the Maastricht Treaty's amendments to the EEC Treaty (then Articles 3(n) and 129b of the renamed EC Treaty). This shared competence means that both the Union and Member States may legislate in the relevant area, but the latter can do so only to the extent that the EU has not exercised its conferred competence and only in a manner which is consistent with EU measures. In addition, the Union has also been conferred the power to enter into agreements with States or international organisations under certain circumstances (Article 216 TFEU), which is particularly relevant for the EU's external energy relations.

[111] Treaty of Lisbon amending the Treaty on European Union and the Treaty establishing the European Community, signed at Lisbon, 13 December 2007, OJ C 306, 17.12.2007, pp. 1–271.

Significantly, the conferral of competence to the EU on energy matters is subject to important limitations regarding Members' sovereignty over their energy resources and their sovereign prerogative to decide their energy mix. Article 194(2) TFEU states, indeed, that EU measures 'shall not affect a Member State's right to determine the conditions for exploiting its energy resources, its choice between different energy sources and the general structure of its energy supply, without prejudice to Article 192(2)(c)'. The latter reservation concerns the possibility for the Council to adopt measures affecting the energy mix to advance the Union's environmental competence but only acting unanimously. With this significant caveat, the reservation of Member States' sovereign prerogatives defines a distribution between them and the Union akin to the distinction, made in Chapters 2 and 3, between, on the one hand, the 'entitlements' part of energy transactions and, on the other hand, both the facilitation of energy transactions and the regulation of their negative externalities. States retain the first component of the transaction, whereas the Union is conferred legal powers over the second component of the transaction and the regulation of its externalities. The powers retained by States in this regard remain the rule, rather than the exception. By way of illustration, Denmark, which is the main oil producer of the 27-Member post-Brexit EU, has decided that it will phase out oil production entirely by 2050.[112]

Article 194(1) TFEU confers powers on the EU by reference both to their context and their purposes:

> 1. In the context of the establishment and functioning of the internal market and with regard for the need to preserve and improve the environment, Union policy on energy shall aim, in a spirit of solidarity between Member States, to:
>
> (a) ensure the functioning of the energy market;
> (b) ensure security of energy supply in the Union;
> (c) promote energy efficiency and energy saving and the development of new and renewable forms of energy; and
> (d) promote the interconnection of energy networks.

The contexts and aims in this provision give expression to the three aforementioned overarching purposes of security, competitiveness and

[112] See M. Buttler, 'Denmark to End North Sea Oil Production in Milestone Deal', 3 December 2020, www.bloomberg.com

sustainability, and they have found legal expression in numerous measures, as discussed next.

4.2.3 Exercise of Normative Powers: The Energy 'Packages'

Since the mid 1990s, the security, competitiveness and sustainability purposes have been pursued through sets of measures, often referred to as 'packages'. The legal bases in the founding treaties together with their development through the instruments forming these packages are the most striking illustration of the extensive normative powers enjoyed by the EU in energy matters.

Table 7.1 summarises these packages identifying the most representative instruments of each of them and their focus.

The policies underlying the current package were introduced and explained in a 2016 Communication from the European Commission.[113] In the conception expounded in this Communication, the sustainability dimension clearly shapes the other two goals (international competitiveness and energy security). The 'Energy Union' is presented as a strategy for the modernisation of the EU economy as a necessary step in the transition to a low-carbon economy. The three main goals identified in the Communication, i.e. energy efficiency, global leadership in renewable energies, and a 'fair deal' for consumers, highlight this focus as well as the interconnections between the three goals. There is a noticeable shift in this package from a focus on the organisation of the internal energy market to the global role of the EU as a leader in climate policy and, it is planned, renewable energy markets. In many ways, it conveys the understanding that the transition will indeed happen, and that the EU needs to position itself as an early mover. The outward shift had received a substantial impulsion during the implementation of the third package already, embodied in the Commission's Communication 'The EU Energy Policy: Engaging with Partners beyond our Borders', which connected the internal market and external energy policy.[114]

Another significant aspect in the construction of the energy union is the progressive development of an institutional component, mainly with the creation of ACER, ENTSO-E and ENTSO-G in the third energy

[113] European Commission, *Communication – Clean Energy for All Europeans*, 30 November 2016, COM(2016) 860 Final.

[114] European Commission, Communication – The EU Energy Policy: Engaging with Partners beyond our Borders, 7 September 2011, COM(2011) 539 final.

Table 7.1. *The EU energy packages*

Package	Main instruments	Main focus
First energy package (1996/1998)	*Directive 96/92/EC* of 19 December 1996 concerning common rules for the internal market in electricity *Directive 98/30/EC* of 22 June 1998 concerning common rules for the internal market in natural gas	Liberalisation of the internal markets of electricity and gas, mainly through (1) functional (management and accounting) unbundling of vertically integrated utilities, i.e. separation of production/supply from transmission; and (2) negotiated or regulated third-party access to networks.
Second energy package (2003)	Directive 2003/54/EC of 26 June 2003 concerning common rules for the internal market in electricity and repealing Directive 96/92/EC Directive 2003/55/EC of 26 June 2003 concerning common rules for the internal market in natural gas and repealing Directive 98/30/EC Regulation (EC) No 1228/2003 of 26 June 2003 on conditions for access to the network for cross-border exchanges in electricity	Pursued the liberalisation of the internal markets of electricity and gas, mainly through (1) legal unbundling, (2) regulated third-party access, (3) choice of supplier, (4) requirement for Member States to establish independent national regulatory agencies (NRAs) and (5) a regulatory framework for cross-border interconnectors
Third energy package (2009)	Directive 2009/72/EC of 13 July 2009 concerning common rules for the internal market in electricity and repealing Directive 2003/54/EC Directive 2009/73/EC of 13 July 2009 concerning common rules for the internal market in natural	Further pursued the liberalisation of the internal markets of electricity and gas through (1) ownership unbundling, (2) regulation of third-party access to electricity and gas networks, (3) strengthening of NRAs, (4) enabling the adoption by the EU of

Table 7.1. (*cont.*)

Package	Main instruments	Main focus
	gas and repealing Directive 2003/55/EC Regulation (EC) No 713/2009 of 13 July 2009 establishing an Agency for the Cooperation of Energy Regulators (ACER) Regulation (EC) No 714/2009 of 13 July 2009 on conditions for access to the network for cross-border exchanges in electricity and repealing Regulation (EC) No 1228/2003 Regulation (EC) No 715/2009 of 13 July 2009 on conditions for access to the natural gas transmission networks and repealing Regulation (EC) No 1775/2005	network codes, (5) establishment of an EU agency (ACER) and (6) creation of two EU Networks of Transmission System Operators (ENTSO-E and ENTSO-G)
Fourth energy package (2019): Clean Energy for All Europeans Package	Directive (EU) 2018/844 of 30 May 2018 amending Directive 2010/31/EU on the energy performance of buildings and Directive 2012/27/EU on energy efficiency Directive (EU) 2018/2002 of 11 December 2018 amending Directive 2012/27/EU on energy efficiency Directive (EU) 2018/2001 of 11 December 2018 on the promotion of the use of energy from renewable sources Directive (EU) 2019/944 of 5 June 2019 on common	The Fourth package focusses on (1) electricity, (2) renewable energies and (3) efficiency. It is the first to leave out gas, which is being addressed by a separate gas package which was to be adopted in 2020. It strengthens the cross-border and coordination role of ACER, and it introduces a new energy governance system whereby Member States must adopt an integrated ten-year (2021–2030) National Energy and Climate Plan (NECP),

Table 7.1. (*cont.*)

Package	Main instruments	Main focus
	rules for the internal market for electricity and amending Directive 2012/27/EU Regulation (EU) 2018/1999 of 11 December 2018 on the Governance of the Energy Union and Climate Action Regulation (EU) 2019/943 of 5 June 2019 on the internal market for electricity Regulation (EU) 2019/941 of 5 June 2019 on risk-preparedness in the electricity sector and repealing Directive 2005/89/EC Regulation (EU) 2019/942 of 5 June 2019 establishing a European Union Agency for the Cooperation of Energy Regulators	including a projection up to 2050.

package and, more recently, with the new Regulation (EU) 2018/1999 on the Governance of the Energy Union and Climate Action. Together with the general bodies of the EU, mainly the Commission, these energy-specific structures embody the institutional component of this peculiar illustration of a regional centralised approach.

4.2.4 Institutional Architecture of the EU Energy Union

The institutional architecture of the EU energy union has both grown and become more energy-specific over time. Generally speaking, it relies on three layers of institutions.

4.2.4.1 General EU Bodies The first layer is provided by the general EU bodies, mainly the Commission but also the Council and the

Parliament, which through the co-decision procedure, have adopted most of the instruments relating to energy and the environment.

The Commission has some Directorates-General with a specific focus on energy (DG Energy or ENER), environmental protection (DG Environment or ENV) or climate change (DG Climate Action or CLIMA). As the executive body of the EU, it performs a major impulsion role, which can be illustrated by the use of 'Green' and 'White' Papers and Communications as catalysts for energy packages. As noted above, a 1995 White Paper on 'An Energy Policy for the European Union'[115] led to the adoption of the First Package. Similarly, a 2006 Green Paper on a 'A European Strategy for Sustainable, Competitive and Secure Energy',[116] followed by a 2007 Communication on an 'Energy Policy for Europe'[117] catalysed the Third Package. The Fourth package also resulted from a 2016 Communication on 'Clean Energy for All Europeans'.[118]

The measures proposed by the Commission in these and other initiatives are, in most cases, adopted following the co-decision procedure involving both the Council and the European Parliament as decision-makers and the Commission as proponent. This procedure, introduced in the 1992 Maastricht Treaty[119] and subsequently extended, has been renamed by the Lisbon Treaty as the 'ordinary legislative procedure' (Article 294 TFEU).

4.2.4.2 Energy-Specific Bodies: ACER, ENTSO-E and ENTSO-G The main component of the energy-specific architecture of the EU is the Agency for Cooperation of Energy Regulators (ACER), introduced by a 2009 Regulation[120] and effectively starting operations in 2011. Before ACER, cooperation among national energy regulators was organised

[115] European Commission, *White Paper – An Energy Policy for the European Union*, Brussels, 13 December 1995, COM(95) 682 Final.

[116] European Commission, *Green Paper – A European Strategy for Sustainable, Competitive and Secure Energy*, 8 March 2006, COM(2006) 105 Final.

[117] European Commission, *Communication – An Energy Policy for Europe*, 10 January 2007, COM(2007) 1 Final.

[118] European Commission, *Communication – Clean Energy for All Europeans*, 30 November 2016, COM(2016) 860 Final.

[119] Treaty of Maastricht on European Union, 7 February 1992, *OJ C 191*, 29.7.1992, pp. 1–112. Now TEU.

[120] Regulation (EC) No. 713/2009 of 13 July 2009 establishing an Agency for the Cooperation of Energy Regulators (ACER).

under the European Regulators Group for Electricity and Gas (ERGEG),[121] which remained in operation until 2011.[122]

ACER acts as a regulators coordinator of the internal electricity and gas markets.[123] Its normative power[124] finds expression inter alia through the drafting of guidelines, at the request of the Commission, which provide the basis for network codes,[125] the adoption of non-binding opinions and recommendations, and the taking of individual binding decisions on certain matters, including those relating to cross-border transactions where the national regulators involved have not been able to reach agreement.[126]

In addition to ACER, the Third Package introduced two European networks of Transmission System Operators, one for electricity (ENTSO-E)[127] and one for gas (ENTSO-G).[128] Their goal is to harmonise the rules for cross-border exchanges by means of draft network codes and long-term network development planning.[129] From a legal standpoint, ENTSOs are organised under the domestic laws of Belgium as non-profit associations.

The same applies to another regulator coordinating body established in March 2000 on the initiative of ten national regulatory agencies, the Council of European Energy Regulators (CEER).[130]

121 Commission *Decision* 003/796/EC of 11 November 2003 on establishing the European Regulators Group for Electricity and Gas.

122 Commission Decision 2011/280/EU of 16 May 2011 on repealing Decision 2003/796/EC on establishing the European Regulators Group for Electricity and Gas.

123 See R. Heffron, '"Shared Governance": ACER and the Roles of the National Energy and Competition Regulators in the EU', in P. Cameron, R. Heffron (eds.), *Legal Aspects of EU Energy Regulation* (Oxford: Oxford University Press, 2nd ed. 2016).

124 The acts that ACER is empowered to adopt are specified in Article 2 of the Regulation (EU) 2019/942 of 5 June 2019 establishing a European Union Agency for the Cooperation of Energy Regulators [Regulation (EU) 2019/942].

125 Regulation (EU) 2019/942, Article 5.

126 Regulation (EU) 2019/942, Article 6(10). On the decision-making power of ACER see more generally Article 2(d), Regulation (EU) 2019/942.

127 Regulation (EC) No. 714/2009 of 13 July 2009 on conditions for access to the network for cross-border exchanges in electricity and repealing Regulation (EC) No. 1228/2003 [Regulation (EC) No. 714/2009], Article 5.

128 Regulation (EC) No. 715/2009 of 13 July 2009 on conditions for access to the natural gas transmission networks and repealing Regulation (EC) No. 1775/2005 [Regulation (EC) No. 715/2009], Article 5.

129 Regulation (EC) No. 714/2009, Article 8(1)–(2) and (10); Regulation (EC) No. 715/2009, Article 8(1)–(2) and (10).

130 CEER was established by means of a *Memorandum of Understanding for the establishment of the Council of European Energy Regulators*. The Statute of CEER, as of 2020, is available at: www.ceer.eu/.

4.2.4.3 Multi-Stakeholder Fora Aside from the bodies identified so far, energy governance in the EU relies on a number of multi-stakeholder fora, which bring together the public sector (national regulators, government officials, the European Commission), the private sector (transmission operators, network users, power exchanges and traders) and consumers.

The main two fora are the Electricity Regulatory Forum (known as the 'Florence Forum'),[131] established in 1998, and the Gas Regulatory Forum (known as the 'Madrid Forum'), established in 1999. In addition to electricity and gas, two other fora created in 2004 focus on renewable energies and efficiency (the Sustainable Energy Forum, known as the 'Amsterdam Forum') and on fossil fuels (the Fossil Fuel Forum, known as the 'Berlin Forum').[132] A fifth forum, established in 2008, focusses on consumer-related matters (the Citizen's Energy Forum or 'London Forum'). These fora meet annually or biannually, and they serve as multi-stakeholder mechanisms to facilitate consensual and participative harmonisation of the internal market rules, but they also address many other energy-related matters, such as climate change and energy security.

As the foregoing discussion shows, the EU energy union has a degree of centralisation that clearly exceeds that of any other regime found in international law, including the one on nuclear energy. Its peculiarity stems from the nature of the European integration process, which makes the EU a supranational organisation based on international law but operating as a highly integrated system more akin to a pyramidal domestic legal system. As discussed next, the contrast between the EU integration and other regional efforts is stark. From this perspective, the latter provide a more representative illustration of regional proto-centralisation.

4.3 *The Latin American Energy Organization (OLADE)*

4.3.1 Origins of the OLADE

Much like other institutional initiatives of the 1970s, the establishment of the Latin American Energy Organization (OLADE, from its Spanish acronym) was catalysed by the oil crisis of October 1973.[133]

[131] On this forum see Q. C. Trinh and L. Meeus, '*From Florence Forum to Florence Process*: a look back', *Conference Paper: 6th International Conference on the European Electricity Market EEM09*, Leuven.

[132] See E. Ehlers, 'The Amsterdam and Berlin Fora and the Forum Process in European Energy Policy', in M. Roggenkamp, U. Hammer (eds.), *European Energy Law Report IV* (Intersentia, 2007), pp. 109–134.

[133] See C. Joyner, 'Latin America's Communal Response to the Energy Crisis: The Latin American Energy Organization (OLADE)' (1974) 6 *Lawyer of the Americas* 637. There is scant literature on the OLADE. The available materials are mostly in the form of reports

The seeds of the organisation precede the crisis, however. They were sowed in a series of consultative meetings held by the region's ministers of energy and petroleum starting in August 1972, in Caracas (Venezuela), then in April 1973, in Quito (Ecuador), leading eventually to the adoption of the Lima Agreement on 2 November 1973 establishing the OLADE.[134]

The OLADE pursued, since its inception, several objectives, all related to the promotion of energy cooperation among participating States to achieve energy independence and security, increase production and exports, and aim for energy integration, which has yet to materialise in any meaningful manner.

Here, I briefly discuss two aspects of OLADE. First, I describe its institutional structure, functions and power, from the perspective of the proto-centralised approach examined in this chapter. Second, I briefly survey some of the main iterations of the Latin American energy integration initiatives, up until the 2019 Lima Declaration adopted under the aegis of the OLADE.[135]

4.3.2 Structure and Powers

The OLADE was formally established as an intergovernmental organisation (Articles 28, 29 and 30 of the Lima Agreement), which, at the end of 2020, had twenty-seven Members and one permanent observer (Algeria).

The fundamental purpose of OLADE is stated in Article 2 of the Lima Agreement:

> The Organization is an instrument for cooperation, coordination, and consultation, with its own juridical identity, whose fundamental purpose is the integration, protection, conservation, rational utilization, marketing, and defence of the energy resources of the Region.

or brochures. See e.g. L. A. Marciano da Fonseca, 'The Latin American Energy Organization (OLADE)' (1980) 9 *Energy* 861; A. Cruz, 'Latin American Energy Cooperation and its Extension to other Developing Countries' (1985) 10 *Journal of Energy and Development* 273; *OLADE: Historia y perspectiva energética de una región* (Santa Fe de Bogotá: OLADE, 1991). The main source of information remains OLADE's website, available at: www.olade.org/en/about-olade/.

[134] Convenio Constitutivo de la Organización Latinoamericana de Energía [Agreement Establishing the Latin American Energy Organization], 2 November 1973, 1000 UNTS 129 [Lima Agreement].

[135] Declaración de Lima de la XLIX Reunión de Ministros de la Organización Latinoamericana de Energía, 14 November 2019 [Lima Declaration].

Read in the light of the preamble, the 'defensive' dimension of the initiative comes across very clearly. The preamble mentions such dimension twice by reference to 'all kinds of pressures brought to bear against any of them [State parties' in their just struggle to exercise fully their sovereign rights' and then to the need to defend their own energy policies 'in the face of actions, sanctions or coercions'. Thus, like the OPEC a decade earlier, OLADE was born largely as a 'permanent sovereignty' as well as a development organisation. This is further emphasised in Article 3 of the Lima Agreement, which lists many objectives pursued by the organisation and begins, in letter (a), by restating the defensive objective. Of note, no single form of energy is preferred. Instead, the references are to 'natural' or 'energy resources' and a diverse portfolio of resources was central since the early days of the organisation.

The institutional structure of the organisation rests on three main bodies (Article 4): the Meeting of Ministers, the Council of Experts, and a Permanent Secretariat. A limited measure of normative powers is vested on the Meeting of Ministers in Article 10, letters (a) and (b), for the adoption of general policies, internal regulations and recommendations on how to respond to 'unfavourable situations affecting the Member States'. The Meeting of Ministers adopts its decisions with the affirmative vote of at least two-thirds of the Member States (Article 14). The other two bodies have more executive functions, either of impulsion (Article 18(b) vests this function in the Council of Experts) or support (which is generally entrusted to the Permanent Secretariat, directed by an Executive Secretary appointed by the Meeting (Article 10 (g)).

The Permanent Secretariat has been organised, since the 1970s, in four main divisions, the scope and remit of which has varied over time reflecting the focus of the organisation. At present, these divisions are (1) administration, finance and shared services, (2) studies, projects and information, (3) sustainable energy development and (4) energy integration, access and security. The latter two highlight the current focus on sustainability, access and security.

4.3.3 The OLADE and the Latin American Energy Integration Context

As regards integration, it has been an objective of OLADE since the adoption of the Lima Agreement, although an elusive one. Regional integration of and through energy markets features in the preamble as well as in Articles 2 and 3, letters (l) and (m) of the Lima Agreement. It was at the heart of the Pronouncement of San José, a general policy statement adopted in July 1979 by the first Extraordinary Meeting of Ministers,[136] and it is still a key objective stated in 2019 Lima Declaration. Indeed, the third postulate of the Lima Declaration aims to strengthen regional energy integration 'recognising' the role of OLADE in the process, and its fourth postulate confers the character of 'regional priority' on regional energy integration. Such recognition is a frequent feature of such policy statements.

To understand its context, it must be recalled that OLADE operates within a broader network of diverse and sometimes competing organisations at the regional level. As noted by one early observer, 'energy cooperation has had as a frame of reference Latin America's socioeconomic integration process'.[137] Aside from OLADE, some degree of energy-specific institutionalisation was developed for some energy resources and products,[138] such as the 1965 Latin American State Oil Reciprocal Assistance (ARPEL),[139] which brings together the region's national oil companies, the 1964 Regional Electrical Integration Commission (CIER),[140] an association of national electricity committees and utilities, or the 1979 Central American Electrification Council (CEAC).[141] Over time, OLADE has entered into cooperation agreements with these and many other bodies.[142] In addition, the integration context represented by OLADE competes, more generally, with a broader hemispheric-wide model illustrated by the failed US-led Hemispheric Energy Initiative[143] as well as with other Latin American-specific models which are based on a regional hegemony design. This aspect can be illustrated by Venezuela's efforts, throughout the 2000s, to become the

[136] Pronouncement of San José, First Extraordinary Meeting of Ministers, 7 July 1979, English version reproduced in Marciano da Fonseca, The Latin American Energy Organization, Appendix II, para. 11, emphasising the external aspects of a joint Latin American position.

[137] Cruz, *Latin American Energy Cooperation*, at 273.

[138] See Cruz, *Latin American Energy Cooperation*, at 274–276. For a more recent study on regional energy integration see A. Ruiz-Caro, *Cooperación e integración energética en América Latina y el Caribe* (Santiago de Chile: CEPAL, 2006).

[139] Asociación Regional de Empresas de Petróleo y Gas Natural en Latinoamérica y El Caribe: a https://arpel.org/

[140] Comisión de Integración Energética Regional: www.cocier.org

[141] Consejo de Electrificación de América Central: www.ceaconline.org/

[142] For a list of OLADE partnerships see: www.olade.org/en/about-olade/

[143] Summit of the Americas Plan of Action, First Summit of the Americas Miami, Florida, 9–11 December 1994, Initiative 12 (Energy Cooperation).

regional hegemon through its recovered economic strength due to the high price of oil.[144]

It is in such politically complex context that must be read the 2019 Lima Declaration's reaffirmation of OLADE as 'the most suitable space' to develop a high-level energy dialogue (second postulate) and recognition of 'the need to support and strengthen the role of OLADE' in the integration process 'as a regional entity that has the institutional capacity and expertise necessary to propose, accompany and promote the initiatives that are generated in energy integration among its Member Countries' (third postulate).

4.4 ASEAN Energy Cooperation

4.4.1 Origins of ASEAN Energy Cooperation

Much like for other regions and blocs, the October 1973 oil crisis prompted an institutional response from the South-East Asian Nations that a few years earlier had organised themselves under the Association of South-East Asian Nations (ASEAN).

This response came in the form of an ASEAN Council on Petroleum (ASCOPE), established on 15 October 1975[145] on the proposal of Indonesia, with the aim to support ASEAN Ministerial Conferences and, more specifically, to facilitate the sharing of oil in case of a sudden shortage. Prompted by a decision recorded in the Declaration of ASEAN Concord issued by the heads of State and Government meeting in Bali in February 1976,[146] an emergency sharing scheme akin to that of the IEA

[144] See generally A. Ruiz-Caro, 'La cooperación e integración energética en América Latina y el Caribe' in *Puente Europa: Dinámicas productivas de la integración: comercio, moneda, trabajo e industria* (2010), pp. 62–67, at 64–65; P. Singh, 'The Politics of Energy Cooperation in Latin America' (2009) 46 *International Studies* 457; C. Malamud, 'The South American Energy Summit and Regional Integration: A Path Paved with Good (and Not So Good) Intentions', *Working Paper – Real Instituto Elcano* (4 June 2007).

[145] See Memorandum of Understanding on the ASEAN Council on Petroleum, Jakarta, Indonesia, 15 October 1975; Declaration of the ASEAN Council on Petroleum, Jakarta, Indonesia, 15 October 1975.

[146] Declaration of ASEAN Concord, Bali, Indonesia, 24 February 1976, at para. 1(i): 'Member states shall assist each other by according priority to the supply of the individual country's needs in critical circumstances, and priority to the acquisition of exports from member states, in respect of basic commodities, particularly food and energy'.

was developed the following years[147] and eventually formalised in the 1986 ASEAN Petroleum Security Agreement.[148]

Starting in the mid 1980s, this narrow focus on the short-term security of oil supply started to give way to a much broader focus on energy cooperation,[149] first embodied (1) in a number of cooperation treaties, with a limited institutional dimension, and later developed (2) through a range of multi-year plans of action framing energy cooperation as a key component of economic integration.

4.4.2 Legal Framework

Regarding the treaty base, a framework ASEAN Energy Cooperation Agreement was adopted in June 1986[150] with the broad aim to 'cooperate in the efficient development and use of all forms of energy, whether commercial, non-commercial, renewable or non-renewable' (Article 1). This agreement had only a thin institutional basis, in the form of a Consultative Committee of 'Senior Officials' tasked with 'promot[ing] and keep[ing] under review the various cooperation activities envisaged in the framework agreed by the Member Countries' (Article 8).

In 1995, Article 8 of the agreement was amended to strengthen this institutional component by (1) including a specific reference to an annual ASEAN Ministers on Energy Meeting (AMEM) in charge of giving 'guidance' and approving 'policies, strategies and action programmes envisaged in this Agreement', (2) clarifying the executive role of the consultative meeting of senior officials, now called Senior Officials Meeting on Energy (SOME) and (3) entrusting the secretarial aspects to

147 On this process see B. A. Hamzah, 'Petroleum Security Scheme in ASEAN: The Constraints of ASCOPE' (1982) *ASEAN Forecast (Special Supplement)* 37.

148 ASEAN Petroleum Security Agreement Manila, 24 June 1986, establishing the ASEAN Emergency Petroleum Sharing Scheme. This agreement was subsequently superseded by the 2009 ASEAN Petroleum Security Agreement, Cha-am, 1 March 2009, Article 7.7. The 2009 Agreement introduced more flexibility in the response system, following the model of the IEA, through both 'Coordinated Emergency Response Measures' (CERMs) (Article 3.2) and medium/longer-term measures (Article 3.3) based on regional energy cooperation.

149 See e.g. F. Nicolas, *ASEAN Energy Cooperation. An Increasingly Daunting Challenge* (Paris, Institut Français des Relations Internationales, 2009); E. Thompson, 'ASEAN and Northeast Asia Energy Security' (2006) 23 *East Asia* 1; E. Thompson, 'ASEAN and Northeast Asian energy security: cooperation or competition' (2006) 23 *East Asia* 67; A. Symon, 'Fuelling Southeast Asia's growth: the energy challenge' (2004) 21 *ASEAN Economic Bulletin* 239.

150 Agreement on ASEAN Energy Cooperation Manila, 24 June 1986, subsequently amended by protocols of 1995 and 1997.

the ASEAN Secretariat.[151] Within this context, the AMEM has adopted a range of multi-year action plans that are discussed in the next section.

In addition to the framework agreement, over time several other agreements have been concluded to advance energy cooperation within the ASEAN context. A key instrument is the agreement establishing the ASEAN Centre for Energy,[152] which builds upon a prior initiative undertaken in cooperation with the then European Community.[153] The Centre is to 'serve as a catalyst for the economic growth and development of the ASEAN region by initiating, coordinating and facilitating national as well as joint and collective activities on energy' (Article 2). It is expressly granted domestic and international legal personality (Article 1(3)) and it is managed by a Governing Council (partly overlapping the SOME) and an Executive Director.

Other illustrations include Memoranda of Understanding on the development of a Trans-ASEAN Gas Pipeline[154] and an ASEAN Power Grid,[155] or cooperative arrangements with the IEA[156] and IRENA.[157]

151 Protocol Amending the Agreement on ASEAN Energy Cooperation Bangkok, 15 December 1995.

152 Agreement on the Establishment of the ASEAN Centre for Energy, 22 May 1998, subsequently amended in 2013.

153 Agreement on the Establishment of the ASEAN – EC Energy Management Training and Research Centre Brussels, Belgium, 8 September 1988, subsequently amended in 1995. At the fourteenth AMEM, in 1996, Ministers had decided to transform the entity established by the 1988 agreement into an ASEAN Centre on Energy.

154 The ASEAN Memorandum of Understanding (MoU) on the Trans-ASEAN Gas Pipeline, Bali, 5 July 2002, extended until May 2024 by an MoU of 25 September 2013. The development of this major infrastructure project has proved to be more difficult than initially expected. See B. K. Sovacool, 'Energy policy and cooperation in Southeast Asia: The history, challenges, and implications of the trans-ASEAN gas pipeline (TAGP) network' (2009) 37 *Energy Policy* 2356. At the thirty-eighth AMEM, held in November 2020, Ministers reaffirmed 'the continuing role of natural gas in the region's cleaner energy future and the need to continue the pursuit of a common gas market for ASEAN by enhancing connectivity and accessibility of gas', Energy Transition Towards Sustainable Development, Joint Ministerial Statement of the thirty-eighth ASEAN Ministers on Energy Meeting, 19 November 2020 [2020 AMEM Statement], para. 9.

155 Memorandum of Understanding on the ASEAN Power Grid, 23 August 2007. Progress on this initiative has been more substantial, as recorded in the 2020 AMEM Statement, paras. 6–8, including the development of an ASEAN Interconnection Master Plan Study (AIMS) and the launch of a Lao PDR-Thailand-Malaysia-Singapore Power Integration Project (LTMS-PIP).

156 Memorandum of Understanding on Energy Cooperation between the Association of Southeast Asian Nations and the International Energy Agency, 22 September 2011.

157 Memorandum of Understanding between the Association of Southeast Asian Nations and the International Renewable Energy Agency, 30 October 2018.

4.4.3 The Broader ASEAN Economic Integration Context

The cooperative efforts reviewed so far have been extended by several five-year plans of action adopted by the AMEM, starting in the early 1990s. Following an initial programme of action for the period 1991–1995, endorsed by the 1991 AMEM, an ASEAN Medium-Term Programme of Action on Energy Cooperation (1995–1999) focussing on the areas of cooperation initially identified in the 1986 ASEAN Energy Cooperation Agreement.

Since then, a series of ASEAN Plans of Action for Energy Cooperation (APAECs) have been proposed by the SOME and adopted by the AMEM, most recently the APAEC 2016–2025 Phase I: 2016–2020.[158] At its thirty-eighth Meeting in November 2020, the AMEM expressed satisfaction on the achievements of phase I[159] and endorsed the move to phase II, which has a stronger emphasis on accelerating the energy transition.[160] Yet, the APAEC remains committed to different forms of energy, expressly including gas, coal and nuclear alongside renewables, as reaffirmed by the AMEM in its November Statement. This is a typical feature of regional organisations, whether highly (the EU) or loosely integrated (the OLADE and the ASEAN).

158 See ASEAN Centre for Energy, *ASEAN Plan of Action on Energy Cooperation (APAEC) 2016–2025 Phase I: 2016–2020* (Jakarta: ACE, 2015).

159 2020 AMEM Statement, para. 18.

160 See ASEAN Centre for Energy, *ASEAN Plan of Action on Energy Cooperation (APAEC) 2016–2025 Phase II: 2021–2025* (Jakarta: ACE, 2020).

8

International Law and the Energy Transformation

I Overview

In Chapter 1, I introduced the internationalisation of energy transactions by reference to three inflexion points in a narrative, three deep and broad processes which both drive and are driven by the legal organisation of society. As I mentioned then as well as throughout this book, the third process is unfolding before our eyes driven in complex ways by technological, socioeconomic and environmental forces. The overall account provided in this book reflects, at the level of international law, this process of energy transition which in turn is driving a more profound socioeconomic transformation.

But law is not exactly a mirror reflecting technological and socioeconomic developments in 'real-time'. Legal adjustment may be delayed or hindered for a variety of reasons ranging from simple institutional inertia or process complexity to political confrontation to normative choices about the direction of travel. Such choices can either seek to resist or even combat certain social developments or, conversely, try to steer society in certain directions. Understanding the implications of the energy transformation for international law as well as those of the latter for the former requires not only a description of the main manifestations of the energy transformation or of certain legal developments but also an account of how these two layers are interconnected.

In this final chapter, I begin with an account of the interconnections between technological transformation and institutional structures, which I draw from the theory of socio-technical transitions (II). Then, I discuss the main manifestations of the energy transformation, broadly understood as encompassing the technological transition and its wider socioeconomic and geopolitical implications (III). Finally, I analyse the interactions between the process of energy transformation and the international law of energy, drawing upon the more detailed analysis of the rules, processes and institutions conducted in previous chapters (IV).

II Socio-Technical Transitions

To understand the interactions between the process of energy transformation and the international law of energy it is necessary to situate them within a broader account of technological development and the place of institutions in it.

The prevailing understanding of the evolution of energy systems is broadly organised in phases dominated, respectively, by animal/human strength, wind and water mills, combustion of wood, coal and hydrocarbons as the main energy resource, punctuated by phase transitions.[1] From the 1950s and 1960s onwards, contrary to the views of those who believed that nuclear energy would become the prevailing form of energy,[2] fossil fuels consolidated their dominant position albeit in a now more diversified matrix including nuclear, hydroelectricity and a small share of non-hydro renewable sources (then called 'alternative'), particularly after the oil crisis of 1973. Today, we still live under the umbrella of the thermo-industrial revolution, largely based on the combustion of fossil fuels (coal, oil and gas and their derivates) as the main form of energy used for electricity, thermal and transportation purposes.[3]

[1] See V. Smil, 'World History and Energy', in R. U. Ayres (ed.), *Encyclopedia of Energy*, vol. 6 (Amsterdam/Boston: Elsevier, 2004), pp. 549–561. Smil is widely considered the foremost authority in the global history of energy. His 2004 chapter provides a concise outline of this history, which Smil has explored in several previous and subsequent works. For a recent general account see V. Smil, *Energy and Civilization. A History* (Cambridge MA: MIT Press, 2017). 'Sequential' understandings of energy transitions must be handled with caution to avoid the impression of rigid technological determinism. Smil himself warns against such impression: 'When seen from a strictly biophysical point of view, energy may have an unchallenged primacy among the variables determining the course of history, but when it is considered from broader cultural and social perspectives, it may not even rank as primus inter pares. In addition to all of those indisputable energy imperatives, there are a multitude of nonenergy factors that initiate, control, shape, and direct human decisions to harness and use energies in a myriad of specific ways', *World History and Energy*, at 559. This warning is important because legal organisation is one such variable. See further I. J. Miller, P. Warde, 'Energy Transitions as Environmental Events' (2019) 24 *Environmental History* 464, at 467–468.

[2] For a historical account of this projected transition which did not happen see R. D. Lifset, 'Nuclear Power in America: The Story of a Failed Energy Transition' (2019) 24 *Environmental History* 524.

[3] Most energy is consumed by thermal services, heating and cooling (51 per cent), then by transportation (32 per cent), and finally by power generation (17 per cent). The share of renewable energies is still relatively small, particularly in transportation (only 3.3 per cent), whereas in thermal services it accounts for 10 per cent and for 26 per cent in power generation. Importantly, however, this share is growing rapidly. Between 2013 and 2018, total final energy consumption increased by 7.2 per cent. The amount of demand met by

In this context, the term socio-technical transition is used to describe the variation, over time, of a range of technologies, such as those used to generate energy. The 'energy transition' and the wider socioeconomic 'transformation' it entails are examples of a socio-technical transition.[4]

The development and diffusion of new technologies at the heart of socio-technical transitions tends to follow four main stages. The first is a long but critical experimentation and learning phase at the level of technology units (e.g. steam engines, nuclear reactors, photovoltaic panels). This is the phase where technological 'innovation', as it is commonly understood, takes place, although innovations relating to production processes, marketing and strategy may be no less important and they take place at a later stage. In the second phase, the production of these units is scaled up to benefit from economies of scale, which results in more competitive units. In a third phase, increased production allows the new technology to expand its market share and become dominant in the core markets. Finally, the now established technology propagates from core to rim markets through trade and investment and thereby consolidates the new socio-technical regime.[5] In the post 1750 energy transitions, the emergence and diffusion of new forms of generating energy in early adopters was a long process spanning some 130 years (for the adoption and consolidation of coal and steam power) and 80 years (for the adoption of oil, gas and electricity).[6] Late adopters tend to undergo a much faster transition, relying on the experience of early adopters,[7] hence the expression 'first in, last out; last in,

fossil fuels, nuclear and traditional biomass grew at a slower pace (5.7 per cent) whereas that of renewable energy grew much faster (21.4 per cent). Yet, the overall of renewable energy remains below of third of demand growth. See REN21, *Renewables 2020. Global Status Report* (2020).

4 See F. W. Geels, 'Socio-technical transitions to sustainability: a review of criticisms and elaborations of the Multi-Level Perspective' (2019) 39 *Current Opinion in Environmental Sustainability* 187; F. W. Geels, J. Schot, 'Typology of sociotechnical transition pathways' (2007) 36(3) *Research Policy* 399; F. W. Geels, B. K. Sovacool, T. Schwanen, S. Sorrell, 'Sociotechnical transitions for deep decarbonization' (2017) 357(6357) *Science* 1242.

5 A. Grubler, 'Energy transitions research: Insights and cautionary tales' (2012) 50 *Energy Policy* 8, at 14 (discussing the work of C. Wilson, *Meta-analysis of Unit and Industry Level Scaling Dynamics in Energy Technologies and Climate Change Mitigation Scenarios* (Laxenburg: IIASA Interim Report IR-09–029, 2009).

6 Grubler, *Energy transitions research*, at 11–12.

7 See M. Frankel, 'Obsolescence and technological change in a maturing economy' (1955) 45 (3) *American Economic Review* 296; A. Grubler, 'Time for a change: On the patterns of diffusion of innovation' (1996) 125/3 *Daedalus* 19; B. Gales et al, 'North versus south:

first out'.[8] By way of illustration, the United Kingdom and Germany were early adopters of coal and steam (as compared to late adopters such as Italy and Sweden) and it took longer for them to move away from this energy matrix.[9] Throughout these transitions, one socio-technical regime deeply entrenched in terms of sunk investments, power relations, but also legal institutions, was challenged, progressively undermined and finally replaced with another. That entailed a major redistribution of power across market players with important effects for States.

Today, the world is undergoing a socio-technical transition of similar proportions to the thermo-industrial revolution. The financial and technological manifestations of the transition are complex. As noted earlier, total final energy consumption has followed a medium- and long-term upward trajectory, interrupted in 2020 by the measures to manage the COVID-19 pandemic, but likely to continue. The increase in energy consumption has led to an increase in the overall consumption of fossil fuels, nuclear and traditional biomass (again, with the important caveat of the pandemic, which has massively affected transportation). A 2020 Report by REN21 quantifies this increase at approximately 5.7 per cent, which is lower than the increase of 7.2 per cent in overall energy demand over the same period (2013–2018), but an increase nevertheless.[10] It is therefore not in the absolute figures that the transition is most visible but in the relative shares. In the same period, modern renewables (mainly solar and wind) grew much faster (21.5 per cent) than both energy consumption and other energy sources. When one looks at new financial investment (annual) in new energy generation capacity, the growth of modern renewables is also striking. Between 2018 and 2019, the capacity to generate electricity (measured in gigawatts) increased from 512 to 627 GW for solar photovoltaic (22 per cent) and from 591 to 651 GW for wind power (10 per cent). The leading country at the level of investment and new capacity in solar PV and wind is China, followed by the United States, and then other countries such as Japan (for overall investment and solar PV), India (for overall investment, solar PV and wind power) and the United Kingdom (only for wind power). According to the *World Energy Outlook* 2020, an influential annual report produced by the IEA,

energy transitions and energy intensity in Europe over 200 years' (2006) 11/2 *European Review of Economic History* 219; Wilson, *Meta-analysis.*

[8] Grubler, *Energy transitions research*, at 12.

[9] Grubler, *Energy transitions research*, at 13 (figure 2).

[10] See generally REN21, *Renewables 2020. Global Status Report* (2020).

solar power schemes in most major countries can now produce electricity at a cost which is lower than coal and gas.[11] Another important conclusion from this report is that the gains from cheaper and cleaner electricity (with electricity gaining ground in the provision of thermal and transportation services)[12] puts great pressure on the need for suitable electricity networks (grids and transmission lines), at a time when the COVID-19 shock has financially weakened the utilities undertaking such infrastructure developments. Thus, 'electricity grids could prove to be the weak link in the transformation of the power sector'.[13] The technological transition is therefore clear when seen from the perspective of modern renewable energies. The broader implications of the transition, however, are far more difficult to determine.

III The Energy Transformation

3.1 From Transition to Transformation

An attempt at mapping the profound implications of – i.e. the 'transformation' driven by – the energy transition is provided in a January 2019 report from the Global Commission on the Geopolitics of the Energy Transformation,[14] convened by the Director of IRENA and chaired by the former President of Iceland, Ólafur Ragnar Grímsson.

This is the first mainstream attempt to map and assess the implications of the ongoing energy transition (the report refers to these wider socio-economic implications of the transition as the 'energy transformation') from the perspective of global power redistribution. As noted in the introduction to the report:

> [t]he accelerating deployment of renewables has set in motion a global energy transformation that will have profound geopolitical consequences. Just as fossil fuels have shaped the geopolitical map over the last two centuries, the energy transformation will alter the global distribution of

[11] IEA, *World Energy Outlook* (2020), Executive Summary, at 18 ('With sharp cost reductions over the past decade, solar PV is consistently cheaper than new coal- or gas-fired power plants in most countries, and solar projects now offer some of the lowest cost electricity ever seen').

[12] On this specific issue see M. Grubb, P. Drummond, N. Hughes, *The Shape and Pace of Change in the Electricity Transition: Sectoral Dynamics and Indicators of Progress* (UCL/We mean business coalition, October 2020).

[13] IEA, *World Energy Outlook* (2020), Executive Summary, at 19.

[14] Global Commission on the Geopolitics of the Energy Transformation, *A New World: The Geopolitics of the Energy Transformation* (IRENA, 2019).

> power, relations between states, the risk of conflict, and the social, economic and environmental drivers of geopolitical instability.[15]

The drivers of this transformation, according to the report (which summarises a wider body of work appearing in major peer-reviewed publications), are the declining costs of electricity produced from non-hydro renewable sources, the problems of pollution and climate change caused by fossil fuels, the spread of renewable energy promotion policies, technological innovation, shareholders' increasing demands, and a major shift in public opinion.[16]

Regarding the reasons why this transformation affects geopolitics, they relate to the broader availability of renewable energy resources (by contrast with the geographically concentrated fossil fuels), the fact that they are 'flows' rather than 'stocks' (hence not exhaustible), the ability to deploy renewables at any scale, from a macro to a micro level (the so-called democratising effects of renewable energies), and their rapidly decreasing marginal costs, which requires however stable regulatory and market conditions.[17]

3.2 *The Geopolitics of Stranded Fossil Fuel Assets*

An example can bring these rather abstract geopolitical considerations into focus. A widely reported study published in 2018 in *Nature Climate Change* showed that, due specifically to the diffusion of renewable energy, electric transportation systems and efficiency measures, the demand (not the supply) for fossil fuels may peak and then decline sometime between 2030 and 2040.[18] From the perspective of countries producing at a comparatively high cost, such as Canada and Venezuela but also the United States and Russia, the decline in demand is estimated to have major effects on the viability of their entire fossil fuel industry, as such demand will be satisfied by low-cost producers (e.g. Gulf countries). By contrast, for net fossil fuel importers such as China and Japan, the effect of this phenomenon on their gross domestic product would be positive.

[15] *The Geopolitics of the Energy Transformation*, at 12.

[16] *The Geopolitics of the Energy Transformation*, at 18–23. For an analysis based on modelling techniques see J.-F. Mercure et al, 'Reframing incentives for climate policy action' (2021) 6 *Nature Energy* https://doi.org/10.1038/s41560-021-00934-2

[17] *The Geopolitics of the Energy Transformation*, at 23–24.

[18] J.F. Mercure et al, 'Macroeconomic impact of stranded fossil fuel assets' (2018) 8 *Nature Climate Change* 588.

These results were based on the use of high-resolution integrated assessment modelling techniques.[19] The study identified possible 'winners' and 'losers' of this transition.

Unlike previous studies, the projections in this study are not based on whether new climate policies are adopted but entirely driven by decisions and investment that has already occurred in the past, and which has set the world into a broad and possibly irreversible technological trajectory. Yet, if new climate policies to reach the 'well below' 2C target of the Paris Agreement are indeed adopted and low-cost fossil fuel producers continue their production at current levels, the adverse impact on high-cost fossil fuel producers would be much deeper and more disruptive (the entire fossil fuel industries of Canada, Russia and the United States may collapse). The study was widely reported in the media, circulated by influential figures such as former US Vice President Al Gore, taken up in domestic political processes (e.g. divestment campaigns and opposition to new fossil fuel development), and relied upon in major institutional reports such as the *Special Report on the 1.5C target* issued by the Intergovernmental Panel for Climate Change (IPCC),[20] the 2018 *New Climate Economy Report*,[21] and the aforementioned 2019 *Report on the Geopolitics of the Global Energy Transformation*.[22] It remains, of course, an attempt at anticipating possible future scenarios and, as such, subject to caution. But it is, at the very least, worth considering.

Two potential extensions of this study concern power redistribution at the international and domestic levels. At the international level, China would gain significantly from accelerating the energy transition, not only because it would help it address its critical air pollution problem but also because it would promote the competitiveness of its own renewable energy industry abroad and, by undermining the economic strength of the United States and Russia, it would strengthen its strategic position with respect to two key geopolitical competitors. The EU, as a major importer of fossil fuels and a resolute supporter of the low-carbon

[19] J.-F. Mercure et al, 'Environmental impact assessment for climate change policy with the simulation-based integrated assessment model E3ME-FTT-GENIE' (2018) 20 *Energy Strategy Reviews* 195 (describing in detail the model used for this type of simulation and scenario building).

[20] IPCC, *Special Report: Global warming of 1.5°C* (2018), chapter 4, at 319, 373–375.

[21] Global Commission on the Economy and Climate, *New Climate Economy: Unlocking the inclusive growth story of the 21st century: Accelerating climate action in urgent times* (2018), at 12, 39.

[22] *The Geopolitics of the Energy Transformation*, at 64–65, 82.

transition through its industrial policy would also gain much from the acceleration of the transition, both in terms of cheaper imports and competitiveness in international markets. However, domestically, the structural adjustment entailed by the energy transition in countries with (comparatively) uncompetitive fossil fuel industries may severely affect certain specific sectors of the population, particularly workers in these industries. Depending on which political forces are supported by these constituencies, these important implications of the transition could generate a fertile ground for populist politics in key countries, with the attendant volatility for international relations. Even in countries such as China, which have spearheaded the move to renewables, the massive implications of moving away from fossil fuels would have a massive impact on domestic workers in this sector.

3.3 The Geopolitics of Critical Raw Materials

A dimension of the new energy geopolitics which is not adequately captured in the work discussed so far concerns so-called critical raw materials (CRMs), namely certain mineral components which are strategically important for renewable energy technologies (Li-ion batteries, fuel cells, wind energy, electric traction motors, PV technology), artificial intelligence, the digital economy and defence. The EU, Japan and the United States have established specific lists of CRMs, which are regularly updated.[23] The geographical distribution of the production of CRMs is highly concentrated in a number of countries. That introduces an important dimension of mineral geopolitics, akin to the concentrations of oil and gas in certain large producers. Between 2021 and 2016 China

[23] EU: European Commission, *Critical Raw Materials Resilience: Charting a Path towards greater Security and Sustainability*, 3 September 2020, COM/2020/474 final; G.-A. Blengini et al, *Study on the EU's List of Critical Raw Materials* (European Commission, 2020) [*Study on the EU CRMs List*]; S. Bobba et al, *Critical Raw Materials for Strategic Technologies and Sectors in the EU. A Foresight Study* (European Commission, 2020) [*CRMs Foresight Study*]; Japan: Resource Securement Strategies, Prime Minister of Japan and His Cabinet, 2012, www.kantei.go.jp/jp/singi/package/dai15/sankou01.pdf (in Japanese); H. Hatayama, K. Tahara, 'Criticality Assessment of Metals for Japan's Resource Strategy' (2015) 56 *Materials Transactions* 229; United States: Department of the Interior, Final List of Critical Minerals 2018, 18 May 2018, Federal Register, vol. 83, No. 97, pp. 23295–23296; M. Humphries, *Critical Materials and US Public Policy* (Congressional Research Service, 18 June 2019).

alone was the main global supplier of 66 per cent of CRMs[24] and of 44 per cent of those supplied to the EU.[25]

For certain CRMs, widely used in wind energy and electric vehicles,[26] such as Heavy Rare Earth Elements (HREEs[27]) and Light Rare Earth Elements (LREEs[28]), China alone accounted for 86 per cent of global supply and for almost all (98–99 per cent) of those imported by the EU.[29] As regards PV technology, it relies on CRMs such as borate, gallium, germanium, indium and silicon metal.[30] With the exception of borate, whose main global supplier is Turkey, the main global supplier of all these other CRMs is China (gallium: 80 per cent, germanium: 80 per cent, indium: 48 per cent, silicon metal: 66 per cent).[31] To manage risks of potential supply disruption, the EU sources most of these CRMs from countries other than China (Turkey, Germany, Finland, France and Norway).[32] As for batteries, which is a key technology for both electricity storage and electric vehicles, their production relies on materials such as cobalt, lithium, natural graphite, niobium, silicon metal and titanium, as well as on non-critical materials such as copper, manganese and nickel.[33] The main global suppliers of these inputs are scattered around the globe, but not all are equally important. Cobalt and nickel (as a base for cathodes), lithium (as an electrolyte material) and natural graphite (as a base for anodes) are key. China is the main global supplier of natural graphite (69 per cent) and the Democratic Republic of the Congo that of cobalt (59 per cent).[34] Regarding the latter, there have been concerns that China's Belt and Road Initiative (BRI) may lead to Chinese economic control over the reserves of strategic minerals in Africa, including cobalt in the DRC.[35] Lithium, which is a key component, is mainly produced in

[24] *Study on the EU CRMs List*, at 6.
[25] *Study on the EU CRMs List*, at 8.
[26] *CRMs Foresight Study*, at 17, 29–33 (wind energy), 34–37 (electric vehicles).
[27] Dysprosium, erbium, europium, gadolinium, holmium, lutetium, terbium, thulium, ytterbium, yttrium.
[28] Cerium, lanthanum, neodymium, praseodymium and samarium.
[29] *Study on the EU CRMs List*, at 5 and 8.
[30] *CRMs Foresight Study*, at 17, 38–42.
[31] *Study on the EU CRMs List*, at 5.
[32] *Study on the EU CRMs List*, at 8.
[33] *CRMs Foresight Study*, at 17, 19–23.
[34] *Study on the EU CRMs List*, at 5.
[35] See J. Lee et al, 'Reviewing the material and metal security of low-carbon energy transitions' (2020) 124 *Renewable and Sustainable Energy Reviews*, https://doi.org/10.1016/j.rser.2020.109789 (at 8).

Argentina (16 per cent), Australia (29 per cent) and Chile (40 per cent), but 45 per cent of the lithium hard rock mineral refining is based in China.[36]

The latter point raises a dimension which is well covered in the reports commissioned by the EU to update its CMRs list, namely flow disruption as a result of bottlenecks in the supply chain. Keeping with the example of batteries, China has a pre-eminent role not only at the level of raw material supply but, even more so at those of material processing (for cathodes and anodes), component development (cathodes, anodes, electrolytes, separators) and assemblies (e-ion cells).[37] In such a context, the governance of the continued flow of materials within the global supply chains remains a major issue, much like in the classical geopolitics of oil and gas. The claims against China's export restrictions of raw materials and rare earths brought in the last decade before WTO dispute settlement organs, some foreign investment disputes relating to prospection of rare earths, and the scramble for the deep seabed mining of such minerals[38] are but some illustrations of the role of international law with regard to this dimension of the new geopolitics of critical materials.

[36] *CRMs Foresight Study*, at 19.

[37] *Study on the EU CRMs List*, at 20.

[38] For trade disputes see e.g. *China – Measures Related to the Exportation of Various Raw Materials*, AB Report, 30 January 2012, WT/DS394/AB/R WT/DS395/AB/R WT/DS398/AB/R 30 (dispute relating to a complaint by the United States regarding restrictions on exports of certain critical and non-critical materials, specifically bauxite, coke, fluorspar, magnesium, manganese, silicon carbide, silicon metal, yellow phosphorus and zinc) [*China – Raw Materials*]; *China – Measures Related to the Exportation of Rare Earths, Tungsten, and Molybdenum*, AB Report, 7 August 2014, WT/DS431/AB/RWT/DS432/AB/RWT/DS433/AB/R (dispute relating to a complaint by the United States regarding restrictions on exports of certain critical and non-critical materials, specifically various forms of rare earths, tungsten and molybdenum) [*China – Rare Earths*]; *China – Duties and other Measures concerning the Exportation of Certain Raw Materials – Request for the establishment of a panel by the European Union*, 27 October 2016, WT/DS509/6 (the dispute concerns restrictions on exports of certain critical and non-critical materials, specifically antimony, chromium, cobalt, copper, graphite, indium, lead, magnesia, talc, tantalum and tin) [*China – Duties on Raw Materials*]. Regarding foreign investment disputes see e.g. *Metal-Tech Ltd. v. Republic of Uzbekistan*, ICSID Case No. ARB/10/3, Award (4 October 2013) (the dispute concerned a molybdenum processing project); *Stans Energy Corp. and Kutisay Mining LLC v. Kyrgyz Republic*, PCA Case No. 2015–32, Award (20 August 2019) (the dispute concerned licenses for the exploration of rare earths, bismuth, molybdenum and silver in the Kutisay II deposit); *Cortec Mining Kenya Limited, Cortec (Pty) Limited and Stirling Capital Limited v. Republic of Kenya*, ICSID Case No. ARB/15/29, Award (22 October 2018) (the dispute concerned prospecting licenses for rare earths and niobium); *Navodaya Trading DMCC v. Gabon*, UNCITRAL Rules (OIC Investment Agreement), filed in 2018, pending (dispute

IV International Law as a Battle Front

4.1 *Introductory Observations*

In the power shifts described in the foregoing paragraphs, international law (and law in general) is a critical battle front. As I noted earlier by reference to the literature on socio-technical transitions, socio-technical regimes tend to consolidate through their deep entrenchment in terms of sunk investments, power relations but also legal institutions, domestic and international. Challengers of a socio-technical regime must therefore overcome a whole set of 'rules of the game' which have been designed or which otherwise suit the prevailing socio-technical regime.

The process of moving from one socio-technical regime to another can therefore be especially turbulent from a legal standpoint and, more specifically, from a regulatory change perspective. We can expect the legal institutions that give expression to the entrenchment of a given socio-technical regime (e.g. the ad hoc regimes for the joint development of hydrocarbons and the pipeline agreements for their transportation discussed in Chapters 4 and 5) to co-exist with new expressions which open trails for the new regime to grow. Such trails may find expression at the broad level of 'purposes', as discussed in Chapter 1 by reference to the

concerning the non-renewal of a manganese exploration permit in East Gabon); *Montero Mining and Exploration Ltd. v. United Republic of Tanzania* (Canada–Tanzania BIT), Notice of Intent to Submit a Claim to Arbitration (17 January 2020) (dispute concerning Montero's investment in the Wigu Hill rare earth element project). As for deep seabed mining, the main targets are polymetallic nodules (PMN), cobalt-rich ferromanganese crusts (CFCs) and seafloor massive sulphides (SMS) (containing a range of critical and non-critical materials from cobalt, manganese, nickel, tungsten to lithium, germanium, molybdenum and rare earths used in batteries, renewable energy technologies and electric vehicles). On the exploration contracts concerning these resources see the website of International Seabed Authority (ISA), listing the contracts for PMN, CFCs and polymetallic sulphides: www.isa.org.jm/exploration-contracts. On deep seabed mining see: European Commission, *Communication: Blue Growth – Opportunities for marine and maritime sustainable growth*, 13 September 2012, COM(2012) 494 final, section 5.4; ECORYS, *Study to investigate the state of knowledge of deep-sea mining* (2014); K. Miller et al, 'An Overview of Seabed Mining Including the Current State of Development, Environmental Impacts, and Knowledge Gaps' (2018) 4 *Frontiers in Marine Science*, doi: 10.3389/fmars.2017.00418; I. Feichtner, 'Sharing the Riches of the Sea: The Redistributive and Fiscal Dimension of Deep Seabed Exploitation' (2019) 30 *European Journal of International Law* 601; I. Feichtner, 'Mining for humanity in the deep sea and outer space: The role of small states and international law in the extraterritorial expansion of extraction' (2019) 32 *Leiden Journal of International Law* 255; S. Ranganathan, 'Ocean Floor Grab: International Law and the Making of an Extractive Imaginary' (2019) 30 *European Journal of International Law* 573.

emergence and consolidation of 'access' and 'sustainability' as purposes of energy governance, as well as in Chapters 6 and 7 by reference to the reorientation of the mandates and functions of centralised (e.g. the IAEA or EU energy policy) and proto-centralised regimes (e.g. the reorientation of the IEA mandate and the establishment of IRENA). They can also be supported by the development of new legal frameworks, either general (such as the multilateral environmental agreements discussed in Chapter 3) or project-specific (such as the ad hoc regimes developed to support offshore windfarms and cross-border transmission lines discussed in Chapter 5). The latter are noteworthy because, rather than limiting themselves to the regulation of negative externalities, they specifically organise new transactions. But the consolidation of a new socio-technical regime needs to go a step further and reach much deeper into the general legal frameworks organising the heart of those transactions that define the prevailing socio-technical regime. This is where the battle front between the prevailing energy regime and the emerging one lies today.

My goal in the following sections is to examine the current front lines by providing some specific and representative illustrations of how such power struggles are finding expression in international law. For presentation purposes, these examples can be grouped in three broad categories, namely the use of international law: to challenge or delay the transition (3.2); to outperform competitors trying to grasp the opportunities of the transition or, at least, to navigate its complexities (3.3); and to secure some level of inclusiveness both in the decisions relating to the transition and in its social effects (3.4).

4.2 Hindering the Transition

4.2.1 Introduction

Regarding the first category of examples, different norms and institutions can be used to hinder or delay the transition or at least recoup part of the cost incurred by those sectors and countries deeply entrenched in the fossil fuel economy. The operation of existing rules in this context can be illustrated by reference to several legal debates.

Here, I focus on three of them: the debate about the regulation of different types of energy-related subsidies under trade law, the debate surrounding the progressive extension of the Emissions Trading Directive to cover new sectors, and the use of foreign investment claims by fossil fuel and nuclear energy companies to recover part of the value lost as a result of energy transition policies.

4.2.2 Fossil Fuel and Renewable Energy Subsidies under Trade Law

The debate on the trade-compatibility of, on the one hand, subsidies to fossil fuels and, on the other hand, subsidies to renewable energies, has become increasingly important as a result of the magnitude and implications of the former as compared to the latter.

According to a study from IRENA,[39] the world's total direct (financial transfers) energy subsidies to fossil fuels, renewables and nuclear energy amounted to at least USD 634 billion in 2017. Fossil fuel subsidies accounted for USD 447 billion, whereas subsidies to renewable energy accounted for USD 128 billion (for electricity generation) and USD 38 billion (for biofuels). Unpriced negative externalities from subsidies to fossil fuels (negative effects caused by fossil fuel transactions and not borne – internalised – by transaction participants) amounted to a staggering USD 3.1 trillion in the same year, which is nineteen times the subsidies to renewable energies (electricity and biofuels taken together).

In this context, one would expect trade law to either favour the shift away from fossil fuel subsidies or, at the very least, to place them legally and practically on an equal footing with subsidies to renewable energy. Yet, the conclusions of a detailed study on the treatment of these two types of subsidies under trade law suggest that trade law is more permissive and lenient for subsidies to fossil fuels than for subsidies to renewable energy.[40] In essence, renewable energy subsidies are more vulnerable to challenges under trade law because the support schemes used are more specific (hence more 'actionable' in trade law terminology) and they often rely (for political reasons) on local content requirements (LCRs).[41] By contrast, fossil fuel subsidies are consumer-targeted and

[39] M. Taylor, *Energy Subsidies: Evolution in the Global Energy Transformation to 2050* (Abu Dhabi: IRENA, April 2020), at 8ff.

[40] See H. B. Asmelash, 'Energy Subsidies and WTO Dispute Settlement: Why only Renewable Energy Subsidies are Challenged' (2015) 18 *Journal of International Economic Law* 261. See also J. P. Trachtman, *Fossil Fuel Subsidies Reduction and the World Trade Organization* (Geneva: ICTSD, 2017).

[41] See J.-C. Kuntze, T. Morenhout, *Local Content Requirements and the Renewable Energy Industry – A Good Match?* (Geneva: ICTSD, 2013) (discussing the use of LCRs in renewable energy support schemes in a dozen countries, namely Argentina, Brazil, Canada, China, Croatia, France, India, Italy, South Africa, Turkey and the United

introduce no clear differentiation across recipients, which makes them more difficult to challenge under existing trade law. These conclusions illustrate how trade law can hinder the move from one socio-technical regime to another although, as the author notes, fossil fuel subsidies have been addressed to some extent in WTO accession negotiations[42] and, occasionally, in free trade agreements.[43] It must also be noted that it is not renewable energy subsidies at large which are targeted in the few cases heard by WTO dispute settlement organs so far, but only certain specific schemes (LCRs in feed-in-tariff schemes supporting domestic producers of equipment),[44] the structure of which is largely determined for political reasons.

For present purposes, the different regime – in practice – of fossil fuel subsidies and of certain renewable energy subsidies in use suggest that some core rules of trade law (e.g. the national treatment standard,[45] the more specific prohibition of LCRs[46] or the Agreement on Subsidies and Countervailing Duties[47]) are being construed in such a way as to restrict industrial policy, including the so-called green industrial policy, i.e. the policies adopted by a State to provide targeted support to certain industries and sectors as a way of realising latent comparative advantages.[48] By contrast, as discussed in Chapter 2, the sweeping fossil fuel subsidies provided by many States were overlooked or implicitly grandfathered or, still, deliberately left unclearly regulated under the trade regime.

States). On LCRs for renewable energy see generally G. C. Hufbauer, J. J. Schott, C. Cimino-Isaacs, M. Vieiro and and E. Wadam, *Local Content Requirements: A Global Problem* (New York: Columbia University Press, 2013).

42 Asmelash, *Energy Subsidies*, at 281–282.

43 See E. Cima, 'Promoting Renewable Energy Through FTAs? The Legal Implications of a New Generation of Trade Agreements' (2018) 52 *Journal of World Trade* 663, at 672 (referring to the FTA between the EU and Singapore, Articles 7.3 and 13.11(3)).

44 On this key point see I. Espa, G. Marin Duran, 'Renewable Energy Subsidies and WTO Law: Time to Rethink the Case for Reform Beyond Canada – Renewable Energy/Fit Program' (2018) 21 *Journal of International Economic Law* 621, at 624–628.

45 GATT, Article III.

46 GATT, Article III(4)–(5), and Agreement on Trade-Related Investment Measures, 15 April 1994, Marrakesh Agreement Establishing the World Trade Organization, Annex 1A, 1868 UNTS 186, Articles 2.1, 2.2 and Annex (Illustrative List), para. 1(a).

47 Agreement on Subsidies and Countervailing Measures, 15 April 1994, Marrakesh Agreement Establishing the World Trade Organization, Annex 1A, 1869 UNTS 14, Article 3.1(b).

48 See generally M. Wu, J. Salzman, 'The Next Generation of Trade and Environment Conflicts: The Rise of Green Industrial Policy' (2014) 108 *Northwestern University Law Review* 401.

The issue came to prominence only after the 1973 oil crisis and, despite some reference to it during the Tokyo round (1973–1979), it was not until the Uruguay round that it was addressed in some detail (1986–1994). The attempts to constrain States' margin of manoeuvre in this area were, however, resisted and ultimately unsuccessful.

4.2.3 The Extension of the ETS Directive to New Sectors

Another useful illustration is provided by the progressive extension of the ambit of regulated sectors and entities under the EU Emissions Trading Scheme (ETS),[49] which ends its third phase in 2020 and will be starting its fourth phase (2021–2030).[50] The ambit of the ETS has been expanded in phases, and some carbon-intensive operators adversely affected by the extension have – unsurprisingly – challenged the scheme.

One early dispute during the first phase concerned the inclusion of certain sectors (steel) while others (aluminium and chemicals) were left outside. In the *Arcelor Mittal* cases,[51] Arcelor, a large steel producer, challenged the application of the ETS Directive and the French implementing measures to its operations as contrary to the equal treatment clause in the EU founding treaties. The heart of the challenge was whether the ETS Directive could – without unlawful discrimination – apply to the steel sector but not to chemical and aluminium sectors. The ECJ concluded that the three sectors at stake were 'in a comparable position' but that the differential treatment was justified as a valid exercise of the Community's 'broad discretion' based on 'objective criteria appropriate to the aim pursued'.[52] In this case, there is no clear 'brown versus green' element in the dispute, but there is certainly an attempt to use legal instruments to challenge energy transition measures.

[49] Consolidated Text of Directive 2003/87/EC of 13 October 2003 establishing a system for greenhouse gas emission allowance trading within the Union, last amended on 18 May 2020 [ETS Directive].

[50] The documentation on this ongoing revision process is available at: https://ec.europa.eu/clima/policies/ets/revision_en#tab-0-1.

[51] The ECJ was seized in two ways, namely through a reference procedure from the French *Conseil d'Etat* (*Société Arcelor Atlantique et Lorraine et al. V. Premier Ministre, Ministre de l'Economie, des Finances et de l'Industrie, Ministre de l'Ecologie et du Développement Durable*, ECJ Case C-127/07, Judgment (16 December 2008) [*Arcelor reference*]) and through an action for annulment brought by Arcelor (*Arcelor SA v. European Parliament and Council*, ECJ Case T-16/04, Judgment (2 March 2010) [*Arcelor annulment*]).

[52] See *Arcelor reference*, paras. 38, 57–58, 69 and 72.

A clearer example emerged when the EU sought to extend the third phase of the ETS to cover the aviation sector, including companies from non-EU countries insofar as they maintained flights taking off from or landing in EU territory.[53] The extraterritorial aspects of this extension led to a legal challenge by a group of US aviation companies[54] and, concomitantly, to great diplomatic pressure from the United States as well as some emerging economies, most notably China, to limit the scope of the extension.[55] The decision of the ECJ's grand chamber addressed several important questions of international law, most notably the nature of the obligations arising from the Kyoto Protocol and the scope of certain customary principles (State sovereignty over its own airspace, prohibition of appropriation of the high seas, freedom to fly over the high seas), which had been invoked by the claimant to argue that the extension was unlawful.[56] But the Court concluded otherwise.

Yet, eventually, the EU gave in to political pressure and limited the ETS extension to flights within the European Economic Area (EEA: EU countries plus Iceland, Lichtenstein and Norway),[57] while the regime applicable to aviation was addressed by the International Civil Aviation Organization (ICAO).[58] Negotiations within ICAO led to a system of emissions reduction (CORSIA) applicable as of 2021[59] and, as a result, the EU maintained the scope limitation of the ETS Direction only to intra-EEA flights.[60]

53 Directive 2008/101/EC of 19 November 2008 amending Directive 2003/87/EC so as to include aviation activities in the scheme for greenhouse gas emission allowance trading within the Community.

54 *Air Transport Association of America and others v. Secretary of State for Energy and Climate Change*, CJEU Case C-366/10 (21 December 2011) [*Aviation case*].

55 See L. Rajamani, J. Scott, 'EU Climate Unilateralism' (2012) 23 *European Journal of International Law* 469.

56 *Aviation case*, paras. 73–78 (on Kyoto) and 101–111 (principles of international customary law).

57 See Regulation (EU) No. 421/2014 of 16 April 2014.

58 See Consolidated statement of continuing ICAO policies and practices related to environmental protection, adopted at the thirty-eighth Session of the Assembly of the ICAO, 4 October 2013.

59 The Carbon Offsetting and Reduction Scheme for International Aviation (CORSIA), is based on ICAO Assembly, Resolution A39/3 'Consolidated statement of continuing ICAO policies and practices relating to environmental protection – Global Market-Based Measure (GMBM) scheme', 6 October 2016, Doc. ICAO/A/39-WP/530, para. 5.

60 Regulation (EU) 2017/2392 of 13 December 2017 amending Directive 2003/87/EC to continue current limitations of scope for aviation activities and to prepare to implement a global market-based measure from 2021.

4.2.4 Recouping Lost Value

The third illustration where the tension between 'brown' and 'green' is more visible is provided by certain investment claims brought by companies adversely affected by energy transition policies. It is difficult to ascertain exactly whether the measures at stake in different disputes are aimed to pursue the energy transition or are triggered by other considerations. The fact that the measure has no environmental aim is not necessarily relevant because, as discussed earlier, the energy transition is driven by a range of considerations, including purely economic ones. In this section, I provide two representative examples of such disputes, which concern nuclear energy and coal-fired electricity generation.

The first example concerns a series of claims by Swedish investor Vattenfall against Germany in connection with measures restricting its coal-fired electricity generation activities[61] and the phaseout of nuclear energy.[62] The first claim has been settled and the second is still pending, but they both reflect the use of certain legal instruments, *in casu* the investment protection standards of the Energy Charter Treaty,[63] to challenge regulatory change at the level of domestic, EU and international law. The second case arises, more specifically, from the nuclear phaseout enacted by Germany in 2011, following the Fukushima accident,[64] which set 2022 as the deadline to shut down all remaining nuclear energy reactors, including those of Vattenfall. Although, at the time of writing, the foreign investment claim against Germany was still pending, on 29 September 2020 the German Constitutional Court ruled[65] in favour of Vattenfall, concluding that the compensation clause of the nuclear phaseout law was partially unconstitutional and that a 2018 amendment to this law,[66] required by a 2016 decision, was not sufficient to bring the law into conformity with the constitution. In its December 2016, the Court had considered that the fixed shutdown dates

[61] *Vattenfall AB, Vattenfall Europe AG, Vattenfall Europe Generation AG v. Federal Republic of Germany*, ICSID Case No. ARB/09/6, Award (11 March 2011) (embodying the parties' settlement agreement of the same date) [Vattenfall I].

[62] *Vattenfall AB and others v. Federal Republic of Germany*, ICSID Case No. ARB/12/12, pending [Vattenfall II].

[63] Energy Charter Treaty, 17 December 1994, 2080 UNTS 100. See Chapter 2.

[64] Thirteenth Act Amending the Atomic Energy Act (13. Gesetzes zur Änderungdes Atomgesetzes, 31 July 2011, Bundesgesetzblatt 2011 Seite 1704).

[65] Order of the Federal Constitutional Court (29 September 2020), 1 BvR 1550/19.

[66] Sixteenth Act Amending the Atomic Energy Act (16. Gesetz zur Änderung des Atomgesetzes – 16. AtG-Novelle, 16th AtG Amendment), Article 1.

set in 2011 were inconsistent with the right to property protected by Article 14(1) of the German Constitution[67] because inter alia it did not provide adequate compensation for unused residual electricity volumes. Aside from procedural aspects relating to the conditioning of the entry into force of the 2018 amendment upon a binding State aid-related determination of the European Commission, the heart of the decision lies in a proportionality assessment. According to the Court, subordinating compensation for unused residual electricity volumes (unsold electricity as a result of the shutdown) to reasonable efforts by Vattenfall to sell that capacity to another company was only admissible if the conditions of the sale were sufficiently clear, which they were not under the law. The developments in this case so far illustrate an important dimension of transitional processes, which, from a legal standpoint, must address previously acquired rights.

The second example provides a clearer illustration of how foreign investment law may be used to seek to recoup the value of assets which have lost value as a result of the low-carbon transition. It concerns a US coal mining company, Westmoreland Coal Co., which as other coal mining companies, has struggled financially as a result of the transition away from coal.[68] The complaint challenges a climate change–driven policy by the government of Alberta, in Canada, which shortens the lifespan of coal-fired electricity generation and thereby affects the profitability of mines supplying coal to adjacent power-generation plants. The claim is expressly framed as one focussing on regulatory change driven by the low-carbon transition:

> In 2012, the Government of Canada decided to take action with respect to the greenhouse effects of burning coal. It enacted regulations that committed to closing down all power utilities that relied on coal within fifty years. These regulations ensured that existing coal-burning power utilities would be phased out over time, giving stability and predictability to both the power plants and the coal companies that provide the fuel. [...] In 2013–2014, Westmoreland acquired a number of coalmines, including the

[67] Judgment of the Federal Constitutional Court (6 December 2016), BVerfGE 143, 246, paras. 1, 2 and 4 (operative part).

[68] The company, which was the United States' largest independent coal producer, went into joint administration in according with the US Bankruptcy Code (chapter 11, under the caption *In re Westmoreland Coal Company, et al.*, 18–35672 (DRJ) (Bankr. S.D. Tex.)), and it re-emerged in early 2019 as a privately held company owned and operated by a group of its former creditors. See 'Westmoreland emerges from Chapter 11', Westmoreland News Release, 15 March 2019, KL2 3116482.5.

> 'mine-mouth' operations in Alberta at issue in this dispute. For mine-mouth operations, coalmines are developed adjacent to and in conjunction with a power so that the coal can be delivered to the power plant economically. [...] The logic and value of Westmoreland's investment was threatened with change in November 2015 when a new Alberta provincial government announced its 'Climate Leadership Plan'. Alberta, which historically had relied primarily on its abundant coal supply to fuel its power plants, decided that it wanted to eliminate all power emanating from coal by 2030.[69]

Subsequently, the investor refers to the compensation scheme designed by Alberta and claims that it was discriminatorily excluded from it due to the fact that it is not from Alberta. Of particular note, the investor does not seem to challenge the phaseout itself but rather the allegedly discriminatory compensation policy: 'Westmoreland recognizes and does not dispute that Canada and Alberta are entitled to enact regulations for the public good. However, when they do, the must be fair to foreign investors'.[70] It claims a minimum of USD 470 million, plus interest.[71] The dispute is pending and, irrespective of its merits, which will be evaluated

69 *Westmoreland Coal Company v. Government of Canada*, UNCITRAL Rules (NAFTA Dispute), Notice of Arbitration and Statement of Claim, 19 November 2018 [*Westmoreland NoA*], paras. 4–6. Another dispute arising from the environmental focus on the Albertan government elected in 2015 has been reportedly announced by a Czech investor, Lama Energy Group, in connection with a stalled tar sands project in Alberta. See D. Charlotin, 'Frustrated by delays in licensing process Czech oilsands investor puts Canada on notice of a claim under bilateral investment treaty', *IAR Reporter* (8 April 2019). Other known disputes relating to the phasing out of fossil fuel projects include *Uniper SE, Uniper Benelux Holding B.V. and Uniper Benelux N.V. v. Netherlands*, ICSID Case No. ARB/21/22, introduced on 30 April 2021, and *RWE AG and RWE Eemshaven Holding II BV v. Netherlands*, ICSID Case No. ARB/21/4, registered on 2 February 2021 (these two claims challenge aspects of the Dutch phase-out policy); *TransCanada Corporation and TransCanada PipeLines Limited v. The United States* of America, ICSID Case No. ARB/16/21, discontinued on 24 March 2017 (the initial claim concerned the lack of approval of a pipeline project to carry oil from Canadian tar sands to refineries in the United States. The project required presidential approval, which was withheld for environmental reasons but then granted, after the 2016 US presidential elections brought a new incumbent to power. Executive orders signed by the Biden administration in January 2020 may reignite the dispute). Two other claims may be attempts at recovering failed investment but there is no public information on the specificities of the dispute: *Eni International B.V., Eni Oil Holdings B.V. and Nigerian Agip Exploration Limited v. Nigeria, ICSID* Case No. ARB/20/41, registered on 9 October 2020; *Shell Petroleum N.V. and The Shell Petroleum Development Company of Nigeria Limited v. Nigeria*, ICSID Case No. ARB/21/7, registered on 10 February 2021.

70 *Westmoreland NoA*, para. 12.

71 *Westmoreland NoA*, para. 105.

in due course, it provides a clear illustration of how foreign investment claims can be used specifically to recoup investments in the previous socio-technical regime.

However, this is not the only use of either trade or investment law. As discussed next, the challengers of a socio-technical regime can also rely on trade and investment law in order to advance their own economic interests. Some of the disputes examined in the foregoing paragraph can indeed be seen from a different perspective.

4.3 *Harnessing Existing Rules in Support of the Transition*

4.3.1 Introduction

International law is providing a battleground not only for competition between 'brown' and 'green' sectors but also, within the latter, for tactical competition among different strands of the renewable energy industry. The more ground the 'flow' energy matrix gains, i.e. the more flows of electricity, renewable energy equipment and critical raw materials become important, the stronger the competition within the emerging socio-technical regime. The examples reviewed in the following sections concern several 'uses' of international law by the sectors driving the emerging socio-technical regime.

The first example focusses on disputes over renewable energy subsidies but seen from the angle of competition between different producers of renewable energy equipment. I then discuss how the renewable energy industry as well as many financial investors owning shares of renewable energy companies are harnessing foreign investment law to optimise their return on investment by means of claims against States having implemented support schemes. Finally, I briefly refer to an emerging category of disputes which are only noteworthy, for present purposes, because they illustrate the global search for the mineral basis of the energy transition.

4.3.2 Competition within the Emerging Socio-Technical Regime

'Green industrial policies' providing support to producers of electricity from renewable sources and, through LCRs, also to local producers of renewable energy equipment, remain limited in number. Yet, they epitomise the front line of the transition struggle not only between 'brown' and 'green' sectors, but also between different competitors within the latter. Such policies gained ground following the 2008 world economic crisis, which – together with the run-up to the 2009 Conference of the Parties of the UNFCCC in Copenhagen – prompted the adoption of stimulus packages benefitting renewable energies.[72] They are likely to gain further ground with the green stimulus packages announced by many governments around the world to relaunch their economies after the COVID-19 pandemic of 2020–2021.[73]

Competition struggles within the broad renewable energy sector are relevant because they illustrate another facet of international law as a key battle front in the energy transition, which could be called the scramble for market share in the new 'green economy'. These disputes typically concern alleged discrimination amongst producers of renewable energy equipment (LCRs in a range of support schemes) or the treatment of an energy resource/product (biofuels), which are frequent green industrial policy instruments. Table 8.1 lists the 14 green industrial policy-related disputes brought to date (out of 598 brought before the WTO since 1995).

The listing in Table 8.1 is organised according to the date in which consultations were requested by a WTO Member. The reference to 'green industrial policy-related' disputes is only intended to emphasise that these disputes concern sectors of the emerging socio-technical regime in the energy sector. Other disputes relevant for the transition (e.g. those concerning more efficient appliances and vehicles) are not included, as they would blur the focus on the analysis.

Whereas 14 disputes out of a total of 598 represent only a small share of the dispute settlement activity, a number of observations can be derived from them. First, it is significant that all these disputes emerged in the aftermath of the 2008 world economic crisis and, mainly, against measures encompassed by green recovery strategies. A causal link between 'recovery' or the 'transition' to a low-carbon economy would be difficult to establish for each and every measure at stake, but a general

[72] See IEA, *Green stimulus after the 2008 crisis* (Paris: IEA, 2020) at: www.iea.org/articles/green-stimulus-after-the-2008-crisis. See also Wu/Salzman, *The Next Generation*.

[73] See S. Evans, J. Gabbatiss, 'Coronavirus: Tracking how the world's 'green recovery' plans aim to cut emissions', Carbon Brief – International Policy (16 June 2020), available at: www.carbonbrief.org/coronavirus-tracking-how-the-worlds-green-recovery-plans-aim-to-cut-emissions. For a comparison of stimulus packages in 2008–2009 and those planned for the post-pandemic period see J. Jaeger, M. I. Westphal, C. Park, 'Lessons Learned on Green Stimulus: Case Studies from the Global Financial Crisis', *WRI Working Paper* (November 2020).

Table 8.1. *Green industrial policy disputes before the WTO*

Filing year	Dispute	Main issues
2010	*Canada – Certain Measures Affecting the Renewable Energy Generation Sector* (Complainant – Japan), Request for consultation (Japan), 13 September 2010, AB Report, 6 May 2013, WT/DS412/AB/RWT/DS426/AB/R (proceedings also addressed a separate complaint from the EU filed 2011)	LCRs FIT schemes for the generation of wind and PV-based electricity
2010–2011	*China – Measures Concerning Wind Power Equipment*, DS419, Request for consultations (United States), 22 December 2010; Request for consultations (Japan), 19 January 2011	Support schemes for manufacturers of wind power equipment conditional on the use of domestic inputs
2012	*European Union and Certain Member States – Certain Measures Affecting the Renewable Energy Sector*, DS452, Request for consultations (China), 5 November 2012	LCRs FIT schemes for the generation of PV-based electricity
	United States – Countervailing Duty Measures on Certain Products from China (Complainant: China), Request for consultations, 25 March 2012, AB Report, 18 December 2014, WT/DS437/AB/R, AB Report on Article 21.5 DSU, 16 July 2019, WT/DS437/AB/RW	Trade remedies imposed on certain Chinese products, including solar panels and wind towers
	European Union and a Member State – Certain Measures Concerning the Importation of Biodiesels, DS443, Request for consultations (Argentina), 17 August 2012	Measures concerning the allocation of biodiesel quantities to meet an EU mandatory renewable energy target

Table 8.1. (*cont.*)

Filing year	Dispute	Main issues
2013	*India – Certain Measures Relating to Solar Cells and Solar Modules* (Complainant: United States), Request for consultations, 6 February 2013, AB Report, 16 September 2016, WT/DS456/AB/R, WT/DS456/AB/R/Add.1	LCRs FIT schemes for the generation of PV-based electricity
	European Union and Certain Member States – Certain Measures on the Importation and Marketing of Biodiesel and Measures Supporting the Biodiesel Industry, DS459, Request for consultations (Argentina), 15 May 2013	Fiscal advantages given to EU-produced biofuels
	European Union – Anti-Dumping Measures on Biodiesel from Argentina (Complainant: Argentina), Request for consultations, 19 December 2013, AB Report, 6 October 2016, WT/DS473/AB/R	Trade remedies imposed on biodiesel from Argentina
2014	*European Union – Anti-Dumping Measures on Biodiesel from Indonesia* (Complainant: Indonesia), Request for consultations, 10 June 2014, Panel Report, 25 January 2018, WT/DS480/R	Trade remedies imposed on biodiesel from Indonesia
2016	*United States – Certain Measures Relating to the Renewable Energy Sector* (Complainant: India), Request for consultations, 9 September 2016, Panel Report, 27 June 2019, WT/DS510/R, WT/DS510/R/Add.1	Fiscal advantages to renewable energy producers conditional on domestic equipment and input, and fiscal advantages to locally produced biofuels

Table 8.1. (*cont.*)

Filing year	Dispute	Main issues
2018	*United States – Safeguard Measure on Imports of Crystalline Silicon Photovoltaic Products*, DS545, Request for Consultations (Korea), 14 August 2018	Trade remedies imposed on foreign PV equipment
	United States – Certain Measures Related to Renewable Energy, DS563, Request for consultations (China), 14 August 2018	Subsidies and LCRs in the energy sector
	Peru – Anti-dumping and countervailing measures on biodiesel from Argentina, DS572, Request for consultations (Argentina), 29 November 2018	Trade remedies imposed on biodiesel from Argentina
2019	*European Union – Certain Measures concerning Palm Oil and Oil Palm Crop-based Biofuels*, DS593, Request for consultations (Indonesia), 16 December 2019	Limits on the use of palm oil for biofuels unless it can be certified as presenting low risk of indirect land-use change

trend is sufficiently discernible. Secondly, the identity of the respondents and complainants in these disputes is also informative. They include major producers of the relevant 'goods', such as China, the United States, the EU, India, Japan and Indonesia.[74] Thirdly, the measures all concern efforts to give an economic advantage to a certain green sector over another. In some cases, the dispute is handled through consultations

[74] In 2019, the top five countries in term of investment in new solar-PV capacity were China, the United States, Japan, India and Chinese Taipei; those in wind power capacity were China, the United States, the United Kingdom, India and Spain; and those in biofuels production were the United States, Brazil, China, India, Canada (for ethanol) and Indonesia, the United States, Brazil, Germany and France (for biodiesel). See REN21, *Renewables 2020*, at 36.

without resort to the more legalised steps in the WTO dispute settlement procedure. Although it is not possible to state exactly whether – and how many – other disputes have been handled through consultations before even reaching the WTO level, it is likely that formal requests for consultations are only resorted in cases where an arrangement or modus vivendi cannot be otherwise found.

The political economy considerations underpinning each measure, dispute and sector vary significantly. Trade remedies or LCRs adopted by a State to protect its renewable energy equipment industry may adversely affect the renewable energy electricity generation industry, as such measures may increase the equipment costs. Even among the power generators, competition for the award of lucrative contracts (e.g. for participation in the feed-in-tariff scheme) may lead to disputes based on international law. An example is provided by *Mesa v. Canada*.[75] This investment claim, brought under the North American Free Trade Agreement (NAFTA),[76] concerned the design and implementation of the very feed-in-tariff scheme challenged in *Canada – Renewables*. The claimant argued that, as a result of shortcomings in such design and implementation, it had not been awarded any contract to sell electricity to Ontario. The tribunal (by a majority decision) dismissed the claims because inter alia the scheme fell under the public procurement carve-out in Article 1108(7)(1) of the NAFTA.[77] Another example is *Windstream v. Canada*.[78] A US investor claimed inter alia that Ontario authorities had treated a Korean investor, Samsung, more favourably because, unlike the claimant, Samsung had not been subject to a moratorium on offshore wind energy developments. The tribunal rejected the claim for breach of the NAFTA's non-discrimination standards (Articles 1102 and 1103) on the grounds that the two investors were not in like circumstances (Samsung's investment did not concern offshore wind).[79]

[75] *Mesa Power Group, LLC v. Government of Canada*, UNCITRAL, PCA Case No. 2012–17, Award (24 March 2016).

[76] North American Free Trade Agreement, 17 December 1992, 32 ILM 289 and 605 (1993).

[77] The tribunal dismissed all claims. The claimant filed a petition to vacate the award before US courts, but it was rejected. See *Mesa Power Group LLC v. Government of Canada*, US District Court for the District of Columbia, 15 June 2017, Case 1:16-cv-01101-JDB.

[78] *Windstream Energy LLC v. Government of Canada*, PCA Case No. 2013–22, Award (27 September 2016).

[79] The tribunal concluded, however, that Canada had failed to accord fair and equitable treatment to the investor in breach of Article 1105 NAFTA.

The disputes reviewed in this section all suggest the growing presence of the sectors embodying the emerging socio-technical regime. Front lines in the socio-technical transition struggle thus exist not only between the prevailing and the emerging regimes but also within the latter. Such 'internal' struggles provide an indication of the 'phase' at which the transition process is at present. As noted earlier in this chapter (see Section II), the third phase of a socio-technical transition process is characterised by increased production of new technology, which allows it to expand its market share in the core markets until it becomes dominant. From an empirical standpoint, renewable energies are clearly not dominant yet in any one of the main drivers of energy consumption, thermal services, transportation and electricity generation. But their share is growing at a very fast pace, and massive investment in both generation and equipment is being made and supported in 'core markets' such as China, India, the EU and the United States. The struggles illustrated in this section provide a clear indication – at the level of international law – of how advanced this process is. Yet, even if one were to consider these trade disputes are merely the tip of an iceberg, these fourteen disputes represent only an indication of the direction of travel. As discussed next, this indication is corroborated when we turn our attention from trade to another major area of dispute settlement, namely foreign investment claims challenging regulatory change.

4.3.3 The 'Stability' Struggle: Investment Claims in the Renewable Energy Sector

Between 1972 and 2020, at least 178 foreign investment claims with environmental components were filed,[80] out of a total of 1061 known disputes (concluded and pending).[81] Claims with environmental components are defined as those which arise from the operation of foreign investors (1) in environmental markets (e.g. land-filling, waste treatment, garbage collection, pesticides/chemicals, energy efficiency, renewable energy, emissions reduction, biodiversity compensation) and/or (2) in other activities, where their impact on the environment or on certain minorities through it is part of the dispute (e.g. tourism,

[80] I rely here on my own dataset of disputes. Disputes decided or discontinued, as of the timing of writing, are reproduced in Table 8.4. The figures in this section are based on this dataset.

[81] See UNCTAD's Investment Dispute Settlement Navigator (as of 5 January 2021): https://investmentpolicy.unctad.org/investment-dispute-settlement

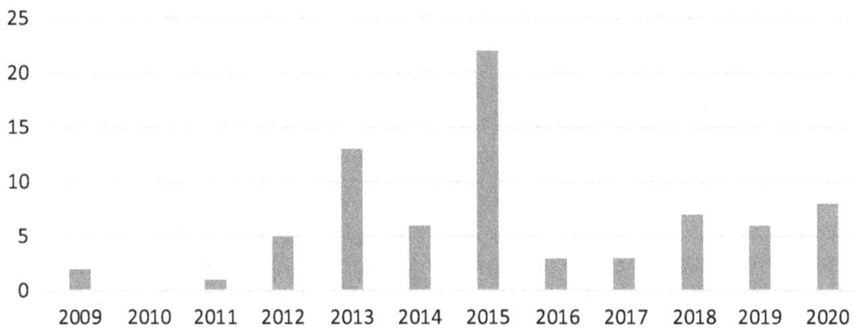

Figure 8.1 Temporal distribution of investment claims arising from the energy transition.

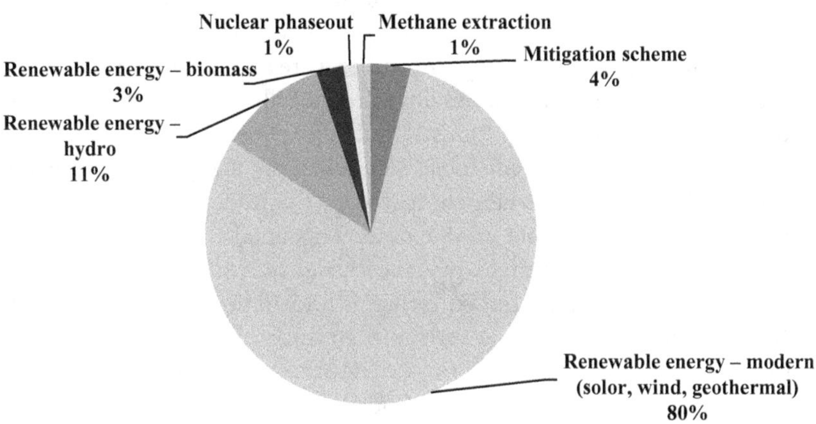

Figure 8.2 Sectoral distribution of investment claims arising from the energy transition.

extractive industries, pesticides/chemicals, water extraction or distribution) and/or (3) when the application of domestic or international environmental law is at stake.[82] Approximately 80 per cent (143) of these disputes have been brought after 2008, and over half of them (76) concern the energy transition, mostly (61) modern renewable energy projects (solar, wind and geothermal). Figures 8.1 and 8.2 show

[82] See J. E. Viñuales, *Foreign Investment and the Environment in International Law* (Cambridge: Cambridge University Press, 2012), at 17.

the temporal distribution of these seventy-six disputes as well as the relative share of each sector in them:

The main legal issues at stake in the overwhelming majority of these disputes are the challenges involved in navigating the changing conditions of markets, such as the renewable energy generation market, which is not only regulated but rests on a market built by regulation. There are over seventy foreign investment disputes challenging adjustments of the renewable energy regulatory framework in countries such as Albania, Bulgaria, Canada, the Czech Republic, Germany, Italy, Kenya, Romania, Spain or Tanzania, and possibly many more undisclosed ones. The geographically wide span of the countries facing such challenges provides an indication of the scope of the phenomenon. Table 8.2 is the equivalent of Table 8.1 for the much longer list of investment disputes arising from the energy transition.

Despite their many differences, the broad underlying question raised by these disputes is analogous. In the aftermath of the 2008 economic crisis, when good investment opportunities were scarce, many companies but also financial intermediaries invested heavily in renewable energy projects supported by green industrial policies. These policies were seen as offering a relatively predictable, safe and very significant return on investment, particularly when compared to the underwhelming investment alternatives available at the time. The uptake was so high that several countries struggled to pay the subsidies, which, depending on the cases, could have represented genuine windfall profits for investors at a time of national economic restraint. In such a context, a range of measures were adopted to limit the return on investment to more sustainable levels. Such measures included taxes, levies as well as adjustments in the tariff rate, volume and time-horizon of the investments. That, in turn, hit the profitability of many investors, who sought to rely on investment agreements to recoup the expected profits.

The outcomes of these cases vary significantly across countries, measures, legal instruments relied upon and specific factual circumstances. Overall, however, they provide two indications which are important to understand the link between international law and the energy transition. First, foreign investment claims are increasingly being brought by the sectors embodying the emerging socio-technical regime. In most cases, they do not concern the lawfulness under international law of measures constraining the transaction to limit its negative externalities but, quite to the contrary, they concern the protection of a new type of energy transaction against fluctuations in the regulatory framework on which they rely. This sets energy transition disputes apart from the broader set

Table 8.2. *Energy transition disputes before investment arbitration tribunals*

Filing year	Dispute	Main issue
2009	*Naftrac Limited v. National Environmental Investment Agency (Ukraine)*, PCA Arbitration (Optional Environmental Rules), Award (4 December 2012)	Mitigation scheme
	Vattenfall AB, Vattenfal Europe AG, Vattenfall Europe Generation AG v. Germany, ICSID Case No. ARB/09/6 Award (11 March 2011)	Mitigation scheme
2011	*Mesa Power Group, LLC v. Canada*, UNCITRAL Rules, PCA Case No. 2012–17, Award (24 March 2016)	Renewable energy – modern
2012	*Vattenfall AB and others v. Germany*, ICSID Case No. ARB/12/12 (pending)	Nuclear energy phaseout
	Mercer International Inc. v. Canada, ICSID Case No. ARB(AF)/12/3, Award (6 March 2018)	Renewable energy – hydro
	Windstream Energy LLC v. Canada, UNCITRAL Rules, Award (27 September 2016)	Renewable energy – modern
	Charanne and Construction Investments v. Spain, SCC Rules, Award (21 January 2016)	Renewable energy – modern
	The PV Investors v. Spain, PCA Case No. 2012–14, Final Award (28 February 2020)	Renewable energy – modern
2013	*Transglobal Green Energy, LLC and Transglobal Green Panama, S.A. v. Panama*, ICSID Case No. ARB/13/28, Award (2 June 2016)	Renewable energy – hydro
	EVN AG v. Republic of Bulgaria, ICSID Case No. ARB/13/17, Award (18 July 2013)	Renewable energy – modern
	Natland Investment Group N.V. and others v. Czech Republic, PCA Case No. 2013–35, Partial Award (20 December 2017)	Renewable energy – modern
	Antaris Solar GmbH and others v. Czech Republic, UNCITRAL Rules, Award (2 May 2018)	Renewable energy – modern
	Voltaic Network GmbH v. Czech Republic, UNCITRAL Rules, Award (15 May 2019)	Renewable energy – modern
	I.C.W. Europe Investments Limited v. Czech Republic, UNCITRAL Rules, Award (15 May 2019)	Renewable energy – modern

Table 8.2. (*cont.*)

Filing year	Dispute	Main issue
	Photovoltaik Knopf Betriebs-GmbH v. Czech Republic, UNCITRAL Rules, Award (15 May 2019)	Renewable energy – modern
	WA Investments-Europa Nova Limited v. Czech Republic, UNCITRAL Rules, Award (15 May 2019)	Renewable energy – modern
	Mr Jürgen Wirtgen, Mr Stefan Wirtgen, and JSW Solar (zwei) GmbH & Co.KG v. Czech Republic, UNCITRAL Rules, Final Award (11 October 2017)	Renewable energy – modern
	RREEF Infrastructure (G.P.) Limited and RREEF Pan-European Infrastructure Two Lux S.à r.l. v. Spain, ICSID Case No. ARB/13/30, Award (11 December 2019)	Renewable energy – modern
	Antin Infrastructure Services Luxembourg S.à.r.l. and Antin Energia Termosolar B.V. v. Spain, ICSID Case No. ARB/13/31, Award (15 June 2018), Decision on the rectification of the award (29 January 2019)	Renewable energy – modern
	Eiser Infrastructure Limited and Energia Solar Luxembourg S.a.r.l. v. Spain, ICSID Case No. ARB/13/36, Award (4 May 2017)	Renewable energy – modern
	Isolux Netherlands, B.V. v. Spain, SCC Case V2013/153, Final Award (17 July 2016)	Renewable energy – modern
2014	*Alpiq AG v. Romania*, ICSID Case No. ARB/14/28, Award (9 November 2018)	Renewable energy – hydro
	Blusun S.A., Jean-Pierre Lecorcier and Michael Stein v. Italy, ICSID Case No. ARB/14/3, Final Award (27 December 2016), Decision on Annulment (13 April 2020)	Renewable energy – modern
	RWE Innogy GmbH and RWE Innogy Aersa S.A.U. v. Spain, ICSID Case No. ABR/14/34, Decision on jurisdiction, liability and certain issues of quantum (30 December 2019)	Renewable energy – modern
	InfraRed Environmental Infrastructure G.P. Limited and others v. Spain, ICSID Case No. ARB/14/12, Award (2 August 2019)	Renewable energy – modern

Table 8.2. (*cont.*)

Filing year	Dispute	Main issue
	Masdar Solar & Wind Cooperatief U.A. v. Spain, ICSID Case No. ARB/14/1, Award (16 May 2018)	Renewable energy – modern
	NextEra Energy Global Holdings B.V. and NextEra Energy Spain Holdings B.V. v. Spain, ICSID Case No. ARB/14/11, Decision on Jurisdiction, Liability and Quantum Principles (12 March 2019), Final Award (31 May 2019)	Renewable energy – modern
2015	*ČEZ, a.s. v. Republic of Bulgaria*, ICSID Case No. ARB/16/24 (pending)	Renewable energy – biomass
	Hydro S.r.l. and others v. Albania, ICSID Case No. ARB/15/28, Award (24 April 2019)	Renewable energy – hydro
	ENERGO-PRO a.s. v. Bulgaria, ICSID Case No. ARB/15/19 (pending)	Renewable energy – hydro
	Hydro Energy 1 S.à r.l. and Hydroxana Sweden AB v. Spain, ICSID Case No. ARB/15/42, Decision on Jurisdiction, Liability and Directions on Quantum (9 March 2020)	Renewable energy – hydro
	9REN Holding S.a.r.l v. Spain, ICSID Case No. ARB/15/15, Award (31 May 2019)	Renewable energy – modern
	BayWa r.e. Renewable Energy GmbH and BayWa r.e. Asset Holding GmbH v. Spain, ICSID Case No. ARB/15/16, Decision on Jurisdiction, Liability and Directions on Quantum (2 December 2019)	Renewable energy – modern
	Cube Infrastructure Fund SICAV and others v. Spain, ICSID Case No. ARB/15/20, Decision on Jurisdiction, Liability and Partial Decision on Quantum (19 February 2019), Final Award (26 June 2019)	Renewable energy – modern
	Mathias Kruck and others v. Spain, ICSID Case No. ARB/15/23 (pending)	Renewable energy – modern
	STEAG GmbH v. Spain, ICSID Case No. ARB/15/4, Decision on Jurisdiction, Liability and Principles on Quantum (8 October 2020)	Renewable energy – modern
	SolEs Badajoz GmbH v. Spain, ICSID Case No. ARB/15/38, Award (31 July 2019)	Renewable energy – modern

Table 8.2. (*cont.*)

Filing year	Dispute	Main issue
	OperaFund Eco-Invest SICAV PLC and Schwab Holding AG v. Spain, ICSID Case No. ARB/15/36, Award (6 September 2019)	Renewable energy – modern
	E.ON SE, E.ON Finanzanlagen GmbH and E.ON Iberia Holding GmbH v. Spain, ICSID Case No. ARB/15/35 (pending)	Renewable energy – modern
	Cavalum SGPS, S.A. v. Spain, ICSID Case No. ARB/15/34, Decision on Jurisdiction, Liability and Directions on Quantum (31 August 2020)	Renewable energy – modern
	KS Invest GmbH and TLS Invest GmbH v. Spain, ICSID Case No. ARB/15/25 (pending)	Renewable energy – modern
	JGC Corporation v. Spain, ICSID Case No. ARB/15/27 (pending)	Renewable energy – modern
	Stadtwerke München GmbH, RWE Innogy GmbH et al. v. Spain, ICSID Case No. ABR/15/1, Award (2 December 2019)	Renewable energy – modern
	Eskosol S.p.A. in liquidazione v. Italy, ICSID Case No. ARB/15/50, Award (4 September 2020)	Renewable energy – modern
	WalAm Energy Inc. v. Kenya, ICSID Case No. ARB/15/7, Award (10 July 2020)	Renewable energy – modern
	CEF Energia B.V. v. Italy, SCC Case No. 158/2015, Award (16 January 2019)	Renewable energy – modern
	Belenergia S.A. v. Italy, ICSID Case No. ARB/15/40, Award (6 August 2019)	Renewable energy – modern
	Greentech Energy Systems A/S & Ors. v. Italy, SCC Arbitration V (2015/095), Award (23 December 2018)	Renewable energy – modern
	Watkins Holdings S.à r.l. and others v. Spain, ICSID Case No. ARB/15/44, Award (21 January 2020)	Renewable energy – modern
2016	*Amlyn Holding B.V. v. Croatia*, ICSID Case No. ARB/16/28) (pending)	Renewable energy – biomass
	ESPF Beteiligungs GmbH, ESPF Nr. 2 Austria Beteiligungs GmbH, and InfraClass Energie 5 GmbH & Co. KG v. Italy, ICSID Case No. ARB/16/5, Award (14 September 2020)	Renewable energy – modern

Table 8.2. (*cont.*)

Filing year	Dispute	Main issue
	Kinangop Wind Park v. Kenya, ICC Arbitration (Contract-based), Award (2 July 2018)	Renewable energy – modern
2017	*Agro EcoEnergy Tanzania Limited, Bagamoyo EcoEnergy Limited, EcoDevelopment in Europe AB, EcoEnergy Africa AB v. Tanzania*, ICSID Case No. ARB/17/33 (pending)	Renewable energy – modern
	Cluff Geothermal Company and Great Rift Drilling v. Geothermal Development Company, LCIA Case, Award (3 June 2019)	Renewable energy – modern
	Tennant Energy, LLC v. Canada, PCA Case No. 2018–54 (pending)	Renewable energy – modern
2018	*Hydrika 1 S.A.C. and others v. Peru*, ICSID Case No. ARB/18/48 (pending)	Renewable energy – hydro
	European Solar Farms A/S v. Spain, ICSID Case No. ARB/18/45 (pending)	Renewable energy – modern
	ACF Renewable Energy Limited v. Bulgaria, ICSID Case No. ARB/18/1 (pending)	Renewable energy – modern
	LSG Building Solutions GmbH and others v. Romania, ICSID Case No. ARB/18/19 (pending)	Renewable energy – modern
	Veolia Propreté SAS v. Italy, ICSID Case No. ARB/18/20 (pending)	Renewable energy – modern
	KLS Energy Lanka Sdn. Bhd. and KLS Energy Lanka (Private) Ltd v. Sri Lanka, ICSID Case No. ARB/18/39 (pending)	Renewable energy – modern
	Invenergy v. Poland. Invenergy Renewables LLC and Others v. Republic of Poland PCA Case No. 2018–40 (pending)	Renewable energy – modern
2019	*Energy Utility Corporation Limited v. KivuWatt Limited*, ICSID Case No. ARB/19/3 (pending)	Methane extraction
	Orazul International España Holdings S.L. v. Argentina, ICSID Case No. ARB/19/25 (pending)	Renewable energy – hydro
	Latam Hydro LLC and CH Mamacocha S.R.L. v. Peru, ICSID Case No. ARB/19/28 (pending)	Renewable energy – modern
	Sapec, S.A. v. Spain, ICSID Case No. ARB/19/23 (pending)	Renewable energy – modern

Table 8.2. (*cont.*)

Filing year	Dispute	Main issue
	Canepa Green Energy Opportunities I, S.á r.l. and Canepa Green Energy Opportunities II, S.á r.l. v. Spain, ICSID Case No. ARB/19/4 (pending)	Renewable energy – modern
	Strabag, Erste Nordsee-Offshore Holding and Zweite Nordsee-Offshore Holding v. Germany, ICSID Case No. ARB/19/29 (pending)	Renewable energy – modern
2020	*Koch Industries, Inc. and Koch Supply & Trading v. Canada*, ICSID Case No. ARB/20/52 (pending)	Mitigation scheme
	Hamburg Commercial Bank AG v. Italy, ICSID Case No. ARB/20/3 (pending)	Renewable energy – modern
	Campos de Pesé, S.A. v. Panama, ICSID Case No. ARB/20/19 (pending)	Renewable energy – modern
	Mitsui & Co., Ltd. v. Spain, ICSID Case No. ARB/20/47 (pending)	Renewable energy – modern
	Fin.Doc S.r.l. and Others ("PV Investors") v. Romania, ICSID Case No. ARB/20/35 (pending)	Renewable energy – modern
	Encavis and others v. Italy, ICSID Case No. ARB/20/39 (pending)	Renewable energy – modern
	Arka Energy B.V. v. Albania, ICSID Case No. ARB/20/54 (pending)	Renewable energy – modern
	EP Wind Project (Rom) Six Ltd. v. Romania, ICSID Case No. ARB/20/15 (pending)	Renewable energy – modern

of investment disputes with environmental components. Secondly, the main focus of these energy transition disputes is the stability of the rules that facilitate the advent and consolidation of the new socio-technical regime. Thus, the old investment law developed to protect the fossil fuel-based socio-technical regime is now being used to protect the laws and institutions created to make room for a new regime.

Taken together, these two indications corroborate the tentative conclusion of the previous section that the process has already reached the third phase of a socio-technical transition, characterised by increased market share of the new technology in the core markets. By looking at the somewhat turbulent legal process through which this expansion happens, it is possible to better understand the role of international law in the energy transition. In the next section, one aspect which has so far been left outside of the legal analysis, i.e. disputes concerning the mineral basis of the emerging socio-technical regime, is re-introduced by reference to both trade and investment disputes.

4.3.4 Disputes Concerning Critical and Other Raw Materials

A discussion of disputes arising from either trade in minerals or investment in extractive industries[83] may not seem directly relevant to the energy transition. It is only once the mineral needs of the technologies driving such transition are made explicit (see Section 3.3) that the link can be readily understood. Even from this standpoint, a caveat must be introduced to the extent that the minerals at stake in these disputes can be used for a wider range of purposes besides renewable energy and batteries, including the digital economy, robotics and defence technology. With these caveats in mind, the purpose of this section is to briefly examine the relevance of two sets of disputes brought, respectively, before WTO dispute settlement organs and investment tribunals.

The first set of disputes all concern the dominant position of China as the main global supplier of a wide range of both critical and non-critical raw materials. Even when certain raw materials have other major suppliers, China often plays a major role in subsequent stages of their supply chain, such as material processing and/or component development and/or assemblies. The more a supply chain for a given raw material is dominated by one country, the higher the risk of bottlenecks and flow disruptions. Hence the importance, as in the geopolitics of oil and gas, of the regulation of exports discussed in Chapter 2. The three main cases brought before WTO dispute settlement organs in this area concern export measures, and they were triggered by complaints from either the United States, in *China – Raw Materials* and *China – Rare Earths*, or the EU, in *China – Duties on Raw Materials*, who follow very closely the geopolitical risks associated with China's dominant position in the global supply chain of critical raw materials (see Section 3.3). The materials at stake in each case include some which are key inputs of energy transition technologies, such as silicon metal and indium (for solar PV), rare earths (for wind energy and electric vehicles), and cobalt and graphite (for batteries). Yet, the disputes cannot be said to be linked only to the energy transition given

[83] For the references of the disputes discussed in this section, see n. 38.

the wider set of materials involved and their much wider application beyond energy transition technologies. For example, the metal molybdenum, which was at stake in *China – Rare Earths*, is mostly used in metallurgy to make metal alloys for a range of uses including drills, jet engines and power-generation turbines. In the chemical industry, molybdenum is also used as a catalyst for petroleum processing. Fluorspar, at stake in *China – Raw Materials*, is used for batteries but also for the production of aluminium and in the chemical industry to produce hydrogen fluoride, a raw material for refrigerants, gasoline, plastics and herbicide, among other applications. Hence the need to distinguish the disputes discussed in this section from those examined in Sections 4.3.2 and 4.3.3.

The same important caveat applies to the investment claims arising from mining projects relating to some critical and non-critical raw materials. In three of them (*Stans Energy v. Kyrgystan*; *Cortec v. Kenya* and the notice of dispute filed by Montero Mining against Tanzania), rare earths mining featured prominently. But often, the focus on metallurgical inputs, such as molybdenum (*Metal-Tech v. Uzbekistan*; *Stans Energy v. Kyrgyzstan*) or manganese (*Nabodaya Trading v. Gabon*), significantly blurs the connection between the dispute and the energy transition. In all cases, however, the underlying transaction illustrates the search for new deposits of these materials in countries (e.g. Kenya, Kyrgyzstan, Tanzania, Uzbekistan) other than the main suppliers, mostly China (for rare earths and molybdenum). A more detailed analysis of these and possibly many other disputes could bring into focus another manifestation of the energy transition at the level of mining disputes. By way of illustration, in late 2018, a dispute arose between Chile and a US investor, Albemarle Corp ALB.N, regarding the discounted price offered by the latter to companies producing battery metals in Chile. Lithium is a key component in battery production and both Chile and Albemarle are major global players in the lithium supply chain. Chile threatened to bring a commercial arbitration claim to enforce the terms of a 2016, which required the discounted price, but eventually the dispute was managed through negotiations.[84] Yet, in 2020, tensions arose again, this time in a way that more clearly unveils the deep geopolitical implications of such disputes. As noted by a commentator:

> The high-stakes feud comes as Albemarle pushes to expand production in Chile and take control of Australia's Greenbushes, the world's largest

[84] A. De la Jara, 'Exclusive: Chile to delay arbitration with top lithium producer Albemarle', *Reuters* (27 December 2018).

> lithium mine, to meet an expected tripling in demand for the key battery metal by 2025 as automakers produce more electric vehicles.[85]

Lithium reserves are highly concentrated in South America within the so-called lithium triangle (Argentina, Bolivia and Chile), followed by Australia and China.[86] A dispute such as this one and the legal regime applicable to it have therefore wider significance for the energy transition. Again, it illustrates a deeper level ('phase three') of the socio-technical transition to the extent that the transactions themselves have undergone a transformation process.

4.4 Limiting the Adverse Implications of the Transition

Additional corroboration of the current phase of the socio-technical transition can be derived from a different angle. As may be expected, the more the emerging socio-technical regime expands in phase three, the clearer its own adverse implications (its 'negative externalities') become. The recognition of such implications and their deliberate regulation can be taken as yet another sign of the progressive consolidation of the new socio-technical regime. International law has a bearing on what could be broadly called the inclusiveness of the transition, which involves both the participatory and transparency dimensions of the many processes manifesting the transition and the need to provide new opportunities to those populations adversely affected by the measures driving the energy transition (e.g. workers in the old model who may lose their jobs). From this perspective, international law is relevant in two main ways.

First, the very activities through which the transition is to be effected may be subject to a range of participatory requirements, such as the rights of access to environmental information, participation in environmental decision-making and access to justice under the 1998 Aarhus Convention[87] or the 2018 Escazú Agreement,[88] or the prior informed consent requirement conditioning the relocation of indigenous and tribal

[85] D. Sherwood, 'Exclusive: Lithium giant Albemarle locks horns with Chile over reserves data', *Reuters* (10 September 2020).

[86] See S. Kalantzakos, 'The Race for Critical Minerals in an Era of Geopolitical Realignments' (2020) 55 *The International Spectator* 1, at 7.

[87] Convention on Access to Information, Public Participation in Decision-Making and Access to Justice in Environmental Matters, 25 June 1998, 2161 UNTS 447.

[88] Regional Agreement on Access to Information, Public Participation and Justice in Environmental Matters in Latin America and the Caribbean, Escazú, 4 March 2018, C.N.195.2018.TREATIES-XXVII.18.

peoples, e.g. in the context of hydroelectricity projects.[89] Much like the rules concerning trade, investment and transit (see Chapter 2), those regulating negative externalities (see Chapter 3) are also, to a large extent, unspecific and therefore potentially applicable to projects of the emerging socio-technical regime. That is a defining feature of what I called the foundational approach, although not every rule and/or instrument will be equally conducive to specific transactions of the contending socio-technical regimes.

The second way in which international law addresses the inclusiveness dimension of the energy transition is by placing limits on the very measures adopted to promote the transition. Of particular note in this context is the reference, in the preamble of the Paris Agreement, to 'the imperatives of a just transition of the workforce and the creation of decent work and quality jobs in accordance with nationally defined development priorities' as well as the expectation that:

> Parties should, when taking action to address climate change, respect, promote and consider their respective obligations on human rights, the right to health, the rights of indigenous peoples, local communities, migrants, children, persons with disabilities and people in vulnerable situations and the right to development, as well as gender equality, empowerment of women and intergenerational equity.[90]

This paragraph is ambiguously drafted, but it does refer, at least in part, to the protection of human rights not only against climate change but also against the measures adopted to tackle climate change, which include energy transition policies. Under this broad umbrella, the Green Climate Fund has adopted an Environmental and Social Policy, the purpose of which is:

> In carrying out its mandate of promoting a paradigm shift towards low-emission and climate-resilient development pathways in the context of sustainable development, GCF will effectively and equitably manage environmental and social risks and impacts, and improve outcomes of all GCF-financed activities.[91]

[89] See e.g. Convention (No. 169) concerning Indigenous and Tribal Peoples in Independent Countries, 27 June 1989, 28 ILM 1382 (1989) (ILO Convention 169), Arts. 16(2) and 6; 'United Nations Declaration on the Rights of Indigenous Peoples', 2 October 2007, UN Doc. A/RES/61/295 (UNDRIP), Annex, Arts. 10 and 19.

[90] Adoption of the Paris Agreement, Decision 1/CP.21, 12 December 2015, FCCC/CP/2015/L.9, Annex, Paris Agreement, paras. 10 and 11.

[91] Green Climate Fund Board, 'Environmental and Social Policy', GCF/B.19/43 titled 'Decisions of the Board' – nineteenth meeting of the Board, 26 February–1 March 2018, section 3.1 (Policy objectives), chapeau.

This policy is about mitigating not only climate change but also the adverse impact of activities that promote the 'paradigm shift towards low-emission and climate-resilient development pathways'. Other manifestations of this issue are a number of policy statements emphasising the 'just transition'.[92] One is the 'Silesia Solidarity and Just Transition Declaration' adopted by some States during the twenty-fourth meeting of the parties of the UN Framework Convention on Climate Change, held at Katowice, Poland, in December 2018.[93] Paragraph 5 of this declaration specifically recognises the 'challenges faced by sectors, cities and regions in the transition from fossil fuels and high emitting industries, and the importance to ensure a decent future for workers impacted by the transition'. At the very time this declaration was being adopted, the implications of these words were very keenly felt as a result of the 'yellow vests' demonstrations in France, which were triggered by a planned tax on fossil fuels.[94] Work on the just transition is integral to the process to achieve SDG 7, discussed in Chapter 1.

As suggested by the different illustrations provided in this chapter, international law is becoming an important battle front in the ongoing energy transition. Significantly, the answers one can find in the relevant rules, instruments and processes with respect to a given case or issue are not necessarily aligned. A subsidy consistent with a given investment discipline may be inconsistent with a trade discipline or vice-versa. That very measure may be required or justified by an environmental or a human rights treaty. Moreover, action consistent with an environmental treaty (e.g. mitigation action) can conflict with human rights obligations. As noted in Chapter 1 of this study, the purposes pursued by different rules are diverse and not necessarily consistent. As shown in this chapter, a 'branch-by-branch' analysis the link between international law and the energy transition is both necessary and insufficient. It is necessary because it provides issue- or context-specific answers and lays the

[92] For an overview of these statements see International Institute for Sustainable Development, *NGO Brief: Just Transition in Focus*, 31 May 2018, available at: https://sdg.iisd.org/commentary/policy-briefs/ngo-brief-just-transition-in-focus/.

[93] The text is available at: https://cop24.gov.pl/presidency/initiatives/just-transition-declaration/. On this political context of this declaration see K. E. H. Jenkins, B. K. Sovacool, A. Blachowicz, A. Lauer, 'Politicising the Just Transition: Linking global climate policy, Nationally Determined Contributions and targeted research agendas' (2020) 115 *Geoforum* 138.

[94] See A. Chrisafis, 'Who are the gilets jaunes and what do they want?', *The Guardian* (7 December 2018).

foundations for more integrative perspectives. But it is also insufficient because it leaves out many relevant norms and fails to capture the interactions between different sets of norms pursuing different goals. Admittedly, the suitability of the vantage point depends upon the type of question one is trying to answer. Specific questions regarding the violation of participatory rights or of trade or investment disciplines or, still, the requirements of environmental agreements or the powers conferred by the law of the sea over marine spaces, can be usefully accommodated within a single- or multi-branch approach. In some cases, certain partial vantage points can be combined to encompass a wider expanse, as it has been done with the trade-environment, trade-human rights, investment-environment, investment-human rights and human rights-environment interfaces.[95]

These efforts are useful, but their scope cannot adequately capture what a phenomenon as vast as the energy transition means for international law as a whole. For such an inquiry, a wider, integrated and transversal analytical vantage point is needed. Such an approach must be capable of accommodating this more general inquiry while, at the same time, connecting a wide range of more specific dots that have been explored using a 'branch-by-branch' coding. Higher abstraction is not necessarily integrative if the significant developments made in the international law of energy, whether from a topical or a branch perspective, cannot be 'integrated', i.e. brought to bear in the more general inquiry. Using a term that will be familiar to some readers, what is needed is a 'metalanguage', a language such as a 'grammar' capable of analysing, comparing and possibly integrating other languages (the 'object languages'). The analytical framework introduced in this book is an attempt to connect these widely different 'dots' and, thereby, to lay more solid foundations for the study of the international law of energy and its relevance for the ongoing energy transition.

[95] On these different interfaces see e.g. E. Vranes, *Trade and the Environment: Fundamental Issues in International Law, WTO Law, and Legal Theory* (Oxford: Oxford University Press, 2009); T. Cottier, J. Pauwelyn, E. Burgi (eds.), *Human Rights and International Trade* (Oxford: Oxford University Press, 2005); Viñuales, *Foreign Investment and the Environment*; P.-M. Dupuy, E.-U. Petersmann, F. Francioni (eds.), *Human Rights in International Investment Law and Arbitration* (Oxford: Oxford University Press, 2009); D. K. Anton, D. Shelton, *Environmental Protection and Human Rights* (Cambridge: Cambridge University Press, 2012).

Conclusion

The account provided in this study leads to two overall conclusions: the international law of energy must be understood as the entirety of international law seen from the prism of energy as a legal object; and the energy transition, indeed the energy transformation, is being organised through a combination of both old and new rules spanning the entirety of international law.

The main reason sustaining the first conclusion is quite simply that the legal organisation of international energy transactions can only be understood if international law as a whole is brought into sight. To do so, it is useful to rely on some conceptual categories extracted from a general analysis of the field and characterising: energy as a legal object, the purposes of global energy governance, the structure of international energy transactions, and the main approaches or patterns followed in their regulation. These categories have been introduced in Chapter 1 and applied in the remaining chapters. International law frames energy as certain 'resources' converted into 'products' through a range of 'activities' relying on certain 'technologies'. The geographical mismatch between the countries where the energy resources characterising the 'mineral fuel' economy are mainly located and those where they are consumed has been the main driver of the internationalisation of energy transactions. The international rules and processes governing such transactions are mainly concerned with conferring and allocating entitlements over energy, enabling and protecting the investment, trade and transit flows entailed by such transactions, and regulating their negative externalities on humans and the environment. Over time, these rules have pursued a number of sometimes related purposes, mainly availability, security of supply, diversification, efficiency, safety, access and sustainability. An examination of the entire field leads to the identification of certain patterns in the way international energy transactions are governed, which I have called the 'foundational', 'ad hoc' and 'centralised' approaches.

Through these analytical lenses it is possible to bring into view a vast expanse of rules and processes that shape international energy transactions. The rules conferring and allocating entitlements over energy encompass matters as diverse as territorial sovereignty, powers over maritime spaces, maritime delimitation, international watercourses, the rights of peoples, human rights and even the law of occupation.[1] Those enabling and protecting the transaction are mainly found in the regulation of foreign investment, trade and transit.[2] And the adverse effects of such transactions are regulated by a range of rules found not only in instruments relating to the latter areas but also in a wider body of rules and processes concerning the protection of human rights and the environment.[3] Taken together, these rules and processes, whether they specifically refer to energy or not, constitute the 'foundations' of the international law of energy. Other rules, much more specific, govern a narrower object, namely deposits or projects. These rules are developed to meet the specific needs of each situation. They are *ad hoc*. The main examples concern the regimes developed over time to govern the joint development of hydrocarbon deposits,[4] the hydroelectrical potential of shared watercourses, the transportation of oil and gas through pipelines, that of electricity through transmission lines, and the development of windfarms offshore.[5] Between these very general and very specific regulatory layers, a certain degree of institutionalisation has also developed to promote cooperation on specific energy resources. In some cases, the very purpose of the regime is such that it has taken the form of a highly centralised regime, such as the one governing nuclear energy.[6] In other cases, the degree of centralisation is lower and narrower, focussing on the defence of certain specific interests (e.g. those of producers – such as OPEC or GECF – or consumers – such as the IEA – of oil or gas) or on the promotion of certain forms of energy (e.g. renewable energies promoted by IRENA, and increasingly also by the IEA) or on cooperation at a regional level (whether highly integrated, as in the EU, or more loosely so, as in Latin America and South-East Asia).[7] Looking through these analytical lenses it is possible to keep in sight both the trees and the

[1] See the first part of Chapter 2.
[2] See the second part of Chapter 2.
[3] See Chapter 3.
[4] See Chapter 4.
[5] On these types of *ad hoc* regimes see Chapter 5.
[6] See Chapter 6.
[7] On these various forms of energy pro-centralisation see Chapter 7.

wood; and it is also possible to assess at these two levels the implications of the energy transformation from the perspective of international law.

International law is a battleground in the energy transformation driven by the transition from a socio-technical regime to another. This means not only that the structure and content of international law are at stake in the competition and confrontation between and within socio-technical regimes, but also that international law is one of the key mediums shaping the process. The energy transformation is indeed being organised through a combination of both old and new rules spanning the entirety of international law. Analytically, the conceptual categories introduced in Chapter 1 and used throughout the book can be used to describe the transformation at the level of the purposes of energy governance, the rules regulating the negative externalities of international energy transactions, and the rules organising the very core of such transactions, in that order.

The purposes of energy governance have changed to make room for 'access' and 'sustainability' without, however, excluding the pursuit of more traditional purposes.[8] This is manifested not only by how goals (e.g. SDG 7) are framed but also in the reorientation of the mandates and functions of centralised (e.g. the IAEA or even the EU energy policy starting with the 'Third Package') and proto-centralised regimes (most notably the reorientation of the IEA mandate and the establishment of IRENA).[9] The emergence and consolidation has been part of the struggle to redefine the content and structure of international law to support the socio-technical transition.

New technologies for achieving such purposes have both steered and been steered by the rules regulating the negative externalities of international energy transactions. This is manifested mainly by the re-elaboration of energy questions in instruments aimed at curbing emissions of greenhouse gases, reducing environmental degradation, and advancing human rights.[10] It is also manifested to a lesser extent in the operation of provisions protecting these objectives and included in instruments enabling and protecting energy transactions. At this level, which is closer to the organisation of the transaction

8 See the discussion of the purposes of energy governance in Chapter 1.
9 See the discussion of these organisations and their evolution in Chapters 6 and 7.
10 See the discussion of these instruments in the second part of Chapter 3.

itself, the degree of resistance is stronger, even in provisions specifically focussing on non-economic objectives.[11]

When we move to the rules and processes organising the transaction itself, the landscape is blurred. On the one hand, ad hoc regimes are now been increasingly employed to organise not only joint development or transportation of hydrocarbons but also offshore windfarms and long-distance electricity transmission lines.[12] Similarly, the sector-neutral rules on foreign investment protection are being widely relied upon by the renewable energy sector to defend its competitiveness against other energy generation processes.[13] On the other hand, the green industrial policies enacted to sustain the development of renewable energy sectors have been successfully challenged before trade panels, whereas fossil fuel subsidies and other production subsidies have so far escaped trade disciplines.[14] Largely beyond reach is the deepest legal layer, the rules conferring entitlements over energy, even in a highly integrated context such as the EU. This is most likely due to sovereignty considerations, which extend not only to the minerals of the fossil fuel economy but also to those underpinning the very technologies driving the energy transition. The exercise of such sovereignty must unfold within bounds set by the rules enabling and protecting international energy transactions, both old and new, but the very conferral and allocation of the entitlement remains firmly in the grip of States.

From the standpoint of the social practice and technology we call international law, the socio-technical transition and the transformation it entails seem well advanced. Within the four broad phases of a transition (technological innovation, scaling up of production, expansion of market share in core markets, propagation and consolidation throughout), the emerging socio-technical regime appears to be well into the third phase. Its position is, as shown before, supported both by new purposes, rules and organisations and by old rules, on foreign investment and, to a lesser extent, trade. The trading system is one of the main front lines in the struggle for market share among companies of the emerging

[11] See the discussion of these instruments in the first part of Chapter 3.

[12] See the discussion of the ad hoc regimes of offshore windfarms and cross-border transmission lines in Chapter 5. Ad hoc hydroelectricity regimes are also relevant but, given their long history, they cannot as such be considered as manifestations of the energy transformation.

[13] See the discussion in Chapter 8.

[14] See the discussion in Chapter 8.

socio-technical regime. Such struggle is telling of the level of consolidation of the sectors representing the new socio-technical regime.

But a transition is not a replacement. It is a process through which the relative shares of different energy technologies – and their related transactions – undergo a substantial, sometimes fundamental readjustment. The technologies – and the rules – of the previous socio-technical regime do not disappear; they co-exist with those of the emerging regime. This is important because the full range of the international law of energy can be expected to remain relevant, and also to remain a battlefront, provided of course that humanity is afforded the time to tackle the underlying causes of the transition.

INDEX

CAMBRIDGE STUDIES IN INTERNATIONAL AND COMPARATIVE LAW

Books in the Series

164 *The International Law of Energy* Jorge Viñuales
163 *The Three Ages of International Commercial Arbitration* Mikaël Schinazi
162 *Repetition and International Law* Wouter Werner
161 *State Responsibility and Rebels: The History and Legacy of Protecting Investment Against Revolution* Kathryn Greenman
160 *Rewriting Histories of the Use of Force: The Narrative of 'Indifference'* Agatha Verdebout
159 *The League of Nations and the Protection of the Environment* Omer Aloni
158 *International Investment Law and Legal Theory: Expropriation and the Fragmentation of Sources* Jörg Kammerhofer
157 *Legal Barbarians: Identity, Modern Comparative Law and the Global South* Daniel Bonilla Maldonado
156 *International Human Rights Law Beyond State Territorial Control* Antal Berkes
155 *The Crime of Aggression under the Rome Statute of the International Criminal Court* Carrie McDougall
154 *Minorities and the Making of Postcolonial States in International Law* Mohammad Shahabuddin
153 *Preclassical Conflict of Laws* Nikitas E. Hatzimihail
152 *International Law and History: Modern Interfaces* Ignacio de la Rasilla
151 *Marketing Global Justice: The Political Economy of International Criminal Law* Christine Schwöbel-Patel
150 *International Status in the Shadow of Empire* Cait Storr
149 *Treaties in Motion: The Evolution of Treaties from Formation to Termination* Edited by Malgosia Fitzmaurice and Panos Merkouris
148 *Humanitarian Disarmament: An Historical Enquiry* Treasa Dunworth
147 *Complementarity, Catalysts, Compliance: The International Criminal Court in Uganda, Kenya, and the Democratic Republic of Congo* Christian M. De Vos
146 *Cyber Operations and International Law* François Delerue
145 *Comparative Reasoning in International Courts and Tribunals* Daniel Peat
144 *Maritime Delimitation as a Judicial Process* Massimo Lando
143 *Prosecuting Sexual and Gender-Based Crimes at the International Criminal Court: Practice, Progress and Potential* Rosemary Grey
142 *Capitalism As Civilisation: A History of International Law* Ntina Tzouvala
141 *Sovereignty in China: A Genealogy of a Concept Since 1840* Adele Carrai
140 *Narratives of Hunger in International Law: Feeding the World in Times of Climate Change* Anne Saab
139 *Victim Reparation under the Ius Post Bellum: An Historical and Normative Perspective* Shavana Musa

138 *The Analogy between States and International Organizations* Fernando Lusa Bordin

137 *The Process of International Legal Reproduction: Inequality, Historiography, Resistance* Rose Parfitt

136 *State Responsibility for Breaches of Investment Contracts* Jean Ho

135 *Coalitions of the Willing and International Law: The Interplay between Formality and Informality* Alejandro Rodiles

134 *Self-Determination in Disputed Colonial Territories* Jamie Trinidad

133 *International Law as a Belief System* Jean d'Aspremont

132 *Legal Consequences of Peremptory Norms in International Law* Daniel Costelloe

131 *Third-Party Countermeasures in International Law* Martin Dawidowicz

130 *Justification and Excuse in International Law: Concept and Theory of General Defences* Federica Paddeu

129 *Exclusion from Public Space: A Comparative Constitutional Analysis* Daniel Moeckli

128 *Provisional Measures before International Courts and Tribunals* Cameron A. Miles

127 *Humanity at Sea: Maritime Migration and the Foundations of International Law* Itamar Mann

126 *Beyond Human Rights: The Legal Status of the Individual in International Law* Anne Peters

125 *The Doctrine of Odious Debt in International Law: A Restatement* Jeff King

124 *Static and Evolutive Treaty Interpretation: A Functional Reconstruction* Christian Djeffal

123 *Civil Liability in Europe for Terrorism-Related Risk* Lucas Bergkamp, Michael Faure, Monika Hinteregger and Niels Philipsen

122 *Proportionality and Deference in Investor-State Arbitration: Balancing Investment Protection and Regulatory Autonomy* Caroline Henckels

121 *International Law and Governance of Natural Resources in Conflict and Post-Conflict Situations* Daniëlla Dam-de Jong

120 *Proof of Causation in Tort Law* Sandy Steel

119 *The Formation and Identification of Rules of Customary International Law in International Investment Law* Patrick Dumberry

118 *Religious Hatred and International Law: The Prohibition of Incitement to Violence or Discrimination* Jeroen Temperman

117 *Taking Economic, Social and Cultural Rights Seriously in International Criminal Law* Evelyne Schmid

116 *Climate Change Litigation: Regulatory Pathways to Cleaner Energy* Jacqueline Peel and Hari M. Osofsky

115 *Mestizo International Law: A Global Intellectual History 1842–1933* Arnulf Becker Lorca

114 *Sugar and the Making of International Trade Law* Michael Fakhri

113 *Strategically Created Treaty Conflicts and the Politics of International Law* Surabhi Ranganathan

112 *Investment Treaty Arbitration As Public International Law: Procedural Aspects and Implications* Eric De Brabandere
111 *The New Entrants Problem in International Fisheries Law* Andrew Serdy
110 *Substantive Protection under Investment Treaties: A Legal and Economic Analysis* Jonathan Bonnitcha
109 *Popular Governance of Post-Conflict Reconstruction: The Role of International Law* Matthew Saul
108 *Evolution of International Environmental Regimes: The Case of Climate Change* Simone Schiele
107 *Judges, Law and War: The Judicial Development of International Humanitarian Law* Shane Darcy
106 *Religious Offence and Human Rights: The Implications of Defamation of Religions* Lorenz Langer
105 *Forum Shopping in International Adjudication: The Role of Preliminary Objections* Luiz Eduardo Salles
104 *Domestic Politics and International Human Rights Tribunals: The Problem of Compliance* Courtney Hillebrecht
103 *International Law and the Arctic* Michael Byers
102 *Cooperation in the Law of Transboundary Water Resources* Christina Leb
101 *Underwater Cultural Heritage and International Law* Sarah Dromgoole
100 *State Responsibility: The General Part* James Crawford
99 *The Origins of International Investment Law: Empire, Environment and the Safeguarding of Capital* Kate Miles
98 *The Crime of Aggression under the Rome Statute of the International Criminal Court* Carrie McDougall
97 *'Crimes against Peace' and International Law* Kirsten Sellars
96 *Non-Legality in International Law: Unruly Law* Fleur Johns
95 *Armed Conflict and Displacement: The Protection of Refugees and Displaced Persons under International Humanitarian Law* Mélanie Jacques
94 *Foreign Investment and the Environment in International Law* Jorge E. Viñuales
93 *The Human Rights Treaty Obligations of Peacekeepers* Kjetil Mujezinović Larsen
92 *Cyber Warfare and the Laws of War* Heather Harrison Dinniss
91 *The Right to Reparation in International Law for Victims of Armed Conflict* Christine Evans
90 *Global Public Interest in International Investment Law* Andreas Kulick
89 *State Immunity in International Law* Xiaodong Yang
88 *Reparations and Victim Support in the International Criminal Court* Conor McCarthy
87 *Reducing Genocide to Law: Definition, Meaning, and the Ultimate Crime* Payam Akhavan
86 *Decolonising International Law: Development, Economic Growth and the Politics of Universality* Sundhya Pahuja

85 *Complicity and the Law of State Responsibility* Helmut Philipp Aust
84 *State Control over Private Military and Security Companies in Armed Conflict* Hannah Tonkin
83 *'Fair and Equitable Treatment' in International Investment Law* Roland Kläger
82 *The UN and Human Rights: Who Guards the Guardians?* Guglielmo Verdirame
81 *Sovereign Defaults before International Courts and Tribunals* Michael Waibel
80 *Making the Law of the Sea: A Study in the Development of International Law* James Harrison
79 *Science and the Precautionary Principle in International Courts and Tribunals: Expert Evidence, Burden of Proof and Finality* Caroline E. Foster
78 *Transition from Illegal Regimes under International Law* Yaël Ronen
77 *Access to Asylum: International Refugee Law and the Globalisation of Migration Control* Thomas Gammeltoft-Hansen
76 *Trading Fish, Saving Fish: The Interaction between Regimes in International Law* Margaret A. Young
75 *The Individual in the International Legal System: Continuity and Change in International Law* Kate Parlett
74 *'Armed Attack' and Article 51 of the UN Charter: Evolutions in Customary Law and Practice* Tom Ruys
73 *Theatre of the Rule of Law: Transnational Legal Intervention in Theory and Practice* Stephen Humphreys
72 *Science and Risk Regulation in International Law* Jacqueline Peel
71 *The Participation of States in International Organisations: The Role of Human Rights and Democracy* Alison Duxbury
70 *Legal Personality in International Law* Roland Portmann
69 *Vicarious Liability in Tort: A Comparative Perspective* Paula Giliker
68 *The Public International Law Theory of Hans Kelsen: Believing in Universal Law* Jochen von Bernstorff
67 *Legitimacy and Legality in International Law: An Interactional Account* Jutta Brunnée and Stephen J. Toope
66 *The Concept of Non-International Armed Conflict in International Humanitarian Law* Anthony Cullen
65 *The Principle of Legality in International and Comparative Criminal Law* Kenneth S. Gallant
64 *The Challenge of Child Labour in International Law* Franziska Humbert
63 *Shipping Interdiction and the Law of the Sea* Douglas Guilfoyle
62 *International Courts and Environmental Protection* Tim Stephens
61 *Legal Principles in WTO Disputes* Andrew D. Mitchell
60 *War Crimes in Internal Armed Conflicts* Eve La Haye
59 *Humanitarian Occupation* Gregory H. Fox
58 *The International Law of Environmental Impact Assessment: Process, Substance and Integration* Neil Craik

57 *The Law and Practice of International Territorial Administration: Versailles to Iraq and Beyond* Carsten Stahn
56 *United Nations Sanctions and the Rule of Law* Jeremy Matam Farrall
55 *National Law in WTO Law: Effectiveness and Good Governance in the World Trading System*Sharif Bhuiyan
54 *Cultural Products and the World Trade Organization* Tania Voon
53 *The Threat of Force in International Law* Nikolas Stürchler
52 *Indigenous Rights and United Nations Standards: Self-Determination, Culture and Land* Alexandra Xanthaki
51 *International Refugee Law and Socio-Economic Rights: Refuge from Deprivation* Michelle Foster
50 *The Protection of Cultural Property in Armed Conflict* Roger O'Keefe
49 *Interpretation and Revision of International Boundary Decisions* Kaiyan Homi Kaikobad
48 *Multinationals and Corporate Social Responsibility: Limitations and Opportunities in International Law* Jennifer A. Zerk
47 *Judiciaries within Europe: A Comparative Review* John Bell
46 *Law in Times of Crisis: Emergency Powers in Theory and Practice* Oren Gross and Fionnuala Ní Aoláin
45 *Vessel-Source Marine Pollution: The Law and Politics of International Regulation* Alan Khee-Jin Tan
44 *Enforcing Obligations* Erga Omnes *in International Law* Christian J. Tams
43 *Non-Governmental Organisations in International Law* Anna-Karin Lindblom
42 *Democracy, Minorities and International Law* Steven Wheatley
41 *Prosecuting International Crimes: Selectivity and the International Criminal Law Regime* Robert Cryer
40 *Compensation for Personal Injury in English, German and Italian Law: A Comparative Outline* Basil Markesinis, Michael Coester, Guido Alpa and Augustus Ullstein
39 *Dispute Settlement in the UN Convention on the Law of the Sea* Natalie Klein
38 *The International Protection of Internally Displaced Persons* Catherine Phuong
37 *Imperialism, Sovereignty and the Making of International Law* Antony Anghie
36 *Principles of the Institutional Law of International Organizations* C. F. Amerasinghe
35 *Necessity, Proportionality and the Use of Force by States* Judith Gardam
34 *International Legal Argument in the Permanent Court of International Justice: The Rise of the International Judiciary* Ole Spiermann
33 –
32 *Great Powers and Outlaw States: Unequal Sovereigns in the International Legal Order* Gerry Simpson
31 *Local Remedies in International Law (second edition)* Chittharanjan Felix Amerasinghe

30 *Reading Humanitarian Intervention: Human Rights and the Use of Force in International Law* Anne Orford

29 *Conflict of Norms in Public International Law: How WTO Law Relates to Other Rules of International Law* Joost Pauwelyn

28 –

27 *Transboundary Damage in International Law* Hanqin Xue

26 –

25 *European Criminal Procedures* Edited by Mireille Delmas-Marty and J. R. Spencer

24 *Accountability of Armed Opposition Groups in International Law* Liesbeth Zegveld

23 *Sharing Transboundary Resources: International Law and Optimal Resource Use* Eyal Benvenisti

22 *International Human Rights and Humanitarian Law* René Provost

21 *Remedies against International Organisations* Karel Wellens

20 *Diversity and Self-Determination in International Law* Karen Knop

19 *The Law of Internal Armed Conflict* Lindsay Moir

18 *International Commercial Arbitration and African States: Practice, Participation and Institutional Development* Amazu A. Asouzu

17 *The Enforceability of Promises in European Contract Law* James Gordley

16 *International Law in Antiquity* David J. Bederman

15 *Money Laundering: A New International Law Enforcement Model* Guy Stessens

14 *Good Faith in European Contract Law* Reinhard Zimmermann and Simon Whittaker

13 *On Civil Procedure* J. A. Jolowicz

12 *Trusts: A Comparative Study* Maurizio Lupoi and Simon Dix

11 *The Right to Property in Commonwealth Constitutions* Tom Allen

10 *International Organizations before National Courts* August Reinisch

9 *The Changing International Law of High Seas Fisheries* Francisco Orrego Vicuña

8 *Trade and the Environment: A Comparative Study of EC and US Law* Damien Geradin

7 *Unjust Enrichment: A Study of Private Law and Public Values* Hanoch Dagan

6 *Religious Liberty and International Law in Europe* Malcolm D. Evans

5 *Ethics and Authority in International Law* Alfred P. Rubin

4 *Sovereignty over Natural Resources: Balancing Rights and Duties* Nico Schrijver

3 *The Polar Regions and the Development of International Law* Donald R. Rothwell

2 *Fragmentation and the International Relations of Micro-States: Self-Determination and Statehood* Jorri C. Duursma

1 *Principles of the Institutional Law of International Organizations* C. F. Amerasinghe

For EU product safety concerns, contact us at Calle de José Abascal, 56–1°,
28003 Madrid, Spain or eugpsr@cambridge.org.

www.ingramcontent.com/pod-product-compliance
Lightning Source LLC
LaVergne TN
LVHW010339220926
848484LV00004BB/936

* 9 7 8 1 1 0 8 4 1 5 8 3 5 *